The American Drug Scene

An Anthology

Fourth Edition

James A. Inciardi
University of Delaware

Karen McElrath
Queen's University

Roxbury Publishing Company
Los Angeles, California

Library of Congress Cataloging-in-Publication Data

The American drug scene / [edited by] James A. Inciardi, Karen McElrath—4th ed.
p. cm.
Includes bibliographical references.
ISBN 1-931719-08-X
1. Drug abuse—United States. I. Inciardi, James A. II. McElrath, Karen, 1959–
HV5825.A696 2004
362.29′12′0973—dc22   2003064640
                                    CIP

The American Drug Scene, 4th ed.

Publisher: Claude Teweles
Managing Editor: Dawn VanDercreek
Production Editor: Monica K. Gomez
Copy Editor: Jackie Estrada
Cover Design: Marnie Kenney
Typography: Robert Leuze

Printed on acid-free paper in the United States of America. This paper meets the standards for recycling of the Environmental Protection Agency.

ISBN 1-931719-08-X

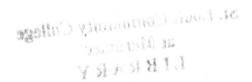
ROXBURY PUBLISHING COMPANY
P.O. Box 491044
Los Angeles, California 90049-9044
Voice: (310) 473-3312 • Fax: (310) 473-4490
E-mail: roxbury@roxbury.net
Website: www.roxbury.net

Contents

  Andrew Weil suggests that drug use results from people's natural
  desire to alter their levels of consciousness.

  The late Dr. Lindesmith argues that opiate addiction results from
  the conscious awareness that continued drug use is necessary to
  prevent the pain associated with opiate withdrawal.

  The author outlines addiction theory, rhetoric, and treatment outcomes and weighs the evidence that drug addiction is a chronic,
  relapsing disease influenced by biological, psychosocial, and environmental factors.

  A generation ago, sociologist Howard Becker believed that deriv-
  ing pleasure from marijuana was a learned process. He suggested
  also that marijuana users progressed through a series of stages.
  Hirsch and his colleagues test Becker's theory in their study of
  marijuana users, many of whom are college students.

---

* Indicates chapters that are new to the Fourth Edition.

---

* Indicates chapters that are new to the Fourth Edition.

---

* Indicates chapters that are new to the Fourth Edition.

* Indicates chapters that are new to the Fourth Edition.

* Indicates chapters that are new to the Fourth Edition.

---

* Indicates chapters that are new to the Fourth Edition.

Preface

The *American Drug Scene, Fourth Edition,* is a collection of both classic and contemporary essays and articles on the changing patterns, problems, perspectives, and policies related to both legal and illicit drug use. In these 41 selections, as well as in the commentaries that precede them, the information presented is both contemporary and historical, theoretical and descriptive.

The breadth of coverage includes all the major drugs of abuse (amphetamines, narcotics, marijuana, cocaine, hallucinogens, and "club drugs"), as well as such legal drugs as alcohol and tobacco.

Other areas covered include such topics as: drugs, violence, and street crime; substance abuse prevention and treatment; HIV/AIDS and injection drug use; and the drug legalization debate.

One of the many strengths of *The American Drug Scene, Fourth Edition,* is the inclusion of the social contexts that frame and influence drug use. Moreover, thought-provoking introductions to each section and each article guide the reader by identifying and explaining central issues, key concepts, and relationships among topics.

The Fourth Edition includes 11 new articles that address recent and emerging patterns of drug use and policy debates, such as: MDMA/Ecstasy, marijuana for medicinal purposes, Ketamine, and the role of clubs in promoting harm reduction.

Of special interest are the original essays, which focus on topics of current concern and controversy. Examples include the relationship between "club drugs" and sexual violence, cocaine and the criminalization of pregnancy, and what the media has referred to as an "epidemic" of OxyContin abuse.

Discussion questions and suggested readings also expand the usefulness of this edition.

If anything has been learned about the drug problem in the United States, it is an awareness that the problem is continually shifting and changing. There are fads, fashions, and even rages in the drugs of abuse. Heroin, marijuana, cocaine, LSD, and numerous other drugs have all had their periods of currency. And although one substance may be a drug of choice for just a few months, the popularity of others often endures for years, or even generations. Drug "epidemics" (periods during which there are many new users) seem to come and go as well. The United States experienced an epidemic of cocaine use during the 1880s and 1890s, followed by a decline in popularity early in the twentieth century and the reemergence in the 1970s. Several heroin epidemics occurred during the second half of the twentieth century, and a crack-cocaine epidemic began in the mid-1980s. In the 1990s, heroin and methamphetamine—previously popular drugs—were in the news once again. And now there are the "club drugs" or "dance drugs"—Rohypnol, Ecstasy, GHB, and Ketamine.

The tenor and direction of drug control policies tend to shift as well. Although major changes in drug policy are infrequent, intermittent fads and fashions have characterized periodic "wars on drugs." Such initiatives as "zero tolerance," asset forfeiture, mandatory minimum sentences for small-time traffickers, compulsory treatment for drug-involved offenders, and numerous others have experienced periods of acceptance and disfavor. And not surprisingly, the public, political, and ideological reactions to the policies of White House incumbents are abundant, ardent, and enduring.

We hope that readers find the material interesting, stimulating, and instructive. ✦

James A. Inciardi
University of Delaware

Karen McElrath
Queen's University
Belfast, Ireland

About the Editors

James A. Inciardi, Ph.D., is the Director of the Center for Drug and Alcohol Studies at the University of Delaware; a professor in the Department of Sociology and Criminal Justice at Delaware; an adjunct professor in the Department of Epidemiology and Public Health at the University of Miami School of Medicine; and a guest professor in the Department of Psychiatry at the Federal University of Rio Grande do Sul in Porto Alegre, Brazil. Dr. Inciardi received his Ph.D. at New York University and has a background in law enforcement, corrections, drug abuse treatment, and research. He is currently involved in the development, implementation, and evaluation of prison-based treatment programs for drug-involved offenders, as well as HIV/AIDS epidemiology and prevention studies in the United States, Latin America, and the Caribbean. Finally, he is the author, co-author, or editor of some 50 books and 300 articles and chapters in the areas of substance abuse, criminology, criminal justice, history, folklore, public policy, HIV/AIDS, medicine, and law.

Karen McElrath is a reader in the School of Sociology and Social Policy, Queen's University of Belfast, Ireland. She is the author of several articles pertaining to drug use, risk behaviors for HIV infection, and drug policy and is the editor of the book *HIV and AIDS: A Global View* (Greenwood). She was a co-investigator of a large ethnographic study of Ecstasy users and currently is involved in a research project that investigates risk behaviors and barriers to treatment among injecting drug users. A second project examines drug use lifestyles and injecting behaviors among Nubain users. ✦

About the Contributors

Harry J. Anslinger (deceased) was the first U.S. Commissioner of Narcotics and presided over the Federal Bureau of Narcotics from 1930 through 1962.

Mark A. Bellis is affiliated with the Birkenhead and Wallasey Primary Care Trust in England.

Robert S. Broadhead is a professor of sociology at the University of Connecticut.

Archie Brodsky is a research associate in psychology at Harvard Medical School.

John J. Casey is president and managing partner at Evans Hagen and Company.

Michael C. Clatts is the Director of the Institute for Research on Youth at Risk at National Development and Research Institutes, Inc.

William Cloud is an associate professor in the Graduate School of Social Work at the University of Denver.

Randall W. Conforti is an associate at the Ranch Rehabilitation Service in Menomonee Falls, Wisconsin.

Courtney Ryley Cooper (deceased) was a journalist and author of such "true crime" classics as *Ten Thousand Public Enemies* (1935), *Here's to Crime* (1937), and *Designs in Scarlet* (1939).

Kathleen Daly is an associate professor at the School of Criminology and Criminal Justice at Griffith University, Brisbane.

Erik F. Dietz is with the Federal Bureau of Prisons in Washington, D.C.

Vincent P. Dole is a professor and senior physician emeritus with Rockefeller University in New York City and founder of the methadone maintenance treatment modality for narcotics addiction.

William N. Elwood is with the Center for Public Health and Evaluation Research in Key West, Florida.

Donald Franklin is affiliated with the HIV Neurobehavioral Research Center at the University of California at San Diego.

Samuel R. Friedman is with the National Development and Research Institutes in New York City.

Paul J. Goldstein is a sociologist, ethnographer, and professor at the School of Public Health of the University of Illinois.

Jennifer L. Goode is a research specialist at the Center for Drug and Alcohol Studies of the University of Delaware.

Carolyn J. Graney is affiliated with the Department of Sociology at Lawrence University in Appleton, Wisconsin.

Robert Granfield is an assistant professor of sociology at the University of Denver and served as project evaluator for the Faculty Training Program in Drug Dependency at the Graduate School of Social Work.

Lester Grinspoon is an emeritus professor of psychiatry at Harvard Medical School and has published widely in the area of drug abuse.

Karen Bettez Halnon is an assistant professor of sociology at Pennsylvania State University.

Thomas E. Hanlon is affiliated with the Friends Research Institute in Baltimore, Maryland.

Douglas D. Heckathorn is a professor of sociology at Cornell University.

Michael L. Hirsch is the Barker-Oakes Distinguished Professor of Sociology and Chair of the Sociology Department at Central Methodist College in Fayette, Missouri.

HNRC Group (San Diego HIV Neurobehavioral Research Center) is affiliated with the University of California at San Diego, the Naval Hospital San Diego, and the San Diego Veterans Affairs Healthcare System.

Karen Hughes is with the Centre for Public Health at Liverpool John Moores University in England.

Dana Hunt is a senior scientist with Abt Associates Inc.

James A. Inciardi, Ph.D.: See "About the Editors."

Philip Jenkins is a distinguished professor of history and religious studies at Pennsylvania State University.

Mara L. Keire is affiliated with the Rothermere American Institute of the University of Oxford in England.

Timothy W. Kinlock is affiliated with the Friends Research Institute in Baltimore, Maryland.

Meichun Kuo is affiliated with the Department of Health and Social Behavior at the Harvard School of Public Health.

Stephen E. Lankenau is an assistant professor in the Department of Sociomedical Sciences at Columbia University's Mailman School of Public Health.

Hang Lee is affiliated with the Center for Vaccine Research and Department of Pediatrics at the University of California Los Angeles School of Medicine in Torrance.

Jae-Eun Lee is the director of the Office of Decision Science at the Mississippi State Department of Health.

Alfred R. Lindesmith (deceased) was a professor of sociology at Indiana University and one of the first researchers to conduct sociological studies of addiction.

Helen Lowey is with the Centre for Public Health at Liverpool John Moores University in England.

Lisa Maher is a senior lecturer at the School of Public Health and Community Medicine of the University of New South Wales in Sydney.

Andrew M. Mattison is affiliated with the HIV Neurobehavioral Research Center at the University of California at San Diego.

Karen McElrath, Ph.D.: See "About the Editors."

Marissa A. Miller is the Antimicrobial Resistance Program Director at the National Institute of Allergy and Infectious Diseases.

Nicole L. Mott is with the National Center for State Courts in Washington, D.C.

David F. Musto is a professor of psychiatry and social history at Yale University.

Ethan A. Nadelmann is the director of the Lindesmith Center in New York City.

Mark Nichter is affiliated with the Department of Anthropology at the University of Arizona.

David N. Nurco (deceased) was a research professor in the Department of Psychiatry of the University of Maryland School of Medicine.

Marie Nyswander (deceased) was a physician and clinician with Rockefeller University in New York City and co-founder of the methadone maintenance treatment modality for narcotics addiction.

Stanton Peele is a professor, consultant, psychologist, and attorney who has published widely in the area of addiction.

Todd G. Pierce is a medical anthropologist and ethnographer who has published in the areas of drug abuse and HIV risk behaviors.

Anne E. Pottieger is a former scientist with the Center for Drug and Alcohol Studies of the University of Delaware and now conducts research as an independent consultant.

Edward Preble (deceased) was an anthropologist and ethnographer with Manhattan State Hospital and spent much of his career conducting street studies of the New York City drug scene.

Peter Reuter is a professor at the School of Public Affairs and the Department of Criminology of the University of Maryland.

Marsha Rosenbaum is the Director of The Lindesmith Center–West in San Francisco and the author of the classic work *Women on Heroin* (1981).

Michael W. Ross is with the WHO Center for Health Promotion and Prevention Research, School of Public Health at the University of Texas–Houston Health Science Center.

Christine A. Saum is an associate scientist at the Center for Drug and Alcohol Studies of the University of Delaware.

Harvey A. Siegal is a sociologist, ethnographer, and professor and director of Substance Abuse Intervention Programs at Wright State University School of Medicine in Dayton, Ohio.

Hilary L. Surratt is an associate scientist at the Center for Drug and Alcohol Studies of the University of Delaware.

Yaël Van Hulst is a research assistant in the sociology department at the University of Connecticut.

Henry Wechsler is a lecturer in social psychology at Harvard University and is affiliated with the Department of Health and Social Behavior of the Harvard School of Public Health.

Andrew Weil is a clinical professor of internal medicine and founder and director of the Program in Integrative Medicine at the University of Arizona Health Sciences Center in Tucson.

James Q. Wilson taught at Harvard University and the University of California at Los Angeles before joining the School of Public Policy at Pepperdine University.

Tanya Wolfson is affiliated with the HIV Neurobehavioral Research Center at the University of California at San Diego. ✦

Introduction

The American drug scene has a long and enduring history. To begin with, the drinking of alcohol to excess is centuries old. In *The Life and Times of the Late Demon Rum*, the celebrated American social historian and biographer J. C. Furnas suggests that alcohol came to the colonies with the first English and Dutch settlers and that the drinking of "spirits" and "strong waters" was a problem since the first days of the emerging American republic. Tradition had taught that rum, gin, and brandy were nutritious and healthful. Distilled spirits were viewed as foods that supplemented limited and monotonous diets; as medications that could cure colds, fevers, snakebites, and broken legs; and as means of relaxation that would relieve depression, reduce tension, and enable hardworking laborers to enjoy a moment of happy, frivolous camaraderie. By the early 1700s nearly all Americans of every occupation and social class drank alcoholic beverages in quantity, sometimes to the point of intoxication; and by the end of the eighteenth century the daily per capita drinking of Americans was almost a half pint of hard liquor.

The use of other drugs for the enhancement of pleasure and performance or for the alteration of mood also dates back several centuries. Perhaps it all began with Thomas Dover, who developed a form of medicinal opium sold as Dover's Powder. Introduced in England in 1709 and in the colonies several years later, it contained one ounce each of opium, ipecac (the dried roots of a tropical creeping plant), and licorice, combined with saltpeter, tartar, and wine. The attraction of Dover's Powder was in the euphoric and anesthetic properties of opium. For thousands of years opium had been a popular narcotic. A derivative of the oriental poppy (*Papaver somniferum L.*), it was called the "plant of joy" some 4,000 years ago in the "fertile crescent" of Mesopotamia.

The introduction of Dover's Powder in the colonies apparently started a trend. By the later part of the eighteenth century, medications containing opium were readily available throughout urban and rural America. They were sold over the counter in pharmacies, in grocery and general stores, at traveling medicine shows, and through the mail. They were marketed under such labels as Ayer's Cherry Pectoral, Mrs. Winslow's Soothing Syrup, McMunn's Elixir, Godfrey's Cordial, Scott's Emulsion, and Dover's Powder. Many of these remedies were seductively advertised as "painkillers," "cough mixtures," "soothing syrups," "consumption cures," and "women's friends." Others were promoted for the treatment of such varied ailments as diarrhea, dysentery, colds, fever, teething, cholera, rheumatism, pelvic disorders, athlete's foot, and even baldness and cancer. The drugs were produced not only from imported opium but also from white opium poppies that were being legally grown in the New England states, Florida and Louisiana, the West and Southwest, and the Confederate States of America during the Civil War.

For thousands of years, opium had been the only known product of the oriental poppy. In 1803, however, a young German pharmacist, Frederick Serturner, isolated the chief alkaloid of opium. Serturner had hit upon morphine, which he named after Morpheus, the Greek god of dreams. The discovery had profound effects on both medicine and society, for morphine is the greatest single pain reliever the world has ever known. After the hypodermic syringe was invented in 1853, the use of morphine by injection in military medicine during the Civil War and the Franco-Prussian War granted the procedure legitimacy and familiarity to both physicians and the public.

Furthermore, hypodermic medication had its pragmatic aspects—it brought quick local relief, its dosage could be regulated, and it was effective when oral medication was impractical. The regimen, however, was used promiscuously, for many physicians were anxious to illustrate their ability to quell the pain suffered by their patients, who, in turn, expected instant relief from discomfort.

Beyond opium and morphine, the over-the-counter medicine industry expanded even further in the 1880s to include cocaine and heroin. By the close of the nineteenth century, it was estimated that millions of Americans were addicted to the over-the-counter medications, and agitation had begun for controls over the manufacture and distribution of products containing cocaine, opium, and their various derivatives.

One result was the passage of the Pure Food and Drug Act in 1906, which prohibited the interstate transportation of adulterated or misbranded food and drugs. The act brought about the decline of over-the-counter medications because the proportions of alcohol, opium, morphine, heroin, cocaine, and a number of other substances in each preparation now had to be indicated. As a result, most of the remedies lost their appeal.

The Pure Food and Drug Act merely imposed standards for quality, packaging, and labeling; it did not actually outlaw the use of cocaine and opiate drugs. Public Law No. 47, 63rd Congress (H.R. 1967), more popularly known as the Harrison Act, sponsored by New York Representative Francis Burton Harrison and passed in 1914, ultimately served that purpose. At the same time, the new legislation went a long way toward altering public and criminal justice responses to drug use in the United States for generations to come. The Harrison Act required all people who imported, manufactured, produced, compounded, sold, dispensed, or otherwise distributed cocaine and opiate drugs to register with the Treasury Department, pay special taxes, and keep records of all transactions. As such, it was a revenue code designed to exercise some measure of public control over drugs rather than to penalize all the users of narcotics in the United States. In effect, however, penalization is specifically what occurred. Although subcultures and criminal cultures of drug users already existed prior to the passage of the Harrison Act, the legislation served to expand their membership. Since then, drug use has generally been viewed not only as a social problem in the United States but as a criminal problem as well.

From the 1920s through the beginning of the twenty-first century, there have been many drugs of abuse—heroin, cocaine, crack, LSD, PCP, Ecstasy, the amphetamines and methamphetamines, and numerous others—all of which are discussed in the following articles. In addition to describing the drugs, their patterns of use, and their impact on society, chapters examine such other topics as the links between drug use and crime, the AIDS/drug connection, treatment and prevention initiatives, and alternative drug control policies.

Before proceeding with this material, however, it is important that readers have some understanding of the variety of drug-related terms whose meanings are often taken for granted. As such, this introduction closes with a short glossary of the most important definitions.

Basic Drug Groups

Drugs: any natural or artificial substances (aside from food) that by their chemical nature alter the functioning of the body.

Psychoactive drugs: drugs that alter perception and consciousness, including analgesics, depressants, stimulants, and hallucinogens.

Analgesics: drugs used for the relief of varying degrees of pain without rendering the user unconscious. There are both narcotic and non-narcotic varieties of analgesics.

Depressants: drugs that act on and lessen the activity of the central nervous system (CNS), diminishing or stopping vital functions.

Sedatives: CNS depressant drugs that produce calm and relaxation. Alcohol, barbiturates and related compounds, and minor tranquilizers are sedative drugs.

Hypnotics: CNS depressant drugs that produce sleep. Barbiturates, methaqualone, and chloral hydrate are hypnotic drugs. As such, a number of drugs are both sedatives and hypnotics.

Stimulants: drugs that stimulate the central nervous system and increase the activity of the brain and spinal chord. Amphetamines and cocaine are CNS stimulant drugs.

Hallucinogens: drugs that act on the central nervous system, producing mood and perceptual changes varying from sensory illusions to hallucinations. Sometimes referred to as "psychedelics," hallucinogenic drugs include marijuana, hashish, LSD, PCP, and psilocybin.

Use, Abuse, and Dependency Terms

Drug misuse: the inappropriate use of a prescription or nonprescription drug; that is, using it in greater amounts than, for purposes other than, or for longer than it was intended.

Drug abuse: any use of an illegal drug, or the use of a legal drug in a manner that can cause problems for the user.

Addiction: drug craving accompanied by physical dependence, which motivates continuing usage, resulting in a tolerance to the drug's effects and a syndrome of identifiable symptoms when the drug is abruptly withdrawn. Narcotics, barbiturates, and cocaine are addicting drugs.

Dependence: a concept that indicates the central role that a substance has come to play in an individual's life, with evidence of problems relating to control of intake and the development of physical and psychological difficulties, despite which the individual continues to use the substance.

Neuroadaptation: the chemical and biological changes that occur in the brain in response to the use of psychoactive drugs.

Tolerance: a state of acquired resistance to some or all of the effects of a drug. Tolerance develops after the repeated use of certain drugs, resulting in a need to increase the dosage to obtain the original effects.

Cross-tolerance: among certain pharmacologically related drugs, tolerance of the effects of one carrying over to most or all others. For example, a person who has become tolerant of the euphoric effects of secobarbital is likely to be tolerant of the euphoric effects of all other short-acting barbiturates.

Cross-addiction: also referred to as cross-dependence, a situation in which dependence on drugs of the same pharmacological group is mutual and interchangeable. For example, persons addicted to heroin can use methadone or some other narcotic in place of the heroin without experiencing withdrawal.

Withdrawal: the cluster of reactions and behavior that ensue upon the abrupt cessation of a drug on which the user's body is dependent.

Detoxification: the removal of physical dependency.

Drug Reactions

Potentiation: the ability of one drug to increase the activity of another drug when the two are taken simultaneously. Potentiation can be expressed mathematically as $a + b = A$. For example, aspirin (a) plus caffeine (b) increases the potency of the aspirin (A).

Synergism: similar to potentiation, a situation in which two or more drugs are taken together and the combined action dramatically increases the normal effects of each drug. A synergistic effect can be expressed mathematically as $1 + 1 = 5$; it typically occurs with mixtures of alcohol and barbiturates.

Antagonism: a situation in which two drugs taken together have opposite effects on the body. An antagonistic reaction can be expressed mathematically as $1 + 1 = 0$; it typically occurs with certain mixtures of depressants and stimulants.

Idiosyncrasy: an abnormal or peculiar response to a drug, such as excitation from a depressant or sedation from a stimulant.

Side effect: any effect other than what the drug was intended for, such as stomach upset from aspirin.

Routes of Drug Administration

Intravenous: injected into the vein.

Intramuscular: injected into the muscle.

Cutaneous: absorbed through the skin.

Subcutaneous: inserted under the skin.

Insufflation (inhalation): drawn into the lungs through the nose or mouth.

Oral: swallowed and absorbed through the stomach.

Vaginal: absorbed through vaginal tissues.

Anal: absorbed through rectal tissues.

Sublingual: absorbed through the tissues under the tongue.

Drug Schedules Under the Controlled Substances Act

The Comprehensive Drug Abuse and Control Act of 1970 brought together under one law most of the federal drug control legislation that had been enacted since the early part of the nineteenth century. Title II of the law, known as the Controlled Substances Act, categorized certain substances into five "schedules" and defined the offenses and penalties associated with the illegal manufacture, distribution, dispensation, and possession of any drug in each schedule.

Schedule I includes drugs with a high potential for abuse, with no currently accepted medical use in the United States, and with a lack of accepted safety when used under medical supervision. Schedule I lists a variety of opiates and their deriva-

tives, numerous hallucinogenic substances, and a variety of other substances, including heroin, LSD, marijuana, mescaline, peyote, psilocybin, methaqualone (Quaalude), Ecstasy, and GHB.

Schedule II includes drugs for which there is a high potential for abuse; these are drugs that are currently used for medical treatment in the United States and that if abused could lead to dependence. Examples of Schedule II drugs include opium, morphine, cocaine, methadone, Ritalin, methamphetamine, amphetamine, and OxyContin.

Schedule III includes drugs that have a potential for abuse less than those in Schedules I and II, that are currently accepted for medical use in the United States, and that may lead to moderate or low physical dependence or high psychological dependence. Examples of Schedule III drugs include anabolic steroids; any compound or mixture containing amobarbital, secobarbital, or pentobarbital; and hydrocodone.

Schedule IV includes drugs that have a low potential for abuse and are currently accepted for use in the United States. If abused, these drugs could lead to limited physical or psychological dependence. Examples of Schedule IV drugs include the long-acting barbiturates such as phenobarbital; minor tranquilizers such as Librium, Valium, Xanax, and Miltown; and chloral hydrate.

Schedule V includes drugs that have a potential for abuse and dependence lower that those listed in Schedule IV. Examples of Schedule V drugs are those that contain limited quantities of narcotics, such as codeine cough syrup.

References

Furnas, J. C. (1965). *The Life and Times of the Late Demon Rum*. New York: Putnam.

Inciardi, J. A. (2002). *The War on Drugs III: The Continuing Saga of the Mysteries and Miseries of Intoxication, Addiction, Crime, and Public Policy*. Boston: Allyn and Bacon. ✦

Part I

Theoretical Perspectives on Drug Use and Addiction

Why do people take drugs? For the enhancement of pleasure or performance? To relieve anxiety or boredom? As an escape from reality? To suppress feelings of sorrow, inadequacy, guilt, or other emotional pain? Likely for all of these reasons and many more. In fact, there may be as many reasons for taking drugs as there are people who use them. Moreover, theories of drug use and abuse are legion—so much so that one publication of the National Institute on Drug Abuse devoted its entire 488 pages to outlining the major views.

Although many early explanations of substance abuse considered it to be a moral weakness, a number of modern investigators have described drug users as maladjusted, hostile, immature, dependent, manipulative, and narcissistic individuals, suggesting that drug use is just one more symptom of their disordered personalities. Others suggest that because drug use is an integral part of the general culture that surrounds the user, it is learned behavior. And there are other explanations: the bad-habit theory, disruptive-environment theory, cognitive-control theory, social-deviance theory, biological-rhythm theory, subcultural theory, social-neurobiological theory, and many, many more.

Quite popular for many years was the theory of the "addiction-prone personality," elucidated by Dr. Kenneth Chapman of the U.S. Public Health Service several decades ago:

> . . . the typical addict is emotionally unstable and immature, often seeking pleasure and excitement outside of the conventional realms. Unable to adapt comfortably to the pressures and tensions in today's speedy world, he may become either an extremely dependent individual or turn into a hostile "lone wolf" incapable of attaching deep feelings toward anyone. In his discomfort, he may suffer pain—real or imaginary. The ordinary human being has normal defense machinery with which to meet life's disappointments, frustrations, and conflicts. But the potential addict lacks enough of this inner strength to conquer his emotional problems and the anxiety they create. In a moment of stress, he may be introduced to narcotics as a "sure-fire" answer to his needs. Experiencing relief from his pain, or an unreal flight from his problems, or a puffed-up sense of power and control regarding them, he is well on the road toward making narcotics his way of life.

Stated differently, when "stable" people are introduced to drugs, they will discard them spontaneously before becoming dependent. Those who have "addiction-prone" personalities, because of psychoses, psychopathic or psychoneurotic disorders, or predispositions toward mental dysfunctioning, "become transformed into the typical addict."

For a number of contemporary theorists, drug use is related to a more basic need for *pleasure*, plain and simple. For example, there is extensive physiological, neurological, and anthropological evidence to suggest that we are members of a species that has been honed for pleasure. Nearly all people want and enjoy pleasure, and the pursuit of drugs—whether caffeine, nicotine, alcohol, opium, heroin, marijuana, or cocaine—seems to be universal and inescapable. It is found across time and across cultures. The process of evolution has for whatever reasons resulted in a human neurophysiology that responds both vividly and avidly to a variety of common substances. The brain has pleasure centers—receptor sites and cortical cells—that react to "rewarding" dosages of many substances. Or, as University of California pharmacologist Larry Stein explained it in 1989,

> The fact that we respond to a reward shows just how deeply embedded in the design of the brain this reinforcement mechanism is. Dopamine and the opioid peptides are transmitters in very powerful control systems based on a certain chemistry. . . . Along come poppy seeds and coca leaves that have chemicals very similar to these central systems. They go right in, do not pass GO. To say that cocaine or amphetamines, or heroin or morphine, should be highly appealing is an understatement.

Regardless of the theory put forth, it would appear that drug users are of four basic types: *experimenters, social-recreational users, involved users,* and *dysfunctional abusers.*

The *experimenters* are by far the largest group of drug users (not including alcohol users). They most frequently try one or more drugs once or twice in a social setting, but the drug does not play a significant role in their lives. They use their drug of choice experimentally because their social group finds the drug's effects pleasurable. Experimenters do not seek out a drug but may use it when someone presents it to them in an appropriate setting. In this situation, they may smoke marijuana or "snort" cocaine once or twice because the drug does something to them. As a college senior commented about his first cocaine experience,

> I generally don't use drugs, except maybe a little grass now and then. My only experience with coke was a few weeks ago in the dormitory. My roommate came in with a couple of other guys and started getting high on it. They kept trying to get me to do some, and finally I snorted some just for the heck of it. When I did, it was quite a blast at first, from my head all the way down, and then I felt like I was floating. After, I felt a little weird. . . . It was good.

Social-recreational users differ from experimenters primarily in terms of frequency and continuity of consumption. For example, they may use drugs when they are at a party and someone presents the opportunity. Drugs still do not play a significant role in these users' lives. They do not actively seek out drugs but use them only because it does something to them—it makes them feel good. A 28-year-old Miami woman related,

> Partying can be even more fun with a few lines of coke. I never have any of my own, but usually I'll tie in with some guy who does. We'll get a little stoned, and maybe go to bed. It's all in good fun. . . . Another time I was on a double date and this guy had some good toot. We drove up to Orlando and went into Disney World. Do you know what it's like goin' through the haunted mansion stoned like that? It's a whole different trip.

The great majority of alcohol use occurs in a social-recreational context.

For *involved users*, a major transition has taken place since the individual engaged in social-recreational use. As users become "involved" with a particular drug, they also become drug seekers, and their drug of choice becomes significant in their lives. Although they are still quite able to function—in school, on the job, or as a parent or spouse—their proficiency in many areas begins to decline markedly. Personal and social functioning tends to be inversely related to the amount of time involved users spend using drugs. They still have control over their behavior, but their use of the drug occurs with increasing frequency for some adaptive reason; their drug does something *for* them.

Involved users are of many types. Some use drugs to deal with an unbearable work situation, indulging in controlled amounts several times a day. Others use drugs to enhance performance or bolster their self-esteem. And still a third group regularly use drugs to deal with stress, anxiety, or nagging boredom. As one involved cocaine user, a self-employed accountant, put it,

> I seem to be always uptight these days with almost everything I do. Everybody seems to always want something—my clients, my wife, the bank, the world. . . . A few lines [of cocaine] every two-three hours gets me through the day—through the tax returns, the tension at home, the bills, sex, whatever. Without the coke I'd probably have to be put away somewhere.

The *dysfunctional abusers* are what have become known as the "cokeheads," "alcoholics," and "addicts." For them, drugs have become the significant part of their lives. They are personally and socially dysfunctional and spend all of their time involved in drug seeking, drug taking, and other related activities. Moreover, they no longer have control over their drug use.

In the six chapters that follow, a variety of perspectives on drug use and addiction are presented, including the natural mind view of Andrew Weil and the sociological work of Alfred R. Lindesmith. The disease concept of addiction is reviewed, the theory and research on how marijuana use is learned behavior is explored, and a historical view of the "femininity of addiction" is presented. Part I concludes with a sociopharmacological perspective of drug use that focuses on how social, economic, and health inequalities create conditions conducive to drug use, and how the social order needs to change in order to effectively reduce harmful drug consumption.

Reference

Chapman, K. (1951). "A Typical Drug Addict." *New York State Health News,* August 28, 1951.

Additional Readings

Durrant, Russil, and Jo Thakker (2003). *Substance Use and Abuse: Cultural and Historical Perspectives.* Thousand Oaks, CA: Sage Publications.

McLellan, A. Thomas, David C. Lewis, Charles P. O'Brien, and Herbert D. Kleber. (2000). "Drug Dependence, a Chronic Medical Illness: Implications for Treatment, Insurance, and Outcomes Evaluation." *Journal of the American Medical Association,* 284(13): 1689–1695.

Schivelbusch, Wolfgang. (1992). *Tastes of Paradise: A Social History of Spices, Stimulants, and Intoxicants.* New York: Pantheon.

Zoha, Luigi. (2000). *Drugs, Addiction, and Initiation: The Modern Search for Ritual.* Santa Rosa, CA: Daimon Publishers. ✦

1
Why People Take Drugs

Andrew Weil

Andrew Weil, a graduate of Harvard Medical College, believes that people of all cultures are born with the desire to periodically alter their consciousness. He suggests that this desire can be observed in children at very young ages; but because adults frown upon these actions, children learn to suppress or conceal their urges through socialization. According to Dr. Weil, the use of alcohol and other drugs is a natural expression of our innate desire to experience different states of consciousness. He describes his own experiences with mescaline as well as those of others who have used the drug. Finally, he notes the importance of "set" and "setting," suggesting that these two factors may have a greater influence on an individual's drug experience than the drug itself.

The use of drugs to alter consciousness is nothing new. It has been a feature of human life in all places on the earth and in all ages of history. In fact, to my knowledge, the only people lacking a traditional intoxicant are the Eskimos, who had the misfortune to be unable to grow anything and had to wait for white men to bring them alcohol. Alcohol, of course, has always been the most commonly used drug, simply because it does not take much effort to discover that the consumption of fermented juices produces interesting variations from ordinary consciousness. The ubiquity of drug use is so striking that it must represent a basic human appetite. Yet, many Americans seem to feel that the contemporary drug scene is something new, something qualitatively different from what has gone before. This attitude is peculiar, be-

cause all that is really happening is a change in drug preference. There is no evidence that a greater percentage of Americans are taking drugs, only that younger Americans are coming to prefer illegal drugs, like marijuana and hallucinogens, to alcohol. Therefore, people who insist that everyone is suddenly taking drugs must not see alcohol in the category of drugs. Evidence that this is precisely the case is abundant, and it provides another example of how emotional biases lead us to formulate unhelpful conceptions. Drug taking is bad. We drink alcohol. Therefore, alcohol is not a drug. It is, instead, a "pick-me-up," a "thirst quencher," a "social lubricant," "an indispensable accompaniment to fine food," and a variety of other euphemisms. Or, if it is a drug, at least it is not one of those bad drugs that the hippies use.

This attitude is quite prevalent in the adult population of America, and it is an unhelpful formulation for several reasons. In the first place, alcohol is very much a drug by any criterion and causes significant alterations of nervous functioning, regardless of what euphemistic guise it appears in. In fact, of all the drugs being used in our society, alcohol has the strongest claim to the label *drug,* in view of the prominence of its long-term physical effects. In addition, thinking of alcohol as something other than a drug leads us to frame wrong hypotheses about what is going on in America. We are spending much time, money, and intellectual energy trying to find out why people are taking drugs; but, in fact, what we are doing is trying to find out why some people are taking some drugs that we disapprove of. No useful answers can come out of that sort of inquiry; the question is improperly phrased.

Of course, many theories have been put forward. People are taking drugs to escape, to rebel against parents and other authorities, in response to tensions over foreign wars or domestic crises, in imitation of their elders, and so on and so on. No doubt, these considerations do operate on some level (for instance, they may shape the forms of illegal drug use by young people), but they are totally inadequate to explain the universality of drug use by human beings. To come up

4

with a valid explanation, we simply must suspend our value judgments about kinds of drugs and admit (however painful it might be) that the glass of beer on a hot afternoon and the bottle of wine with a fine meal are no different in kind from the joint of marijuana or the snort of cocaine; nor is the evening devoted to cocktails essentially different from the day devoted to mescaline. All are examples of the same phenomenon: the use of chemical agents to induce alterations in consciousness. What is the meaning of this universal phenomenon?

It is my belief that the desire to alter consciousness periodically is an innate, normal drive analogous to hunger or the sexual drive. Note that I do not say "desire to alter consciousness by means of chemical agents." Drugs are merely one means of satisfying this drive; there are many others, and I will discuss them in due course. In postulating an inborn drive of this sort, I am not advancing a proposition to be proved or disproved but simply a model to be tried out for usefulness in simplifying our understanding of our observations.

The model I propose is consistent with observable evidence. In particular, the omnipresence of the phenomenon argues that we are dealing not with something socially or culturally based, but rather with a biological characteristic of the species. Furthermore, the need for periods of non-ordinary consciousness begins to be expressed at ages far too young for it to have much to do with social conditioning. Anyone who watches very young children without revealing his presence will find them regularly practicing techniques that induce striking changes in mental states. Three- and four-year-olds, for example, commonly whirl themselves into vertiginous stupors. They hyperventilate and have other children squeeze them around the chest until they faint. They also choke each other to produce loss of consciousness.

To my knowledge these practices appear spontaneously among children of all societies, and I suspect they have done so throughout history as well. It is most interesting that children quickly learn to keep this sort of play out of sight of grownups, who instinctively try to stop them. The sight of a child being throttled into unconsciousness scares the parent, but the child seems to have a wonderful time; at least, he goes right off and does it again. Psychologists have paid remarkably little attention to these activities of all children. Some Freudians have noted them and called them "sexual equivalents," suggesting that they are somehow related to the experience of orgasm.

But merely labeling a phenomenon does not automatically increase our ability to describe, predict, or influence it; besides, our understanding of sexual experience is too primitive to help us much.

Growing children engage in extensive experimentation with mental states, usually in the direction of loss of waking consciousness. Many of them discover that the transition zone between waking and sleep offers many possibilities for unusual sensations, such as hallucinations and out-of-the-body experiences, and they look forward to this period each night. (And yet, falling asleep becomes suddenly frightening at a later age, possibly when the ego sense has developed more fully. We will return to this point in a moment.) It is only a matter of time before children find out that similar experiences may be obtained chemically; many of them learn it before the age of five. The most common route to this knowledge is the discovery that inhalation of the fumes of volatile solvents in household products induces experiences similar to those caused by whirling or fainting. An alternate route is introduction to general anesthesia in connection with a childhood operation—an experience that invariably becomes one of the most vivid early memories.

By the time most American children enter school, they have already explored a variety of altered states of consciousness and usually know that chemical substances are one doorway to this fascinating realm. They also know that it is a forbidden realm, in that grownups will always attempt to stop them from going there if they catch them at it. But, as I have said, the desire to repeat these experiences is not mere whim; it looks like a real drive arising from the neurophysiological structure of the human brain. What, then, happens to it as the child becomes more and more involved in the process of socialization? In most cases, it goes underground. Children learn very quickly that they must pursue anti-social behavior patterns if they wish to continue to alter consciousness regularly. Hence, the secret meetings in cloakrooms, garages, and playground corners where they can continue to whirl, choke each other, and, perhaps, sniff cleaning fluids or gasoline.

As the growing child's sense of self is reinforced more and more by parents, school, and society at large, the drive to alter consciousness may go underground in the individual as well. That is, its indulgence becomes a very private matter, much like masturbation. Furthermore, in view of the overwhelming social pressure against such indulgence and the strangeness of the experiences from the point of view of normal, ego-centered consciousness, many children become quite frightened of episodes of non-ordinary awareness and very unwilling to admit their occurrence. The development of this kind of fear may account for the change from looking forward to falling asleep to being afraid of it; in many cases, it leads to repression of memories of the experiences.

Yet, co-existing with these emotional attitudes is always the underlying need to satisfy an inner drive. In this regard, the Freudian analogy to sexual experience seems highly pertinent. Like the cyclic urge to relieve sexual tension (which probably begins to be felt at much lower ages than many think), the urge to suspend ordinary awareness arises spontaneously from within, builds to a peak, finds relief, and dissipates all in accordance with its own intrinsic rhythm. The form of the appearance and course of this desire is identical to that of sexual desire. And the pleasure, in both cases, arises from relief of accumulated tension. Both experiences are thus self-validating; their worth is obvious in their own terms, and it is not necessary to justify them by reference to anything else. In other words, episodes of sexual release and episodes of suspension of ordinary consciousness feel good; they satisfy an inner need. Why they should feel good is another sort of question, which I will try to answer

toward the end of this chapter. In the meantime, it will be useful to keep in mind the analogy between sexual experience and the experience of altered consciousness (and the possibility that the former is a special case of the latter rather than the reverse).

Despite the accompaniment of fear and guilt, experiences of non-ordinary consciousness persist into adolescence and adult life, although awareness of them may diminish. If one takes the trouble to ask people if they have ever had strange experiences at the point of falling asleep, many adults will admit to hallucinations and feelings of being out of their bodies. Significantly, most will do this with a great sense of relief at being able to tell someone else about it and at learning that such experiences do not mark them as psychologically disturbed. One woman who listened to a lecture I gave came up to me afterward and said, "I never knew other people had things like that. You don't know how much better I feel." The fear and guilt that reveal themselves in statements of this sort doubtless develop at early ages and probably are the source of the very social attitudes that engender more fear and guilt in the next generation. The process is curiously circular and self-perpetuating.

There is one more step in the development of adult attitudes toward consciousness alteration. At some point (rather late, I suspect), children learn that social support exists for one method of doing it—namely, the use of alcohol—and that if they are patient, they will be allowed to try it. Until recently, most persons who reached adulthood in our society were content to drink alcohol if they wished to continue to have experiences of this sort by means of chemicals. Now, however, many young people are discovering that other chemicals may be preferable. After all, this is what drug users themselves say: that certain illegal substances give better highs than alcohol. This is a serious claim, worthy of serious consideration.

At this point, I would like to summarize the main ideas I have presented so far and then illustrate them with personal examples. We seem to be born with a drive to experience episodes of altered consciousness. This drive expresses itself at very early ages in all children in activities designed to cause loss or major disturbance of ordinary awareness. To an outside, adult observer, these practices seem perverse and even dangerous, but in most cases adults have simply forgotten their own identical experiences as children. As children grow, they explore many ways of inducing similar changes in consciousness and usually discover chemical methods before they enter school. Overwhelming social pressures against public indulgence of this need force children to pursue anti-social, secretive behavior patterns in their explorations of consciousness. In addition, the development of a strong ego sense in this social context often leads to fear and guilt about the desire for periods of altered awareness. Consequently, many youngsters come to indulge this desire in private or to repress it. Finally, older children come to understand that social support is available for chemical satisfaction of this need by means of alcohol. Today's youth, in their continuing experimentation with methods of changing awareness, have come across a variety of other chemicals which they prefer to alcohol. Thus, use of illegal drugs is nothing more than a logical continuation of a developmental sequence going back to early childhood. It cannot be isolated as a unique phenomenon of adolescence, of contemporary America, of cities, or of any particular social or economic class.

I feel confident about this developmental scheme for two reasons. First, I have seen it clearly in the histories of many hundreds of drug users I have interviewed and known. Second, I have experienced it myself. I was an avid whirler and could spend hours collapsed on the ground with the world spinning around—this despite the obvious unpleasant side effects of nausea, dizziness, and sheer exhaustion (the only aspects of the experience visible to grownups). From my point of view, these effects were incidental to a state of consciousness that was extraordinarily fascinating—more interesting than any other state except the one I entered at the verge of sleep. I soon found out that my spinning made grownups upset; I learned to do it with other neighborhood children in out-of-

the-way locations, and I kept it up until I was nine or ten. At about the age of four, like most members of my generation, I had my tonsils out, and the experience of ether anesthesia (administered by the old-fashioned open-drop method) remains one of my strongest memories of early life. It was frightening, intensely interesting, and intimately bound up with my thoughts about death. Some years later, I discovered that a particular brand of cleaning fluid in the basement of my house gave me a similar experience, and I sniffed it many times, often in the company of others my age. I could not have explained what I was doing to anyone; the experience was interesting rather than pleasant, and I knew it was important to me to explore its territory.

Alcohol was not forbidden in my home; I was even allowed occasional sips of cocktails or after-dinner cordials. Because I never liked the taste of alcohol, I was unable to understand why grownups drank it so often. I never connected it with my own chemical experiences. I did not discover a real alcohol high until I was a senior in high school; then, at age sixteen, it suddenly became clear to me that alcohol was another method, apparently a powerful one, of entering that interesting realm of consciousness. Soon, I fell into a pattern of weekend drinking parties, at which everybody consumed alcohol in order to get drunk. These highs were enjoyable for a time, but once their novelty wore off, I indulged in them for purely social reasons. Before long, I began to find the objective, physical effects of alcohol unpleasant and hard to ignore. I hardly knew of the existence of illegal drugs and would not have considered trying them. To me, marijuana was a narcotic used by criminals, and I had no idea why anyone would take amphetamines or opiates.

In the summer of 1960, just before I entered Harvard College as a freshman, I read an article in the Philadelphia *Evening Bulletin* about the death of a student at a southern California college, supposedly from an overdose of mescaline. He had been taking it "to get inspiration for papers in a creative-writing course." A paragraph from a recent paper was quoted—a visionary description of "galaxies of exploding colors." Mescaline was identified as an experimental drug, largely unknown, said to produce visions. My curiosity was aroused at once, and I resolved to devote my ingenuity to getting and trying mescaline.

At Harvard, excessive weekend consumption of alcohol by students and faculty was the rule rather than the exception, and I went along with the majority, even though the experience of being high on alcohol had long since ceased being interesting to me in my explorations of consciousness. Use of illegal drugs was non-existent except in a very submerged underground. I read everything I could find in scientific journals about mescaline, then came across Aldous Huxley's famous essay, *The Doors of Perception*. The little book convinced me that my intuitions about mescaline as something to be checked out were right. For example, I read:

. . . [mescaline] changes the quality of consciousness more profoundly and yet is less toxic than any other substance in the pharmacologist's repertory.[1]

And:

. . . it had always seemed to me possible that, through hypnosis, for example, or autohypnosis, by means of systematic meditation, or else by taking the appropriate drug, I might so change my ordinary mode of consciousness as to be able to know, from the inside, what the visionary, the medium, the mystic were talking about.[2]

Huxley made a convincing case that mescaline was the appropriate drug. Coincidentally, he appeared at the Massachusetts Institute of Technology that fall to give a series of Saturday lectures on visionary experience that were broadcast on the Harvard radio station. I listened carefully to Huxley's thesis that altered states of consciousness included the highest forms of human experience and that chemicals like mescaline were the most direct means of access.

That humanity at large will ever be able to dispense with Artificial Paradises seems very unlikely. Most men and women lead lives at the worst so painful, at the best so monotonous, poor, and lim-

ited, that the urge to escape, the longing to transcend themselves, if only for a few moments, is and has always been one of the principal appetites of the soul. Art and religion, carnivals and saturnalia, dancing and listening to oratory—all these have served, in H. G. Wells' phrase, as Doors in the Wall. And for private, for everyday use, there have always been chemical intoxicants. All the vegetable sedatives and narcotics, all the euphorics that grow on trees, the hallucinogens that ripen in berries or can be squeezed from roots—all, without exception, have been known and systematically used by human beings from time immemorial. And to these natural modifiers of consciousness, modern science has added its quota of synthetics. . . .[3]

As a project for David Riesman's course on American society, I began to write a long study of psychoactive drugs and social attitudes toward them. An instructor in the course suggested that I look up a psychologist, Timothy Leary, who, he thought, was actually doing research with hallucinogens. I first talked with Leary in his tiny office in the Center for Personality Research on Divinity Avenue. He spoke with sincerity, conviction, and enthusiasm about the potential of drugs like LSD, psilocybin, and mescaline. He envisioned a graduate seminar based on regular consumption of hallucinogens, alternating with intensive periods of analysis to identify and apply the insights gained while high. He predicted that within ten years everyone would be using the drugs "from kindergarten children on up." And he did not anticipate strong opposition by society. I asked whether I could be a subject in his psilocybin studies. He said no, he was sorry, but he had promised the university administration not to use undergraduates. He encouraged me to try to get mescaline, which he thought would be possible.

It took two months and only moderate ingenuity to obtain legally a supply of mescaline from an American chemical firm. Then seven other undergraduates and I began taking mescaline and evaluating our experiences with great care. A dozen experiences I had with the drug in 1961 (in half-gram doses) were highly varied. Most were nothing more than intensifications of preexisting moods with prominent periods of euphoria. Only a small percentage of the time did the sensory changes (such as constant motion of boundary lines and surfaces or vivid imagery seen with the eyes closed) seem worth paying much attention to. In a few instances, great intellectual clarity developed at the peak of the experience, and insights were gained that have had lasting importance. After a dozen trips (we called them "sessions"), I was able to see that much of the mescaline experience was not really so wonderful: the prolonged wakefulness, for example, and the strong stimulation of the sympathetic nervous system with resultant dilated eyes, cold extremities, and stomach butterflies. Yet, its potential for showing one good ways of interpreting one's own mind seemed enormous. Why was that potential realized so irregularly?

During the year that our drug ring operated out of Claverly Hall, I had a chance to watch perhaps thirty mescaline experiences of other undergraduates, and, again, what was most striking was the variability of these sessions. All of the experiences were mostly pleasant, with no bad reactions, but no two were alike, even in the same person. What we were seeing was also being noted by Leary and Alpert in their continuing studies with psilocybin. They gave the drug to large numbers of intellectuals, artists, alcoholics, prisoners, addicts, and graduate students; reported that the vast majority of the experiences were positive; and pointed out the importance of "set" and "setting" in determining the subject's reaction. Set is a person's expectations of what a drug will do to him, considered in the context of his whole personality. Setting is the environment, both physical and social, in which a drug is taken. Leary and Alpert were the first investigators of the hallucinogens to insist on the importance of these two variables. Without them, we are unable to explain simply why the drug varies so unpredictably in its psychic effects from person to person and from time to time in the same person. With these variables, the observations become suddenly clear; hence, the usefulness of the concept of set and setting.

I will discuss this concept and its implications when I talk about marijuana. At this point, I will merely note that the combined effects of set and setting can easily overshadow the pharmacological effects of a drug, as stated in a pharmacology text. One can arrange set and setting so that a dose of an amphetamine will produce sedation or a dose of a barbiturate, stimulation. The first time I tried mescaline, my set included so much anxiety (a roomful of people sat around watching to see what would happen) that I felt nothing whatever for four hours after swallowing the dose and, thereafter, only strong physical effects. There were simply no psychic effects to speak of. This phenomenon has been reported often with marijuana (which I did not try until two years later) and is of great significance, for it argues that the *experience* associated with use of a drug may not be as causally related to the drug as it appears to be.

It is not my purpose here to recount my drug experiences. I write of them to indicate that the route to mescaline, for me and others, was a highly logical one traceable back to earliest childhood. My desire to try mescaline, once I had learned of its existence, was as natural as my desire to whirl myself into dizziness, hallucinate while falling asleep, sniff cleaning fluid, or get drunk in high school. I did not take mescaline because I went to Harvard, met Timothy Leary, rebelled against my parents, was motivated, or sought escape from reality. I took it because I was a normal American teenager whose curiosity had survived thirteen years of American education. And it is instructive to note that the way mescaline first came to my attention was through a scare story in a newspaper describing a fatal reaction to the drug (a most improbable event, as it turns out).

Now, when I say that people take drugs in response to an innate drive to alter consciousness, I do not make any judgment about the taking of drugs. The drive itself must not be equated with the forms of its expression. Clearly, much drug taking in our country is negative in the sense that it is ultimately destructive to the individual and, therefore, to society. But this obvious fact says nothing about the intrinsic goodness or badness of altered states of consciousness or the need to experience them. Given the negativity of much drug use, it seems to me there are two possibilities to consider: (1) altered states of consciousness are inherently undesirable (in which case, presumably, the drive to experience them should be thwarted); or (2) altered states of consciousness are neither desirable nor undesirable of themselves but can take bad forms (in which case the drive to experience them should be channeled in some "proper" direction). Do we have enough evidence to make an intelligent choice between these possibilities?

Primarily, we need more information about altered states of consciousness. Altered from what? is a good first question. The answer is: from ordinary waking consciousness, which is "normal" only in the strict sense of "statistically most frequent"; there is no connotation of "good, " "worthwhile," or "healthy." Sleep and daydreaming are examples of altered states of consciousness, as are trance, hypnosis, meditation, general anesthesia, delirium, psychosis, mystic rapture, and the various chemical "highs." If we turn to psychology or medicine for an understanding of these states, we encounter a curious problem; Western scientists who study the mind tend to study the objective correlates of consciousness rather than consciousness itself. In fact, because consciousness is non-material, there has been great reluctance to accord it the reality of a laboratory phenomenon; psychologists, therefore, do not study consciousness directly, only indirectly, as by monitoring the physiological responses or brain waves of a person in a hypnotic trance or in meditation. Non-material things are considered inaccessible to direct investigation, if not altogether unreal. Consequently, there has been no serious attempt to study altered states of consciousness as such.

In the East, psychological science has taken a very different turn. Subjective states are considered more directly available for investigation than objective phenomena, which, after all, can only be perceived through our subjective states. Accordingly, an experiential science of consciousness has developed in the Orient, of which yoga is a magnificent example. It is a science as brilliantly articulated as Western conceptions of neurophysiology, but no attempt has been made to correlate it carefully with the physical realities of the nervous system as demonstrated by the West.

Therefore, Eastern science should be helpful in understanding altered states of consciousness, but it must always be checked against empirical knowledge of the objective nervous system. Now, one of the puzzling and unifying features of altered states of consciousness is their relative absence of physical correlates. For example, there are really no significant physiological differences between a hypnotized person and an unhypnotized person, or even any way of telling them apart, if the hypnotized subject is given appropriate suggestions for his behavior. As we shall see, the same holds true for the person high on marijuana—he is not readily distinguishable from one who is not high. Consequently, research as we know it in the West really cannot get much of a foothold in this area, and the scientific literature is dreadfully inadequate.

Nevertheless, I think it is possible to come to some useful conclusions about altered states of consciousness from what we can observe in ourselves and others. An immediate suggestion is that these states form some sort of continuum, in view of how much they have in common with each other. For example, trance, whether spontaneous or induced by a hypnotist, is simply an extension of the daydreaming state, in which awareness is focused and often directed inward rather than outward. Except for its voluntary and purposeful character, meditation is not easily distinguished from trance. Masters of meditation in Zen Buddhism warn their students to ignore *makyo*, sensory distortions that frequently resemble the visions of mystics or the hallucinations of schizophrenics. In other words, there is much cross-phenomenology among these states of consciousness, and, interestingly enough, being high on drugs has many of these same features, regardless of what drug induces the high.

The sense of physical lightness and timelessness so often reported by drug users is quite common in trance, meditation, and mystic rapture, for instance. Great ease of access to unconscious memories is also common in these states. Hypnotic subjects capable of sustaining deep trances can be "age regressed"—for example, made to reexperience their tenth birthday party. In deepest trances, awareness of present reality is obliterated, and the subject is amnesic for the experience when he returns to normal consciousness. In lighter trances, age-regressed subjects often have a sense of dual reality—the simultaneous experience of reliving the tenth birthday party, while also sitting with the hypnotist. Exactly the same experience is commonly reported by users of marijuana, who often find themselves spontaneously reliving unconscious memories as present realities; I have had this sense of dual reality myself on a number of occasions when I have been high on marijuana in settings that encouraged introspective reverie.

I want to underline the idea that these states form a continuum beginning in familiar territory. When we watch a movie and become oblivious to everything except the screen, we are in a light trance, in which the scope of our awareness has diminished but the intensity of it has increased. In the Oriental scientific literature, analogies are often drawn between consciousness and light: intensity increases, as scope decreases. In simple forms of concentration, like movie-watching or daydreaming, we do not become aware of the power of focused awareness, but we are doing nothing qualitatively different from persons in states of much more intensely focused consciousness where unusual phenomena are the rule. For example, total anesthesia sufficient for major surgery can occur in deep trance; what appears to happen is that the scope of awareness diminishes so much that the pain arising from the body falls outside it. The conscious experience of this state is that "the pain is there, but it's happening to someone else." (Patients given morphine sometimes report the same experience.) I have myself seen a woman have a baby by Caesarean section with no medication; hypnosis alone was used to induce anesthesia, and she remained conscious, alert, in no discomfort throughout the operation.

I have also seen yogis demonstrate kinds of control of their involuntary nervous systems that my medical education led me to believe were impossible. One that I met could make his heart go into an irregular pattern of beating called fibrillation at will and stop it at will. Such men ascribe their successes in this area solely to powers of concentration developed during regular periods of meditation. There is no need, I think, to point out the tremendous implications of these observations. Because we are unable to modify consciously the operations of a major division of our nervous system (the autonomic system), we are prey to many kinds of illnesses we can do nothing much about (cardiovascular diseases, for example). The possibility that one can learn to influence directly such "involuntary" functions as heart rate, blood pressure, blood flow to internal organs, endocrine secretions, and perhaps even cellular processes by conscious use of the autonomic nervous system, is the most exciting frontier of modern medicine. If, by meditation, a man can learn to regulate blood flow to his skin (I have seen a yogi produce a ten-degree-Fahrenheit temperature difference between right and left hands within one minute of getting a signal; the warmer hand was engorged with blood and dark red, the cooler hand was pale), there is no reason why he could not also learn to shut off blood flow to a tumor in his body and thus kill it.

Another chief characteristic of all these states is a major change in the sense of ego, that is, in awareness of oneself as a distinct entity. Thus, when we catch ourselves daydreaming, we wonder where we were for the past few minutes. Now, it is most interesting that many systems of mind development and many religions encourage their adherents to learn to "forget" themselves in precisely this sense. For example, in Zen archery (an application of Zen technique that can be used as a spiritual exercise) the meditating archer obliterates the distinction between himself and the bow; hitting the bull's eye with the arrow then becomes no more difficult than reaching out and touching it, and the shot is always a bull's eye. D. T. Suzuki, who brought Zen to the attention of the West, has written of this process: "The archer ceases to be conscious of himself as the one who is engaged in hitting the bull's eye which confronts him."[4] In fact, the ability to forget oneself as the doer seems to be the essence of mastery of any skill. And since the observing ego is the center of normal waking consciousness, the essence of mastery of any skill is the ability to forsake this kind of consciousness at will.

Furthermore, mystics from all religious traditions testify that this same loss of sense of self is an essential aspect of the highest of human experiences—an assertion the Christian might associate with Jesus' words: "Whoever loses his life for my sake will gain it."[5] In higher forms of yogic or Buddhist meditation, the aim is to focus consciousness on a single object or thought and then to erase all notion of anyone doing the meditation. Patanjali, the ancient writer who first codified and recorded the principles of the much more ancient science of yoga, wrote of *samadhi* (the highest state of consciousness envisioned in yoga): "When alone, the object of contemplation remains and one's own form is annihilated, this is known as *samadhi*."[6] *Samadhi* is a real experience that has been attained by many.

It is noteworthy that most of the world's highest religious and philosophic thought originated in altered states of consciousness in individuals (Gautama, Paul, Mohammed, etc.). It is also noteworthy that creative genius has long been observed to correlate with psychosis, and that intuitive genius is often associated with daydreaming, meditation, dreaming, and other non-ordinary modes of consciousness.

What conclusions can we draw from all this information? At the least, it would seem, altered states of consciousness have great potential for strongly positive psychic development. They appear to be the ways to more effective and fuller use of the nervous system, to development of creative and intellectual faculties, and to attainment of certain kinds of thought that have been deemed exalted by all who have experienced them.

So there is much logic in our being born with a drive to experiment with other ways of experiencing our perceptions, in particular to get away periodically from ordinary, ego-centered consciousness. It may even be a key factor in the present evolution of the human nervous system. But our immediate concern is the anxiety certain expressions of this drive are provoking in our own land, and we are trying to decide what to make of altered states of consciousness. Clearly, they are potentially valuable to us, not inherently undesirable, as in our first hypothesis. They are also not abnormal, in that they grade into states all of us have experienced. Therefore, to attempt to thwart this drive would probably be impossible and might be dangerous. True, it exposes the organism to certain risks, but ultimately it can confer psychic superiority. To try to thwart its expression in individuals and in society might be psychologically crippling for people and evolutionarily suicidal for the species. I would not want to see us tamper with something so closely related to our curiosity, our creativity, our intuition, and our highest aspirations.

If the drive to alter consciousness is potentially valuable and the states of altered consciousness are potentially valuable, then something must be channeling that drive in wrong directions for it to have negative manifestations in our society. By the way, I do not equate all drug taking with negative manifestations of the drive to alter consciousness. Drug use becomes negative or abusive only when it poses a serious threat to health or to social or psychological functioning. Failure to distinguish drug use from drug abuse—another unhelpful conception arising from emotional bias—has become quite popular, especially in federal government propaganda. The National Institute of Mental Health continues to label every person who smokes marijuana an abuser of the drug, thus creating an insoluble marijuana problem of enormous proportions. Professional, legal, and medical groups also contribute to this way of thinking. In fact, the American Medical Association has gone so far as to define drug abuse as any use of a "drug of abuse" without professional supervision—

an illustration of the peculiar logic necessary to justify conceptions based on emotional rather than rational considerations.

Certainly, much drug use is undesirable, despite the claims of drug enthusiasts, although this problem seems to me much less disturbing than the loss to individuals and to society of the potential benefits of consciousness alteration in positive directions. But let us not get ahead of ourselves. Our inquiry in this chapter is directed to the question of why people take drugs. I have tried to demonstrate that people take drugs because they are means of satisfying an inner need for experiencing other modes of consciousness and that whether the drugs are legal or illegal is an unimportant consideration. To answer the question most succinctly: people take drugs because they work.

Or, at least, they seem to.

Notes

1. Aldous Huxley, *The Doors of Perception* (New York: Perennial Library, 1970), pp. 9–10.

2. *Ibid.*, p. 14.

3. *Ibid.*, pp. 62–63.

4. D. T. Suzuki, Introduction to *Zen in the Art of Archery* by Eugene Herrigel (New York: Vintage Books, 1971), p. 10.

5. Matthew 16:26; compare Luke 10:24.

6. Patanjali, *Yoga Aphorisms* III:3, quoted by James Hewitt in *A Practical Guide to Yoga* (New York: Funk and Wagnalls, 1968), p. 146. Further commentary on this aphorism may be found in *How to Know God: The Yoga Aphorisms of Patanjali*, translated by Swami Prabhavananda and Christopher Isherwood (New York: Signet Books, 1969), pp. 122–123.

For Discussion

If drug use can result from the natural desire to alter one's consciousness, why do we punish drug offenders for something over which they have little control?

Reprinted from: Andrew Weil, "Why People Take Drugs" in *The Natural Mind*, pp. 17–38. Copyright © 1972, 1986 by Andrew Weil. Reprinted by permission of Houghton Mifflin Company. ✦

2

A Sociological Theory of Drug Addiction[1]

Alfred R. Lindesmith

Various theories have been developed to explain drug use and addiction. Current explanations are grounded in the sociological, psychological, or biological sciences. Some theories are interdisciplinary in that they seek to combine two or more of these perspectives. Regardless of where they originate, theories of addiction are important in that they contribute to our understanding of the causal factors that lead to drug dependence. If we are able to identify the causal processes, we are in a better position to develop social policies and treatment initiatives that can serve addicts more effectively.

In this essay, dating back to 1938, the late Alfred R. Lindesmith criticizes the psychiatric explanation of opiate addiction. Psychiatrists, he argues, attach moral labels (e.g., "psychopaths") to addicts and assume that the continued use of opiates results from the addict's need to "escape from life." Although Lindesmith recognizes that users experience euphoria during their early stages of narcotics use, he disagrees with psychiatrists' assertions that the continuous use of opiate drugs is always for the sake of a "high." His sociological theory assumes that opiate addiction results from the conscious awareness that continued drug use is necessary to eliminate or prevent the pain associated with opiate withdrawal. Addicts do not use opiates to escape from life; rather, they do so to avoid withdrawal.

The problem of drug addiction has been an important one in this country for several decades and has proved to be a difficult one to handle from a theoretical, as well as from a therapeutic, standpoint. In spite of more than a half-century of experimentation with "cures," the drug addict has continued to relapse and thereby aroused the wonder and ire of those who have attempted to treat him. It has frequently been said that the drug user cannot be cured "if he doesn't want to be cured"; but this appears to beg the question, for it is the very essence of addiction that the victim desires to use the drug—and also, at the same time, desires to be free of it. An indication of the strength of the addict's attachment to his drug is furnished by the fact that when the Japanese government in 1929 permitted unregistered opium-smokers in Formosa to register and gave them the choice of applying for either a cure or a license, only thirty out of approximately twenty-five thousand asked for the cure.[2]

Current explanations of the drug habit appear to center about a few general conceptions and modes of approach, none of which have led to convincing results. Psychiatrists have often regarded the use of opiates as an escape from life and have viewed addicts as defective persons seeking to compensate for, or avoid, their inferiorities and mental conflicts.[3] As would be expected, addicts have been labeled as "psychopaths," with the assumption that the attachment of this ambiguous label in some mysterious way explained the phenomenon. Various statements, as to the percentage of defective persons among addicts, have not been accompanied by any comparison with the percentage of defective persons in the general, non-addicted population. In fact, the need or desirability of this sort of comparison does not seem to have occurred to the majority of these writers.

This point of view contrasts the "psychopath," who is assumed to be susceptible to addiction, with "normal" persons, who are presumed by implication to be immune, or, if they accidentally become addicted, they are said to quit and remain free. No evidence has been produced, however, which indicates that any but an exceedingly small percentage of addicts ever remain free of the drug for long periods of years,[4] and no "normal" person has ever been shown to be immune to the subtle influence of the drug. It appears from an examination of the literature that all "normal" persons who have been foolhardy enough to imagine themselves immune and have consequently experimented upon themselves and taken the drug steadily for any length of time, have become addicts, or "junkers," as they usually style themselves.[5] The contention that any type of person can be readily cured of the drug habit in a permanent sense is without any support in terms of actual evidence. We have found that narcotic agents and others who are in close contact with the actual problem ordinarily acquire a wholesome fear of the drug and do not delude themselves concerning their own capacity to resist its influence.

A French medical student,[6] in the course of writing a thesis on morphine, decided to experiment upon himself. For five consecutive days, he took an injection each evening at about nine o'clock. He reported that after three or four injections he began to desire the next ones, and that it cost him a decided effort to refrain from using it the sixth night. He managed to carry out his plan, but clearly implied that, if he had continued the experiment for a short time longer, he believed that he would have become addicted. The addict, in his opinion, is *un homme perdu*, who is rarely able ever again to retain his freedom. This account constitutes an interesting document for the individual who believes that he or anyone else is immune to addiction by reason of a superabundance of will-power or because of an absence of psychopathy. In 1894, Mattison advised the physician as follows:

> Let him not be blinded by an underestimate of the poppy's power to ensnare. Let him not be deluded by an over-confidence in his own strength to resist; for along this line, history has repeated itself with sorrowful frequency, and—as my experience will well attest—on these two treacherous rocks hundreds of promising lives have gone awreck.[7]

Sir William Willcox states:

> We know people who say: "I am a man, and one having a strong will. Morphine or heroin will not affect me; I can take it as long as I like without becoming an addict." I have known people—sometimes medical men—who have made that boast, and without exception they have come to grief.[8]

The conception of opiates as affording an escape from life also does not appear to be satisfactory or correct in view of the well-known fact that the addict invariably claims that all the drug does is to cause him to feel "normal." It is generally conceded that the euphoria associated with the use of opiates is highly transitory in character, and, while it is true that during the initial few weeks of use the drug may cause pleasure in some cases and may function as a means of escape, still, when addiction is established, this no longer holds true. The drug addict, who is supposed to derive some mysterious and uncanny pleasure from the drug, not only fails to do so as a rule but is also keenly aware of the curse of addiction and struggles to escape it. Far from being freed from his problems, he is actually one of the most obviously worried and miserable creatures in our society.

Finally, we may call attention to the fact that the current conception of the addict as a "psychopath," escaping from his own defects by the use of the drug, has the serious defect of being admittedly inapplicable to a certain percentage of cases. L. Kolb, for example, finds that 86 percent of the addicts included in a study of his had defects antedating and presumably, explaining the addiction. One may, therefore, inquire how addiction is to be explained in the other 14 percent of the cases. Are these persons addicts, because they are free from defects? The assumption is sometimes made that those in whom defects cannot be found have secret defects which explain the addiction. Such an assumption obviously places the whole matter beyond the realm of actual research. Moreover, one may ask, who among us does not have defects of one kind or another, secret or obvious?

In general, it appears that the conception of the drug addict as a defective psychopath prior to addiction is more in the nature of an attempt to place blame than it is an explanation of the matter. It is easy and cheap to designate as "inferior" or "weak" or "psychopathic" persons whose vices are different from our own and whom we consequently do not understand.[9] Similarly, the "causes" of addiction as they are often advanced—"curiosity," "bad associates," and the "willingness to try anything once"—suffer from the same moralistic taint. Undoubtedly, these same factors "cause" venereal disease; yet, science has ceased to be concerned with them. In the case of drug addiction, we still are more interested in proving that it is the addict's "own fault" that he is an addict than we are in understanding the mechanisms of addiction.

It was noted long ago that not all persons, to whom opiate drugs were administered for sufficiently long periods of time to produce the withdrawal symptoms, became addicts. It frequently occurs in medical practice that severe and chronic pain makes the regular administration of opiates a necessity.[10] Some of the persons who are so treated show no signs of the typical reactions of addicts and may even be totally ignorant of what they are being given. Others to whom the drug is administered in this way return to it when it has been withdrawn, and become confirmed addicts. This fact caused German and French students of the problem to adopt distinct terms for the two conditions—those who received the drug for therapeutic reasons and who showed none of the symptoms of the typical "craving" of addicts were spoken of as cases of "chronic morphine poisoning," or "morphinism"; whereas, addicts in the ordinarily accepted sense of the word were called "morphinomanes" or, in German, *Morphiumsüchtiger*.[11]

Attempts have been made to introduce such a usage in this country, though without success, and it is consequently awkward to try to refer to these two conditions. In this paper, the term "habituated" will be used to refer to the development of the mere physiological tolerance; whereas, the term "addiction" will be reserved for application to cases in which there is added to the physiological or pharmacological tolerance a psychic addiction, which is marked by the appearance of an imperious desire for the drug and leads to the development of the other characteristic modes of behavior of the drug addict, as he is known in our society. For persons who are merely habituated to the drug without being addicted, there is no need for special conceptual treatment any more than persons who have had operations need to be set off as a distinct class. Once the drug has been removed, these persons show no craving for it or any tendency to resume its use, unless, perhaps, the disease for which the opiate was originally given reappears.

Any explanation of the causation of drug addiction must attempt to account for this fact, that not all persons who are given opiates become addicts. What are the factors which cause one man to escape, while the next, under what appear to be the same physiological conditions, becomes an incurable addict? Obviously, the factor of the patient's knowledge of what he is being given is an important one, for clearly, if he is ignorant of the name of the drug, he will be unable to ask for it or consciously to desire it. The recognition of the importance of keeping the patient in ignorance of what drugs he is being given is quite general. Various devices which serve this end, such as giving the drug orally rather than hypodermically, keeping it out of the hands of the patient and permitting no self-administration, mixing the dosage of opiates with other drugs whose effects are not so pleasant and which serve to disguise the effects of the opiate, etc., have been advocated and have become more or less routine practice. But in some cases, individuals who are fully aware that they are receiving morphine (or some other opium alkaloid) may also not become addicted, even after prolonged administration.[12] Other factors, besides ignorance of the drug administered, must therefore operate to prevent the occurrence of addiction in such cases. What seems to account for this variability—and this is the crux of the theory being advanced—is not the knowledge of the drug administered, but the knowledge of the true significance of the withdrawal symptoms when they appear and the use of the drug thereafter for the consciously understood motive of avoiding these symptoms.[13] As far as can be determined, there is no account in the literature of anyone's ever having experienced the full severity of the withdrawal symptoms in complete knowledge of their connection with the absence of the opiate drug, who has not also become an addict. Addiction begins when the person suffering from withdrawal symptoms realizes that a dose of the drug will dissipate all his discomfort and misery. If he then tries it out and actually feels the almost magical relief that is afforded, he is on the way to confirmed addiction. The desire for the drug, and the impression that it is necessary, apparently become fixed with almost incredible rapidity, once this process of using the drug to avoid the abstinence symptoms has begun. Among confirmed addicts, it appears to be the general rule also that those who have the greatest difficulty in obtaining regular supplies of narcotics ("boot and shoe dope fiends") are precisely those who develop the most intense craving for it and use it to excess when the opportunity presents itself. In other words, deprivation is the essential factor both in the origin of the craving and in its growth.

In order to prove the correctness of the theory advanced, it is necessary to consider, first, its applicability to the general run of cases—that is, to determine whether or not addicts become addicted in any other way than through the experience with withdrawal—and whether there are non-addicts, in whom all of the conditions or causes of addiction have occurred without actually producing addiction. We do not have the space here to go into an extended analysis and explanation of any large number of cases. We can only state that, from our analysis of the cases that have come to our attention, both directly and in the literature, it appears to be true without exception that addicts do, in fact, become addicted in this manner and that addiction does invariably follow whenever the drug is used for the conscious purpose of alleviating withdrawal distress. That this is the case is strikingly brought out by the addict's own argot. The term "hooked" is used by drug users to indicate the fact that a person has used the drug long enough so

that, if he attempts to quit, withdrawal distress will force him to want to go on using the drug. At the same time, "to be hooked" means to be addicted, and anyone who has ever been "hooked" is forever after classified by himself, as well as by other addicts, as belonging to the in-group, as an addict, a "user" or "junker," regardless of whether he is using the drug at the moment or not.[14] Similarly, a person who has not been "hooked," regardless of whether he is using the drug or not, is not classified as an addict.[15] It is a contradiction in terms of addict argot, therefore, to speak of "a junker who has never been hooked" or of an individual who has been "hooked" without becoming an addict. Addict argot admits no exceptions to this rule. We found that drug users invariably regard any query about a hypothetical addict who has not been compelled to use the drug by the withdrawal distress, or about a hypothetical non-addict who has, as incomprehensible nonsense. To them, it is self-evident that to be "hooked" and to be an addict are synonymous.[16]

As we have indicated, our own experience is in entire accord with this view of the addict, as it is crystallized in his vernacular. In addition, we have found certain types of cases which bear more directly upon the theory and which offer conclusive and, we may say, experimental verification of the theory. It is upon cases of this type which we wish to concentrate our attention.

Crucial instances which strongly corroborate the hypothesis are those cases in which the same person has first become habituated to the use of the drug over a period of time and then had the drug withdrawn without becoming addicted; and then, later in life, under other circumstances, become a confirmed addict. Erwin Strauss[17] records the case of a woman:

[W]ho received morphine injections twice daily for six months, from February to July of 1907, on account of gall stones. After her operation in July, the drug was removed and the patient did not become an addict[18] but went about her duties as before, until 1916, nine years later, when her only son was killed at the Front. She was prostrated by her grief and, after intense anguish and thoughts of suicide, she thought of the morphine which had been administered to her nine years before. She began to use it, found it helpful, and soon was addicted. *What is particularly noteworthy is that, when asked if she had suffered any withdrawal symptoms when the drug was withdrawn the first time in 1907, she stated that she could not recall any.* [Italics are mine.]

Another case of the same kind was interviewed by the writer.

A man, Dr. H., was given morphine regularly for a considerable period of time when he underwent three operations for appendicitis with complications. He was not expected to live. As he recovered, the dosage of morphine was gradually reduced and completely withdrawn without any difficulty. Although the patient suffered some discomfort during the process and knew that he had been receiving morphine, he attributed this discomfort to the processes of convalescence. Dr. H. had occasion to see drug addicts in his medical practice and had always felt a horror of addiction and had sometimes thought he would rather shoot himself than be one. This attitude of horror remained unaltered during the hospital experience just related. Several years later, Dr. H. contracted gall-stone trouble and was told that an operation would be necessary. Opiates were administered, and Dr. H., who wished to avoid another operation at all costs, administered opiates to himself, hoping that the operation might not be necessary. He began to use the drug for pains of less and less significance, until he found himself using it every day. He became apprehensive during this process, but reasoned with himself that there was nothing to be alarmed about, inasmuch as drug addiction was certainly not the horrible thing it was supposed to be and he was certain that he would have no difficulty in quitting. His horror of addiction disappeared. When he attempted to quit, he found that it was more difficult than he had supposed. He, of course, noticed the regular recurrence of the withdrawal illness and *then realized in retrospect that he had experienced the same symptoms, without recognizing them, several years before.* [Italics are mine.]

A third case of the same kind is briefly mentioned by Dansauer and Rieth,[19] and two others have come to the attention of the writer. Obviously, the number of instances in which a coincidence of this kind is likely to occur is very small, but those that have been found, unequivocally and without exception, indicate that, if morphine is withdrawn carefully, without the patient's recognizing or noticing the symptoms of abstinence, no craving for the drug develops. The typical phenomena which signalize addiction, such as the tendency to increase the dose inordinately, to exhibit and feel a powerful desire to obtain the drug at any cost, and to be unhappy without it—these phenomena do not put in their appearance, until the patient has discovered that there are withdrawal symptoms of a persistent severe character and has used the drug for a time, solely or chiefly to prevent these symptoms from appearing. In the argot of the addict, when this has occurred, the person is "hooked"; he "has a habit." If he quits before it occurs or if he resolutely refrains from using the drug to alleviate the abstinence symptoms the first time he experiences them, he may still escape. If the symptoms occur in their full intensity, however, the impulse to seek relief in the drug, when it is known that only the drug will give relief, is irresistible—especially since the patient is not likely to realize that the danger of addiction is present. He thinks only of the fact that he can obtain relief from those terrible symptoms, which, to the uninitiated, may be genuinely terrifying.

As an illustration of the process of the establishment of addiction which we are attempting to isolate, another case of a man who became addicted in medical practice may be cited.

Mr. G. was severely lacerated and internally injured as the result of an accident. He spent thirteen weeks in a hospital, during which time he received frequent doses of morphine, some hypodermically and some orally. He paid no attention to what it was that was being used on him and felt no effects of any unusual character, except that the medicine to some extent relieved him of pain. He was discharged from the hospital and, after several hours, began to develop considerable discomfort and irritability and the other symptoms of morphine withdrawal. He had no idea what was the matter. In about twelve hours, he was violently nauseated and, during his first night at home, called his family physician in at two o'clock in the morning, fearing that he was about to die. The physician also was not certain what was wrong, but gave him some mild sedatives and attempted to encourage him. The violence of the symptoms increased during the next day, to such an extent that Mr. G. began to wish that he would die. During the course of the second night, the family physician decided that he was perhaps suffering from withdrawal of opiates and gave Mr. G. an injection of morphine to find out. The effect was immediate; in about twenty minutes, Mr. G. fell asleep and slept on in perfect comfort for many hours. He still did not know what he had been given, but when he woke up the next day the doctor told him and said, "Now we are going to have a time getting you off!" The dosage was reduced and in a week or two the drug was entirely removed, but Mr. G., during this short time, had become addicted. After the drug had been removed for a few days, he bought himself a hypodermic syringe and began to use it by himself.[20]

It may seem surprising, at first glance, that many addicts do not know what is wrong with them the first time that the abstinence symptoms occur. This is not difficult to understand when one realizes that many persons seem to think that withdrawal symptoms are purely imaginative or hysterical in character. Even in spite of the occurrence of these symptoms in animals, which have been subjected to the prolonged administration of opiates, and in spite of their occurrence in patients who have no idea what opiates are or that they have been given any, students of drug addiction have sometimes asserted that these symptoms have no physiological basis. In view of this belief among the instructed, it is easy to understand the layman who believes the same thing when he begins to experiment with the drug. Furthermore, there is nothing whatever in the initial effects of the drug to furnish the slightest

clue as to what happens later. As the use of the drug is continued, in the same proportion that tolerance appears, and the positive effects diminish, the withdrawal symptoms increase, until they obtrude themselves upon the attention of the individual, and finally become dominant. In most cases of confirmed addiction, the drug appears to serve almost no other function than that of preventing the appearance of these symptoms.

One of the most difficult features of addiction to account for, by means of any explanation of the drug habit in terms of the positive effects, or euphoria, supposed to be produced by it, is the fact that during the initial period of use there takes place a gradual reversal of effect, so that the effects of the drug upon an addict are not only not the same as their effects upon a non-addicted person, but they are actually, in many respects, the precise opposite.[21] This is true both of the physiological and of the psychological effects. The initial dose causes one to feel other than normal; whereas in the case of the addict, the usual dose causes him to feel normal when he would feel below normal without it. The euphoria initially produced by the drug has often been emphasized as a causative factor, but inasmuch as this euphoria, or "kick," disappears in addiction, the continuation of the drug habit cannot be explained in this way.[22] Moreover, when administered therapeutically to allay pain, there is often absolutely no euphoria produced even in the initial period, and the patient may nevertheless become addicted. In fact, it is possible for a person to be unconscious during the entire initial stage when tolerance is established and still become addicted, as a consideration of the implications of the case of Mr. G. shows. It is this reversal of effect which accounts at one and the same time for the seductive aspect of opiates, as well as for their insidiousness. As they cease to produce pleasure, they become a necessity and produce pain if removed. The euphoria produced by the drug at first makes it easy to become addicted, but does not account for the continuance of the habit when the euphoria is gone. A theory which makes the withdrawal distress central in addiction takes account of this reversal of effects.

It follows, if one believes that the drug habit is to be accounted for on the basis of the extraordinary or uncanny state of mind it is sometimes supposed to produce, that addicts should be able to recognize such effects immediately and easily. It is a notorious fact, however, and one that baffles the addicts, as well as those who study them, that under certain conditions the drug user may be completely deceived for varying periods of time into believing that he is receiving opiates, when he actually is not, or that he is not receiving any when, as a matter of fact, he is. We shall not elaborate this point any more than to call attention to the fact that it has been put into practice as a principle in a number of gradual reduction cures, wherein, without the addict's knowledge, the amount of the drug was gradually reduced and finally withdrawn entirely, while injections of water or a saline solution were continued.[23] Then, when the addict had been free of opiates for several days, or a week, or even more, he was told that he had not been getting any of his drug for some time and usually discharged, sometimes in the vain hope that this experience might prove to him that it was only his "imagination" which led him to think he needed his drug! The fact that such a thing is possible is evidence that the direct positive effects per se are not sufficiently extraordinary to make addiction intelligible.

The tendency of the addict to relapse may be readily explained in terms of the viewpoint outlined as arising from the impression that is made upon him when he observes the remarkable and immediate effects the drug has in dissipating unpleasant physical or mental states. What the addict misses when he is off the drug is not so much the hypothetical euphoria as the element of control. On the drug, he could regulate his feeling tone; when he is not using it, it appears to him that he is the passive victim of his environment or of his changing moods. During the initial period of use, the only effects of an injection to which attention is paid are ordinarily the immediate ones lasting but a few minutes or, at most, a half-hour or an hour or so. This episodic significance of injections changes into a continuous

twenty-four-hour-a-day sense of dependence upon the drug only after the addict has learned from the recurrence of the beginnings of withdrawal symptoms, as the effects of each shot wore off, that the drug was necessary to the continuance of his well-being. He learns to attribute effects to the "stuff," which are in part imaginary—or rather, projections of the need for it which he feels. When he is off, every vicissitude of life tends to remind him of his drug, and he misses the supporting and sustaining sense of its presence. And so, the ordinary pleasures of life are dulled, something seems to be amiss, and the unhappy addict eventually relapses—either deliberately or otherwise. If he does not relapse, it appears that he nevertheless remains susceptible to it for long periods of years. Cases of relapse after as long as ten or more years of abstinence are recorded.[24]

The thesis of the paper is that addiction to opiate drugs is essentially based upon the abstinence symptoms which occur when the effects of the drug are beginning to wear off rather than upon any positive effects or uncanny or extraordinarily pleasurable state of mind erroneously supposed to be produced by the drug in continued use. Addiction is established in the first instance in a process involving:

1. The interpretation of the withdrawal symptoms as being caused by the absence of opiates. . . .[25]

2. The use of the drug for the consciously understood purpose of alleviating these symptoms or of keeping them suppressed.

As a result of this process there is established in the addict the typical desire for the drug, a constant sense of dependence upon it, and the other attendant features of addiction. The attitudes which arise in this experience persist when the drug has been removed and predispose toward relapse. When the point is reached at which withdrawal symptoms intrude themselves upon the attention of the individual and compel him to go on using the drug, he also has forced upon him the unwelcome definition of himself as a "dope fiend." He realizes then what the craving for drugs means and, applying to his own conduct the symbols which the group applies to it, he is compelled to readjust his conception of himself to the implications of this collective viewpoint. He struggles against the habit and then eventually accepts his fate and becomes "just another junker." Obviously, when the withdrawal distress has entered into the conscious motives of the person, and he realizes that he must anticipate the recurrence of these terrible symptoms, if he does not assure himself of a supply of the drug, and when the definition of self as an addict has occurred, the drug user becomes ripe for assimilation into the culture of drug addiction, as it exists chiefly in our underworld.

The proposed theory has advantages and implications beyond those already mentioned. It is applicable in form to all cases and, as indicated, an extensive exploration of the literature, as well as many interviews with addicts, has so far failed to uncover a single negative case, even of a hearsay type. Moreover, it harmonizes and rationalizes various aspects of the habit which have often been regarded as paradoxical or contradictory in character—as, for example, the fact that addicts claim they do not obtain pleasure from the drug, the initial reversal of effects, and the strange tendency of addicts to relapse when, from a medical standpoint, they appear to be cured.

A number of further implications of the point of view presented seem to have important bearings on certain theories of social psychology and of sociology. Thus, students of the writings of George H. Mead will notice that the hypothesis follows the lines of his theory of the "significant symbols" and its role in human life. According to the view presented, the physiological effects of the drug do not become effective in influencing the psychic and social life of the person, until he has applied to them the "significant symbols" (or perhaps, in Durkheimian language, "collective representations") which are employed by the group to describe the nature of these effects. Addiction, in other words, appears as a process which goes on, on the level of "significant symbols"—it is, in other words, peculiar to man living in organized society in communication with his fellows.[26]

This theory rationalizes and explains the reasons for the ordinary rules-of-thumb employed in the therapeutic administration of morphine to prevent addiction. Some of these rules and practices include (1) keeping the patient in ignorance of the drug being used, (2) mixing other drugs with different and less pleasing effects with the opiate, (3) varying the mode of administration and disguising the drug in various kinds of medicines. The significance of these practices appears to be that they prevent the patient from attributing to morphine the effects which it in fact produces—in other words, they prevent the patient from applying certain collective symbols to his own subjective states, prevent the whole experience from being associated with the patient's preconceptions of drug addiction, and so prevent addiction.

The proposed hypothesis has the further advantage of being essentially experimental in character, in the sense that it is open to disproof, as, for example, by anyone who doubts it and is willing or foolhardy enough to experiment on himself with the drug. As has been indicated, the writer has been unable to find any record in the literature of an experiment of this character which, prolonged enough to be a test—that is, which lasted long enough so that the withdrawal distress upon stoppage of the drug was pronounced—did not result in addiction. This appears to constitute an exception to what is often assumed to be true of knowledge in the field of the social sciences—namely, that it confers, *ipso facto*, the ability to control. It is in accord with the well-known fact that addiction to narcotic drugs is peculiarly prevalent in those legitimate professions in which theoretical knowledge of these drugs is most general—that is, in the medical and allied professions.

A further significant implication of the viewpoint presented is that it offers a means of relating phenomena of a purely physiological variety to cultural or sociological phenomena. The interpretation of withdrawal distress, which we have emphasized as a basic factor in the beginning of addiction, is, it should be emphasized, a cultural pattern, a social interpretation present in a formulated fashion in the social milieu exactly like other knowledge or beliefs. When the organic disturbances produced by the withdrawal of the drug intrude themselves upon the attention of a person, they impede his functioning and assume the nature of a problem, demanding some sort of rationalization and treatment. The culture of the group supplies this rationalization by defining the situation for the individual and, in so doing, introduces into the motives and conceptions which determine his conduct other factors which lead to addiction whenever the drug is continued beyond the point at which this insight occurs.

Finally, we should like to emphasize again the methodological implications of the study. A great deal of argumentation has taken place in sociology on the matter of methodology—whether universal generalizations are possible or not, concerning the role of statistical generalizations and of quantification generally, and concerning the so-called case method. Most of these arguments have tended to take place on an abstract level; whereas, it would seem that in the final analysis, they can be settled only in terms of actual results of research. We, therefore, regard it as significant that the theory advanced in this study is not quantitative in form, nor is it a purely intuitive generalization which is not subject to proof, but that it is experimental in form, in spite of the fact that it is based upon the analysis of data secured largely in personal interviews. It is, moreover, stated in universal form and is, therefore, not dependent upon or relative to a particular culture or a particular time. As such, it provides the possibility of its own continuous reconstruction and refinement, in terms of more extended experience and of more elaborated instances. In other words, it provides a place for the exceptional or crucial case, which George H. Mead has described as the "growing point of science."[27]

Comment

The writer does not state whether his study relates to any one form of drug addiction, but it seems he is concerned chiefly, if not solely, with morphine addiction. At least, he discusses addiction in which withdrawal symptoms are prominent, and so his theory does not seem to apply to types of addiction, such as cocaine, hasheesh, and others, in which withdrawal symptoms are absent or of a minor nature.

It is stated that "addiction begins when the person suffering from withdrawal symptoms realizes that a dose of the drug will dissipate all his discomfort and misery." And, furthermore: "If he fails to realize the connection between the distress and the opiate, he escapes addiction." How often does this occur? Conceivably, in some patients who have received such drugs to alleviate pain or as sedatives. But we presume that the author does not intend to suggest that many drug addicts are established in the course of medical treatment. Apart from such cases, may we not consider that an individual who persists in securing drugs and administering them to himself, until he is likely to suffer withdrawal symptoms of any degree, is in fact already an addict? And that withdrawal symptoms are then a complication in the course of drug addiction, dependent on the fact that tolerance for the drug has been acquired? But that does not explain why the individual became an addict, although it might be offered as a reason for the difficulty in giving up the addiction, if he so desires or is requested. We would again recall the forms of drug addiction, in which there are few or no withdrawal symptoms.

The cases quoted by the author as crucial for the corroboration of his hypothesis are not convincing. The case quoted from Strauss does not seem to lend any support to the hypothesis. This woman did not become an addict because of withdrawal symptoms, but in an effort to secure relief from a state of acute mental depression. As the case report states: "She began to use it, found it helpful, and soon was addicted." When it is stated that persons may relapse "after as long as ten or more years of abstinence," then surely the renewal of addiction is not due to withdrawal symptoms.

Throughout the paper, there are several statements which call for comment. Thus, it is said that current theories of drug addiction tend to be moralistic, rather than scientific. This does not seem a correct interpretation of the many physiological and psychiatric studies on the subject. Again, references should be given for the statement—in regard to the nature of withdrawal symptoms—that "students of drug addiction have sometimes asserted that these symptoms have no physiological basis." It is stated that "the victim desires to use the drug—and also at the same time desires to be free of it." In what proportion of cases? Too often, one has found the addict seeking a "cure" with the aim of having his tolerance cut down because of financial difficulties, or because the dosage was too high for practical purposes. The author talks of "the drug," but experience with drug addicts shows so often that they have been addicted to several drugs, depending on available supplies and, after a period of abstinence through failure of supplies, would start in afresh on drugs of which they had no previous experience. What were they seeking, if not some form of satisfaction or pleasure or relief from a state of emotional distress or difficulty of life?

One cannot pass over a striking statement: "This appears to constitute an exception to what is often assumed to be true of knowledge in the field of the social sciences—namely, that it confers, *ipso facto*, the ability to control." We are reminded of the musings of one, Burns, who had knowledge but had not always the ability to control—and had knowledge of that also. Thus, in the "Unco Guid, or the Rigidly Righteous":

One point must still be greatly dark,
The moving why they do it;
And just as lamely can ye mark
How far perhaps they rue it.

Rejoinder

Comment section by:
David Slight
Department of Psychiatry
University of Chicago

A considerable portion of Dr. Slight's comments are based upon an implicit conception of method which is fundamentally different from our own. We assume, and stated in our article, that a scientific expla-

nation must be stated in terms of factors or processes which are present in all the members of the class to which the generalization is supposed to apply. There is no evidence in Dr. Slight's comments that he has taken any account of this principle, and it is for this reason that he has failed to discuss the main issues. When he asserts, concerning the case given by Strauss, "This woman did not become an addict because of withdrawal symptoms, but in an effort to secure relief from a state of acute mental depression," he does not take into account a fact which is known to all—that many addicts begin to use the drug under circumstances which have no connection whatever with "mental distress." Some addicts, for example, first tried the drug in connection with a sex affair with a prostitute, and others first learn about the drug in medical practice. One may also ask if it would not be reasonable to suppose that the woman in this case experienced mental depression at some time during her six-month attack of disease nine years before she became an addict? Why did she not become addicted then? Dr. Slight does not touch this problem.

In the sentence beginning "Apart from such cases . . ." Dr. Slight appears to imply either that no addicts are created in medical practice or that, if they are, they should be excluded from the argument. Medical practice today does create new addicts—not many, but some. They are addicts in precisely the same sense as others are, and any generalization must include them. Concerning the latter part of this same sentence, we may say for a rather large percentage even of addicts on the street that the withdrawal symptoms are not at first understood. This was true in about 50 percent of our cases. A number of them had to have the symptoms explained to them by addicts or by doctors.

The implication that knowledge of the drug being given and of the withdrawal symptoms is irrelevant, and that the sheer brute fact of having used the drug long enough to produce withdrawal symptoms in itself constitutes addiction is directly contradicted in medical practice itself. The patient who is given morphine in hospitals is kept in ignorance of what is happening to him, and this is done for the explicit purpose of preventing addiction. Medical men quite generally maintain that this practice has, in fact, been very effective. Several decades ago, when such techniques were not as widely employed, medical practice did, in fact, create many new addicts.

The principle that an explanation must be applicable to *all*, rather than to some, of the cases is again ignored when he asks, "What are they [the addicts] seeking if not some form of satisfaction or pleasure or relief from a state of emotional distress or difficulty in life?" This view is simply the current common-sense misconception of the problem, and it explains nothing. It entirely ignores those cases in which addiction is a consequence of the sheer accident of disease. In terms of this view, how is one to account for continued addiction in that group of addicts for whom the major "emotional distress or difficulty in life" is the addiction itself?

The questions of fact which Dr. Slight raises cause us to wonder where he obtained the information upon which he bases his statements. He is correct when he surmises that we were concerned only with opiate addiction, but he repeatedly refers to the use of other drugs and says that addicts shift readily from one drug to another, depending upon available supply. This is incorrect. Opiate addicts shift only from one opiate to another. Chicago addicts use mainly heroin, for which they may pay as much as two hundred dollars an ounce. As a consequence, they cannot afford to use other drugs, and very few do. If an addict is utterly unable to obtain an opiate, he does only one thing—he "kicks his habit"; that is, he breaks the continuity of his addiction. During abstinence, some addicts may try other drugs or drink whiskey, but that does not prove that all forms of drug-taking are alike any more than the fact that some disappointed lovers turn to drink proves that sex activity and alcoholism are alike.

Notes

1. The study on which this paper is based was carried out at the University of Chicago under the direction of Dr. Herbert Blumer.

2. Report to the Council of the League of Nations by the Committee of Enquiry into the Control of Opium Smoking in the Far East, II (1930), p. 420.

3. This general view is not only widespread among psychiatrists, but is popularly held as well. The great majority of writers in medical journals on this subject assume it. It may be found elaborated in a typical form in the following articles by L. Kolb: "Pleasure and Deterioration from Narcotic Addiction," *Jour. Ment. Hyg.*, Vol. IX (October, 1925); "Drug Addiction in Relation to Crime," *ibid.*, (January, 1925); "The Struggle for Cure and the Conscious Reasons for Relapse," *Jour. Nerv. and Ment. Dis.*, Vol. LXVI (July, 1927); and "Drug Addiction—A Study of Some Medical Cases," *Arch. Neurol. and Psychiat.*, Vol. XX (1928). It is also developed by Dr. Schultz in "Rep. of the Comm. on Drug Addicts to Hon. R. C. Patterson, etc.," as reported in *Amer. Jour. Psychiat.*, Vol. X (1930–31).

4. Dansauer and Rieth ("über Morphinismus bei Kriegsbeschädigten," in *Arbeit und Gesundheit Schriftenreihe zum Reichsorbeitsblatt*, Vol. XVI [1931]), found that 96.7 percent of 799 addicts had relapsed within five years after taking a cure. Relapse after more than ten years is sometimes mentioned. We ourselves were acquainted with an addict who stated that he had abstained for fifteen years before resuming the drug. We have never encountered or read an authentic account of any so-called cured addict who did not show by his attitudes toward the drug that the impulse to relapse was actively present.

5. It is characteristic of practically all addicts, prior to their own addiction, that they do not expect or intend to become addicts.

6. L. Faucher; *Contribution de l'étude du rêve morphinique et de la morphinomanie* (Thèse de Montpellier; No. 8 [1910–11]).

7. *JAMA*, Vol. XXIII.

8. *Brit. Jour. Inebriety* XXXI, 132.

9. The aim of this paper is to present a sociologial theory of opiate addiction which appears to offer possibilities for a rational and objective understanding of the problem without any element of moralization. This theory is based upon informal and intimate contact over a long period of time with approximately fifty drug addicts. The main points of the theory have been tested in the material available in the literature of the problem, and no conclusions have been drawn from case materials collected, unless

these materials were clearly corroborated by case materials in the literature.

10. Dansauer and Reith (*op. cit.*) cite two hundred and forty such cases. Many of these cases had used the drug for five or more years without becoming addicts.

11. See e.g., Levinstein, *Die Morphiumsucht* (1877); F. McKelvey Bell, "Morphinism and Morphinomania," *N.Y. Med. Jour.*, Vol. XCIII (1911); and Daniel Jouet, *étude sur la morphinisme chronique* (Thèse de Paris [1883]).

12. The case of Dr. H., cited later in this paper, is such a case.

13. Withdrawal distress begins to appear after a few days of regular administration but does not ordinarily become severe until after two, three, or more weeks, when its severity appears to increase at an accelerated rate. In its severe form, it involves acute distress from persistent nausea, general weakness, aching joints and pains in the legs, diarrhea, and extreme insomnia. In isolated cases, death may result from abrupt withdrawal of the drug.

14. We have checked this point with addicts who had voluntarily abstained for as long as six years. They unhesitatingly declared themselves to be addicts who happened not to be using drugs at the time—i.e., "junkers" or "users" who were "off stuff."

15. A type of individual who uses the drug without being hooked, is the one who uses it, say once a week, and thus avoids the withdrawal distress. Such a person is called a "joy-popper" or "pleasure-user" and is not regarded as an addict, until he has used the drug steadily for a time, experienced withdrawal distress, and became hooked. He then permanently loses his status as a "pleasure-user" and becomes a "junker." An addict who has abstained for a time and then begins to use it a little bit now and then is not a "pleasure-user"—he is just "playing around." See D. W. Maurer's article in the April, 1936, issue of *American Speech*.

16. As the other evidence which indicates how central and how taken for granted the role of withdrawal distress in addiction is, we may mention that the addict's word "yen" refers simultaneously to withdrawal distress *and* to the desire for the drug. Also, "to feel one's habit" means to feel the withdrawal distress. Addicts call cocaine non-habit-forming, because it does not cause withdrawal distress when stopped.

17. "Zuer Pathogenese des chronischen Morphinismus," *Monatschr. fur Psychiat. und Neruol.*, Vol. XLVII (1920).

18. As defined, e.g., in the *Report of the Departmental Committee on Morphine and Heroin Addiction to the British Ministry of Health*: "A person who, not requiring the continued use of a drug for the relief of the symptoms of organic disease, has acquired, as a result of repeated administration, an overwhelming desire for its continuance, and in whom withdrawal of the drug leads to definite symptoms of mental or physical distress or disorder."

19. *Op. Cit.*, p. 103.

20. Interviewed by the writer.

21. This had been partially emphasized by Erlenmeyer, as quoted by C. E. Terry and Mildred Pellens, *The Opium Problem* (1928), pp. 600 ff.; and it has been noted, in one way or another, in much of the physiological research that has been done on morphine effects.

22. The English Departmental Committee in 1926 (*op. cit.*) stated that, whatever may have been the original motive, the use of the drug is continued not so much from that original motive as "because of the craving created by the use" (quoted in Terry and Pellens, *ibid.*, pp. 164–65).

23. *Ibid.*, pp. 577 ff., quoting C. C. Wholey; *ibid.*, pp. 572 ff., quoting M. R. Dupony. A number of addicts have somewhat sheepishly admitted to us that they had been deceived in this manner for as long as ten days.

24. Rolb, "Drug Addicts—A Study of Some Medical Cases," *loc. cit.*

25. It is significant to note that this belief that withdrawal distress is caused by the absence of the opiate is not adequate or correct from the standpoint of physiological theory.

26. Very young children, the feeble-minded, and the insane would not be expected to have the necessary sophisticated conception of causality or the ability to manipulate "significant symbols" which, as we have indicated, are necessary preconditions of addiction.

    Dr. Charles Schultz, in a study of 318 cases found only 14 patients, or less than five percent, who were "probably high-grade morons, and even these gave the impression of having their dull wits sharpened by the use of drugs" (*loc. cit.*). Regarding insanity—it has been noted that it confers immunity to addiction, and that insanity appears to occur less frequently among the blood realtions of addicts than among the blood relatives of samples of the general population. O. Wuth, "Zur Erbanlage der Süchtigen," *Z. für die Ges. Neur. und Psychiat.*, CLIII (1935), pp. 495 ff.; Alexander Pilcz, "Zur Konstitution der Süchtigen," *Jahrb. für Psychiat.*, LI (1935), pp. 169 ff.; Jouet, *op. cit.*; Sceleth and Kuh, *JAMA*, LXXXII, p. 679; P. Wolff, *Deutsche medizinische Wochenschrift*, Vol. LVII, in his report on the results of a questionnaire, etc. Note the testimony of Gaupp, Bratz, and Bonhoeffer.

On the immunity of children, see R. N. Chopra et al., "Administration of Opiates to Infants in India," *Indian Med. Gaz.*, LXIX (1934), pp. 489 ff.; "Opium Habit in India," *Indian Jour. Med. Research*, Vol. XV (1927);

"Drug Addiction in India and Its Treatment," *Indian Med. Gaz.*, LXX (1935), pp. 121 ff.

27. In an essay, "Scientific Method and Individual Thinker," in *Creative Intelligence* (1917).

For Discussion

Can Lindesmith's theory apply to drug users for whom the drug of choice is not accompanied by withdrawal symptoms? Why or why not?

3

Some Considerations on the Disease Concept of Addiction

Jennifer L. Goode

In *this essay, the author considers the evidence that drug addiction is a chronic and relapsing disease influenced by a complex array of biological, psychosocial, and environmental factors. Although addiction shares many characteristics with other medical diseases, it is has not traditionally been regarded as such. The history of addiction theory is reviewed, and special consideration is given to its fluid nomenclature, including what precisely constitutes an addiction diagnosis. Etiologic agents are defined and detailed, and treatment outcomes are measured. Even though relapse is a common occurrence, studies suggest that treatment can produce beneficial, even if incremental, results. Challenges to conventional conceptualization, treatment, and assessment have been increasingly raised, suggesting that addiction research and clinical practice will continue to evolve into the future.*

Drug addiction is a chronic and relapsing disease, characterized by changes in the brain, compulsive drug taking, and other drug-related behaviors (National Institute on Drug Abuse [NIDA] 1999). Addiction manifests in a loss of control, craving, distortions in perception and thought, and continued drug use despite serious adverse consequences. While the term *drug abuse* refers to the use of psychoactive drugs that leads to impaired functioning, including potentially risky and hazardous behaviors (Landry 1994), abuse differs from addiction in that an abuser can choose whether or not to use drugs, but an individual suffering from addiction increasingly loses that choice (Leshner 1998).

A central feature of addiction is a phenomenon known as *salience*. Salience refers to the degree of focus on a particular activity as compared with other activities; that is, for drug-addicted individuals, the use of drugs becomes a compulsively important priority in their lives, even at the expense of other activities and interests (Loonis, Apter, and Sztulman 2000; Gardner 2001). Another common feature of addiction is ambivalence, or the inability to decide between two equally powerful, opposing choices. Periods of denial tend to alternate with periods of attempting to stay clean; the tension between these two polar opposite choices likely explains why most addicted individuals vacillate between periods of addiction and abstinence throughout their drug-using lives (Senay 1998). These phenomena, along with the compulsivity of use even in the face of grave consequences, are essential to understanding the nature of addiction.

The initiation, development, and progression of addiction are synergistically influenced by a wide range of biological, psychosocial, and environmental factors. Because of its complex etiology and characteristics, drug addiction has a particularly strong association with relapse (Curry et al. 1988). Relapse in itself is complex and can be initiated by multiple and interactive risk factors that vary in their influence on the process (Donovan 1996). Generally, relapse refers to the resumption of pretreatment patterns of drug use or the development of new patterns of drug use after an unspecified period of abstinence, but exact definitions vary. Although relapse is common, treatment can play an important role in facilitating recovery (Tims, Leukefeld, and Platt 2001).

The designation of drug addiction as a chronic and relapsing disease is a central theme in addiction literature (Landry 1994; O'Brien and McLellan 1996; Hser et al. 1997; McLellan et al. 2000; White, Boyle, and Loveland 2002). However, the disease concept of drug addiction has evolved considerably over the past two centuries in the context of medicine, public health, and clinical diagnosis (Meyer 1996). Addiction rhetoric has evolved over time as well to reflect innovations in the conceptualization of addiction. The words used to portray drug addiction are important on multiple levels: language serves cultural, social, and economic agendas and conveys deeper symbolic meaning when applied to individuals of varying backgrounds and circumstances. For example, the context of language can lend understanding as to why some drug users are seen as suffering from a disease and are subsequently offered treatment, while others may be seen as criminals who deserve to do time for their misbehavior (White 2000a). Knowledge of the history of addiction theory and its ever-evolving lexicon fosters a better understanding of the modern concept of addiction.

A Brief History

References to chronic intoxication as a disease of the body and soul can be traced back to ancient civilizations of Egypt and Greece, but in America, the disease concept of addiction is relatively new (White 2000a). The view of addiction as a disease rather than a vice first arose in the late eighteenth century, in conjunction with a sudden increase in the consumption of alcohol in America (White et al. 2002). Early writings in the late eighteenth and early nineteenth centuries debated between theories of chronic alcohol exposure as either a vice or a sickness. Early disease concept advocates viewed chronic drunkenness as a symptom of a disease, rather than as a disease in its own right. However, expanding knowledge of the physical manifestations of consistent alcohol consumption offered credence to the medical perspective. The Swedish physician Magnus Huss' revolutionary scientific work identified the physical manifestations resultant of chronic alcohol exposure and new

terms were coined in 1849: *alcoholism*, to mean a chronic state of alcohol intoxication characterized by physical pathology and impaired social functioning, and its accompanying descriptor, *alcoholic*, to describe the individual afflicted with this condition (White 1998). Huss bolstered the theory of "alcoholism" as a disease and called for health professionals to study and offer treatment for the condition (White 2000a). Other late-eighteenth- and nineteenth-century professional literature agreed, and numerous writings during that time conceptualized alcoholism as a chronic and progressive disease. By extension, drugs other than alcohol would begin to share in the disease concept (White et al. 2002).

Narcotic abuse surfaced in nineteenth-century America due to a number of factors, including indiscriminate prescribing of opiates by physicians, widespread availability, and an influx of opium-smoking immigrants from Asia. Going further, innovations such as the isolation of morphine and the introduction of the hypodermic syringe led to more severe and compulsive drug use (White 2000a; Reisine and Pasternak 1996). The cultural perception of opiate use was transformed from health misfortune, to vice, to disease in and of itself. Initially, the perception of opiate addiction was tainted by the cultural climate of the time: the predominantly white middle-class users who mostly ate and injected opiates were increasingly thought of as suffering from a "disease," while Chinese immigrants who mostly smoked opium were subjected to persecution and racism and stigmatized as having a "vice" (White 1998, 2000a). Professional literature first introduced the idea of opiate addiction as a chronic and relapsing disease, and as evidence of the addictive potential of narcotics accumulated, the media began to accept and perpetuate a medical concept of opiate addiction into the mainstream as well (White 1998, 2000a).

The disease concept of drug addiction gained wide acceptance as the nineteenth century wore on. Professionals began to specialize in the treatment of alcohol, opium, morphine, and cocaine "inebriety," a term that emerged to encompass a wide spectrum of problematic drug use, and hundreds of disease-themed articles and medical texts were published during this period. However, the concept began to wane in popularity in the early decades of the twentieth century, as the recognition of fraudulent patent medicine cures and pessimism regarding long-term recovery contributed to a dramatic shift in the cultural perception of addiction. As a result, treatment programs decreased and restrictive laws governing the use of alcohol and drugs increased. Further, the Harrison Act of 1914 essentially criminalized drug use, redefining the addict from an individual who needs treatment for a disease to a degenerate who deserves punishment for his or her intolerable vice (White 2000b).

However, a resurgence of thought in the mid-twentieth century refocused attention on the disease concept of addiction. A growing professional advocation for medical research and a public health approach toward addiction treatment and evaluation has since taken root, and professionals in the field today widely agree that addiction is a primary, chronic disease. For example, the National Council on Alcoholism and Drug Dependence as well as the American Society of Addiction Medicine have adopted the view that addiction is a chronic and relapsing disease, and this stance is central to their policy positions (White et al. 2002). Now that we've reached the general consensus that addiction is a "disease," it is important to understand how the concept of "addiction" is defined and how it differs from other forms of drug misuse.

Defining Addiction

Over time, there have been countless attempts to operationalize the concept of drug addiction. Numerous revisions and disagreements over definitions have persisted because abuse and addiction are conditions that exist along a continuum of symptoms and manifestations, from occasional use, to abuse, to chronic addiction (O'Brien 1996). Further, definitions of "drug addiction" are as widely varying as the underlying ambitions of those who propose such definitions (Gardner 2001). Although there remain serious conceptual problems, some developments have proven useful in terms of research and clinical practice (Tims et al. 2001). Clinical assessment tools and new linguistic frameworks have been developed over time, leading to a better understanding of the diagnosis, treatment, and conceptualization of the disease.

The first attempts to categorize forms of drug abuse occurred in the late nineteenth century in conjunction with a rise in the use of narcotics (Grant and Dawson 1999). During this time period, a mixture of medical and moral language was common throughout the literature (White 2000a). New classifications emerged; along with *inebriety*, common terms included *morphinism*, *narcomania*, and *narcotism*—the "ism" referring to perpetual states of drug use and the "mania" referring to craving and subsequent bingeing. Around the same time, the term *dope fiend* became popular slang, reflecting the general public's negative perception of chronic drug use: "dope" referred to products containing heroin or cocaine and "fiend" is actually a derivative of a German word meaning diabolical or hated (White 1998).

Clearly there was a need for a more encompassing, compassionate, and scientific drug lexicon. The word *addiction*, derived from the Latin word *addicere*, meaning to admire or surrender to a master, first appeared in the literature in the mid-1890s. The term *addict* appeared around 1910 to replace an earlier term, *habitué*, to designate an individual suffering from the chronic, progressive disease (White 1998). With the term *alcoholism* popularized in reference to drinking, the words "addiction" and "addict" came to symbolize issues pertaining to drugs other than alcohol (White 2000a). Historically, addiction has referred to physical dependence and withdrawal and repeated behaviors to avoid or get rid of the withdrawal. In addition, because the behavior associated with obtaining and using drugs incites a wide range of negative consequences for the user and others, the term "addiction" came to imply a behavioral health disorder characterized by compulsive, continued use of drugs in a manner harmful to the user and/or others (Tims et al. 2001).

Currently, the most influential definitions of the terms we're discussing are those of the American Psychiatric Association's (APA) *Diagnostic and Statistical Manual of Mental Disorders, Fourth Edition* (DSM-IV; APA 1994) and the World Health Organization's (WHO) *International Classification of Diseases-10* (ICD-10; WHO 1992). Significantly, both of these diagnostic tools use the word *substance dependence* as a synonym for addiction, although it wasn't always that way. In 1968, the term *drug dependence* replaced the term *drug addiction* in both assessment tools. Prior to this, drug dependence had not been used in reference to compulsive drug use (Maddux and Desmond 2000). Theoretically, the idea was to avoid confusion and produce a term applicable to drug abuse in general. The verdict is still out.

Overall, both diagnostic systems attempt to define and quantify the multidimensional aspects of the same condition. The DSM-IV, most commonly used in the United States, assesses *substance-related disorders*, which are broken down into two categories: substance use disorders and substance-induced disorders. *Substance use disorders* comprise syndromes related to the pathological use of substances, including substance abuse and dependence (addiction); *substance-induced disorders* refer to disorders created by substance use, such as intoxication and withdrawal, and psychiatric syndromes, including anxiety, mood disorders, and dementia. *Substance or drug dependence* (addiction) is defined as a pathologic condition manifested by three or more of seven criteria, which fall into three general categories: physiological states (tolerance and withdrawal), behavior with negative consequences (preoccupation with use, substantial time using or recovering from the effects, continuing use in the face of physical and emotional problems), and a loss of psychological freedom (inability to quit or cut down, or to use more often or for longer than intended) (APA 1994).

Several key definitions and related concepts merit discussion before proceeding. Pharmacologic definitions of dependence are often confused with addiction and abuse, but clinically, physical dependence, tolerance, and addiction are all separate phenomena (Kowal 1999; Savage et al. 2001). *Physical dependence* is a state of adaptation by the body to a specific drug class, and *withdrawal* is the physical process the body goes through when administration of the drug is abruptly ceased or lowered. *Tolerance* describes the state of adaptation in which the same amount of a drug has progressively less effect on an individual or when increasingly higher doses of a drug are needed to achieve the same effect (Landry 1994). Physical dependence and withdrawal can develop with the repeated administration of several classes of drugs, including antidepressants, antipsychotics, and opiates; these are the body's normal physiologic responses to certain classes of drugs (Kirsh et al. 2002). In DSM-IV terminology, the physical dependence and withdrawal that develop from certain drug categories constitute a *drug-induced disorder*, that is, symptoms brought on by the use of a particular substance. On the other hand, drug addiction (or *drug dependence* in proper DSM terminology) is a *drug use disorder*, which may or may not include tolerance and withdrawal symptoms (Senay et al. 2003).

The confusion in addiction nomenclature is especially sensitive regarding the use of pain medication, such as opioid analgesics. Although special considerations do need to be made for those with a history of drug abuse, the prevailing concern among many in the medical field is that the prescription of pain medication to patients will unintentionally breed a new generation of "addicts." Consequently, patients who suffer from chronic pain are often undertreated. Further complicating matters is the concept of *pseudoaddiction*, or the abuse of medications brought on by unrelieved pain (Kirsh et al. 2002). On the surface, it may be appear that the patient is exhibiting behaviors consistent with a diagnosis of addiction, but pseudoaddiction is distinguished from the true disease of addiction in that the abusive behaviors cease once the pain has been effectively treated (Savage et al. 2001). In reality, drug addiction—the biopsychosocial disease and topic of this essay—is a rare development among patients prescribed pain medication with no prior history of drug abuse (Kowal 1999).

In sum, physiologic adaptation is not in itself sufficient to warrant a diagnosis of addiction (McLellan et al. 2000). Addiction (or drug dependence) implies much more. The disease is characterized by an element of compulsion in the individual's drug use; the overarching concept of addiction implies persistent substance use, despite physical, psychological, and social implications for the user (McLellan et al. 2000; Tims et al. 2001).

Scientists, researchers, and clinicians continue to disagree on a universal standard of "addiction" or "dependence" in reference to the chronic, relapsing medical disease that we are evaluating. The debate, long-lived and unlikely to be resolved in the immediate future, probably has just as many proponents on one side as the other, and there are probably just as many reasons to argue one preference over the other. Some even contend that neither term is sufficient. Perhaps in the future a new word will be invented to displace both *addiction* and *dependence* that will more eloquently capture the essence of this complex, chronic, and relapsing disease.

As far as debate over the current choices is concerned, many argue that the distinction between physical dependence and drug dependence is unnecessarily muddled. On the other side, it has been suggested that the word addiction promotes social stigmatization. In a study dating back to 1978, participants found the verbal concept of drug dependence to be less negative than drug addiction. The author suggested that a shift to the word dependence, as advocated in the then recently revised DSM and ICD diagnostic manuals, would promote less emotionally charged discussion on the topic (Rippere 1978). However, recent literature suggests that not everyone has heeded the call to adopt the diagnostic nomenclature espoused by the APA and WHO. Maddux and Desmond (2000) conducted a search of the Medline database and found that of the 272 articles that incorporated addiction or de-

pendence in the title, 41 percent used addiction and 59 percent chose dependence, demonstrating a wide acceptability of both terms. The authors of the essay (an editorial in the well-respected journal *Addiction*) advocate the use of the word addiction, noting, "Terms that are intrinsically useful, clear and appropriate tend to survive. Those that are less useful or clear . . . tend to fade away."

Already, social scientists have expanded upon the current terms in order to provide a better linguistic framework in which to understand the multiple layers of the disease. Since addiction tends to vacillate between periods of use and abstinence that occur over an extended period of time, researchers have designated this process an "addiction career" or "dependence career" (Hser et al. 1997). A career perspective advances the theory that perception, action, skills, thought processes, and the like change and develop at different stages throughout an individual's career. During career development, decisions occur when old roles are replaced with new or modified roles. The career concept of addiction takes a longitudinal approach, recognizing that drug use and its effects are a dynamic and permanent feature in the individual's life (Hser et al. 1997). In other words, once addiction has taken hold, it is something that requires constant attention. Even if the addiction has been in remission for many years, the threat of relapse is always real. The idea is to build upon the stage in an addiction career in which drug use does not play a salient role in the individual's life.

Now that we've defined addiction and better understand the complexities that constitute a diagnosis, how exactly does it develop and progress? What gives the disease its chronicity and idiosyncrasy?

Risk Factors and the Etiology of Addiction

Drug addiction develops and intensifies through the synergistic interaction of multiple variables. O'Brien (1996) breaks down these variables into three main categories: agent (drug), host (user), and environment, which provide a useful framework to unravel the complex etiology of drug addiction.

Agent

The initial choice of whether or not to try drugs is volitional, but the drug of choice is often influenced by external factors, such as price and availability (O'Brien and McLellan 1996). Drug availability varies by region, as do the effects of the specific drugs chosen for consumption.

Pharmacologic factors, the effects of drugs on the body, increase one's risk for continued use and the development of an addiction. Drugs that produce particularly euphoric results are more reinforcing to the user (O'Brien 1996). Going further, the route of administration can potentiate a drug's effect, which has a significant impact on abuse potential (Landry 1994; O'Brien 1996). Inhaled drug vapors reach the brain within 7 seconds; injecting into the veins produces effects in 20 seconds; injecting into the muscle takes 4 minutes; snorting takes 3 to 5 minutes; and liquid or solid ingestion takes 20 to 30 minutes; the faster the drug reaches the brain and the higher the concentration of a drug that reaches the brain, the more intense the euphoria, and therefore, the greater the risk of developing an addiction (Landry 1994).

Host

The effects of drugs tend to vary among individuals (O'Brien 1996) and literature suggests that genetic makeup plays a significant role in the risk of developing addiction (McLellan et al. 2000; Meyer 1996). Genetics influence the effects of the initial use of a drug, and any pleasurable effects are in turn likely to reinforce further use of the substance (O'Brien and McLellan 1996). Studies with alcoholics, which likely bear relevance to other drug users, suggest that genetics increase the risk for developing addiction, but do not necessarily determine the outcome. For example, genetic influences account for approximately 40 to 60 percent of the risk of developing an alcohol use disorder (Schuckit 2000). Research also indicates that the first-degree relatives of alcoholics

have a three to fourfold higher prevalence of alcoholism than those who do not have a history of alcoholism in their family (Schuckit 1999).

An addicted brain is physically and chemically different than a normal brain. A host of neurobiological changes accompany the progression from voluntary to compulsive drug use, and research suggests that chronic drug use leads to long-term and permanent changes in the brain, even after an individual has ceased using drugs (NIDA 1999; Gardner 2001; Begley 2001; O'Brien and McLellan 1996). The compulsive aspect of drug addiction in and of itself is likely a consequence of drug-induced alterations in brain functioning (NIDA 1999). Significantly, once addiction has taken hold, these brain changes lock an addict into a perpetual risk for relapse (O'Brien and McLellan 1996).

Drug use permanently alters the pleasure and reward circuits in the brain, creates a vulnerability to other drugs that stimulate the reward system even if the individual has no experience using them, and renders an addict vulnerable to internal and external cues associated with drug taking (Gardner 2001). The integration of the reward circuitry with emotional, motivational, and memory centers in the brain enable the individual to experience the pleasure from drugs while simultaneously learning to recognize the signals associated with the rewards. For example, repeatedly associating a friend, a place, or even an emotional state with using drugs can result in a conditioned learning process (McLellan et al. 2000), not unlike Pavlov's famous experiment with salivating dogs. These cues can also trigger relapse, even among persons who have been abstinent for long periods of time (McLellan et al. 2000; Gardner 2001).

Chronic drug use also permanently affects the release and reuptake of dopamine in the reward pathways of the brain. Different drugs affect dopamine functioning differently, but all abusable drugs seem to stimulate it in some manner (Gardner 2001). Dopamine is a neurochemical deep within the brain responsible for inducing pleasure; essentially, when people use drugs they are turning on their brain's pleasure circuit.

Eventually, however, chronic drug use starts to have the opposite pleasure-producing effects and not only do dopamine levels in the brain actually decrease, the brain begins to have trouble producing it at all. The lack of dopamine then begins to evoke feelings of depression and drug craving (Leshner 1998).

Comorbid psychiatric conditions in individuals may play an important role in the development of addiction as well. For example, early antisocial and delinquent behavior may be indicative of problems with addiction later on (Landry 1994). However, the use of drugs can exacerbate or even create new psychiatric symptoms and behavioral problems that may not have developed otherwise (O'Brien 1996). Another theory posits that the more unconventional and risk-taking the individual, the more likely he or she is to experiment with drugs; by extension, the more extreme these personality traits, the more severe the involvement with drugs and the more dangerous the drugs of choice (Goode 1999).

The inability to cope with stress, negative self-image, depression, anxiety, and even shyness are also common cofactors that can initiate substance use, which may later progress into an addiction (Landry 1994; O'Brien 1996). Stress in particular has been shown to play a key role in perpetuating patterns of use, especially relapse (NIDA 2002; Sinha 2001). In fact, many of the host factors that initially contribute to the addiction process are also important in the relapse process. Sometimes individuals will "lapse" or "slip," engaging in a minor indulgence of their former drug-taking activities without fully reverting to their former drug use patterns. However, sometimes a lapse (or two) can initiate what is often referred to as "reinstatement." That is, one or two doses can essentially reinstate the whole addiction process. In order to cope with the negative feelings the lapse brought on, the individual reverts to his or her old coping behavior (drug use), at which point the relapse process is already under way (Gardner 2001).

Although various drugs and their interaction with an individual's biology and personality can influence the onset and course of addiction, a range of environmental factors can also contribute to the course of the disease and can potentially threaten one's efforts to recover from it (NIDA 1999).

Environmental Factors

Environmental factors encompass the physical, economic, political, and socio-cultural aspects of the drug user's life. As such, an individual's potential for addiction is complicated by variables such as cultural traditions, economic conditions, social controls, and the influence of other drug users (Bakalar 2001). Environmental influences, "cues" that become associated with drugs—people, places, and things—can reinforce drug use and can also trigger cravings that sustain an individual's risk for relapse, even after treatment (Gardner 2001; Bakalar 2001).

Since drug use is learned and reinforced through socialization (Goode 1999), peer influences and social pressures are important environmental factors that can influence the course of addiction (O'Brien and McLellan 1996). For example, adolescents are influenced by their peers' use of drugs and attitudes regarding such use. Those whose friends have access to drugs have an increased exposure and consequently, an increased risk of becoming users. Family influences, including substance abuse by parents or other family members, inconsistent discipline, and lack of warmth and emotional support are all conducive to the onset of drug use as well (Landry 1994).

Unequal social, economic, and health policies are macroissues responsible for creating conditions in which drug use thrives (Friedman 2002). Studies suggest that inner-city inhabitants, who often live in a culture of violence and economic and educational disadvantage, have an increased likelihood of developing an addiction (Landry 1994; O'Brien 1996). Several developments over the past few decades have exacerbated the drug problem in many of these areas: the deterioration of the economic structure of the lower sector of the working class, a growing economic polarization, and the political and physical decay of many of the minority communities can all translate into feelings of despair, hopelessness, and depression, making drug abuse an attractive escape (Goode 1999). But a culture of drug-induced escapism is not limited to urban landscapes, as similarly socioeconomically disadvantaged rural areas, for example, have been associated with prescription drug addiction (Clancy 2000; Alcoholism and Drug Abuse Weekly, 2002; Department of Justice 2002a,b).

Recovery and Treatment Outcomes

Given the complex nature of addiction, it is not surprising that relapse is a common occurrence. In fact, relapse may even be considered a part of the learning process that ultimately initiates permanent recovery (Tims et al. 2001). Relapse does not mean that addicts must start all over again, especially if they continue with treatment rather than drop out, return to abstinence as soon as possible, and move forward from the point in their recovery process where they previously left off. The relapse itself can provide key information as to what precisely instigated the behavior in the first place. That information can then be used to formulate strategies to prevent it from happening again (Washton 1989).

It is important to recognize that while there are general strategies that have proven successful for many individuals, no single type of treatment is guaranteed successful for everyone. Effective treatment must address issues beyond the drug use itself. Complications in treating drug abusers include poly-drug use, comorbid psychiatric conditions, criminal activity, and social issues, such as homelessness and unemployment (Anglin and Hser 1990). Recovery requires a multidimensional approach, and often long-term monitoring and multiple experiences in treatment in order to prevent relapse and achieve lasting results (NIDA 1999).

The American Society of Addiction Medicine [ASAM] promotes a continuum of care model, which acknowledges that episodes of addiction manifest with different severity and circumstances among individuals, and that treatment needs to address the multiple and changing needs of the individual at dif-

ferent points in time (ASAM 1996). The basic guiding principles of placement criteria include clinical objectivity and a choice of four general treatment levels: outpatient, intensive outpatient, residential, and intensive inpatient. Within each of these four levels lies a continuum of care options that address and respond to the variation in patients' needs over time. ASAM discourages using previous treatment failure as a condition for placement, and instead relies on clinically determined need to fit the patient into the most optimal treatment. While there are no specific criteria for the length of stay in treatment, patients with more severe problems need to have the option of extended care. Finally, 12-step and self-help groups are important dimensions in care; ASAM recognizes that the spiritual component in the recovery process can be significant in all levels of the recovery process, but does not make any specific recommendations within the specific levels of care. The ASAM continuum of care is the ideal way that addicted patients should be treated, but it is not necessarily how they really are treated in practice. As addiction medicine advances, the field will increasingly recognize the need to incorporate these guidelines and ideas into treatment (Senay 1998).

Just as addiction treatment is evolving, so too are the methods to evaluate the success of such episodes of care. Significantly, recent literature has called into question conventional evaluation methods and calculations of "success" among drug treatment outcomes (McLellan et al. 2000; O'Brien and McLellan 1996; McLellan 2002; White et al. 2002; Hser et al. 1997; Miller 1996). If drug addiction is a chronic, relapsing disease that can be controlled but not cured, then why is care provided and outcome measured in predominantly acute terms? Relapse rates depend on the exact definition of "relapse" and at what point in time the follow-up study is conducted; therefore, inconsistencies plague addiction literature. It has been suggested that researchers and clinicians abandon the notion of relapse entirely and instead employ terminology that more accurately describes the normal course of events that take place in recovering from addiction (Miller 1996).

Since many drug addicts experience multiple episodes of treatment, abstinence, and subsequent reentry into treatment, researchers have built upon the "career" concept to designate this process as a "treatment career." Treatment careers can be lengthy, especially if initiated early, and are often punctuated with periods of sobriety in between phases of drug use. Again, the career framework proves useful in conceptualizing the chronic nature of addiction and the cyclical processes of treatment and relapse (Hser et al. 1997). Further, White and colleagues (2002) have proposed implementing a "recovery management" model in addiction treatment, which requires a shift in thinking from a dichotomous concept of treatment outcome to instead focus on the processes involved in long-term recovery and improvement in the quality of life for the patient. It shifts the focus to the *management* of the disease, instead of the *cure* or acute *treatment* of the disease. This appears to build upon ASAM's continuum of care model in practice, and extends Hser and colleagues' (1997) career concepts to include "recovery career" in addition to addiction and treatment careers in linguistic conceptualization.

Although most of the addiction literature deals with predictors of relapse (Brewer et al. 1998; Dekimpe et al. 1998), treatment retention (Zhang, Friedmann, and Gerstein 2003; Grella et al. 1999; Greenfield and Fountain 2000), ethnicity and gender issues (Prendergast and Hser 1998; Fiorentine and Hillhouse 1999; Comfort and Kaltenbach 2000; Petry 2003), the relationship of social support (Dobkin et al. 2002), and counseling (Joe et al. 2001; Etheridge et al. 1999) to treatment success, and treatment outcomes for specific drugs like narcotics (Bailey and Hser 1994; Gruber, Chutuape, and Stitzer 2000; Katz et al. 2001; Booth, Crowley, and Zhang 1996; Ghodse et al. 2002) and cocaine (Siegal, Li, and Rapp 2002; Simpson et al. 1999), there are a few valuable studies that shed some perspective on the specific topic of drug addiction as a chronic and relapsing disease.

Overall, treatment outcomes of drug addiction display success rates similar to those of other chronic diseases. McLellan et al. (2000) undertook a literature review to compare drug dependence with other chronic illnesses, including diabetes, hypertension, and asthma. Each condition is a chronic, medical disease that shares common etiological agents, including genetic influence, personal choice, and environmental factors, which in turn influence the course and outcome of the disease. They found that success rates and incidence of relapse were remarkably similar across all four diseases. For example, one-year follow-up studies showed that 40 to 60 percent of addiction patients remain continuously abstinent. Like diabetics who do not adhere to their diet and medication, drug addicts who do not remain in treatment or who discontinue recommended measures such as self-help groups, typically have a poor prognosis. Low socioeconomic status, lack of social support, and comorbid psychiatric conditions were found to be significant contributors among all four diseases in predicting low adherence to treatment and consequently, poor treatment outcome.

Although treatment utilization and adherence varies among drug users, multiple treatment admissions are very common. A comprehensive study by Anglin, Hser, and Grella (1997) looked at prior treatment episodes among a sample of 10,010 clients enrolled in the Drug Abuse Treatment Outcome Study (DATOS) from 1991 to 1993 in 96 treatment programs across 11 U.S. cities. Approximately half of the patients entered treatment for the first time, whereas the other half had at least one prior treatment episode, and in many cases multiple prior treatments and lengthy periods of time involved in treatment. Clients averaged a history of 2.9 prior drug treatment episodes before enrolling in DATOS, though it varied by treatment modality; outpatient methadone treatment (OMT) clients had the highest number of previous treatments at 7.1, whereas outpatient drug-free (ODF) and short-term inpatient (STI) clients had the lowest number of previous treatments, averaging 2.3. Concordantly, the length of clients' "treatment careers," measured by the time between first treatment and current enrollment, varied by modality. The average treatment career was 3.1 years, with OMT averaging careers of 7.1 years and ODF and STI both averaging careers of 2.1 years.

In terms of predisposing factors, male clients were less likely than female clients to have had previous treatment, as were African Americans compared with whites. Increasing years of education were positively associated with previous treatment history. The drug of choice was also related to previous drug treatment, as users of heroin or cocaine or both were more likely to have had prior treatment compared with users of alcohol. Years of heroin or cocaine use, total number of drugs ever used, cigarette smoking, HIV risk behaviors (using needles and engaging in sex work), criminal behavior, and having ever received inpatient mental health treatment were all significantly associated with prior treatment episodes among clients of DATOS. Overall, severe addiction characteristics and engagement in risky behavior were associated with a greater number of previous treatment episodes (Anglin et al. 1997).

Prior treatment influences current treatment adherence and outcome, which impacts future treatment utilization and effectiveness (Hser et al. 1997). Research suggests that treatment processes differ among patients with and without previous experience (Hser, Joshi, et al. 1999) and, although evidence is limited, it is likely that incremental gains are achieved through multiple treatment episodes (Hser et al. 1997). For example, a study of 276 drug abusers seeking treatment referral showed that successful abstinence for at least three months after a previous episode of treatment was among the factors that significantly increased the subject's likelihood of actually reentering treatment. Among a sample of 789 cocaine-abusing DATOS patients, those with prior treatment experience had greater perceived needs in many aspects of their lives besides their drug problems, were less likely to have received one-on-one counseling, and were less likely to have followed program rules and regulations. Ac-

cordingly, the impact of increasing individual counseling and fostering greater program compliance had a greater impact on those with prior treatment histories, compared with those who had no prior treatment experience (Hser, Joshi, et al. 1999). Another study conducted by Hser, Grella, Hsieh, Anglin, and Brown (1999) among clients in DATOS long-term residential programs found that individuals with prior treatment histories were generally more difficult to treat, but that their likelihood of abstinence was similar to individuals with no prior treatment experience, as long as they remained in treatment for a sufficient time period.

In general, strategies that encourage entry into treatment, prolong the time spent in treatment, and facilitate reentry into treatment when warranted are more apt to produce better posttreatment outcomes (Hser et al. 1997).

Final Thoughts

Overcoming drug addiction is not easy. It is imperative to understand that biological, psychological, social, economic, and cultural factors vary among individuals and influence the initiation, progression, and ultimate recovery from addiction in profound ways.

Treatment should be individualized to address the multidimensional aspects of drug addiction. Further, adherence to a prescribed treatment regimen is essential, and individual effort must extend beyond the acute episode of intervention. Even though relapse is a common occurrence, it does not render treatment ineffective. In fact, it may be the way in which we evaluate treatment outcomes that is ineffective. As McLellan et al. (2000) observe, when patients with diabetes, hypertension, and asthma do not maintain their treatment regimen and symptoms reemerge ("fall off the wagon" in addiction slang), it is considered a demonstration of how treatment is a "success." Yet, when addicted individuals fall back into drug use after not complying with their treatment regimen, it is most often viewed as "failure" of the treatment, and by extension, a failure of the individual.

The process of recovery should be recognized as just that—a process, similar to a gray scale, and not simply black and white in terms of success and failure. Does smoking a joint within the first three months of recovery from cocaine addiction necessarily mean that treatment "failed"? Is that statistically a failure, or realistically a step in the right direction that the individual can build upon? Future research and clinical practice should continue to highlight the processes that facilitate recovery, rather than fixate on the assignment of an arbitrary treatment outcome. A focus on long-term, holistic recovery from drug addiction and the lifestyle changes and strategies of patients are important future considerations in the field.

Recent calls for change in how we treat individuals and evaluate outcomes demonstrate that the addiction field is continually evolving in interdisciplinary thought and practice. New additions to the addiction lexicon—the "career" perspective, for example—have given rise to a more realistic framework in which to understand the complex, multidimensional components of addiction and the processes that underlie sustained recovery. Perhaps a completely new nomenclature will arise to replace the ambiguity and disagreement that carry on over the very words *addiction* and *drug dependence*. Hopefully, the innovative ideas, research methods, and clinical practice of the future will engender a more complete understanding of the chronic, relapsing nature of the disease and will ultimately give rise to the most effective strategies yet to help individuals overcome addiction once and for all.

References

Alcoholism and Drug Abuse Weekly. (2002). Maine Analysis Demonstrates Far-Reaching Harm From OxyContin. (2002, February 11) *Alcoholism and Drug Abuse Weekly*, 14: 1–3.

American Psychiatric Association. (1994). *Diagnostic and Statistical Manual of Mental Disorders* (4th ed.). Washington, DC: Author.

American Society of Addiction Medicine (ASAM). (1996). *Patient Placement Criteria for the Treatment of Substance Related Disorders*, ed 2 (ASAM PPC-2). Chevy Chase, MD: Author.

Anglin, M. D. and Hser, Y.-I. (1990). Treatment of Drug Abuse. In M. Tonry and J. Q. Wilson (Eds.), *Drugs and Crime* (pp. 393–458). Chicago: The University of Chicago Press.

Anglin, M. D., Hser, Y.-I., and Grella, C. E. (1997). Drug Addiction and Treatment Careers Among Clients in the Drug Abuse Treatment Outcome Study (DATOS). *Psychology of Addictive Behavior*, 11(4): 308–323.

Bailey, R. C., and Hser, Y.-I. (1994). Influences Affecting Maintenance and Cessation of Narcotics Addiction. *Journal of Drug Issues*, 24(1/2): 249–273.

Bakalar, J. (2001). The Varieties of Addiction. In S. Chen and E. Skidelsky (Eds.), *High Time for Reform: Drug Policy for the 21st Century* (pp. 39–50). London: The Social Market Foundation.

Begley, S. (2001). How It All Starts in Your Brain. *Newsweek*, 137(7): 40–42.

Booth, R. E., Crowley, T. J., and Zhang, Y. (1996). Substance Abuse Treatment Entry, Retention and Effectiveness: Out-of-Treatment Opiate Injection Drug Users. *Drug and Alcohol Dependence*, 42, 11–20.

Brewer, D. D., Catalano, R. F., Haggerty, K., Gainey, R. R., and Fleming, C. B. (1998). A Meta-analysis of Predictors of Continued Drug Use During and After Treatment for Opiate Addiction. *Addiction*, 93(1): 73–92.

Clancy, Mary Anne. (2000, May 13). Down East High: Washington County Pill Addicts Have Health Officials Worried. *Bangor Daily News*. Retrieved January 2003 from Lexis-Nexis online subscription.

Comfort, M., and Kaltenbach, K. A. (2000). Predictors of Treatment Outcomes for Substance-Abusing Women: A Retrospective Study. *Substance Abuse*, 21(1): 33–45.

Curry, S., Marlatt, G. A., Peterson, A. V., and Lutton, J. (1988). Survivial Analysis and Assessment of Relapse Rates. In D. M. Donovan and G. A. Marlatt (Eds.), *Assessment of Addictive Behaviors* (pp. 454–473). New York: The Guilford Press.

Dekimpe, M. G., Van de Gucht, L. M., Hanssens, D. M., and Powers, K. I. (1998). Long-Run Abstinence After Narcotics Abuse: What Are the Odds? *Management Science*, 44(11): 1478–1492.

Department of Justice (DOJ). (2002a, July). *Kentucky Drug Threat Assessment*. National Drug Intelligence Center. Product No. 2002-S0382KY-001. Retrieved February 2003.

Available: *http://www.usdoj.gov/ndic/pubs/1540/index.htm*

———. (2002b, April). *Maine Drug Threat Assessment*. National Drug Intelligence Center. Product 2002-S0377ME-001. Retrieved February 2003. Available: *http://www.usdoj.gov/ndic/pubs/909/index.htm*

Dobkin, P. L., De Civita, M., Paraherakis, A., and Gill, K. (2002). The Role of Functional Social Support in Treatment Retention and Outcomes Among Outpatient Adult Substance abusers. *Addiction*, 97: 347–356.

Donovan, D. M. (1996). Assessment Issues and Domains in the Prediction of Relapse. *Addiction*, 91(Suppl.): S29–S36.

Etheridge, R. M., Craddock, S. G., Hubbard, R. L., and Rounds-Bryant, J. L. (1999). The Relationship of Counseling and Self-Help Participation to Patient Outcomes in DATOS. *Drug and Alcohol Dependence*, 57: 99–112.

Fiorentine, R., and Hillhouse, M. P. (1999). Drug Treatment Effectiveness and Client-Counselor Empathy: Exploring the Effects of Gender and Ethnic Congruency. *Journal of Drug Issues*, 29(1): 59–74.

Friedman, S. R. (2002). Sociopharmacology of Drug Use: Initial Thoughts. *International Journal of Drug Policy*, 13: 341–347.

Gardner, D. (2001). Addiction and Free Will. In S. Chen and E. Skidelsky (Eds.), *High Time for Reform: Drug Policy for the 21st Century* (pp. 29–38). London: The Social Market Foundation.

Ghodse, A. H., Reynolds, M., Baldacchino, A. M., Dunmore, E., Byrne, S., Oyefeso, A., Clancy, C., and Crawford, V. (2002). Treating an Opiate-Dependent Inpatient Population: A One-Year Follow-up Study of Treatment Completers and Noncompleters. *Addictive Behaviors*, 27: 765–778.

Goode, E. (1999). *Drugs in American Society*, Fifth Edition. Boston: McGraw-Hill College.

Grant, B. F., and Dawson, D. A. (1999). Alcohol and Drug Use, Abuse, and Dependence: Classification, Prevalence and Comorbidity. In B. S. McCrady and E. E. Epstein (Eds.), *Addictions: A Comprehensive Guidebook* (pp. 9–29). New York: Oxford University Press.

Greenfield, L., and Fountain, D. (2000). Influence of Time in Treatment and Follow-up Duration on Methadone Treatment Outcomes. *Journal of Psychopathology and Behavioral Assessment*, 22(4): 353–364.

Grella, C. E., Hser, Y.-I., Joshi, V., and Anglin, M. D. (1999). Patient Histories, Retention, and Outcome Models for Younger and Older Adults in DATOS. *Drug and Alcohol Dependence*, 57: 151–166.

Gruber, K., Chutuape, M. A., and Stitzer, M. L. (2000). Reinforcement-Based Intensive Outpatient Treatment for Inner City Opiate Abusers: A Short-Term Evaluation. *Drug and Alcohol Dependence*, 57: 211–223.

Hser, Y.-I., Anglin, M. D., Grella, C., Longshore, D., and Prendergast, M. L. (1997). Drug Treatment Careers: A Conceptual Framework and Existing Research Findings. *Journal of Substance Abuse Treatment*, 14(6): 543–558.

Hser, Y.-I., Grella, C. E., Hsieh, S., Anglin, M. D., and Brown, B. S. (1999). Prior Treatment Experience Related to Process and Outcomes in DATOS. *Drug and Alcohol Dependence*, 57: 137–150.

Hser, Y.-I., Joshi, V., Anglin, M. D., and Fletcher, B. (1999). Predicting Post-Treatment Cocaine Abstinence: What Works for First-Time Admissions and Treatment Relapsers? *American Journal of Public Health*, 89(15): 666–671.

Joe, G. W., Simpson, D. D., Dansereau, D. F., and Rown-Szal, G. A. (2001). Relationships Between Counseling Rapport and Drug Abuse Treatment Outcomes. *Psychiatric Services*, 52(9): 1223–1229.

Katz, E. C., Gruber, K., Chutuape, M. A., and Stitzer, M. L. (2001). Reinforcement-Based Outpatient Treatment for Opiate and Cocaine Abusers. *Journal of Substance Abuse Treatment*, 20(1): 93–98.

Kirsh, K. L., Whitcomb, L. A., Donaghy, K., and Passik, S. D. (2002). Abuse and Addiction Issues in Medically Ill Patients With Pain: Attempts at Clarification of Terms and Empirical Study. *Clinical Journal of Pain*, 18(Suppl. 4): S52–S60.

Kowal, N. (1999). What Is the Issue?: Pseudoaddiction or Undertreatment of Pain. *Nursing Economic$*, 17(6): 348–350.

Landry, M. J. (1994). *Understanding Drugs of Abuse: The Processes of Addiction, Treatment, and Recovery*. Washington, DC: American Psychiatric Press.

Leshner, A. I. (1998). Addiction as a Brain Disease: What the Research Shows. *Brain Work: The Neuroscience Newsletter*, 8(3): 6–8.

Loonis, E., Apter, M. J., and Sztulman, H. (2000). Addiction as a Function of Action System Properties. *Addictive Behavior*, 25(3): 477–481.

Maddux, J. F., and Desmond, D. P. (2000). Addiction or Dependence? [Editorial]. *Addiction*, 95(5): 661–665.

McLellan, A. T. (2002). Have We Evaluated Addiction Treatment Correctly? Implications From a Chronic Care Perspective [Editorial]. *Addiction*, 97: 249–252.

McLellan, A. T., Lewis, D. C., O'Brien, C. P., and Kleber, H. D. (2000). Drug Dependence, a Chronic Medical Illness: Implications for Treatment, Insurance, and Outcome Evaluation. *JAMA*, 284(13): 1689–1695.

Meyer, R. E. (1996). The Disease Called Addiction: Emerging Evidence in a 200-Year Debate. *The Lancet*, 347(8995): 162–167.

Miller, W. R. (1996). What is Relapse? Fifty Ways to Leave the Wagon. *Addiction*, 91(Suppl.): S15–S27.

National Institute on Drug Abuse (NIDA). (1999). *Principles of Drug Addiction Treatment: A Research-Based Guide*. Bethesda, MD: National Institutes of Health Publication No. 99-4180.

——. (2002). NIDA Community Drug Alert Bulletin—Stress & Substance Abuse. Accessed September 2, 2003. Available online: *http://165.112.78.61/StressAlert/StressAlert.html*

O'Brien, C. P. (1996). Drug Addiction and Drug Abuse. In J. G. Hardman and L. E. Limbird (Eds.-in-Chief); P. B. Molinoff and R. W. Ruddon (Eds.); and A. G. Gilman (Consulting Ed.), *Goodman & Gilman's The Pharmacological Basis of Therapeutics*, Ninth Edition (pp. 557–577). New York: McGraw-Hill, Health Professions Division.

O'Brien, C. P., and McLellan, A. T. (1996). Myths About the Treatment of Addiction. *The Lancet*, 347(8996): 237–240.

Petry, N. M. (2003). A Comparison of African American and Non-Hispanic Caucasian Cocaine-Abusing Outpatients. *Drug and Alcohol Dependence*, 69: 43–49.

Prendergast, M. L., and Hser, Y.-I. (1998). Ethnic Differences in Longitudinal Patterns and Consequences of Narcotics Addiction. *Journal of Drug Issues*, 28(2): 495–517.

Reisine, T., and Pasternak, G. (1996). Opioid Analgesics and Antagonists. In J. G. Hardman and L. E. Limbird (Eds-in-Chief); P. B. Molinoff and R. W. Ruddon (Eds.); and A. G. Gilman (Consulting Ed.), *Goodman & Gilman's The Pharmacological Basis of Therapeutics*, Ninth Edition (pp. 521–555). New York: McGraw-Hill, Health Professions Division.

Rippere, V. (1978). "Drug Addiction" and "Drug Dependence": A Note on Word Meanings. *British Journal of Addiction*, 73(4): 353–358.

Savage, S., Covington, E. C., Heit, H. A., Hunt, J., Joranson, D., and Schnoll, S. H. (2001). *Definitions Related to the Use of Opioids for the Treatment of Pain*. American Academy of Pain Medicine, American Pain Society and American Society of Addiction Medicine. Accessed November 12, 2003. Available: *www.asam.org*.

Schuckit, M. (1999). New Findings on the Genetics of Alcoholism. *Journal of the American Medical Association*, 281(20): 1875–1876.

——. (2000). Genetics of the Risk of Alcoholism. *American Journal on Addictions*, 9(2): 103–112.

Senay, E. C. (1998). *Substance Abuse Disorders in Clinical Practice*. New York: W. W. Norton & Company.

Senay, E. C., Adams, E. H., Geller, A., Inciardi, J. A., Muñoz, A., Schnoll, S. H., Woody, G. E., and Cicero, T. J. (2003). Physical Dependence on Ultram (Tramadol Hydrochloride): Both Opioid-like and Atypical Withdrawal Symptoms Occur. *Drug and Alcohol Dependence*, 69: 233–241.

Siegal, H. A., Li, L., and Rapp, R. C. (2002). Abstinence Trajectories Among Treated Crack Cocaine Users. *Addictive Behavior*, 27(3): 437–449.

Simpson, D. D., Joe, G. W., Fletcher, B. W., Hubbard, R. L., and Anglin, M. D. (1999). A National Evaluation of Treatment Outcomes for Cocaine Dependence. *Archives of General Psychiatry*, 56 (6): 507–514.

Sinha, R. (2001). How Does Stress Increase Risk of Drug Abuse and Relapse? *Psychopharmacology*, 158: 343–359.

Tims, F. M., Leukefeld, C. G., and Platt, J. J. (2001). Relapse and Recovery. In F. M. Tims, C. G. Leukefeld, and J. J. Platt (Eds.), *Relapse + Recovery in Addictions* (pp. 3–17). New Haven, CT: Yale University Press.

Washton, A. M. (1989). *Cocaine Addiction: Treatment, Recovery, and Relapse Prevention*. New York: W. W. Norton & Company.

White, W. L. (1998). *Slaying the Dragon: The History of Addiction Treatment and Recovery in America*. Bloomington, IL: Chestnut Health Systems.

——. (2000a). Addiction as a Disease: Birth of a Concept. *Counselor*, 1(1): 46–51, 73.

——. (2000b). The Rebirth of the Disease Concept of Alcoholism in the 20th Century. *Counselor*, 1(2): 62–66.

White, W. L., Boyle, M., and Loveland, D. (2002). Alcoholism/Addiction as a Chronic Disease: From Rhetoric to Clinical Reality. *Alcoholism Treatment Quarterly*, 20(3/4): 107–130.

World Health Organization (WHO). (1992). *International Classification of Diseases and Related Health Problems* (10th Rev.). Geneva: Author.

Zhang, Z., Friedmann, P. D., and Gerstein, D. R. (2003). Does Retention Matter? Treatment

Duration and Improvement in Drug Use. *Addiction*, 98: 673–684.

For Discussion

1. Should drug addiction be treated, evaluated, and insured just like diabetes, hypertension, and asthma? If addiction is a chronic, medical disease that shares similar etiologic agents with other chronic diseases like diabetes, why is there such a stigma attached to addiction and not the others?

2. Is applying the term "career" to concepts of drug addiction, treatment, and recovery a useful approach to understanding the nature of the disease? In what ways is an addiction career similar to and dissimilar from other "careers"?

3. Which term is more appropriate to describe the biopsychosocial disease we have evaluated, "addiction" or "dependence"? What are some possible arguments for and against each one? What are some alternative terms to addiction and dependence that would better characterize the disease?

4

The Use of Marijuana for Pleasure

A Replication of Howard S. Becker's Study of Marijuana Use

Michael L. Hirsch
Randall W. Conforti
Carolyn J. Graney

Howard S. Becker was perhaps the first of many researchers to examine the sociological aspects of marijuana use. His major efforts in this regard appear in his classic work Outsiders: Studies in the Sociology of Deviance *(Free Press, 1963). Based on interviews with 50 marijuana users, Becker proposed that gleaning pleasure from marijuana smoking occurs through a learning process. Further, he noted that marijuana users progress through a series of stages. Beginners learn to master techniques (e.g., inhalation, appropriate dosage) from experienced users. Occasional users smoke marijuana intermittently; that is, when the opportunity arises. More frequent use characterizes regular users who must arrange for a steady supply of marijuana for self-use.*

In the following essay, Michael L. Hirsch, Randall W. Conforti, and Carolyn J. Graney report on an attempt to replicate Becker's original study. Their research was based on interviews with 50 marijuana users, half of whom were college undergraduates. Although they found some support for Becker's model, they also noted some discrepancies.

It seems an historic truism that the presence of drugs or drug use within a given culture engenders controversy or public debate about the relationship of drugs to the larger social order (Braudel 1981). American culture is no exception. Within recent historical memory, our culture has both criminalized and decriminalized the production and use of alcoholic beverages. We currently are involved in a debate about drug use that ranges from those who would declare a war on the traffickers and users of materials deemed illicit, to the suggestion that drug use generally should be decriminalized (Ridding 1989; Keer 1988).

Historically, sociologists (and other social scientists) have contributed to the debate surrounding drug use. This is done not by choosing sides, but rather by providing interested parties with explorations of the relationship between social context and drug use (Conforti, Hirsch, and Graney 1989; Yamaguchi and Kandel 1985; Seeman and Anderson 1983; Radosevich et al. 1979; Alexander 1963). This includes understandings of how drug use is related to cultural belief systems (Room 1976; Mulford and Miller 1959), typologies of drug users (Bloomquist 1971), and conceptualizations of drug addiction (McAuliffe and Gorden 1974; Ray 1964).

In the field of sociology, the work of Howard S. Becker stands out as both the touchstone of sociologically inspired drug research (Becker 1953) and the work responsible for the development of what has come to be known as labelling theory in the study of deviance (Becker 1963, 1964). In part, Becker's work has remained relevant because of the enduring nature of the drug debate itself. Questions of individual predispositions to drug use/criminal behavior, challenged by Becker as early as 1953, have re-emerged as behavioral explanations today (e.g., Walters and White 1989). In addition, Becker's thesis that an understanding of marijuana use could be obtained by approaching the drug as an object from which individuals learn to derive pleasure is itself worthy of re-examination. The utility of such a conception is likely to extend beyond the use of marijuana to drugs such as cocaine and crack.

It is because of the explanatory power of Becker's initial approach and the needs of policy makers/drug counselors today that a re-examination of Becker's work is warranted. In doing such a re-examination, the authors have chosen as their vehicle a replication of Becker's original work. Though the value of replicative work has generally been noted (e.g., Denzin 1989; Schwartz and Jacobs 1979), attempts at replication are particularly important (and rarely attempted) when dealing with contextual models (given the fluidity of contextual reality). In what follows, recent efforts to corroborate Becker's work will be discussed. General points of confirmation will be noted, as well as extensions of his original work, reasons for these extensions, and suggestions for further research.

Method

In Becker's original research (1953), the snowball-sampling method was utilized as the means of obtaining 50 marijuana users willing to be interviewed. Snowball sampling, noted for its strength in penetrating relatively closed populations and its utility in network analysis but not for yielding representative samples (True 1989), yielded a mixed demographic sample in Becker's work. (His sample was somewhat heavily weighted toward musicians who made up approximately ½ of the subjects. In a recent phone interview Becker reported not having kept any more detailed information about his sample than what is reported above.) Site selection, determined by Becker's Chicago residency, was not stated as a methodological issue in the original research.

Becker's interviews were conducted informally, with no set questionnaire format being utilized. Interviewees were asked general questions by Becker regarding their initiation to and use of the drug. They were not directed toward any specifics by Becker, as he took notes of their commentary (Becker's recollection in a recent phone interview). It is from such an informal conversational style that Becker gathered his data, and it is upon this data that Becker bases his stage theory/typology of users.

Like Becker's, our research is based upon data gathered from 50 marijuana users. Also, like Becker's, our respondents were obtained through the use of the snowball-sample method. However, whereas Becker's respondents were all derived within one municipal area (Chicago), our respondents are split between two municipal areas, Milwaukee and the Fox River Valley in Wisconsin (the respective homes of the authors).

Demographically, more information is available regarding our respondents than for Becker's. In comparison to Becker's sample, in which musicians account for 50 percent of the sample, 50 percent of our sample is made up of undergraduate students from both metropolitan areas. The remaining 25 respondents come from a wide range of social positions which include house painters, mechanics, nurses, lawyers, teachers, and middle managers. Respondents in our sample ranged in age from 18 to 44 and included 32 men and 18 women. All of our respondents were of European descent. The greatest methodological difference between Becker's work and our own is in the interview process itself. Whereas Becker's interview process was informal in nature, we took a number of set questions into the interview. Our questions, drawn from the discussions reported by Becker, were designed to yield data similar to that which he obtained (Becker 1953, 1963). Thus, whereas Becker abstracts a "becoming-a-user pattern" from his informal interviews, we specifically questioned respondents about their earliest contacts with the drug and asked them to reconstruct chronologically their relationship to the drug. Such reconstruction was to include both behavioral and attitudinal aspects, and when such information was not forthcoming in a given interview, respondents were specifically asked to fill in omissions, if possible.

Within the format of this more formal interview procedure, several questions were included with the hope of extending Becker's original work. One advantage of replicative research in this instance was the possibility of asking questions designed to extend the research in the direction where deficiencies in the original work were suspected. In this case we questioned Becker's "becoming-a-user" pattern for what we perceived as its neglect of the period of time which preceded the point of an individual's stated willingness to try the drug. Other questions were asked about projections toward future use on the part of reporting individuals, fears they associated with the use of the drug, opinions on legalization, etc. This was information absent from Becker's original work, yet deemed of interest by our research team.

Results

Becker's Path to Pleasurable Usage and Stages of Marijuana Use

Becker's original work (1953) surrounds his belief that the use of marijuana could be constructively approached, if the drug itself was conceived of as an object from which pleasure could be derived. Unless an individual develops "a conception of the drug as an object which could be used for pleasure . . . marijuana use was considered meaningless and did not continue" (Becker 1953). Beginning his life histories of marijuana use with individuals at a "point of willingness to use the drug," Becker outlines a three-stage process through which individuals obtain a conception of the drug as an object from which pleasure may be derived. This process includes: 1) learning a technique which supplies "sufficient dosage for the effects of the drug to appear"; 2) both experiencing and recognizing the effects of the drug; and 3) learning to enjoy the effects (Becker 1953). In addition, Becker notes that, at each juncture on the way toward pleasurable use of the drug, the initiate is aided by and dependent upon the guidance of others.

In subsequent discussions of the same data, Becker (1963) utilizes the concept "career" as a way to understand behavioral patterns related to marijuana use. For Becker, a behavioral career is a ". . . sequence of movements (on the part of the individual) from one position to another" within the social milieu (Becker 1963). Here, focusing on the individual, Becker constructs a three-stage model to describe the changes an individual goes through on the path to becoming a

bona fide user of the drug (Figure 4.1). His stages include: 1) the beginner, a person involved in initial encounters with the drug (the stage within which the above three steps are subsumed); 2) the occasional user, one whose drug use is sporadic or determined by chance; and 3) the regular user, one whose systematic (daily) use has led him or her to procure personal supplies of the drug [it is important to note that Becker views stages 1 and 2 as transitional, stage 3 seemingly the only stable use pattern] (Becker 1963).

Figure 4.1

Our Construction

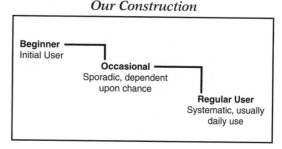

Verification of Becker's Path and Stages of Marijuana Use

Whereas Becker begins his life histories "with the person having arrived at the point of willingness to try marijuana" (Becker 1953), we have included in our life histories the orientations individuals had to the drug before an opportunity to use the drug arose in their life. Our logic for doing so is as follows: as it seems unlikely that those who "arrived at the point of willingness to try marijuana" have reached that point by the same path, it should be of interest to those studying drug-use patterns how different people "arrive" at this same point of willingness.

Preconceptions of the Drug

One half of our respondents held what may be considered negative preconceptions about the drug, the remaining one half being split between those with neutral preconceptions (37 percent) and positive preconceptions (13 percent). Among those holding negative positions were those who recounted anti-drug instruction, knowledge of family members who had varying drug problems, and those who associated the use of marijuana with the socially undesirable. Among those holding neutral positions were those who had no real knowledge of the drug (positive or negative reports), those who held some intellectual curiosity regarding its use, and those who saw it as relatively harmless, equating its use with the use of tobacco and/or alcohol. Among those holding positive views of the drug were those who thought it was "cool" to smoke the drug, had hearsay evidence regarding its "enjoyable" effects, and had early in their lives seen people enjoying themselves with the drug.

Becoming Willing to Use the Drug

How individuals come to be willing to use the drug of course varies with their original preconceptions. For those who were positively oriented to the drug, a willingness to experiment already existed; they lacked only the opportunity. For those with neutral orientations to the drug, "willingness to use the drug" per se often didn't develop. Instead, opportunities to try the drug arose (most often in situations where peers or siblings were using it) and respondents found themselves trying the drug without any forethought regarding its use. Those with negative preconceptions went through the greatest changes on their way toward a willingness to try the drug. Among this group, two avenues were associated with the change in their orientations to the drug. For some, willingness first appeared after encounters with others who commanded their respect and who either used the drug in front of them or discussed its use with them. For others, a willingness to use the drug arose as part of a more general movement away from an unquestioned willingness to uphold the status quo.

First Encounters

All of the respondents in our study reported first-use encounters as having involved other individuals closely associated with and important to their day-to-day life activities. Of those cited as involved in initia-

tions were close friends, boyfriends or girlfriends, family members [siblings and cousins (one person reported smoking with her mother sometime after her initial use)], classmates, and roommates. Initiation gatherings ranged from experimentation with only one other present, to contexts of larger social groupings, here parties being most often cited. It is important to note that none of our respondents spoke of initially using the drug while alone or alone with a stranger or group of strangers.

The Path to the Pleasurable Usage of Marijuana

Our respondents generally corroborate Becker's description of the elements making up the path toward the pleasurable usage of marijuana (as well as the importance others play in learning the proper use of the drug, recognition of its effects, and their enjoyment of the effects). Our research suggests that Becker's three-step presentation is simplistic. There is much to be learned by more closely examining the variance that exists between individual paths to pleasurable usage.

Experiences on the way toward pleasurable use of the drug vary a great deal. There are those who get high, perceive that they are high, and enjoy the high the first time they smoke; and those that smoke 30–40 times over the course of a 2–3-year period before they get high for the first time. Although Becker (1953) states that "(T)he novice does not ordinarily get high the first time he smokes marijuana . . ." we found that 34 percent of our respondents reported getting high the first time they used the drug. The majority of these reported favorable encounters (although two reported the ill effects of nausea and vomiting; there were a few neutral reactions reported as well). An additional 32 percent reported getting high after the first 2–3 attempts, 30 percent after several attempts and the remaining 6 percent after 30–40 uses.

Our respondents' reasons for continued experimentation with the drug after the initial encounter varied in relation to the results of the first experience and the original reasons for their use of the drug. Others did not get high the first time and defined the feeling of "being high" enjoyable. An attempt to recreate that state was motivation enough to try the drug again, for those who did not get high the first time, as well as those who got high but had neutral or negative reactions. When their original willingness to try the drug was associated with a positive motivation toward its use (including those whose original preconception had been negative), this motivation continued even after the failure of the first attempt. Most had anticipated the possibility of "not getting high" their first attempt. Among this group, second and third attempts at using the drug tended to be more deliberately planned and executed than were their initial attempts. One respondent continued his experimentation by stealing small amounts of the drug from his parents' supply.

Such planned attempts by the above group were in sharp contrast to those who had neutral orientations to the drug at the time of its first use. For this group, later attempts at "getting high" proved to be much more passive and haphazard. Whereas the above mentioned group had been more likely to seek out the drug after their initial use, further experimentation by this latter group was often as unexpected as was their initial use. However, regardless of original motivations and results of initial use, once an individual's own experience with the drug proved to be favorable, continued use was predicated on the desire to re-experience pleasurable sensations.

Career Patterns of Use

In our attempt to corroborate this part of Becker's work, our respondents were asked to reconstruct chronologically their relationship to the drug, beginning with their preconceptions and moving to present use. In comparing Becker's model to our information, we find that his model is somewhat descriptive of the behavioral transitions experienced by individuals experimenting with the drug's use. As it now stands, however, his model is both sequentially incomplete and conceptually limited. Conceptual limitations become evident, as we attempt to

place our respondents into his classification system.

The first sequential limitation is the most obvious; we have already discussed its absence. This is Becker's exclusion of a stage, wherein individuals develop a willingness to experiment with the drug. Given its importance to an understanding of drug use, the addition of an orientation stage to Becker's model seems to be reasonable.

Other sequential limitations, blurred with the model's conceptual limitations, become evident when we look beyond the beginner stage and attempt to place respondents into the occasional and regular use categories. Becker's criteria for placement . . . occasional use being chance usage and regular use being systematic usage with self-procuring behaviors . . . makes it difficult to place those whose occasional use is at times systematic (e.g., attending parties hoping the drug will be available), and those whose regular use is at times augmented by chance occurrence (e.g., a weekend user who happens to smoke during the week, if confronted with an unexpected opportunity). We must also ask if it is meaningful to extend the regular use category from those who systematically procure and use the drug 2–4 times per month or year to those whose systematic procurement translates into a daily use frequency of 4–9 times. Would it be at all meaningful to create an abuse/addiction category to deal with those whose use may be self-defined as problematic? If so, how would we place such a category into the current model? Also, though Becker's work suggests that both the beginner and the occasional use categories are transitional stages, the majority of our respondents seem to have maintained a use pattern which falls in between his occasional and regular use categories. How do we account for such non-transition within his framework?

It is at this point in our attempt to replicate Becker's work that we are faced with our greatest challenge. If we stay with Becker's model, we find that we are unable to categorize individuals who consider themselves to be drug abusers, who have quit using the drug, who have never used the drug and are orienting toward its use (or not orienting toward its use, for that matter), or whose patterns fall between his occasional and regular use categories. If we respond to these limitations by constructing a typology of present career use patterns, an approach that would allow for the classification of all respondents, we risk losing the temporal progression of the original model.

Discussion

A comparison of our work with Becker's reveals a general corroboration of his thesis, i.e., the utility of understanding marijuana as an object from which individuals learn to derive pleasure, as well as points of contention regarding the process through which individuals learn to derive enjoyment from the drug, and regarding his typology/stage theory of drug use patterns. We will begin our discussion with points of contention, move to points of confirmation, and conclude with suggestions regarding the direction of future research.

Points of Contention

As noted above, in his analysis of the data, Becker derives a three-step process through which individuals learn to derive pleasure from the use of marijuana. Our research leads us to question the reliability of Becker's description of this process for, as we note above, a large percentage of our respondents reported both getting high and enjoying the high at the time of their first use. As we look to explain the discrepancy between the two studies, several factors come to our attention, all of which relate to the time lapse between the original work and our replicative efforts.

First, we must recognize the existence of both the availability of technologies specifically designed to increase the drug dosage an individual is able to take in a single encounter and the availability of more powerful strains of the plant marijuana. Both the technologies for the smoking of the drug and the nature of the drug being smoked have increased the likelihood that an individual's first encounter will result in the presence of the drug's effects.

In addition to the above changes, cultural attitudes have changed to the extent that first encounters themselves may have taken place in settings that were less clandestine or anxiety-provoking than was true of the time Becker did his research. It is likely that all of these factors taken together have changed first encounters to such an extent that we may no longer rely on Becker's model to understand the reality of initial encounters.

Our next departure from Becker's work is more critical and relates to the utility of his typology/stage theory of use patterns. As noted above, Becker's typology (Figure 4.1) suggests that those who come to enjoy the effects of the drug progress in their use of the drug to the point of regular use. The suggestion that all marijuana smokers are or will become regular (daily) users of the drug is not corroborated by the information provided by our informants, many of whom have used the drug for years but do not fit into his regular use category. It is possible that marijuana users in Becker's time all progressed to regular use of the drug, but we find this to be unlikely. Instead, we believe it is time to abandon Becker's model altogether and consider a more recent alternative offered by Van Dijk (1972).

Van Dijk's model (Figure 4.2) begins with initial contact with the drug and moves through three possible stages, experimentalism, integrated use, and excessive use, toward the possibility of addiction. The advantages of such a model over Becker's relates both to the inclusion of the stated possibility of an addictive use category (the initial three categories here being equated to Becker's three stages in order) but also the possibility of stabilized intermediate use patterns. In addition, Van Dijk's model explicitly allows for the return to earlier patterns of drug use, as well as the discontinuing of drug use at any stage.

Though such a model of use is superior to Becker's in terms of its explanatory power, both models neglect that stage prior to first contact with the drug which has been pointed to in our research of users' preconceptions. If we were to amend Van Dijk's model to include such a stage (Figure 4.3), we would have a model which not only al-

Figure 4.2

Van Dijk's Model

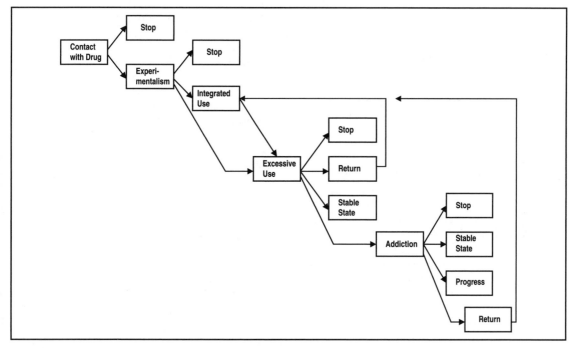

Figure 4.3

Revised Model

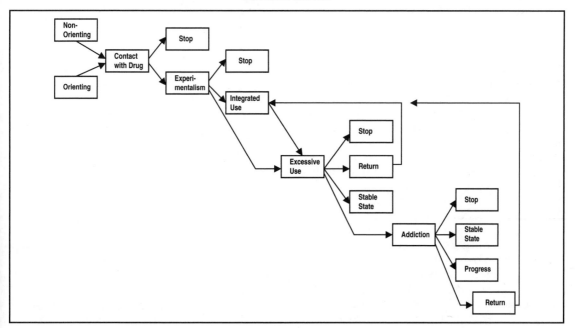

lows us to place all of our respondents within stated categories, but would also allow us to visualize how preconceptions influence the continuation of experimentation after initial contact with the drug.

Points of Convergence

The major point of convergence between Becker's work and our own lies in our belief in the utility of approaching marijuana as an object from which individuals must learn to derive pleasure, before drug use behavior will be evidenced. It is in the reconstruction of our respondents' relationships to the drug that we are able to gain an understanding of the motivations which led both to initial experimentation with the drug and subsequent or continued use. The explanatory power of such an approach derives from the focus upon the interactive environment, within which individuals learn to use and enjoy the drug. Such a focus argues against, then and now, theoretical positions which seek to explain drug use by positing predispositions toward drug use/criminal behavior in the individuals themselves.

Directions of Future Research

Though our review of Becker's work is not without criticisms, we believe his work has raised questions that need to be answered. First, his structural/interactive approach to understanding marijuana use does point to the normative components of the learning situation which influence drug use. What Becker does not address (nor do we in this work) is the way in which other individuals, in similar situations to those who become marijuana users, do not become users themselves. If the structural/interactive model is to gain in the power of explanation, we must be willing to explore the life worlds of both the user as well as the non-user, in an attempt to understand the movement of some toward drug use and the continued non-use on the part of others.

Second, we believe that there is great utility in the manner of research Becker began and we have continued. We believe much could be learned, if we expanded our study of drug use by undertaking similar research

of other drugs, both legal (e.g., alcohol and tobacco) and illegal (e.g., crack, cocaine, LSD, etc.). Though we may assume similar "becoming-user" patterns will hold for all drugs, differences may exist between them as well. In any event, much may be gained by just such a comparison.

Finally, we believe much could be gained by cross-cultural studies of drug use as well. In particular, it would be of interest to study the differences in drug use experience between cultures which hold the same drug to be licit and illicit. Such comparisons may yield information regarding the role cultural norms play in the regulation of drug use and, perhaps, the control of drug effects.

Conclusion

There is no doubt that Becker's work will continue to serve as a benchmark for those generally interested in drug use. Our attempt to replicate his work was motivated both by a desire to venerate an old master and a desire to continue to improve our stock of knowledge regarding drug use. In the comparative dialogue created by our replicative attempt, we have noted cultural changes that contributed to the variance between our respective results, attempted to correct what we believe to have been inadequacies in the original work, and also raised questions which go beyond the scope of this research.

References

Alexander, C. N., Jr. (1963). Consensus of mutual attraction in natural cliques: A study of adolescent drinkers. *The American Journal of Sociology* 69, 395–403.

Becker, H. S. (1953). Becoming a marijuana user. *The American Journal of Sociology* 59, 235–242.

——. (1963). *Outsiders: Studies in the sociology of deviance.* New York: The Free Press.

——. (1964). *The other side.* London: The Free Press.

Bloomquist, E. R. (1971). *Marijuana: The second trip.* Beverly Hills: Glencoe Press.

Braudel, F. (1981). *The structures of everyday life* (Vol. 1). New York: Harper and Row.

Conforti, R. W., and Hirsch, M. L., Graney, C. (1989). *The use of marijuana for pleasure.*

Conference paper, Spring 1990 Midwest Sociology Convention.

Denzin, N. K. (1989). *The research act.* Englewood Cliffs: Prentice-Hall.

Keer, P. (1988). The unspeakable is debated: Should drugs be legalized? *The New York Times.*

McAuliffe, W. E., and Gorden, R. (1974). A test of Lindesmith's theory of addiction: The frequency of euphoria among long-term addicts. *American Journal of Sociology* 79, 795–801.

Mulford, H., and Miller, D. (1959). Drinking behavior related to definitions of alcohol: A report of research in progress. *American Sociological Review* 24, 385–389.

Radosevich, M., Lanza-Kaduce, L., Akers, R. L., Krohn, M. D., et al. (1979). The sociology of adolescent drug and drinking behavior: A review of the state of the field. *Deviant Behavior* 1, 15–35.

Ray, M. B. (1964). The cycle of abstinence and relapse among heroin addicts. In H. S. Becker (ed.), *The other side* (pp. 163–178). London: The Free Press.

Ridding, A. (1989). Western panel is asking end to all curbs on drug traffic. *The New York Times.*

Room, R. (1976). Ambivalence as a sociological explanation: The case of cultural explanations of alcohol problems. *American Sociological Review* 41, 1047–1062.

Schwartz, H., and Jacobs, J. (1979). *Qualitative sociology: A method to the madness.* New York: The Free Press.

Seeman, M., and Anderson, C. S. (1983). Alienation and alcohol: The role of work, mastery, and community in drinking behavior. *American Sociological Review* 48, 60–77.

True, J. A. (1989). *Finding out: Conducting and evaluating social research.* Belmont: Wadsworth.

Van Dijk, W. K. (1972). *Complexity of the dependence problem: Interaction of biological with psychogenic and sociogenic factors. Biochemical and pharmacological aspects of drug use.* Haarlem: DeErven F. Bohn.

Walters, G. D., and White, T. (1989). The thinking criminal: A cognitive model of lifestyle criminality. *Criminal Justice Research Bulletin* 4, 1–10.

Yamaguchi, K., and Kandel, D. B. (1985). On the resolution of role incompatibility: A life event history analysis of family roles and marijuana use. *American Journal of Sociology* 90, 1284–1293.

For Discussion

Hirsch and his colleagues expand upon Becker's theory of marijuana use. To what extent can their theory apply to other drug use?

Reprinted from: Michael L. Hirsch, Randall W. Conforti, and Carolyn J. Graney, "The Use of Marijuana for Pleasure: A Replication of Howard S. Becker's Study of Marijuana Use" in *Handbook of Replication Research.* Copyright © 1990 by Select Press. Reprinted by permission. ✦

5

Dope Fiends and Degenerates

The Gendering of Addiction in the Early Twentieth Century

Mara L. Keire

In the late nineteenth century, the majority of "addicts" in the United States were women from middle-class backgrounds who used drugs for medicinal purposes. This profile changed significantly in the twentieth century, when most "addicts" were men from lower- or working-class backgrounds. In the next article, Mara Keire discusses these major demographic changes. She introduces the concept of the "femininity of addiction" and argues that our perception of addicts and addiction continued into the twentieth century, despite the demographic changes in the profile of drug users. She also argues that these cultural perceptions served as powerful influences in the area of drug policy.

As historian David Courtwright describes in *Dark Paradise: Opiate Addiction in America Before 1940*, the typical addict of the late nineteenth century was an older middle-class woman who first started taking drugs for medical reasons, while the typical twentieth-century addict was a young man of the urban lower classes who had originally experimented with drugs for pleasure.[1] This demographic shift was dramatic, and Courtwright convincingly argues that the contrast between the ailing matron and the hustling junkie was significant in shaping our national narcotics policy.[2] But in the face of these undeniable demographic differences, important cultural continuities re-

mained. These cultural continuities bridged the demographic shift and connected the medical addicts of the 1880s and 1890s to the dope fiends of the 1910s and 1920s.

The most important cultural continuity was the perceived femininity of addiction. Starting in the 1870s, doctors injected women with morphine to numb the pain of "female troubles," or to turn the willful hysteric into a manageable invalid. Up through the turn of the century, morphine was a literal prescription for bourgeois femininity.[3] Thus, by the 1890s, when the first drug epidemic peaked, approximately two-thirds of the medical addicts were women, making women medical addicts almost half of all addicts in the United States. As a result of this thirty-year association of women with addiction, both users and observers saw drug addiction as something feminine as late as the 1930s, long after men had become the majority of users.[4]

To show how the femininity of addiction connected the older medical addicts to the nascent urban drug culture of the early twentieth century, this article will focus on drug use among the sporting class in the urban red-light district. I have two reasons for analyzing drugs in the vice district. First, the urban tenderloin was the location of cities' disreputable leisure, and as such it was the site of the new addiction.[5] Second, the new addicts either came from the sporting class, which was comprised of prostitutes, pimps, thieves, gamblers, gangsters, entertainers, fairies, and johns; or, they were youths who admired the sporting men and women. In their efforts to join the ranks of the sporting class, the new addicts emulated the sporting class's manners and mores—including their drug use.[6] By focusing on drug use by prostitutes, pimps, and the gay men known as fairies, I will demonstrate how the continued cultural association of addiction with femininity shaped the perception of addiction throughout society, and influenced the decision of men to incorporate drug use into their rejection of conventional male gender roles.[7]

This article is divided into four parts, including a theoretical intermission. The first section is a brief description of drugs in the vice district. In the second section, I focus on opiate use by pimps and prostitutes, paying particular attention to reformers' interpretations of the meaning of underworld addiction. After the section on pimps and prostitutes, I halt the historical narrative in order to discuss subcultures and subcultural style. When I re-engage the narrative, I conclude by analyzing cocaine use among fairies as exemplary of how the nineteenth-century feminization of drugs shaped twentieth-century male drug use.

Drugs in the District

Although never as prevalent as drinking, drug taking was an integral part of life in the urban vice districts. At the turn of the century, the members of the sporting class who took drugs mostly smoked opium. They bought their opium at Chinese restaurants, laundries, and opium dens, but the drug was also readily available in brothels.[8] Indeed, a 1905 study on prostitution found it just as noteworthy when opium was absent as when it was present.[9] By the early teens, both the urban vice districts, and drug use within them, had become more diverse. No longer just saloons, parlor houses, and cribs, the vice districts included dance halls, poolrooms, cabarets, gambling dens, movie theaters, and cigar shops. Concurrent with this diversification of services, there was a diversification in drug use. Anti-vice investigators were as likely to hear about people using morphine, heroin, and cocaine as smoking opium. While brothels and Chinese establishments continued as mainstays to the drug trade, saloons, dance halls, and disreputable pharmacies became increasingly important sites of supply.[10] These circumstances changed dramatically during World War I, when the war fervor enabled reformers to close the red-light districts and Federal officials to strengthen the enforcement of narcotics laws.[11]

As drug use diversified between 1910 and 1920, different cliques within the sporting world distinguished themselves through the types of drugs they used. As the price of opium rose, opium smoking, once so ubiquitous, became associated with the upper echelons of the sporting world—actors and actresses, high-rolling gamblers, and wealthy slummers.[12] Prostitutes and their pimps continued to consume opiates, although it became more likely that they were taking cheaper drugs like morphine than that they were smoking opium.[13] Meanwhile, reformers observed with growing alarm the gangs of boys who were adding cocaine and heroin use to their delinquent activities.[14] It was in the face of these continuities—opium smoking by prostitutes, gamblers, and entertainers—and changes—heroin and cocaine use within the growing youth culture—that members of the sporting class and outside observers interpreted the new patterns of drug use. They did so by drawing on, but altering, an older cultural reference: the femininity of drug use.

Prostitutes and Pimps

With prostitutes, the association of addiction with women was literal and direct. Prostitutes were women and prostitutes took drugs.[15] In his 1880 study of Chicago opiate addicts, Charles W. Earle observed that nearly three quarters of the addicts were women, and that fully a third of these women were prostitutes.[16] Thus the cultural continuity in the early twentieth century was twofold. Prostitutes had taken drugs in the earlier period and women had taken drugs for medical reasons. Like nineteenth-century matrons, prostitutes took drugs to treat a whole range of problems euphemistically called "female troubles." These ailments included dysmenorrhea, injuries from childbearing, ovarian cysts, uterine cancer, and venereal diseases.[17] The Chicago Vice Commissioners believed that a high percentage of prostitutes became addicts, either as a result of self-medication or a doctor's prescription, because their work increased their vulnerability to venereal diseases.[18]

In addition to the medical explanation, there was a moral explanation for prostitutes' addiction that also drew on "common sense" assumptions about women's nature. Like most of their contemporaries, anti-vice reformers believed that women were inherently modest and sexually unaggressive.[19]

For women to act so contrary to their natures—to submit to sex with countless strangers—something must have undermined their essential purity. Anti-vice reformers found the cause in drugs, alcohol, and the imperatives of addiction—but not always the culprits. Many reformers asserted that prostitutes had no choice in either their addiction or their work: "white slavers" used intoxicants to trick young women into prostitution, and then they forced their prostitutes to continue drinking or taking drugs so that they would not resist their sexual servitude. Anti-vice reformers interpreted prostitutes' dependence on drugs and alcohol as proof that prostitutes found their work distasteful. They believed that prostitutes' addiction was a sign of the extremes to which the agents of vice had to go to overcome women's innate morality.[20]

While the medical and moral explanations had a logical coherence, prostitutes' behavior challenged reformers' image of them as passive victims. The occasional report of a prostitute helpless within a brothel, stupefied by "a deadly drug," and covered with abscesses, reinforced reformers' conception of the world.[21] More often than not, however, the stories from the street called into question the morality tales that reformers sought to tell. For example, in a 1908 report to the United States delegation of the International Opium Convention, a "newspaper detective" described the daily routine of a Baltimore streetwalker. She solicited until two or three in the morning, at which time she took her earnings, bought the night's supply of opium, returned home to her pimp, and together they smoked for the next few hours. She then slept until six or seven in the evening, took a shot of morphine, and went back out on the street to earn more money so that she and her pimp could have more opium.[22] This story was shocking in part because of its role inversion—it was the woman who was leaving the house, earning the money, and providing for the man. Yet, despite the role inversion, this story had a domestic inevitability that the detective did not find as horrifying as what a different investigator witnessed six years later in New York City. In a saloon at the corner of Fourth

Avenue and Thirteenth Street, an investigator watched two women crush tablets of heroin and snort them with no self-consciousness about the other patrons. That these women took drugs in a public place, not a private room, was part of what the investigator found so repugnant.[23] The difference between the private opium smoking in 1908 and the public heroin consumption in 1914 challenged reformers' explanations of prostitutes' addiction. The more active and public role that prostitutes displayed in acquiring and taking their drugs in the 1910s called the prostitutes' assumed powerlessness into question.

Evidence that prostitutes introduced young men to drugs was even more damaging to their image as passive victims than the agency they exhibited in acquiring their drugs. One of the most scandalous discoveries made by the Chicago Vice Commissioners was that messenger boys working in the Levee, Chicago's red-light district, were learning drug use from prostitutes.[24] The messenger boys' stories probably resembled the one that an addict told sociologist Bingham Dai in the early 1930s. In his youth, the man had worked as a messenger boy in Butte, Montana's restricted district. There he attracted the attention of several prostitutes who were looking for pimps. At first he was bashful, but eventually the messenger boy raised his courage to talk to one of them. After confirming with a fellow messenger that the prostitute was a good money-maker, he agreed to be her pimp, and started living with her. In the course of their relationship, she slept with him, gave him money, and taught him to smoke opium.[25] It was stories like these that led researchers to sum up the causes of the new addicts' habits with phrases like "bad associates" and "tenderloin life."[26]

While the investigative reports gradually undermined the progressive-era portrayal of prostitutes, urban reformers generally remained sympathetic to prostitutes, even addicted prostitutes, but reviled their pimps. Reports of the pimps' addiction only increased this antipathy. With pimps and prostitutes alike, their drug use was a sign of how far they had fallen, but for prostitutes it rein forced a victimization that was consistent with gender roles in mainstream society. Women were supposed to be helpless, ailing, and even addicted—after all, it is likely that some reformers had older female relatives who were themselves addicts.[27] The pimps' addiction, however, was an affront to American masculinity, for as Surgeon General H. S. Cumming asserted in 1925, "opium makes a man effeminate."[28]

If the dominant nineteenth-century image of a female addict was the ailing middle-class matron, the stereotyped male addict of that period was the pig-tailed Chinese coolie or perhaps an aesthete inspired by Thomas De Quincey or Samuel Taylor Coleridge. Either image implied an orientalized decadence at odds with middle-class masculinity.[29] In the early twentieth century, these images translated into a feminization of male addicts, including pimps. Exhibiting their biases about the nature of men and addicts, contemporary commentators did not believe that boys became addicts because they aspired to be pimps, but rather that they became pimps because drug use made them unfit for any kind of active work. According to public health official Lawrence Kolb, "the ultimate effect [of opiates] is to create a state of idleness and dependency which naturally enhances the desire to live at the expense of others and by anti-social means."[30] In other words, addiction made men less manly.

The pimp's addiction represented just one aspect of his deviation from mainstream male gender roles. Pimps lived off the earnings of "immoral women"—and the more money that their prostitutes earned, the better they could dress, the more drinks they could buy for their fellows, and the higher the stakes at which they could gamble.[31] The flamboyance of the pimp's life had a direct correlation with how much money his prostitutes were earning. As such, the pimp's relationship to prostitutes resembled an inversion of the bourgeois gender relations that Thorstein Veblen described.[32] Women's work supported men's conspicuous consumption. Thus, the pimp did not just deviate from the bourgeois masculine ideal: he lived its inverse.

Nevertheless, as historian Natalie Zemon Davis reminds us in her 1975 essay, "Women on Top," inversions are rarely simple and they "*undermine* as well as reinforce" hierarchies of power.[33] The pimp threatened conventional gender roles because he offered a masculine model that linked male domination to supposedly feminine patterns of consumption and idleness. The pimp inverted middle-class conventions, but he was not an invert in the emerging medical sense of the term—he was a heterosexual male. The pimp retained his masculinity because he retained his power over women. Although the pimp transgressed bourgeois gender roles, his gender relations were consistent with identity.[34] Thus, even though middle-class reformers portrayed the pimp as a feminized villain, within the sporting class, pimps were the height of suave masculinity.

Middle-class reformers recognized this conundrum and feared that pimps provided a viable, although perverse, alternative for working-class youths. They believed that young men in the ghetto would eschew the bourgeois values of hard work and restraint and embrace the sporting class's leisure and free-spending conviviality.[35] Some observers, including sociologist Frederic M. Thrasher, warned that the increasing drug use among boys in urban gangs was an indication that they were choosing to emulate the sporting class.[36] Like the messenger boy in Butte, Montana, urban youths were trying drugs because they were "part and parcel of the role of a successful pimp."[37] By the early 1920s, the majority of new drug users were urban youths who imitated the lifestyle of the sporting class. These young men took drugs despite their long-standing association with femininity, because ironically that association was an integral part of the pimp's heightened masculinity.[38]

Theoretical Intermission

Up to this point, I have interpreted the femininity of drug use from the perspective of middle-class observers. I will now switch perspectives and address how a particular group within the sporting class—fairies—used cocaine as a way to signal their social and sexual identity. In order to do so, I must discuss at greater length subcultures and the transmission of cultural style.[39]

The sporting class was a distinct urban subculture. Although contemporaries defined the people associated with the urban vice district as a separate class, values and style, not income or family, defined membership. The elements that set the sporting class apart from respectable society were not only how they spent their time, but also their clothing and public presentation. The members of the sporting class, like those of other subcultures, adopted distinctive clothes and body language in order to announce their participation in that subculture. These stylistic elements were their signifiers.[40] Signifiers were not only physical objects—for example, a prostitute's ankle-flashing short skirt—they were also cultural messages: at the turn of the century, a short skirt equaled sexual availability. Thus a pimp's flashy clothing and jewelry were signifiers of his group identity, his wealth, the quality of his prostitutes, and his rejection of the work ethic of respectable men.

The sporting class, however, also had distinct divisions. The most notable distinction was between those who worked in the district and those who played in it. For prostitutes, their revealing dress and cosmetics were literal advertisements of who they were and what they were selling. Thus the adoption of the prostitute's distinctive trademarks of short skirts, cigarettes, a slow saunter, and bold eye contact, were "professional" signifiers. Other members in the sporting class— the consumers—had choices in their identification. The gang members, fairies, and charity girls (sexually-active young women who were not prostitutes) adopted certain types of dress and gestures to signal what were usually leisure-time identities.[41] This distinction is crucial. Although the sporting class consisted of both consumers and producers, these two groups had vastly different reasons for adopting their cultural signifiers. Producers used signifiers to make their living, consumers used them to express their identity.

The people who set the tone and offered the cultural models within the tenderloin were the madams, pimps, and prostitutes— the people who worked in the district. The prostitutes provided, while pimps and madams enabled, the sexual commerce that was the foundation upon which all other activities in the district were built. As a result of their centrality, the successful madams, pimps, and prostitutes had the highest status within the district and established the cultural styles. Charity girls, fairies, and other groups who were socializing in the district by choice rather than financial necessity looked up to the sporting-class elite. In forming their own group identities, gang members, fairies, and charity girls often appropriated elements of the sporting elite's style as signifiers of their own subcultural identity.[42] Fairies, for example, borrowed heavily from the "professional" signifiers of prostitutes to create their leisure-time identities—signifiers they later carried beyond the district into the general culture.

Fairies

The keynote of fairies' subcultural identity was their effeminacy. In *Gay New York*, historian George Chauncey has ably described fairies and their subcultural style. He argues that fairies, who socialized in the urban tenderloin and the most transgressive commercial dance halls, self-consciously rejected masculine gender roles by selectively adopting "feminine" signifiers. As he observes, "In the right context, appropriating even a single feminine—or at least unconventional—style or article of clothing might signify a man's identity as a fairy." These cultural cues could be suede shoes or a red tie, plucked eyebrows or bleached hair, and most stereotypically an exaggerated walk, a limp wrist, or arms akimbo.[43] Cocaine was another signifier that some fairies adopted to distinguish themselves from conventional society. These fairies chose cocaine because, like their contemporaries, they associated drug use with femininity.

Fairies took prostitutes as their model of femininity. Chauncey argues that fairies purposely adopted prostitutes' style and slang. An important element of prostitutes' style was drug use, which fairies copied as well.

New York Police Commissioner Theodore A. Bingham described this cultural transmission when he wrote to public health reformer Hamilton Wright that:

> the classes of the community most addicted to the habitual use of cocaine are the parasites [sic] who live on the earnings of prostitutes, prostitutes of the lowest order, and young degenerates who acquire the habit at an early age through their connection with prostitutes and parasites [sic].[44]

While fairies may have taken prostitutes as their feminine model, these "degenerates" reinterpreted that femininity in the process of making it their own. Like all cultural transfers, there was an alteration in the process. Prostitutes used a range of drugs, but they were best known as opiate addicts. Fairies, on the other hand, were most closely associated with cocaine.

There are two possible explanations for why fairies incorporated cocaine, instead of the opiates, into their subcultural style. The first is functional: cocaine provided an excuse for "trade," conventionally masculine men who were sexually interested in fairies, to approach fairies. As an anti-drug reformer noted, "the practice of sniffing also leads to more social contagion, since the offer of a pinch of cocaine may be as simple a gesture as to offer a cigarette." In saloons and dance halls, cocaine functioned in much the same way as cigarettes did when men were picking up each other.[45] Other drugs, which involved more paraphernalia, could not function in this simple fashion.[46] The second reason for fairies' choice of cocaine was its physical effects. Prostitutes may have taken opiates to anesthetize themselves to their work, but fairies' identities were tied to their leisure, not to their work. One of the keynotes of their leisure identity was a bright flamboyance which suggests why fairies favored cocaine over the opiates. Cocaine could produce a brittle effervescence that made it more attractive to fairies than the effects of opiates, which suggested a laid-back "hipness" inconsistent with fairies' cultural style.[47] These functional and physical explanations of fairies' cocaine use explain why fairies chose cocaine over other drugs,

but not why they incorporated drug use into their cultural style. Fairies made cocaine part of their subculture because it was a feminine signifier.

One of the best examples of the association of a fairy with cocaine use was in the story of Daisy, a regular at Martin's Saloon in Brooklyn. At Martin's, Daisy flirted with the patrons, borrowed a powder puff from investigator Natalie Sonnichsen, sang a dirty song, and performed a dance imitating sodomy with Elsie, another fairy. In order to confirm the disreputable goings-on, the general secretary of the Committee of Fourteen, an anti-vice association, sent out a male investigator, S. M. Auerbach, to determine whether the fairies were soliciting. When Auerbach approached Daisy, he began the conversation by asking Daisy whether he was a "cocaine fiend," and if he had any "coca" to spare. Although Daisy was all out, he readily admitted that he was a "fiend." While Auerbach did not use this exchange as the first step to setting up a date, Daisy let Natalie know that he "had designs on Mr. A.[48] Daisy's story illustrates the subcultural style that fairies adopted. Daisy signaled that he was a fairy by using feminine gestures such as borrowing Natalie Sonnichsen's powder puff. Daisy's style was not, however, a demure femininity—his outrageous antics were more playful versions of prostitutes' public sexuality. Moreover, Daisy's frenetic sociability suggested to Auerbach that Daisy was a "cocaine fiend" which gave Auerbach, who was quintessentially "trade," an excuse to approach Daisy. In other words, for Daisy, cocaine was one of a range of feminine signifiers that he adopted in order to communicate his identity as a fairy.[49]

Fairies' adoption of cocaine as a signifier meant that cocaine eventually became a general gay signifier, and with that shift the association of drugs and femininity became increasingly tenuous. By the 1920s, the association of drugs with homosexuality had spread beyond the urban vice district. When the Hollywood Scandals of the early twenties revealed that movie stars were using drugs, the media began speculating about the sexual orientation of leading actors and directors.[50] It was the association of drugs with fairies that informed John Dos Passos' characterization of Tony Garrido in *The Big Money*, the final book of his U.S.A. trilogy. Tony was an attractive Cuban expatriate, but it was his addiction as much as his "mincing walk" that confirmed his homosexuality to his wife Margo Dowling.[51] Whether they were playing off of these associations or informing them, members of wealthy gay artistic circles continued using cocaine into the 1930s.[52]

Although the connection between drug use and homosexuality became increasingly tenuous after World War II, drugs continued to appeal to people disaffected with conventional society, including gay men like William Burroughs and Allen Ginsberg. Even though the hustling junkie now seems more masculine than feminine, William Burroughs was "queer," and it was through his infamous addiction, as well as his sexual preference, that he communicated his rejection of mainstream masculinity.[53] The Beats were a long way from the ailing matrons of the nineteenth century, but the fairy and the pimp—alternative masculine models from the progressive-era vice districts—provide the genealogical link that spans the seemingly unbridgeable demographic difference between nineteenth- and twentieth-century addicts.

Conclusion

Since the 1970s, historians have argued that the demographic differences between the ailing matrons of the late nineteenth century and the dope fiends of the early twentieth century powerfully influenced Federal enactment of anti-drug laws. Historians have not, however, recognized how the femininity of addiction—the cultural continuity that connected the old and new addicts—shaped the early enforcement of narcotics laws. The perception in the 1920s that addicts were unmanly—weak, untrustworthy, and constitutionally flawed—informed how agents enforced, judges interpreted, and the public supported narcotics laws as ad hoc responses hardened into long-term Federal policy.

The "deviant" gendering of drug addicts tipped the balance from uneasy toleration to unquestioned prohibition. David Musto has argued that the passage of narcotics laws and their stringent enforcement required a reviled "other" in order to create an anti-drug consensus.[54] These "others" have included the "cocaine-crazed" Southern black men at the turn of the century, the marijuana-smoking Mexican migrant of the late 1930s, and, most recently, the pregnant crack whore. In each of these cases, however, race and class alone were not enough to create public consensus—it was their alternative, and often threatening, sexual roles that decisively alienated drug users from the mainstream. This process of "othering" was necessarily multivalenced, and the allegations of deviant sexuality and the transgression of conventional gender roles critically reinforced other, more obvious, racial and class antipathies toward drug users.

Ironically, this process of "othering" often strengthened the cultural appeal of drug use. Media representation made casual drug use within subcultures an emblematic signifier of those cultures. Criminal prosecution turned drug users into romantic outlaws, while labeling simplified complicated subcultural rituals into easily imitated affectations. As a result, people who felt disaffected with conventional society could express their alienation by taking drugs and—however tenuous their connection—signal their affinity for the reviled others. Thus, the association of drugs with transgressive subcultures has meant that although the particular cultural connotations have changed, the overriding reason for drug experimentation in the twentieth century has been rebellion against the restrictions of conventional society. The gendering of addiction at the turn of the century continues to haunt reform efforts, for the recurring tension between othering and embracing the other remains the central conundrum of America's ongoing "war on drugs."

Notes

The research for this paper was partially funded by a grant-in-aid from the American

Institute of Pharmacy History and a travel fellowship to the Rockefeller Archive Center. I would like to thank my advisers Ronald G. Walters, Dorothy Ross, and David Musto for their support. I owe scholarly debts to David Courtwright, Nadja Durbach, Chris McKenna, Laura Street, Cheryl Warsh, and the anonymous reviewers. I presented earlier versions of this paper at the Conference on Historical Perspectives on the Use and Abuse of Illicit Drugs in the United States held at the Yale School of Medicine and the Conference on Historical Perspectives on Alcohol and Drug Use in American Society, 1800–1997 at the College of Physicians of Philadelphia. I would like to thank both the conference organizers and participants for their insights and their encouragement.

1. David T. Courtwright, *Dark Paradise: Opiate Addiction in America Before 1940* (Cambridge, Mass., 1982), 1–4.

2. David T. Courtwright, Herman Joseph, and Don Des Jarlais, *Addicts Who Survived: An Oral History of Narcotic Use in America, 1923–1965* (Knoxville, Tenn., 1989), 3–5.

3. For a discussion of bourgeois feminine ideals, hysteria, and the ailments of women's reproductive system, see Carroll Smith-Rosenberg, "Puberty to Menopause: The Cycle of Femininity in Nineteenth-Century America," and "The Hysterical Woman: Sex Roles and Role Conflict in Nineteenth-Century America," in *Disorderly Conduct: Visions of Gender in Victorian America* (New York, 1985), 182–216. Smith-Rosenberg beautifully describes nineteenth-century doctors' understanding of female health and their resulting advice, but she does not examine the therapeutic measures that doctors adopted to treat their patients. On doctors's use of opiates to treat hysteria and "female troubles," see H. H. Kane, *Drugs That Enslave: The Opium, Morphine, Chloral and Hashisch Habits* (Philadelphia, 1881; reprint, New York, 1981), 18, 25; Charles F. Terry and Mildred Pellens, eds., *The Opium Problem* (New York, 1928), 96–100; David T. Courtwright, "The Female Opiate Addict in Nineteenth-Century America," Essay in *Arts and Sciences* 10 (1982): 163–4; H. Wayne Morgan, *Drugs in America: A Social History, 1800–1980* (Syracuse, 1981), 39–40. For the congruence between addiction and gender roles for middle-class women, compare Smith-Rosenberg's descriptions with Kane, *Drugs That Enslave*, 49; T. D. Crothers, *Morphinism and Narcomanias From Other Drugs: Their Etiology, Treatment, and Medicolegal Relations* (Philadelphia, 1902; reprint, New York, 1981), 104; and F. E. Oliver, "The Use and Abuse of Opium," Massachusetts State Board of Health, *Third Annual Report* (Boston, 1872), 162–177 in *Yesterday's Addicts: American Society and Drug Abuse, 1865–1920*, ed. H. Wayne Morgan (Norman, Okla., 1974), 49.

4. David Courtwright argues that during the "first wave" of American drug use, 1870–1940, the peak of opiate addiction was in the mid-1890s. At that point, he estimates that in the United States there could have been no more than 313,000 addicts or 4.59 per thousand. Within the addict population, almost half were women medical addicts from the middle class. After the effective prohibition of narcotics in the late 1910s, and the creation of the Federal Bureau of Narcotics, the available numbers become so politically loaded and statistically unreliable, that Courtwright, even after an exhaustive search, was not able to produce equivalent numbers for the later period. He does posit, however, that in 1920 there could have been no more than 210,000 addicts, or approximately 2 addicts per thousand. Moreover, the number of addicts kept declining through World War II. From contemporary observations, it is clear that from 1900 onwards, there were progressively fewer medical addicts and that there were proportionally more recreational addicts—most of whom were young men from the city. Courtwright, *Dark Paradise*, 28, 36, 34, 113–115.

5. John Phillips, "Prevalence of the Heroin Habit: Especially the Use of the Drug by 'Snuffing,'" *Journal of the American Medical Association* 59 (1912): 2147; Clifford B. Fan, "The Relative Frequency of the Morphine and Heroine Habits: Based Upon Some Observations at the Philadelphia General Hospital," *New York Medical Journal* 101 (1915): 893; Courtwright, *Dark Paradise*, 90, 192 n22; Morgan, *Drugs in America*, 57, 91.

6. Richard Dewey to Hamilton Wright, 5 November 1908, file: "U.S. Data: Rhode Island to Wyoming," box 2, entry 47, Record Group 43, National Archives at College Park, Maryland (hereafter, NARG followed by the record group number); Joseph McIver and George E. Price, "Drug Addiction: Analysis of One Hundred and Forty-Seven Cases at the Philadelphia General Hospital," *Journal of the American Medical Association* 66 (1916): 477; L. L. Stanley, "Morphinism and Crime," *Journal of the American Institute of Criminal Law*

and Criminology 8 (1918): 749–56 in *Yesterday's Addicts*, 83.

7. I use the term "fairies" deliberately. Historian George Chauncey has convincingly argued that in the early decades of this century, people did not see sexuality as a binary heterosexual/homosexual split. Instead, he argues, it was not just sexual preference, but also style that determined sexual labels. Fairies—a self-description—were flamboyantly effeminate men who took the "woman's role." There was also a class dimension to this category. Fairies were usually from the working class, while "queers," who were less overt in their sexual display, were from the middle class. See George Chauncey, *Gay New York: Gender, Urban Culture, and the Making of the Gay Male World, 1890–1940* (New York, 1994), 12–23.

8. "Prostitution in Precinct XV," 119011, 2, Committee of Fifteen, Rare Books and Manuscripts Division, New York Public Library; "Several Raids Made on 'Joints' Last Night," *New York News*, 17 March 1901, Newspaper Clippings, Committee of Fifteen; "Quan Yick Nam," 19 February 1901, Committee of Fifteen; "Arthur F. Wilson States," 1 March 1901, Committee of Fifteen.

9. "Parlor Houses," file 6.8, box 91, Lillian Wald Papers, Columbia University.

10. *New Orleans Item*, 9 August 1907, 25 July 1914, 13 November 1915, 23 December 1910, and 22 January 1915.

11. On the closing of the red-light districts as a wartime measure, see Allan M. Brandt, *No Magic Bullet: A Social History of Venereal Disease in the United States Since 1880, With a New Chapter on AIDS* (New York, 1987), 70–77. On how concerns about war preparedness influenced the more stringent interpretation of the Harrison Act, see David F. Musto, *The American Disease: Origins of Narcotic Control, Expanded Edition* (New York, 1987), 135, 328 n35.

12. Frank A. McGuire and Perry M. Lichtenstein, "The Drug Habit," *Medical Record* 90 (1916): 185; McIver and Price, "Drug Addiction," 478; Courtwright, *Dark Paradise*, 83–84.

13. [Vice Commission of Newark, New Jersey], *Report on the Social Evil Conditions of Newark, New Jersey to the People of Newark* (n.p., ([1914]), 126–30; Courtwright, *Dark Paradise*, 2.

14. Jane Addams, *The Spirit of Youth and the City Streets* (New York, 1909; reprint, Urbana, 1972), 63–67; Pearce Bailey, "The Heroin

Habit," *The New Republic* 6 (1916): 314–16 in *Yesterday's Addicts*, 172.

15. Male prostitution was a barely recognized phenomenon during the Progressive era.

16. Charles W. Earle, "The Opium Habit: A Statistical and Clinical Lecture," *Chicago Medical Review* 2(1880): 442–46 in *Yesterday's Addicts*, 53. In Earle's sample of 235 addicts, 169 were women. Earle wrote that a third of these women were prostitutes, which would mean that approximately 56 women were addicts—making prostitutes approximately a quarter of all drug users in the sample.

17. Courtwright, *Dark Paradise*, 52.

18. Vice Commission of Chicago, *The Social Evil in Chicago: A Study of Existing Conditions, with Recommendations* (Chicago, 1911), 84–87, 289. See also Ruth Rosen, "Introduction" in *The Maimie Papers*, ed. by Ruth Rosen and Sue Davidson (Old Westbury, 1977), xiv, xli n5. Interestingly, at the municipal maintenance clinic in Shreveport, Louisiana, which was open from 1919 to 1923, the most frequently given explanation for opiate addiction was venereal disease. Of the 449 patients, 28.5 percent (121 men, 8 women) said they had started taking opiates because of "venereal disease" or "gonorrhea." When "blood poisoning" and "french fever," both of which were euphemisms for sexually transmitted diseases, are added to the tally the percentage increases to 30.0 percent (127 men, 8 women), History Sheets. Narcotics Division, Louisiana State Board of Health, Willis Butler Papers, Department of Archives and Special Collections, Noel Memorial Library, Louisiana State University in Shreveport.

19. On nineteenth-century feminine ideals, see Nancy F. Cott, "Passionlessness: An Interpretation of Victorian Sexual Ideology," *Signs* 4 (1978): 219–236 in *Women and Health in America*, ed. Judith Walzer Leavitt (Madison, 1984), 57–69; Carroll Smith-Rosenberg and Charles Rosenberg, "The Female Animal: Medical and Biological Views of Woman and Her Role in Nineteenth-Century America," *Journal of American History* 60 (1973): 332–356 in *Women and Health*, 12–27; and Ronald G. Walters, ed., *Primers for Prudery: Sexual Advice to Victorian America* (Englewood Cliffs, 1974), 6.

20. *The Social Evil in Chicago*, 285; Sara Graham-Mulhall, "Experiences in Narcotic Drug Control in the State of New York," *New York Medical Journal* 113 (1921): 106–11 in *Yesterday's Addicts*, 211; The Vice Commission of Phila-

delphia, *A Report on Existing Conditions with Recommendations to the Honorable Rudolph Blankenburg, Mayor of Philadelphia* (n.p., 1913), 34; George J. Kneeland, *Commercialized Prostitution in New York City* (New York, 1917; reprint Montclair, N.J., 1969), 15–16. This explanation also had a racist version in which authors asserted that opium smoking was the only way that white prostitutes could endure having sex with Chinese men; for a typical example, see I. L. Nascher, *The Wretches of Povertyville: A Sociological Study of the Bowery* (Chicago, 1909), 134.

21. Christina Kuppinger, "Report for May, To the Officers and Directors of the Midnight Mission," May 1911, file 2, box 5, Ernest Bell Papers, Chicago Historical Society.

22. "Baltimore Notes," 17 July 1908, file: "Miscellaneous Correspondence," box 2, entry 48, NARG 43; "Philadelphia Notes," 20–21 July 1908, 2, 5–6, file: "Miscellaneous Correspondence," box 2, entry 48, NARG 43.

23. "135 Fourth Avenue—Saloon Hangout—Drugs," box 28, Committee of Fourteen Papers, Rare Books and Manuscripts Division, New York Public Library. See also "317 West 41st Street—Black and Tan Saloon—Drugs," box 28, Committee of Fourteen.

24. *The Social Evil in Chicago*, 242–244. Although he did not state whether they were messenger boys, L. L. Stanley found in a study of 100 prisoners in San Quentin that 15 had learned drug use from prostitutes; Stanley, "Morphinism and Crime," in *Yesterday's Addicts*, 80–83. This pattern continued into the 1940s; see Teddy's interview in Courtwright et al., *Addicts Who Survived*, 51.

25. Bingham Dai, *Opium Addiction in Chicago* (1937; reprint, Montclair, N.J., 1970), 144–148. See also L. L. Stanley, "Morphinism and Crime," in *Yesterday's Addicts*, 85.

26. S. Dana Hubbard, "The New York City Narcotic Clinic and Differing Points of View on Narcotic Addiction," New York City Department of Health, *Monthly Bulletin* 10 (1920) in *The Opium Problem*, 123–124; "The First Annual Summary of the Clinical Work on Opium Addiction in Philadelphia General Hospital for the Philadelphia Committee by the Clinical Staff," Part II (1926), 6–7, file 552, box 1, sub-series 1, series IV, Bureau of Social Hygiene Papers, Rockefeller Archive Center, Tarrytown, New York.

27. Ann Douglas Wood, "'The Fashionable Disease': Women's Complaints and Their Treatment in Nineteenth-Century America," *The*

Journal of Interdisciplinary History 4 (1973): 25–52 in *Women and Health*, 227; Barbara Ehrenreich and Deirdre English, *For Her Own Good: 150 Years of the Experts' Advice to Women* (Garden City, 1978), 23, 92–96, 103; Brian Dijkstra, *Idols of Perversity: Fantasies of Feminine Evil in Fin-de-Siècle Culture* (New York, 1985), 25–37. Harriet Beecher Stowe's daughter Georgiana is an example of an addict within a reform family; Courtwright, "The Female Opiate Addict," 163–164.

28. H. S. Cumming, "Control of Drug Addiction Mainly a Police Problem," *The American City Magazine* (November 1925), file 126, box 3, sub-series 1, series III, Bureau of Social Hygiene; John S. Haller, Jr. and Robin M. Haller, *The Physician and Sexuality in Victorian America* (Carbondale, IL., 1974), 302. One of the physical effects of opiate addiction is male impotence. Knowledge of this side effect may be one reason that people associated addiction with effeminacy; see Kane, *Drugs That Enslave*, 45; W. M. Kraus, "An Analysis of the Action of Morphine upon the Vegetative Nervous System of Man," *Journal of Nervous and Mental Diseases* 48 (1918) in *The Opium Problem*, 461; and W. Hale White, *Materia Medica, Pharmacy, Pharmacology and Therapeutics* (1924) in *The Opium Problem*, 462; Morgan, *Drugs in America*, 189 n56.

29. Morgan, *Drugs in America*, 35–37, 54–55. On turn-of-the-century conceptions of manliness and fears about the "feminized male," see E. Anthony Rotundo, "Roots of Change: The Women Without and the Woman Within," in *American Manhood: Transformations in Masculinity from the Revolution to the Modern Era* (New York, 1993), 247–283.

30. Clifford G. Roe and Clare Teal Wiseman, *The Prosecutor: A Four-Act Drama* (n.p., 1914), 33–34; W. A. Bloedorn, "Studies of Drug Addicts," *U.S. Naval Medical Bulletin* 11 (1917) in *The Opium Problem*, 494; Lawrence Kolb, "Drug Addiction in Its Relation to Crime," *Mental Hygiene* 9 (1925): 75.

31. Ruth Rosen, *The Lost Sisterhood: Prostitution in America, 1900–1918* (Baltimore, 1982), 109.

32. Thorstein Veblen, *Theory of the Leisure Class*, with an introduction by Robert Lekachman (1899; reprint, New York, 1979), 80–82.

33. Natalie Zemon Davis, "Women on Top," in *Society and Culture in Early Modern France* (Stanford, 1975), 131. Emphasis in original.

34. In turn-of-the-century medical literature, "invert" was the term for gay men who trans-

gressed gender boundaries and were more like women than men; see John D'Emilio and Estelle B. Freedman, *Intimate Matters: A History of Sexuality in America* (New York, 1988), 226; Chauncey, *Gay New York*, 48–49.

35. "The White Slavery Films: A Review," *The Outlook* 106 (1914): 345–50; James Bronson Reynolds to Frederick H. Whitin, 24 October 1914, box 3, Committee of Fourteen. Bruce Raeburn of the William Ransom Hogan Jazz Archive at Tulane University has observed that jazz great Jelly Roll Morton's boast that he was a pimp exemplifies the pimp's prestige in the early twentieth century.

36. Frederic M. Thrasher, "Drug Addiction and Adolescent Behavior (Study Completed July 5, 1929)" (typescript), 15, 28, file 128, box 3, sub-series 1, series III, Bureau of Social Hygiene. Although John Devon was not a pimp, the things that Leroy Street admired about him—his leisure, his dress, and his worldliness—were the kinds of things that urban youths admired in pimps. It was as a result of this type of hero worship that Leroy Street and others picked up their idols' drug habits; Leroy Street in collaboration with David Loth, *I Was a Drug Addict* (New York, 1953), 11–13.

37. Dai, *Opium Addiction in Chicago*, 149.

38. McIver and Price, "Drug Addiction," 477; C. Edouard Sandoz, "Report on Morphinism to the Municipal Court of Boston," *Journal of Criminal Law, Criminology, and Police Science* 13 (1922): 24, 36; "The First Annual Summary of the Clinical Work on Opium Addiction in Philadelphia General Hospital for the Philadelphia Committee by the Clinical Staff," Part II (1926), 3, file 552, box 1, sub-series 1, series IV, Bureau of Social Hygiene; Terry and Pellens, eds., *The Opium Problem*, 474. The argument can be made that pimps were the antecedents for hipster jazz musicians; Jill Jonnes, "The Sky Is High and So Am I," in *Hep-Cats, Narcs, and Pipe Dreams: A History of America's Romance With Illegal Drugs* (New York, 1996), 119–140. Howard Becker's description of dance musicians and marijuana smoking also shows the clear continuities between drug use and alternate masculine models; Howard S. Becker, *Outsiders: Studies in the Sociology of Deviance* (New York, 1963).

39. For an excellent discussion of subcultures and group identity, see Dick Hebdige, *Subculture: The Meaning of Style* (London, 1979).

See also Ken Gelder and Sarah Thornton, eds., *The Subcultures Reader* (London, 1997).

40. For a further explanation of signifiers, see "Myth Today," in Roland Barthes, *Mythologies*, trans. Annette Lavers (Paris, 1957; reprint, New York, 1972), 109–159.

41. Frederic M. Thrasher, *The Gang: A Study of 1,313 Gangs in Chicago*, 2d rev. ed. (Chicago, 1927), 68–69, 79; Chauncey, *Gay New York*, 44, 51–56; Kathy Piess, *Cheap Amusements: Working Women and Leisure in Turn-of-the-Century New York* (Philadelphia, 1986), 57, 62–67.

42. Thrasher, *The Gang*, 252, 255–257, 262; Peiss, *Cheap Amusements*, 66.

43. George Chauncey, *Gay New York*, 51–55, quotation on page 51.

44. Chauncey, *Gay New York*, 60–61, 69, 286; Theo. A. Bingham to Hamilton Wright, 23 June 1909, file: "United States Data, New York," box 1, entry 47, NARG 43. See also the story of a fairy who started taking morphine on the advice of prostitutes in Dai, *Opium Addiction in Chicago*, 163. It is important to note that although "degenerate" had a variety of meanings in the medical literature, in common parlance it generally denoted homosexuality; Charles Johnston, alias Hattie Ross, to Robert S. Bickerd, 29 July 1910, box 1, Committee of Fourteen.

45. The quotation is from page 9 of an unidentified report in file 51, box 7, Bureau of Social Hygiene, Rockefeller Boards, Record Group 2, Rockefeller Family Archives, Rockefeller Archive Center; Chauncey, *Gay New York*, 64, 188. See also, *The Social Evil in Chicago*, 290.

46. Courtwright et al., *Addicts Who Survived*, 97.

47. The term "hip" was originally associated with opium smoking which occurred "on the hip;" see Jonnes, *Hep-Cats, Narcs, and Pipe Dreams*, 125.

48. "Martin's Saloon. Opposite Jackson Avenue Park," 1 August 1912; "Martin's Saloon," 8 August 1912; and "Martin's Saloon. Jackson Avenue," 14 August 1912, box 29; and "Dance Hall and Martin's Saloon," 15 August 1912, box 28, Committee of Fourteen. Cocaine and fairies were associated with other transgressive places where "anything went," see "Memo," 18 August 1913, box 3, Committee of Fourteen; "Re saloons etc., Queens Boro," 24 July 1913, 5–6, box 29, Committee of Fourteen; George Chauncey, Jr., "Christian Brotherhood or Sexual Perversion? Homosexual Identities and the Construction of Sexual

Boundaries in the World War I Era," *Journal of Social History* 19 (1985): 189–212 in *Hidden From History: Reclaiming the Gay and Lesbian Past*, eds. Martin Bauml Duberman, Martha Vicinus, and George Chauncey, Jr. (New York, 1989), 297. I would like to thank George Chauncey for bringing it to my attention that the Newport investigation targeted sexual perversion and cocaine use, see U.S. Senate, 67th Cong., 1st sess., Committee on Naval Affairs, *Alleged Immoral Conditions at Newport (R.I.) Naval Training Station* (Washington, D.C., 1921), 17 reprinted in Jonathan Katz, ed., *Government Versus Homosexuals* (New York, 1975).

49. There are a number of examples of cocaine functioning as a gay signifier in German and Swiss medical literature. For an overview of this literature, see Oriana Josseau Kalant, ed. and trans., *Maier's Cocaine Addiction (Der Kokainzsmus)* (1926; reprint, Toronto, 1987), 43, 50–54, 160–162, 167, 182–185.

50. *Sins of Hollywood: A Group of Actual Happenings Reported and Written by a Hollywood Newspaper Man* (Hollywood, 1922) in *The Movies in Our Midst: Documents in the Cultural History of Film in America*, ed. Gerald

Mast (Chicago, 1982), 177, 180; "Slain Film Director Believed Victim of Love Revenge Plot," *New York Herald*, 3 February 1922, William Desmond Taylor Clippings, Library of the Performing Arts at Lincoln Center.

51. John Dos Passos, *The Big Money* (1933; reprint, New York, 1969), 287–90, 402–403.

52. Barry Paris, *Louise Brooks* (New York, 1989), 239, 367–369.

53. Jonnes, *Hep-Cats, Narcs, and Pipe Dreams*, 208–210; William S. Burroughs, *Queer* (New York, 1985).

54. Musto, *The American Disease*, 5–8, 11, 43–44, 219–223.

For Discussion

Discuss whether the "gendering of addiction" applies in contemporary society.

Reprinted from: Mara L. Keire, "Dope Fiends and Degenerates: The Gendering of Addiction in the Early Twentieth Century" in *Journal of Social History* 31(4), pp. 809–822. Copyright © 1998 by *Journal of Social History*, George Mason University. Reprinted by permission. ✦

6

Sociopharmacology of Drug Use

Initial Thoughts

Samuel R. Friedman

Samuel Friedman introduces the concept of "sociopharmacology" as it relates to drug use. A sociopharmacological approach to drug use takes into account the particular social, economic, and political context in which drug use occurs. By using several examples, Friedman illustrates the importance of sociopharmacology in terms of its ability to explain drug use. He suggests that social order and social context, rather than the individual, represent the underlying "causes" of drug use.

Introduction

Much research on drug use has focused on individual characteristics of the drug users and the psychopharmacology of drug use. Such research investigates how the psychological traits of drug users and chemical traits of drugs lead to addiction and to its associated problems. At its 'best', this research medicalises addiction and its associated problems. At its worst, it legitimates the demonising of drug users and a war on drugs that, in the United States alone, spends $11 billion annually on law enforcement and interdiction without reducing heroine or cocaine availability or purity or increasing their prices. This drug war approach has, however, helped mask the consequences of social structures based on racial and gender inequality and on economic exploitation by leading millions to see their consequences for local communities and individuals to be the product, instead, of individual criminality and drug use. Millions of drug users have

been incarcerated as a result of this scapegoating policy; and it has not prevented the spread of injection drug use, and its related lethal blood-borne infections such as HIV, hepatitis B and C, and endocarditis around the world (Friedman, 1998a; Schiraldi, Holman & Phillip, 2000; Stimson, 1993; Stimson, Ball & Des Jarlais, 1998).

Whether through medicalisation or demonisation, such research defines the user as the problem, and thus ignores socioeconomic and other issues that create vulnerabilities to harmful and/or chronic drug use among individuals, neighbourhoods, and population groups. We offer the concept of 'sociopharmacology of drug use' as a partial contribution to developing an alternative way of thinking and acting on drug-related issues.

Our concept of 'sociopharmacology' attempts to locate drug use in a broader socioeconomic context, as it intersects with the histories and physiologies of individuals, the social, political and economic histories and current realities of different populations, communities and countries, and the pharmacology of drugs. We thus look at the social 'causation' of drug use patterns, where our concept of 'causation' is not one of forces with deterministic impact on individuals, but rather one in which social structures and processes effect the likelihood that individuals will use various drugs. Human subjectivity and agency are important; but what Durkheim (1982) called 'social facts' nonetheless emerge out of the play of multilevel influences and individual and collective dialectical reactions to these forces. Here, then, our argument parallels those of other students of the social epidemiology of disease, morbidity, and mortality (Armstrong, Barnett, Casper & Wing, 1998; Armstrong & Castorina, 1998; Berkman & Kawachi, 2000; Casper, Wing & Strogatz, 1991; Diez-Roux, Nieto, Muntaner, et al., 1997; Diez-Roux, Nieto, Caulfield, Tyroler, Watson & Szklo, 1999; Elreedy, Krieger, Ryan, Sparow, Weiss & Hu, 1999; Fife & Mode, 1992; Hu, Frey, Costa, Massey, Ryan, Flemming, D'Errico, Ward & Buechler, 1994; Kaplan, Pamuk, Lynch, Cohen & Balfour, 1996; Kennedy, Ichiro, Kawachi & Prothrow-Stith, 1996;

Lynch, Kaplan, Pamuk, Cohen, Heck, Balfour & Yen, 1998; O'Campo, Xue, Wang & O'Brien Caughy, 1997; Simon, Hu, Diaz & Kerndt, 1995; Wallace & Wallace, 1999; Zierler & Krieger, 1997), as well as of substance use (Bell, Carlson & Richard, 1998; Brugal, Domingo-Salvany, Maguire, Cayla, Villalbi & Hartnoll, 1999; Faris & Dunham, 1939; Chein, Gerard, Lee & Rosenfeld, 1964; Diez-Roux et al., 1997; Kleinschmidt, Hills & Elliot, 1995; Nurco, 1972; Nurco, Shaffer & Cisin, 1984; Redlinger & Michel, 1970).

This concept of sociopharmacology differs from Rhodes' (1996) concept of 'social pharmacology'. Rhodes, like Becker (1977), focuses on how social and cultural forces affect 'knowledge about the perceived and expected 'pharmacological' effects of drugs'. Rhodes also discusses the cultural concept of disinhibition due to drug use, and its potential as an excuse for engaging in unsafe sex, in terms of social contexts (or what Mills, 1940 referred to as a 'vocabulary of motives'). We, by contrast, focus on social causation of drug use patterns in populations and subpopulations rather than on perceptions of drug effects.

Similarly, our concept differs from analyses of small group, role, and folk cultural regulatory mechanisms that shape how drug users use their drugs or that help them maintain controlled levels of use or safer injection practices (Friedman et al., 1998b; Friedman, Curtis, Neaigus, Jose & Des Jarlais, 1999; Friedman, Kang, Deren, Robles, Colón, Andia, Oliver-Valdez & Finlinson, 2002; Neaigus, Friedman, Curtis, Des Jarlais, et al., 1994; Southgate & Hopwood, 2001; Zinberg, 1984). It may have more in common with the way in which Southgate and Hopwood (2001) discuss the social roots of their 'folk pharmacology' in the economic and social structures of gay life in Sydney, Australia (see below).

To What Degree Is There Drug Use That Is Not Socially Caused?

As will be discussed below, our theory of drug use is based on the hypothesis that certain parts of the social order are more likely to use drugs; and, beyond that, the drugs which are used in a given social location will be those which seem to them to produce moods or consciousness that help people deal with problems with which society confronts them. Thus, we posit that much harmful drug use is socially caused by ways in which the social order itself causes pain or other reactions in some people that they attempt to medicate with the drugs. To some degree, however, there is probably a residual degree of drug use, including harmful drug use, which would be present in any social order. One way to think about this is that, even in a truly decent society, many people would use some potentially addictive substances during particular social or cultural events. Some of these people might, as a consequence, become addicted and come to use drugs in ways harmful to themselves or others. In addition, some harmful drug use, including the use of potentially-addictive drugs, would be likely to occur because some substances are fun or otherwise pleasing enough so some people will knowingly risk the dangers. Additional drug use might arise as a form of pain medication by people who have undergone traumatic experiences.

What would be done in such a society to help those who develop drug problems? It is difficult to imagine the details of a decent society—but we suspect that human solidarity, values of human respect and equality, the possibility for a desirable future, science, and love would be mobilized to reduce and prevent such harm. (Similar needs might exist in relationship to the dangers of other dangerous pursuits, such as over-devotion to down-hill skiing.)

Social Factors Which May Underlie Harmful Drug Use: Preliminary Thoughts

Unfortunately, the world as it is seems to be far from ideal. Billions of people have real pressures on them that are almost insupportable, whether as a consequence of living in a poor nation; being part of an oppressed people or community; having been sexually or physically abused as a child; having an uncertain, degrading, boring, or highly risky employment situation; or living with a spouse, child, parent, or other person in a relationship that is fraught with tension or violence. We suggest that such pressures are likely to lead some of those exposed to them to use particular drugs in harmful ways. Other factors will also be involved in determining which individuals among those exposed to the pressures actually take up various forms of drug use. The study of this aspect of the problem is important, and has been the major focus of prior research in the field to such an extent that these issues of social causation have been inadequately studied.

For the lucky and wealthy, such social pressures are episodic. For the overwhelming majority of the population, however, they are chronic. Members of the blue, pink, or white collar working class generally face more of these problems than do the corporate rich or those of otherwise wealthy family (Mishel, Schmitt & Bernstein, 1999; UNDP, 1999), although other problems, such as sexual abuse, may be more equally distributed among economic categories. Racial/ethnic stratification, such as the subordination of African Americans, Latino/as, and others in United States and, generally, the Americas, or of non-whites in South Africa, or of Catholics in Ulster, is usually associated with worse health and living conditions for the subordinated groups (Geschwender, 1978; Omi & Winant, 1994). Gender relationships are deeply complicated by issues of class and race/ethnicity, but the greater burdens and stresses that women face even if they do not have an explicit history of sexual abuse and/or violation, domestic violence, and/or survival sex work, have been widely documented (Albeda & Tilly, 1997; Folbre, 1993a, b; Goldberg & Kremen, 1990; Zierler & Krieger, 1997). Elsewhere, Friedman (1991) suggested that 'dignity-denial' is deeply rooted in such social structures of modern capitalism as the workplace, racial and gender subordination, and organisational structures. One possible result of such dignity-denial is the use of drugs or other substances as a source of solace or self-medication against the pain of not being respected as an equal human being.

Although such pressures may be chronic, their intensity varies over time. Recent decades may have been a period in which these pressures have intensified. Economic conditions worsened during the period from approximately 1970–1999 in a great many countries. Relevant data from a number of countries are presented in Table 6.1 and in Fig. 6.1 and Fig. 6.2. These show that profit rates have been decreasing, unemployment increasing, and inequality increasing over recent decades. As described elsewhere (Friedman, 1998a, b; Friedman, Southwell, Bueno, Paone, Byrne & Crofts, 2001), these economic pressures and their associated politics of scapegoating have contributed to overwork, cutbacks in social and health services, a sense of increasing inequality, widespread imprisonment of scapegoated groups including racial/ethnic minorities and drug users, and the weakening of community social ties all over the world.

We hypothesise that large numbers of people use pharmacologically active substances to help them deal with these pressures and, perhaps, to deal with trauma or with mental illness (which may be derived from these or related pressures). Some use occurs among people who may (also) enjoy using pharmacologically active substances—at least at first. Such substances include marijuana, tobacco, heroin, alcohol, amphetamines, cocaine, and caffeine. Some

Table 6.1

Differences Between Postwar Boom Period and Since in Selected Economic Characteristics of G-7 Industrialised Countries

Net profit of private business	
1950–1969	18.0%
1970–1990	13.0%
Unemployment rate	
1950–1973	3.1%
1973–1993	6.2%

G-7 countries: Canada, France, Germany, Italy, Japan, United Kingdom, United States.
Source: Brenner, 1998, p. 5.

of these substances, of course, are tolerated, others celebrated, and still others are proscribed. A major focus of a sociopharmacology of drugs should be to study what kinds of socially derived pressures are associated with what kinds of substance use. One potentially important aspect of such research will be to study if and how occupational and industrial characteristics of job are associated with particular kinds of drug use in both formal and informal work sectors. There is some literature suggesting that occupation is associated with use of specific psychoactive substances (Ebie & Pela, 1981; Mongkolsirichaikul, Mokkhavesa & Ratanabanangkoon, 1988; Philpot, Harcourt & Edwards, 1989; Roberts & Lee, 1993; Stratford, Ellerbrock, Akins & Hall, 2000; Watts & Short, 1990). Winnick (1964) shows that narcotic addiction among physicians, and perhaps jazz musicians, is associated with the occupational characteristics of

their jobs. There has been considerable speculation that caffeine and amphetamines are used to stay alert in some jobs such as truck driving; that other drugs (nicotine, marijuana) are used to deal with boredom in occupations such as routine assembly line work; that opiates are used to cope with painful or otherwise insufferable working conditions such as those associated with sex work; and that steroids and amphetamines are sometimes used to enhance performance in professional sports. Southgate and Hopwood (2001) describe drug use in Sydney as a form of socially regulated pleasure seeking based on the economic and social structures of the gay community. Left implicit in their discussion is the extent to which social stigmatisation of gays, and struggles against this, also structure these mores and behaviors.

Living in a local area that is socioeconomically deprived may be related to sub-

Figure 6.1

Income inequality: Deciles D9/D1

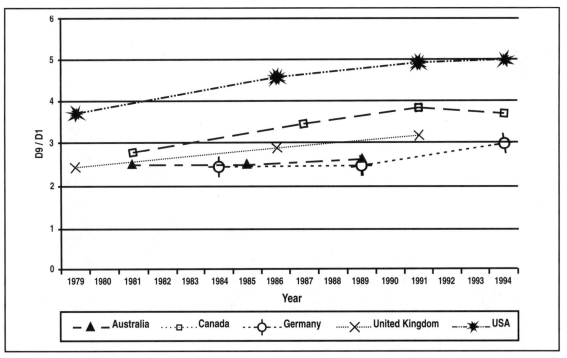

Source: Ruiz-Huerta, Martinez, Ayala. Earnings inequality, unemployment and income distribution in the OECD, Working Paper number 214, LIS. 1999.

stance use and its related harms. Bell et al. (1998) review a number of studies which show that census tract level analysis of drug use and of its potential socioecological causes provide useful insight into drug use (Faris & Dunham, 1939; Chein et al., 1964), heroin or narcotics addiction (Redlinger & Michel, 1970; Nurco, 1972), and multiple indices of social pathology (Nurco et al., 1984). Bell et al. (1998) themselves show that, in Houston, four identifiable socioecological factors help differentiate census tracts (social disorganisation, economic success, threat of violence, and chronic disease); and that narcotic offenses load heavily (0.50) on a social disorganisation factor. Brugal et al. (1999) report that unemployment rates in small areas within Barcelona are associated with neighborhood population-prevalences of opiod addiction. Diez-Roux et al. (1997) showed that deprived neighbourhoods have

higher levels of smoking, as well as higher cholesterol and body mass index. Kleinschmidt et al. (1995) also showed that smoking is influenced by neighbourhood deprivation.

These data, however, are merely indicative. More research is clearly needed on ways in which social statuses, pressures, and locations are related to drug use and to drug related harm.

There are probably also important cultural and marketing elements in much substance use (in addition to the social and economic ones already discussed). In some areas, psychoactive substances such as coca leaves, mushrooms, or poppy derivatives are part of traditional cultures. In others, these same substances are deeply stigmatised—which may lead them to seem attractive to the rebellious or alienated. Marketing dynamics, as shaped by interactions among

Figure 6.2

Ratio of Chief Executive Officer pay to Facatory Worker pay. United States of America.

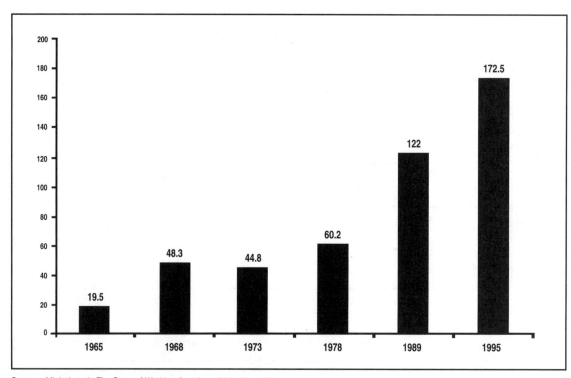

Source: Mishel et al., The State of Working America, 1996–97, p. 227.

producers, distributors, and police forces, affect where which drugs are available at given times. Examples of this are the diffusion of heroin use in Southeast Asia and cocaine use in South America after attempts to disrupt drug trafficking (Friedman et al., 1998a; Stimson et al., 1998; Stimson, 1993). This may help explain why some substances are used more in some localities than in others.

Implications for Theory, Research, and Action

These thoughts have implications for future research that embrace both macro-social issues and the links between the macro and the micro.

First, research is needed to determine the social distribution of the use of various drugs among different social and socioeconomic categories of the populations of different countries. This should include consideration of routes of administration, frequency and patterns of use, and other variables that may affect the likelihood of drug-related harm. These data will allow testing and exploration of the underlying theory of (partial) social causation of drug use.

Second, if the underlying theory is correct, then data on drug-related harm are likely to point to the ills and contradictions of society. Research should be conducted on how such data might identify nations, communities, occupations, and populations whose conditions create vulnerability to drug-related harm. Such data can concomitantly help identify points of social strain or contradiction within populations. The large extent of substance use in the United States probably suggests serious social dysfunction at the macro level. Research is also needed on how social, economic and health policies, or a lack thereof, create conditions that increase demand for harmful drug use and/or make it more likely that large numbers of people will engage in drug production, distribution, and sale.

Individualistic theories of drug use have been used to stigmatise and even demonise individual drug users as being weak or criminal. The sociopharmacological approach, by way of contrast, suggests that if anyone or anything should be demonised, it should be the social order, not the individual user. Whereas individualistic perspectives have justified blaming and incarcerating hundreds of thousands of people in ways that divert attention from and exacerbate serious socioeconomic problems and contradictions, a sociopharmacological view suggests that action should be focused on social change rather than on blaming the victim. This argument, of course, parallels arguments against 'blaming the victim' in other fields of research and action (Chambliss, 1999; Ryan, 1976).

Nonetheless, current drug use patterns do cause misery among drug users, their families, and their neighbors. Although it can be argued that many of these harms are a consequence of legal repression and/or social stigmatisation of drug users, the current pains remain to be addressed. Research and programmes are needed to reduce these harms. Such programmes should help them deal with chemistry-related issues, health-related issues, and issues that concern how they can get along better with family members and neighbours. To the extent that the harmful drug use is the result of social pressures, programs to ameliorate these harms should probably include a mixture of training in ways to more safely deal with these social pressures by personal adjustment and training, and organising for individual and social collective self-defense against these pressures and their causes. Research is needed on how best to provide resources to individuals, communities, and other social groups that they can use to ameliorate both the conditions that lead to harmful drug use and also to reduce harmful drug use among drug users.

To the extent that drug use is the result of social contradictions or occupational necessity, laws that punish users and dealers are at best mistaken efforts based on misdiagnosis of the roots of the problem. However, such laws should not usually be seen as 'mistakes' by well-meaning lawmakers but as serving the function of scapegoating the vulnerable. This serves to remove accountability both from the socioeconomic system and also from those people who benefit from the existing social order by dividing and weakening opposition to the nearly insupportable pressures the system puts on most people (Friedman, 1998a, b; Friedman et al., 2001).

Finally, to the extent that drug-related harm stems from basic social structures and processes, the highest-priority research and action should probably focus on social change and how to get it. This might include research on 'noncompliant elites and ruling classes' and how they can be induced or coerced into needed social changes (or, failing that, replaced). That is, the primary research focus should be on changing society rather than on changing drug users.

Acknowledgements

I would especially like to acknowledge Sara Kershnar, Generation Five, San Francisco, CA. She helped work on this paper and made many contributions to it, but ultimately her other responsibilities precluded her being an author. Her contributions to what is good in this paper were many; its faults are undoubtedly those of the paper's author. We would also like to acknowledge assistance from Kevin Anderson, Rachel Anderson, Patricia Case, Nick Crofts, Fabio Mesquita, Regina Bueno, and Mat Southwell. Support for this research was provided by United States National Institutes on Drug Abuse grant P30 DA11041 (Center for Drug Use and HIV Research).

References

Albeda, R., & Tilly, C. (1997). (Eds.). *Glass ceilings and bottomless pits: women's work, women's poverty*. Boston: South End Press.

Armstrong, D. L., & Castorina. (1998). Community occupational structure, basic services, and coronary mortality in Washington State, 1980–1994. *Annals of Epidemiology 8*, 370–377.

Armstrong, D. L., Barnett, E., Casper, M., & Wing, S. (1998). Community occupational structure, medical and economic resources, and coronary mortality among US blacks and whites, 1980–1988. *Annals of Epidemiology 8*, 184–191.

Becker, H. (1977). Knowledge, power and drug effects. In P. E. Rock (Ed.), *Drugs and politics*, (pp. 167–190). Somerset, NJ: Transaction Books.

Bell, D. C., Carlson, J. W., & Richard, A. J. (1998). The social ecology of drug use: a factor analysis of an urban environment. *Substance Use and Misuse 33*, 2201–2217.

Berkman, L. F., & Kawachi, J. (2000). *Social epidemiology*. New York: Oxford.

Brenner, R. (1998). The economics of global turbulence. *New Left Review 229*, 1–264.

Brugal, M. T., Domingo-Salvany, A., Maguire, A., Cayla, J. A., Villalbi, J. R., & Hartnoll, R. (1999). A small area analysis estimating the prevalence of addiction to opioids in Barcelona, 1993. *Journal of Epidemiology and Community Health 53*, 488–494.

Casper, M., Wing, S., & Strogatz, D. (1991). Variation in the magnitude of black-white differences in stroke mortality by community occupational structure. *Journal of Epidemiology and Community Health 45*, 302–306.

Chambliss, W. (1999). *Power, politics and crime*. Boulder, CO: Longview Press.

Chein, I., Gerard, D. L., Lee, R. S., & Rosenfeld, E. (1964). *The road to H*. New York: Basic.

Diez-Roux, A. V., Nieto, F. J., Caulfield, L., Tyroler, H. A., Watson, R. L., & Szklo, M. (1999). Neighborhood differences in diet: The Atherosclerosis In Communities (ARIC) Study. *Journal of Epidemiology and Community Health 53*, 55–63.

Diez-Roux, A. V., Nieto, F. J., Muntaner, C., et al. (1997). Neighborhood environments and coronary heart disease: a multilevel analysis. *American Journal of Epidemiology 146*, 48–63.

Durkheim, E. (1982). *The rules of the sociological method*. New York: Free Press (W. D. Halls, Trans.).

Ebie, J. C., & Pela, O. A. (1981). Some sociocultural aspects of the problem of drug abuse in Nigeria. *Drug and Alcohol Dependence 8* (4), 301–306.

Elreedy, S., Krieger, N., Ryan, P. B., Sparrow, D., Weiss, S. T., & Hu, H. (1999). Relations between individual and neighborhood-based measures of socioeconomic position and bone lead concentrations among community-exposed men. *American Journal of Epidemiology 150*, 129–141.

Faris, R. E., & Dunham, H. W. (1939). *Mental disorders in urban areas*. Chicago: University of Chicago Press.

Fife, D., & Mode, C. (1992). AIDS incidence and income. *Journal of Acquired Immune Deficiency Syndrome 5*, 1105–1110.

Folbre, N. (1993a). *Who pays for the kids? Gender and the structures of constraint.* London: Routledge.

——. (1993b). *Women's work in the world economy.* New York: New York University Press.

Friedman, S. R., Curtis, R., Neaigus, A., Jose, B., & Des Jarlais, D. C. (1999). *Social networks, drug injectors' lives, and HIV/AIDS.* New York: Kluwer/Plenum.

Friedman, S. R., Friedmann, P., Telles, P., Bastos, F., Bueno, R., Mesquita, F., & Des Jarlais, D. C. (1998a). New injectors and HIV-1 risk. In G. V. Stimson, D. C. Des Jarlais, & A. L. Ball (Eds.), *Drug injecting and HIV infection: global dimensions and local responses* (pp. 76–90). London: UCL Press.

Friedman, S. R., Furst, R. T., Jose, B., Curtis, R., Neaigus, A., Des Jarlais, D. C., Goldstein, M., & Ildefonso, G. (1998b). Drug scene roles and HIV risk. *Addiction 93* (9), 1403–1416.

Friedman, S. R., Kang, S.-Y., Deren, S., Robles, R., Colón, H. M., Andia, J., Oliver-Velez, D., & Finlinson, A. (2002). Drug-scene roles and HIV risk among Puerto Rican injection drug users in East Harlem, New York City and Bayamón, Puerto Rico. *Journal of Psychoactive Drugs*, in press.

Friedman, S. R., Southwell, M., Bueno, R., Paone, D., Byrne, J., & Crofts, N. (2001). Harm reduction—a historical view from the left. *International Journal of Drug Policy 12,* 3–14.

Friedman, S. R. (1991). Alienated labor and dignity denial in capitalist society. In B. Berberoglu (Ed.), *Critical perspectives in sociology* (pp. 83–91). Kendall/Hunt.

——. (1998a). The political economy of drug-user scapegoating—and the philosophy and politics of resistance. *Drugs: Education, Prevention and Policy 5* (1), 15–32.

——. (1998b). HIV-related politics in long-term perspective. *AIDS Care 10* (Supplement 2), S93–S103.

Geschwender, J. (1978). *Racial stratification in America.* Dubuque, IA: William C. Brown.

Goldberg, G. S., & Kremen, E. (Eds.). (1990). *The feminization of poverty: only in America?* New York: Praeger.

Hu, D. J., Frey, R., Costa, S. J., Massey, J., Ryan, J., Fleming, P. L., D'Errico, S., Ward, J. W., & Buehler, J. (1994). Geographical AIDS rates and sociodemographic variables in the Newark, New Jersey, metropolitan area. *AIDS and Public Policy 9,* 20–25.

Kaplan, G. A., Pamuk, E. R., Lynch, J. W., Cohen, R. D., & Balfour, J. L. (1996). Inequality in income and mortality in the United States. *British Medical Journal 312,* 999–1003.

Kennedy, B. P., Ichiro Kawachi, I., & Prothrow-Stith, D. (1996). Income distribution and mortality: cross-sectional ecological study of the RobinHood index in the United States. *British Medical Journal 312,* 1004–1007.

Kleinschmidt, I., Hills, M., & Elliott, P. (1995). Smoking behaviour can be predicted by neighborhood deprivation measures. *Journal of Epidemiology and Community Health 49* (Suppl. 2), S72–S77.

Lynch, J. W., Kaplan, G. A., Pamuk, E., Cohen, R. D., Heck, K., Balfour, J. L., & Yen, I. H. (1998). Income inequality and mortality in metropolitan areas of the United States. *American Journal of Public Health 88,* 1074–1080.

Mills, C. W. (1940). Situated actions and vocabularies of motives. *American Sociological Review 5,* 904–913.

Mishel, L., Schmitt, J., & Bernstein, J. (1999). *The State of Working America, 1998–1999.* Ithaca, NY: Cornell University Press.

Mongkolsirichaikul, D., Mokkhavesa, C., & Ratanabanangkoon, K. (1988). The incidence of amphetamine use among truck drivers from various regions of Thailand. *Journal of the Medical Association of Thailand 71* (9), 471–474.

Neaigus, A., Friedman, S. R., Curtis, D. C., Des Jarlais, D. C., et al. (1994). The relevance of drug injectors' social networks and risk networks for understanding and preventing HIV infection. *Social Science and Medicine 38* (1), 67–78.

Nurco, D. N., Shaffer, J. W., & Cisin, I. H. (1984). An ecological analysis of the interrelationships among drug abuse and other indices of social pathology. *International Journal of the Addictions 19,* 441–451.

Nurco, D. N. (1972). An ecological analysis of heroin addicts in Baltimore. *International Journal of the Addictions 7,* 341–353.

O'Campo, P., Xue, X., Wang, M. C., & O'Brien Caughy, M. (1997). Neighborhood risk factors for low birthweight in Baltimore: a multilevel analysis. *American Journal of Public Health 87,* 1113–1118.

Omi, M., & Winant, H. (1994). *Racial formation in the United States.* New York: Routledge.

Philpot, C. R., Harcourt, C. L., & Edwards, J. M. (1989). Drug use by prostitutes in Sydney. *British Journal of Addiction 84* (5), 499–505.

Redlinger, L. J., & Michel, J. B. (1970). Ecological variations in heroin abuse. *Sociological Quarterly 11,* 219–229.

Rhodes, T. (1996). Culture, drugs and unsafe sex: confusion about causation. *Addiction 91*, 753–758.

Roberts, R. E., & Lee, E. S. (1993). Occupation and the prevalence of major depression, alcohol, and drug abuse in the United States. *Environmental Research 61* (2), 266–278.

Ryan, W. (1976). *Blaming the victim*. New York: Random House.

Schiraldi, V., Barry, H., & Phillip, B. (2000). *Poor prescriptions: the cost of imprisoning drug offenders in the United States*. Washington, DC: Justice Policy Institute.

Simon, P. A., Hu, D. J., Diaz, T., & Kerndt, P. R. (1995). Income and AIDS rates in Los Angeles County. *AIDS 9* (3), 281–284.

Southgate, E., & Hopwood, M. (2001). The role of folk pharmacology and lay experts in harm reduction: Sydney gay drug using networks. *International Journal of Drug Policy 12*, 321–335.

Stimson, G. V. (1993). The global diffusion of injecting drug use: implications for human immunodeficiency virus infection. *Bulletin on Narcotics XLV* (1), 3–17.

Stimson, G. V., Ball, A., & Des Jarlais, D. C. (1998). *Drug injecting and HIV infection*. London: UCL Press.

Stratford, D., Ellerbrock, T. V., Akins, J. K., & Hall, H. L. (2000). Highway cowboys, old hands, and Christian truckers: risk behavior for human immunodeficiency virus infection among long-haul truckers in Florida. *Social Science and Medicine 50* (5), 737–749.

United Nations Development Programme. (1999). *Human development report 1999*. New York: Oxford.

Wallace, D., & Wallace, R. (1999). *A plague on your houses: how New York was burned down and national public health crumbled*. New York: Verso.

Watts, W. D., & Short, A. P. (1990). Teacher drug use: a response to occupational stress. *Journal of Drug Education 20* (1), 47–65.

Winnick, C. (1964). Physician narcotic addicts. In H. S. Becker (Ed.), *The other side: perspectives on deviance* (pp. 261–279). New York: The Free Press.

Zierler, S., & Krieger, N. (1997). Reframing women's risk: social inequalities and HIV infection. *Annual Review of Public Health 18*, 401–436.

Zinberg, N. E. (1984). *Drug, set and setting: the basis for controlled intoxicant use*. New Haven, CT: Yale University Press.

For Discussion

1. How is drug use attributable to social disorder? How could more egalitarian social, economic, and health policies help decrease the illegal drug market?

2. Do you think there is a link between occupation and the choice of drug? By extension, what kind of connection exists between being a student and engaging in substance use?

Part II

Alcohol and Tobacco

A major element in the American drug scene is the use and abuse of *legal* drugs—alcohol, tobacco, prescription stimulants and sedatives, anabolic steroids, and other substances as well—as a response to boredom, frustration, stress, and loneliness or, as in the case of steroids, for the enhancement of physical performance. Because these drugs are legal, they are potentially available to everyone, and the use of alcohol and tobacco is particularly widespread.

Alcohol is the most widely used drug in the United States. Estimates of people aged 12 and over who have used alcohol in their lifetime hover around the 83 percent range.[1] Moreover, in 2002 almost 120 million people from that same category (over 50 percent of the population) reported having had at least one drink in the past month. Of that number, about 23 percent, or 54 million people, had five or more drinks on the same occasion at least once in the past month (binge drinkers), and almost 16 million Americans had five or more drinks during one sitting on at least five different days in the past month (heavy drinkers).[2]

These high numbers are even more telling when statistics on alcohol-related mortality are considered. More than 100,000 deaths each year are connected to alcohol consumption.[3] Causes of these alcohol-related deaths run the gamut from drunk driving, homicide and suicide, and certain alcohol-related illnesses to 12 ailments solely attributable to alcohol abuse, such as alcoholic cirrhosis of the liver and alcohol dependence syndrome.

Although the majority of those who use alcohol are social recreational drinkers, problem drinking is widespread, and the costs of drinking are staggering—well in excess of $100 billion annually. Despite these costs, alcohol remains something of a social enigma. On the one hand, alcohol is the biggest killer drug in the United States; it causes more havoc, violence, damage, and death than all other drugs combined, legal *and* illegal. On the other hand, when used responsibly and in moderation, it can be a relatively safe and pleasant drug for the majority. In fact, there is evidence suggesting that when used regularly in small amounts, alcohol can even be healthful, reducing blood cholesterol.[4]

The "problem" seems not to lie with alcohol per se but with its misuse. Because alcohol is legal, it is readily available to anyone deemed to be of age. Moreover, alcohol has had numerous roles—social, medical, and religious—in human cultures around the globe for thousands of years. For these reasons, many users fail to understand that it is a dangerous drug, with a high addiction potential and the prospect of severe physical harm through overuse.

While the use of alcohol in moderation may be beneficial to the body, such is not the case with tobacco. Consider the numbers:

- In 2002, almost 29 percent of men aged 12 and over in the United States re-

71

ported having smoked cigarettes in the past month.[5]

- For the same year, 23 percent of women aged 12 years and over reported having smoked cigarettes in the past month.[6] Together the figures represent 26 percent of the U.S. population aged 12 and over.

- Each year in the United States, there are more than 440,000 tobacco-related deaths, the great majority of which are from cardiovascular disease and lung cancer. However, a significant number of these deaths are among nonsmokers, the result of chronic inhalation of secondhand smoke.

- Eighty percent of all smokers began smoking before age 20, and the average age when smoking begins is 15.4 years.

Like alcohol, tobacco is something of a social enigma. Cigarette smoking is considered the most important preventable cause of death in the United States, yet cigarettes are one of the most heavily advertised products. Cigarette advertising themes typically associate smoking with high-style living, healthy activities, and economic, social, and professional success. And interestingly, cigarette advertising campaigns increasingly target women, minorities, and blue-collar workers—groups that account for an increasing proportion of the cigarette smoking population.

If cigarettes were outlawed in the United States, there would be both costs and benefits. On the positive side, a ban on cigarettes would result in

- **Longer lives.** There is strong evidence supporting links between smoking and heart disease, lung cancer, and a shortened life span. A ban could reduce human suffering, lengthen life, and increase productivity.

- **Health care savings.** Studies suggest that the billions of dollars now spent each year on smoking-related diseases could be saved.

- **Less illness.** It is generally agreed that smokers are ill more often, and remain ill longer, than nonsmokers. A ban would reduce smoking-related absenteeism, saving companies billions of dollars each year.

- **Increased productivity.** Without cigarette breaks, smokers would gain a month's work each year.

- **Fewer fires.** The costs from smoking-related accidental fires are considerable, whether measured in lives, lost productivity, or property damage.

On the other hand, a ban on producing, manufacturing, using, and exporting tobacco products would result in numerous costs for the U.S. economy:

- **Job losses.** Farm sales of tobacco total $1 billion annually in North Carolina, accounting for more than a third of the tobacco grown in the United States. Tobacco product manufacturing is a $14.8 billion industry with a payroll of more than $500 million. A ban could devastate the state's economy.[7]

- **Reduced tax revenues.** In 2002, cigarette taxes generated approximately $17 billion in state and federal taxes. This revenue would vanish.

- **Reduced exports.** Even though its use has declined, tobacco still generated over one billion dollars in trade surplus in 2002.

- **Farm reductions.** Tobacco farming would disappear, and the potential for replacement crops is uncertain.

- **Reduced pension funds.** Because over 400,000 people die prematurely each year as a result of tobacco-related illnesses, they do not live long enough to collect all or part of their accumulated social security and other pension benefits. As such, reductions in the number of tobacco-related deaths would put considerable pressure on government and private pension funds.

Completely outlawing tobacco products is unlikely. It would be unworkable, and few Americans, smokers and nonsmokers alike, support the idea. In a 2003 Gallup poll, for example, 84 percent of the adult population (smokers and nonsmokers) felt that smoking should remain a legal, personal choice. Interestingly, however, in terms of smoking in the workplace, 97 percent felt that it should be banned, or at least limited to special smoking areas.

In the chapters that follow, the focus is on alcohol and tobacco.

Notes

1. *National Household Survey on Drug Abuse* (Rockville, MD: National Institute on Drug Abuse, 2002).

2. *National Household Survey on Drug Abuse* (Rockville, MD: National Institute on Drug Abuse, 2002).

3. Nidus Information Services, Inc., *Well Connected Report: Alcoholism* (December 1998).

4. Substance Abuse Resource Center, "Moderate Drinking for Your Health" (Connecticut Clearing House, 1998).

5. *National Household Survey on Drug Abuse* (Rockville, MD: National Institute on Drug Abuse, 2002).

6. *National Household Survey on Drug Abuse* (Rockville, MD: National Institute on Drug Abuse, 2002).

7. *Tobacco in North Carolina: What's in Store for Our Economy, Our Communities?* (Raleigh, NC: North Carolina Rural Economic Development Center, August 8, 2000).

Additional Readings

Brower, Aaron M. (2002). "Are College Students Alcoholics?" *Journal of American College Health*, 50: 253–255.

Furnas, J. C. (1965). *The Life and Times of the Late Demon Rum*. New York: Capricorn Books.

Goodman, Jordan. (1993). *Tobacco in History: The Cultures of Dependence*. London: Routledge.

Landman, Anne, Pamela M. Ling, and Stanton A. Glantz. (2002). "Tobacco Industry Youth Smoking Prevention Programs: Protecting the Industry and Hurting Tobacco Control." *American Journal of Public Health*, 92: 917–930.

Perkins, Wesley H. (2002). "Surveying the Damage: A Review of Research on Consequences of Alcohol Misuse in College Populations." *Journal of Studies on Alcohol*, suppl. 14: 91–100.

Yen, Karl L., Elizabeth Hechavarria, and Susan B. Bostwick. (2000). "Bidi Cigarettes: An Emerging Threat to Adolescent Health." *Archives of Pediatrics & Adolescent Medicine*, 154(12): 1187–1189. ✦

7

A Brief History of Alcohol

Harvey A. Siegal
James A. Inciardi

Alcohol has had an enduring history. In the following essay, Harvey A. Siegal and James A. Inciardi contemplate the likely origins of alcohol use and its early evolution. A number of interesting facts about alcohol are also examined, including the different kinds of alcohol, the meanings of "proof" and "blood alcohol content," and how alcohol affects the body.

The desire to temporarily alter how our minds process the information brought by our senses is perhaps one of the oldest and most pervasive of humanity's wishes. In fact, some researchers have suggested that the need to do so is as powerful and permanent as the in-born drives of self-preservation, hunger, and security (Weil 1972). In its pursuit, people have, at various times and in various places, subjected their bodies to beatings and mutilation, starvation and sensory deprivation; they have focused their minds solely on a single object, or let consciousness expand without direction; and they have often pursued a more direct route, changing the brain's chemistry by ingesting a chemical substance. Of all of these, the chemical that has probably been used by more of the earth's people in more places and times is one of the by-products of a simple organism's conversion of sugar and water into energy. It is ethanol, or beverage alcohol. Each year, countless millions of people experience, both positively and negatively, the effects of this domesticated drug we call alcohol.

More is known about alcohol than any other drug; yet, it staggers the imagination about how much more there remains to learn. Our experiences with this most familiar and comfortable of drugs could readily constitute a social history of civilization. We've lauded and vilified it. We've brought it into our most important religious rituals and have included it as part of our significant rites-of-passage. Conversely, we've discouraged its use; even prohibited its manufacture and sale by constitutional amendment. Wars have been fought over it and underworld empires have been built on the proceeds from its sales. It's been acclaimed as having the power to comfort and cure and is held responsible for thousands of deaths each year, billions of dollars in losses, and an incalculable amount of human suffering. All of us, in some way, have been touched or influenced by this drug, so let's take a brief look at its history.

Early History

Like many significant inventions, the specifics of alcohol's discovery are not known. We conjecture that it likely occurred during the neolithic age. Perhaps someone left wild berries, fruit, or even grapes in a vessel for a few days. When they returned, airborne yeasts had already begun fermenting the mixture. The result—which we call "wine"—undoubtedly proved to be more interesting and enjoyable than the original fruit, and, like other innovations, it did not take people long to improve their invention.

As people settled into communities and began cultivating plants and domesticating animals instead of just simply hunting and gathering their food, they found that a surplus often ensued. Surplus grains could also be fermented once the starch in them—which by itself would not ferment—could be rendered into sugar. To accomplish this, as is still done in parts of the world today, these early agriculturists found that chewing the grain somehow changes it into a fermentable mixture. We know now that the chemical responsible for this transformation—ptyalin—is found naturally in saliva. Other societies discovered that by allowing the grain to germinate, then roasting the new shoots, the fermentation process could be initiated. In this way, the beverage we know as "beer" came into being. People discovered that not only fruits, berries, and grains could be used to produce alcohol, but leaves, tubers, flowers, cacti, and even honey could be fermented as well.

These early concoctions (roughly designated as wines or beers), however, were limited in their alcoholic strength. As yeasts metabolize the sugar, carbon dioxide (which is what makes bread rise, wine bubble, or gives beer a head) and alcohol are released as by-products. When the alcoholic content of the mixture exceeded 11 percent or 12 percent the process slowed markedly; as it approached 14 percent, the yeasts were rendered inactive (i.e., killed), and the process of fermentation stopped entirely. In addition to the limitation imposed by the biology of the yeasts, the alcoholic content could be affected by the producers themselves. For example, including more sugar (or fermentable material) would increase the amount of alcohol that would be produced. Whether the producers were willing to allow the yeasts the time necessary to complete the fermentation process or were too eager to consume the brew to wait, this influenced its alcohol content.

It was not until the time of the Crusades that Europeans were able to consume alcoholic beverages more potent than beer or wine. The Crusaders returned from the Holy Lands having learned a process known as distillation. To distill wine, it first would be heated. Because alcohol has a lower boiling point than water, it would vaporize first. Then, as this vapor cooled, it condensed back into liquid form. This distillate made a considerably more potent beverage. In fact, beverages of quadruple potency now became possible. These were known as "distilled spirits" or "liquors," referring to the essence of the wine.

Aqua Vitae: The Water of Life

What is this drug which has been called by some the "water of life"—*aqua vitae*, in scholastic Latin, or *ambrosia*, the nectar of the gods—and "the corrupter of youth" and the "devil's own brew" by others? Ethyl alcohol or ethanol (whose chemical formula is C_2H_5OH) is a clear, colorless liquid with little odor but a powerful burning taste. Ethanol is just one of many alcohols such as methyl (wood) and isopropyl (rubbing) alcohol. All others are poisonous and cannot be metabolized by the body.

In addition to ethanol and water, alcoholic beverages generally contain minute amounts of substances referred to as "congeners." Many of these chemicals are important to the flavor, appearance, and aroma of the beverage. Brandy, for example, is relatively rich in congeners while vodka contains relatively few. Alcoholic beverages differ in strength. Beer generally has an alcoholic content of 5 percent; malt liquors are slightly higher. Natural wine varies in alcoholic content between 6 percent and 14 percent. Fortified wines—i.e., those that have had additional alcohol added—contain between 17 percent and 20 percent alcohol. Liquor or spirits contain approximately 40 percent ethanol. The common designation of "proof" originated centuries ago in Britain as a test for the potency of a beverage. To accomplish this test, if gun powder saturated with alcohol burned upon ignition, this was taken as "proof" that the liquor was more than half pure alcohol. In the United States, proof is calculated as being roughly twice the proportion of ethanol by unit volume of beverage; for example, an 86-proof Scotch is 43 percent alcohol.

Although the relative strengths of the beverages differ, current standard portions that are consumed actually provide the same amount of ethanol to the drinker. For example, the same quantity of alcohol is consumed if someone drinks either a 12-ounce can or bottle of beer, a three- to four-ounce glass of wine, or a mixed drink made with one and one-half ounces (i.e., one shot) of distilled spirits. Thus, the claim that "I don't drink much alcohol, but I do drink a lot of beer" is simply not true.

Alcohol's Effects

Unlike most other foods, alcohol is absorbed directly into the bloodstream without digestion. A small amount passes directly through the stomach lining itself; most, however, progresses on to the small intestine, where it is almost entirely absorbed. The feeling of warmth that one experiences after taking a drink results from the irritating effect that alcohol has on the tissues of the mouth, esophagus (food-tube), and stomach. Alcohol does not become intoxicating until the blood carrying it reaches the brain. The rapidity with which this occurs is in large measure determined by the condition of the stomach. An empty stomach will facilitate the absorption of the alcohol, while a full stomach retards it. To some degree, the type of beverage consumed has an effect on absorption, as well. Beer, for example, contains food substances which tend to retard this absorption. Drinks which are noticeably carbonated—such as champagne—seem to "quickly go to one's head," since the carbon dioxide facilitates the passage of alcohol from the stomach to the small intestine.

Alcohol is held in the tissues of the body before it is broken down (i.e., metabolized), like any other food or chemical substance. The body metabolizes alcohol at a steady rate, with the individual being able to exercise virtually no control over the process. Therefore, a healthy man who weighs approximately 160 pounds, drinking no more than three-fourths of an ounce of distilled spirits every hour, could consume more than a pint in a day's time without experiencing any marked intoxication. If the same quantity was consumed over an hour or two, however, the person would be very drunk. Today, much research is directed at finding an "antidote" for alcohol: a chemical that would either break down the alcohol itself, or accelerate the body's metabolic process. Although several promising lines of research are under way, it will likely be many years before something is commercially available. Finally, the belief that black coffee (i.e., caffeine) is an "antidote" is without fact. What the caffeine does do, however, is to stimulate the drinker—the intoxicated person is still "drunk," but he or she may, after several cups of black coffee, feel more awake.

Ethanol is broken down (metabolized) by the liver. In experiments, animals have had their livers removed, and then were given ethyl alcohol. The alcohol remained, much like wood (methyl) alcohol, in their bodies without being metabolized and exhibited the toxic effects—such as nerve damage—brought on by unpotable alcohols. How does this process work? The liver produces and holds the enzymes responsible for alcohol metabolism. Once in the liver, alcohol combines with its enzymes. Alcohol is initially transformed into acetaldehyde, a chemical considerably more toxic than alcohol. Almost instantaneously, other enzymes convert the acetaldehyde into acetic acid (the same compound that constitutes vinegar), an essentially innocuous substance. The acetic acid is then further metabolized into carbon dioxide and water. Interestingly, one of the treatment strategies for managing alcoholism employs this metabolic process itself. In it, Disulfiram (Antabuse), a chemical which compromises the body's capacity to convert acetaldehyde to acetic acid, is used as an adversive agent. By itself, Disulfiram has little effect on a patient who takes a daily dose of it. If alcohol is consumed while Disulfiram remains in the body, the produced acetaldehyde collects quickly, much to the great discomfort of the drinker. The patient is warned of this unpleasant effect, and the consequent fear of it can help increase his or her motivation to abstain from alcohol.

Alcohol does have some nutritional value. The primitive brews and concoctions were probably richer in nutritional value, especially carbohydrates, vitamins, and minerals, than the highly refined beverages we consume today. Alcohol itself is a rich source of calories which are converted into energy and heat. An ounce of whiskey, for example, provides approximately 75 calories, the equivalent of a potato, an ear of corn, a slice of dark bread, or a serving of pasta. The caloric content of mixed drinks is greater, since the sweeteners of the mixer provide additional calories. These extra calories are, of course, fattening, if the drinker does not reduce his or her intake of other foods.

The fact that alcohol provides sufficient calories for subsistence provides an additional health hazard. Many heavy drinkers express a preference to "drink their meals." While alcohol does provide calories, other nutrients, such as proteins, vitamins, and minerals vital to health and well-being, are entirely lacking. These heavy drinkers often suffer from chronic malnutrition and vitamin-deficiency diseases. In fact, adult malnutrition apart from heavy drinking is extremely rare in the United States.

Alcohol exerts its most profound effects on the brain. The observable behavior produced by drinking is as much a result of the social situation in which a person drinks as it is the drinker's mood and expectations about what the drinking will do and the actual quantity of alcohol consumed. For example, after drinking the identical quantity and type of beverage one might experience euphoria or depression, while another may feel full of energy or simply wish to sleep; or a drink found initially stimulating might encourage sleep. Pharmacologically, alcohol is a central nervous system depressant drug. Currently, neuroscientists are studying the operation of specific biochemical mechanisms, but some research has suggested that alcohol acts most directly on those portions of the brain which control sleep and wakefulness.

The amount of alcohol within a person is conventionally described as Blood Alcohol Content (B.A.C.). This measures the proportion of alcohol that might be found within an individual's bloodstream and can be assessed by analyzing body substances such as blood, breath, or urine. Although, as we mentioned, the effects vary by both drinking situation and the experience that the drinker has had, we can roughly expect to see some of the following occur. After two or three drinks in a short period of time, a person of about 160 lbs. will begin to feel the effects of the drug. These include feelings of euphoria, freeing of inhibitions, and perhaps impaired judgment. Such a person would have an approximate B.A.C. of 0.04 percent.

If our subject has another three drinks in a short period, his or her B.A.C. will elevate to around 0.1 percent. Now, besides affecting the higher centers of thought and judgment located in the cerebral cortex, the alcohol is beginning to act on the lower (more basic) motor areas of the brain. By law, in virtually all the states, this person would now be judged incapable of operating a motor vehicle and, if caught doing so, would be charged with Driving Under the Influence (DUI). The person would have some difficulty walking and appear to lurch somewhat; there would be noticeable decline in activities requiring fine hand-eye coordination; and one's speech would be somewhat slurred.

At higher concentrations of alcohol, from 0.2 percent B.A.C. and up (resulting from the consumption of at least 10 ounces of spirits), more of the central nervous system is affected. The drinker has difficulty coordinating even the simplest of movements and may need assistance to even walk. Emotionally, he or she appears very unstable and readily changes from rage to tears and then back again. At 0.40 percent to 0.50 percent B.A.C., alcohol depresses enough of the central nervous system's functions that the drinker may lapse into a coma. At concentrations of 0.60 percent B.A.C. and above, the most basic centers of the brain—those that govern respiration—are so suppressed that death may occur.

Alcohol and Health

Abusive drinking has a profoundly negative influence on virtually every one of the body's organ systems. This negative impact occurs directly through the irritating and inflaming properties the drug has, and indirectly as an effect of alcohol's metabolism by the liver. Further, like many other drugs, tolerance (both physiologic and psychologic) to alcohol occurs. As such, one needs to drink more to achieve the desired effects. Naturally, the more one drinks, the greater the (potential and actual) damage caused by alcohol.

Alcohol irritates the lining of the stomach, which in turn causes an increase in the amount of gastric juices secreted. These irritate, inflame, and ultimately can chemically abrade the stomach's lining, causing ulcers. Alcohol can damage the small intestine itself, compromising the organ's ability to absorb nutrients, especially vitamins. Other organs that are involved in the digestive process, such as the pancreas, are damaged as well; adult-onset diabetes is typically linked to abusive drinking.

Because the liver is responsible for metabolizing the alcohol consumed, it is this organ which is most affected. Not only is the liver abused by the irritating and inflaming properties of alcohol, but, as it metabolizes the drug, proteins broadly described as "free fatty acids" are released. These settle throughout the liver and other internal organs, ultimately compromising their function by blocking blood and other vessels. The livers of alcohol abusers are characterized by fatty deposits, dead and dying tissues, and evidence of scarring. Ultimately, the organ may be so compromised that it fails entirely, and death follows.

Although there is support for the notion that very moderate alcoholic consumption—i.e., never more than two glasses of wine a day—has healthful benefits, heavy drinkers have increased rates of cardiovascular problems. Heart disease is more prevalent among this group—who are more likely to be heavy cigarette smokers as well—than the general population.

Chronic abuse of alcohol can have disastrous effects on the central nervous system. Alcohol is a tolerance-producing and ultimately addicting drug. For the addicted person, withdrawal distress can be life threatening. Longer term, permanent damage can include dementia, profound memory loss, the inability to learn, and impaired balance and coordination. Alcoholic people have higher rates of depression, suicide, and evidence of other mental illnesses.

Alcohol abuse is linked with automobile accidents, especially among adolescents. It is estimated that almost one-half of fatal crashes involve drinking. Other accidents, drownings, burns, and trauma are strongly associated with drinking. Drinking has been associated with violence, especially domestic violence and child abuse. Finally, when consumed by a pregnant woman, alcohol can cause profound damage to the fetus. Babies born suffering from fetal alcohol syndrome are less likely to survive, more likely to fail to thrive, and manifest both physiologic and psychologic developmental problems.

Alcohol, humanity's oldest domesticated drug, is also one of its greatest enemies. In the United States, we estimate that there are almost 10 million alcohol dependent or alcoholic people and perhaps twice that proportion of "problem drinkers." We estimate that each year alcohol abuse costs our nation well in excess of one hundred billion dollars in terms of loss, health care, and decreased productivity. We do pay a large personal and societal price for this chemical comfort.

A Note on the Social History of Alcohol in the United States

Most societies have used alcohol medicinally, ritually, or recreationally. Colonial America was no exception. Beer and wine were made and universally consumed. Distilling grain into "ardent spirits" as a way of promoting the production, storage, and shipment of agricultural products was encouraged. Drunkenness seldom occurred in public and was reportedly not widespread. As the country moved from colonial to revolutionary America, the scene changed; towns grew and social-control mechanisms became more formal. Intoxication was reviled, and drunkenness was defined as a private weakness and a social ill. Thus, America's "drinking problem" began to emerge.

Shortly thereafter, the beginnings of a temperance movement appeared. Initially dominated by a New England aristocracy interested in maintaining the old social order, the movement was concerned about alcohol use at all levels of society. Calvinist temperance preachers expressed fear of the common man who, with drink, spoke profanely, engaged in infidelities, and did not work as he should. By the 1830s, the temperance movement had lost its aristocratic air and became more egalitarian (and middle class) with the inclusion of Methodist, Baptist, and Presbyterian preachers. From the Civil War until the 1890s, the movement attempted to sell the virtues of the well-regulated middle-class life to the working and lower classes. The message was simple: remain sober, work hard, and become a member of the middle class (Gusfield 1962).

At the forefront of the temperance movement in the late 1890s was the Women's Christian Temperance Union (WCTU) and its dynamic leader, Frances Willard. While leading the WCTU in its crusade to abolish drink, she was simultaneously involved in a variety of progressive social reform movements, ranging from women's suffrage to the labor unions' right to strike, to calls for universal childhood education. The WCTU, along with the Anti-Saloon League and the Methodists' Board of Temperance, spearheaded the drive that led to the passage of the Eighteenth Amendment to the U.S. Constitution. When ratified in 1920, the amendment prohibited the manufacture, sale, and transportation of intoxicating liquors (Gusfield 1962).

Prohibition was deemed successful, at first. Hospital admissions related to alcohol consumption—liver disease—declined as many people practiced abstinence. Nevertheless, heavy drinkers continued to drink, and a newly created crime—bootlegging—emerged and took hold. In fact, it is generally conceded that American organized crime was born out of the era of prohibition. By the early 1930s, abstinence was no longer the social norm. A movement to repeal the Eighteenth Amendment grew. Supporters of the repeal argued that the Eighteenth Amendment violated personal liberties, was in fact unenforceable, and created crime (R. W. Howland and T. W. Howland 1978). The noble experiment came to an end on December 5, 1933, when the Twenty-first Amendment repealed the Eighteenth. Although prohibition resulted in fewer alcohol-related illnesses, it was a miserable failure in almost every other aspect. Hoping to restore a moral order to America, its chief contribution was to foster crime and support a profound disrespect for the law.

The lessons learned from alcohol are both valuable and complex. There is, simultaneously, great good and danger in psychoactive drugs. The challenge to us all lies in learning as much about them as we can. If we choose to imbibe, we should do so in a responsible manner that will not endanger the health and well-being of others or ourselves.

References

Gusfield, J. R. (1962). "Status conflicts and the changing ideologies of the American temperance movement." In *Society, Culture, and Drinking Patterns*, D. J. Pittman and C. R. Snyder (eds.), New York: John Wiley and Sons.

Howland, R. W., and T. W. Howland. (1978). "200 years of drinking in the United States." In *Drinking: Alcohol and American Society—Issues and Current Research*, J. A. Ewing and B. A. Rouse (eds.), Chicago: Nelson-Hall.

Weil, A. (1972). *The Natural Mind*. Boston: Houghton Mifflin.

For Discussion

1. Compare the role of bars with the role of shooting galleries discussed in Chapter 18.

2. Review the health consequences of alcohol use. How is it that alcohol use has remained legal for most of the past century at a time when legislation sought to control the use of other drugs?

8

Gateway to Nowhere

How Alcohol Came to Be Scapegoated for Drug Abuse

Stanton Peele
Archie Brodsky

Stanton Peele and Archie Brodsky argue that some United States drug policies are guided by the assumption that alcohol, tobacco, and marijuana serve as "gateways" to "harder" substances, such as cocaine and heroin. Citing data that dispute the theoretical assumptions of the gateway theory, the authors provide critical commentary about the alleged cause-and-effect relationship between "soft" and "hard" substances. Moreover, the authors suggest that drug policies based on the gateway theory may in fact be counterproductive.

The "gateway" theory of drug use holds that exposure to "entry" drugs—notably alcohol, cigarettes, and marijuana—reliably predicts deeper and more severe drug involvements. U.S. drug czar Barry McCaffrey has incorporated the gateway theory as an integral part of the country's drug policy. However, although most heavier drug users undoubtedly were once lighter drug users, this association does not establish a causal connection. Few young people progress from lighter to heavier drug use; in fact, the dominant trend is for young people to reduce illicit drug use and to stabilize drinking with maturity. The gateway theory may actually be counterproductive if we consider that in non-temperance cultures that manage alcohol successfully, alcohol is generally intro-duced to young people at an early age. Other evidence suggests that moderate-drinking and drug-using young people, even when such behavior is illegal, are better off psychologically and are more likely to make a successful transition to adulthood than abstainers. Overriding all such profiles of moderate and abusive users of drugs and alcohol are social-epidemiologic models which indicate that the best predictors of abusive substance use are social, family, and psychological depredations that occur independent of supposed gateway linkages.

The National Drug Control Strategy for 1997 unveiled by U.S. drug czar Gen. Barry R. McCaffrey (Office of National Drug Control Policy, 1997) adopts a "zero-tolerance" policy toward youthful alcohol, tobacco, and marijuana use. The strategy regards all of these as "gateway behaviors" leading to serious drug abuse. In support of this contention, the strategy cites a report by the Center on Addiction and Substance Abuse (CASA, 1994) entitled *Cigarettes, Alcohol, Marijuana: Gateways to Illicit Drug Use.* The CASA report has been widely influential, in part because CASA president Joseph A. Califano, Jr., is a former Secretary of the U.S. Department of Health, Education, and Welfare.

Califano and CASA relied on data from a 1991 government survey to show that both adolescents and adults who have used cigarettes, alcohol, and marijuana are hundreds of times more likely to use cocaine than those who have never used any of the three substances. Califano's conclusion: The most critical step in stamping out dangerous drug abuse is to prevent young people from embarking on the road to perdition through the gateway of smoking, drinking, or using marijuana.

According to *The National Drug Control Strategy,* "Drug policy must be based on science, not ideology." This pronouncement is belied by the document's uncritical reliance on the "gateway" concept, whose enthusiastic acceptance by public officials and agencies has not been accompanied by any real scientific scrutiny. For example, the findings of the annual national surveys of high-school student drug use conducted at the University of Michigan over the past two decades offer little support for the gateway theory; instead, they show historical fluctuations in drug use. No one has shown a consistent pattern of youthful alcohol, marijuana, and cigarette use trends that presages cocaine and heroin use trends (Zimmer and Morgan, 1997).

The 1996 survey results (Johnston et al., 1997) continued a recent mild upward trend in use of marijuana, but not other illegal drugs. Along with a slight upturn in marijuana use among high school seniors, tobacco use was also up, while "binge" drinking (five or more drinks at one time within the past two weeks) remained at roughly the same level (30 percent of high school seniors) in 1996. Although the incidence of such drinking is lower than the highs of over 40 percent in the late seventies and early eighties, this does not signify a lessening of overall alcohol excess among young Americans. Researchers at the Harvard School of Public Health have labeled 44 percent of U.S. college students as binge drinkers (50 percent of men had 5+ drinks, 39 percent of women had 4+ drinks) (Wechsler et al., 1994). What lies in store for these young people as they mature?

When young people get away from home by going to college, their binge drinking rises; in time, however, their drinking declines (as does their drug use) as they assume adult roles (Bachman et al., in press). Given that so many young people ultimately do moderate their drinking, why are we failing so badly with the prohibitionist alcohol-education message in which Gen. McCaffrey places such confidence? This failure has more than temporary consequences. Unfortunately, despite the overall drop-off from early problem drinking, a higher than average percentage of those who display unhealthy early drinking will develop adult drinking problems (Schulenberg et al., 1996).

The Reign of Ideology

It is not news that the government and government-related agencies want to prevent everyone from using illegal drugs and young people from sampling legal substances, such as alcohol, as well. As a part of this campaign, the Califano report marked a well-worn tendency to oversimplify complex matters and to tell people what they want and expect to hear. Remember that Robert L. DuPont, an anti-drug activist (he testifies, for example, on behalf of school systems seeking to implement drug tests), former White House drug chief, and the first director of the National Institute on Drug Abuse, was the first to popularize the gateway concept in 1985, with his book, *Getting Tough on Gateway Drugs: A Guide for the Family.*

Warnings against gateway or "stepping-stone" drugs are standard practice by educators, the media, and public-health advocates. These alarmist warnings fuel the War on Drugs in its most indiscriminate form. Hearing of the gateway theory, we may hesitate to teach teenage children to drink responsibly. We begin to fear that exposing them to mild, positive drinking will open the floodgate and sweep them into the crack house.

What makes far more sense is to acknowledge the obvious to children—that there is healthy and unhealthy drinking. Both research and common sense tell us that the young people least likely to drink disruptively are those who were introduced to alcohol by moderate-drinking parents, rather than being initiated into drinking by their peers. Vaillant (1983) found that young Italian-American men tracked from adolescence were only one-seventh as likely to become alcoholics in adulthood as neighboring Irish-Americans in Boston. Yet, it was the Italian-American families who introduced children to alcohol in a family context early in life, while the Irish-Americans urged children to abstain. Likewise, children who learn to drink wine at family social and religious ceremonies are not likely to be found taking crack on our city streets.

But reasonable souls who wouldn't mind having their kids learn in school that alcohol is a normal amenity of life for adults who can use it in moderation are out of luck, at least in the United States. Although Prohibition ended in the United States sixty years ago, only drug-education programs with an uncompromisingly prohibitionist message—

even toward alcohol—can be federally funded. On Main Streets across America, billboards and banners proclaim to our young that "Alcohol Is a Liquid Drug." This announcement provides no useful guidance for coming to terms with a substance that is legal, and that most Americans currently use.

The gateway theory also leads to the coercive treatment of many adolescents. In his book *The Great Drug War*, Arnold Trebach (1987) described how 19-year-old Fred Collins was pressured into residential treatment at Straight Inc. in Florida. Confined for four months, Collins was subjected to constant surveillance and indoctrination, accompanied by sleep and food deprivation. Collins escaped, and a jury awarded him $220,000 from Straight. At the trial, Collins was shown to have occasionally indulged in beer and marijuana. But to many in the treatment community, this "proved" he was headed for the disaster of addiction.

Collins embodies the gateway model's credibility gap—the disparity between the image and the reality of mainstream youth who start down the supposed primrose path to chemical enslavement. He illustrates, too, the costs of trying to make the relatively benign reality conform to the malign image. Among these costs are needless grief for parents and children and money wasted on unnecessary or ineffective treatment. At the same time, frightening warnings that young people can plainly see are untrue lead most to dismiss useful and realistic messages about harmful alcohol or drug use. After all, today's college students, nearly half of whom are binge drinkers, have been shaped by years of anti-drug and anti-alcohol education programs.

A Misleading Oversimplification

The cause-and-effect relationships that Califano's report took to be self-evident are in fact the subject of much scholarly debate. As (New York) City University Medical School pharmacologist John Morgan and his colleagues (1993, p. 217) noted, "This gateway concept seems to resemble driving slowly and safely as a gateway to driving recklessly and unlawfully. The reckless driver has always driven carefully at some point. How often does careful driving proceed to recklessness and does the careful driving cause the recklessness?"

It is true that users of narcotics and cocaine typically smoke cigarettes, drink alcohol (often to excess), and use other drugs as well. That is hindsight; looking from the other direction, adolescents and young adults who have had some experience with tobacco, alcohol, and marijuana are somewhat more likely to try "hard" drugs as well. But these generalizations do not mean that "soft" drug use causes, or even predisposes, a young person to use "hard" drugs.

One of the most prominent gateway advocates is epidemiologist Denise Kandel of Columbia University. But Kandel (1989) takes pains to point out that most youths stop at some point on the progression to hard drugs. Even among those who misbehave with drugs and alcohol, most eventually stop using drugs and moderate their alcohol use. Few of the teenagers who drink, even with the problems this causes, will turn into chronic problem drinkers, let alone crackheads. What we really need to figure out is who those few are who progress to extreme drug use, and what distinguishes them from the majority who would never even consider passing through the gateway.

An Enduring Myth

For what is at best a shallow half-truth, the notion of an inexorable progression from tasting forbidden fruit to self-destruction has had a remarkably enduring appeal for Americans. Its roots lie in the nineteenth-century temperance movement's image of "the fatal glass of beer"—that first sip taken by the innocent farm boy in the sinful city. The Currier & Ives print "The Drunkard's Progress" was one of many temperance tales that began with a man tippling and ended in suicide or murder.

Although Prohibition's repeal discredited the idea that alcohol addicts any and every user, this magical potency was then transferred to narcotics. At the same time, marijuana was misclassified as a narcotic. When marijuana became a staple on college campuses in the 1960s and 1970s, however, this myth also had to be discarded. But marijuana continued to be demonized—only now as a stepping stone to heroin addiction. Eventually, alcohol and cigarettes were made additional stepping stones to drug addiction. Thus, we still see the shadow of "the fatal glass of beer" in the title of an article by Kandel and Yamaguchi (1993) in *The American Journal of Public Health*, "From Beer to Crack."

But this model of drug use succeeds little better than the temperance version. In the Harvard alcohol survey, seven in ten students drank in the last month. But according to a 1994 government survey, only 12 percent of 18–25-year-olds and 6 percent of 12–17-year-olds had taken marijuana during the past month, only 1 percent of 18–25-year-olds and 0.3 percent of 12–17-year-olds had taken cocaine, and far fewer had taken crack or heroin (National Household Survey on Drug Abuse, 1996). Based on such information, the stepping-stone theory had to be watered down into the notion of gateway drugs. In this view, alcohol and cigarettes—along with marijuana—don't guarantee, but only make it more likely, that some will use harder drugs.

But even this revision doesn't work. If a substantial segment of Americans have used marijuana for years without getting involved with other illegal drugs, then not only is the old stepping-stone theory a shibboleth, but so too the weaker gateway version. What is true of marijuana is even more true of alcohol, since such a large majority of Americans drink. And a study from the National Development and Research Institutes (Golub and Johnson, 1994) found that the relationship between alcohol use and more serious drug abuse has been *decreasing* during the past three decades.

Alcohol, which can be used in a variety of healthy and unhealthy ways, is just too mainstream to be connected reliably to drug use. This has been truer the more illicit drugs have been marginalized. Cultural myths die hard, but the fatal-glass myth has lingered particularly long. It is time to pull the plug on it. To do something about the destructive consequences of drug abuse, we need to jettison entirely our temperance mentality.

Easy Image, Hard Reality

The Califano report conjures up an "Invasion of the Body Snatchers" image of America, as beer and cigarettes steal the souls of innocent children. This latter-day "Demon Rum" scenario is just another case of looking for our keys under the street light rather than where we actually lost them. For the hard reality to which all research points is that some young people are more vulnerable to destructive habits than others. They are more vulnerable because of psychological maladjustment, family disruption, and economic and social deprivation. For example:

- Kandel (1989) identified depressive symptoms, parental drug use, and the lack of a close parent-child relationship as risk factors for progressing to more serious drug use.

- Sociologist Richard Clayton (1985) found that truancy was a strong prior predictor of cocaine use among high-school students *independent of any other substance use.*

- Grace Barnes (1987) of the New York State Division of Alcoholism and Alcohol Abuse found that children from broken homes were far more likely to use illicit drugs. However, single parents could overcome this risk by providing "appropriate levels of nurturance and control."

The focus should not be on gateway drugs but on the highly dysfunctional lives of adolescent drug abusers. Two UCLA psychologists, Michael Newcomb and Peter Bentler (1989), found that the most destructive teenage drug use occurred among youths whose lives were characterized by limited opportunities (often resulting from inner-city conditions), internal emotional distress, and unhappiness. Among those in the inner city, even when they were able to stop taking drugs, their lives in other respects (e.g., crime, early pregnancy) did not improve. UC Berkeley psychologists Jonathan

Shedler and Jack Block (1990) actually found that young people who experimented with drugs were better adjusted than frequent users and abstainers. These researchers were also able to predict drug problems for teens based on psychological profiles constructed when the subjects were small children! More recently, Pape and Hammer (1996) found a similar pattern with respect to alcohol use by male adolescents in Norway: that those who got drunk for the first time at either a very early or a late age had elevated levels of psychological problems; those who first got drunk in mid-adolescence were most likely to develop normally.

The lives of young people at serious risk for drug abuse have been best described by the problem-behavior theory of University of Colorado psychologist Richard Jessor (1987). Jessor has shown that drug abuse is one of a cluster of problem behaviors that also include truancy, delinquency, unhealthy eating habits, excessive TV watching, reckless driving, and premature or reckless sexual behavior. These behaviors do not cause one another; rather, they are common manifestations of traumatized and aimless lives.

Looked at from the opposite direction, Donovan and Jessor (1985) find the risk of problem behavior is reduced by high self-esteem, a sense of personal control, placing a high value on health, and participation in constructive mainstream activities such as school and church. Jessor and his colleagues summed up some of these positive factors as "an orientation toward, commitment to, and involvement with the prevailing values, standards of behavior, and established institutions of American society" (Costa, Jessor, and Donovan, 1989, p. 842).

Direction for Policy

A drug policy based on the mechanistic "gateway" model is a policy badly in need of reconsideration. It should be replaced by one grounded in a real understanding of why people use and abuse drugs. After decades of continuous effort, we still face substantial drug use among young people, including periodic rises like that noted in the Michigan survey. Obviously, the ultimate solution for youthful drug abuse and much else ailing America is to strengthen personal values and family lives and to allow more people to buy into the American dream. But, while we struggle to achieve this elusive goal, we can try to do the following:

- Acknowledge the difference between exposure to drugs and drug abuse, and especially between controlled and destructive drinking.

- With those young people most at risk for becoming involved with drugs, warnings to avoid any use of drugs, alcohol, and cigarettes have thus far been futile. It is more useful to require (and help) them to take responsibility for their actions, to escape destructive situations, and to contribute to society.

No drug makes people use it or other drugs. The causes of drug abuse are life conditions that motivate people to act destructively toward themselves and others. Liberals identify these as social and economic circumstances involving a loss of opportunity and hope. Conservatives identify them as a breakdown of moral standards and public order. Either of these explanations has a lot more going for it than Demon Rum.

Acknowledgments

Preparation of this article was supported by a small grant from the Weinberg Consulting Group.

References

Bachman, J. G., Wadsworth, K. N., O'Malley, P. M., Johnston, L. D., and Schulenberg, J. E. (in press). *Smoking, Drinking and Drug Use in Young Adulthood: The Impacts of New Freedoms and Responsibilities*. Mahwah, NJ: Erlbaum.

Barnes, G. M., and Windle, M. (1987). "Family factors in adolescent alcohol and drug abuse," *Pediatrician* 14: 13–18.

Center on Addiction and Substance Abuse at Columbia University. (1994). *Cigarettes, Alcohol, Marijuana: Gateways to Illicit Drug Use*. New York: Author.

Clayton, R. R. (1985). "Cocaine use in the United States: In a blizzard or just being snowed?" In N. J. Kozel and E. H. Adams (eds.), *Cocaine*

Use in America: Epidemiologic and Clinical Perspectives. Rockville, MD: National Institute on Drug Abuse, 8–34.

Costa, F. M., Jessor, R., and Donovan, J. E. (1989). "Value on health and adolescent conventionality: A construct validation of a new measure in Problem-Behavior Theory," *Journal of Applied Social Psychology* 19: 841–861.

Donovan, J. E., and Jessor, R. (1985). "Structure of problem behavior in adolescence and young adulthood," *Journal of Consulting and Clinical Psychology* 53: 890–904.

DuPont, R. L., Jr. (1985). *Getting Tough on Gateway Drugs: A Guide for the Family.* Washington, DC: American Psychiatric Press.

Golub, A., and Johnson, B. D. (1994). "The shifting importance of alcohol and marijuana as gateway substances among serious drug users," *Journal of Studies on Alcohol* 55: 607–614.

Jessor, R. (1987). "Problem-Behavior Theory, psychosocial development, and adolescent problem drinking," *British Journal of Addiction* 82: 331–342.

Johnston, L. D., O'Malley, P. M., and Bachman, J. G. (1997). *National Survey Results on Drug Use from the Monitoring the Future Study, 1975–1996.* Vol. I.—*Secondary School Students.* Rockville, MD: U.S. Department of Health and Human Services, National Institute on Drug Abuse.

Kandel, D. B. (1989). "Issues of sequencing of adolescent drug use and other problem behaviors." In B. Segal (ed.), *Perspectives on Adolescent Drug Use.* New York: Haworth, 55–76.

Kandel, D. B., and Yamaguchi, K. (1993). "From beer to crack: Developmental patterns of drug involvement," *American Journal of Public Health* 83: 851–855.

Morgan, J. R., Riley, D., and Chesher, G. B. (1993). "Cannabis: Legal reform, medicinal use and harm reduction." In N. Heather, A. Wodak, E. Nadelmann, and P. O'Hare (eds.), *Psychoactive Drugs and Harm Reduction.* London: Whurr, 211–229.

National Household Survey on Drug Abuse: Main Findings 1994. (1996). Rockville, MD: U.S. Department of Health and Human Services, Substance Abuse and Mental Health Services Administration.

Newcomb, M. D., and Bentler, P. M. (1989). "Substance use and abuse among children and teenagers," *American Psychologist* 44: 242–248.

Office of National Drug Control Policy (1997). *The National Drug Control Strategy: 1997.* Washington, DC: Author.

Pape, H., and Hammer, T. (1996). "Sober adolescence—Predictor of psychological maladjustment in young adulthood?" *Scandinavian Journal of Psychology* 37: 362–377.

Schulenberg, J. E., O'Malley, P. M., Bachman, J. G., Wadsworth, K. N., and Johnston, L. D. (1996). "Getting drunk and growing up: Trajectories of frequent binge drinking during the transition to young adulthood," *Journal of Studies on Alcohol* 57: 289–304.

Shedler, J., and Block, J. (1990). "Adolescent drug use and psychological health," *American Psychologist* 45: 612–629.

Trebach, A. S. (1987). *The Great Drug War.* New York: Macmillan.

Vaillant, G. E. (1983). *The Natural History of Alcoholism: Causes, Patterns, and Paths to Recovery.* Cambridge, MA: Harvard University Press.

Wechsler, H., Davenport, A., Dowdall, G., Moeykens, B., and Castillo, S. (1994). "Health and behavioral consequences of binge drinking in college: A national survey of students at 140 campuses," *Journal of the American Medical Association* 272: 1672–1677.

Zimmer, L., and Morgan, J. P. (1997). *Marijuana Myths, Marijuana Facts.* New York: The Lindesmith Center.

For Discussion

1. What criteria can best differentiate between "soft" and "hard" drugs?

2. Is it possible that the "gateway theory" might serve the interests of public officials involved in the drug war? If so, how?

9

College Binge Drinking in the 1990s

A Continuing Problem

Henry Wechsler
Jae-Eun Lee
Meichun Kuo
Hang Lee

Henry Wechsler and his colleagues examine alcohol consumption across several college campuses, and for three different time periods in the 1990s. The authors discuss the various categories (e.g., abstainers; binge drinkers) used in their study and offer descriptions of those individuals who fall within these categories. Binge drinking continues to present problems both for persons who engage in this behavior and for other individuals with whom they come in contact. The authors suggest that binge drinking might be best addressed through a comprehensive approach.

In 1993, the Harvard School of Public Health College Alcohol Study (CAS) surveyed a random sample of students at 140 colleges in 39 states and the District of Columbia. The survey constituted the first attempt to study drinking patterns in a nationally representative sample of college students. The findings, first published in December 1994,[1] received widespread national attention.

The study's authors described a style of drinking that they designated as "binge" drinking, defined as the consumption of five or more drinks in a row for men and four or more for women, at least once in the two weeks preceding the survey. The term *binge drinking* was used by Wechsler and colleagues several years before in a study of Massachusetts college students' alcohol use.[2] The term is now used in the media as a catchword to designate college drinking that leads to serious problems. Following the publication of the initial CAS results, there was greater media attention to alcohol-related tragedies among college students, including deaths in a variety of circumstances: acute alcohol poisonings, falls, drownings, automobile collisions, fires, and hypothermia resulting from exposure. Such drastic consequences underscore the multitude of other, less severe, outcomes of binge drinking.

Heightened public interest in binge drinking prompted changes in the way colleges addressed the problem. Until the mid-1990s, student drinking issues were largely the responsibility of alcohol educators and deans of students. Since then, in association with extensive media coverage and the release of several national studies of drinking behavior, college presidents are often involved. Many of them are frequently included in statewide and regional coalitions that address the problem jointly.

Other indications that college alcohol issues have been placed on the national agenda are such developments as passage of a resolution by the U.S. House of Representatives and the Senate to address binge drinking; a National Institute on Alcoholism and Alcohol Abuse special task force on college drinking, as well as a special grant program to focus on this issue; a Centers for Disease Control and Prevention (CDC) health risk survey for college students; and frequent features on binge drinking in major television network news magazine programs. The Robert Wood Johnson Foundation has established an initiative, the Matter of Degree program, which provides funding to universities to develop comprehensive environmental-change approaches by establishing college/community coalitions to address the problem of student drinking.

In 1997, the CAS survey of students was repeated at the original colleges with new samples. That survey found little change in the intervening four years in the overall rates of binge drinking. For the 116 colleges in that analysis, a minor drop occurred in the proportion of binge drinkers, from 44.1% in 1993 to 42.7% in 1997. However, the study uncovered an increase in the prevalence of both frequent binge drinking and abstention. A polarization effect was observed, resulting in two sizable groups of students on campus: those who did not drink at all (19%) and those who binge drank three or more times in a two-week period (21%). Students in the latter group of frequent binge drinkers were found to consume a median of 14.5 drinks per week, and this group accounted for 68% of all the alcohol consumed by college students.[3]

Despite all of the attention focused on binge drinking by colleges and the media and the initial actions to reduce alcohol-related problems, little change in student drinking levels occurred on the national level between 1993 and 1997. The CAS was repeated in 1999 to examine overall levels of binge drinking and to determine whether the trend toward increased polarization of drinking behavior on campus had continued.

Method

Sample of Colleges

In 1999, we resurveyed 128 schools from the original list of 140 colleges that were surveyed in 1993 and the 130 colleges surveyed in 1997. The 128 schools were located in 39 states and the District of Columbia. The original 1993 sample was selected from a list of accredited four-year colleges provided by the American Council on Education. The sample was selected using probability sampling proportionate to the size of undergraduate enrollment at each institution. In 1999, we obtained student samples using the same procedures we had used in the first two surveys. Details of the sample and research design of the 1993 and 1997 surveys are described elsewhere.[1,4]

In 1999, as in the previous surveys, we asked administrators at each college to provide a random sample of 225 undergraduates drawn from the total enrollment of full-time students. The attrition of ten colleges in 1997 and two colleges in 1999 was primarily the result of the college administrators' inability to provide a random sample of students and their mailing addresses to us within the time requirements for the study.

In conducting the data analyses, we excluded schools that failed to meet the minimal criteria for response rate. To be part of the three-year comparison sample described in this report, a school had to have a response rate of at least 50% in two of the three surveys and a rate of at least 40% in the third. For all three survey years, 119 schools met these criteria, and we dropped nine from the analyses. When we compared the binge-drinking rates of the 119 retained in 1999 with the corresponding rates of all 128 participating in 1999, we found that they were identical. Dropping the low-response schools did not change the results of the survey. Similar comparisons for the 1997 and 1993 rates of these schools with those of the total samples in those years also revealed no differences.

The sample of 119 colleges presents a national cross-section of four-year colleges. Two thirds of the colleges sampled are public institutions, and one third are private. In terms of student enrollments, two fifths of the schools (44%) are large (more than 10,000 students), one fifth (23%) are medium sized (5,001 to 10,000 students), and one third (34%) are small (5,000 students or fewer). About two thirds are located in an urban or suburban setting and one third are in small-town or rural settings. Fifteen percent are affiliated with a religious denomination, and 5% enroll women only.

Questionnaire

The 1999 survey repeated standard questions used in 1993 and 1997 about alcohol, tobacco, and other drug use, as well as lifestyle, demographic, and other background characteristics. These questions were adapted from previous large-scale, national studies.[2,5,6] The questionnaire instructed participants to define a drink in equivalent amounts of alcohol: a 12-oz. (360 ml) bottle or can of beer, a 4-oz. (120 ml) glass of wine, a 12-oz. (360 ml) bottle or can of wine cooler, or a shot of liquor (1.25 oz. or 37 ml), either straight or in a mixed drink. Questions also inquired about students' experiences with prevention programs and school alcohol and tobacco policies.

The Measure of Binge Drinking

Heavy episodic or *binge drinking* was defined as the consumption of at least five drinks in a row for men or four drinks in a row for women during the two weeks before the completion of the questionnaire. In the past decade, large-scale epidemiologic studies of youth alcohol use have employed five drinks in a row as a measure of heavy drinking, and this has become a standard measure in both secondary school populations [the University of Michigan's National Institute of Drug Abuse (NIDA)-sponsored Monitoring the Future study[5]] and college populations (Core Institute Survey,[7] National College Health Risk Behavior Survey[8]). In an analysis of the 1993 CAS data,[9] a gender-specific definition ("five/four") of binge drinking provided a measure of equivalent alcohol-related problems for college men and women.

The CAS gender-specific measure of binge drinking was constructed from responses to four questions: (a) gender; (b) recency of last drink; (c) drinking five or more drinks during the past two weeks; and (d) drinking four or more drinks during the past two weeks. Missing data for any of these questions resulted in the exclusion of that student's responses from the analysis of binge drinking. We excluded 2.6% of the responses in 1993, 1.4% in 1997, and 2.3% in 1999.

We defined *frequent binge drinkers* as those students who had binged three or more times in the past two weeks (or more than once a week, on average), *occasional binge drinkers* were those students who had binged one or two times in the same period. *Nonbinge drinkers* were those students who had consumed alcohol in the past year but had not binged in the previous two weeks,

and *abstainers* were those students who had consumed no alcohol in the past year.

Students who had consumed alcohol in the past 30 days were asked to report on the number of occasions they had a drink of alcohol in the past month. The response categories were one to two occasions, three to five occasions, six to nine occasions, 10 to 19 occasions, 20 to 39 occasions, and 40 or more occasions. In response to a question asking whether getting drunk was a reason for drinking, students who responded *very important, important,* or *somewhat important,* as opposed to *not important,* were considered to have the drinking style of "drinking to get drunk." High school binge drinking was defined as *the amount of alcohol usually consumed during the last year of high school,* using the same five/four measure.

Students who drank alcohol in the past year were asked a series of questions about their experiences with alcohol-related problems during the current school year, including 12 health and behavioral consequences of one's own drinking. All students were asked eight questions about the consequences of other students' drinking (secondhand effects). We examined these secondhand effects among students who were not binge drinkers (nonbinge drinkers and abstainers) and lived on campus (i.e., were residents of on-campus dormitories or fraternity/sorority houses).

In this article, data on alcohol-related sexual assaults and unwanted sexual advances, problems that most frequently affect women, are presented for women only. We divided colleges into high-binge institutions (more than 50% of students are binge drinkers); middle-binge level (36%–50%), and low-binge (35% or lower) on the basis of the aggregated binge-drinking behavior of their students.

Mailing and Response Rate

In all three surveys, questionnaires were mailed directly to students at the end of February. Three separate mailings were sent within a three-week period: first a questionnaire, then a reminder postcard, followed by a second questionnaire. Mailings were timed to avoid the period immediately preceding and following spring break so that students would be responding to questions concerning their behavior during a time when they were on campus. The students' responses were voluntary and anonymous. The study therefore received exempt status from the institutional review committees. To encourage students to respond, we offered an award of one $1,000 prize to a student whose name was drawn from among students responding within one week; a $500 award and ten $100 awards were offered to students whose names were drawn from a pool of all who responded.

Response rates varied among the colleges that participated in the 1993, 1997, and 1999 surveys. Average response rates were 60% in 1999 (range = 49%–83%), 60% in 1997 (range = 40%–88%), and 70% in 1993 (range = 41%–100%).

We used two procedures to examine potential bias introduced by nonresponders. The response rates at individual colleges were not associated with their binge-drinking rates. The Pearson correlation coefficient between a college's binge rate and its response rate was $-.029$ ($p = .753$) in 1999, $.006$ ($p = .949$) in 1997, and $-.014$ ($p = .879$) in 1993. In addition, we adjusted for response rates in the multiple logistic regression models in all of the analyses.

Data Analysis

We used chi-square analysis to compare student characteristics and outcomes of interest between the three survey years. Prevalence of outcomes over the three survey years was indicated by percentages and their percentage changes, and tested for significance, using the chi-square test. We employed logistic regression to assess the odds of an alcohol-related problem or behavior for binge drinkers compared with nonbinge drinkers. In this article, we report adjusted odds ratios (ORs) and 95% confidence intervals for student and college characteristics, based on the logistic regression model. In addition, we employed the generalized estimating equations (GEE)[10,11] approach to fitting the logistic regression models. Because it uses the clustered outcomes appropriate to our sampling scheme, the GEE provides more robust standard errors of the OR esti-

mates. The GEE procedure resulted in little or no difference in the estimated ORs, compared with the ordinary logistic regression models, and provided slightly greater standard errors of the estimate. When appropriate, we used the GEE-based standard errors to perform the significance tests. We also used this method in the time-trend analysis of frequent binge drinking and abstaining over the three surveys, adjusting for class year, sex, and race.

Four percent of the participants were sampled in both the 1997 and 1999 surveys. However, we found no statistical evidence of reduced variation in the sample resulting from these duplicated respondents, and therefore they remained in the analysis. To facilitate comparisons between the 1993, 1997, and 1999 data, we used data from only those respondents at the 119 schools that met the inclusion criteria for relatively high response rates in all survey years. Thus, the 1999 findings are slightly different (usually 1% or less) from those previously reported in articles reporting data for the 140 colleges in 1993[1] and the 116 colleges[3] in 1997.

Results

Composition of the Student Samples

In 1999, three of five (61%) respondents were women. This was higher than the national rates (55%) of undergraduate women at four-year institutions.[12] Perhaps this was attributable, at least in part, to the inclusion of six women's colleges. Four of five (78%) of the respondents were White, and 15% were more than 23 years of age. The background characteristics of the students at the 119 colleges were similar to those found in 1993 and 1997. However, because each of the three survey samples consisted of more than 14,000 students, even small differences were statistically significant (Table 9.1).

In 1999, the proportion of women in the CAS was higher than in 1993 and 1997, and the proportion of white and older students in 1999 was lower than in 1993 and 1997. Because both of these demographic characteristics were associated with drinking outcome, we controlled the multivariate comparisons of

Table 9.1

General Characteristics of Student Samples, 1993, 1997, 1999

	Sample			χ^2		
	1993	1997	1999	'93 v '99	'93 v '97	'97 v '99
Characteristic	(N = 15,403) %	(N = 14,724) %	(N = 14,138) %	p	p	p
Gender						
Male	42.6	39.8	38.7	< .0001	< .0001	.0710
Female	57.4	60.2	61.3			
Ethnicity						
Hispanic	6.5	7.9	7.3	.0055	< .0001	.0396
Non-Hispanic	93.5	92.1	92.7			
White	82.7	78.9	78.0	< .0001	< .0001	.0021
Black/African American	4.8	5.1	5.9	.0001	.3214	.0042
Asian/Pacific Islander	6.5	7.6	8.3	< .0001	.0003	.0490
Native American Indian/Other	6	8.4	7.9	< .0001	< .0001	.0706
Age						
< 24 y	83.5	83.6	84.8	.0015	.8603	.0030
≥ 24 y	16.5	16.4	15.2			
Years in School						
Freshman	20.2	23.7	23.0	< .0001	< .0001	.2775
Sophomore	19.3	21.5	22.4	< .0001	< .0001	.0243
Junior	24.3	23.4	24.6	.8105	.0126	.0073
Senior	25.5	22.3	22.0	< .0001	< .0001	.2775
5th	10.8	9.1	8.1	< .0001	< .0001	.0044

Table 9.2

College Student Patterns of Alcohol Use, 1993, 1997, 1999

	Prevalence (%)			Change(%)		
	1993	1997	1999			
Category	(N = 14,995)	(N = 14,520)	(N = 13,819)	'93 v '99	'93 v '97	'97v '99
Abstainer (past y)	15.4	18.9	19.2	24.7***	22.6***	1.7
Nonbinge drinker[†]	40.1	38.2	36.6	−8.6***	−4.7***	−4.1**
Occasional binge drinker[‡]	24.7	22.0	21.4	−13.1***	−11.0***	−2.4
Frequent binge drinker[§]	19.8	20.9	22.7	14.5***	5.6*	8.5***

Note. Sample sizes vary from those in Table 9.1 because of missing values.
[†]Students who consumed alcohol in the past year but did not binge.
[‡]Students who binged one or two times in a 2-week period.
[§]Students who binged three or more times in a 2-week period.
*p < .05; **p < .01; ***p < .001.

drinking and other behaviors in the three survey samples for those characteristics.

Even though the overall rate of binge drinking did not change between 1993 and 1999, other changes were evident. In 1999, drinking on college campuses continued a trend toward becoming more strongly polarized: almost one in five students (19%) was an abstainer, and almost one in four (23%) was a frequent binge drinker. The numbers of students in these two groups increased over the three survey years. To examine the 1993 to 1999 trends among abstainers and frequent binge drinkers, adjusting for year in class, race, and sex, we used the GEE. The result showed a significant increase in ab-

Table 9.3

Changes in Prevalence of Binge Drinking, 1993, 1997, 1999 by Student Characteristics

| Characteristic | Prevalence (%) | | | Change (%) | | |
	1993 (N = 15,403)	1997 (N = 14,724)	1999 (N = 14,138)	'93 v '99	'93 v '97	'97 v '99
Total	44.5	42.9	44.1	−0.8	−3.6**	2.9*
Gender						
Male	50.7	48.3	50.7	0.0	−4.6*	4.8*
Female	39.9	39.3	40.0	0.3	−1.5	1.8
Ethnicity						
Hispanic	39.0	37.9	39.5	1.1	−2.8	4.1
Non-Hispanic	44.8	43.3	44.5	−0.7	−3.4*	2.8*
White	48.4	46.9	49.2	1.7	−3.1*	5.0**
Black/African American	15.7	19.1	15.5	−1.5	21.5	−18.9
Asian/Pacific Islander	22.1	25.3	23.1	4.5	14.7	−8.9
Other	38.8	37.4	39.6	2.1	−3.6	5.9
Age						
< 24 y	47.5	45.6	47.0	−1.2	−4.0**	2.9*
≥ 24 y	29.0	28.8	28.1	−2.9	−0.6	−2.4
Year in school						
Freshman	43.5	43.3	42.1	−3.3	−0.4	−3.0
Sophomore	45.7	43.8	44.5	−2.6	−4.2	1.6
Junior	44.7	44.5	45.9	2.8	−0.3	3.2
Senior	44.0	41.3	44.9	2.0	−6.1*	8.7**
5th	45.2	41.8	42.5	−5.9	−7.7	1.8
Residence						
Dormitory	47.3	45.3	44.5	−5.8**	−4.2*	−1.7
Fraternity/sorority house	83.1	81.6	78.9	−5.1	−1.9	−3.3
Off campus	41.1	40.2	43.7	6.2***	−2.3	8.7***
Fraternity/sorority member	67.4	65.5	64.7	−4.0	−2.8	−1.3
Binged in high school						
No	32.3	30.9	31.1	−3.8	−4.5*	0.7
Yes	69.7	70.7	73.9	6.0***	1.3	4.6***
Marital status						
Never married	47.5	45.7	46.9	−1.3	−3.7**	2.5
Married	20.5	18.7	18.3	−10.5	−8.9	−1.7

*$p < .05$; **$p < .01$; ***$p < .001$.

stainers during the four-year period from 1993 to 1997 (OR = 1.21, $p < .0001$) and no change (OR = 0.97, $p = .51$) during the two-year period from 1997 to 1999. Overall, we observed a significant increase in the number of abstainers from 1993 to 1999 (OR = 1.18, $p < .0001$). The number of frequent binge drinkers significantly increased during the 4-year period, 1993 to 1997 (OR = 1.11, $p < .0126$), and continued to increase significantly during the 2-year period, 1997 to 1999 (OR = 1.01, $p = .024$). Overall, we noted a significant increase in frequent binge drinkers from 1993 to 1999 (OR = 1.20, $p < .0001$).

When we took student characteristics into account, the rise in abstention and frequent binge drinking was significant between 1993 and 1999 in most student subgroups. The growth in abstention between 1993 and 1997 was significant in both men ($p < .001$) and women ($p < .001$). However, an increase in the numbers of women who abstained occurred in 1997, whereas the increase in men's abstaining was significant in both 1997 and 1999 ($p < .001$, see Table 9.4). A significant

Table 9.4

College Student Patterns of Alcohol Use, 1993, 1997, 1999, by Student Characteristics

	Abstainers						Frequent bingers					
	Prevalence (%)			Change (%)			Prevalence (%)			Change (%)		
	1993	1997	1999	'93 v '99	'93 v '97	'97 v '99	1993	1997	1999	'93 v '99	'93 v '97	'97 v '99
Total	15.4	18.9	19.2	24.7***	22.6***	1.7	19.8	20.9	22.7	14.5***	5.6*	8.5
Gender												
Male	14.9	18.4	20.1	34.9***	24.0***	8.8*	22.8	23.8	26.0	13.7***	4.0	9.3**
Female	15.8	19.2	18.7	18.2***	21.5***	-2.7	17.5	19.0	20.6	17.4***	8.5*	8.2*
Ethnicity												
Hispanic	14.8	19.1	20.5	38.9***	29.4***	7.3	15.4	17.2	16.6	7.7	11.6	-3.4
Non-Hispanic	15.4	18.9	19.1	23.8***	22.2***	1.3	20.1	21.3	23.2	15.3***	5.7*	9.1***
White	13.1	16.1	15.6	19.2***	23.3***	-3.4	22.0	23.6	26.3	19.4***	7.1**	11.5***
Black/African American	32.6	35.3	38.0	16.6*	8.2	7.8	6.4	6.6	6.5	2.8	3.3	-0.5
Asian/Pacific Islander	32.1	33.2	36.7	14.1*	3.3	10.4	7.6	9.4	8.4	10.9	24.3	-10.9
Other	15.2	20.7	19.8	30.0**	36.3***	-4.6	15.4	17.2	17.4	13.1	11.8	1.1
Age												
< 24 y	14.8	18.7	18.4	24.4***	26.2***	-1.5	22.0	23.1	24.8	12.8***	5.2*	7.3**
≥ 24 y	18.7	20.3	24.1	29.3***	8.9	18.8**	8.8	9.7	10.8	23.0*	10.5	11.3
Year in school												
Freshman	22.0	24.7	24.7	12.4*	12.4*	0.0	21.1	23.1	22.3	5.5	9.5	-3.7
Sophomore	17.5	20.1	21.0	20.0***	15.1**	4.2	20.1	22.5	24.1	20.1***	11.7*	7.5
Junior	13.5	17.9	17.4	28.5***	32.1***	-2.7	20.2	20.9	23.2	15.1**	3.8	10.9*
Senior	12.3	14.9	15.2	24.4***	21.4**	2.5	19.4	18.7	22.3	14.7**	-3.8	19.2***
5th	11.1	14.2	15.8	41.9***	27.5*	11.3	17.2	18.9	20.5	19.2*	10.0	8.4
Residence												
Dormitory	17.3	19.3	19.9	14.9***	11.4*	3.1	22.5	22.5	23.0	2.2	0.2	2.0
Fraternity/sorority house	1.2	3.0	4.4	257.7**	146.3	45.2	49.4	52.5	51.1	3.5	6.4	-2.7
Off campus	15.3	18.9	18.6	21.9***	23.8***	-1.6	17.0	18.8	22.1	29.9***	10.5**	17.5***
Fraternity/sorority member	5.6	8.1	8.5	53.2***	45.8***	5.1	34.3	38.6	39.6	15.3***	12.3**	2.7
Binged in high school												
No	21.2	25.5	26.4	24.6***	20.1***	3.8	10.9	11.3	12.2	11.5**	3.9	7.3
Yes	3.3	3.7	2.8	-15.4	9.9	-23.0*	38.2	43.3	46.7	22.1***	13.4***	7.7**
Marital status												
Never married	14.4	17.8	18.2	25.9***	23.3***	2.1	21.7	22.8	24.4	12.3***	4.8*	7.2***
Married	22.9	28.0	29.1	27.4***	22.3***	4.1	4.7	5.3	6.4	38.1*	13.6	21.6

*p <.05; **p <.01; ***p <.001.

rise in abstention was reported among Hispanic (*p* < .001), African American (*p* < .05), Asian (*p* < .05), freshmen students (*p* < .05), and in residents of dormitories (*p* < .001) and fraternity/sorority houses (*p* < .01). In the meantime, a significant rise in frequent binge drinking occurred among students who were binge drinkers in high school.

The data in Table 9.5 show changes in the prevalence of binge drinking in terms of college characteristics. In comparing colleges in various categories according to characteristics of the institution, we found that the prevalence of binge drinking at most types of colleges did not change between 1993 and 1999. Where significant changes emerged, as in the case of competitive standings of institutions, there was no clear pattern or direction of change. The abstainer and frequent

binge-drinker rates at most types of colleges increased between 1993 and 1997 and did not change between 1997 and 1999. The rise in both abstention and frequent binge drinking between 1993 and 1999 occurred in most college subgroups (Table 9.6).

From 1993 to 1999, an increase in binge-drinking rates was observed at 53% of the 119 participating colleges but was statistically significant at only seven schools (6%). A decrease in binge-drinking rates was observed at almost an equal number of participating colleges (47%) and was statistically significant for only eight schools (7%). Thus, the results indicating no change among students at all colleges are reinforced when individual colleges are examined.

The polarization in college drinking appeared when we examined data from indi-

Table 9.5

Changes in Prevalence of Binge Drinking, 1993, 1997, 1999, by College Characteristics

College characteristic	N 1999	Prevalence (%) 1993	1997	1999	Change (%) '93 v '99	'93 v '97	'97 v '99
Total	119	44.5	42.9	44.1	−0.8	−3.6**	2.9*
Commuter school[†]	17	30.9	31.9	31.4	1.5	3.1	−1.5
Not commuter school	102	46.9	44.7	46.2	−1.6	−4.7***	3.3*
Not competitive[‡]	25	39.5	38.2	39.5	0.1	−3.3	3.5
Competitive	43	46.2	44.7	42.2	−8.7***	−3.3	−5.6*
Very competitive	31	45.9	44.3	49.8	8.6***	−3.5	12.5***
Highly competitive	19	46.2	43.7	45.1	−2.4	−5.4	3.2
Small < 5000	40	43.3	42.3	41.1	−5.1*	−2.3	−2.9
Medium 5001–10 000	27	42.9	41.7	45.0	4.8	−2.8	7.9*
Large > 10 001	52	45.6	43.6	45.8	0.5	−4.3*	5.0*
Public	82	45.0	43.3	44.6	−0.9	−3.7*	2.9
Private	37	43.2	42.0	43.1	−0.3	−3.0	2.7
Northeast	28	50.1	45.5	47.9	−4.3	−9.2***	5.4*
South	35	43.2	40.7	42.4	−1.8	−5.7*	4.2
North Central	35	48.1	48.0	48.6	0.9	−0.2	1.1
West	21	33.6	34.3	34.4	2.6	2.1	0.5
Religious affiliation	19	41.3	41.3	42.9	3.7	0.0	3.7
Nonreligious	100	45.0	43.2	44.6	−1.0	−4.0**	3.2
Rural/small town	34	49.7	46.2	48.9	−1.6	−7.1***	5.8**
Suburban/urban	85	41.8	41.1	42.2	0.9	−1.7	2.6
Women only	6	28.9	30.6	31.3	8.4	6.1	2.1
Not women's college	113	45.0	43.6	44.9	−0.4	−3.2*	2.9*

Note: College characteristics may vary slightly from those reported in the 1993 and 1997 studies.
[†]Commuter schools were defined as schools with ≥90% of students living off campus.
[‡]Competitiveness is based on ACT and SAT scores and percentage of applicants accepted, as reported in *Barron's Profiles of American Colleges.*[20]
*p <.05; **p <.01; ***p <.001.

vidual colleges from 1993 to 1999. An increase in abstention was observed at three out of four colleges (77%), and was statistically significant for 19 (16%) schools. This was in contrast to decreases in abstainers at only 23% of the colleges; none of the decreases reached statistical significance. An increase in frequent binge drinkers was observed at eighty-three (70%) out of 119 colleges and was statistically significant for 11% of schools. On the other hand, we observed a decrease in frequent binge drinkers at only 30% of colleges. It was statistically significant for only three (3%) schools.

Drinking Style

The data in Table 9.7 indicate changes in drinking style among students who drank alcohol in the past year. The intensity of their drinking increased significantly between 1993 and 1999. In 1999, a greater percentage of both male and female students drank on 10 or more occasions; usually binged when they drank; were drunk three or more times in the past month; and drank to get drunk. Although we found a general increase in drinking intensities from survey to survey, the strongest increase had occurred by 1997.

Prevalence of Alcohol-Related Problems

In 1999, the prevalence of each of 12 alcohol-related educational, interpersonal, health, and safety problems among college men and women who drank any alcohol in the past year was significantly higher than in 1993. These increases had occurred by 1997, and additional increases did not appear between 1997 and 1999. In fact, some prob-

Table 9.6

College Student Patterns of Alcohol Use, 1993, 1997, 1999, by College Characteristics

| | Abstainers | | | | | | Frequent bingers | | | | | |
| | Prevalence (%) | | | Change (%) | | | Prevalence (%) | | | Change (%) | | |
College characteristic	1993	1997	1999	'93 v '99	'93 v '97	'97 v '99	1993	1997	1999	'93 v '99	'93 v '97	'97 v '99
Commuter school[†]	17.1	21.5	24.3	42.2***	26.2***	12.6*	11.2	11.9	12.8	14.0	5.9	7.7
Not commuter	15.1	18.5	18.4	21.8***	22.1***	−0.3	21.3	22.4	24.3	13.8***	5.0*	8.4***
Not competitive[‡]	17.4	21.8	19.9	14.9**	25.4***	−8.4	15.9	17.9	18.5	16.7***	12.7*	3.6
Competitive	13.8	17.2	21.2	53.5***	24.4***	23.4***	22.0	22.6	21.9	−0.3	3.1	−3.3
Very competitive	17.3	20.3	15.4	−10.9*	17.7***	−24.3***	20.5	21.5	26.7	29.9***	4.9	23.9***
Highly competitive	12.8	15.5	20.3	58.3***	21.2*	30.6***	19.0	20.7	23.6	23.9***	8.7	14.0*
Small < 5001	16.3	19.8	19.7	20.7***	21.1***	−0.3	19.0	20.8	20.2	6.0	9.2*	−2.9
Medium 5001–10000	15.1	19.2	18.4	21.7***	27.3***	−4.4	18.7	19.1	22.9	22.5***	2.0	20.0***
Large > 10 001	15.1	18.3	19.4	28.2***	21.3***	5.7	20.6	21.7	24.4	18.4***	5.4	12.4***
Public	14.5	17.9	18.6	28.3***	23.4***	4.0	20.1	21.2	23.1	14.9***	5.6*	8.8**
Private	17.8	21.1	20.7	16.4***	18.9***	−2.1	19.1	20.3	21.8	14.0**	6.1	7.5
Northeast	12.2	15.3	14.9	21.8**	25.3***	−2.7	23.5	22.3	24.7	5.1	−5.4	11.1*
South	17.4	21.0	20.8	20.1***	20.9***	−0.7	19.4	20.6	22.6	16.6***	5.9	10.1*
NorthCentral	12.4	16.3	16.4	32.2***	31.0***	0.9	21.6	24.1	25.6	18.8***	11.8**	6.2
West	21.3	24.6	26.9	26.4***	15.5**	9.4	12.9	14.3	15.2	17.8*	10.9	6.2
Religious affiliation	23.1	25.7	25.0	8.5	11.3*	−2.5	19.9	21.8	22.8	14.7*	9.6	4.7
Nonreligious	14.2	17.6	18.2	28.5***	23.9***	3.7	19.8	20.7	22.7	14.4***	4.8	9.3***
Rural/small town	13.8	18.3	17.9	30.1***	32.8***	−2.0	23.2	23.9	26.1	12.6***	2.8	9.4**
Suburban/urban	16.3	19.3	17.8	9.3***	18.3***	−7.6	18.1	19.3	21.3	17.9***	7.1*	10.1*
Women only	20.8	18.6	18.7	−10.5	−10.7	0.3	7.4	11.1	14.1	90.2***	50.3*	26.5
Not women's college	15.2	18.9	19.3	26.4***	24.3***	1.7	20.2	21.5	23.2	14.6***	6.1*	8.0***

[†]Commuter schools were defined as schools with ≥90% of students living off campus.
[‡]Competitiveness is based on ACT and SAT scores and percentage of applicants accepted, as reported in *Barron's Profiles of American Colleges*.[20]
*p <.05 **p <.01 ***p <.001

Table 9.7

Drinking Styles of Students Who Consumed Alcohol, 1993, 1997, 1999, by Gender

| Drinking style | Prevalence (%) | | | Change (%) | | |
	1993	1997	1999	'93 v '99	'93 v '97	'97 v '99
Drank on 10 or more occasions in the past 30 days						
Total	17.9	20.6	22.2	24.2***	15.5***	7.5**
Male	24.1	28.2	30.7	27.1***	17.0***	8.6*
Female	12.8	15.2	16.5	28.6***	18.7***	8.4
Usually binges when drinks						
Total	40.4	41.6	44.5	10.2***	2.9	7.0***
Male	43.2	43.2	47.3	9.7***	0.0	9.6***
Female	38.2	40.5	42.6	11.7***	6.0*	5.3*
Was drunk three or more times in the past month						
Total	23.1	28.0	29.3	26.5***	21.1***	4.5
Male	28.3	33.7	35.9	26.9***	19.1***	6.5*
Female	18.9	23.9	24.8	30.9***	26.3***	3.6
Drinks to get drunk[†]						
Total	39.7	52.4	47.2	18.9***	32.0***	−9.9***
Male	45.0	58.5	54.4	20.9***	29.8***	−6.9***
Female	35.6	48.3	42.7	19.7***	355.0***	-11.6***

Note. Only students who drank alcohol in the last year are included.
[†]Say that getting drunk is an important reason for drinking.
*p <.05; **p <.01; ***p <.001.

lems decreased significantly between 1997 and 1999 but were still significantly higher than in 1993.

Risk of Alcohol-Related Problems

In the 1999 study, as in the previous studies, occasional binge drinkers and frequent binge drinkers were more likely to experience alcohol-related problems than those who drank alcohol but did not binge (Table 9.8). Occasional binge drinkers were five times as likely as nonbinge drinkers to report they had experienced five or more of 12 different alcohol-related problems, whereas frequent binge drinkers were 21 times as likely to do so. This result is consistent with previous years. Frequent binge drinkers, in contrast to nonbinge drinkers, were four to 15 times more likely to experience a particular problem as a result of their drinking.

Secondhand Binge Effects

We examined the secondhand binge effects experienced by nonbinge drinkers and abstainers who lived in dormitories or fraternity or sorority residences. In 1999, as in 1993 and 1997, the most frequent problems were (a) being interrupted while studying or being awakened at night (58%), (b) having to take care of a drunken fellow student (50%), and (c) being insulted or humiliated (29%). About three out of four students (77%) experienced at least one secondhand effect.

We found no clear pattern of change in the rates of secondhand effects in the three survey years. Some problems, such as experiencing an unwanted sexual advance and having to take care of a drunken student, increased significantly. Other problem experiences, such as being pushed, hit, or assaulted, or being the victim of sexual assault or date rape, decreased significantly.

Secondhand Binge Effects at High-Binge, Medium-Binge, and Low-Binge Campuses

In 1999, as in the previous study, students who did not binge drink and who lived in a dormitory or fraternity or sorority house on high-binge campuses were twice as likely as nonbinge drinkers and abstainers on low-binge campuses to report experiencing any of the secondhand effects listed in the study. In addition, they were three times as likely to report at least one such effect (Table 9.9).

Comment

A Cautionary Note About Student Surveys

The CAS is based on self-reported responses to a mail survey and is subject to sources of error associated with this approach. First, respondents may intentionally or unintentionally distort their answers. However, a number of studies support the validity of self-reports of alcohol use.[13,14,15] The same pattern of responses among different student subgroups is present in all three years of the study, as well as in other, major studies of college alcohol use.[5,7,16]

Second, another possible source of bias may be introduced through sample attrition or nonresponse. Although we received responses from 60% of the students in the random samples in 1999 and 1997, these rates were lower than the 1993 rate (70%). However, the binge-drinking rates in the CAS in all three survey years were almost identical to rates obtained by other researchers who used different sampling methods.[5,7,8] Furthermore, the statistical controls we used to examine potential bias revealed no association between student nonresponse and binge-drinking rates in any of the three survey years.

The CAS did not have an equivalent time period in investigating change over the six-year period. It is possible that changes during the two-year period from 1997 to 1999 may be more difficult to detect than changes over the years from 1993 to 1997. We urge readers to use caution in interpreting our finding that the rates changed more between 1993 and 1997 than between 1997 and 1999.

Finally, the data presented in this article describe all colleges in the sample or college subgroupings. Within these national norms, individual colleges may vary extensively. For example, although the national binge-drinking rate is 44%, the rate ranged from less than 1% at the lowest binge school to 76% at the highest.

Table 9.8

Risk of Alcohol-Related Problems Among Students in Different Binge Drinking Categories, 1999

Problem	Nonbinge drinkers (n = 5063) %	Occasional binge drinkers (n = 2962) %	Adjusted OR	95% CI	Frequent binge drinkers (n = 3135) %	Adjusted OR	95% CI
Miss a class	8.8	30.9	4.70	4.01, 5.51	62.5	16.86	14.40, 19.80
Get behind in schoolwork	9.8	26.0	3.17	2.70, 3.72	46.3	7.94	6.81, 9.28
Do something you regret	18.0	39.6	2.85	2.50, 3.25	62.0	6.94	6.08, 7.93
Forget where you were or what you did	10.0	27.2	2.82	2.41, 3.29	54.0	8.36	7.22, 9.71
Argue with friends	9.7	23.0	2.68	2.28, 3.14	42.6	6.24	5.37, 7.26
Engage in unplanned sexual activities	7.8	22.3	3.17	2.68, 3.76	41.5	7.04	6.00, 8.28
Not use protection when you had sex	3.7	9.8	2.88	2.29, 3.64	20.4	6.13	4.95, 7.63
Damage property	2.3	8.9	2.92	2.20, 3.90	22.7	9.75	7.57, 12.72
Get into trouble with campus or local police	1.4	5.2	3.00	2.08, 4.39	12.7	8.07	5.84, 11.40
Get hurt or injured	3.9	10.9	2.67	2.10, 3.39	26.6	8.16	6.60, 10.16
Require medical treatment for an alcohol overdose	0.3	0.8	2.73	1.17, 6.73	0.9	3.40	1.42, 8.72
Drove after drinking alcohol	18.6	39.7	2.87	2.53, 3.27	56.7	7.64	6.75, 8.66
Have five or more different alcohol-related problems	3.5	16.6	4.59	3.69, 5.74	48.0	21.11	17.25, 26.04

Note: Only students who drank alcohol in the past year are included. Problems did not occur at all or occurred one or more times. Sample sizes vary slightly for each category because of missing values. OR = odds ratio; CI = confidence interval. Adjusted ORs of occasional binge drinkers *v* nonbinge drinkers are significant at p <.001 (OR adjusted for age, sex, marital status, race/ethnicity, and parental college education). Adjusted ORs of frequent binge drinkers *v* nonbinge drinkers are significant at p <.001 (OR adjusted for age, sex, marital status, race/ethnicity, and parental college education).

Findings and Conclusion

Surveys of representative samples of college students at 119 colleges in 39 states in 1993, 1997, and 1999 have yielded remarkably similar rates of binge drinking over the past six years. Two of five college students were classified as binge drinkers in each of the three surveys. Although no change occurred in the overall binge-drinking rate, the nature of drinking among students who drink has become more extreme, with a significant increase in heavier drinking throughout the entire six years. We noted increases in the number of frequent binge drinkers between 1993 and 1999, as well as in the proportion of students who were drunk three or more times, who drank on 10 or more occasions,

who usually binged when they drank, and who drank to get drunk. Among drinkers, the proportion of frequent binge drinkers increased from 23.4% in 1993 to 28.1% in 1999. During the same six years, the rates of abstaining from alcohol increased from 15.4% to 19.2%.

Most of the increase in abstention had occurred by 1997. These patterns of change have resulted in greater polarization in drinking behaviors on campuses. Although two out of three students who live in fraternity or sorority houses are binge drinkers, one in three (33.2%) students who lives in a campus residence hall or dormitory lives in an alcohol-free residence. An additional 12.6% of the respondents who did not currently live in such

Table 9.9

Risk of Experiencing Secondhand Binge Drinking Effects by Students at Low-, Middle-, or High-level Binge Drinking Campuses

	Low (n = 963) %	Medium (n = 934) %	Adjusted OR	95% CI	High (n = 1019) %	Adjusted OR	95% CI
Been insulted or humiliated	20.5	29.3	1.65	1.23, 2.19	35.8	2.06	1.57, 2.73
Had a serious argument or quarrel	13.7	18.6	ns	—	22.6	1.60	1.18, 2.19
Been pushed, hit, or assaulted	5.5	9.5	2.16	1.35, 3.51	10.9	1.94	1.19, 3.15
Had your property damaged	7.4	13.6	2.60	1.72, 4.02	16.0	2.76	1.81, 4.19
Had to take care of a drunken student	37.3	53.6	1.92	1.50, 2.46	57.2	2.11	1.65, 2.69
Had your studying/sleeping interrupted	43.2	60.5	2.32	1.82, 2.97	70.5	2.98	2.33, 3.81
Experienced an unwanted sexual advance[†]	14.7	20.1	ns	—	22.6	1.73	1.26, 2.38
Been a victim of sexual assault or date rape[†]	0.6	1.3	ns	—	1.0	ns	—
Experienced at least one of the above problems[‡]	63.7	81.3	2.44	1.85, 3.24	86.3	3.24	2.43, 4.32

Note: Analyses are limited to nonbinge drinkers and abstainers who lived in dormitory or fraternity or sorority residences. School binge levels were divided as follows: low binge = 37%, medium = 37%–50%, and high › 50%. OR = odds ratio; CI = confidence interval; ns = not significant. Adjusted ORs of students at schools with middle-level binging *v* students at lower-level schools are significant at p 05, and adjusted ORs of students at schools with high levels of binge drinking *v* students at schools with low levels are also significant at *p* .‹ .05 (OR adjusted for age, sex, marital status, race/ethnicity, and parents' college education).
[†]Analyses are based on responses of women only.
[‡]Available marital status was excluded from the adjusted OR.

housing indicated that they would like to live in alcohol-free quarters.

From 1993 to 1999, the proportion of binge drinkers remained very similar for almost all subgroups of students and in all types of colleges. The same types of students who had the highest rates of binge drinking in 1993 and 1997 continued to have those high rates in 1999. Among the students most likely to binge drink were fraternity or sorority house residents and members of Greek organizations and students who were white, male, and were binge drinkers in high school. The students least likely to binge drink continued to be African American or Asian, aged 24 years or older, married, and who were not binge drinkers in high school.

The only exception to the lack of change in binge drinking during the six-year period related to place of residence. Binge-drinking rates decreased among students living in dormitories and increased among students living off campus. This finding may be important in understanding current efforts at prevention of high-risk drinking.

In recent years, some debate has occurred about the five/four measure of binge drinking (five drinks for men, four for women).[17] Does it overstate the problem or label normative behavior as deviant? Findings from this study continue to show that students who drink at these levels, particularly those who do so more than once a week, experience a far higher rate of problems than other students. For example, frequent binge drinkers are likely to miss classes (OR = 16.9), to vandalize property (OR = 9.7), and to drive after drinking (OR = 7.6). Indeed, the frequent binge drinkers are also more likely to experience five or more different alcohol-related problems (OR = 21.1).

Students on campuses that have many binge drinkers experienced higher rates of secondhand problems, compared with students on campuses with lower rates of binge drinking. Students who did not binge drink and lived on high-binge campuses were twice as likely to report being assaulted, awakened, or kept from studying by drinking students than were nonbinge drinkers and abstainers at low-binge campuses. A student who did not binge drink on a high-binge campus was three times more likely than his or her counterpart on a low-binge campus to report at least one secondhand effect. These findings indicate that students who drink at the binge level create problems for themselves and for other students at their colleges. Indeed, we have previously reported that frequent binge drinkers consumed two thirds of all the alcohol college students drink. They also accounted for more than three fifths of the most serious alcohol-related problems on campus.

Some Future Thoughts: Going Beyond the Data

In [another] article . . . we report on a survey of college administrators' views and actions in dealing with binge drinking.[18] Their responses indicate that they have a great deal of concern about student drinking and that most colleges are taking actions to address the problem. Why, then, do rates of binge drinking continue to be this high? Why do we find an increase in the most extreme forms of drinking? Perhaps not enough time has passed since the initial studies attracted attention to the serious problem of college alcohol abuse for change to occur.

Another explanation may be related to the types of actions college officials are taking. Almost all colleges employ educational approaches to effect change. Certainly that is an appropriate strategy for academic institutions. Yet, we know that most students have received information about drinking and that those groups with the highest binge-drinking rates (athletes and fraternity members) have received the most information (Wechsler, Nelson, and Weitzman, unpublished data, 1999).[19] Although these educational programs are reaching the right target audiences, they have not resulted in

decreased binge drinking and we cannot expect this strategy to accomplish this difficult task by itself.

The apparent inadequacy of even targeted educational efforts to change problem drinking among high-risk groups is not surprising. Public health is increasingly recognizing that education and information alone are not enough to change behavior. In our opinion, we need more support from additional, complementary initiatives. Prevention efforts must work on the alcohol supply, and they must increase the involvement of role models, those who shape opinions, and policymakers beyond the college campus, including community members and students' families.

The finding that binge drinking decreased among students living on campus but increased among those living off campus may reflect the current focus of prevention efforts. Without involving the community and the way alcohol is marketed, efforts to decrease binge drinking may simply displace it.

A comprehensive approach to student binge drinking should consider such factors as

- Alcohol marketing, outlet density, price, special promotions, and the volume in which alcohol is sold.

- Drinking history of students before they come to college. Working with high schools to decrease binge drinking should result in reducing the problem in colleges.

- Assuring alcohol-free social and recreational activities for students on weekends so that they have more to do than just "party."

- Increasing educational demands in terms of Friday classes and exams to reduce the length of the weekend and provide full-time education for full-time tuition.

- Enacting control policies and enforcing them, recognizing that the heaviest binge drinkers will not change unless forced to do so. These students do not think they have a drinking problem. They consider themselves moderate drinkers, and they are not ready to change. They may require an offer they cannot refuse. "Three strikes and you're out" (a punishment appropriate to the level of the violation) and parental notification may be strategies needed for these students. Although social marketing may be effective for some students (e.g., those who are less committed to the binge-drinking lifestyle), it may not succeed with others.

Finally, there are no magic solutions. Just as no single technique applies to all students, no single approach applies to all colleges. Colleges differ in the roles that factors such as fraternities, intercollegiate athletics, and drinking traditions play on campus, as well as in the academic demands they make on student performance and the options that students have for recreation and social life. Alcohol control laws and their enforcement differ in the state and local communities in which colleges are located. All of these factors must be taken into consideration in planning a comprehensive response to student binge drinking.

Acknowledgements

This study was supported by the Robert Wood Johnson Foundation. We gratefully acknowledge the assistance of the Center for Survey Research of the University of Massachusetts, Boston; Dr. Anthony M. Roman, for conducting the mail survey; Jeff Hansen and Mark Seibring, for the preparation of the data; and Toben Nelson and Dr. Elissa Weitzman, for the preparation of the manuscript.

For further information, please address communications to Henry Wechsler, Ph.D., Department of Health and Social Behavior, Harvard School of Public Health, 677 Huntington Avenue, Boston, MA 02115 (e-mail: *hwechsle@hsph.harvard.edu*)

Notes

1. Wechsler, H., Davenport, A., Dowdall, G., Moeykens, B., Castillo, S. Health and behavioral consequences of binge drinking in college: A national survey of students at 140 campuses. *JAMA*. 1994; 272(21): 1672–1677.

2. Wechsler, H., Isaac, N. "Binge" drinkers at Massachusetts colleges: Prevalence, drinking style, time trends, and associated problems. *JAMA*. 1992; 267: 2929–2931.

3. Wechsler, H., Molnar, B., Davenport, A., Baer, J. College alcohol use: A full or empty glass? *J Am Coll Health*. 1999; 47(6): 247–252.

4. Wechsler, H., Davenport, A., Dowdall, G., Grossman, S., Zanakos, S. Binge drinking, tobacco, and illicit drug use and involvement in college athletics: A survey of students at 140 American colleges. *J Am Coll Health*. 1997; 45(5): 195–200.

5. Johnston, L. D., O'Malley, P. M., Bachman, J. G. *National Survey Results on Drug Use From the Monitoring the Future Study, 1975–1995. Vol II, College Students and Young Adults*. US Dept of Health and Human Services; NIH Publication number 98–4140; 1997.

6. Wechsler, H., Dowdall, U. W., Maenner, G., Gledhill-Hoyt, J., Lee, H. Changes in binge drinking and related problems among American college students between 1993 and 1997. *J Am Coll Health*. 1998; 47: 57–68.

7. Presley, C. A., Meilman, P. W., Cashin, J. R., Lyerla, R. *Alcohol and Drugs on American College Campuses. Use, Consequences, and Perceptions of the Campus Environment. Vol IV: 1992–94*. Carbondale, IL: Southern Illinois University; 1996.

8. Douglas, K. A., Collins, J. L., Warren, C., et al. Results from the 1995 National College Health Risk Behavior Survey. *J Am Coll Health*. 1997; 46(2): 55–66.

9. Wechsler, H., Dowdall, G., Davenport, A., Rimm, F. A gender-specific measure of binge drinking among college students. *Am J Public Health*. 1995; 85: 982–985.

10. Liang, K. Y., Zeger, S. L. Longitudinal data analysis using generalized linear models. *Biometrik*. 1992; 73: 12–22.

11. Zeger, S. L., Liang, K. Y., Albert, P. S. Models for longitudinal data: A generalized estimating equation approach. *Biometrics*. 1988; 44: 1049–1060.

12. U.S. Dept. of Education. *Digest of Education Statistics*. Washington, DC: National Center of Educational Statistics; 1998.

13. Frier, M. C., Bell, R. M., Ellickson, P. L. *Do Teens Tell the Truth? The Validity of Self Report Tobacco Use by Adolescents*. Santa Monica, CA: RAND; 1991. RAND publication N-3291-CHF.

14. Cooper, A. M., Sobell, M. B., Sobell, L. C., Maisto, S. A. Validity of alcoholics' self-re-

ports: Duration data. *Int J Addict*. 1981; 16: 401–406.

15. Midanik, L. Validity of self-report alcohol use: A literature review and assessment. *Brit J Addict*. 1988; 83: 1019–1030.

16. Centers for Disease Control and Prevention. Youth Risk Behavior Surveillance: National College Health Risk Behavior Survey, United States. *MMWR*. 1997; 46(SS-6): 1–54.

17. Wechsler, H., Austin, S. B. Binge drinking: The five/four measure. *J Stud Alcohol*. 1998; 59(1): 122–124.

18. Wechsler, H., Kelly, K., Weitzman, E. What colleges are doing about student binge drinking: A survey of college administrators. *J Am Coll Health*. 2000; 48: 219–226.

19. Wechsler, H., Nelson, T., Weitzman, E. From knowledge to action: How Harvard's college alcohol study can help your campus design a campaign against student alcohol abuse. *Change*. In press.

20. *Barron's Profiles of American Colleges*. Hauppauge, NY: Barron's Educational Series; 1996.

For Discussion

1. What explanations might be offered for the fairly large number of students who fell into the categories of either (a) abstainers or (b) frequent binge drinkers?

2. Discuss possible explanations for the findings with respect to ethnicity and drinking.

10
Smoking

What Does Culture Have to Do With It?

Mark Nichter

Ethnicity and culture are two important concepts in sociological study. Mark Nichter deconstructs these concepts and describes their importance in the study of tobacco smoking. He suggests that culture has many significant dimensions and that tobacco smoking is just one dimension of symbolic behavior. Nichter suggests that tobacco smoking is best understood through the interaction of individual and wider social, political, and economic factors. He poses a number of significant questions for future research into tobacco smoking.

Abetter understanding of tobacco uptake, trajectories of use, expressions of dependence and quitting attempts requires a careful consideration of the interaction between individual and contextual factors, the way in which nested social contexts interface and influence one another and an appreciation of risk and protective factors. The study of nested contexts is challenging. A move from the study of additive to interactive factors influencing tobacco use demands both a new vision of what types of data need to be collected and new methods of data analysis. The papers in [*Addiction* 98] go a long way towards summarizing what we know about family, peer, neighborhood, media, economic and political economic influences on tobacco use. Rather than revisit themes already covered . . . I wish to raise a few additional issues related to ethnicity and 'culture' as a context influencing adolescent smoking. Ways will then be suggested in which ethnographic studies of smoking can add to our understanding of smoking behavior as a phenomenon influenced by both structural locations which bound subjective experience and cultural play which involves experimentation with self-image and identity (Pavis et al. 1998).

Let me comment first on the role of 'culture', a factor influencing tobacco use that was raised. . . . When [*Addiction* 98] was first discussed, 'culture' was considered as a context meriting its own review. Given that a Surgeon General's Report (US Department of Health & Human Resources 1998) had recently summarized ethnic differences in rates of smoking, it appeared redundant to restate what is already known and more useful to consider how cultural norms and institutions, gender roles and aesthetics played out in each of the other contexts being addressed. I would urge future researchers investigating 'culture' and tobacco use to continue to look at the interaction between culture and social and economic contexts, and to consider 'culture' on two fronts: (a) culture as it is commonly regarded in relation to ethnic differences, and (b) popular culture as an ongoing project subject to both the identity needs of youth and the influence of an advertising industry that manipulates these needs to sell cigarettes and develop market niches.

Ethnicity and culture are terms that public health researchers need to differentiate and take seriously, especially when studying adolescence (Fergerson 1998).[1] When using the term 'ethnicity' it is important to differentiate between an ethnic identity one assumes in context and an ethnic label that is imposed by others. One's ethnic identity is an identity one chooses to assume on the basis of some sense of social and political affiliation. Far from being fixed or static, which would render ethnicity a reified construct (a 'thing'), ethnic identity may be claimed or distanced in particular contexts, at particular times, and for particular reasons. One's sense of ethnic identity is situational and changes in accord with life-style, residence, etc. At its core, ethnic identity is based on shared meanings that emerge from collective experiences and as such it is produced and reproduced in social interaction. An ethnic label, on the other hand, is a static designation assigned to a person by someone else. It is based on a set of criteria that distinguishes them from others in the eyes of whomever it is that controls the categorization scheme. The history of ethnic categorization in the United States has been politically motivated and has been influenced by a changing agenda (Edmontson & Schultze 1994).

Ethnic labeling, whether by skin color, language or region of origin, lumps people together who may have as many differences as similarities. Lumping has diverse ramifications. It can contribute to misleading and sometimes disempowering stereotypes as well as provide an opportunity for those labeled to gain critical mass and mobilize forces toward particular ends. For example, diverse groups categorized as Hispanic may mobilize as a collective based on the common experience of oppression and assume an ethnic identity as much for political as cultural reasons.

When ethnicity is employed as a category in public health, it is important to be clear about one's assumptions and how ethnic designation is going to be used in data analysis. Is an ethnic label being used to examine the possible role of biological differences? Is ethnicity a proxy for a whole bundle of social and economic factors associated with the position a group of people has been forced to assume as a result of a history of discrimination or oppression (e.g. as a marker of social inequity and structural violence)? Or is ethnicity being examined to determine whether the distinctive characteristics of an ethnic group's 'culture' are protecting or exposing this group to particular types of risk? If the latter is the case, we must bear in mind that 'culture' is one of the most highly debated concepts in cultural anthropology (Sewell 1999).

Culture is commonly thought of as an enduring set of social norms and institutions that organize the life of members of particular ethnic groups giving them a sense of continuity and community. It is often described rather vaguely as an all-encompassing associational field in which ethnicity is experienced. Numerous anthropologists have discussed the limitations of such conceptualization of 'culture', especially in complex societies subject to the forces of modernity. When 'culture' is thought about in terms of consensus and as a template for ideal behavior, the positions of different stakeholders (defined by gender, generation, class, power relations, etc.) are forgotten and heterogeneity is ignored. A processual rendering of culture is more productive. Such an approach directs attention to cultural dimensions of social transactions and asks what is cultural about particular types of behavior in different contexts. Culture is treated more as an adjective than a noun (Appadurai 1996).

Why is a discussion of ethnicity and culture important for tobacco research? There has been mounting criticism of late about the way in which race/ethnicity has been used in public health research as a set of pigeonholes, if not black boxes. This fosters an analysis of 'difference' that focuses on individual and group traits rather than the contexts in which people live (Lillie-Blanton & LaVeist 1996). Despite warnings against reading too much into aggregate (e.g. state, national) data on smoking and ethnicity, it is easy to overlook ethnic heterogeneity and see ethnicity as a risk factor rather than a risk marker. A question often posed in debates about ethnicity and smoking is the following: are cultural factors responsible for ethnic differences in levels of smoking (at different ages by gender), or is ethnicity merely a marker for multiple social and economic factors predisposing one to smoke or abstain from smoking? Adopting an 'action is in the interaction' perspective, I would argue that there is a much better way of framing this important issue. Two questions appear more relevant to ask:

1. Is smoking behavior in particular social and economic contexts influenced by cultural norms and processes and if so, how?

2. What has smoking come to represent to those sharing an ethnic identity in an environment in which the tobacco industry often targets ethnic pride in marketing campaigns?

I would argue that it is far more productive to look for cultural differences in smoking after first accounting for other factors known to predispose an individual to smoke, including education, social class, economic insecurity, stressors (e.g. discrimination), other drug use, etc. Following an analysis which pays credence to the shortcomings of quantitative research—for example, that it often overlooks important differences between socio-economic indices (King 1997)—ethnic differences should be examined more closely. At a minimum the following three issues should be addressed by ethnographic research. What is the role that cultural institutions, values, and processes play in: (1) protecting against smoking in the general population, as well as particular patterns of smoking among males and females, (2) fostering smoking as a normative behavior within particular gender and age cohorts and (3) affecting the distribution of particular smoking trajectories (e.g. early versus late onset of smoking, smoking characterized by rapid versus slow escalation, etc.). This ethnographic analysis would serve as a complement to assessments by researchers who examine intraethnic group differences by examinations of social class, education, residence, racial segregation and acculturation.

What cultural factors might be productive to examine more closely when researching smoking trajectories? Parenting styles and respect for elders are two variables highlighted in the Surgeon General's Report as important factors influencing smoking behavior. Beyond noting that these factors affect smoking uptake and age of initiation, we need to consider how and in what ways they affect youth once they begin smoking. What verbal and non-verbal messages do youth receive from male and female parental figures in different ethnic communities at different points in their smoking trajectories? Once someone becomes a smoker, are they urged to quit or is their behavior accepted? How does respect for elders influence when and where youth may smoke, and how does this differ by not only age and gender, but by employment status? How do cultural sanctions influence patterns and levels of smoking?

The messages youth receive about smoking must not be looked at in isolation. It is not just the content of the message that makes a difference, but the meaning and social relations it evokes. Several publications have suggested that authoritarian parental messages protect African American youth against higher rates of smoking (Koepke, Flay & Johnson 1990; Distefan, Gilpin et al. 1998; Clark, Scarisbrick-Hauser et al. 1999). We need to understand youth response to these messages in terms of their relationships with the people delivering them as well as other messages they receive. What protective role do associated messages play such as those which emphasize maintaining a positive self image in the face of adversity and messages which remind youth that one's behavior reflects not only on their person, but family and community? In what contexts do such messages matter and in what contexts do they fall on deaf ears? In contexts where such messages matter, do they contribute to reported ethnic differences in peer group influence (Unger et al. 2001) or are other factors involved? And, are there gender and age differences in the ways youth respond to both peer influence and the messages of elders?[2]

In addition to examining the influence of family and peers it might be useful to focus attention on the influence of role models which include, but are not limited to these two groups of people. For example, among African American families, senior women (mothers, grandmothers, extended and fictive kin) often, but not always, act as effective role models for the young as providers and survivors. Their message about smoking has been fairly consistent and clear—it does not look good for young African American men or women to smoke and it does not reflect well on their family; but what happens, for example, to the many African American men and women who join the armed forces when they turn 18 years of age? What influence do older officers who smoke have on new recruits in their units? Given high rates of smoking uptake and relapse in the military among young recruits (Bray et al. 1988, 1999), studying the influence of officers as role models would seem worthwhile.

Another issue worth considering is how core cultural values affect smoking behavior once uptake has occurred. For example, the importance accorded to social exchange and reciprocity within different ethnic groups may be an important factor to investigate. Being offered and accepting or refusing a cigarette within Filipino-American communities, for example, may carry a locus of meaning far different than within African American or mainstream Anglo communities, and this meaning may differ by gender (Nichter et al. 2002). Similarly, cultural values may influence peer group norms and boundary setting related to tobacco use. For example, I have observed that peers sometimes play a dual role in both encouraging smoking uptake and limiting where, when and how much friends smoke; that is, they are at once a risk and a protective factor that may affect smoking trajectories (Nichter 1999). The role of peers in establishing boundaries for acceptable behavior has also been noted by Tessler (2000), Kobus (2003) and Maggs (1997) in her research on alcohol use. An issue worth exploring is whether peer relations vary within different ethnic groups such that friends are more or less likely to act as boundary setters circumscribing the behaviors of peers? For example, would Native American youth be less likely to limit friends smoking behavior due to deep-seated cultural norms valuing autonomy than, for example, Mexican Americans?

Another important issue in need of investigation is the meaning that smoking assumes during socially constructed life transitions. The study of smoking transitions in particular ethnic communities would benefit from ethnographies of what else is occurring at times when significant shifts in smoking appear to be taking place. Such research needs to pay special attention to cultural perceptions of age appropriate behavior, normative transgressions and risk taking (Lightfoot 1997; Turbin, Jessor & Costa 2000; Burton et al. 1996), and behaviors associated with assuming greater adult responsibility. In order to understand better the role that smoking plays as a marker of gender and age identity, we need to examine social constructions of adolescence as well as femininity/masculinity. Perceptions of when adolescence begins and ends often differ by gender in accord with roles and expectations, the division of labor within the household and the availability (political economy) of paid work outside the home. While girls in some ethnic group contexts are expected to bear the responsibilities of adult women early (e.g. become child-care providers if not mothers), in other groups young women are encouraged to stay at school for long periods of time; in some contexts, adolescence may be much longer for boys than girls because transitions to employment and marriage take place much later. The point being made is that comparisons of male and female smoking within and across groups need to be contextualized and not merely be based on physical age.

Let me next draw attention to aesthetics and style as important cultural factors influencing smoking, because they are often associated with ethnic identity. At a recent conference I attended, one speaker cited as a reason for lower rates of African American smoking among youth was that smoking was a 'white thing'. An African American woman in the audience corrected the speaker by stating, 'Not acting white isn't what our youth are all about, it is being Black and being proud. Smoking is not a "Black thing"'.[3] The woman went on to suggest that the reason black youth did not take to smoking was 'mostly because it wasn't important to their styling'. Her words echo the findings of a multi-site study in the United States, where researchers found that black girls in comparison to white girls were far more likely to think that 'not smoking' enhanced their self image (Mermelstein 1999). Smoking, put simply, was not equated with style. Ethnographies of African American perceptions of beauty and individual expression have drawn attention to the importance of styling and cool pose to ethnic identity as well as courtship rituals (Majors & Billson 1992; Parker et al. 1995).

Styling can act as both a protective and risk factor for smoking. A better appreciation of cultural aspects of style and the way status is displayed in ethnic communities might provide us with a better understanding of why certain marketing pitches for cigarettes work well in these communities and what kind of tobacco control messages might be best suited for them. It would also be wise to monitor changes in perceptions of 'smoking as stylish' as a barometer of how well the advertising industry is doing in making smoking culturally acceptable in different ethnic groups.[4] In this regard, it is important to bear in mind that the advertising industry is in the business of positioning products to enable people to position themselves as part of an ongoing cultural project.

This brings me to the importance of studying popular culture and the way youth negotiate their identities in consumer society. One of the primary ways we structure time, define who we are and express social relations is through acts of consumption. Consumption events punctuate the flow of everyday life as we move from school or work to leisure time. They help us to rekey our moods and states of mind. Consumption practices also play a role in fantasy and social performance, image experimentation and image management, social affiliation and the expression of group and individual boundaries. In particular, cigarettes serve as symbols as well as props that allow people to imagine as well as act out constantly varying roles on the stage of everyday life (Danesi 1999). Youth create, appropriate and assign meaning to smoking at the same time as they are being primed to interpret smoking in particular ways.

There is nothing new in recognizing all of this. What is called for is a more sophisticated approach to studying the meaning of smoking in popular culture, an approach that accounts for both the expression of agency and the social meaning of smoking performances. Here it is vital to recognize that, although it may be possible to link cigarettes with particular meanings among certain groups and in certain situations, tobacco use is better conceived as a form of imaginative play involving symbols and mutually understandable cues rather than discrete messages sent through a code (Bateson 1972). While it is true that smokers may send messages through their tobacco use, most do not consciously or explicitly set out to send particular messages. The interaction of a smoker's cognitive and emotional situation, their facility in performing smoking routines and the widely distributed cultural imagery that they work off of is glossed over in an analysis of tobacco as a code of meaning (a semiotic). What is required are studies of tobacco use that attend to the stage (context) in which smoking occurs, cultural meanings associated with tobacco, and processes of self expression which involve performance. Smoking is but one part of image management. For this reason it is important to study smoking as it is combined and contrasted with other expressive acts such as sports, substance use and dress in a constantly evolving fashion system. It is entire ensembles of symbolic behavior that make cultural statements more often than single acts such as smoking a cigarette. When one takes up or gives up smoking, they often make shifts in an array of interrelated behaviors.

In this light we need to deepen our understanding of the importance of smoking in movies and community-based marketing strategies where youth are paid to smoke in particular spaces. Most research on smoking in the movies focuses attention on the number of times smoking occurs, whether main characters smoke cigarettes and if smoking occurs in particularly memorable scenes. The assumption is that youth will want to imitate attractive main characters and that a transfer of positive arousal will occur from scenes to products. Another dimension of tobacco use may be just, if not more important. Background smoking as well as smoking featured in the foreground of movies gives youth ideas about when, where and how to smoke in a manner which enables a range of social performances. At a time when smoking is increasingly being regulated, the tobacco industry will need to provide youth with new images of smoking in spaces and at times when it is feasible. Researchers monitoring smoking in the media need to look beyond the cigarette to the context in which it is smoked and what is signaled by particular smoking gestures. Researchers monitoring community-based tobacco strategies need, similarly, to pay more attention to where 'paid smokers' are positioned and the spaces and times in which cigarettes, small cigars, and other tobacco products are being fashioned to appear normative.

Let me turn briefly to a few other issues related to smoking environments and how they may affect smoking trajectories as well as expressions of tobacco dependence. The study of human geography investigates what behaviors and forms of social interaction and identities are associated with place. This discipline might have much to contribute to studies of what types of smoking occur in different smoking environments. Such studies might provide, for example, valuable insights into smoking topography. At a time when constraints on where and when one may smoke are increasing, more attention needs to be focused on the relaxed and pressured manner in which people smoke in different spaces. Chapman, Haddad & Sunhusake (1997) have called our attention rightly to changes in the depth of smoke inhalation and rates of inhalation by those forced to smoke outside of work sites. Payne (2001) has noted further that women are more likely than men to be employed in work sites where smoking bans lead smokers to smoke both harder and faster. She hypothesizes that gender differences in smoking topography may affect trajectories of lung cancer. Whether or not this is the case, gender-sensitive studies of the way people smoke at different times and in different places are worth doing. Given all the restrictions on youth smoking, it might be valuable to investigate not only how many cigarettes youth smoke a day, but also when youth engage in rushed and relaxed smoking. It is worth considering more closely how smoking trajectories among youth are affected by access to times and spaces where smoking can occur in particular ways. For example, are smoking transitions more likely to take place when youth have access to relaxed smoking environment, such as in a car?

It is very important that we consider the impact of smoking opportunities and constraints on expressions of dependence. Recent research suggests that it may be better to conceptualize tobacco dependence in terms of degrees, not absolutes, and as multi-dimensional phenomena (Shadel et al. 2000). It is likely that youth and adult expressions of dependence differ or that the order in which signs of dependence appear may be different for smokers of different ages (Nichter et al. 2002). It is reasonable to hypothesize that expressions of dependence among youth may be associated with smoking opportunities and constraints over the course of the day and week. In order to test this hypothesis, measures of dependence sensitive to youth and their life world will need to be developed (Nichter 2000). Such measures will have to be sensitive to patterns of smoking, the plans youth make to smoke, and the salience of particular cigarettes in their day.

A last point I would like to raise is related to the way modernity itself may be a context we need to consider in relation to tobacco use. Today youth live in an age of increasing time compression, greater opportunities for arousal and diminishing tolerance for 'boredom', and the proliferation of products that promise instant gratification. Cigarettes have been engineered biologically to be a fast and effective nicotine delivery device and engineered socially (advertised) to be an antidote for boredom. There may be biocultural reasons why nicotine, like caffeine, is appealing to youth in today's world. Consider, for example, that a significant percentage of youth are placed in an environment where they are required to multi-task at school when experiencing mild to moderate sleep deprivation (Wahlstrom 1999). Youth today are going to bed later than ever before because they have the opportunity and means to be in constant contact with their friends through cell phones and instant messaging, have access to hundreds of television programs thanks to cable technology, are able to experiment with new identities at will in computer chat rooms, and they can spend hours searching the web to complete school assignments. Yet they are subject to early wake up times demanded by school schedules more geared to the political economy of adults than the lives of youth.

Does the pharmacology of nicotine make tobacco attractive to youth given these conditions? Anthropologists who have studied the history of substance use from coca leaves to sugar, coffee and tea have observed that 'food drugs' tend to become popular when they match the biocultural demands of work cycles as well as facilitate the practice of ideologies at the site of the body, through trade, etc. (Mintz 1985 and 1997; Jankowiak & Bradburd 1996 and 2003; Gladwell 2001; Wolf 1982). If such is the case for tobacco, we need to reflect on both the appeal of tobacco as a symptom of our times and the tobacco industry as the purveyor of a form of ideology. This ideology is clearly a form of capitalism based on the promotion of dependence. Indeed, one could argue that tobacco is the best example of a dependence industry affecting the world on multiple fronts ranging from the micro (cellular) to the macro (society, global relations). Nicotine delivery devices render tobacco as addictive as possible, tobacco agriculture makes farmers more dependent on fertilizers than almost any other crop and politicians and state governments easily become addicted to tobacco generated revenues. The ideology of dependence propagated by the tobacco industry is an important political economic dimension of 'culture' which we must not fail to appreciate.

Notes

1. For a complete discussion of the meaning of 'race,' see Freeman (1998).

2. See for example the study by Simons-Morton et al. (2001), which suggests gender differences in the effect of 'peer pressure' on smoking and drinking among younger adolescents.

3. While it is important to recognize cultural aesthetics as an expression of core values and improvisation, it is also important to recognize that an 'oppositional cultural frame of reference' (Cross 1995; Ogbu 1994) does affect choices in style and self-presentation. This may impact on smoking.

4. Conspicuous consumption among blacks is also an expressive act having collective significance best understood against the backdrop of a history of racism (Lamont & Molnar 2001). This is tapped into and used as a marketing strategy to sell tobacco products.

References

Appadurai, A., ed. (1996) *Modernity at Large: Cultural Dimensions of Globalization*. Minneapolis: University of Minnesota Press.

Bateson, G. (1972) *Steps to an Ecology of the Mind*. New York: Ballantine Books.

Bray, R. M., Sanchaez, R. P., Orenstein, M. L., Lentine, D., Vincus, A. A., Baird, T. V., Walker, J. A., Wheeless, S. C., Guess, L. L., Kroutil, L. A. & Iannacchione, V. G. (1999) *1998 Department of Defense Survey of Health Related Behaviors Among Military Personnel* (Report RTI/70/7034/006-FR). Research Triangle Park, NC: Research Triangle Institute.

Bray, R. M., Marsden, M. E., Guess, L. L., Wheeless, S. C., Iannacchione, V. G. & Kessling, S. R. (1988) *1988 Worldwide Survey of Substance Abuse and Health Behaviors Among Military Personnel* (Report RTI/4000/06-02FR). Research Triangle Park, NC: Research Triangle Institute.

Burton, L., Obeidallah, D. A. & Allison, K. (1996) Ethnographic insights on social context and adolescent development among inner-city African-American teens. In: Jessor, R., Colby, A. & Shweder, R. A., eds. *Ethnography and Human Development: Context and Meaning in Social Inquiry*, pp. 396–418. Chicago: University of Chicago Press.

Chapman, S., Haddad, S. & Sundhusake, D. (1997) Do workplace bans cause smokers to smoke 'harder'? Results from a naturalistic observational study. *Addiction*, 92, 607–610.

Clark, P., Scarisbrick-Hauser, A., Gautam, S. P. & Wirk, S. (1999) Anti-tobacco socialization in homes of African-American and White parents, and smoking and non-smoking parents. *Journal of Adolescent Health*, 24, 329–339.

Cross, W. E., Jr. (1995) Oppositional identity and African American youth: issues and prospects. In: Hawley, W. D. & Jackson, A. W., eds. *Toward a Common Destiny: Improving Race and Ethnic Relations in America*, pp. 185–204. San Francisco: Jossey-Bass.

Danesi, M. (1999) *Of Cigarettes, High Heels, and Other Interesting Things. An Introduction to Semiotics*. New York: St Martin's Press.

Distefan, J., Gilpin, E., Choi, W. S. & Pierce, J. P. (1998) Parental influences predict adolescent smoking in the United States, 1989–93. *Journal of Adolescent Health*, 22, 466–474.

Edmontson, B. & Schultze, C., eds. (1994) *Modernizing the US Census; Panel on Census Requirements in the Year 2000 and Beyond.* National Research Council. Washington, DC: National Academy Press.

Fergerson, G. (1998) Whither 'culture' in adolescent health research [Commentary]? *Journal of Adolescent Health,* 23, 150–152.

Freeman, H. P. (1998) The meaning of race in science—considerations for cancer research. *Cancer,* 82, 219–229.

Gladwell, M. (2001) The critics. A critic at large. Java man: how caffeine created the modern world. *The New Yorker,* 7, 76–80.

Jankowiak, W. M. & Bradburd, D. (1996) Using drug foods to capture and enhance labor performance: a cross-cultural perspective. *Current Anthropology,* 37, 717–720.

Jankwick, W. M. & Bradburd, D., eds. (2003) *Stimulating Trade: Drugs, Governments and Western Economic Expansion.* Columbia University Press, in press.

King, G. (1997) The 'race' concept in smoking: a review of the research on African Americans. *Social Science and Medicine,* 45, 1075–1087.

Kobus, K. (2003) Peer contributions to adolescent smoking. *Addiction,* 98 (Supplement 1), 37–55.

Koepke, D., Flay, B. R. & Johnson, C. A. (1990) Health behaviors in minority families: the case of cigarette smoking. *Family Community Health,* 13, 35–43.

Lamont, M. & Molnar, V. (2001) How blacks use consumption to shape their collective identity: evidence from marketing specialist. *Journal of Consumer Culture,* 1, 31–46.

Lightfoot, C. (1997) *The Culture of Adolescent Risk-Taking.* New York: Guilford Press.

Lillie-Blanton, M. & LaVeist, T. (1996) Race/ethnicity, the social environment, and health. *Social Science and Medicine,* 43, 83–91.

Maggs, J. L. (1997) Alcohol use and binge drinking as goal-directed action during the transition to postsecondary education. In: Schulenberg, J., Maggs, J. L. & Hurrelman, K., eds. *Health Risks and Developmental Transitions During Adolescence,* pp. 345–371. Cambridge, UK: Cambridge University Press.

Majors, R. & Billson, J. M. (1992) *Cool Pose: The Dilemmas of Black Manhood in America.* New York: Lexington Books.

Mermelstein, R. (1999) Explanations of ethnic and gender differences in youth smoking: a multi-site, qualitative investigation. *Nicotine and Tobacco Research,* 1, S91–S98.

Mintz, S. (1985) *Sweetness and Power: The Place of Sugar in Modern History.* New York: Penguin.

Nichter, M. (1999) Anthropology's contribution to the study of tobacco consumption: what do we know, what do we need to find out? Paper presented at the Society for Applied Anthropology Annual Meeting, Tucson, AZ.

——. (2000) Assessing nicotine dependence among adolescents: the devil is in the details. Paper Presented at the 11th World Conference on Tobacco or Health, Washington, DC.

Nichter, M., Nichter, M., Thompson, P. J., Shiffman, S. & Moscicki, A.-B. (2002) Using qualitative research to inform survey development on nicotine dependence among adolescents. *Drug and Alcohol Dependence,* 68, S41–S56.

Ogbu, J. U. (1994) From Cultural Differences to Differences in Cultural Frame of Reference. In: Greenfield, P. & Cocking, R., eds. *Cross Cultural Roots of Minority Child Development,* pp. 365–392. Hillsdale, New Jersey: Erlbaum.

Parker, S., Nichter, M., Nichter, M., Vuckovic, N., Sims, C. & Rittenbaugh, C. (1995) Body image and weight concerns among African American and white adolescent females: differences that make a difference. *Human Organization,* 54, 103–114.

Pavis, S., Cunningham-Burley, S. & Amos, A. (1998) Health related behavioural change in context: young people in transition. *Social Science and Medicine,* 47, 1407–1418.

Payne, S. (2001) 'Smoke like a man, die like a man'?: a review of the relationship between gender, sex and lung cancer. *Social Science and Medicine,* 53, 1067–1080.

Sewell, W. H., Jr. (1999) The concepts of culture. In: Bonnell, V. E. & Hunt, L., eds. *Beyond the Cultural Turn: New Directions in the Study of Society and Culture,* pp. 35–61. Berkeley, CA: University of California Press.

Shadel, W., Shiffman, S., Niaura, R., Nichter, M. & Adams, D. B. (2000) Current models of nicotine dependence: what is known and what is needed to advance understanding of tobacco etiology among youth. *Drug and Alcohol Dependence,* 59, S9–S21.

Simmons-Morton, B., Haynie, D. L., Crump, A. D., Eitel, P. & Saylor, K. E. (2001) Peer and parent influences on smoking and drinking among early adolescents. *Health Education and Behavior,* 28, 95–107.

Tessler, L. (2000) Locations of self in smoking discourses and practices: an ethnography of smoking among adolescents and young adults in the United States. Master's Thesis, Tucson, University of Arizona.

Turbin, M. S., Jessor, R. & Costa, F. M. (2000) Adolescent cigarette smoking: health-related behavior or normative transgression? *Prevention Science,* 1, 115–124.

US Department of Health and Human Resources (1998) *Tobacco Use Among U.S. Racial/Ethnic Minority Groups—African American, American Indians and Alaska Natives, Asian Americans and Pacific Islanders, and Hispanics.* A Report of the Surgeon General. Atlanta, GA: US Department of Health and Human Services, Centers for Disease Control and Prevention: National Center for Chronic Disease Prevention and Health Promotion, Office on Smoking and Health.

Unger, J., Rohrbach, L. A., Cruz, L., Baezconde-Garbanati, K., Ammann, H., Palmer, P. H. & Johnson, C. A. (2001) Ethnic variation in peer influences on adolescent smoking. *Nicotine and Tobacco Research,* 3, 167–176.

Wahlstrom, K. L., ed. (1999) *Adolescent Sleep Needs and School Starting Times.* Bloomington, Indiana: Phi Delta Kappa Educational Foundation.

For Discussion

1. Does the tobacco industry take advantage of ethnic and cultural stereotypes in its advertising? How effective are these strategies?

2. In what ways does popular culture influence smoking, regardless of ethnic identity?

Part III

Marijuana

Marijuana is a derivative of the Indian hemp plant *Cannabis sativa L.*, an annual shrub that flourishes in most warm and temperate climates and varies in height from three to ten feet or more. The leaves are long, narrow, and serrated and form a fan-shaped pattern; each "fan" has from 3 to 15 leaves, but typically only five or seven. The leaves are shiny and sticky, and their upper surfaces are covered with short hairs. Three psychoactive preparations can be derived from cannabis:

1. *Marijuana,* the crushed and dried twigs, leaves, and flowers

2. *Hashish,* the resinous extract obtained by boiling in a solvent the parts of the plant that are covered with the resin or by scraping the resin from the plant

3. *Hashoil,* a dark, viscous liquid produced by a process of repeated extraction of cannabis material

The active ingredient in cannabis is *delta-9-tetrahydro-cannabinol,* or simply THC. The THC content of most marijuana ranges from 1 to 16 percent, depending on where and how it was grown; in hashish, this figure can be as high as 20 to 30 percent, and it is twice that for hashoil.

Cannabis products vary in both name and form in different parts of the world. In Asia, for example, there is "ganja," "charas," and "bhang." *Ganja* consists of the young leaves and flowering tops of the cultivated female plant and its resin, pressed or rolled into a sticky mass, then formed into flat or round cakes. Its color is dark green or greenish brown, and it has a pleasant smell and characteristic taste. *Charas* is the prepared resin separated from the tops of the female plant. It is pounded and rubbed until it is a gray-white powder and then made into cakes or thin, almost transparent sheets, or it is left in dark brown lumps. Bhang consists of the older or more mature leaves of the plant and is often used by boiling it in water and adding butter, to make a syrup. *Bhang* is less potent than ganja, which in turn is considerably weaker than charas.

In the Middle East the word "hashish" is usually applied to both the leaves and the resin or a mixture of the two. In North Africa the resin and tops, usually reduced to a coarse powder, is known as "kif" in Morocco and "takrouri" in Algeria and Tunisia; in Central and Southern Africa "dagga" refers to the leaves and tops.

Despite these many differences in nomenclature, the subjective effects of marijuana are essentially the same, although varying in intensity depending on THC content. At social-recreational use levels, these effects include alteration of time and space perception; a sense of euphoria, relaxation, well-being, and disinhibition; dulling of attention; fragmentation of thought and impaired immediate memory; an altered sense of identity; and exaggerated laughter and increased suggestibility. At doses higher than the typical recreational levels, more pronounced distortions of thought may occur, including a disrupted sense of one's own body, a sense of personal unreality, visual distortions, and sometimes hallucinations, paranoid thinking, and acute psychotic-like symptoms.

Although marijuana is one of the oldest psychoactive drugs, its use in the United States is relatively recent. At the beginning of the twentieth century, what was referred to in Mexico as "marijuana" (also "marihuana" and "mariguana") began to appear in New Orleans and a number of the Texas border towns. By 1920, the use of marijuana had become visible among members of minority groups—blacks in the South and Mexicans in the Southwest. Given the social and political climate of the period, it is not surprising that the use of the drug became a matter of immediate concern. The agitation for reform that had resulted in the passage of the Pure Food and Drug Act in 1906 and the Harrison Act in 1914 was still active, and the movement for national prohibition of alcohol was at its peak. Moreover, not only was marijuana an "intoxicant of blacks and wetbacks" that might have a corrupting influence on white society, but it was considered particularly dangerous because of its alien (spelled "Mexican") and un-American origins.

Through the early 1930s, state after state enacted anti-marijuana laws, usually instigated by lurid newspaper articles depicting the madness and horror attributed to the drug's use. Even the prestigious *New York Times*, with its claim of "All the News That's Fit to Print," helped reinforce the growing body of beliefs surrounding marijuana use. In an article headlined "Mexican Family Go Insane" and datelined Mexico City, July 6, 1927, the *Times* reported:

A widow and her four children have been driven insane by eating the marihuana plant, according to doctors, who say that there is no hope of saving the children's lives and that the mother will be insane for the rest of her life. The tragedy occurred while the body of the father, who had been killed, was still in a hospital. The mother was without money to buy other food for the children, whose ages range from 3 to 15, so they gathered some herbs and vegetables growing in the yard for their dinner. Two hours after the mother and children had eaten the plants, they were stricken. Neighbors, hearing outbursts of crazed laughter, rushed to the house to find the entire family insane. Examination revealed that the narcotic marihuana was growing among the garden vegetables.

Popular books of the era were as colorful as the press in describing marijuana and the consequences of its use. A 1928 book, aptly titled *Dope: The Story of the Living Dead*, by Winifred Black, offered the following about "hasheesh":

And the man under the influence of hasheesh catches up his knife and runs through the streets hacking and killing everyone he meets. No, he has no special grievance against mankind. When he is himself, he is probably a good-humored, harmless, well-meaning creature; but hasheesh is the murder drug, and it is the hasheesh which makes him pick up his knife and start to kill.

Marihuana is American hasheesh. It is made from a little weed that grows in Texas, Arizona, and Southern California. You can grow enough marihuana in a window-box to drive the whole population of the United States stark, staring, raving mad . . . but when you have once chosen marihuana, you have selected murder and torture and hideous cruelty to your bosom friends.

In other reports, the link between the anti-marijuana sentiment and prejudice was apparent. On January 27, 1929, the *Montana Standard* reported on the progress of a bill that amended the state's general narcotic law to include marijuana:

There was fun in the House Health Committee during the week when the Marihuana bill came up for consideration. Marihuana is Mexican opium, a plant used by Mexicans and cultivated for sale by Indians. "When some bean field peon takes a few rares of this stuff," explained Dr. Fred Fulsher of Mineral County, "he thinks he has just been elected president of Mexico so he starts to execute all of his political enemies . . ." Everybody laughed and the bill was recommended for passage.

Although marijuana is neither Mexican opium nor a narcotic of any kind, it was perceived as such by a small group of legislators, newspaper editors, and concerned citizens who were pressuring Washington for federal legislation against the drug. Their demands were almost immediately heard by Harry J. Anslinger, the then recently installed Commissioner of the Treasury Department's Bureau of Narcotics in 1930. Although it would appear that Anslinger was an ultra-right-wing conservative who truly believed marijuana to be a threat to the future of American civilization, his biographer maintained that he was an astute government bureaucrat who viewed the marijuana issue as a mechanism for elevating himself and the Bureau of Narcotics to national prominence. Using the mass media as his forum, Anslinger described marijuana as a Frankenstein drug that was stalking American youth. In an issue of *American Magazine* he wrote, for example,

> The sprawled body of a young girl lay crushed on the sidewalk the other day after a plunge from the fifth story of a Chicago apartment house. Everyone called it suicide, but actually it was murder. The killer was a narcotic known to America as marijuana, and to history as hashish. It is a narcotic used in the form of cigarettes, comparatively new to the United States and as dangerous as a coiled rattlesnake.

Anslinger's crusade resulted in the signing into law of the Marijuana Tax Act on August 2, 1937, classifying "the scraggly tramp of the vegetable world" as a narcotic and placing it under essentially the same controls to which the Harrison Act had subjected opium and coca products.

Currently, marijuana is the most widely used illegal drug in the United States. Government statistics estimate that almost 95 million Americans aged 12 and over (40 percent) have tried it, and of that number, there are over 14 million current users of the drug. In 2002, marijuana was used by 75 percent of illicit drug users.

From 1960 through the end of the decade, the number of Americans who had used marijuana at least once had grown from a few hundred thousand to an estimated 8 million. By the early 1970s, marijuana use had increased geometrically throughout all strata of society, but by the onset of the 1980s evidence indicated that marijuana use was declining. In 1975, for example, surveys showed that some 30 million people were users. By the early 1980s, this figure had dropped to 20 million, with the most significant declines among people ages 25 and under. Perhaps the younger generation had begun to realize that although marijuana was not the "devil drug," "assassin of youth," or "weed of madness" that Harry Anslinger and his counterparts had maintained, it was not a totally innocuous substance either. Perhaps the change occurred because of the greater concern with health and physical fitness that became so much a part of American culture during the 1980s, or as an outgrowth of the antismoking messages that appeared daily in the media. Whatever the reason, it was clear that youthful attitudes had changed. Over the period from 1979 through the beginning of 1990, the proportion of seniors in American high schools who saw "great risk" in using marijuana even once or twice rose from 9.4 percent to 24.5 percent, while the proportion who had ever experimented with marijuana declined from 60.4 percent to 32.6 percent. However, beginning in 1992 national surveys reflected an upswing in marijuana use among youth and a corresponding decrease in perceived harmfulness. Prevalence rates peaked in the late 1990s, and although there has been a modest decline in use among youth since then, the perceived risk associated with using marijuana has continued to decline. The general public's opinion regarding marijuana has also shifted over time: one-third of Americans favor the legalization of marijuana, nearly double the percentage since 1986. Further, according to a 2002 *Time/CNN* poll, 80 percent of Americans believe that adults should be allowed to use marijuana for medicinal purposes.

In the following chapters, a variety of perspectives are presented, ranging from Harry J. Anslinger's "assassin of youth" viewpoint to Lester Grinspoon's thoughts on medical marijuana. There is also a report from Texas on adolescents' use of "fry"—marijuana mixed with embalming fluid. Concluding Part III is an article that first appeared in the magazine *High Times*, "The Power of Four-Twenty." Karen Bettez Halnon presents a sociological analysis of "420" and its various meanings that those "in the know" of the marijuana subculture share.

Additional Readings

Bock, Alan W. (2000). *Waiting to Inhale: The Politics of Medical Marijuana*. Santa Ana, CA: Seven Locks Press.

Russo, E., M. Dreher, and M. L. Mathre. (Eds.). (2002). *Women and Cannabis: Medicine, Science and Sociology*. Binghamton, NY: The Haworth Press.

Sloman, Larry. (1979). *Reefer Madness: The History of Marijuana in America*. Indianapolis: Bobbs-Merrill.

Sussman, Steve, Alan W. Stacy, Clyde W. Dent, Thomas R. Simon and C. Anderson Johnson. (1996). "Marijuana Use: Current Issues and New Research Directions." *Journal of Drug Issues*, 26: 695–733.

Zimmer, Lynn, and John P. Morgan. (1997). *Marijuana Myths, Marijuana Facts: A Review of the Scientific Evidence*. New York: The Lindesmith Center. ✦

11
Marijuana

Assassin of Youth

Harry J. Anslinger
Courtney Ryley Cooper

In the 1930s, Harry J. Anslinger was appointed Commissioner of the Federal Bureau
of Narcotics. The following article is one of
many that he wrote describing marijuana as a
"Frankenstein" drug that was stalking American youth. As a result of Anslinger's crusade,
on August 2, 1937, the Marijuana Tax Act was
signed into law, classifying the scraggly tramp
of the vegetable world as a narcotic and placing it under essentially the same controls as
the Harrison Act had done with opium and
coca products.

The sprawled body of a young girl lay
crushed on the sidewalk the other day after a
plunge from the fifth story of a Chicago
apartment house. Everyone called it suicide,
but actually it was murder. The killer was a
narcotic known to America as marijuana,
and to history as hashish. It is a narcotic
used in the form of cigarettes, comparatively
new to the United States and as dangerous as
a coiled rattlesnake.

How many murders, suicides, robberies,
criminal assaults, holdups, burglaries, and
deeds of maniacal insanity it causes each
year, especially among the young, can be
only conjectured. The sweeping march of its
addiction has been so insidious that, in numerous communities, it thrives almost un-
molested largely because of official
ignorance of its effects.

Here indeed is the unknown quantity
among narcotics. No one can predict its effect. No one knows, when he places a marijuana cigarette to his lips, whether he will

become a philosopher, a joyous reveler in a
musical heaven, a mad insensate, a calm philosopher, or a murderer.

That youth has been selected by the peddlers of this poison as an especially fertile
field makes it a problem of serious concern
to every man and woman in America.

There was the young girl, for instance,
who leaped to her death. Her story is typical.
Some time before, this girl, like others of her
age who attend our high schools, had heard
the whispering of a secret which has gone
the rounds of American youth. It promised a
new thrill, the smoking of a type of cigarette
which contained a "real kick." According to
the whispers, this cigarette could accomplish wonderful reactions and with no harmful aftereffects. So the adventurous girl and a
group of her friends gathered in an apartment, thrilled with the idea of doing "something different" in which there was "no
harm." Then a friend produced a few cigarettes of the loosely rolled "homemade" type.
They were passed from one to another of the
young people, each taking a few puffs.

The results were weird. Some of the party
went into paroxysms of laughter; every re-
mark, no matter how silly, seemed excruciat-
ingly funny. Others of mediocre musical
ability became almost expert; the piano
dinned constantly. Still others found themselves discussing weighty problems of youth
with remarkable clarity. As one youngster
expressed it, he "could see through stone
walls." The girl danced without fatigue, and
the night of unexplainable exhilaration
seemed to stretch out as though it were a
year long. Time, conscience, or consequences
became too trivial for consideration.

Other parties followed, in which inhibitions vanished, conventional barriers de-
parted, all at the command of this strange
cigarette with its ropy, resinous odor. Finally
there came a gathering at a time when the
girl was behind in her studies and greatly
worried. With every puff of the smoke the
feeling of despondency lessened. Everything
was going to be all right—at last. The girl was
"floating" now, a term given to marijuana intoxication. Suddenly, in the midst of laughter and dancing, she thought of her school
problems. Instantly they were solved. With-

out hesitancy she walked to a window and leaped to her death. Thus can marijuana "solve" one's difficulties.

The cigarettes may have been sold by a hot tamale vendor or by a street peddler, or in a dance hall or over a lunch counter, or even from sources much nearer to the customer. The police of a Midwestern city recently accused a school janitor of having conspired with four other men, not only to peddle cigarettes to children, but even to furnish apartments where smoking parties might be held.

A Chicago mother, watching her daughter die as an indirect result of marijuana addiction, told officers that at least fifty of the girl's young friends were slaves to the narcotic. This means fifty unpredictables. They may cease its use; that is not so difficult as with some narcotics. They may continue addiction until they deteriorate mentally and become insane. Or they may turn to violent forms of crime, to suicide or to murder. Marijuana gives few warnings of what it intends to do to the human brain.

The menace of marijuana addiction is comparatively new to America. In 1931, the marijuana file of the United States Narcotic Bureau was less than two inches thick, while today the reports crowd many large cabinets. Marijuana is a weed of the Indian hemp family, known in Asia as *Cannabis Indica* and in America as *Cannabis Sativa*. Almost everyone who has spent much time in rural communities has seen it, for it is cultivated in practically every state. Growing plants by the thousands were destroyed by law-enforcement officers last year in Texas, New York, New Jersey, Mississippi, Michigan, Maryland, Louisiana, Illinois, and the attack on the weed is only beginning.

It was an unprovoked crime some years ago which brought the first realization that the age-old drug had gained a foothold in America. An entire family was murdered by a youthful addict in Florida. When officers arrived at the home they found the youth staggering about in a human slaughterhouse. With an ax he had killed his father, his mother, two brothers, and a sister. He seemed to be in a daze.

"I've had a terrible dream," he said. "People tried to hack off my arms!"

"Who were they?" an officer asked.

"I don't know. Maybe one was my uncle. They slashed me with knives and I saw blood dripping from an ax."

He had no recollection of having committed the multiple crime. The officers knew him ordinarily as a sane, rather quiet young man; now he was pitifully crazed. They sought the reason. The boy said he had been in the habit of smoking something which youthful friends called "muggles," a childish name for marijuana.

Since that tragedy there has been a race between the spread of marijuana and its suppression. Unhappily, so far, marijuana has won by many lengths. The years 1935 and 1936 saw its most rapid growth in traffic. But at least we now know what we are facing. We know its history, its effects, and its potential victims. Perhaps with the spread of this knowledge the public may be aroused sufficiently to conquer the menace. Every parent owes it to his children to tell them of the terrible effects of marijuana to offset the enticing "private information" which these youths may have received. There must be constant enforcement and equally constant education against this enemy, which has a record of murder and terror running through the centuries.

The weed was known to the ancient Greeks and it is mentioned in Homer's *Odyssey*. Homer wrote that it made men forget their homes and turned them into swine. Ancient Egyptians used it. In the year 1090, there was founded in Persia the religious and military order of the Assassins, whose history is one of cruelty, barbarity, and murder, and for good reason. The members were confirmed users of hashish, or marijuana, and it is from the Arabic *"hashshashin"* that we have the English word "assassin." Even the term "running amok" relates to the drug, for the expression has been used to describe natives of the Malay Peninsula who, under the influence of hashish, engage in violent and bloody deeds.

Marijuana was introduced into the United States from Mexico, and swept across America with incredible speed. It began with the whispering of vendors in the Southwest that marijuana would perform miracles for those who smoked it, giving them a feeling of physical strength and mental power, stimulation of the imagination, the ability to be "the life of the party." The peddlers preached also of the weed's capabilities as a "love potion." Youth, always adventurous, began to look into these claims and found some of them true, not knowing that this was only half the story. They were not told that addicts may often develop a delirious rage during which they are temporarily and violently insane; that this insanity may take the form of a desire for self-destruction or a persecution complex to be satisfied only by the commission of some heinous crime.

It would be well for law-enforcement officers everywhere to search for marijuana behind cases of criminal and sex assault. During the last year a young male addict was hanged in Baltimore for criminal assault on a ten-year-old girl. His defense was that he was temporarily insane from smoking marijuana. In Alamosa, Colo., a degenerate brutally attacked a young girl while under the influence of the drug. In Chicago, two marijuana-smoking boys murdered a policeman.

In at least two dozen other comparatively recent cases of murder or degenerate sex attacks, many of them committed by youths, marijuana proved to be a contributing cause. Perhaps you remember the young desperado in Michigan who, a few months ago, caused a reign of terror by his career of burglaries and holdups, finally to be sent to prison for life after kidnapping a Michigan state policeman, killing him, then handcuffing him to the post of a rural mailbox. This young bandit was a marijuana fiend.

A sixteen-year-old boy was arrested in California for burglary. Under the influence of marijuana he had stolen a revolver and was on the way to stage a holdup when apprehended. Then there was the nineteen-year-old addict in Columbus, Ohio, who, when police responded to a disturbance complaint, opened fire upon an officer, wounding him three times, and was himself killed by the returning fire of the police. In Ohio a gang of seven young men, all less than

twenty years old, had been caught after a series of 38 holdups. An officer asked them where they got their incentive.

"We only work when we're high on 'tea,' " one explained.

"On what?"

"On tea. Oh, there are lots of names for it. Some people call it 'mu' or 'muggles' or 'Mary Weaver' or 'moocah' or 'weed' or 'reefers'—there's a million names for it."

"All of which mean marijuana?"

"Sure. Us kids got on to it in high school three or four years ago; there must have been twenty-five or thirty of us who started smoking it. The stuff was cheaper then; you could buy a whole tobacco tin of it for fifty cents. Now these peddlers will charge you all they can get, depending on how shaky you are. Usually though, it's two cigarettes for a quarter."

This boy's casual story of procurement of the drug was typical of conditions in many cities in America. He told of buying the cigarettes in dance halls, from the owners of small hamburger joints, from peddlers who appeared near high schools at dismissal time. Then there were the "booth joints" or Bar-B-Q stands, where one might obtain a cigarette and a sandwich for a quarter, and there were the shabby apartments of women who provided not only the cigarettes but rooms in which girls and boys might smoke them.

"But after you get the habit," the boy added, "you don't bother much about finding a place to smoke. I've seen as many as three or four high school kids jam into a telephone booth and take a few drags."

The officer questioned him about the gang's crimes: "Remember that filling-station attendant you robbed—how you threatened to beat his brains out?"

The youth thought hard. "I've got a sort of hazy recollection," he answered. "I'm not trying to say I wasn't there, you understand. The trouble is, with all my gang, we can't remember exactly what we've done or said. When you get to 'floating,' it's hard to keep track of things."

From the other youthful members of the gang the officer could get little information. They confessed the robberies as one would vaguely remember bad dreams. "If I had killed somebody on one of those jobs, I'd never have known it," explained one youth. "Sometimes it was over before I realized that I'd even been out of my room."

Therein lies much of the cruelty of marijuana, especially in its attack upon youth. The young, immature brain is a thing of impulses, upon which the "unknown quantity" of the drug acts as an almost overpowering stimulant. There are numerous cases on record like that of an Atlanta boy who robbed his father's safe of thousands of dollars in jewelry and cash. Of high school age, this boy apparently had been headed for an honest, successful career. Gradually, however, his father noticed a change in him. Spells of shakiness and nervousness would be succeeded by periods when the boy would assume a grandiose manner and engage in excessive, senseless laughter, extravagant conversation, and wildly impulsive actions. When these actions finally resulted in robbery the father went at his son's problem in earnest—and found the cause of it a marijuana peddler who catered to school children. The peddler was arrested.

It is this useless destruction of youth which is so heartbreaking to all of us who labor in the field of narcotic suppression. No one can predict what may happen after the smoking of the weed. I am reminded of a Los Angeles case in which a boy of seventeen killed a policeman. They had been great friends. Patrolling his beat, the officer often stopped to talk to the young fellow, to advise him. But one day the boy surged toward the patrolman with a gun in his hand; there was a blaze of yellowish flame, and the officer fell dead.

"Why did you kill him?" the youth was asked.

"I don't know," he sobbed. "He was good to me. I was high on reefers. Suddenly I decided to shoot him."

In a small Ohio town, a few months ago, a fifteen-year-old boy was found wandering the streets, mentally deranged by marijuana. Officers learned that he had obtained the dope at a garage. "Are any other school kids getting cigarettes there?" he was asked.

"Sure. I know fifteen or twenty, maybe more. I'm only counting my friends."

The garage was raided. Three men were arrested and 18 pounds of marijuana seized. "We'd been figuring on quitting the racket," one of the dopesters told the arresting officer. "These kids had us scared. After we'd gotten 'em on the weed, it looked like easy money for a while. Then they kept wanting more and more of it, and if we didn't have it for 'em, they'd get tough. Along toward the last, we were scared that one of 'em would get high and kill us all. There wasn't any fun in it."

Not long ago a fifteen-year-old girl ran away from her home in Muskegon, Mich., to be arrested later in company with five young men in a Detroit marijuana den. A man and his wife ran the place. How many children had smoked there will never be known. There were 60 cigarettes on hand, enough fodder for 60 murders.

A newspaper in St. Louis reported after an investigation this year that it had discovered marijuana "dens," all frequented by children of high-school age. The same sort of story came from Missouri, Ohio, Louisiana, Colorado—in fact, from coast to coast.

In Birmingham, Ala., a hot tamale salesman had pushed his cart about town for five years, and for a large part of that time he had been peddling marijuana cigarettes to students of a downtown high school. His stock of the weed, he said, came from Texas and consisted, when he was captured, of enough marijuana to manufacture hundreds of cigarettes.

In New Orleans, of 437 persons of varying ages arrested for a wide range of crimes, 125 were addicts. Of 37 murderers, 17 used marijuana, and of 193 convicted thieves, 34 were "on the weed."

One of the first places in which marijuana found a ready welcome was in a closely congested section of New York. Among those who first introduced it there were musicians, who had brought the habit northward with the surge of "hot" music demanding players of exceptional ability, especially in improvisation. Along the Mexican border and in seaport cities it had been known for some time that the musician who desired to get the "hottest" effects from his playing often turned to marijuana for aid.

One reason was that marijuana has a strangely exhilarating effect upon the musical sensibilities (Indian hemp has long been used as a component of "singing seed" for canary birds). Another reason was that strange quality of marijuana which makes a rubber band out of time, stretching it to unbelievable lengths. The musician who uses "reefers" finds that the musical beat seemingly comes to him quite slowly, thus allowing him to interpolate any number of improvised notes with comparative ease. While under the influence of marijuana, he does not realize that he is tapping the keys with a furious speed impossible for one in a normal state of mind; marijuana has stretched out the time of the music until a dozen notes may be crowded into the space normally occupied by one. Or, to quote a young musician arrested by Kansas City officers as a "muggles smoker":

Of course I use it—I've got to. I can't play any more without it, and I know a hundred other musicians who are in the same fix. You see, when I'm "floating," I own my saxophone. I mean I can do anything with it. The notes seem to dance out of it—no effort at all. I don't have to worry about reading the music—I'm music-crazy. Where do I get the stuff? In almost any low-class dance hall or night spot in the United States.

Soon a song was written about the drug. Perhaps you remember:

Have you seen
That funny reefer man?
He says he swam to China;
Any time he takes a notion,
He can walk across the ocean.

It sounded funny. Dancing girls and boys pondered about "reefers" and learned through the whispers of other boys and girls that these cigarettes could make one accomplish the impossible. Sadly enough, they can—in the imagination. The boy who plans a holdup, the youth who seizes a gun and prepares for a murder, the girl who decides suddenly to elope with a boy she did not even know a few hours ago, does so with the confident belief that this is a thoroughly logical action without the slightest possibility of disastrous consequences. Command a person "high" on "mu" or "muggles" or "Mary Jane" to crawl on the floor and bark like a dog, and he will do it without a thought of the idiocy of the action. Everything, no matter how insane, becomes plausible. The underworld calls marijuana "that stuff that makes you able to jump off the tops of skyscrapers."

Reports from various sections of the country indicate that the control and sale of marijuana has not yet passed into the hands of the big gangster syndicates. The supply is so vast and grows in so many places that gangsters perhaps have found it difficult to dominate the source. A big, hardy weed, with serrated, swordlike leaves topped by bunchy small blooms supported upon a thick, stringy stalk, marijuana has been discovered in almost every state. New York police uprooted hundreds of plants growing in a vacant lot in Brooklyn. In New York State alone last year 200 tons of the growing weed were destroyed. Acres of it have been found in various communities. Patches have been revealed in back yards, behind signboards, in gardens. In many places in the West it grows wild. Wandering dopesters gather the tops from along the right of way of railroads.

An evidence of how large the traffic may be came to light last year near La Fitte, La. Neighbors of an Italian family had become amazed by wild stories told by the children of the family. They, it seemed, had suddenly become millionaires. They talked of owning inconceivable amounts of money, of automobiles they did not possess, of living in a palatial home. At last their absurd lies were reported to the police, who discovered that their parents were allowing them to smoke something that came from the tops of tall plants which their father grew on his farm. There was a raid, in which more than 500,000 marijuana plants were destroyed. This discovery led next day to another raid on a farm at Bourg, La. Here a crop of some 2,000 plants was found to be growing between rows of vegetables. The eight persons arrested confessed that their main source of income from this crop was in sales to boys and girls of high-school age.

With possibilities for such tremendous crops, grown secretly, gangdom has been hampered in its efforts to corner the profits of what has now become an enormous business. It is to be hoped that the menace of marijuana can be wiped out before it falls into the vicious protectorate of powerful members of the underworld.

But to crush this traffic we must first squarely face the facts. Unfortunately, while every state except one has laws to cope with the traffic, the powerful right arm which could support these states has been all but impotent. I refer to the United States government. There has been no national law against the growing, sale, or possession of marijuana.

As this is written a bill to give the federal government control over marijuana has been introduced in Congress by Representative Robert L. Doughton of North Carolina, Chairman of the House Ways and Means Committee. It has the backing of Secretary of the Treasury Morgenthau, who has under his supervision the various agencies of the United States Treasury Department, including the Bureau of Narcotics, through which Uncle Sam fights the dope evil. It is a revenue bill, modeled after other narcotic laws which make use of the taxing power to bring about regulation and control.

The passage of such a law, however, should not be the signal for the public to lean back, fold its hands, and decide that all danger is over. America now faces a condition in which a new, although ancient, narcotic has come to live next door to us, a narcotic that does not have to be smuggled into the country. This means a job of unceasing watchfulness by every police department and by every public-spirited civic organization. It calls for campaigns of education in every school, so that children will not be deceived by the wiles of peddlers, but will know of the insanity, the disgrace, the horror which marijuana can bring to its victim. And, above all, every citizen should keep constantly before him the real picture of the "reefer man"—not some funny fellow who, should he take the notion, could walk across the ocean.

In Los Angeles, Calif., a youth was walking along a downtown street after inhaling a marijuana cigarette. For many addicts, merely a portion of a "reefer" is enough to induce intoxication. Suddenly, for no reason, he decided that someone had threatened to kill him and that his life at that very moment was in danger. Wildly he looked about him. The only person in sight was an aged bootblack. Drug crazed nerve centers conjured the innocent old shoe-shiner into a destroying monster. Mad with fright, the addict hurried to his room and got a gun. He killed the old man, and then, later, babbled his grief over what had been wanton, uncontrolled murder.

"I thought someone was after me," he said. "That's the only reason I did it. I had never seen the old fellow before. Something just told me to kill him!"

That's marijuana!

For Discussion

This article was published a few years after alcohol prohibition was repealed. Is it likely that the United States government will always keep some drugs illegal? How might the government benefit from certain drug prohibitions?

Reprinted from: Harry J. Anslinger and Courtney Ryley Cooper, "Marijuana: Assassin of Youth" in *American Magazine*, July 1937. ✦

12
Medical Marihuana In a Time of Prohibition

Lester Grinspoon

The use of marijuana for medicinal purposes has been debated for several years. In this article, Lester Grinspoon describes the legal debates and legislation regarding marijuana. He discusses various methods and sources for accessing marijuana for medical purposes and describes the problems associated with these sources of access. He argues that marijuana has great potential for treating various illnesses and symptoms but notes that current legislation is restrictive and actually impedes our understanding of the full benefits of medicinal marijuana. He also suggests that laws regarding marijuana should mirror the laws regarding the regulation of alcohol.

> "A new scientific truth does not triumph by convincing its opponents and making them see the light, but rather because its opponents eventually die and a new generation grows up that is familiar with it."
> —Max Planck

The medical value of marihuana has become increasingly clear to many physicians and patients. There are three reasons for this. First, it is remarkably non-toxic. Unlike most of the medicines in the present pharmacopeia, it has never caused an overdose death. Its short-term and long-term side effects are minimal compared with medicines for which it will be substituted. Second, once patients no longer have to pay the prohibition tariff, it will be much less expensive than the medicines it replaces. Third, it is remarkably versatile. Case histories and clinical experience suggest that it is useful in the treatment of more than two dozen symptoms and syndromes, and others will undoubtedly be discovered in the future.

As clinical evidence of marihuana's medical efficacy and safety accumulates and firsthand experience of its value becomes more common, the discussion is turning to how it should be made available. When I first considered this issue in the early 1970s, I thought the main problem was its classification in Schedule I of the Comprehensive Drug Abuse and Control Act of 1970, which describes it as having a high potential for abuse, no accepted medical use in the United States, and lack of accepted safety for use under medical supervision. At that time I naively believed that a change to Schedule II would overcome a major obstacle, because clinical research would be possible and prescriptions would eventually be allowed.

I was the first witness at a joint meeting of the Drug Enforcement Administration and the Food and Drug Administration that was convened to consider a petition for rescheduling introduced by the National Organization for the Reform of Marijuana Laws in 1972. At that time I had already come to believe that the greatest harm in recreational use of marihuana came not from the drug itself but from the effects of prohibition. But I saw that as a separate issue; I thought that, like opiates and cocaine, cannabis could be used medically while remaining outlawed for other purposes. I also thought that once it was transferred to Schedule II, research on marihuana would be pursued eagerly, since it had shown such interesting therapeutic properties. From this research we would eventually be able to determine how it should be used medicinally, how prescriptions could be provided, and who would be responsible for quality control. I have begun to doubt this, 25 years later. It would be highly desirable if marihuana could be approved as a legitimate medicine within the present federal regulatory system, but it now seems to me unlikely.

First, I should note that cannabis has already been a legally accepted medicine in the United States several times. Until 1941, when it was dropped after the passage of the Marihuana Tax Act, it was one of the drugs listed in the U.S. Pharmacopeia. If it had not been removed at that time, it would have been grandfathered into the Comprehensive Drug Abuse and Control Act as a prescription drug, just as cocaine and morphine were. Again, in the late 1970s and early 1980s, cannabis was used medically by hundreds of patients (mainly in the form of synthetic tetrahydrocannabinol) in projects conducted by several of the states for the treatment of nausea and vomiting in cancer chemotherapy. This episode ended because each state program had to comply with an enormous federal paperwork burden that was more than the physicians and administrators involved could bear. The federal government itself approved the use of cannabis as a medicine in 1976 by instituting the Compassionate IND program, under which physicians could obtain an individual Investigational New Drug application (IND) for a patient to receive cannabis. This program too was so bureaucratically burdened that in the course of its history only about three dozen patients ever received marihuana, and only eight are still receiving it. When the program was discontinued permanently in 1992, James O. Mason, the chief of the Public Health Service, gave the following reason: "If it is perceived that the Public Health Service is going around giving marihuana to folks, there would be a perception that this stuff can't be so bad. It gives a bad signal. I don't mind doing that if there is no other way of helping these people . . . But there is not a shred of evidence that smoking marihuana assists a person with AIDS." In effect, this action was analogous to the recall of a prescription drug, without any evidence of toxic effects to support it.

Today, even transferring marihuana to Schedule II would not be enough to make it available as a prescription drug. Such drugs must undergo rigorous, expensive, and time-consuming tests before they are approved by the Food and Drug Administration for marketing as medicines. The purpose is to protect the consumer by establishing safety and efficacy. Because no drug is completely safe or always efficacious, an approved drug has presumably satisfied a risk-benefit analysis. When physicians prescribe for individual patients they conduct an informal analysis of a similar kind, taking into account not just the drug's overall safety and efficacy, but its risk and benefits for a given patient with a given condition. The formal drug approval procedures help to provide physicians with the information they need to make this analysis.

This system is designed to regulate the commercial distribution of drug company products and protect the public against false or misleading claims about their efficacy and safety. The drug is generally a single synthetic chemical the company has developed and patented. It submits an application to the Food and Drug Administration and tests it first for safety in animals and then for clinical efficacy and safety. The company must present evidence from double-blind controlled studies showing that the drug is more effective than a placebo and as effective as available drugs. Case reports, expert opinion, and clinical experience are not considered sufficient. The standards have been tightened since the present system was established in 1962, and few applications that were approved in the early 1960s would be approved today on the basis of the same evidence.

Certainly we need more laboratory and clinical research to improve our understanding of medicinal cannabis. We need to know how many patients and which patients with each symptom or syndrome are likely to find cannabis more effective than existing drugs. We also need to know more about its effects on the immune system in immunologically impaired patients, its interactions with other medicines, and its possible uses for children.

But I have come to doubt whether the FDA rules should apply to cannabis. There is no question about its safety. It is one of humanity's oldest medicines, used for thousands of years by millions of people with very little evidence of significant toxic effects. More is known about its adverse effects than about those of most prescription drugs. The American government has conducted a decades-long multimillion-dollar research program in a futile attempt to demonstrate toxic effects that would justify the prohibition of cannabis as a non-medical drug. Should time and resources be wasted to demonstrate for the FDA what is already so obvious?

As for efficacy, some believe that has been proven too, although most disagree. During the 1970s and 1980s several of the state-sponsored research projects I mentioned suggested that marihuana had advantages over both oral tetrahydrocannabinol and other medicines in the treatment of nausea and vomiting from cancer chemotherapy. But as long as the imprimatur of science can be given only to rigorous double-blind controlled studies, the case for marihuana has not been made. The assertion that it is a useful medicine rests almost entirely on case reports and clinical experience, just as it did in the late 19th and early 20th centuries.

A double-blind controlled study may be the best way to prove the relative value of a new medicine whose advantages over established drugs are not obvious. But it is not the only way to demonstrate efficacy. The focus of controlled trials is usually statistical differences in effects in groups of patients, but medicine has always been concerned mainly with individuals, whose needs can be obscured in such experiments, especially when little effort is made to identify distinctive characteristics that affect their responses. The value of case reports and clinical experience is often underestimated. They are the source of much of our knowledge of synthetic medicines as well as plant derivatives. Controlled experiments were not needed to recognize the therapeutic potential of chloral hydrate, barbiturates, aspirin, curare, or lithium. The therapeutic value of penicillin was widely recognized after it had been given to only six patients. Similar evidence revealed the use of propranolol for hypertension, diazepam for status epilepticus, and imipramine for childhood enuresis. These drugs had originally been approved by regulators for other purposes.

As early as 1976 several small and imperfect studies, not widely known in the medical community, had shown that an aspirin a day could prevent a second heart attack. In 1988 a large-scale experiment demonstrated effects so dramatic that the researchers decided to stop the experiment to publish the life-saving results. On one estimate, as many as 20,000 deaths a year might have been prevented from the mid 1970s to the late 1980s if the medical establishment had been quicker to recognize the value of aspirin. The lesson is suggestive: marihuana, like aspirin, is a substance known to be unusually safe and with enormous potential medical benefits. There is one contrast, however; it was impossible to be sure about the effect of aspirin on heart attacks without a long-term study involving large numbers of patients, but innumerable reports show that cannabis often brings immediate relief of suffering that can be measured in a single person.

Case histories are, in a sense, simply the smallest research studies, and the case reports on marihuana are numerous and persuasive. There is an experimental method known as the N-of-1 clinical trial, or the single-patient randomized trial. In this type of experiment, active and placebo treatments are administered randomly in alternation or succession to a patient. The method is often useful when large-scale controlled studies are impossible or inappropriate because the disorder is rare, the patient is atypical, or the response to the treatment is idiosyncratic.

Some medical marihuana patients I know of carried out similar experiments on themselves by alternating periods of cannabis use with periods of no use. They had such symptoms as nausea and vomiting, muscle spasms, compromised vision, seizures, and debilitating pruritus. It is certain that cannabis won its reputation as a medicine partly because many other patients around the world have carried out the same kind of experiment. Admittedly, in these experiments cannabis could not be administered completely at random and there was no placebo, but in any case its psychoactive effects are usually unmistakable, and few patients or observers could be deceived by a placebo. Case histories and other reports of clinical experience are sometimes disparagingly dismissed as merely "anecdotal" evidence, which is said to be irrelevant because only apparent successes are counted and failures are ignored. It is true that cannabis may be useful for some people with, say, multiple sclerosis, chronic pain, or depression, and not for others. But cannabis is so safe that if even a few patients with a given symptom could get that kind of relief, they should be allowed access to it.

Even if it made sense to put marihuana through the FDA process, there would be other problems in taking the conventional route to medical legitimacy. As I have mentioned, FDA procedures are designed for single chemical compounds, but marihuana is a plant material containing many chemicals. Also, it is taken chiefly by smoking, and no other drug in the present pharmacopeia is delivered by this route. Furthermore, thousands of people are already getting relief from cannabis, and they would not be risking severe penalties if they did not believe that it was more useful than conventional medicines. Can we expect them to put their pain and suffering on hold for years while the established procedures grind away?

Patients, their families, and others are becoming increasingly impatient for a legal means of obtaining medical cannabis. The most dramatic manifestation of this impatience has been the referenda allowing distribution of medicinal cannabis that have been passed in several states. In 1996 California became the first state to approve such a law. Within weeks of the vote, more than a dozen cannabis clubs opened to help sick people in need of relief, and the membership of one quickly grew to 8000. Many Americans believe that this is the best temporary approach to the problem of making medical cannabis available.

Among those who understand the present importance of the cannabis clubs or cooperatives, there are two views on their organization. One model follows the conventional delivery system for medicine: the patient who needs medicinal cannabis (read medicine) goes to the buyers club (read pharmacy) and presents a note from a physician which certifies that the patient has a condition for which the physician recommends cannabis (read prescription) to the staff of the buyers club (read pharmacist). If both the doctor and the buyers club behave responsibly and ethically, only those who have a certified need for the medicine can receive it, and those who are certified now have a reliable source. They are relieved of the anxiety of having to find it on the street or grow their own.

In a buyers club of this kind, the patient is of course not expected to take the medicine on the premises. In contrast, the second distribution model resembles a social club more than a pharmacy. The dispensing area is plastered with menus offering types, grades, and prices. Large rooms are filled with brightly colored posters, lounge chairs and sofas, tables, magazines, and newspapers. While some people remain only long enough to buy their medicine, most stay to smoke and talk. There are animated conversations, laughter, music, and the pervasive pungent odor of cannabis. The atmosphere is informal, welcoming, and warm, providing support for patients who may be socially isolated and have little opportunity to share concerns and feelings about their illnesses. This type of club is a blend of Amsterdam-style coffeehouse, American bar, and medical support group.

Most people who recognize the importance of the buyers clubs believe that the first model, epitomized by the now closed Oakland Club, is preferable to the second model, represented by the now closed San Francisco Cultivators' Club. The San Francisco model, largely because of the on-site cannabis smoking and relaxed atmosphere, seems more casual in its commitment to confirming medical need, and this has made even the supporters of buyers clubs a little nervous. Yet the importance of the social aspect cannot be underestimated. It is becoming increasingly clear that emotional support—contacts with and help from friends, family, co-workers, and others—plays an important role in battling illness. This support improves the quality of life and may even prolong the life of people with various illnesses, including cancer. The San Francisco buyers club was not designed by psychiatrists and social scientists to provide supportive group therapy, but there is reason to believe it did. One of the properties of marihuana may have contributed to its effectiveness: when people use cannabis, they tend to be more sociable and find it easier to share difficult thoughts and feelings. If there is even a kernel of truth to the idea that talking about the stress, setbacks, and triumphs in the battle against an illness can help a patient cope and recover, it is clear that the San Francisco model provides the best kind of environment for the dispensing of marihuana.

Unfortunately, even many supporters of medical cannabis regarded the language of California Proposition 215 as permitting the legal use, cultivation, and distribution of marihuana too broadly. The initiatives passed more recently in several states have more tightly drawn limitations. They will not permit cannabis clubs with the medical and psychiatric advantages of the San Francisco model, and they allow such a short list of medical uses that only a few of the patients who could find marihuana helpful will be allowed to use it. But in any case, buyers clubs have to be regarded as a stopgap measure. The federal government is not going to allow the development of a separate distribution system for one medicine. It has already succeeded in closing most of the California buyers clubs, and if it is as successful elsewhere, they will not long endure.

Other present approaches to making marihuana medically available have even more serious drawbacks. Marihuana is now classified as a Schedule I drug, which means that it is legally defined as too dangerous for use even under medical supervision. But for the sake of argument, let us suppose that the government comes to its senses and marihuana is moved to Schedule II. This would allow investigators to do the studies which lead to FDA approval for medical use. But where will the money to finance these studies come from? New medicines are usually introduced by drug companies, which spend an estimated US$200,000,000 or more on the development of each product. They are willing to undertake these costs only because they hope for large profits during the 20 years they own the patent. Obviously pharmaceutical companies cannot patent marihuana and, in fact, may oppose its acceptance as a medicine because it will compete with their own products. Only the U.S. government has sufficient resources to explore medical marihuana. But its record on the matter is, to put it mildly, not reassuring. The government has opposed any loosening of restrictions on clinical research with cannabis, including the research needed for FDA approval. I believe the government will ultimately have to provide some support for this research because of public pressure, but it will arrive slowly. A study of marihuana in the treatment of the AIDS wasting syndrome has recently been approved and funded after 4 years of obstruction. But this happened only because the political climate had changed after the California initiative, and even so, the main subject of the study had to be changed from medical efficacy to safety.

But let us suppose that studies are somehow completed showing that marihuana is safe and effective as a treatment for the weight reduction syndrome of AIDS, and physicians are able to prescribe it for that condition. This will present unique problems. When a drug is approved for one medical purpose, physicians are generally free to write off-label prescriptions—that is, prescribe it for other conditions as well. Dronabinol (Marinol), a synthetic form of tetrahydrocannabinol, was approved as a prescription drug in 1986 for the treatment of nausea and vomiting in cancer chemotherapy, and later for the treatment of the weight reduction syndrome of AIDS. However, presumably because it was thought to be susceptible to medically questionable use, it became the first FDA-approved drug for which off-label use was forbidden. The ban has proved too difficult to enforce, and doctors have prescribed it off-label, although somewhat timidly. If marihuana is approved as a medicine, how will this concern about off-label prescriptions be dealt with?

Present state and federal schemes for making cannabis medically available invariably specify that it must be used for the treatment of illnesses defined as "serious," "life-threatening," "terminal," or "debilitating." Which of the many symptoms and syndromes for which cannabis is useful should be considered "serious"? For example, what about premenstrual syndrome? Surely women who suffer from this disorder consider it a serious problem, and many of them find that marihuana is the most useful treatment. What about intractable hiccups or the loss of erectile capacity in paraplegics? The people who suffer from these rare problems know how debilitating they can be.

Generally speaking, the more dangerous a drug is, the more serious or debilitating must be the symptom or illness for which it is approved. Conversely, the more serious the health problem, the more risk is tolerated. If the benefit is very large and the risk very small, the medicine is distributed over the counter (OTC). OTC drugs are considered so useful and safe that patients are allowed to use their own judgment without a doctor's permission or advice. Thus, today anyone can buy and use aspirin for any purpose at all. This is permissible because aspirin is considered so safe; it takes "only" 1000–2000 lives a year in the United States. The remarkably versatile ibuprofen and other NSAIDs can also be purchased over the counter, because they too are considered very safe; "only" 7000 Americans lose their lives to these drugs annually. Acetaminophen, another useful OTC drug, is responsible for about 10% of cases of end-stage renal disease. The public is also allowed to purchase many herbal remedies whose dangers have not been determined and which probably have only placebo effects.

Compare these drugs with marihuana. Today no one can doubt that it is, as DEA Administrative Judge Francis L. Young put it, "among the safest therapeutic substances known to man." If it were now in the official pharmacopeia, it would be a serious contender for the title of least toxic substance in that compendium. In its long history, marihuana has never caused a single overdose death. Yet government schemes for its medi-

cal use are always cloaked in language suggesting that it is too dangerous to be used except under the most stringent limitations. In several states, medical marihuana initiatives require patients to register, and in two states they will need identification cards to protect them from arrest.

As a Schedule II drug, marihuana would be classified as having a high potential for abuse and limited medical use. Restrictions on these drugs are becoming tighter. Nine states now require doctors to make out prescriptions for many of them in triplicate so that one copy can be sent to a centralized computer system that tracks every transaction. In 1989 New York State added the benzodiazepines (Valium and related drugs) to the list of substances monitored in this way. Research has shown that since then many patients in New York who have a legitimate need for benzodiazepines are being denied them, and less safe and effective drugs are being substituted. Increased regulation caused by fear of drug abuse has been to the disadvantage rather than the advantage of patients.

In such situations physicians are often afraid to recommend what they know or suspect to be the best medicine because they might lose their reputations, licenses, and careers. Pharmacies might be reluctant to carry marihuana as a Schedule II drug, and physicians would hesitate to prescribe it. Through computer-based monitoring, the DEA could know who was receiving prescription marihuana and how much. It could hound physicians who by its standards prescribed cannabis too freely or for off-label purposes the government considered unacceptable. The potential for harassment would be extremely discouraging. Unlike other Schedule II drugs such as cocaine and morphine, cannabis has many potential medical uses. Many patients might try to persuade their doctors that they had a legitimate claim to a prescription. Physicians would not want the responsibility of making such decisions if they were constantly under threat of discipline by the state. A physician who prescribed marihuana for chronic pain, for example, might be subjected to the same harassment as those whom the DEA considers to be dispensing opioids too liberally. Since the passage of the medical marihuana initiative in California, I have heard from many patients who say their doctors are afraid to recommend (not prescribe) marihuana because of threats from the federal government—even though those threats have been declared by the courts to be legally baseless.

There is actually no case for the present restrictions—unless third-party reefer-madness anxiety counts as a risk. The Schedule II classification of cannabis would not be accurate. It does not have a high potential for abuse, and above all, it does not have limited medical uses. For example, a physician might sensibly and safely prescribe it for muscle spasms and chronic pain resulting from a variety of conditions, from paraplegia to premenstrual syndrome. If the government and medical licensing boards insist on tight restrictions, challenging physicians as though cannabis were a dangerous drug every time it is used for any new patient or any new purpose, there will be constant conflict with one of two outcomes: patients do not get all the benefits they should from this medicine, or they get the benefits by abandoning the legal system for the black market or their own outdoor or closet gardens.

Then there is the question of who will provide the cannabis. The federal government now provides cannabis from its farm in Mississippi to eight patients who have residual Compassionate INDs. But surely the government could not or would not produce marihuana for many thousands of patients receiving prescriptions, any more than it does for other prescription drugs. But if production is contracted out, will the farmers have to enclose their fields with security fences? How would the marihuana be distributed? If through pharmacies, how would they provide secure facilities capable of keeping fresh supplies? When urine tests are demanded for workers, how would patients who use marihuana legally as a medicine be distinguished from those who use it for other (disapproved) purposes?

If the full potential of cannabis as a medicine were to be achieved in the setting of the present prohibition system, all of these prob-lems and more would have to be addressed. A delivery system that successfully navigated this minefield would be so cumbersome, inefficient, and bureaucratically top-heavy that patients would continue to grow their own or buy it on the illicit market. The authorities could claim that a legal medical distribution apparatus existed, but most patients would find themselves in the same situation they are in today. The Compassionate IND program, the federal government's last scheme to satisfy these needs, lasted from 1976 to 1992 but never supplied more than a few dozen patients with cannabis.

Some believe a solution to the "medical marihuana problem" (restricting the use of cannabis for medical purposes only) will be found in the isolation of individual cannabinoids, the manufacture of synthetic cannabinoids, and the development of analogs (chemical cousins of cannabinoids). Supposedly, these drugs, sometimes in combination, will make the natural product superfluous. Their use in the form of parenterals, nasal sprays, vaporizers, skin patches, pills, and suppositories will allegedly make it unnecessary to expose the lungs to the particulate matter in marihuana smoke. Furthermore, the commercial products may lack psychoactive effects, which is apparently very important to some people. A pain researcher at the Memorial Sloan-Kettering Cancer Institute recently said that he was excited by the new analogs because "the euphoria sparked by cannabinoids . . . is undesirable in chronically ill patients." Not everyone will agree that freedom from the psychoactive effects is an advantage, but some cannabinoids and analogs may be preferable to whole smoked or ingested marihuana for other reasons. For example, cannabidiol may be more effective as an anti-anxiety drug when it is taken without THC, which sometimes generates anxiety. Other cannabinoid analogs may occasionally prove more useful than marihuana because they can be administered intravenously. For example, loss of consciousness occurs in 15–20% of patients who suffer a thrombotic or embolic stroke, an even higher proportion after a hemorrhagic stroke, and some who develop a brain syndrome after a severe blow to the head. The cannabinoid analog dexanabinol (HU 211) has recently been shown to limit brain swelling and protect brain cells from damage in these circumstances. It is apparently not psychoactive and can be given intravenously to an unconscious person.

The modern pharmaceutical laboratory will undoubtedly develop other cannabinoid-related products with properties that whole marihuana and marihuana extracts lack. There are already two known receptors for cannabinoids with different anatomical distributions and only partially overlapping functions. New agonists, antagonists, and inverse agonists will be developed for these receptors (and possibly for others still to be discovered), some of which may have therapeutic potential. For example, tetrahydrocannabinol and possibly other cannabinoids enhance appetite. Perhaps pharmacologists will develop cannabinoid inverse agonists which inhibit appetite and act as non-toxic weight reduction medicines. A better understanding of brain functions will also result from this kind of research.

But these encouraging developments have a worrisome downside. South American Indians have chewed the coca leaf for thousands of years with little apparent abuse and few ill effects, but since the isolation of methylbenzoylecgonine (cocaine) from the leaf's other natural alkaloids, some users have developed serious problems. Similarly, opium in its natural form is less risky than, say, the potent synthetic opioid fentanyl. HU 211 (dexanabinol) is not psychoactive, but its stereoisomer, HU 210, synthesized in the same laboratory, is hundreds of times more psychoactive than THC. Other analogs may be equally potent. The danger is that they will bear the same relationship to marihuana that fentanyl bears to opium.

There are other reasons why isolated cannabinoids and cannabinoid analogs will probably never completely displace marihuana itself as a medicine. It was once widely believed that the availability of dronabinol would make medical marihuana superfluous. Dronabinol is packed in sesame oil, partly for easier absorption, but also because it makes smoking impossible and therefore was thought to make non-medical use unlikely. But patients have generally not found dronabinol to be nearly as useful as whole smoked marihuana. Even among those who judge it equally effective, many find that street marihuana is less expensive. If the advent of prescribable dronabinol did not make marihuana medically obsolete, it is hard to believe that the arrival of new analogs will do so. I believe that many if not most patients who could get benefits from the new analogs will choose instead to smoke the more easily accessible and less expensive marihuana.

In evaluating the prospects for cannabis analogs, we must consider what a pharmaceutical product requires for economic success:

1. It must be as useful as or more useful than competitive medicines for a particular symptom or syndrome, or it must have a wide variety of approved medicinal uses.

2. It must not have more undesirable side effects than competitive medicines.

3. It must have a mode of delivery which is as good as or better than available alternatives.

4. It must be priced competitively.

5. It must have a risk-benefit ratio which is at least as good as that of competitive medicines.

6. It must not be restrictively scheduled under the federal Comprehensive Drug Abuse and Control Act. The more restrictive the schedule, the more serious the impact on marketability and the cost of development.

Now compare the anticipated analogs with whole marihuana:

1. Except in a few situations, such as intravenous injection in an unconscious person, analogs or combinations of analogs are unlikely to be more useful than natural cannabis for most specific symptoms. Nor are they likely to have a much wider spectrum of therapeutic uses than the natural product, which contains the cannabinoids (and synergistic combinations of cannabinoids)

from which the analogs are derived. In fact, one result of the development of new analogs may be to identify new medical uses for marihuana in its natural form. Shortly after dexanabinol, which is both a potent antoxidant and an NMDA antagonist, was found to protect brain cells against damage after a stroke or trauma, it was shown that THC and cannabidiol, also potent antioxidants, provide the same kind of protection. In fact, given the urgency of retarding the pathological process set in motion by a stroke or brain trauma, it may be more medically sensible to allow patients with closed head injuries to smoke the more accessible marihuana immediately upon regaining consciousness as they await transportation to a hospital to receive dexanabinol.

2. The analogs may not cause such minor side effects as inflammation of the sclera of the eyes or increased heart rate, but these are not medically significant. Except for infrequent orthostatic hypotension (faintness on standing up), pulmonary exposure to smoke and, in the opinion of some, the psychoactive effect (the high), marihuana has few medically significant side effects.

3. Inhalation devices now being perfected protect the lungs by separating the cannabinoids in whole marihuana from burnt plant products. When these devices are manufactured in large numbers, they will provide an inexpensive, safe, and highly effective means of delivery. Again, except for a few situations such as unconsciousness and pulmonary impairment, it is doubtful that a better means of delivery will be available for analogs.

4. Given the cost of development, the new analogs will be expensive. They will probably cost much more than whole smoked marihuana even at the inflated prices imposed by the prohibition tariff. Suppose, for example, that a new analog is an antinauseant comparable with the prescription drug ondansetron in effectiveness and price. Today a pa-

tient suffering from the nausea of cancer chemotherapy might require from one to four 8 mg ondansetron pills at $30–40 apiece. Many patients will probably get equally effective relief from a few puffs of a marihuana cigarette—cost $5 at today's street price, 30 cents if marihuana is produced as a medicine.

5. The potential benefits of whole smoked marihuana are extraordinarily high compared with the risks. For example, the therapeutic ratio of marihuana is not known because it has never caused an overdose death. It has been estimated on the basis of extrapolation from animal data to be 20,000–40,000:1. Even if the therapeutic ratio of a new analog is also high, it is unlikely to be as safe as whole marihuana because it will be physically possible to ingest much more of the analog.

6. Any new cannabinoid analog with psychoactive properties would presumably have to be placed in a restricted schedule by the federal government. The Unimed Corporation, which makes dronabinol, is now attempting to have it transferred from Schedule II to Schedule III. That would allow physicians to write prescriptions which could be refilled up to three times, reducing the inconvenience and cost to the patient. Yet THC in the form of dronabinol is chemically the same as the THC in whole marihuana, which remains in Schedule I. It will become increasingly difficult to justify such inconsistencies, which might be regarded as hypocritical.

Ultimately, I do not believe the full potential of cannabinoids as medicines can be realized through the use of prescription analogs as long as the crushing, costly prohibition on natural marihuana is maintained. Will prescription analogs be approved for all of the present and future medical uses of whole cannabis? If not, will off-label prescriptions of the analogs be allowed? And if prescription drugs are available, will they always be sought? For example, minor stomach upset is almost always quickly relieved with a few puffs of cannabis. Will people suffering from this symptom go to the trouble and expense of seeking a prescription? When it is generally appreciated that marihuana usually relieves not only gastric distress, but many other common symptoms such as headache, insomnia, tension, pain and dysphoria, it may come to be regarded much as aspirin is today.

In fact, the range of beneficial uses of marihuana is so broad that it may ultimately be wrong to single out the strictly medical uses for approval. Many people use it not only to ease everyday discomforts, but also to heighten creativity or help them in their work. It can serve as an intellectual stimulant, promote emotional intimacy, or enhance the appreciation of food, sex, natural beauty, music, and art. Cannabis use simply cannot be made to conform to the boundaries established by present medical institutions. In this case the demand for legal enforcement of a distinction between medical and non-medical use may be incompatible with the realities of human need. I know that to say this is to invite the charge that medical marihuana advocates are only using medicine as a stalking horse for the legalization of non-medical use. This false accusation is actually a mirror image of the view taken by enemies of marihuana. They are unwilling to admit that it can be a safe and effective medicine largely because they are committed to exaggerating its dangers when used for other purposes. Nevertheless, it would be hypocritical to deny that there is a connection. For 28 years I have been urging the legalization of marihuana for general use. At one time I thought medical use could be treated as a distinct issue, because even people who might never see the urgency of legalizing non-medical use would respond to medical need. Now I have changed my mind. On the contrary, I believe that making marihuana fully available as a medicine is one of the reasons for general legalization.

Ideally, cannabis should be available under more or less the same rules now applied to alcohol. At present, I fear, the political and legal system is too ossified to accommodate that change. But I believe enforcement of the laws against marihuana will be increasingly neglected because of the same kind of public pressure that has led to the enactment of the medical marihuana initiatives in five states. If I am correct, anti-marihuana statutes will come to resemble the laws against oral sex which still exist in several states but are ignored so totally that most people do not even know they exist. As the number of people arrested for possession declines, cannabis in its natural form, along with isolated cannabinoids and analogs, will be used more freely as a medicine. As a result, the public will be in a better position to learn about its virtues, and our understanding of those virtues will in turn make the laws more difficult to enforce. I hope and expect that this process will bring the era of prohibition to a de facto end. Only then will it be possible to realize the full potential of this remarkable substance, and its medical potential in particular.

For Discussion

1. Is medical marijuana a distinct issue apart from the wider legalization debate? Can medical marijuana be legal without easing the drug laws in general?

2. What do you consider to be the most important forces prohibiting marijuana from gaining medical legitimacy?

13

'Fry'

A Study of Adolescents' Use of Embalming Fluid With Marijuana and Tobacco

William N. Elwood

In the early 1990s, media reports in Texas suggested the emergence of marijuana joints that were laced with embalming fluid. Referred to in street slang as "fry" and "fry sticks," William Elwood discusses this drug variation in the following article. His study, based on in-depth interviews with 20 adolescents of various ethnic backgrounds, includes description of the dangers of using embalming fluid inappropriately, the "manufacture" of "fry sticks," methods of obtaining embalming fluid, ease of purchase, the social context surrounding consumption patterns, and effects of this drug combination, as reported by users.

Adolescent use of marijuana and tobacco has continued to rise throughout the 1990s (Liu, 1997; Mathias, 1997). Perhaps as a part of this trend, there have been growing reports of adolescents who use marijuana or tobacco cigarettes dipped in embalming fluid. Unfortunately, most of these reports involve young people presenting for drug treatment, many of whom were incoherent. The purpose of this report is to increase our knowledge of embalming fluid by synthesizing the literature on the subject; reporting on interviews with law enforcement officials, funeral directors, and other community members; and interviewing 20 Houston adolescents who use embalming fluid. The findings that emerge from this investigation are that the embalming fluid compound found on the street contains PCP and that adoles-

cents do not know this. Treatment providers are also hampered from knowing how to treat people who have overdosed or who are suffering from long-term effects. In its pure form, embalming fluid is often diverted from morgues and funeral homes, although the substance also may be purchased directly from chemical companies. The report closes with recommendations including alerts for treatment professionals and education for users who receive treatment.

Introduction

Adolescent use of marijuana has escalated throughout this decade. The National Household Survey on Drug Abuse found a 140 percent jump in marijuana use by youths aged 12 to 17 between 1992 and 1995 (Johnson, 1997). In fact, the increase in current marijuana use by Texas eighth grade students was higher than national trends (Liu, 1997, p. 24). Although lifetime tobacco use among Texas secondary students remained relatively stable in the 1990s, both annual and current tobacco use increased by 14 percent between 1990 and 1996, particularly among tenth grade users (Liu, p. 29). Given this increase in the use of the "gateway" drugs—tobacco and marijuana, it is perhaps not surprising that there has been an increase in the use of other illegal drugs by young people. Among these drugs is "fry," a generic term referring to marijuana cigarettes, marijuana-laced cigars, or tobacco cigarettes or cigars soaked in embalming fluid laced with PCP. This report includes the following sections: description of the study, data and method, presentation of data, and discussion in which the study's limitations and implications will be discussed.

Data and Method

Data for this report come from various sources. First, a comprehensive literature search of medical, psychological, and social sciences journals and local print media was conducted. Second, the author interviewed knowledgeable members of the community, including law enforcement officials, news reporters, funeral home directors and employees, treatment providers, and nail stylists. Third, the author conducted in-depth guided interviews (Parker & Carballo, 1990) with 20 adolescents (ages 15–22) who smoked embalming fluid with marijuana in the month prior to their interviews. An in-depth guided interview is a semi-structured interview that uses an open-ended question format. This interviewing structure acknowledges the ethnographic inquiry tenet that, except under unusual circumstances, the research participant is the instrument (Lincoln & Guba, 1985, p. 250). Nevertheless, data also must be collected systematically; the in-depth guided interview provides a balance between the two. Within this format, the investigator encourages the respondent to expand on topics mentioned by the respondent that may provide additional insight into the use of embalming fluid with tobacco or marijuana, and the consumption of other drugs. In this manner, guided in-depth interviews collect data standardized with regard to subject matter and also allow collection of data that may not have been anticipated. The audiotaping of interviews allows the investigator to reproduce the data exactly as it was collected (Lincoln & Guba, 1985) and, thus, analyze the research participants' actual descriptions. The investigator used an interview guide of issue areas formulated by the author and TCADA officials, and received informed consent from all participants before data collection commenced.

Data were collected using a semi-structured interview guide, which included questions concerning sociodemographic characteristics, drug history, the making of marijuana cigarettes and cigars, and embalming fluid use and its effects. While the semi-structured guide served as a prompt and guide for the interviewer, participants were encouraged to elaborate on topics that appeared to contain information relevant to the study. Interviews were audio recorded and transcribed verbatim into text files. Text files were content coded using a subjective/objective analytical strategy (Maxwell, 1996). The coding scheme itself was derived from the Outline of Cultural Materials (OCM), "a manual which presents a compre-

hensive subject classification system pertaining to all aspects of human behavior and related phenomena" (Murdock et al., 1985, p. xi). Although originally created by and for anthropologists, the OCM was revised in its fifth edition for research in "psychology, sociology, political science, economics, geography, and general science," and can be adapted for use on individual studies (p. xi). For example, the OCM includes only one code, 276, for "narcotics and stimulants—drugs consumed for nontherapeutic purposes" (p. 33). We expanded this one code through additional letters and numbers for such phenomena as "effects/actions attributed to drug use" (276A), "marijuana" (276B6), and "embalming fluid" (276B7e).

Interviews were coded searching expressly for sociodemographic characteristics, drug history, the making of marijuana cigarettes and cigars, and embalming fluid use and its effects. Subjective analytical coding criteria were developed based on the principles of grounded theory (Glaser & Strauss, 1967). Coded data were assessed for behavioral patterns that became apparent as data were analyzed. Data that best illustrate analytical patterns were excerpted for presentation in the text below. In presentation of the data, the one or two-digit codes following data excerpts represent unique participant identifiers, such as (6) or (11).

Presentation of Data

What Is Embalming Fluid?

Embalming fluid, which is used in conjunction with marijuana or tobacco, is a compound of formaldehyde, methanol, ethyl alcohol or ethanol, and other solvents. The embalming fluid compound that we found on the streets, however, also contained PCP. Given these components, it is not surprising that the users we interviewed reported great euphoria or rage, psychedelic apparitions, sleepiness, and forgetfulness regarding many of their behaviors once the users recovered from the substance's effects.

In its purest form, formaldehyde is a simple organic molecule and exists only as a dilute vapor. While a relatively stable gas in moderate temperatures, formaldehyde spontaneously polymerizes at lower temperatures to form trioxane, a paraformaldehyde, from the linking of eight monomeric units. Above 300°C, it breaks down to form carbon monoxide and water. It is very unstable in water and also is photodegradable. For these reasons, it is marketed alone as formalin, an aqueous solution that is 37 percent to 50 percent formaldehyde by weight with 10 percent to 15 percent methanol added to prevent spontaneous polymerization (Bardana & Montanaro, 1991; Gullickson, 1990).

Methanol, also called methyl alcohol or wood alcohol, is a volatile, pungent, poisonous, flammable alcohol used chiefly as a solvent, antifreeze and in the synthesis of formaldehyde and other chemicals. When consumed, methanol can cause poisoning. When inhaled, the substance has effects similar to other volatile inhalants.

Embalming fluid is a compound liquid whose predominant components also include formaldehyde and ethyl alcohol or ethanol, the psychoactive ingredient in alcoholic beverages. In embalming fluid products, the percentage of formaldehyde can range from 5 to 29 percent; ethyl alcohol content can vary from 9 to 56 percent. Embalming fluid also can contain phenol, ethylene glycol, and glutaraldehyde. While most of these components are both flammable and irritants, it is interesting to note that ethyl alcohol is a flammable, central nervous system depressant (Wessels, 1997; see also French, 1983). Despite the synthesis of chemicals which increases the stability of embalming fluid, safety instructions strictly direct its storage between the degrees of 35°F and 120°F (Wessels, 1997). The effects from exposure to embalming fluid include bronchitis, body tissue destruction, brain damage, lung damage, impaired coordination, and inflammation and sores in the throat, nose, and esophagus (Bardana & Montanaro, 1991; State of Connecticut, 1994a; Wessels, 1997).

Purchasing embalming fluid on the street is rather difficult, likely because dealers can make substantially more money by selling individual fluid-soaked joints for $10–$20 each. Nevertheless, we purchased one, two-ounce sample of embalming fluid on the street from a drug dealer for $50. The substance was analyzed by both high temperature and low temperature gas chromatography/mass spectroscopy by Lewis Nelson, MD, of the Poison Control Center in New York. The low temperature version identified volatile solvents including methanol, and found ether and bromobenzene—both starting compounds in PCP (phencyclidine) synthesis. The high temperature analysis expressly found phencyclidine components (Nelson, 1997a). Two samples obtained and analyzed in Connecticut found similar results (Pestana, 1997; State of Connecticut, 1994 a&b).

It is important to realize that PCP is not a normal component of embalming fluid, rather an ingredient that has been added to the embalming fluid compound before its distribution on the street. This study could not confirm exactly when or who added PCP to the embalming fluid compound distributed on the street to make fry, although participant reports suggest that independent individuals add PCP to the embalming fluid compound between the stage at which it is diverted and when fry is sold on the streets. . . .

Phencyclidine (PCP) is a dissociative anesthetic with hallucinogenic properties. The drug was previously used as an anesthetic in humans in the 1950s but discontinued because patients became agitated and disoriented after its use. The drug was also used as an animal tranquilizer but discontinued in 1979. Illegal supplies on the street are manufactured in clandestine labs where supplies are of dubious quality and may contain impurities. Among drug users, PCP can be found as a pure white, crystal-like powder, tablet, capsule, or bitter-tasting, clear liquid that is consumed orally, injected, sniffed, or smoked on tobacco or marijuana products. The drug intensifies the effects of other depressants and can cause hallucinations, frightening "out of body" experiences, impaired motor coordination, depression, extreme anxiety, disorientation, paranoia, aggressive behavior and violence, seizures, and respiratory arrest. The drug can cause dependence, and is known on the street as angel dust, crystal, and horse tranquilizer among others (Johnson, 1997).

The use of marijuana dipped in PCP-laced embalming fluid was reported in the early 1970s in and around Trenton, New Jersey (French, 1983). More recently, use of the substance was reported in Hartford and the surrounding state of Connecticut (Capers, 1994; Borrero, 1996). Known there as "illy" (from "Philly" Blunts cigars, or from the knowledge that the combination can make one "ill") or "clickems," the epidemic peaked in 1993–1994. Use by adolescents became so problematic that one gang, the Latin Kings, asked the State Department of Public Health to intervene (Pestana, 1997). Concurrently in 1994, reports to the National Institute on Drug Abuse's Community Epidemiology Work Group from Philadelphia and Washington, D.C. indicated that the increased use of PCP was associated with the growing use of marijuana cigarettes and marijuana-laced cigars, increasingly laced with PCP. At the same time, Los Angeles reported PCP-sprayed tobacco, parsley, or marijuana, and Chicago reported the use of "sherm sticks," cigarettes dipped in PCP and "happy sticks," home-rolled marijuana or tobacco cigarettes sprayed with PCP. PCP was known on the street as "water" (NIDA, 1994). In New York City, PCP was sprinkled on mint or parsley leaves and sold by the bag, while dealers allowed individuals to dip a cigarette into a small container of embalming fluid for $20 per dip (Frank & Galea, 1994, pp. 152–153). Whether the New York embalming fluid itself contained PCP is unclear.

Use of the PCP-laced embalming fluid and marijuana combination has also reached Texas. In a 1994 survey of youth entering Texas Youth Commission facilities, 3.8 percent reported ever using "wack/fry," while 2.3 percent of participants reported using the substance within their last month of freedom (Fredlund, Farabee, Blair, & Wallisch, 1995, p. 22).

In Houston, the use of "marijuana cigarettes laced with embalming fluid" appeared in the news in 1992. At that time, it was reported that users had turned to the substance because of increased police surveillance regarding cocaine and crack use (Milling, 1992). These treated joints or cigarettes are called most frequently "amp," "fry," or "wa-ter-water" (see also Elwood, 1997). Less common names include "formaldehyde," "wet-wet," "wetdaddy," and "drank." Street names apparently have become so commonly used that they have usurped the chemical names. One participant swore she smoked fry, not marijuana and embalming fluid, because, "I've heard what that stuff [embalming fluid] can do, and I'm not going to touch it" (6).

Reports of the effects of consuming marijuana soaked with the embalming fluid compound are consistent with the effects of tetrahydrocannabinol or THC (the primary psychoactive ingredient in marijuana), PCP, and the chemicals in embalming fluid. It is surprising, however, that none of the adolescents we interviewed listed PCP as one of the psychoactive components in fry, although the hallucinations they reported could not have been the results of the other components. When asked specifically what components they thought caused the effects they recounted, participants listed marijuana and formaldehyde. When asked what other substances they thought were contained in embalming fluid, not one participant listed PCP or any other psychoactive substance. Participants did, however, suspect that embalming fluid was diluted, because, "They cut everything" (17). The most commonly mentioned substance for diluting was an essential substance: "Well, you know they're cutting it with something. Why do you think they call it 'water'?" (11).

Embalming Fluid and Marijuana: How Is the Combination Distributed?

Although we were able to purchase a small, two-ounce bottle of embalming fluid on the street for $50, most young people we interviewed purchased "fry sticks," marijuana joints dipped in embalming fluid laced with PCP, or "fry sweets," Swisher Sweets or Philly Blunt cigars in which the tobacco is replaced with marijuana and dipped in embalming fluid laced with PCP. The price for fry sticks is $10 per joint, also called a "square," and $15–$20 per Swisher Sweet. One purchases "fry sticks" (treated joints) and "fry sweets" (treated Swishers) at the "fry house," a neighborhood house usually used only for drug sales. These establishments are frequently furnished; some adolescents choose to stay and smoke their purchases, particularly if the fry house has video games. The negative aspect of consuming one's purchase at the fry house is that one is expected to share a fry stick with other drug users. Given this community norm, many young people we interviewed chose to purchase their fry sticks and go elsewhere to smoke, particularly if they had planned to share the fry stick with select others.

To make fry sticks, an individual places a number of joints or Swishers (marijuana-laced cigars) on a tray or grate. Having poured embalming fluid into a larger-sized container (e.g., washtub, small aquarium), the dealer dunks the fry sticks into the solution until they are completely saturated. Once the fry sticks have drained sufficiently, and the drainage has been returned to the vat, the sticks are wrapped in aluminum foil until purchased. Purchasers frequently find enough drainage on the aluminum foil to treat another joint on their own. An alternate method of selling fry sticks involves dipping the joint or Swisher into a small jar of embalming fluid upon purchase; if a dealer likes a purchaser, he also might dip a ready-made fry stick into a jar for an additional dose. Only three participants, however, mentioned this prerequisite (1, 6, 8). Dealers reported similar preparation processes, and also reported diluting the embalming fluid they purchase with ethyl alcohol or water.

According to two participants whose friends sold fry sticks, dealers obtain embalming fluid from distributors on Houston's Near North Side, a working-class neighborhood populated mostly with African Americans and Hispanics, which also has a fair share of commercial strips, warehouses, and industry. These dealers pay individuals who bring them embalming fluid, generally people who work in hospital or government morgues, and funeral homes (6, 11). This conduct is corroborated by reports from individuals who work in morgues and funeral homes, who informed us that they siphoned small quantities of embalming fluid from 55-gallon drums. When we asked independent and chain funeral home directors about embalming fluid thefts or diversion, they reported that no such activity occurred at their respective establishments. They had received reports from professional associations or fellow directors, however, warning them of the possibility. Two participants, however, reported break-ins at funeral homes and theft of embalming fluid (6, 17). Some directors reported receiving requests from women who wanted to purchase small quantities for their fingernails; they reported denying all such requests (see also Milling, 1992). Consistent with those reports, funeral home employees also rebuffed all telephone or in-person inquiries to purchase embalming fluid by the investigator and one colleague.

Women who reported diverting embalming fluid reported keeping some of it to use on their fingernails, as women from many racial/ethnic communities believe that embalming fluid strengthens fingernails. And, many commercial products sold to strengthen fingernails contain formaldehyde. They also said that they shared some with friends and relatives, sold it to nail salons, and gave it to their boyfriends, husbands, or spouses. Men who reported diverting embalming fluid stated that they would sell it "to some guys off North Main" street (2).

A logical, if unanticipated, method to obtain embalming fluid is through legal purchase. Indeed, an 18-year-old Hispanic male told us that "some stores actually sell it. You tell 'em it's for science class" (11). We used one Anglo male and two females (Anglo and African American) in their 30s to telephone chemical companies to inquire about purchasing formaldehyde. Chemical company representatives stated that they would not sell the substance to individuals. Given women's requests of funeral homes for formaldehyde, we sent the two women to call on chemical companies to see if they could purchase formaldehyde without making previous telephone inquiries. On their first stop, these women inadvertently called on a chemical firm's corporate office. The receptionist inquired as to the women's interest in purchasing formaldehyde; they responded with the desire to use formaldehyde on their fingernails. The receptionist gave these women the phone number of the firm's warehouse and allowed them to phone from the corporate office. Warehouse personnel offered, without question, to sell the women a 55-gallon drum of formaldehyde. When the women responded that such a drum would not fit in their sedan, warehouse personnel gave them the telephone number of a retail chemical seller to whom they sold formaldehyde in large quantities. At this last establishment, the clerk asked one woman her name, which she placed on the cash receipt, and sold her a one-gallon jug of formaldehyde for $13.95 plus tax. This clerk followed OSHA procedures and provided the customer with a material safety data sheet; however, she did not request identification or any other information regarding this purchase.

Regrettably, we were unable to interview the underground distributors reported to be on Houston's Near North Side; however, it is suspected that the distributors add PCP to embalming fluid at this step. Neither the people who diverted embalming fluid nor the fry stick dealers reported adding any psychoactive substances to the solution. Oddly, the street dealers did not suspect the presence of any substances in embalming fluid. In fact, the only substance participants thought provided a psychoactive effect was formaldehyde. Clearly the inclusion of PCP, methanol, and ethyl alcohol in the embalming fluid cocktail are three of the secrets kept regarding the consumption of marijuana with embalming fluid in Houston.

Who Uses Fry?

For this report, 20 adolescents who had smoked embalming fluid at least once in the month prior to their participation were interviewed. Of these, six were Anglo, eight were African American, and six were Hispanic. Eleven males and nine females were interviewed; 10 were between the ages of 15 and 17, and 10 were between the ages of 18 and 22. Many of the African Americans we interviewed believed that fry was a "Black thing" (4), or a substance smoked mainly by "hoodlums" (9) and gang members. According to a 16-year-old African American female, "All the kids in Third Ward smoke it;

you can even get it at school" (1). Unlike their African American counterparts, however, Anglo and Hispanic adolescents were more likely to believe that fry was something most young people smoked or at least tried: "Kids are just more likely to try stuff, unlike old folks," according to a 16-year-old Anglo female (7).

Fry also appears to be used by adolescents with substantial drug histories. For example, the 16-year-old female who said kids just want to try new drugs reported that the first substance she used was tobacco at age seven and had her first drink of alcohol, Jack Daniels, on her own at age 11. She smoked at least two packs of menthol cigarettes and drank at least three, 40-ounce bottles of beer per day (7). A 20-year-old African American male started smoking cigarettes at 15, drinking 40-ounce bottles of beer at 16, and smoked at least one pack of cigarettes per day and three, 40-ounce bottles of beer on 15 of the last 30 days (10). All of the participants had smoked marijuana at least regularly before smoking fry sticks. Other substances consumed by these individuals include primos (marijuana joints plus crack or cocaine), cocaine, crack, heroin, inhalants, depressants, tranquilizers including Valium and Rohypnol, cold medicine (e.g., Nyquil), non-prescription cough syrup, and cough syrup with codeine.

Most participants could explain precisely how to roll a joint or to make a Swisher, although most dealers currently sell ready-made joints and Swishers. Participants stated, however, that the quality of ready-made joints and Swishers paled compared to those that they or their friends made. The following description of making Swishers was corroborated by at least 10 descriptions.

First, one must obtain a package of cigars. Swisher Sweets is the preferred brand among these adolescents because of its sweet taste; however, King Edward or Philly Blunt brands are acceptable substitutes. Minors either knew which convenience stores would sell to them, or usually could find adults—friends, acquaintances, or even strangers about to enter the store—to purchase cigars for them. Second, one slices a straight line down the cigar with a razor blade, opening the cigar to remove the tobacco. Third, once the tobacco is removed, one refills the cigar paper with marijuana one of two ways. A few of the smokers who were interviewed did not like the taste the tobacco residue imparts on the marijuana; these individuals re-rolled the cigar in reverse—having the outside of the newly formed cigar be the side of the paper that once touched tobacco. Most of those interviewed, however, simply re-rolled the cigar the way it was originally made and licked both edges to reseal the cigar.

To make a candyblunt, a cigar filled with marijuana plus codeine cough syrup (see also Elwood, 1997), participants either poured the syrup onto the marijuana before rolling the cigar, or they coated the outside of the paper once the cigar was re-rolled. If the latter method is used, the cigar must be dried before consuming. Participants listed microwave cooking the cigar for 30 seconds, holding the cigar under a lighter, or simply waiting as means to dry the cigar. Adolescents who liked the combination but found the drying method too cumbersome reported simply drinking cough syrup while smoking the Swisher. Among the benefits of a syrup-dipped and dried Swisher marijuana cigar were the extended burning time, deeper relaxation, and euphoria.

How Is Fry Consumed?

Fry is generally consumed in a small group of three to five people. As one participant said, "You don't want to be alone when you smoke this" (7). At least 10 participants expressly stated that they usually drink alcohol when they smoke fry. According to a 17-year-old Hispanic female, drinking beer "increases the numbing sensation" that embalming fluid and marijuana provide (5). Other alcoholic beverages mentioned include Cisco (fortified wine); Alizé, the brand name for a bottled blend of passion fruit juice and cognac; and "thug passion," Alizé self-mixed with Hennessy cognac (1–3, 6, 17–20). Alizé and thug passion were mentioned only by African Americans; beer, usually in 20- or 40-ounce bottles, was the most frequently mentioned alcoholic beverage consumed with fry, regardless of race/ethnicity. Marijuana was used extensively in fry;

tobacco use was cited only as a substitute due to lack of money.

What Are the Immediate Effects?

Respondents report that the actual smoking of fry is not a pleasant experience. According to one participant, it "tastes like rubbing alcohol" (2) and "smells like gasoline" (5). Other descriptions included "nasty" (10), "dirty" (8), "like chemicals" (12), and "I just don't know, but I don't like it" (19).

Reported highs lasted between 30 minutes to one hour, "two hours if you don't share too much" (10). The high for a 20-year-old Hispanic male who smoked one fry stick by himself lasted five days (14). These extended periods may be due not only to the embalming fluid mixture and the number of comrades who shared it, but also to the fact that a joint or cigar treated in embalming fluid burns more slowly than one that was not treated, according to seven respondents. Respondents thus have longer opportunities to absorb the THC, solvents, and PCP.

Toxic psychosis, hallucinations and delusions, is a common effect of the PCP-embalming fluid-dipped marijuana combination (see also State of Connecticut, 1994 a&b). Hallucinating was the effect mentioned by 12 of the 20 participants in this study. They reported seeing "colors and designs" (1, 2, 3, 6, 12), and "things that aren't there" (10). Perhaps because fry makes one "messed up" and forgetful (5, 9, 10, 19), these adolescents found it difficult to describe their hallucinations in detail. Nevertheless, they mentioned seeing "really cool images" (15), such as a "yellow sky, purple clouds, [and] red trees" (6), "like fireworks" (18). Another description of these "really cool images" was seeing "light pinks and purples, yellows, and dots, which kept stretching like it all was chewing gum" (17). Participants admitted that the psychoactive effect was "a trip" (10), "like tripping . . . [an] altered reality" in which the "walls moved" (16). One 20-year-old Hispanic male put it succinctly: "It can't compare to LSD, though" (14). Although these participants listed and described hallucinations as one of the effects from smoking fry, not one suspected that there was a hallucinogenic psychoactive substance in the embalming fluid compound. Those interviewed attributed all additional effects—other than those normally associated with plain marijuana consumption—to the embalming fluid itself.

Negative effects of fry included feelings of panic, paranoia, and disorientation (6, 14, 15)—one reason why participants indicated that fry should not be smoked alone. Smoking fry in groups did not prevent respondents from engaging in embarrassing behavior, however. Four participants reported taking off their clothes and running naked down the street (1–3, 6). Intense anger was also cited: "I was hot, mad, aggravated, trying to hold back my frustration" (17). In response to this anger, respondents reported engaging in or witnessing serious physical confrontations (1–3, 6, 11, 17). An Hispanic female reporting attacking her mother with a knife while on fry; unable to restrain her, the young woman's family called the police. The girl awoke two days later in the Harris County Psychiatric Center, naked, restrained, and disoriented. She told her treatment providers that she had smoked embalming fluid. As neither she nor the treatment staff likely knew that fry also contained PCP, they did not prescribe anti-psychotic drugs for her, and the young woman had to endure her detoxification without assistance from prescription medication.

Smoking fry can also lead to losing consciousness (4). This effect may be why two respondents expressly described fry as a "dangerous drug" (20), "especially for a girl" (14). According to a Hispanic male, fry "can control a girl, more than roofies [Rohypnol]" (14). Two participants stated that fry heightens women's sexual appetites (6, 14), while one reported witnessing group sex with one female who had smoked fry (14). Moreover, one 19-year-old African American male participant reported that young women traded sex for fry sticks (6). Less frequently mentioned effects were making the brain hurt (6), making one feel methodical rather than angry (9), and numbing the entire body (11), although many participants reported numbing of the lips as a minor side effect from smoking fry.

What Are the Short-Term Effects?

The most frequently mentioned short-term effect was blurred or impaired vision (4, 5, 17, 19, 20), a symptom that begins during the "high" and frequently endures into the next day. One participant stated that his depth perception was so impaired that he walked right in the path of a Cadillac. Apparently, he thought he was farther away from traffic than he actually was (17). Another short-term effect is a headache the day following fry consumption. According to participants, the headache is worse than one from a hangover, and more difficult to overcome (5, 11, 12). They are all too knowledgeable regarding why they endure headaches: "After all, I know why they call it fry—it fries your brain!" (2).

Increased forgetfulness the following day also was cited. This short-term memory loss was described as even more extensive than after smoking marijuana alone (1, 2, 5, 9). Vomiting, depression or sadness, and facial/bodily edema also were reported.

What Are the Long-Term Effects?

In commonplace parlance, the long-term effects of smoking fry are not pretty. Participants recalled seeing long-term fry smokers who muttered to themselves as they walked in bizarre fashions (1, 3, 17, 18, 19). Such fry-impaired individuals also ceased their personal grooming habits and were dirty and disheveled. Five adolescents reported that smoking fry causes brain damage; two knew friends who were in mental health/mental retardation facilities because they had overdosed on fry use (9, 19). One friend had smoked enough fry sticks to consume three, one-ounce bottles of fry and was sent to a state mental facility in Rusk county.

Two additional long-term effects were that the embalming fluid "accumulates in the spinal cord" and makes the "back break down" (10). Apparently, it also "stops the maturation process" (11). Additional effects listed by the State of Connecticut include high fever, heart attacks, high blood pressure, kidney damage, destruction of muscle tissue, brain damage, coma, convulsions, coughing, pneumonia, anorexia, and death.

Consistent with adolescents' optimistic bias regarding health beliefs, none of the respondents believed that they would suffer from any of these effects.

Discussion

The consumption of marijuana with a PCP-laced embalming fluid compound clearly has become problematic among adolescents in Houston. Not the least of the problems involved with the consumption of this substance is that young people do not know exactly what they are consuming. This may account for their surprise at "tripping" upon consuming fry, and for the frustration of treatment providers to care adequately for adolescents who either overdose or who present for treatment (Nelson, 1997b; Pestana, 1997; Taggart, 1997).

One positive note is that fry does not appear to be a gateway drug to other illicit drug use among these Houston adolescents. All participants had used at least tobacco, alcohol, and marijuana before smoking fry; many had experimented previously with other drugs including cocaine, crack, heroin, LSD or acid, and prescription medicines purchased on the street. This trend is different from the "illy" epidemic in Hartford, in which the substance was promoted to elementary school children as an introduction to drug use, according to Pestana (1997). Furthermore, illy was promoted by dealers as a marijuana cigarette laced with embalming fluid and PCP. In contrast to Houston users, at least Connecticut adolescents and children knew more exactly what they were smoking.

To recognize signs of fry consumption, parents, teachers, and social service providers may look for elevated levels of anger and forgetfulness among adolescents. Reports of increased fighting, and even physical signs such as bruises and sores, may suggest the use of fry by adolescents. Clearly such adults should not attempt to handle episodic rages and physical violence independently. Such behavior should be handled as psychotic episodes, including informing law enforcement or health care providers that the individual likely has consumed a large amount of PCP.

Reports of group sex and of trading sex for fry sticks, while infrequent, is troublesome. Increased rates of syphilis, gonorrhea, and even HIV infection among teenagers in Houston has increased throughout this decade (Houston HIV Prevention, 1997). Increases in the use of fry and in the incidence of sexual intercourse in relation to the substance may facilitate the increased transmission of STDs, including HIV, among young people.

Study Limitations

There are two limitations regarding this study. First, readers should be advised that the small convenience sample used for this study might not reflect the use of fry among all adolescents in the Houston metropolitan area. Participants were mostly Anglo, Hispanic, and African American street youth recruited in the Montrose area, and African American adolescents from the Third Ward and South Park neighborhoods. These data may not be generalizable to other adolescents regardless of renegade or traditional lifestyles. However, these qualitative data do suggest an emerging drug trend; more extensive research may uncover whether Texas is poised for a fry epidemic similar to that experienced in Connecticut.

Second, reports of distributing embalming fluid could not be substantiated by any individuals actually engaged in such trading. This stage in the embalming fluid distribution process is surmised from reports by people who smoke fry and/or divert embalming fluid. As PCP is not a normal component in embalming fluid, and as street sellers and smokers reported ignorance of PCP as an ingredient, it is only an assumption that the reported distributors on the Near North Side are the individuals who add PCP to the fluid before selling it to street dealers.

Implications

Implications for action should be tempered with the limitations mentioned above. Nevertheless, treatment alerts should be issued to drug treatment and detoxification providers that drug users who report smoking marijuana or tobacco soaked in embalming fluid likely also consumed PCP, even if they deny or do not report it. Such alerts also should include recommendations to treat extreme behaviors such as those mentioned above with anti-psychotic medications such as haloperidol and sedatives such as diazepam (Valium).

While it is unclear whether the use of fry has become so extensive that it warrants a broadly based campaign as in Connecticut, it is clear that education about this substance is necessary so that the general public is informed of this dangerous additive in some marijuana cigarettes. Marijuana smokers need to know that adulterated marijuana may contain another, hazardous substance that can put them at extreme, immediate risk of adverse effects.

At the very least, fry smokers who receive treatment should be informed that they also have consumed PCP. Many of the problems involved with smoking fry may stem from incomplete or misinformation. For example, one participant knew the dangers of smoking embalming fluid but did not know that fry was the same substance; none of the participants knew or cared about the ingredients in fry. Additionally, there is a need for more stringent controls of embalming fluid and its component chemicals. Nevertheless, this report serves as a first step toward informing the public about this dangerous pattern of use, and alerting medical and mental health professionals to provide appropriate treatment.

Acknowledgments

The author thanks Daphne Moore, Faith Foreman, and Shanna Barnett for their assistance with this project.

References

Bardana, E. J., & Montanaro, A. (1991). Formaldehyde: An analysis of its respiratory, cutaneous, and immunologic effects. *Annals of Allergy, 66,* 441–452.

Borrero, M. (1996, January 3). Illy: Dangerous new street drug. *The Hartford Courant*, A9.

Capers, R. S. (1994, April 5). Latin Kings join in warnings about new drug use. *The Hartford Courant*, A7.

Elwood, W. N. (1997). Boy and girl are back in "the Bottom," and other substance abuse trends in Houston. In Texas Commission on Alcohol and Drug Abuse (Ed.), *Current trends in substance use: Texas 1997* (pp. 93–102). Austin: Texas Commission on Alcohol and Drug Abuse.

Frank, B., & Galea, G. (1994). Current drug use trends in New York City. In *Epidemiologic trends in drug abuse. Community Epidemiology Work Group, June 1994. Vol. II: Proceedings* (pp. 145–153). Rockville, MD: National Institute on Drug Abuse.

Fredlund, E. V., Farabee, D., Blair, L. A., & Wallisch, L. S. (1995). *Substance use and delinquency among youths entering Texas Youth Commission facilities: 1994.* Austin, TX: Texas Commission on Alcohol and Drug Abuse.

French, John. (1983). The drug scene in Newark. In *Trends, patterns, and issues in drug abuse. Community Epidemiology Work Group Proceedings: Vol. II* (pp. 1–6). Rockville, MD: National Institute on Drug Abuse.

Friedman, S. (1986, March 8). "Sky" high: Embalming fluid's popularity as a drug a dangerous trend. *Houston Chronicle*, sect. 1, p. 22.

Glaser, B. G., & Strauss, A. L. (1967). *The discovery of grounded theory: Strategies for qualitative research.* Chicago: Aldine Publishing Company.

Gullickson, G. M. (1990). Formaldehyde. In K. R. Olson (Ed.), *Poisoning and drug overdose* (pp. 160–161). Norwalk, CT: Appleton & Lange.

Houston HIV Prevention Community Planning Group. (1997, September). *City of Houston 1998 HIV prevention comprehensive plan.* Houston: Houston Department of Health and Human Services.

Johnson, J., Maxwell, J., & Leitnerschmidt, M. (1997). *A dictionary of slang drug terms, trade names, and pharmacological effects and uses.* Austin: Texas Commission on Alcohol and Drug Abuse.

Johnson, K. (1997, August 6). Report: Youth marijuana use shows slight decline. *USA Today*, 3A.

Lincoln, Y. S., & Guba, E. G. (1985). *Naturalistic inquiry.* Newbury Park, CA: Sage Publications.

Liu, L. Y. (1997, Spring). *1996 Texas school survey of substance use among students: Grades 7–12.* Austin: Texas Commission on Alcohol and Drug Abuse.

Mathias, R. (1997, March/April). Marijuana and tobacco use up again among eighth and tenth graders. *NIDA Notes*, 12–13.

Maxwell, J. A. (1996). *Qualitative research design: An interactive approach*. Thousand Oaks, CA: Sage Publications.

Milling, T. J. (1992, February 29). Pressure on cocaine traffic pushes abusers to a new high: Dopers said to be smoking pot laced with embalming fluid. *Houston Chronicle*, C9.

Murdock, G. P., Ford, C. S., Hudson, A. E., Kennedy, R., Simmons, L. W., & Whiting, J. W. M. (1985). *Outline of cultural materials* (5th edition). New Haven, CT: Human Relations Area Files, Inc.

National Institute on Drug Abuse. (1994, June). *Epidemiologic trends in drug abuse. Vol. I: Highlights and executive summary* (pp. 64–65). Rockville, MD: National Institute on Drug Abuse.

Nelson, L. (1997a, October 31). *Report on analysis of embalming fluid sample by official of the New York Poison Control Center*. lnelson@pol.net.

——. (1997b, October-December). *E-mail conversations with official of Bellevue Hospital and the New York Poison Control Center*. lnelson@pol.net.

Parker, R. G., & Carballo, M. (1990). Qualitative research on homosexual and bisexual behavior relevant to HIV/AIDS. *Journal of Sex Research*, 27, 497–525.

PCP (Phencyclidine). (1997, September). *NIDA Capsules*. National Institute on Drug Abuse. www.nida.nih.gov/NIDACapsules/NCPCP.html

PCP-dipped marijuana turns teenagers into "zombies." (1996, January 27). *Houston Chronicle*, sect. 1, p. 9.

Pestana, E. (1997, November–December). Telephone conversations with Connecticut public health official who coordinated campaign against embalming fluid use.

State of Connecticut, Department of Public Health and Addiction Services. (1994a). *Illy contains embalming chemicals that will poison you!* [brochure series]. Hartford, CT: Department of Public Health and Addiction Services.

State of Connecticut, Department of Public Health and Addiction Services. (1994b). Letter to emergency medical department directors on the "illy" epidemic.

Stinebaker, J. (1994, December 5). New drug "fry" starting to sizzle in popularity. *Houston Chronicle*, A15.

Swartz, M. K., & Moriarty, A. L. (1996). What's "new" in street drugs: "Illy." *Journal of Pediatric Health Care*, 10, 41–43.

Taggart, M. (1997). Telephone conversations regarding symptoms and treatment of fry-using adolescents at the Texas Youth Commission intake facility, Marlin.

Tschirgi, T. (1990). General information about phencyclidine. [Web site]. Center for Substance Abuse Research, University of Maryland Office of Substance Abuse Studies. www.bsos.umd.edu/cesar/pcp.html.

Wessels, L. W. (1997, November 18). *Material safety data sheets on embalming fluid products*. Pleasant Ridge, MI: Wessels and Associates.

Zuniga, J. A. (1993, September 25). Man gets a life term for shooting spree. *Houston Chronicle*, A32.

For Discussion

1. Discuss possible explanations for the emergence of new variations of drug-taking.

2. Discuss the difficulties in prohibiting legal substances to certain subgroups.

14

The Power of 420

Karen Bettez Halnon

I*n this article, Karen Halnon describes marijuana users' perceptions of the concept of "420." Although it has various meanings for users, Halnon suggests that the phrase offers a collective identity for users. She traces the folklore associated with 420 and explores users' perceptions of the origins of the phrase. Although she concludes that its origins are unclear, she notes that 420 has important symbolic meaning for users, many of whom incorporate "cherished rituals" in drug use lifestyles.*

Marijuana smokers, like other close-knit groups, have a special language. But often people in the straight-and-narrow world just don't understand it. Strange and alien to outsiders are words such as *nugs, dank, permagrin, wake n' bake, blunt, bogarting, Rastafarian, Towlie,* or even *coffee shops.* After 30 years of full-blown marijuana counterculture, outsiders still remain oblivious to the most special marijuana catchphrase of all: "Four hundred and twenty what?"

What outsiders miss, the discerning (and very possibly slightly reddened) eye can find all around. The 420 imprimatur is on bongs, T-shirts, patches, and coffee mugs. Marijuana fans find it frequently in stoner magazines, headshops, and in music lyrics. They feel lucky if they have 420 phone numbers, street addresses, or birthdays. This number is found at smoker Websites, on *Saturday Night Live,* and in news media on or around every April 20. For many smokers, 420 is guiding light and inspiration. Basically, for those with a raised consciousness of it, 420 is part of everyday life.

Curious about this hidden yet vibrant phenomenon, I did some research. The results of my sociological investigation were fascinating. Especially intriguing was the potency of 420, unique in the multiple ways it inspires and cultivates identity, community, and even reality.

It's difficult to even think of another *single numerical expression* that compares. 411 or 911? Lucky 7? Demonic 666? Trinitarian 3? Sexual 69? Tragic 9/11? LSD-25? Or even the infinite 3.1416 . . . ? While these numbers are significant, none by themselves embrace and reflect a community to the extent that 420 does.

In documenting 420, I hope to express the sociological "surprise" of 420. However, sociological surprises do not necessarily provide new information. The surprise of sociology comes when it shines new light on our everyday behaviors and experiences. Everyone on the inside knows that 420 is a most special number. My goal is to explain some of the sociological reasons for its special status as spirit and guide for marijuana smokers. In doing so, I drew upon the insights of nearly a hundred 420 smokers.

Learning the 'Secret Code'

Learning is extremely important in achieving an identity. In fact, it is the basic and necessary way any identity is achieved. And, if learning takes place with friends or family, achieving that identity is even more likely.

Following this pattern, most pot-smokers first learn about 420 from high-school or college friends, or from brothers or sisters. One smoker learned about it from "good friends in the military" who "introduced 4:20 as an alternative to 16:20 military time." Others explained that they "became part of the 'crew' by hitting 420," or learned about it when "sharing marijuana with new friends" at rock concerts—Phish shows in particular.

One of the first lessons smokers learn is that while the meaning of 420 is obvious to insiders as universal or as an international symbol for marijuana, marijuana smoking, and marijuana subculture, it's also a "secret code" or "secret advertiser." Smokers recounted comedic stories, such as where a high school teacher asked a student what time it was, and he replied "Four-twenty,"eliciting the laughter of in-group classmates and the bewilderment of his teacher. Another smoker explained that 420's "secret" quality allowed him to get a pro-marijuana symbol past high-school authorities, sneaking a criminal-style number-420 mug shot in the yearbook without the faculty editor noticing. Others explained that it allowed them to wear blatant symbols of marijuana to school (420 written on hats, T-shirts, and the like) without encountering the negative sanctions associated with less obscure symbols, such as marijuana leaves. Still others explained that 420, as secret code, allowed them to safely and accurately identify others who smoke marijuana. For example, one smoker explained, "420 is like a secret advertiser . . . a good way to keep scattered tabs on who puffs."

All of this is fascinating to the sociologist because secrets and humor are very effective means of binding groups closer together. Secrets create a social boundary between outsiders and insiders. Humor, at least for those who share in it, enhances feelings of relaxation and [warmth]. Together, secrets and humor cultivate closeness, commitment, and group solidarity.

420 'Time'

Smokers explained that 420 is "a time that is in-between day and night, a break . . . a good time to relax and chill." Others said, "If my friends and I are ever up at 4:20 A.M., we always celebrate by smoking a bowl or joint. It is simply a justified reason to smoke."

For novices, 420 motivated smoking behavior by organizing time. The newly inducted learn that 420 means "a" or "the" "time to smoke." For example, smokers explained how they learned that 4:20 in the afternoon was "prime time" for smokers, the "pot smoker's happy hour," the "best time to smoke," or the "international smoke time." One smoker expressed the general sentiment of the novice: "You have to smoke at 4:20 if you have herb." Smokers explained how they set their alarm clocks, or how clocks in gen-

eral served as reminders to smoke at 4:20. Nearly all smokers agreed that for the novice, 420 becomes an excuse or a reason to smoke, and frequently involves excessive smoking.

This pattern is sociologically significant, because a crucial ingredient in the recipe for identity achievement is immersion into identity-shaping activities. In other words, smoking lots of weed in the beginning normalizes getting high and increases the chances of defining oneself as a smoker of weed. The sociologist would also take important note of the fact that the organization of time is one of the most basic frameworks that supports and legitimates a "reality." Stated otherwise, 420 time lends legitimacy or a sense of truthfulness to pot-smoker reality.

Putting such sociological value aside, more seasoned smokers complained and resisted. They complained that such time structuring created a "ritualistic use of 420" or that it turned "marijuana-smoking into a joke." One smoker, who described himself as "patriotic to the weed," claimed that 420 should not be guided by time, but rather a more spontaneous "pledge and a tribute."

Whether a novice or seasoned user, what nearly everyone agreed upon is that 4:20 (P.M. or A.M.) means a source of unity or oneness in the pot-smoker community. It was variously described as a "time to unite with all smokers," a "smoker's club," and a way to "bring users together for smoking, community and solidarity." Smokers repeatedly claimed that 420 created a "common bond" among friends and fellow smokers. They know that when they light up at 4:20, thousands, if not millions, of others are doing the same for the same reason.

420 'Origin' Conversations

Most pot-smokers would probably accept as fact that 420 originated in San Rafael, CA, with the "Waldo Family," and Steve Waldo who used the expression "420 Louie" in high school. Waldo used it as a secret code to remind friends to meet for smoking sessions at the Louis Pasteur statue, 70 minutes after the 3:10 dismissal. However, regardless of whether or not the smokers I talked with actually knew about the veracity of Waldo's claim, they were generally uninterested in determining 420's true origin. One expressed a typical view: "The actual meaning of 420, or where it came from, seems unimportant to me compared to the feeling of 420. That is the true meaning." Another smoker was of a similar opinion: "Most people do not desire to know where 420 came from, but rather enjoy it for its cultural importance." A third, after reviewing a number of possible theories, explained, "While some of these reports are more believable than others, they all represent how important the number is to the marijuana community." Emphasizing the value of learning from talking about 420, a fourth smoker expressed this general point: "I think the most valid meaning of 420 origins is the underlying things you learn."

What fascinated me about origin theories was that while smokers actively discussed and debated them, they didn't care about learning the truth. This apparent contradiction made more sense when I realized that the dozens of theories discussed and debated, though often wrong or unprovable, were equivalent to a 101 course in marijuana cultural literacy. It is, as smokers repeatedly told me, more important to discuss and debate than to discover truth, because of the underlying things that can be learned.

Smokers learn, for example, about taking a defiant attitude toward police enforcement of anti-marijuana laws, and about the meaning and importance of people and things such as Jerry Garcia and the Grateful Dead, Cheech and Chong, Jamaica, Haight-Ashbury, Amsterdam, and THC. While these 101 lessons are an important part of the socialization of new smokers, origin conversations are important for all smokers. They provide a subject for many deep, philosophical and scientific conversations. Smokers said that stoner philosophizing about origins was especially meaningful when sharing a bowl, joint, or bong, and in effect was a learning session. Exploring, but not necessarily proving, origin theories provides many important lessons in marijuana culture. In other words, 420 origins serve as a good, celebratory, and often humorous, teacher.

The most common origin theory proffered by smokers is that 420 is or was a Los Angeles "police code for marijuana-smoking in progress." Researching the validity of this claim, I called the Los Angeles Police Department and asked if 420 was the "real" police code for marijuana smoking in progress. The answering officer explained that 420 in the "penal book" referred to "preventing or obstructing entry upon or passage upon public lands." I then asked what the police code would be for marijuana-smoking in progress. He said the California Health and Safety Code for "any narcotic drug," including marijuana, is 11350.

Steve Waldo, writing in *High Times* ("4:20 & the Grateful Dead," May '01 HT), explained further:

> Although it has often been rumored, 420 is not a police code for drug-law enforcement. Drug enforcement in California, and in San Rafael, is part of the state Health and Safety Code, in which all sections have five-and six-digit numbers, sometimes separated by a decimal point. Pot-related activities and violations fall in the middle [11300s].

The police-code origin theory, while false, calls attention to the fact that marijuana is an illegal substance, pointing to a central value difference between what is law and what is valued among marijuana-smokers. To embrace the police code as smoking symbol is to learn to stand in defiance against laws that make smoking illegal. To call attention to California is to learn about a state that is the leader in the fight to legalize the medical use of marijuana.

A second origin theory is that 420 references THC (delta-9 tetrahydrocannabinol) as "the number of chemicals in THC," the "number of molecules in marijuana," or the "number of elements in the marijuana plant." Skeptical about these biochemistry claims, I solicited evaluation from Peter Webster, Review Editor of the *International Journal of Drug Policy*, who responded to my e-mail query as follows:

> THC, or the principal active ingredient of cannabis, is a single chemical entity, i.e., one chemical. There are however many

other closely-related but less psychoactive chemicals in cannabis, some which may be more important in medical applications. Each, however, is a different chemical since its molecular structure is unique. Again, THC is ONE chemical. "Marijuana" contains perhaps many thousands of different molecular entities, from the couple of hundred cannabinoids such as THC, to chlorophyl, fats, fibers such as lignin, cellulose, sugars, enzymes, and a wide range of other organic chemicals, to minerals, water, etc. [There are a] number of elements: carbon, hydrogen, oxygen, nitrogen, sulfur, chlorine, sodium, potassium, iron, magnesium, phosphorous, many trace metals, and probably many others in trace amounts . . . in effect, most elements in the first part of the periodic table, and probably even some traces of heavy metals—whatever is in the environment in which it grows.

While also false, the THC origin theory aids in learning about the primary psychoactive ingredient in marijuana, which is standard knowledge for any marijuana smoker.

A third set of related theories revolved around Jerry Garcia and the Grateful Dead. Smokers claimed, for example, that 420 was the "address of the Grateful Dead's home at Haight Ashbury," that "pot smoking is almost synonymous with the Grateful Dead," and that 420 refers to the "exact time of Jerry Garcia's death." In researching these claims I found that according to Rebecca Adams in *Deadhead Social Science*, "By late 1966, the Dead were headquartered at 710 Ashbury, near its intersection with Haight, the symbolic heart of the hippie community." And according to the *San Francisco Bay City Guide* (March 2001), "The Grateful Dead were one-time residents of the Haight (710 Ashbury Street)." Finally, while staying in San Francisco, I took a cab to Haight-Ashbury myself to confirm the 710, not 420, address.

In researching the exact time of Jerry Garcia's death, I found that, according to *People* magazine (Aug. 21, 1995) cover story, he died on Wednesday, August 9, 1995 at 4:23 A.M. exactly. Other newspaper articles similarly reported that Garcia passed away in his

bed at Forest Knoll after being found by a nurse who tried to revive him. The time of death again was 4:23 A.M. Thus, a third origin theory, while false again, aids in cultivating marijuana-culture literacy through its focus on classic stoner musician Jerry Garcia, stoner band the Grateful Dead, and the quintessential 1960s drug/hippie community, Haight-Ashbury.

A fourth set of origin theories revolved around times that are, like the theories above, significant to marijuana-smoker culture. One explanation is that 420 means teatime in Amsterdam or Holland. Probably, as in Britain, the time is closer to 4:30. Another explanation was that Tommy Chong (of Cheech and Chong, stars of marijuana cult film *Up in Smoke*) was born on April 20. In fact, he was born May 24, 1938.

Another explanation states that 420 originated from "the date Haille Sallasie visited Jamaica for the first time." The late Ethiopian emperor, venerated by Rastafarians as signifying the rebirth of black rule in Africa, visited Jamaica for three days in April 1966, but he arrived on the 21st.

Thus, a fourth set of origin theories aid smokers in learning about the importance of Amsterdam, a city that tolerates "soft drug" use and where marijuana can be smoked freely in coffeeshops; educates them as to a major marijuana cult film and its figures; and reveals the ritualization of ganja by Rastafarians.

Smokers also claimed that 420 originated from the first recorded use of marijuana. In researching this claim, I found that 2737 B.C. is frequently reported in academic texts as the earliest reference to use of marijuana because of its mention in a Chinese treatise by Emperor Shen Nung. However, Erich Goode (in *Drugs in American Society*, 5th ed.) tells us that "there is no definite date of the earliest recorded use of marijuana, although descriptions of cannabis use can be found in ancient texts from China, India, Persia, Assyria, Egypt, Greece, and Rome. For example, Marijuana is mentioned as a 'healing herb' in *The Divine Husbandman's Materia Medica*, circa first or second century A.D. In 650 B.C. the use of cannabis is mentioned in Persia and Assyria. In 400 B.C. the use of cannabis is mentioned in Rome." This time origin theory, while false or unprovable again, shows that marijuana-smoking has a long and deep historical tradition, and thus naturalizes its use for marijuana smokers.

Drawing more generally upon the illegal drug culture is the theory that 420 originated from the date Albert Hoffman discovered LSD-25. LSD-25 was first synthesized at Sandoz Laboratories in Basel, Switzerland, in 1938. It was re-shelved until April 16, 1943 when Hoffman made a "fresh batch," swallowed 250 micrograms, and experienced the first extremely intense acid trip "for science" (*Acid Dreams*, Martin Lee and Bruce Shalin). This origin theory teaches smokers about Albert Hoffman and LSD, and by doing so asserts the value of using illegal drugs.

Perhaps the most creative but dubious time theory was that 420 originated from the position of a "dangling doobie" in the mouth of a Jamaican getting off work. The position of the joint was said to resemble an analogue clock at 4:20. A final but certainly not exhaustive explanation is that 420 originated from Hitler's birthday. One smoker explained, "Hitler represents in sharp opposite contrast all that the marijuana smoking community stands for." This theory, like the theories above, cannot be proven to have any direct reference to 420. And even though Hitler was in fact born on April 20, 1889, there is no evidence that 420 originated from that date. By learning the dangling doobie and Hitler theories smokers learn about the value of Jamaica and Jamaican weed, and the peaceful, laid-back spirit among smokers.

To summarize, by discussing and debating numerous 420 origin theories marijuana smokers are able to share stories filled with an array of important symbols of marijuana smoker culture: Jamaica, California, Rastafarians, Cheech and Chong, Haight-Ashbury, the Grateful Dead, Jerry Garcia, hippies, THC. Through these conversations, smokers also learn many other lessons about the importance of defying laws and legal authorities that prohibit marijuana-smoking; the value and significance of locales where it is legal or at least tolerated; the deep historical tradition of marijuana-smoking; the spiri-

tual justifications for it; and the easy, relaxed attitude of marijuana smokers.

What is most important is not determining the true origin of 420, but rather engaging in conversations filled with lessons for marijuana-smokers. Because these origin theories are either wrong or unprovable, they provide for an ongoing learning conversation. The sociological significance of ongoing conversations—especially if they are rich in memory, tradition, common beliefs, and values—is that they are a basic and necessary means of maintaining any kind of relationship. The value of 420 origin stories is similar to that of retelling stories in a close-knit family. Stories—whether true, false, or embellished—strengthen the family's sense of belonging, identity and values, bringing it closer together. Even if we suspect that Aunt Lucy or Uncle John is not telling the truth, that doesn't stop us from reveling in their old stories. The retelling itself becomes a cherished ritual and a means of communicating what is valued and important to the family. This said, the definitiveness of the Waldo theory is, at best, a mixed blessing to the pot-smoker community.

The Pot-Smokers' Holiday

April 20—especially at 4:20 P.M.—is the "pot-smokers' holiday," also variously described as the "hippie New Year," "national smoke time," "national pot smoking day," "the holiday," "pot appreciation day," "the ultimate session," or "a day of tribute to the scene." One enthusiastic smoker reported, "Every group has its holidays and pot-smokers are no exception. April 20th is the day of worship observed by smokers around the world." Another said, "It's comforting to know that hundreds of thousands of other people are lighting up with me on 4/20. It's about the community identity of marijuana-smokers."

For marijuana-smokers, April 20 is especially imbued with emotional and spiritual meaning because it produces an intense collective bonding among them. Smokers emphasized the special quality of the Holiday: "We are talking about the day of celebration, the real time to get high, the grand master of all holidays: April twentieth."

That statement also reveals a sense of family within the pot-smoking culture. "Tokers are brothers and sisters, therefore more closely connected than any other association." Another smoker expressed the anticipation and joy of the Holiday: "At 4:19 P.M., everyone suddenly got quiet and the countdown began. When the time turned to 4:20 it was like New Year's. Everyone was cheering and shouting, jumping, hugging, and of course smoking. It really was incredible. I felt connected not only to the people around me, but to everyone else in the world who was doing the same thing at that exact moment."

While 4/20 celebrations give smokers a sense of worldwide community, they also reinforce old friendships, or create new ones at rallies. Friends travel long distances, even across the country, to party together. As a result, friendships are refreshed or "become stronger than ever." And people who might be strangers in other settings bond through their common allegiance to marijuana. One smoker explained, "It is a time when you can approach people that you do not really know and indulge in pot-smoking with them. You develop friendships with people because of the activities on 4/20 and at 4:20."

The sense of worldwide "we-ness" and the friendships established and renewed at 4/20 celebrations are due in large part to the fact that April 20 is a public forum for the fight for legalization. A smoker explained, "It is an exercise in solidarity, all of the pot-smokers coming together to smoke and the police being utterly powerless to do anything about it. I think this is the most valid expression of 420 as it puts the recreational use of marijuana in full view of the public, which is perhaps the first step towards gaining legitimacy." In a sentiment echoed by others, one smoker explained that "4/20 at 4:20 is a time to come together, to share one's lifestyle with others who feel the same way, to come together and stand strong and proud for marijuana." Said another, "Personally, I feel it (April 20) to be a political statement. It is a good time to gather to show one's support of legalization of marijuana."

As a matter of efficient crowd control, police and university authorities generally tolerate the short—and seldom dangerous—yearly public statements by pot-smokers. One smoker said that not only is 4/20 a time to stand proud for marijuana, but that "it's a day of tolerance and the authorities let us 'hippies' have our fun and smoke pot." Another said in proud defiance, "Pronounced 'four twenty,' it is a day of police nonenforcement of drug laws in certain areas, and a day to celebrate a ritual that has survived thousands of years, only to be condemned by our American government . . . It's one of the most liberating feelings to smoke pot in public and not be afraid of being caught."

The experience of such a holiday provides pot-smokers with hope and inspiration—or with a vision of a future when they will be liberated from repressive antimarijuana laws.

The Sociological Surprise of 420

In this article I have attempted to explain the sociological surprise of 420, or how that special number is imbued with the ability to cultivate especially strong marijuana-smoker identity. As "secret code," it creates a social boundary between outsiders and insiders, and enhances a sense of "we-ness" among insiders. As "time," it legitimates smoker reality and structures and motivates excessive smoking behavior among novices, thus providing a valuable "immersion" experience. As "origin conversation," it facilitates learning about many important fundamental facts and values of the marijuana and illegal drug-user cultures. As "pot-smokers' holiday," it provides special family holiday ritual, a "day of tolerance," and a public opportunity to "stand proud for marijuana." Most important, as pot smokers' holiday, 420 creates an intense sense of group belonging among friends, strangers, crowds, and across geographical boundaries. Sociologists call this "collective consciousness," or a kind of mystical, spiritual, or extraordinary sense of belonging, where the group exists as a reality greater than itself.

In sum, the ultimate sociological surprise or fascination of 420 is that a single expression has the unique and powerful ability to cultivate, support, and reinforce pot-smoker identity, community, solidarity, and reality itself. The modest surprise offered here is a more comprehensive explanation of what smokers already know.

For Discussion

1. Do users of other drugs—cocaine, heroin—share a secret subculture similar to that of marijuana smokers? What makes the subculture of marijuana users unique among drug users?

2. Does the sense of belonging that a subculture provides attract people to try drugs? Once a person is initiated, does being a part of a group reinforce continued drug use?

3. How did the concept of 420 become so important if no one really knows what it means?

Part IV

Narcotics, Injection Drug Use, and HIV/AIDS

In pharmacology, a science that focuses on the chemical nature, structure, and action of drugs, *narcotics* include the natural derivatives of *Papaver somniferum L.*—the opium poppy—having both analgesic and sedative properties, and any synthetic derivatives of similar pharmacological structure and action. Thus, the range of substances that can be properly called narcotics is quite limited and encompasses four specific groups:

Natural narcotics

- opium, derived directly from *Papaver somniferum L.*
- morphine and codeine, derived from opium

Semisynthetic narcotics

- heroin
- hydromorphone (Dilaudid)
- oxycodone (OxyContin, Percocet)
- hydrocodone (Vicodin)
- etorphine
- fentanyl

Synthetic narcotics with high potency

- methadone
- meperidine (Demerol)

Synthetic narcotics with low potency

- propoxyphene (Darvon)
- pentazocine (Talwin)

There are many other narcotics, but the examples listed are the best known. The most widely used in the drug culture are methadone and heroin. Methadone was synthesized during World War II by German chemists when supply lines for morphine were interrupted. Although chemically unlike morphine or heroin, it produces many of the same effects. Methadone was introduced in the United States in 1947 and quickly became the drug of choice in the detoxification of heroin addicts.

Since the 1960s methadone has been in common use for the treatment of heroin addiction. Known as "methadone maintenance," the program takes advantage of methadone's unique properties as a narcotic. Like all narcotics, methadone is cross-dependent with heroin. As such, it is a substitute narcotic that prevents withdrawal. More important, however, methadone is orally effective, making intravenous use unnecessary. In addition, it is a longer-acting drug than heroin, with one oral dose lasting up to 24 hours. These properties have made methadone useful in the management of chronic narcotic addiction. Yet on the other hand, methadone is also a primary drug of abuse among some narcotic addicts, resulting in a small street market for the drug. Most illegal methadone is diverted from legitimate maintenance programs by methadone patients. Hence, illegal supplies of the drug are typically available only where such programs exist.

Heroin has a somewhat longer and more curious history. In 1874, British chemist C. R. A. Wright described a number of experiments he had carried out at London's St. Mary's Hospital to determine the effect of combining various acids with morphine. Wright produced a series of new morphine-like compounds, including what became known in the scientific literature as diacetylmorphine. His discovery of *diacetylmorphine* had been the outgrowth of an enduring search for more effective substitutes for morphine. This interest stemmed not only from the painkilling qualities of opiate drugs but also from their sedative effects on the respiratory system. Wright's work went for the most part unnoticed, however.

Some 24 years later, in 1898, pharmacologist Heinrich Dreser reported on a series of experiments he had conducted with diacetylmorphine for Friedrich Bayer and Company of Elberfeld, Germany. He noted that the drug was highly effective in the treatment of coughs, chest pains, and the discomforts associated with pneumonia and tuberculosis. Dreser's commentary received immediate notice, for it had come at a time when antibiotics were still unknown and pneumonia and tuberculosis were among the leading causes of death. He claimed that diacetylmorphine had a stronger sedative effect on respiration than either morphine or codeine, that therapeutic relief came quickly, and that the potential for a fatal overdose was almost nil. In response to such favorable reports, Bayer and Company began marketing diacetylmorphine under the trade name of *heroin*—so named from the German *heroisch*, meaning heroic and powerful.

Although Bayer's heroin was promoted as a sedative for coughs and as a chest and lung medicine, it was advocated by some as a treatment for morphine addiction. This situation seems to have arisen from three somewhat related phenomena. First was the belief that heroin was nonaddicting. Second, since the drug had a greater potency than morphine, only small dosages were required for the desired medical effects, thus

reducing the potential for the rapid onset of addiction. And third, at the turn of the twentieth century, the medical community did not fully understand the dynamics of cross-dependence. *Cross-dependence* refers to the phenomenon that among certain pharmacologically related drugs, physical dependence on one will carry over to all the others. As such, for the patient suffering from the unpleasant effects of morphine withdrawal, the administration of heroin would have the consequence of one or more doses of morphine. The dependence was maintained and withdrawal disappeared, with the two combining to give the appearance of a "cure."

Given the endorsement of the medical community, with little mention of its potential dangers, heroin quickly found its way into routine medical therapeutics and over-the-counter patent medicines. However, the passage of the Pure Food and Drug Act in 1906 and the Harrison Act in 1914 restricted the availability of heroin, and the number of chronic users declined.

Although narcotics use in its various forms has been common throughout United States history, its current and most typical manifestation—the intravenous use of heroin—apparently developed during the 1930s and became widespread after 1945. Between 1950 and the early 1960s, most major cities experienced a low-level spread of heroin use, particularly among the black and other minority populations. Thereafter, use began to grow rapidly, rising to peaks in the late 1960s and then falling sharply. The pattern was so ubiquitous that it came to be regarded as "epidemic" heroin use. More recent "epidemics" occurred in 1973–1974, 1977–1978, and 1982–1983, defined as such on the basis of the number of new admissions to heroin-treatment facilities. Yet interestingly, no one really knew how widespread heroin use was during those years, and even today the estimates are often little more than scientific guesses.

In the 1970s, the National Institute on Drug Abuse developed what it called "heroin trend indicators," relative estimates generated from a composite of reported heroin-related deaths, hospital emergency room visits, heroin-treatment admissions, and high school and household surveys. On the basis of these data, the estimated number of heroin users in the United States in the 1970s ranged from 396,000 to 510,000. From the 1980s onward, government reports maintained that the total number of heroin users in the United States hovered somewhere between 500,000 and 800,000, having been at that level for over two decades.

However, several demographic trends emerged in the 1990s. Government figures again indicated an upsurge in treatment admission rates for heroin addiction: High-purity heroin (which can be inhaled), decreased price, increased availability, and "generational forgetting"—in which a younger generation of drug users had less awareness of the consequences of a particular drug that had been out of fashion—have all been considered factors. Hollywood movies glorifying drug use, strung-out rock musicians, and the "heroin chic" fashion statement promoted by designers all made cultural noise during the decade. Perhaps not surprisingly, government statistics indicate that the proportion of white users and those under the age of 25 admitted to treatment increased between 1992 and 2000, and heroin was the leading illicit drug among substance abuse treatment admissions in 2000. At the beginning of the decade, less than half of new users aged 18 to 24 reported injection as their preferred route of administration; by 2000, almost two-thirds reported injection.

Related to heroin use, and injection in particular, is the AIDS epidemic. Acquired immune deficiency syndrome (AIDS) was first described as a new and distinct clinical entity during the late spring and early summer of 1981. First, clinical investigators in Los Angeles reported five cases to the Centers for Disease Control (CDC) of *Pneumocystis carinii* pneumonia (PCP) among gay men. None of these patients had an underlying disease that might have been associated with PCP or a history of treatment for a compromised immune system. All, however, had other clinical manifestations and laboratory evidence of immunosuppression. Second, and within a month, 26 cases of Kaposi's sarcoma (KS) were reported among gay men in New York and California.

What was so unusual was that prior to these reports, the appearance of both afflictions in populations of previously healthy young men was unprecedented. PCP is an infection caused by the parasite *P. carinii*, previously seen almost exclusively in cancer and transplant patients receiving immunosuppressive drugs. KS, a tumor of the blood vessel walls that often appears as blue-violet to brownish skin blotches, had been quite rare in the United States, occurring primarily in elderly men, usually of Mediterranean origin. Furthermore, like PCP, KS had also been reported among organ transplant recipients and others receiving immunosuppressive therapy. This observation quickly led to the hypothesis that the increased occurrences of the two disorders in gay men were due to some underlying immune system dysfunction. This hypothesis was further supported by the incidence among homosexuals of "opportunistic infections"—infections caused by microorganisms that rarely generate disease in persons with normal immune defense mechanisms. It is for this reason that the occurrence of KS, PCP, or other opportunistic infections in a person with unexplained immune dysfunction became known as the "acquired immune deficiency syndrome," or more simply, AIDS.

With the recognition that the vast majority of the early cases of this new clinical syndrome involved gay and bisexual men, it seemed logical that the causes might be related to the lifestyle unique to that population. The sexual revolution of the 1960s and 1970s was accompanied not only by greater carnal permissiveness among both heterosexuals and gays but also by a more positive social acceptance of homosexuality. The emergence of commercial bathhouses and other outlets for sexual contacts among homosexuals further increased promiscuity, with certain segments of the gay population viewing promiscuity as a facet of "gay liberation." In fact, among the early patients diagnosed with AIDS, their sexual recreation typically occurred within the anonymity of the bathhouses with similarly promiscuous men. Some had had as many as 20,000 sexual contacts and more than 1,100 sex partners. And to complicate matters, sexually active gay men with multiple sex partners were manifesting high rates of sexually transmitted diseases—gonorrhea, syphilis, genital herpes, anal warts, and hepatitis B.

Because of this situation, it is not surprising that such factors as frequent exposure to semen, rectal exposure to semen, the body's exposure to amyl nitrate and butyl nitrate (better known as "poppers" and used to enhance sexual pleasure and performance), and a high prevalence of sexually transmitted diseases were themselves considered potential causes of AIDS. Yet while it was apparent that AIDS was a new disease, most of the gay lifestyle factors were *not* particularly new, having changed only in a relative sense. As such, it was difficult to immediately single out specific behaviors that might be related to the emerging epidemic. Within a brief period, however, the notion that AIDS was some form of "gay plague" was quickly extinguished. The disease was suddenly being reported in other populations, such as injection drug users, blood transfusion patients, and hemophiliacs. And what these reports suggested to the scientific community was that an infectious etiology for AIDS had to be considered.

Almost immediately after the first cases of AIDS were reported in 1981, researchers at the Centers for Disease Control began tracking the disease backward to discover its origins. They ultimately determined that the first cases of AIDS in the United States probably occurred in 1977. By early 1982, AIDS had been reported in 15 states, the District of Columbia, and two foreign countries, but the total number of cases remained extremely low—158 men and one woman. Although more than 90 percent of the men were either gay or bisexual, interviews with all of the patients failed to provide any definite clues about the origin of the disease.

Although it was suspected that AIDS might be transmitted through sexual relations among homosexually active men, the first strong evidence for the idea did not emerge until the completion of a case control study in June 1982 by epidemiologists at the Centers for Disease Control. In that investigation, data were obtained on the sexual partners of 13 of the first 19 cases of AIDS among homosexual men in the Los Angeles area. Within five years before the onset of their symptoms, nine had had sexual contact with people who later developed Kaposi's sarcoma or *P. carinii* pneumonia. The nine were also linked to another interconnected series of 40 AIDS cases in ten different cities by one individual who had developed a number of the manifestations of AIDS and was later diagnosed with Kaposi's sarcoma. Overall, the investigation of these 40 cases indicated that 20 percent of the initial AIDS cases in the United States were linked through sexual contact—a statistical clustering that was extremely unlikely to have occurred by chance.

Even in the face of this evidence, there were those who doubted that AIDS was caused by some transmissible agent. However, when AIDS cases began to emerge in other populations—among individuals who had been injected with blood or blood products but had no other expected risk factors—the transmission vectors for the disease became somewhat clearer. Such cases were confirmed first among people with hemophilia, followed by blood transfusion recipients and injection drug users who shared hypodermic needles, syringes, and other paraphernalia. Then, with the appearance of documented cases of AIDS among the heterosexual partners of male injection drug users, it became increasingly evident that AIDS was a disease transmitted by the exchange of certain bodily fluids—primarily blood, blood products, and semen. "Sexual orientation" was not necessarily the only risk factor.

In 1983 and 1984, scientists at the Institute Pasteur in Paris and the National Institutes of Health in the United States identified and isolated the cause of AIDS: Human T-cell Lymphotropic Virus, Type III (HTLV-III), or Lymphadenopathy—Associated Virus (LAV). Later, this virus would be renamed human immunodeficiency virus, more commonly known as HIV. More specifically, HIV is a "retrovirus," a type of infectious agent that had previously been identified as causing many animal diseases. The designation of "retrovirus" derives from the backward, or "retro" flow of genetic information from RNA to DNA, thus reversing the normal flow of genetic messages. Subsequent studies demonstrated that HIV is transmitted when virus particles or infected cells gain direct access to the bloodstream. This access can occur through all forms of sexual intercourse; the sharing of contaminated needles, blood, and blood products; and the passing of the virus from infected mothers to their unborn or newborn children. Within this context, AIDS involves a continuum of conditions associated with immune dysfunction and is best described as a severe manifestation of infection with HIV.

With respect to the "AIDS/drugs connection," in 1987 the U.S. Public Health Service estimated that there were some 900,000 regular (at least weekly) injection drug users across the nation, 25 percent of whom were already infected with HIV. At the same time, the Centers for Disease Control was reporting that injection drug users, as already noted, were the second highest risk group for AIDS, representing 24 percent of all reported cases in the United States. By early 1988, drug injectors had come to represent 26 percent of known AIDS cases in the United States, and by the 1990s, the statistic was nearly 30 percent. The drug-injector proportion has since declined, currently accounting for 25 percent of all AIDS cases.

The ready transmission of HIV and AIDS among injection drug users is the result of the sharing of injection equipment, combined with the presence of "cofactors." Cofactors include any behavioral practices or microbiological agents that facilitate the transmission of HIV. For injecting heroin, cocaine, and amphetamine users, the blood transmission of HIV may occur as a result of using or sharing contaminated drug injection equipment. Of particular significance is "booting," a practice that increases the amount of residual blood left in drug paraphernalia. Booting involves the aspiration of venous blood back into a syringe for the purpose of mixing the drug with blood, while the needle remains inserted in the vein. The mixed blood/drug solution is then injected back into the vein. Most injection drug users believe that this "premixing" enhances a drug's effects. Since injectors often share needles and syringes, particularly if they are administering the drugs in "shooting galleries"—places where users gather to take drugs—booting increases the probability that traces of HIV from an infected user will remain in a syringe to be passed on to the next user.

Additional risk factors in the AIDS/drug connection are prostitution and exchanges of sex for drugs. There is an extensive body of literature offering a strong empirical basis for the notion that prostitution is a major means of economic support for drug-using women. Moreover, it is well established that there is a high incidence of prostitution among women drug users. As such, the drug-injecting prostitute is not only at high risk for contracting HIV, but for transmitting it as well. Exchanges of sex for drugs, and particularly for crack, also represent risk factors for HIV and AIDS.

Heroin and other injection drug users also represent a population that appears difficult to influence with routine AIDS prevention messages. The potential for HIV acquisition and transmission from infected paraphernalia and "unsafe" sex is likely known to most drug users. Yet most are accustomed to risking death (through overdose or the violence-prone nature of the illegal drug marketplace) and disease (hepatitis and other infections) on a daily basis, and these threats generally fail to eliminate their drug-taking behaviors. For these reasons, warnings that injection equipment sharing or unsafe sex may facilitate an infection that could cause death perhaps five or more years down the road have little impact. It would appear that at least some injection drug users are willing to adjust a few behaviors related to the transmission of HIV, such as purchasing new needles, sterilizing used needles, and reducing the sharing of needles with others. However, the minimal research in this area has tended to be inconclusive, particularly since many of those who adjust their behaviors continue to share needles with friends, relatives, and others who appear healthy. In addition, prevention strategies have had little impact on sexual behaviors.

In recent years, "needle exchange" (or syringe exchange) has emerged as a positive step in reducing the spread of HIV and AIDS among injection drug users. The first needle exchange program began in the Netherlands during 1984. In the United States, state and county government-approved needle exchange programs did not begin until 1988, the delay due mainly to the illegal status of needles and syringes in most parts of the country. In the overwhelming majority of state jurisdictions, injection equipment may not be legally purchased without a doctor's prescription. However, privately funded activist groups began distributing sterile equipment as early as 1986. Since then, numerous legally sanctioned needle exchange schemes have been implemented in the United States, and the overall results have been quite positive.

The chapters that follow explore issues related to narcotics, injection drug use, and the connection with HIV/AIDS. Patterns of heroin use among both street-based and young white users are explored. The emergence of OxyContin, a potent prescription narcotic, is reported on at length, with special attention given to the media hype surrounding the abuse of the drug. A variety of issues in the drugs/AIDS connection, including an extended discussion of needle exchange, are examined as well.

Additional Readings

Courtwright, David T. (2001). *Dark Paradise: Opiate Addiction in America* (2nd ed.). Cambridge: Harvard University Press.

Davenport-Hines, Richard. (2002). *The Pursuit of Oblivion: A Global History of Narcotics, 1500–2000.* New York: W. W. Norton & Company.

Inciardi, James A., and Lana D. Harrison. (Eds.). (1998). *Heroin in the Age of Crack-Cocaine.* Thousand Oaks, CA: Sage Publications.

Kandall, Stephen R. (1996). *Substance and Shadow: Women and Addiction in the United States.* Cambridge: Harvard University Press.

Oliver-Velez, Denise, Ann H. Finlinson, Sherry Deren, Rafaela R. Robles, Michele Shedlin, Jonny Andia, and Hector Colon. (2002). "Mapping the Air-Bridge Locations: The Application of Ethnographic Mapping Techniques to a Study of HIV Risk Behavior Determinants in East Harlem, New York and Bayamon, Puerto Rico." *Human Organization,* 61(3): 262–276.

Spunt, Barry. (2003). "The Current New York City Heroin Scene." *Substance Use & Misuse,* 38(10): 1539–1549. ✦

15
'Dope Fiend' Mythology

Alfred R. Lindesmith[1]

Alfred Lindesmith reviews the public images of drug addicts. For example, common perceptions link addicts with crime, including violence and sexual aggression. Lindesmith argues that many of these images are inaccurate and he attempts to dispel these myths. He suggests, for example, that crimes by drug users tend to be property offenses such as theft. He argues that these crimes are committed largely because drugs are illegal and quite costly. Lindesmith also describes the public image of the drug dealer who entices nonusers into drug initiation. Collectively, these negative images represent what Lindesmith refers to as "dope fiend mythology" and serve to reinforce punitive drug policies.

During the last fifty or so years there has grown up in the United States a body of stereotyped misinformation about drug addicts.[2] Sensational articles and newspaper accounts have harped upon the theme of the "dope-crazed killer" or the "dope fiend rapist" until the public has learned to depend upon this sort of literature as it depends upon the output of fanciful detective mysteries. The fact that the monstrous persons depicted exist mainly as figments of the imagination does not alter the fact that this mythology plays an important role in determining the way in which drug addicts are handled. Among serious students of the problem and among others who have some actual first-hand contact with drug users, as for example prison officials, it has always been recognized that the American public is singularly misinformed on this subject. Nevertheless, the organization of the machinery of justice that deals with this problem is more directly based upon the superstitions of the man on the street than it is upon anything that has been done in the name of impartial and objective analysis. It is the purpose of this paper to indicate and examine some of these popular fallacies, to analyze their function, and to point to the obstacles that stand in the way of a more realistic appraisal of the problem.

Drug addicts are often regarded as the most dangerous and heinous criminals and are linked up with killing and rape. This delusion has been smashed so many times that it is useless to devote serious attention to it.[3] Suffice it to say that students of drug addiction have always been in unanimous agreement that the crimes of rape and murder are rarely committed by drug users. Every publication of crime statistics proves this over and over again for anyone who cares to read.[4] Likewise it has been known in this country for almost a century that the principal drugs of addiction, opium and its derivatives, inhibit rather than stimulate the sex function. The drug addict is ordinarily not interested in sex and is frequently virtually impotent. The overwhelming proportion of law violations committed by drug users is made up of violations of the narcotic laws and petty offenses against property.[5]

The drug user must, of course, violate the narcotic laws. While it is technically true that the use of drugs is not in and of itself a crime, nevertheless, in practice the addict is treated as a criminal and the laws which hedge about him make it virtually impossible for him to avoid violating the narcotic laws daily. His thieving activities are very simply explained in terms of the prices he pays for his drugs. It is frequently estimated that the average cost of a drug habit in this country is somewhere between two and five dollars a day. One must add to this the fact that the drug user must spend a large proportion of his time maintaining his contacts with the peddlers. This means that if he is to maintain a habit he must find some means of making money quickly. The three principal methods utilized by American addicts are theft, prostitution, and drug peddling.

In general, drug users are harmless and not at all dangerous, except that they steal. They rarely carry guns. A gun to most addicts would simply mean another object which could be sold or pawned in order to buy another "bindle of junk." The G men who deal with criminals like Dillinger have dangerous occupations, but the narcotic agent who deals with addicts does not. The vengeance of the drug peddler is directed mainly toward the stool pigeon or informer, not toward the agent. A few years ago a Chicago drug peddler, who was not himself an addict, shot and killed an addict named Max Dent. He did so because the latter had betrayed him to the law. In the terms of the underworld he was a "rat" and according to the code of the underworld no treatment is too harsh for such a person. It is probable that of the relatively few murders attributed to drug law violators, many are of this type. The general public has nothing of this kind to fear. Now and then someone will have his pocket picked or other property stolen by a drug user, and frequently the prostitute is a drug user, but the principal depredations of drug addicts are carried out in stores, and particularly in the large department stores of our cities, where the opportunities for shoplifting are at maximum.

The public stands in virtually no danger of violence at the hands of drug users, except in those relatively rare instances when a user of the drug happens, for example, to be at the same time a professional holdup man. However, addiction is rather infrequent among underworld characters who utilize force or the threat of it. It is more common among such types as pickpockets and shoplifters and other types that do not resort to violence. Even in those cases when an addict is also a gunman, the danger resides not in the use of the narcotics but in the presence of the gun. The use of narcotics probably inhibits more than it encourages the use of violence.

The most substantial effect of the narcotic problem upon the public is the economic one. Aside from direct theft from private citizens, the public pays for the cost of the user's expensive habit and supports the underworld illicit traffic in opiates—one of the big and profitable industries of our country. It does so when it shoulders part of the losses from thefts from merchants when these merchants succeed in passing these losses on to their patrons. The contributions of respectable citizens to prostitutes also frequently serve to give financial support to the illicit traffic. In addition, the public pays for the enforcement of the laws and the penal institutions in which addicts are incarcerated. Instead of being concerned over this invisible and unnecessary form of taxation in the interests of an underworld business, the public has permitted itself to become aroused and indignant over dangers that are often fictitious.

It is often thought that addicts are easily recognizable either by reason of peculiar irresponsible behavior or unusual external appearances or both. This notion is false. Medical men often find it impossible to detect the drug user even after a thorough physical examination. Thus Chopra, a student of addiction in India, who has had experience with thousands of drug users, asserts:

> We know from our extensive experience with opium addicts in India, that it is impossible to detect a person taking opium in small or in moderate quantities, even after a careful physical examination.[6]

E. S. Bishop, a prominent American medical authority, states that if an addict maintains good elimination "he will escape detection."[7] Even when an addict uses large quantities of drugs the matter of determining that fact is often very difficult, the only sure way being to catch him in the act of using it or to find actual traces of the drug in his body. The drug addict driving a car is not a dangerous person—not nearly as dangerous as the respectable citizen who has had a couple of cocktails or a few glasses of beer. Assuming that the addict has his usual dose, there is no evidence to indicate that his skill at driving a car would be any greater if he were not using the drug. Moreover, it is quite well known that many drug users have carried on for many years in occupations requiring skill and intelligence, as for example, the medical profession.

There are certain external indications of drug addiction, but none of these signs is reliable.[8] In fact, it is one of the most remarkable things about drug addiction that the steady use of opiate drugs produces virtually no known significant pathological symptoms. In a recent authoritative study conducted by well-known biochemists, medical men, and physiologists, the results of which were published by the American Medical Association, the following assertions are made:

> The study shows that morphine addiction is not characterized by physical deterioration or impairment of physical fitness aside from the addiction per se. There is no evidence of change in the circulatory, hepatic, renal or endocrine functions. When it is considered that these subjects had been addicted for at least five years, some of them for as long as twenty years, these negative observations are highly significant.[9]

The same authors state:

> In a few recognized cases of opium addiction that have come to autopsy, whether the drug was being taken at the time of death or not, the pathologic changes found have been insignificant.[10]

Concerning the emaciated appearance of some addicts that has sometimes been assumed to be characteristic of drug users, these authorities state:

> We believe that the existence of considerable emaciation in certain cases is caused by the unhygienic and impoverished life of the addict rather than by the direct effects of the drug.[11]

Other students have reached similar conclusions. Thus Terry and Pellens, after an exhaustive and critical examination of an extensive literature, assert:

> Only in cases where large doses of the drug are being consumed can casual observation or even a fairly careful examination determine the existence of the condition ... It has been reported that for many years husbands and wives, to say nothing of other members of the family, have lived in complete ignorance of the existence of this condition in one or the other and that quite possibly the average physician, unaccustomed to dealing with

the condition, might have difficulty in determining its existence.[12]

In view of the above results of research, the belief that a drug addict automatically becomes a moral degenerate, liar, thief, etc., because of the direct influence of the drug, is simply nonsense quite on a par with a belief in witchcraft. It is true that many American addicts belong to underworld or semi-underworld groups and that their behavior, from the viewpoint of a respectable citizen, is often despicable and reprehensible, but it is also true that there are many drug addicts, even in the United States, whose behavior does not fall in these categories and who maintain their self-respect and social status. There is no necessary or invariable connection between the taking of any kind of drug and moral degeneration. This fact is brought out by the consideration of the way in which wealthy addicts with political influence manage to protect themselves from arrest and detection and from a loss of social status. As Dr. Lichtenstein states:

> To call addiction a disease when applied to the wealthy, and a vice when referring to the underworld addict is nothing short of criminal, and such distinction serves but to becloud the situation and to interfere with the ultimate solution of the problem. At present a poor addict is an underworld addict .... We as physicians have no right to refuse treatment to the poor addict. Similarly, hospitals have no right to refuse such people treatment, and we, the general public, are entirely to blame if by forcing the addict to take treatment in a penal institution, we make of him a criminal,—and that is exactly what we are doing.[13]

In other words, it is not the effect of the drug that produces the alleged deterioration of character in the addict, but rather the social situations into which he is forced by the law and by the public's conception of addiction which does the damage. Well-to-do addicts who are in a position to protect themselves against these influences often live useful and productive lives.

It is beyond question that most of the addicts who are arrested and imprisoned in the United States belong to the poor and helpless class known as the "underworld group." Thus W. L. Treadway reports that of a total of 2,407 narcotic law violators studied, a little more than one-third or 925 were regularly employed. Of the same total only about one-seventh, or 352, were reported to have been in "comfortable" economic circumstances before arrest.[14] It is sometimes assumed that this situation is inevitable and natural, but statistical data from other countries reveal that such is not the case. In Formosa, for example, in 1905 more than 90 percent of the addicts are reported as having regular occupations and about 70 percent were reported as married and living with their families.[15] R. N. Chopra, speaking of addicts in India, states:

> Our cases comprised of a fairly large number of good citizens, agriculturists who were working like normal individuals without any appreciable change in their social behavior.[16]

This author also notes a tendency for members of the underworld to seek regular employment and to leave the underworld when they become addicts. It should be remembered that addicts in India are not regarded or treated as criminals. Chopra has the following general comment to make on Indian opium users:

> Opium addicts in this country are not liars or moral wrecks as has been ascribed by some authors elsewhere. Some of our addicts were upright, straight forward and self-respecting individuals. We have observed that moderate consumers of the drug and a majority of those taking even larger doses are generally inoffensive to society . . . . The opium addicts in India are not much objected to by the people at large, but persons taking large doses of the drug, and those who smoke opium, are shunned by respectable citizens lest their children and youths should acquire the habit by force of example. The harm done by an opium addict is mainly confined to himself and not to society.[17]

Chopra found that about two-thirds of Indian addicts showed no appreciable changes in their general behavior as a consequence of the habit, and described the changes in the other one-third of the cases as being mainly of very minor character.[18]

If our addicts appear to be moral degenerates and thieves, it is we who have made them that by the methods we have chosen to apply to their problem. By making it impossible for drug users to obtain low cost legitimate drugs, we have created a huge illicit traffic and impoverished the addict. The price of illicit drugs is ordinarily estimated at anywhere from ten to twenty times the cost of legitimate drugs. It is in the desperate attempt of the drug user to meet these enormous prices that he resorts to theft and prostitution. If we were to set about deliberately to produce thieves and prostitutes we could scarcely improve on this situation.

It may be argued that addicts are thieves and prostitutes before becoming addicts, and no doubt that is sometimes true. A number of investigations indicate, however, that more than half of our addicts have no criminal records of any kind prior to addiction.[19]

An English writer correctly appraised our situation when he wrote:

> In the United States of America a drug habitué is regarded as a malefactor, even though the habit has been acquired through the medicinal use of the drug, as in the case, e.g., of American soldiers who were gassed or otherwise maimed in the Great War. The Harrison Narcotic Law was passed in 1914 by the Federal Government of the United States with general popular approval. It placed severe restrictions upon the sale of narcotics and upon the medical profession, and necessitated the appointment of a whole army of officials. In consequence of this stringent law a vast clandestine commerce in narcotics has grown up in that country. The small bulk of these drugs renders the evasion of the law comparatively easy, and the country is overrun by an army of peddlers who extort exorbitant prices from their hapless victims. It appears that not only has the Harrison Law failed to diminish the number of drug takers—some contend, indeed, that it has increased their numbers—but, far from bettering the lot of the opiate addict, it has actually worsened it; for without curtailing the supply of the drug it has sent up the price tenfold, and this has

had the effect of impoverishing the poorer class of addicts and reducing them to a condition of such abject misery as to render them incapable of gaining an honest livelihood.[20]

The whole blame for addiction is sometimes placed upon the shoulders of the well-known "bogey man," the dope peddler, who is blamed for spreading the habit for the alleged purpose of extending his market.[21] In this connection it should be remembered that the peddler depends upon the enormous prices that he is able to obtain. The situation that makes these prices possible is created directly by our present laws. Prospects of profits of more than a thousand percent inevitably attract business talent in a country like ours. Peddlers and smugglers in such a situation are quite inevitable—as inevitable as bootleggers in the prohibition era. The drug peddler does not create this situation, he only takes advantage of the opportunities that are presented.[22]

The peddler of drugs, contrary to a widespread belief, does not ordinarily attempt to induce non-users to try the drug. Isolated instances of this may occur, but the general rule is quite the opposite. The reasons for this are obvious once they are considered, and it is not because the peddler is virtuous and innocent—he is far from that. He does not try to seduce non-users because it does not pay and because it is too dangerous. The ordinary peddler who makes the actual contacts with consumers leads a very precarious existence outside of prison, living in constant fear of the law. He is arrested and evidence against him is obtained through the use of drug-using stool pigeons posing as bona fide customers.[23] Addict informers must be used for this purpose because peddlers have long since learned the elementary fact that if they did no business with non-addicts it would be impossible for the narcotic agent to obtain direct evidence unaided. If peddlers attempted to extend their markets to non-users, they would facilitate their own arrest. The sentences imposed upon them in such circumstances would also certainly be more severe than they otherwise are.

Inducing non-addicts to try the drug is not profitable because the non-user is not initially interested in paying the high prices. Peddlers cannot give away quantities of the drug sufficient to establish addiction and stay in the business. The drug user is in the business for profit and usually to maintain his own habit. The product he handles often brings as much as $200 an ounce—several times its weight in gold. He can no more afford to give it away than a jewler can afford to give away diamonds. Moreover, most of the peddlers who are arrested and sent to prison are poor. According to W. L. Treadway, of a group of 2,407, 2,055 were not in comfortable economic circumstances prior to arrest.[24] They were, in other words, what is known as "boots" or "boot and shoe dope fiends." Persons of this type living from hand to mouth and spending a large proportion of their time in penal institutions are in no position to give anything away or to take any unnecessary risks.

The large-scale smuggler and peddler likewise cannot promote the wider use of drugs because he must keep the nature of his business secret. He extends his market by "muscling in" on someone else's business and lets the spread of the habit take care of itself, knowing that with our laws as they are and with human beings what they are, there will always be those who will permit their curiosity to overcome their judgment and keep the market lively.[25]

Another current myth is that all addicts, in accordance with the proverb that "misery loves company," have a positive mania for making new addicts. This is nothing but gratuitous slander of an unfortunate and helpless group. This particular myth is current in the United States, but it is curiously absent in other countries of the world. Drug addicts have been observed and studied for at least three-quarters of a century in this country and in Europe, but the idea that each addict makes it his purpose to obtain new recruits is emphasized in only one country—the United States. In England, France, Germany, Russia, India, etc., it has not been noticed.[26] Throughout the nineteenth century it was not noticed in the United States either.[27] Curiously enough, this myth appears to have only local circulation and a very recent origin.

It is true that people become addicts through association with persons who are already addicted, but that does not mean that the user deliberately makes an addict of the non-user. It is through contacts with the user of the drug that the non-addict has his curiosity aroused to the point where he wants to experiment with the drug. Frequently, probably usually, the beginner is warned solemnly against the dangers involved, but he goes ahead in spite of these warnings, believing in his own powers of resistance. The inconsistency of the attempt to blame the addict for making new addicts is indicated by the fact that, once addicted, no one is inclined to excuse the addict on the grounds that he was innocently lured into the habit by another user. In fact, quite a different position is taken. Not only is the user blamed for spreading the habit, but the new addict is immediately declared to be fully responsible for his own addiction and is punished accordingly.

The assumption that all addicts try to spread the habit is given as a justification for imprisoning them under the erroneous assumption that the habit cannot be spread in prison. However, if this is a reason for incarcerating the drug user, he should be tried in court for that offense. Evidence should be presented to prove that he has in fact attempted to induce a non-addict to become an addict. The victims of venereal disease also sometimes deliberately infect others, but that is not regarded as an excuse for sending all the victims of this disease to prison.

Drug addicts in the United States are punished for being addicts. The establishment of narcotic farms has been a gesture in another direction, but is essentially futile as long as the general social and legal situation of the drug user remains what it is. Regardless of attempts to pretend otherwise, the narcotic farms are regarded as prisons by the addicts. They are places where one "does time." The addict who earnestly wishes to break his habit has virtually no other course open to him except to go to prison—unless, of course, he has money. Sending the addict to prison serves no useful purpose. In fact, the stigma of the prison sentence with its resul-

tant social disgrace and loss of employment and position and the extensive acquaintanceships with drug users and peddlers established in prison, merely aggravates the plight of the addict when he is released and makes it harder for him to break away from his habit.[28]

A. M. Turano, in an excellent article on addicts entitled "Punishment for Disease," summarized the official attitude toward treating addicts as follows:

Thus it appears, on the whole, that in begrudgingly offering medical care, the law stands at the bedside of the addict as a fumbling nurse with healing balm in one hand and a primitive tomahawk in the other, unable to decide whether to attack the disease or punish its owner for having acquired it.[29]

As August Vollmer says, "Drug addiction . . . is not a police problem; it never has been, and never can be solved by policemen."[30]

Why then does the situation continue as it is? It is at this point that the mythology surrounding drug addiction plays its part. An ideology, based on the distortion and misrepresentation of fact, has been given a veneer of plausibility, which has made it attractive as well as exciting to the man on the street. This ideology serves to justify the severe treatment generally accorded the drug user, and is utilized by vested interests to frighten the public into appropriating more and more funds to combat the great "dope menace." Solemn discussions are carried on about lengthening the addict's already long sentence and as to whether or not he is a good parole risk. The basic question as to why he should be sent to prison at all is scarcely mentioned. Eventually, it is to be hoped that we shall come to see, as most of the civilized countries of the world have seen, that the punishment and imprisonment of addicts is as cruel and pointless as similar treatment for persons infected with syphilis would be.

However, if we are to continue to punish the drug user for his misfortune, turning him over to the tender mercies of policemen for "treatment," the mythology we have described will be useful. We can continue to offer him the haven of a penitentiary instead of a hospital and justify ourselves by pointing out that, after all, he deserves nothing better. Besides being a vicious and degenerate person seeking to infect others, he is naturally inclined toward theft, prostitution, and any crime whatever. If we throw him into prison, he will only be able to spread the habit to other prisoners. The final ironic touch is the argument that the incarceration of addicts deprives peddlers of their market. On this basis all honest persons should be thrown into prison so that pickpockets would have only each other to steal from.

The "dope fiend" mythology serves, in short, as a rationalization of the status quo. It is a body of superstition, half-truths, and misinformation that bolsters an indefensible repressive law, the victims of which are in no position to protest. The treatment of addicts in the United States today is on no higher plane than the persecution of witches of other ages, and like the latter it is to be hoped that it will soon become merely another dark chapter of history.

Notes

1. Review Editor of the [*"Journal of Criminal Law and Criminology"*]. Professor of Sociology at the State University, Bloomington, Indiana.

2. This article will be concerned only with the users of opiate drugs. Marijuana and cocaine users represent an entirely different problem. One of the reasons for confusion in this field is that the users of totally different types of drugs are not distinguished. The bad reputation of the opiate user is earned for him in part by the cocaine and marijuana users.

3. See, e.g., Dr. Lawrence Kolb. "Drug Addiction in Relation to Crime." *Mental Hygiene* IX (1925), p. 74ff. Also, Terry and Pellens, *The Opium Problem*, 1928.

4. See page 12 of the annual report on the *Traffic in Opium and Other Dangerous Drugs for the Year Ended December 31, 1936*, by the Bureau of Narcotics. Also see Supplement No. 143 to the *Public Health Reports*, "A Statistical Analysis of the Clinical Records of Hospitalized Drug Addicts," by Michael J. Pescor.

5. Thus the annual report of the Bureau of Narcotics for 1936 summarizes approximately 13,000 felonies committed by 4,975 drug users. Of this total, about one-sixth of one per

cent, or 23 cases, are classified as "murder or manslaughter" and rape is not even listed. In contrast, 8,427 of the felonies were classified as "narcotic convictions," 1,898 as "miscellaneous," 1,313 "grand larceny," 609 "burglary," 278 "felonious assault," 278 "highway robbery," 100 "concealed weapons," and 87 "forgery."

6. *The Indian Journal of Medical Research* XX, p. 561.

7. *The Narcotic Drug Problem*, Macmillan, 1921, p. 47.

8. I refer to the external appearance of the skin and to the reactions of the eye.

9. *Opium Addiction*, 1929, p. 115.

10. *Ibid.*, p. 19.

11. *Ibid.*, p. 20.

12. *Op. cit.*, p. 2. On page 514 these authors state: "In spite of frequently repeated statements that the use of opium and its derivatives causes mental and ethical degeneration in all cases, we are inclined to believe that this alleged effect has not been established."

13. Appendix 12 of *Documentation of Fifth Annual Conference of Committees of the World Narcotic Defence Association and International Narcotic Education Association*, held in New York in 1932.

14. "Some Epidemiological Features of Drug Addiction," *British Journal of Inebriety* XXVIII (1930), pp. 50–54.

15. A. Hischman, (1912). *Die Opiumfrage.* p. 46.

16. "The Opium Habit in India," *Indian Journal of Medical Research* XV (1927).

17. *Ibid*. See also the other articles by this author in the same journal and also in *The Indian Medical Gazette*.

18. See also A. H. Lindesmith, "A Sociological Theory of Drug Addiction," *American Journal of Sociology* XLIII (1938), pp. 593–609, for material on the "normality" of the drug user.

19. Thus Michael J. Pescor (*op. cit.*) makes this statement on the basis of the results of the study of 1,036 cases, "If the addict is basically a criminal, it is likely that he would have committed anti-social acts prior to his addiction; yet three-fourths of the patients had no delinquency record prior to addiction." (p. 8). Substantially the same result is reported by Bingham Dai, *Opium Addiction in Chicago*, Shanghai, The Commercial Press, 1937.

20. Harry Campbell, "The Pathology and Treatment of Morphia Addiction," *British Journal of Inebriety* XX (1923), 147–148.

21. Even Terry and Pellens are guilty of repeating this sort of thing of peddlers (*op. cit.*, p. 87). They also say that peddlers give away enough of the drug to addict a person and then charge enough to make up for their losses. No evidence has been produced to show that this sort of thing is actually done.

22. The implication is clear. The way to eliminate the peddler is to eliminate his profit.

23. This use of addicted informers is one of the unfortunate and unpublicized aspects of the enforcement of narcotic laws. The informer uses some of the money that he is paid by the government to buy illicit drugs from peddlers whom he has not betrayed to the law. It is stated that in the past local Narcotic Bureaus actually doled out the drug themselves to the informers working for them. The practice of using stool pigeons has the effect of placing some of the responsibility for the way in which the law is enforced upon one of the most despised underworld types.

24. *Locus cited*. This indicates the significant fact that the profits of the drug traffic do not end up in the pockets of the people who are sent to prison for peddling drugs. It may safely be asserted that the persons who profit from the drug traffic are not addicts and that they do not spend much time in prison.

25. It would be positively silly to suppose that the late Rothstein of New York, who is reputed to have made a great deal of his fortune through handling drugs, would have taken the risk of urging the habit upon someone so as to increase his profit by a few dollars.

26. The literature offers instances in which addicts have deliberately imposed the habit upon someone, but they are rare, and as far as I know no competent student of addiction in European countries has ever maintained that all, or most or even many, addicts sought to do this.

27. See Calkins, *Opium and the Opium Appetite*. Philadelphia, 1871. This is one of the most informative books of the nineteenth century on this subject. Literally hundreds of cases are cited and many different shades of opinion are discussed, but the idea under consideration had obviously not occurred to anyone at that time.

28. Thus there is a population of about 1,600 at the Annex of the Fort Leavenworth Penitentiary. Assuming that there are about 100 new cases admitted each month, an inmate has the opportunity of meeting 2,800 drug peddlers and addicts in the course of a year. When released, he may meet former prison comrades in almost any city in the United States and each such meeting represents a temptation to resume the use of the drug. This situation also facilitates the peddling of drugs and entry into other criminal occupations.

29. *The American Mercury* XXXVI, December, 1935.

30. *The Police and Modern Society*, Berkeley. 1936, p. 118. See also Harry Elmer Barnes, *Society in Transition*, 1939, on this problem.

For Discussion

What are the images of the twenty-first century "dope fiend"? Have these images changed since Lindesmith's article was first published in 1940–1941?

Reprinted from: Alfred R. Lindesmith, "'Dope Fiend' Mythology" in *Journal of Criminal Law and Criminology* 33, pp. 199–208. Copyright © 1940–1941 by Alred R. Lindesmith and *Journal of Criminal Law and Criminology*. Reprinted by permission. ✦

16

OxyContin®

Miracle Medicine or Problem Drug?

James A. Inciardi
Jennifer L. Goode

OxyContin, a powerful prescription painkiller, has generated considerable attention since its introduction to the market in 1996. In this next essay, the authors dissect whether an "epidemic" of OxyContin abuse really exists, or if the media have sensationalized recreational use among a certain segment of the population.

They examine the diversion of OxyContin to the black market for nonprescribed reasons and carefully scrutinize government data to try to ascertain the extent of its misuse. Initial reports of abuse can be traced back to Maine, and the trend subsequently spread down the East Coast into parts of Appalachia. The authors consider the popularity of OxyContin in these areas in the context of the region's cultural and socioeconomic features. Abuse has allegedly infiltrated other parts of the country as well, and many have blamed an onslaught of media coverage for contributing to a national "epidemic." The authors examine the media's coverage of the drug in detail, both from national and international outlets, and reveal striking similarities to media coverage of the "crack epidemic" of the 1980s. While the abuse of OxyContin does indeed exist, it appears to be just the latest drug trend that the media have blown out of proportion.

If anything has been learned about the drug problem in the United States, it is that patterns of drug abuse are continually shifting and changing. Fads and fashions in the drugs of abuse seem to come and go; drugs of choice emerge and then disappear from the American drug scene; and still others are reconstituted, repackaged, recycled, and become permanent parts of the drug-taking and drug-seeking landscape. And as new drugs become visible, there are the concomitant media and political feeding frenzies, followed by calls for a strengthening of the "war on drugs." It happened with heroin in the 1950s, with marijuana and LSD in the 1960s, with Quaalude® and PCP in the 1970s, and with methamphetamine, "ice," ecstasy, crack and other forms of cocaine in the 1980s and 1990s (Jenkins 1999; Inciardi 2002a). The most recent entry to the drug scene to receive this focused attention is OxyContin®, a narcotic painkiller several times more potent than morphine.

Since OxyContin was first introduced to the market in early 1996, it has been hailed as a breakthrough in pain management. The medication is unique in that its time-release formula allows patients to enjoy continuous, long-term relief from moderate to severe pain. For many patients who had suffered for years from chronic pain, it gave them relief from suffering. But during the past few years OxyContin has received a substantial amount of negative attention—not for its medicinal effects, but for its addiction liability and abuse potential. Within this context, this essay examines the brief but eventful history of OxyContin, as well as available data on its use and misuse, media coverage, and the public health consequences that such attention has generated.

OxyContin and Oxycodone

The active ingredient in OxyContin is "oxycodone," a drug that has been used for the treatment of pain for almost 100 years. Oxycodone is a semi-synthetic narcotic analgesic most often prescribed for moderate to severe pain, chronic pain syndromes, and terminal cancers. When used correctly under a physician's supervision, oxycodone can be highly effective in the management of pain, and there are scores of oxycodone products on the market—in various strengths and forms. Popular brands include Percocet® and Percodan,® Roxicet® and Roxicodone,® and Endocet,® OxyIR,® and Tylox® to name but a few. However, no oxycodone product has generated as much attention as OxyContin.

Produced by the Stamford, Connecticut-based pharmaceutical company, Purdue Pharma L.P., OxyContin is unique because unlike other oxycodone products that typically contain aspirin or acetaminophen to increase or lengthen their potency, OxyContin is a single entity product that can provide up to 12 hours of continuous pain relief. Tablets are available in 10, 20, 40, and 80-milligram doses. The company also introduced a 160-milligram dose in July 2000 for its opioid tolerant patients, only to later withdraw it from the market amidst controversy over its alleged abuse (DEA 2002a).

When the clinical trials for OxyContin were reviewed by the Food and Drug Administration (FDA), the drug was demonstrated to be an effective analgesic in individuals with chronic, moderate to severe pain. Yet it was also judged by the FDA to carry a substantial risk of abuse because of its properties as a narcotic. As a result, OxyContin was approved by the FDA but placed in Schedule II of the Controlled Substances Act (CSA), which is the tightest level of control that can be placed on an approved drug for medical purposes. The placement of OxyContin in Schedule II warned physicians and patients that the drug carried a high potential for abuse and that it needed to be carefully managed, particularly among those at risk for substance abuse. In addition, in the *Physicians Desk Reference* and on the drug's package insert, OxyContin carries a boxed warning (more commonly known as the infamous "black box"), which boldly indicates:

WARNING:
OxyContin is an opioid agonist and a Schedule II controlled substance with an abuse liability similar to morphine.

Oxycodone can be abused in a manner similar to other opioid agonists, legal or illicit. This should be considered when prescribing or dispensing OxyContin in situations where the physicians or pharmacist is concerned about an increased risk of misuse, abuse, or diversion.

OxyContin Tablets are a controlled-release oral formulation of oxycodone hydrochloride indicated for the management of moderate to severe pain when a continuous, around-the-clock analgesic is needed for an extended period of time.

OxyContin 80 mg and 160 mg Tablets ARE FOR USE IN OPIOID-TOLERANT PATIENTS ONLY. These tablet strengths may cause fatal respiratory depression when administered to patients not previously exposed to opioids.

OxyContin TABLETS ARE TO BE SWALLOWED WHOLE AND ARE NOT TO BE BROKEN, CHEWED, OR CRUSHED. TAKING BROKEN, CHEWED, OR CRUSHED OxyContin TABLETS LEADS TO RAPID RELEASE AND ABSORPTION OF A POTENTIALLY FATAL DOSE OF OXYCODONE.

Importantly, this "black box," voluntarily inserted in the packaging information by Purdue Pharma in 2001, alerts potential users with the notice that taking broken, chewed, or crushed leads to rapid release and absorption of a potentially fatal dose of the drug. But even before the insertion of the "black box," drug abusers had figured out how to compromise OxyContin's controlled release formula and set off on a powerful high by injecting or snorting dissolved tablets or by crushing and ingesting them.

Despite the numerous controls and warnings required by the FDA, OxyContin has been a major economic success for Purdue Pharma, accounting for some 80% of the company's total business (Greenwald 2003). Prescriptions have risen steadily since the drug's introduction, as the number of prescriptions dispensed increased 20-fold from 1996 through 2000 (Nagel & Good 2001). More than 7.2 million prescriptions were dispensed in 2001 and retail sales totaled more than $1.45 billion, representing a 41% increase in sales between 2000 and 2001 alone. Retail sales increased again in 2002, topping $1.59 billion. In terms of dollar amount, OxyContin now ranks the highest in retail sales of all brand-name controlled substances (DEA 2002a). Federal regulators, however, are put off by these numbers, and focus on the *diversion* of OxyContin to illegal markets, and reports of OxyContin abuse and overdose deaths.

Diversion of OxyContin

Prescription drug diversion involves the unlawful movement of regulated pharmaceuticals from legal sources to the illegal marketplace, and OxyContin's attractiveness to drug abusers has resulted in its diversion in a number of ways. The major mechanisms include the illegal sale of prescriptions by physicians and pharmacists; "doctor shopping" by individuals who visit numerous physicians to obtain multiple prescriptions; the theft, forgery, or alteration of prescriptions by patients; robberies and thefts from pharmacies and pharmaceutical warehouses; and thefts of samples from physicians' offices as well as thefts of institutional drug supplies by health care workers. In all likelihood, OxyContin has been diverted through all of these routes.

Diversion has also occurred by means of fraud, particularly through the abuse of medical insurance programs, a phenomenon observed and investigated most often in a number of rural communities. Medicaid fraud, for example, presents an inexpensive mechanism for abusing drugs and oftentimes an easy route to a lucrative enterprise. For example, a Medicaid patient may pay only $3 for a bottle of a hundred 80-milligram OxyContin tablets. In areas where employment and money are scarce resources, the temptation to sell some of the pills for the going "street price" of $1 per milligram provides an opportunity to earn money. In this example, the $3 bottle from the pharmacy can net the patient up to $8,000 on the illegal market (Moore 2000). If the patient needs more pills before a legitimate refill is possible, he or she may simply "doctor shop" a number of physicians for additional prescriptions and pay cash for the new supplies to avoid having the pharmacist check with the Medicaid people.

Going further, just one corrupt physician, pharmacist, health care worker, or other employee in the healthcare field can have a significant impact on the availability of the product as well. For example, before he was arrested in 2002, a Pennsylvania pharmacist had illegally sold hundreds of thousands of painkillers, including OxyContin, over a three-year period. He made $900,000 on his transactions (only to lose it all in the stock market). Although he operated an independent neighborhood pharmacy, he was reportedly the state's third-largest purchaser of OxyContin (Slobodzian 2002). Similarly, a number of physicians in Eastern Kentucky were arrested in 2003 for a variety of diversion schemes. One saw as many as 150 patients each day, writing narcotic prescriptions for them after a visit of less than three minutes. Another physician traded painkillers for sex with female patients who he had addicted to narcotics. A third opened an office in a shopping mall where he generated prescriptions—one after another—almost as quickly as he could write them (Alford 2003).

As to how much diversion of OxyContin actually occurs is impossible to calculate, because there is not a single national reporting system on pharmaceutical diversion. Furthermore, of the more than 23,000 federal, state, and municipal law enforcement agencies in the United States, well under 10% have a specific focus on prescription drug diversion (Inciardi & Cicero 2002). Nevertheless, some data are available which at least suggest the extent of OxyContin diversion, relative to other drugs of abuse, including narcotic painkillers. In a 2001 survey of 34 police agencies with pharmaceutical diversion units, for example, a total of 5,802 cases of diversion (of any drug) were reported during the calendar year (Inciardi 2002b). The reporting agencies were asked to indicate which drugs were most commonly diverted, and in how many cases each was investigated. The most commonly diverted pharmaceutical drug was hydrocodone (Vicodin,® Lortab,® and similar narcotic analgesics), noted in 31% of the total cases. This was followed by oxycodone in 12% of the cases, and alprazolam (Xanax®) in 6% of the cases. Of the 701 cases involving an oxycodone product, 416 were OxyContin. Overall, OxyContin was represented in only 7% of the drug diversions, a rather small proportion given the attention the drug has received. In addition, the data documented that the diversion of OxyContin was part of a much broader pattern of prescription drug diversion. That is, in the great majority of cases in which OxyContin had been diverted, a wide spectrum of other drugs were being diverted at the same time.

OxyContin Abuse: Do the Figures Add Up?

Although there are several sources of national data on drug abuse that have been operating for decades, the collection of specific data on OxyContin abuse is quite recent. In the Monitoring the Future Survey, a government-sponsored study of drug abuse among high school students and young adults that has been conducted annually since 1975, the collection of information on OxyContin began only in 2002—and this was initiated at the request of Purdue Pharma. The 2002 survey found that 4% of 12th graders, 3% of 10th graders, and 1.3% of 8th graders had used OxyContin at least once during the past year. Interestingly, the use of Vicodin (a brand of hydrocodone) in the past year was at least double that of OxyContin—9.6% for 12th graders, 6.9% for 10th graders, and 2.5% for 8th graders (Johnston, O'Malley & Bachman 2003). In the 2001 National Household Survey on Drug Abuse, another government survey conducted annually, only "lifetime use" (at least once in a person's lifetime "to get high") data were collected for OxyContin. For persons ages 12 and over, less than one half of one percent reported ever using OxyContin to get high (SAMHSA 2002).

Because the Monitoring the Future and the National Household surveys are conducted with a high degree of scientific rigor, the estimates they generate for society's more "stable," at-home and/or in-school populations have a high degree of reliability. These should be contrasted with data from the Drug Abuse Warning Network, which tend to be somewhat problematic. More commonly known as DAWN, this large-scale information collection effort was designed to monitor changing patterns of drug abuse in the United States, and to serve as an early warning system for police, prevention, and treatment agencies. Hundreds of hospital emergency rooms and county medical examiners in major metropolitan areas across the United States report regularly to the DAWN system. However, because of the focus on metropolitan areas, the limitation to drug overdoses and other adverse reactions that result in a trip to the emergency room or county morgue, and the lack of information on specific brands of prescription drugs, DAWN data must be examined with considerable caution. Nevertheless, major pronouncements about drug abuse in the United States are often based solely on DAWN.

With regard to OxyContin, DAWN data indicate that the incidence of emergency room visits related to narcotic analgesic abuse has been on the rise since the mid-1990s, more than doubling between 1994 and 2001. The category with the largest increase during this period was oxycodone, at 352%, and most of the increases in narcotic analgesic mentions occurred toward the end of the decade, after OxyContin had been released to the market. Oxycodone mentions surged 186% from 1999 to 2000 and again by 70% from 2000 to 2001 (Crane 2003). But since DAWN does not publish specific brand names of drugs, it is impossible to ascertain the exact number of episodes specifically related to OxyContin at any given time.

Going further, since many OxyContin overdoses likely occur outside the DAWN reporting system—in rural areas such as Maine, West Virginia, and Kentucky—DAWN data are of no use for estimating the extent of the problem. To fill this gap, the Drug Enforcement Administration (DEA) started actively collecting and analyzing data from medical examiners in an attempt to establish the extent of the "OxyContin problem." Medical examiner reports from 2000–2001 from 32 states reported that 949 deaths were associated with oxycodone, of which almost half (49%) were "likely" related to OxyContin (DEA 2002b). However, careful scrutiny of the data paints a more cautious picture: because there are a multitude of oxycodone products on the market, it is impossible to determine the specific brand of drug found in a cadaver. Nevertheless, out of the 949 deaths, DEA reported that 146 were "OxyContin verified," while another 318 were "OxyContin likely." To make things even more complicated, the majority of the toxicological analyses reported "poly" or "multiple-drug use," suggesting that the death may have been the result of an overdose induced by a combination of substances, not just oxycodone by itself (DEA 2002b). When taking all of these factors into consideration, it is very difficult to establish a direct link between OxyContin and cause of death.

A recent study published in the *Journal of Analytical Toxicology* attempted to more scientifically unravel the questions about OxyContin-related deaths. Based on data from over 1,000 deaths reported by medical examiners and coroner's offices from 23 states from August 27, 1999 through January 17, 2002, the study results were an interesting contrast to those fostered by DEA. The conclusion was that OxyContin alone was found in only 1.3% of the cases examined. Of the 1,014 cases, 90.6% of the deaths involved drug abuse; the remainder were due to other causes. Of the drug abuse deaths, 96.7% were found to have multiple drugs present (Goldberger 2003). DEA officials counter that poly-drug use is often part of patients' overall treatment regimen, such as the co-administration of anti-depressants. They emphasize that it should not be surprising to find that many of the deaths were associated with multiple drugs but insist that this should not override the significance of OxyContin's role in the patient's death (DEA 2002b).

The DEA Office of Diversion Control has attempted to bolster its case against OxyContin by stressing that property and other crimes related to the abuse of the drug increased by as much as 75% in some parts of the United States (DEA 2001a), with new OxyContin-related arrests increasing from 67 in 2000 to 277 in 2001 (DEA 2002a). Although no one is questioning the validity of these arrest figures, there is a problem with this kind of data. The 19th century French sociologist Emile Durkheim once commented that a community has as much crime as it has people to count it (Durkheim

1933). In other words, the DEA arrest data, to a very great extent, follows a "Field of Dreams" scenario—"if you look for it, you will find it." If DEA had placed the same focus on the trafficking and illegal distribution of Xanax or some other highly abusable prescription drug as it had on OxyContin, increasing numbers of arrests would have occurred as well.

An Emerging National Epidemic?

OxyContin abuse first surfaced in rural Maine during the late 1990s, soon after spreading down the east coast and Ohio Valley, and then into rural Appalachia. Communities in western Virginia, eastern Kentucky, West Virginia, and southern Ohio were especially hard hit, and a number of factors characteristic of these areas seem to correlate with their apparent high rates of abuse. In northern Maine and rural Appalachia, for example, there are aspects of the culture that are markedly different from those in other parts of the country. Many of the communities are quite small and isolated, often situated in the mountains and "hollers" (small crevice-like mountain dens and valleys) a considerable distance from major towns and highways. As a result, many of the usual street drugs are simply not available. Instead, locals make due with resources already on hand, like prescription drugs. In addition, isolation impacts heavily on options for amenities and entertainment—a major contrast to the distractions of metropolitan areas. Many substance abuse treatment clients in these rural areas have told their counselors that they started using drugs because of boredom. Many start abusing drugs quite young, as well. According to one treatment counselor in Maine, the average age of drug experimentation and abuse in that state is nine. Young people begin with marijuana and alcohol, progressing on to other drugs as they move into their teenage years (Clancy 2000).

Many adults in these rural areas tend to suffer from chronic illnesses and pain syndromes, born out of hard lives of manual labor in perilous professions—coal mining, logging, fishing, and other blue-collar industries which often result in serious and debilitating injuries. As a result, a disproportionately high segment of the population lives on strong painkillers. The use of pain pills evolves into a kind of coping mechanism, and the practice of self-medication becomes a way for life for many. As such, the use of narcotic analgesics has become normalized and integrated into the local culture (DOJ 2002a).

No one understands this cycle better than the people who live in the region and who are most affected by the problem. As the director of Kentucky's Division of Substance Abuse summarized, there is "a cultural history of solving problems through medication" (Gowda 2003). A Kentucky prosecutor who focuses on drug crimes concurred: "A lot of places, you got a headache, you'll tough it out," he says. "Down here," he continues, "it's like, 'Well, my grandfather's got some drugs. I'll take that and it'll go away.' And it just escalates" (Breed 2001).

Data suggest that the abuse of OxyContin may be escalating in certain areas. For example, the number of patients in Kentucky seeking treatment for oxycodone addiction increased 163% from 1998 to 2000 (DOJ 2002a). While OxyContin is not necessarily always the cause, officials there say that it is one of the most widely abused oxycodone products. Crime statistics seem to support the claim, as Kentucky is one of the leading states for OxyContin-related crimes. Between January 2000 and June 2001 alone, 69 of the state's 1,000 pharmacies reported OxyContin-related break-ins (DOJ 2002a).

Drug treatment admissions from several states may also offer evidence to support a growing trend in OxyContin abuse. Programs in Pennsylvania, Kentucky, and Virginia have reported that 50% to 90% of newly admitted patients identified OxyContin as their drug of choice (Nagel & Good 2001). Figures obtained by DEA from the American Methadone Treatment Association also suggest an increase in the number of patients admitted for OxyContin abuse (DEA 2002a). Moreover, according to the Maine Office of Substance Abuse, the number of narcotics-related (excluding heroin) treatment admissions increased from 73 in 1995 to 762 in 2001 (DOJ 2002b). While OxyContin cannot take all of the blame, officials say it is nonetheless a major contributor and also point out that opiate-based prescription drugs in general outpaced the percentage increases for all other types of drugs in the state. Treatment admissions for these drugs increased 78% from 1998 to 1999 (199 to 355) and another 47% from 1999 through September 2000 (355 to 521), which suggest a possible increase in OxyContin use (DOJ 2002b).

A separate study conducted by Maine's Substance Abuse Services Commission and the Maine Office of Substance Abuse found that treatment admissions for narcotic abuse increased 500% since 1995, and that opiate-related arrests comprised more than 40% of the Maine Drug Enforcement Agency's caseload. The study, commissioned because of the publicity the state received for being one of the first to identify OxyContin abuse, analyzed several aspects of prescription opiate abuse. The study linked the use of narcotics with increased rates of crime, emergency medical treatment, and outbreaks of hepatitis C. While OxyContin was not the only opiate abused in the state at the time, it constituted the centerpiece of the study results published in the *Alcoholism & Drug Abuse Weekly* (Maine Analysis 2002).

Based on these and similar reports in a few other states, it has been suggested in numerous media outlets that the abuse of OxyContin is on the rise, and that its popularity is rapidly spreading beyond the rural East Coast to other parts of the United States. At the same time, however, there is also concern that the media has played an integral role in boosting the drug's popularity.

The Media Frenzy

Media outlets in Maine began reporting on OxyContin abuse in early 2000. The *Bangor Daily News*, for example, ran several features which included information not only about the properties of the drug, but also about: (1) how to compromise its time-release mechanism, (2) the tactics of diversion that people were using to obtain the drug (including Medicaid fraud), and (3) the concerns of the medical profession about the potential for abusing the drug. In addition, numerous examples of alleged OxyContin-related crimes were described in detail.

A smattering of news articles followed in other parts of the nation, but in May of 2000 the *Boston Globe* became the first major daily to focus on OxyContin. The lead commanded readers' attention by reporting that even a town sheriff in rural Maine was "scared" of the situation—because of an unusually large number of people being arrested for drug-related crimes, the sheriff noted, the inmate population at the local jail had grown well over capacity (Gold 2000). The following month, the New Orleans *Times-Picayune* quoted a local DEA supervisor who referred to OxyContin as the "new Vicodin" (hydrocodone). In the same article, an anonymous prescription drug abuser added: "You get kind of a Vicodin feeling, but a little heavier [with OxyContin]" (Cannizaro 2000).

Media coverage changed dramatically after Kentucky's sensational "Operation OxyFest 2001," when more than 100 law enforcement officers from numerous jurisdictions worked together to arrest 207 suspected OxyContin users and dealers throughout the state. The arrests made for good headlines, and many local officials were more than happy to vie for their personal 15 minutes of fame. The most colorful of these was Detective Roger Hall of the Harlan County Kentucky Sheriff's Department, who was quoted as saying that abusers "will kick a bag of cocaine aside to get Oxy" (Kaushik 2001). Never mind that comparing cocaine, a stimulant, to OxyContin, a depressant, is like comparing Mountain Dew to Chamomile tea, the national media had their hook and a sexy sound bite and they certainly ran with it.

A blitz of national media coverage followed. The Associated Press, *Time*, *Newsweek*, *New York Times*, and other media giants, as well as local newspapers across the nation all ran alarming stories about the potentially lethal and dangerous new drug. Much of the initial coverage of OxyContin seemed to follow a similar formula: it started off with the personal tale of a chronically ill patient for whom OxyContin had suddenly made life worth living, followed by a contrasting tale of a lowly, depraved junkie who had become a slave to the drug, all the while littering the piece with both information and misinformation about the drug. And slang labels like "OC's," "Oxys" and "hillbilly heroin" started to permeate the national vocabulary.

As has historically been the case with drugs, coverage of the issue was generally presented in terms of black and white, good vs. evil. "The media presented the drug problem as a war of the holy people against the depraved people, and we haven't gone far past that moralizing tone," noted nationally respected media critic Norman Solomon (Kaushik 2001). Headlines screamed about OxyContin-related crimes, including pharmacy break-ins and terrifying accounts of elderly patients' homes being invaded and raided for the drug. Some stories of robberies appeared in local media outlets, only to be followed by a string of copycat attempts (Kaushik 2001). There were numerous stories of physicians who ran "pill mills" to feed the addiction of their clients, and contrasting stories of other doctors who had been scared off from prescribing the drug. There were numerous reports of pharmacies that had stopped stocking the drug for fear of inviting crime.

The major television networks, not to be outdone, recognized the potential to capitalize on the OxyContin media frenzy. For example, ABC's "20/20" prime time news magazine story was called "What the doctor ordered: Young people hooked on a miracle painkiller." But the story was clearly a set-up. In her opening remarks, Barbara Walters gravely warned that every family with children should pay attention to the impending segment. Then correspondent Lynn Sherr talked about her trip to Portsmouth, Ohio, to document one physician's "pill mill" that fed the addiction of locals and others who said they traveled from as far away as Texas to obtain painkiller prescriptions. The camera showed the orthopedic surgeon's dilapidated office, a broken X-ray machine and even beer cans littering the waiting room. At a dramatic high point in the segment the camera zoomed in on the lengthy list of prescriptions that the aberrant physician had written for his patients. Never mind that most of the scripts had been for Lortab® (hydrocodone) and Soma® (a muscle relaxant); the cameras cleverly focused on but a few OxyContin prescriptions—highlighting and enlarging them for the audience to see. And then, after detailing a sad story of a young, married man's overdose death, blamed on the physician's unscrupulous prescribing practices, and the plea bargain he reached with the local prosecutor, Ms. Sherr closed the story by saying she wasn't sure of the exact statistics, but "several dozen" people in Kentucky had already died from OxyContin overdoses. She called the situation "insidious" (Sherr 2001).

Numerous sources have likened the "OxyContin epidemic" to that of the "crack epidemic" of the 1980s, and as far as the media coverage of the issues is concerned, there are indeed striking similarities. Media hype tends to have a profound influence on the public's perception of the issues.

For example, the journalism watchdog group Fairness and Accuracy In Reporting (FAIR) did an interesting analysis of media coverage and public opinion back in the 1980s, during the height of the crack scare. FAIR reported that in 1985, *The New York Times* published an average of 36 articles per month on drug use and trafficking. In November 1985, crack warranted front-page coverage and the *Times* assigned a full-time reporter to the drug beat. Between July and October 1986, the *Times* increased its coverage to a monthly average of 103 articles, with coverage peaking in September at 169 articles. This coincided with Ronald and Nancy Reagan's infamous "Just Say No" speech, to which Congress responded by approving a new $1.7 billion drug package, apparently appeasing the media and the public alike, as coverage and worries over the drug issue subsided (Fink 1992).

A second wave of public drug fear coincided with coverage of George Bush's presidential election in 1988, in which drug abuse was a central campaign issue. In September of that year, in sync with Bush's Oval Office speech on the evils of drugs, the *Times* published 238 articles on drugs, which breaks down to almost seven per day. By the close of September, 64% of the American public agreed that drugs were more grave a threat than nuclear war, environmental destruction, AIDS, and poverty (Fink 1992).

In a similar manner, the media introduced the OxyContin "epidemic" to the general public. A study printed in the *Journal of Toxicology* tracked articles from two large regional newspapers that associated adverse human health effects with drugs, toxins, or other poisonous chemical substances. Within this criterion, articles on chemical and biological warfare (which dramatically spiked after September 11) were the most prevalent topic, followed by therapeutic drugs. Of the individual non-warfare articles, the two topics with the greatest coverage were medical marijuana (29 stories) and OxyContin abuse (20 stories) (Suchard 2002).

In 2001, the international media began following their American counterparts, as outlets in Europe and more recently Australia began to publish sensational articles about OxyContin. For example, *The Mirror* (England) featured a story that proclaimed, "A dangerous new drug is on the verge of flooding Ireland's inner city," and that "OxyContin is fast replacing other hard drugs as a way for pushers to trap new customers" (Hafford 2001). An *Observer* (England) headline reported in April 2002 that an 18-year-old girl became the UK's first OxyContin overdose victim, a drug that "already killed over 300 in America" (Tough 2002). Interestingly, the story accompanying the headline was actually a feature that had previously appeared in the *New York Times Magazine* in July of 2001. At about the same time, a story called "Epidemic fear as 'hillbilly heroin' hits the streets" accounted the overdose death of the 18-year-old girl, who reportedly drank, smoked and ingested "up to seven oxycodone pills" in a night of partying with her friends. The piece also reported that OxyContin was becoming popular in Manchester and Ireland and reiterated that the drug was responsible for "hundreds of deaths in America . . . prompting fears among police, customs officers and drug workers that it could give rise to a whole new generation of addicts" (Thompson 2002).

Other stories followed, patterning themselves after the media reports seen in the United States. But some readers quickly realized that much of it was media hype. The "Hillbilly Heroin" story in the *Observer* prompted a biting Letter to the Editor from a New Yorker who offered his own perspective on the matter: "The OxyContin scare in the U.S. is as much a product of the media as it is a genuine 'epidemic;' few of the people who become addicted here were taking it for legitimate reasons in the first place. Is it really a surprise that people who already abuse drugs will seek the latest 'stronger than heroin' substance" (Szalavitz 2002)?

While OxyContin stories continue to fill the airwaves and printed page, from the serious to the ridiculous, the frenetic pace began to ease in early 2003. But as Dr. Steven D. Passik wrote in a Letter to the Editor of the *Journal of Pain and Symptom Management* in March 2003: ". . . I have lost even more respect for the media . . . the media's loss of interest in the story shows that they were less concerned about the suffering in places like Eastern Kentucky and Maine, and more concerned about making headlines and capturing the fickle American attention span and demonizing the pharmaceutical industry. The OxyContin story has gone the way of Monica, Mark McGuire's supplements, and countless other pseudo-scandals" (Passik 2003).

Postscript

It would appear that although the abuse of OxyContin is indeed real, it is just one of many drugs that are abused by individuals whose drug taking and drug seeking behaviors focus on prescription painkillers. It also appears that the media stories may have contributed to shifting OxyContin abuse from a regional problem to a national problem. And clearly, OxyContin abuse is anything but an "epidemic." Nevertheless, all of the attention given to OxyContin has prompted U.S. government involvement. In response to the heightened awareness of

OxyContin abuse and diversion, the DEA launched its own comprehensive plan to prevent the illegal distribution of the product. Their broad goals include enforcement and intelligence; regulatory and administrative authority; industry cooperation; and awareness, education and outreach initiatives (DEA 2001b). Industry cooperation is an integral part of the plan, including encouraging Purdue Pharma to adopt a balanced marketing plan. As recently as January 2003, the FDA sent Purdue a letter contending that the company improperly disclosed information on OxyContin's risks, including a "particularly disturbing" ad that ran in the November issue of the *Journal of the American Medical Association*. In response, Purdue has pledged that all future advertisements will balance information about the benefits and risks of their product, as required by the federal Food, Drug and Cosmetic Act (Mishra 2003).

There have also been calls to reformulate the drug, to make it more difficult for abusers to compromise its time-release mechanism. Purdue has pursued alternative formulas, but success has been elusive thus far. Clinical trials found that when naloxone, a narcotic blocker, was added to OxyContin, it sometimes blocked pain relief for patients who ingested the tablets correctly. The company is pursuing an alternate approach by shifting from a tablet to a capsule that contains similar beads of the oxycodone combined with naltrexone, another narcotic blocker. If taken correctly, only the OxyContin beads would dissolve in the system, but if an abuser were to crush the pill, it would crush and activate the naltrexone, therefore masking the drug's effects. The company said complete testing could take as long as five years (Neergaard 2002). Even if this is accomplished, drug abusers are clever people and will likely compromise the new formulation in due course.

In the meantime, Purdue has launched its own public relations offensive. Among the initiatives, they have created educational and outreach materials, including a series of print and television ads and Painfully Obvious,™ a program that provides resources to educate parents, teachers and students about the dangers of prescription drug abuse (Hogen 2002).

Despite the bad press and pressure from the government, the success of OxyContin has not faltered. Only time will tell if the success will be short-lived or if the negative attention will slowly start to chip away at product confidence. In the meantime, those who use it correctly will continue to enjoy consistent pain relief, while those who abuse it will surely continue to inflict pain on the company, law enforcement, the community, and themselves.

References

Alford, Roger. (2003) "Doctors Lured to Help in Appalachia Now Sit in Prison," *Miami Herald,* May 11: 13A.

Breed, Allen G. (2001, June 16) In Appalachia and beyond, OxyContin abuse called 'a plague.' *Associated Press State and Local Wire.* Retrieved January 2003 from Lexis-Nexis on-line subscription.

Cannizaro, Steve. (2000, June 27) Potent new painkiller on the street, cops say; Task force investigating street sales of 'new Vicodin.' The *Times-Picayune.* Retrieved January 2003 from Lexis-Nexis on-line subscription.

Clancy, Mary Anne. (2000, May 13) Down East high: Washington County pill addicts have health officials worried. *Bangor Daily News.* Retrieved January 2003 from Lexis-Nexis on-line subscription.

Crane, Elizabeth. (2003, January) *The DAWN Report: Narcotic Analgesics.* Substance Abuse and Mental Health Services Administration: Office of Applied Studies. Retrieved February 2003. Available: *http://www.samhsa.gov/oas/2k3/pain/DAWNpain.pdf*

Department of Justice (DOJ). (2002a, July) *Kentucky Drug Threat Assessment.* National Drug Intelligence Center. Product No. 2002-S0382KY-001. Retrieved February 2003. Available: *http://www.usdoj.gov/ndic/pubs/1540/index.htm*

——. (2002b, April) *Maine Drug Threat Assessment.* National Drug Intelligence Center. Product 2002-S0377ME-001. Retrieved February 2003. Available: *http://www.usdoj.gov/ndic/pubs/909/index.htm*

Drug Enforcement Administration (DEA). (2001a, July) *Alert: Working to Prevent the Diversion and Abuse of OxyContin.* Office of Diversion Control. Retrieved January 2003. Available: *http://www.deadiversion.usdoj.gov/pubs/brochures/alert_oxycontin/oxybrochure.pdf*

——. (2001b, June 22) *Drugs and Chemicals of Concern: Action Plan to Prevent the Diversion and Abuse of OxyContin.* Diversion Control Program. Retrieved March 2003. Available: *http://www.deadiversion.usdoj.gov/drugs_concern/oxycodone/abuse_oxy.htm*

——. (2002a, June 11) *OxyContin Diversion and Abuse.* Office of Diversion Control. Retrieved January 2003. Available: *http://www.deadiversion.usdoj.gov/drugs_concern/oxycodone/oxy_061102.pdf*

——. (2002b, May 16) *Summary of Medical Examiner Reports of Oxycodone-Related Deaths.* Diversion Control Program. Retrieved January 2003. Available: *http://www.deadiversion.usdoj.gov/drugs_concern/oxycodone/oxycontin7.htm*

Durkheim, Emile. (1933) *The Division of Labor in Society* (New York: Macmillan).

Fink, Micah. (1992, September) *Don't forget the hype: Media, drugs, and public opinion* [Published On-line]. Fairness and Accuracy in Reporting. Retrieved January 2003. Available: *http://www.fair.org/extra/best-of-extra/drugs-hype.html*

Gold, Donna. (2000, May 21) A prescription for crime: Abuse of 2 painkillers blamed for rise in violence in Maine's poorest county. *The Boston Globe.* Retrieved January 2003 from Lexis-Nexis on-line subscription.

Goldberger, Bruce. (2003, February 26) Oxycodone rarely the sole cause of drug abuse deaths, new study finds: Landmark analysis sets standard for interpretation of deaths involving drug abuse. *Journal of Analytical Toxicology.* Retrieved February 2003. Available: *http://www.eurekalert.org/pub_releases/2003-02/pn-ort022603.php*

Gowda, Vanita. (2003, January) Not what the doctor ordered. *Congressional Quarterly DBA Governing Magazine.* Retrieved February 2003 from Lexis-Nexis on-line subscription.

Greenwald, Judy. (2003) Drug maker holds off lawsuits claiming painkiller is unsafe. *Business Insurance;* 31: 4.

Hafford, Rory. (2001, October 27) Hillbilly Heroin; new drug catches gardai on the hop. *The Mirror.* Retrieved February 2003 from Lexis-Nexis on-line subscription.

Hogen, Robin. (2002, February 2) *Purdue launches public service advertising campaign to raise awareness of prescription drug abuse* [On-line Press Release]. Retrieved February 2003. Available: *http://www.pharma.com/pressroom/news/20020402.htm*

Inciardi, James A. (2002a) *The War on Drugs III: The Continuing Saga of the Mysteries and Miseries of Intoxication, Addiction, Crime, and Public Policy* (Boston: Allyn and Bacon).

——. (2002b) "Prescription Drug Diversion," *College on Problems of Drug Dependence,* June 8–12, Quebec City.

Inciardi, James A. and Theodore J. Cicero. (2002) "Research on the Diversion of Prescription Drugs," *First Annual West Coast Training Conference of the National Association of Drug Diversion Investigators,* Marina del Rey, CA, May 21–24.

Jenkins, Philip. (1999) *Synthetic Panics: The Symbolic Politics of Designer Drugs* (New York: New York University Press).

Johnston, L. D., O'Malley, P. M., & Bachman, J. G. (2003) *Monitoring the Future national survey results on drug use: Overview of key findings, 2002.* NIH Publication No. 03-5374. Bethesda, MD: National Institute on Drug Abuse.

Kaushik, Sandeep. (2001, June 4) *OxyCon game: Anatomy of a media-made drug scare* [Published On-line]. Alternet.org: Drug Reporter. Retrieved January 2003. Available: *http://www.alternet.org/story.html?StoryID=10955*

Maine Analysis Demonstrates Far-Reaching Harm from OxyContin. (2002, February 11) *Alcoholism and Drug Abuse Weekly;* 14: 1–3.

Mishra, Raja. (2003, January 24) OxyContin ads to carry prominent warning of risks. *The Boston Globe.* Retrieved February 2003 from Lexis-Nexis on-line subscription.

Moore, Michael O'D. (2000, May 13) Drug abuse spurs pain management debate. *Bangor Daily News.* Retrieved February 2003 from Lexis-Nexis on-line subscription.

Nagel, Laura M. and Good, Patricia M. (2001) *DEA Industry Communicator: Special OxyContin Issue. Vol. 1.* United States Department of Justice Drug Enforcement Administration Office of Diversion Control. Retrieved February 2003. Available: *http://www.deadiversion.usdoj.gov/pubs/nwslttr/spec2001/index.html*

Neergaard, Lauren. (2002, June 18) Abuse-resistant OxyContin hits snag. *The Associated Press.* Retrieved March 2003 from Lexis-Nexis on-line subscription.

Passik, Steven D. (2003) Same as it ever was? Life after the OxyContin media frenzy [Letter to the Editor]. *Journal of Pain and Symptom Management;* 25: 199–201.

Sherr, Lynn. (2001, February 9) What the doctor ordered; Young people hooked on a miracle painkiller. ABC News *20/20* broadcast. Transcript available: *http://www.transcripts.tv/2020.cfm*

Slobodzian, Joseph A. (2002, December 3) Delco pharmacist pleads guilty in illegal drug sales. *The Philadelphia Inquirer.* Retrieved March 2003. Available: *http://www.philly.com/mld/philly/archives/*

Substance Abuse and Mental Health Services Administration (SAMHSA) (2002). *Results from the 2001 National Household Survey on Drug Abuse: Volume III.* Rockville, MD: SAMHSA, Office of Applied Studies. Available: *http://www.samhsa.gov/oas/nhsda.htm*

Suchard, J. (2002) Newspaper Coverage of Clinical Toxicology. *Journal of Toxicology: Clinical Toxicology;* 40: 629.

Szalavitz, Maia. (2002, March 31) Drug Abuse [Letter to the Editor]. *The Observer.* Retrieved March 2003. Available: *http://www.observer.co.uk/letters/story/0,6903,676787,00.html*

Thompson, Tony. (2002, March 24) Epidemic fear as 'hillbilly heroin' hits the streets. *The Observer.* Retrieved March 2003. Available: *http://www.observer.co.uk/uk_news/story/0,6903,672984,00.html*

Tough, Paul. (2002, April 7) Hillbilly Hell: Last month, 18-year-old Samantha Jenkinson from Hull became the first person in the UK to die from an overdose of OxyContin. But the prescription painkiller has already killed 300 in America. Paul Tough traces the spread of 'hillbilly heroin' from the Appalachian backwoods to the teen party scene in Britain. *The Observer.* Retrieved January 2003 from Lexis-Nexis on-line subscription.

For Discussion

1. Are reports of OxyContin abuse overblown by the media? Why has OxyContin been singled out as a problem drug when other prescription drugs are abused in substantial numbers as well?

2. Does media attention pique individuals' curiosity to try drugs, or does it create a certain amount of fear that prohibits experimentation with particular drugs? Does the media's influence even matter?

Adapted from: James A. Inciardi and Jennifer L. Goode, "OxyContin and Prescription Drug Abuse." In *Consumers' Research* 86(7): 17–21. Copyright © 2003 by *Consumers' Research.* Reprinted with permission. ✦

17

Taking Care of Business

The Heroin Addict's Life on the Street

Edward Preble

John J. Casey

"Taking Care of Business," one of the classic papers in the drug field, begins with a brief history of heroin use and distribution in New York City from World War I through the late 1960s. The authors note trends in price, availability, and legitimate opportunities for heroin users. The primary focus of the article, however, is the various levels of heroin distribution. Importantly, Preble and Casey dispel the widely held belief that individuals use heroin as an escape. Rather, they argue, heroin allows individuals to experience purposeful lives. The daily activities in which heroin users are involved are highly rewarding to them, particularly when legitimate opportunities are not generally available.

Introduction

This report is a description of the life and activities of lower-class heroin users in New York City in the context of their street environment. It is concerned exclusively with the heroin users living in slum areas, who comprise at least 80 percent of the city's heroin-using population. They are predominantly Negro and Puerto Rican, with some Irish, Italian, and Jewish.

It is often said that the use of heroin provides an escape for the user from his psychological problems and from the responsibilities of social and personal relationships—in short, an escape from life. Clinical descriptions of heroin addicts emphasize the passive, dependent, withdrawn, generally inadequate features of their personality structure and social adjustment. Most sociological studies of heroin users make the same point. Thus, Chein et al. (1964) reported that street-gang members are not likely to become heroin users, because they are resourceful, aggressive, well-integrated boys who are "reality-oriented" in their street environment. They held that it is the passive, anxious, inadequate boy, who cannot adapt to street life, who is likely to use heroin. Similarly, Cloward and Ohlin (1960) referred to heroin users as "retreatists" and "double failures" who cannot qualify for either legitimate or illegitimate careers. Unaggressive "mamma's boys" is the usual stereotype these days for the heroin addict, both for the students of narcotic use and the public at large. Experienced researchers and workers in the narcotics field know that there is no such thing as "the heroin addict" or "the addict personality." However, most attempts to generalize—the goal of all scientific investigation—result in some version of the escape theory.

The description which follows of the activities of lower-class heroin users in their adaptation to the social and economic institutions and practices connected with the use of heroin contradicts this widely held belief. Their behavior is anything but an escape from life. They are actively engaged in meaningful activities and relationships seven days a week. The brief moments of euphoria after each administration of a small amount of heroin constitute a small fraction of their daily lives. The rest of the time they are aggressively pursuing a career that is exacting, challenging, adventurous, and rewarding. They are always on the move and must be alert, flexible, and resourceful. The surest way to identify heroin users in a slum neighborhood is to observe the way people walk. The heroin user walks with a fast, purposeful stride, as if he is late for an important appointment—indeed, he is. He is hustling (robbing or stealing), trying to sell stolen goods, avoiding the police, looking for a heroin dealer with a good bag (the street retail unit of heroin), coming back from copping (buying heroin), looking for a safe place to take the drug, or looking for someone who beat (cheated) him—among other things. He is, in short, *taking care of business*, a phrase which is so common with heroin users that they use it in response to words of greeting, such as "how you doing?" and "what's happening?" *Taking care of biz* is the common abbreviation. *Ripping and running* is an older phrase which also refers to their busy lives. For them, if not for their middle- and upper-class counterparts (a small minority of opiate addicts), the quest for heroin is the quest for a meaningful life, not an escape from life. And the meaning does not lie, primarily, in the effects of the drug on their minds and bodies; it lies in the gratification of accomplishing a series of challenging, exciting tasks, every day of the week.

Much of the life of the heroin user on the street centers around the economic institutions of heroin distribution. Therefore, this report features a description of the marketing processes for heroin, from importation to street sales. The cost of heroin today is so high and the quality so poor that the street user must become totally involved in an economic career. A description of typical economic careers of heroin users will be presented. Preceding these two sections is a brief historical account of heroin use in New York City from World War I to the present, in which it will be seen that patterns of heroin use have changed at a pace and in a direction in correspondence with the social changes of the past fifty years. Theories and explanations about heroin use, based upon observations of fifty, twenty-five, or even five years ago, are inadequate to account for the phenomenon today. It is hoped that this contemporary account of the social setting for heroin use will provide useful data for the modifications of theory and practice which should accompany any dynamic social process.

Methodology

The data on which this report is based have come from interviews with patients at the Manhattan State Hospital Drug Addiction Unit and from participant observation and interviews with individuals and groups in four lower-class communities in New York City—East Harlem, Lower East Side, Yorkville, Claremont (Bronx). The communities represent the neighborhoods of approximately 85 percent of the addict patients at Manhattan State Hospital. The anthropologist's role and approach to the heroin-using study of informants was in the tradition of Bronislaw Malinowski (1922) and William F. Whyte (1955), which, in Whyte's words, consists of "the observation of interpersonal events." Another dimension was added with the modified use of research techniques, introduced by Abraham Kardiner and his collaborators (1939) in their psychosocial studies of primitive and modern cultures. The main feature of this methodology is the life-history interview with individual subjects. Initial and subsequent contacts with the research informants occurred, in all cases, with their voluntary consent and cooperation. The anthropologist had the advantage of twelve years experience of street work and research in the study neighborhoods, and was able to enlist the assistance of long-time acquaintances for this special project. Four major ethnic groups were represented among the approximately 150 informants: Irish, Italian, Negro, and Puerto Rican.

History of Heroin Use in New York City

The recent history of heroin use in the city can be broken down into six time periods: (1) between World War I and World War II, (2) during World War II, (3) 1947 to 1951, (4) 1951 to 1961, and (6) 1961 to the present.

1. Between World War I and World War II

Prior to World War II the use of heroin was limited, for the most part, to people in the *life*—show people, entertainers, and musicians; racketeers and gangsters; thieves and pickpockets; prostitutes and pimps. The major ethnic groups represented among these users were Italian, Irish, Jewish, and Negro (mostly those associated with the entertainment life). There were also heroin users among the Chinese, who had a history of opium use. The distribution of heroin by those who controlled the market was limited mostly to these people, and there was little knowledge or publicity about it.

2. During World War II

World War II interrupted the trade routes and distributorships for illicit heroin supplies, which resulted in a five-year hiatus in heroin use.

3. 1947 to 1951

When World War II ended, there was a greatly expanded market for heroin in the increased population among Negroes from the South and among migrating Puerto Ricans who came to New York during the war in response to a manpower shortage. In 1940, the Negro population in New York City was 450,000; in 1960, it was over 1 million. In 1940, the Puerto Rican population was 70,000; in 1960, it was over 600,000. As with all new immigrants in New York, they worked at the lowest economic levels, settled in slum neighborhoods, and were the victims of unemployment, poverty, and discrimination. From 1947 to 1951, the use of heroin spread among lower-class Negro and Puerto Rican people and among other lower-class, slum-dwelling people, mainly the Irish and Italians. The increased rate of use was gradual, but steady, and did not attract much attention. Most of the users were young adults in their twenties and thirties. They were more or less circumspect in their drug consumption, which they were able to be because of the relatively low cost and high quality of the heroin.

During this period, heroin was sold in number-five capsules (the smallest capsules used for pharmaceutical products). These *caps* could be bought for about one dollar apiece, and two to six persons could get high on the contents of one capsule. Commonly, four persons would contribute one quarter each and *get down on a cap*. There was social cohesion, identification, and ritual among the users of this period. Sometimes as many as twenty people would get together and, in a party atmosphere, share the powder contents of several capsules which were emptied

upon a mirror and divided into columns by means of a razor blade, one column for each participant. The mirror was passed from person to person and each one would inhale his share through the nose by means of a tapered, rolled-up dollar bill which served as a straw, and was called a *quill*. A twenty, fifty, or hundred dollar bill was used on special occasions when someone wanted to make a show of his affluence. Since heroin was so inexpensive during this time, no addict had to worry about getting his fix; someone was always willing to loan him a dollar or share a part of his drug. The social relationships among these addicts were similar to those found in a neighborhood bar, where there is a friendly mutual concern for the welfare of the regular patrons. The most important economic factor in these early post-war days of heroin use was that heroin users were able to work even at a low-paying job and still support a habit, and many of them did. Relatively little crime was committed in the interest of getting money to buy heroin. A habit could be maintained for a few dollars a day, at little social or economic cost to the community.

4. 1951 to 1957

Around 1951, heroin use started to become popular among younger people on the streets, especially among street-gang members who were tired of gang fighting and were looking for a new high. As heroin use had become more common in the latter days of the previous period, the more street-wise teenagers learned about it and prevailed upon the experienced users to introduce them to it. Contrary to popular reports, experimentation with heroin by youths usually began at their initiative and not through proselytism. The stereotype of the dope *pusher* giving out free samples of narcotics to teenagers in school yards and candy stores, in order to addict them, is one of the most misleading myths about drug use. Also, contrary to professional reports about this development, it was not the weak, withdrawn, unadaptive street boy who first started using heroin, but rather the tough, sophisticated, and respected boy, typically a street-gang leader. Later, others followed his example, either through indoctrination or emulation. By 1955, heroin use among teenagers on the street had become widespread, resulting, among other things, in the dissolution of fighting gangs. Now the hip boy on the street was not the swaggering, leather-jacketed gang member, but the boy nodding on the corner, enjoying his heroin high. He was the new hero model.

As heroin use spread among the young from 1951, the price of heroin began to rise in response to the greater demand, and the greater risks involved in selling to youths. Those who started using heroin as teenagers seldom had work experience or skills and resorted to crime in order to support their heroin use. They were less circumspect in their drug-using and criminal activity, and soon became a problem to the community, especially to those who were engaged in non-narcotic illegal activities, such as bookmaking, loan-sharking, and policy (the gambling game popular among working-class people, in which a correct selection of three numbers pays off at 50 to 1). The activities and behavior of young drug users brought attention and notoriety to the neighborhood, which jeopardized racketeer operations. It was not uncommon for a local racketeer to inform the parents of a young heroin user about his activities, hoping that they would take action.

5. 1957 to 1961

In 1957, the criminal organization, or *syndicate*, which had been mainly responsible for heroin distribution (according to law-enforcement agencies and government investigation committees), officially withdrew from the market. This resulted from two conditions: the passage of stricter federal laws that included provision for conspiracy convictions, and the related fact that illegal drug use was receiving increased attention from the public and officials, especially as a result of the increased involvement of youth with heroin. The risks had become too great, and the syndicate did not want to endanger the larger and more important sources of revenue, such as gambling and loan-sharking. However, the instruction to get out of narcotics was more honored in the breach than in the observance by certain syndicate members. Those who stayed involved in narcotics operated independently. Some made it their primary operation, while others would make only one or two big transactions a year when they needed to recoup quickly from an unexpected financial loss in some other operation. Dealing irregularly in narcotics for this purpose became known as a *fall-back*—a quick and sure way to make money. The syndicate also stayed involved indirectly through loan-shark agreements. In these transactions, large sums of money were lent to narcotic dealers for a period of one month at a fixed rate of return. No questions were asked regarding its use. By this means, the syndicate avoided some of the undesirable aspects of narcotic distribution and still participated in the profits. The official withdrawal of the syndicate from narcotics created opportunities for independent operators, which resulted in a relatively free market.

6. 1961 to the Present

The next major development in the history of heroin use in the city occurred in November 1961, when there was a critical shortage of heroin. Known as a *panic*, this development, whatever its cause, had a profound effect on the course of heroin use in the city. The panic lasted only for a few weeks. During this time, the demand for the meager supplies of heroin was so great that those who had supplies were able to double and triple their prices and further adulterate the quality, thus realizing sometimes as much as ten times their usual profit. By the time heroin became available again in good supply, the dealers had learned that inferior heroin at inflated prices could find a ready market. Since that time, the cost of heroin on the street has continued to climb, through increased prices, further adulteration, and *short counts* (misrepresentation of aggregate weight in a given unit). A few minor panics—about two a year—help bolster the market. Today, an average heroin habit costs the user about $20 a day, as compared to $2 twenty years ago. This fact is responsible for a major social disorder in the city today. It has also had important effects on the personal, social, and family relationships of the heroin users themselves. There is no longer social cohesion among addicts. The competition and struggle necessary to support a habit has turned each one into an independent operator who looks out only for himself. Usually, addicts today will associate in pairs (partners), but only for practical purposes: in a criminal effort which requires two people (as when one acts as lookout, while the other commits a burglary), to share in the price of a bag of heroin, to assist in case of an overdose of drugs, to share the use of one set of works (the paraphernalia used to inject heroin). There is no longer a subculture of addicts, based on social cohesion and emotional identification, but rather a loose association of individuals and parallel couples. Heroin users commonly say, "I have no friends, only associates."

The economic pressures on heroin users today are so great that they prey on each other, as well as on their families and on society at large. An addict with money or drugs in his possession runs a good risk of being *taken off* (robbed) by other addicts. An addict who has been robbed or cheated by another addict usually takes his loss philosophically, summed up by the expression, "That's the name of the game." Referring to a fellow addict who had cheated him, one victim said, "He beat me today, I'll beat him tomorrow." Another addict who specializes in robbing other addicts said, "I beat them every chance I get, which is all the time." Sociability, even among partners, extends no farther than that suggested by the following excerpt: "You might be hanging out with a fellow for a long time, copping together and working as crime partners. You might beat him for a purpose. You might beat him, because maybe you bought a bag together and you know it's not going to do both any good, so you beat him for it. But then you try to go and get some money and straighten him out; make it up to him." Another informant summed up the attitude between partners this way: "I'm looking out for myself—I might be sick tomorrow; anyway, he's got something working for him that I don't know about." Sometimes, a distinction is made between a hustling partner and a crime partner (*crimey*), where it is suggested that the latter is more dependable; however, as one informant put it, "There are larceny-minded crimeys." The causes of these changes in the relationships of heroin users to each other, to family members, and to other members of the community are to be found in the economic practices of heroin distribution.

The Distribution of Heroin in New York City

Heroin contracted for in Europe at $5000 per kilo (2.2 pounds) will be sold in $5 bags on the street for about one million dollars, after having passed through at least six levels of distribution. The following description of the distribution and marketing of heroin, from the time it arrives in New York until it reaches the hands of the heroin user in the street, is a consensus derived from informants in the hospital and in the street representing different ethnic and racial groups from different parts of the city. There are many variations to the account given here at all levels of the marketing process. For example, as in the marketing of any product, a quantity purchase can be made at a lower price; and a dealer who makes a rapid turnover of the product for a wholesaler will receive higher benefits for his work. All the way down the line, the *good customer* is the key to a successful operation. He is one who buys regularly, does a good volume of business, does not ask for credit or try to buy short (offer less than the established price), and can be trusted. The following account does not include all the many variations, but can be taken as a paradigm.

Opium produced in Turkey, India, and Iran is processed into heroin in Lebanon, France, and Italy, and prepared for shipment to the East Coast of the United States. A United States importer, through a courier, can buy a kilogram of 80-percent heroin in Europe for $5000. The quality is represented to him in terms of how many cuts it will hold (that is, how many times it can be adulterated). In earlier days, when the marketing of heroin was a more controlled operation, the word of the European seller was accepted.

Now, it is customary for the importer to test it, either by means of scientific instruments, or through a reliable tester—an addict who makes experimental cuts, uses the drug, and reports on its quality. The importer, who usually never sees the heroin, sells down the line to a highly trusted customer through intermediaries. If it is a syndicate operation, he would only sell to high level, coded men, known as *captains*. These men are major distributors, referred to as *kilo connections* and, generally, as *the people*.

Major Distribution

The *kilo connection* pays $20,000 for the original kilogram (kilo, kee), and gives it a one and one cut (known as *hitting it*); that is, he makes two kilos out of one by adding the common adulterants of milk sugar, mannite (a product from the ash tree, used as a mild laxative), and quinine. The proportions of ingredients used for the cutting vary with the preferences of the cutter. One may use 5 parts milk sugar, 2 parts quinine, and 1 part mannite; while another may use 2 parts milk sugar, 3 parts quinine, and 1 part mannite. All three of these products are quickly soluble with heroin. A match lit under the cooker (bottle cap) will heat and dissolve the mixture into a clear liquid in a few seconds. The milk sugar contributes the bulk, the mannite inflates the volume—described as *fluffing* it up—and the quinine heightens the sensation of the *rush* when, upon injection into the vein, the mixture first registers on the nervous system. In the cutting procedure, the substance to be cut is placed under a fine sieve, often made from a woman's nylon stocking stretched over a coat hanger. The adulterants are sifted on top of it, then the new mixture is sifted through several more times. After the cut, the kilo connection sells down the line in kilos, half kilos, and quarter kilos, depending upon the resources of his customers. He will get approximately $10,000 per half kilo for the now adulterated heroin.

The customer of the kilo connection is known as *the connection* in its original sense, meaning that he knows *the people*, even though he is not one of them. He may also be called an *ounce man*. He is a highly trusted customer. (One common variation here is that the kilo connection may sell to a third line man, known, if a syndicate operation, as a *soldier* or *button man*. He, in turn, will make a one and one cut and sell to the connection.) Assuming that the connection buys directly from a kilo connection, he will probably give the heroin a one and one cut (make two units of each one), divide the total aggregate into ounces, and sell down the line at $700 per ounce. In addition to the adulteration, the aggregate weight of the product is reduced. Known as a *short count*, this procedure occurs at every succeeding level of distribution. At this stage, however, it is called a *good ounce*, despite the adulteration and reduced weight.

The next man is known as a *dealer in weight*, and is probably the most important figure in the line of distribution. He stands midway between the top and the bottom, and is the first one coming down the line who takes substantial risk of being apprehended by law-enforcement officers. He is also the first one who may be a heroin user himself, but usually he is not. He is commonly referred to as one who is *into something* and is respected as a big dealer who has put himself in jeopardy by, as the sayings go, *carrying a felony with him* and *doing the time*; that is, if he gets caught, he can expect a long jail sentence. It is said of him that "he let his name go," or "his name gets kicked around," meaning that his identity is known to people in the street. This man usually specializes in cut ounces. He may give a two and one cut (make three units of each one) to the good ounce from the connection and sell the resulting quantity for $500 per ounce. The aggregate weight is again reduced, and now the unit is called a *piece*, instead of an ounce. Sometimes, it is called a *street ounce* or a *vig ounce* (*vig* is an abbreviation for *vigorish*, which is the term used to designate the high interest on loans charged by loan sharks). In previous years, twenty-five- to thirty-level teaspoons were supposed to constitute an ounce; today, it is sixteen to twenty.

The next customer is known as a *street dealer*. He buys the *piece* for $500, gives it a one and one cut and makes *bundles*, which consist of twenty-five $5 bags each. He can usually get seven bundles from each piece, and he sells each bundle for $80. He may also package the heroin in *half-bundles* (ten $5 bags each), which sell for $40, or he may package in *half-loads* (fifteen $3 bags), which sell for $30 each. This man may or may not be a heroin user.

The next distributor is known as a *juggler*, who is the seller from whom the average street addict buys. He is always a user. He buys bundles for $80 each and sells the twenty-five bags at about $5 each, making just enough profit to support his own habit, day by day. He may or may not make a small cut, known as *tapping the bags*. He is referred to as someone who is "always high and always short"; that is, he always has enough heroin for his own use and is always looking for a few dollars to get enough capital to cop again. The following actual account is typical of a juggler's transactions: he has $25 and needs $5 more to buy a half-load. He meets a user he knows who has $5 and would like to buy two $3 bags; he is short $1. The juggler tells him he needs only $5 to cop, and that, if he can have his $5, he will buy a half-load and give him his two $3 bags—$1, in effect, for the use of the money. When the juggler returns, he gives the person his two bags. In the example here, the person had to wait about two hours for the juggler's return, and it was raining. For taking the risk of getting beat for his money by the juggler, for the long wait and the discomfort of the weather, the juggler was expected to go to the *cooker* with him (share the use of some of the heroin), with the juggler putting in two bags to the other person's one bag and sharing equally in the total. The juggler had his fix and now has eleven bags left. He sells three bags for $9. From the eight bags he has left he uses two himself to get straight—not to get high, but enough to keep from getting sick so that he can finish his business. Now, he sells four bags for $12 and has three left. He needs only $7 more to cop again, so he is willing to sell the last three bags for the reduced price, and he can begin a similar cycle all over again. He may do this three or four times a day. The juggler leads a precarious life, both financially and in the risks he takes of getting robbed by fellow addicts or arrested. Most

arrests for heroin sales are of the juggler. Financially, he is always struggling to stay in the black. If business is a little slow, he may start to get sick or impatient and use some of the heroin he needs to sell, in order to recoup. If he does this, he is in the red and temporarily out of business. A juggler is considered to be doing well if he has enough money left over after a transaction for cab fare to where he buys the heroin. One informant defined a juggler as a "non-hustling dope fiend who is always messing the money up."

Other Specialists

There are ancillary services provided by other specialists in the heroin-marketing process. They are known as: (1) lieutenants, (2) testers, (3) drop-men, (4) salesmen, (5) steerers, (6) taste faces, and (7) accommodators.

1. *Lieutenant:* Very often, a connection or weight dealer will have in his employ a trusted associate who handles the details of transactions with the street-level dealers. He arranges for deliveries, collects the money, and acts as an enforcer, if things go wrong. He may work for a salary or a commission, or both. Sometimes, he will be given some *weight* (part of a kilo) to sell on his own as a bonus.

2. *Tester:* Heroin dealers down the line are likely to keep a trusted addict around to test the quality of the drug for them. In return for this service, he gets all the heroin he needs and pocket money.

3. *Drop-man:* This person, often a young, dependable non-user, is used by sellers to make deliveries. He works for cash and may make as much as $500 for a drop in behalf of a top-level seller. He may also handle the transfer of money in a transaction. He is usually a tough, intelligent, trusted street youth who is ambitious to work his way up in the criminal hierarchy.

4. *Salesman:* Sometimes, the type of person used as a drop-man will be used as a street salesman of heroin for a fairly big dealer. The use of this kind of salesman is growing, because of the unreliability

of addict jugglers and the desirability of having a tough person who can be trusted and not be easily robbed and cheated by addicts. Sometimes, these boys are about 16 to 18 years old and may be going to school. Being young, they usually do not have a police record, and they attract less attention from the police. One informant summed up their attributes this way: "The police won't pay much attention to a kid, but if they do get busted (arrested) they don't talk; they want to be men . . . they (the dealers) trust a guy that don't use it, because they know the guy ain't going to beat him. They got a little gang, and nobody is going to get their stuff, because they're going to gang up on the guy. In that case, they can use a gun in a hurry. The kids that sell the stuff, they don't use it. They buy clothes or whatever they want with the money." They often sell on consignment, starting with a small advance (usually a bundle) and working up to more if they are successful.

5. *Steerer:* The steerer is one who in racetrack parlance would be known as a *tout*, or in a sidewalk sales operation as a *shill*. He is one who tries to persuade users to buy a certain dealer's bag. He may work off and on by appointment with a particular dealer (always a small street dealer or juggler) in return for his daily supply of drugs. Or he may hear that a certain dealer has a good bag and, on a speculative basis, steer customers to him and then go to him later and ask to be taken care of for the service. This is known as *cracking* on a dealer. One of his more subtle selling techniques is to affect an exaggerated-looking high, and, when asked by a user where he got such a good bag, refer him to the dealer. Usually, he is a person who stays in the block all day and is supposed to know what is going on; he is, as they say, *always on the set*.

6. *Taste face:* This is a derogatory term given to one who supports his habit by renting out works—loaning the paraphernalia for injecting heroin—in return for a lit-

tle money or a share of the heroin. Possession of works (hypodermic needle, eyedropper fitted with a baby's pacifier nipple, and bottle cap) is a criminal offense, and users do not want to run the extra risk of carrying them; thus, they are willing to pay something for the service. Although they perform a useful service, these people are held in contempt by other users. Taste refers to the small amount of heroin he is given (known as a *G shot*) and face is a term applied to anyone on the street who is known as a *creep, flunky,* or *nobody.*

7. *Accommodator:* The accommodator is a user who buys at a low level—usually from a juggler—for someone new to the neighborhood who has no connections. These purchases are for small amounts bought by users from other parts of the city or the suburbs. The accommodator receives a little part of the heroin or money for his services. Sometimes, he will also cheat the buyer by misrepresenting the price or the amount, or just by not coming back. However, he has to be somewhat reliable, in order to support his habit regularly in this way. Many selling arrests by undercover narcotics police are of these low-level accommodators.

The Street Bag of Heroin

The amount of heroin in the street bag is very small. A generous estimate of the aggregate weight of a $5 bag is ninety milligrams, including the adulterants. Assuming, as in the above account, that the original kilo of 80-percent heroin is adulterated twenty-four times by the time it reaches the street, the amount of heroin would be about three milligrams. There is considerable fluctuation in the amount of heroin in the retail unit, running the range from one to fifteen milligrams, which depends mainly upon the supply available in the market. The important point is that, no matter how small the amount, heroin users are never discouraged in their efforts to get it. The consensus figure of three milligrams is a good approximation for an average over a one-year period. This is the average analgesic dosage that is used in those countries, such as England, where heroin can be prescribed in medical practice. It is a minimal amount, being considered safe for someone who does not use opiates. It is equivalent to about ten milligrams of either morphine or methadone.

In controlled experiments with opiate addicts, as much as sixty milligrams of morphine have been administered four times a day (Martin, personal communication 1967). Each dosage is equivalent to about twenty milligrams of heroin, which is seven times the amount in the average street bag. In another experiment, it was found that the average heroin addict "recognized" heroin at a minimum level of about fifteen milligrams—five times the amount in the street bag (Sharoff, personal communication 1967). The average dosage of methadone used in opiate-maintenance treatment is one hundred milligrams—about ten times the amount in the street bag. One informant said of the effects of a street bag today: "All it does is turn your stomach over so that you can go out and hustle, and you had better do it fast." Heroin users who are sent to jail report that they are surprised when they do not experience serious withdrawal symptoms after the abrupt cessation of heroin use. Physicians working in the withdrawal wards of narcotic treatment centers refer to the abstinence syndrome among most of their patients today as "subclinical."

The amount of heroin in the street unit has resulted in an institution known as *chasing the bag*. In a community with a high incidence of heroin use, there will be two, three, or four competing bags on the street; that is, bags which have come down through different distributorship lines. Because of the low quality of the heroin, users want to get the best one available on a given day. The number of times it has been cut and the ingredients that were used to cut it are the main considerations. The dealer who has the best bag on the street at a given time will sell his merchandise fast and do a big volume of business. A dealer with a good bag who works hard can sell forty to fifty bundles a day. A good bag dealer can sell seventy-five to one hundred bags a day. By keeping the quality relatively high—for example by giving a one and a half cut to a quantity represented as being able to hold two cuts—he makes less profit on each unit. However, this loss can be offset by the greater volume and the reduced price he gets from his wholesaler, as a result of buying more often and in large quantities. Those with inferior bags on the street do not have a rapid turnover, but they know that sooner or later they can sell their stock, since the demand tends to exceed the supply. There are also other factors operating in their favor. Some users are not known to the dealer of the best bag and cannot buy from him except through the mediation of someone else. This service costs the prospective buyer something and he has to weigh that consideration against the better bag. Usually, however, if he is sure that one bag is much better than another one, he will find the price to pay for the service to get it; the quality of the bag, not the money, is always the primary consideration.

Another condition favorable to the dealers of inferior bags is that a user who hustles for his drugs is too busy to be around all the time waiting for a particular bag to come on the street. He is usually pressed for time and has to take what is available. If the dealer of the good bag is out recopping, the user cannot afford to wait for what may be a long time. The dealer of an inferior bag, whose heroin moves more slowly, is reliable; that is, he is always around and can be depended upon. Even in extreme cases, where a bag is so bad that the dealer builds up a surplus because of slow business, he knows that sooner or later a temporary shortage of heroin—even for a few days—will insure his selling out. Heroin does not spoil and can be easily stored for an indefinite period.

Sometimes, the dealer of an exceptionally good bag will be approached by his competitors, and they will make a deal, whereby he agrees to leave the street on the condition that they buy their bundles from him. In such a deal, those buying the good bundles will *tap the bags* (adulterate them a little more) and put them on the street at the same price. This is one of the many variations in marketing heroin.

It is common practice for a new dealer to come on the street with a good bag and keep it that way, until he has most of the customers. Then, he will start to adulterate the heroin, knowing that his reputation will carry him for a few days; by that time, he has made a good extra profit. When he starts losing customers in large number, he can build the bag up again. Users are constantly experimenting with the products of different dealers, comparing notes with other users, and attempting to buy the best bag that is around. As one informant put it: "You keep searching. If the guy is weak and you buy from him and it's nothing, then you go to Joe or Tom. Like you get a bag over here now, you run over there about in an hour and get another bag from the other guy, and get another from this other guy after a while. You just go in a circle to see. You run in different directions." One informant said, "There are no longer dope addicts on the street, only hope addicts." A report on the street that a heroin user died of an overdose of heroin results in a customer rush on his dealer for the same bag.

Economic Careers of Heroin Users

The nature of the economic careers of heroin users on the street is epitomized in the following quote from a research informant: "I believe in work to a certain extent, if it benefits my profit; but I do believe there is more money made otherwise." Another informant, in referring to a fellow user, said: "He just got no heart to be pulling no scores. He can't steal, he don't know how to steal. You can't be an addict that way. I don't know how he's going to make it."

Virtually all heroin users in slum neighborhoods regularly commit crime, in order to support their heroin use. In addition to the crimes involving violation of the narcotic laws, which are described above, heroin users engage in almost all types of crime for gain, both against property and the person. Because of the greatly inflated price of heroin and because of its poor quality, it is impossible for a heroin user to support even a modest habit for less than $20 a day. Since the typical street user is uneducated, un-

skilled, and often from a minority racial group, he cannot earn enough money in the legitimate labor market to finance his drug use; he must engage in criminal activity. It is a conservative estimate that heroin users in New York City steal $1 million a day in money, goods, and property. About 70 percent of the inmates in New York City Department of Correction institutions are heroin users whose crimes were directly or indirectly connected with their heroin use.

As with non-addict criminals, addict criminals tend to specialize in certain activities, depending upon their personalities, skills, and experience. One of the myths derived from the passivity stereotype of the heroin user is that the heroin user avoids crimes of violence, such as robbery, which involve personal confrontation. This no longer seems to be the case. A 1966 New York City Police Department study of the arrests of admitted narcotic (primarily heroin) addicts for selected felonies, other than violations of narcotic laws, showed that 15.1 percent of the arrests were for robbery (New York City Police Department 1966). This compared with 12.9 percent robbery arrests of all arrests (addict and non-addict) during the same year. Murder arrests among the addicts amounted to 1 percent of the selected felonies, as compared to 1.4 percent of all arrests in the same categories. The biggest differences between addict arrests and all arrests in the seventeen felony categories selected for study were in the categories of burglary and felonious assault. Among the addicts, 40.9 percent were burglary arrests, compared to 19.7 percent of all arrests; felonious assault constituted 5.6 percent among the addicts, compared to 27.9 percent of all arrests. What these figures reveal is not that heroin users avoid crimes of violence, as compared to non-addicts, but that they avoid crimes not involving financial gain, such as felonious assault. Where financial gain is involved, as in robbery, the risk of violence is taken by heroin users in a higher percentage of cases than with non-addicts. These statistics confirm the observations and opinions of street informants, both addict and non-addict. The high percentage of burglaries committed by heroin users is often cited as evidence that, in comparison with non-addict criminals, they prefer non-violent crime. What is overlooked here is that burglary, especially of residences, always involves the risk of personal confrontation and violence. Of the 1745 burglary arrests of admitted addicts in 1966, 975 (51 percent) were residence burglaries.

Analysis of the data from the informants for this study showed the following, with regard to principal criminal occupations, not including those connected with narcotic-laws offenses: burglar—22.7 percent, *flatfooted hustler*—12.2 percent, shoplifter—12.1 percent, robber—9.0 percent. *Flatfooted hustler* is a term used on the street for one who will commit almost any kind of crime for money, depending upon the opportunities. As one self-described flatfooted hustler put it: "I'm capable of doing most things—jostling (picking pockets), boosting (shoplifting), con games, burglary, mugging, or stick-ups; wherever I see the opportunity, that's where I'm at." The main advantage of crimes against the person is that the yield is usually money, which does not have to be sold at a discount, as does stolen property. It is easily concealed and can be exchanged directly for heroin. In the case of stolen goods and property, the person has to carry the proceeds of, say, a burglary around with him, as he looks for a direct buyer or a fence. . . . This exposes him to extra risk of apprehension. When he does find a buyer, he can only expect to get from 10 percent to 50 percent of the value, the average being about 30 percent, depending upon the item—the more expensive the item, the higher the discount.

The distribution and sales of goods and property stolen by heroin users has become a major economic institution in low-income neighborhoods. Most of the consumers are otherwise ordinary, legitimate members of the community. Housewives will wait on the stoop for specialists in stealing meat (known as *cattle rustlers*) to come by, so that they can get a ham or roast at a 60-percent discount. Owners of small grocery stores buy cartons of cigarettes stolen from the neighborhood supermarket. The owner of an automobile places an order with a heroin user for tires, and the next day he has the tires—with the wheels. During the Easter holidays, there is a great demand for clothes, with slum streets looking like the streets of the Garment District.

It has often been noted that retail stores in a slum neighborhood have higher prices than those in more affluent neighborhoods, and this has been attributed to discrimination and profiteering at the expense of poor people with little consumer education and knowledge. Although such charges have some foundation, another major cause of higher prices is the high rate of pilferage by heroin users and others from such stores, the cost of which is passed on to the consumer. One chain store operation which locates exclusively in low-income neighborhoods in New York City is reportedly in bankruptcy due to a 10 percent pilferage rate. This rate compares to about 2 percent citywide.

One economic institution that has resulted directly from the increased criminal activity among heroin users is the *grocery fence*. He is a small, local businessman, such as a candy store owner, bar owner, or beauty parlor owner, who has enough cash to buy stolen goods and property on a small scale and has a place to store them. He then sells the items to his regular customers, both for good will and a profit. He provides a service for the user in providing him with a fast outlet for his goods.

The heroin user is an important figure in the economic life of the slums. In order to support a $20-a-day habit, he has to steal goods and property worth from $50 to $100. Usually, he steals outside his neighborhood, not out of community loyalty, but because the opportunities are better in the wealthier neighborhoods; and he brings his merchandise back to the neighborhood for sale at high discounts. This results, to some extent, in a redistribution of real income from the richer to the poorer neighborhoods. Although non-addict residents in the slums may deplore the presence of heroin users, they appreciate and compete for their services as discount salesmen. The user, in turn, experiences satisfaction in being able to make this contribution to the neighborhood.

The type of criminal activity he engages in, and his success at it, determine, to a large extent, the addict's status among fellow addicts and in the community at large. The appellation of *real hustling dope fiend* (a successful burglar, robber, con man, etc.) is a mark of respect and status. Conversely, *non-hustling dope fiend* is a term of denigration applied to users who stay in the neighborhood begging for money or small tastes of heroin, renting out works, or doing small-time juggling. There are also middle-status occupations, such as *stealing copper*, where the person specializes in salvaging metal and fixtures from vacant tenement buildings and selling to the local junkman. About the only kinds of illegal activity not open to the heroin user are those connected with organized crime, such as gambling and loan sharking. Users are not considered reliable enough for work in these fields. They may be used as a lookout for a dice game or policy operation, but that is about as close as they can get to organized criminal operations.

Respite from the arduous life they lead comes to heroin users when they go to jail, to a hospital, or, for some, when they take short-time employment at resort hotels in the mountains. In the present study, it was found that 43 percent of the subjects were in some type of incarceration at any given period of time. In jail they rest, get on a healthy diet, have their medical and dental needs cared for, and engage in relaxed socialization which centers around the facts and folklore of the heroin user's life on the street.

If a user has been making good money on the street, he eventually builds up a tolerance to heroin which gets to the point where he can no longer finance the habit. He may then enter a hospital for detoxification. If he stays the medically recommended period of time—usually three weeks—he can qualify for Department of Welfare assistance, which eases the economic pressures on him when he resumes his heroin-using life on the street. More often than not, however, he will leave the hospital when his tolerance has been significantly lowered, which occurs in about a week.

Some users solve the problems of too much physical and economic pressure which build up periodically by getting temporary employment out of the city, usually in the mountain resort hotels. There are employment agencies in the Bowery and similar districts which specialize in hiring drifters, alcoholics, and drug addicts for temporary work. In the summer, there is a demand for menial laborers in the kitchens and on the grounds of resort hotels. The agencies are so eager to get help during the vacation season that they go to the street to solicit workers. Some of them provide a cheap suitcase and clothes for those who need them. One informant reported about a particular agency man this way: "He'll grab you out of the street. He'll say, 'Do you want a job, son? I'll get you a good job. You want to work up in the country and get fat? You'll eat good food and everything.' " The agency charges the worker a substantial fee, which is taken out of his first check, and makes extra money by providing private transportation at a price higher than the bus fare. The heroin user usually works through one pay period and returns to the city somewhat more healthy, with a low heroin tolerance, and with a few dollars in his pocket.

It can be seen from the account in this section that the street heroin user is an active, busy person, preoccupied primarily with the economic necessities of maintaining his real income—heroin. A research subject expressed the more mundane gratifications of his life this way:

When I'm on the way home with the bag safely in my pocket, and I haven't been caught stealing all day, and I didn't get beat, and the cops didn't get me—I feel like a working man coming home; he's worked hard, but he knows he done something, even though I know it's not true.

Conclusions

Heroin use today by lower-class, primarily minority-group, persons does not provide for them a euphoric escape from the psychological and social problems which derive from ghetto life. On the contrary, it provides a motivation and rationale for the pursuit of a meaningful life, albeit a socially deviant one. The activities these individuals engage in, and the relationships they have in the course of their quest for heroin, are far more important than the minimal analgesic and euphoric effects of the small amount of heroin available to them. If they can be said to be addicted, it is not so much to heroin as to the entire career of a heroin user. The heroin user is, in a way, like the compulsively hard-working business executive, whose ostensible goal is the acquisition of money, but whose real satisfaction is in meeting the inordinate challenge he creates for himself. He, too, is driven by a need to find meaning in life which, because of certain deficits and impairments, he cannot find in the normal course of living. A big difference, of course, is that with the street user, the genesis of the deficits and impairments is, to a disproportional degree, in the social conditions of his life.

In the four communities where this research was conducted, the average median family income is $3500, somewhat less than that of family Welfare Department recipients. Other average population characteristics for the four communities include: public welfare recipients—four times the city rate; unemployment—two times the city rate; substandard housing—two times the city rate; no schooling—two times the city rate; median school years completed—eight years. Neither these few statistics nor an exhaustive list could portray the desperation and hopelessness of life in the slums of New York. In one short block where one of the authors worked, there was an average of one violent death a month over a period of three years—by fire, accident, homicide, and suicide. In Puerto Rican neighborhoods, sidewalk *recordatorios* (temporary shrines at the scenes of tragic deaths) are a regular feature.

Given the social conditions of the slums and their effects on family and individual development, the odds are strongly against the development of a legitimate, non-deviant career that is challenging and rewarding. The most common legitimate career is a menial job, with no future except in the periodic, statutory raises in the minimum-wage level. If anyone can be called passive in the slums, it is not the heroin user, but the one who submits to and accepts these conditions.

The career of a heroin user serves a dual purpose for the slum inhabitant; it enables him to escape, not from purposeful activity, but from the monotony of an existence severely limited by social constraints, and, at the same time, it provides a way for him to gain revenge on society for the injustices and deprivation he has experienced. His exploitation of society is carried out with emotional impunity on the grounds, for the most part illusory, that he is *sick* (needs heroin to relieve physical distress), and any action is justified in the interest of keeping himself well. He is free to act out directly his hostility and, at the same time, find gratification, both in the use of the drug and in the sense of accomplishment he gets from performing the many acts necessary to support his heroin use. Commenting on the value of narcotic-maintenance programs, where addicts are maintained legally and at no cost on a high level of opiate administration, one informant said:

> The guy feels that all the fun is out of it. You don't have to outslick the cop and other people. This is a sort of vengeance. This gives you a thrill. It's hiding from them. Where you can go in the drugstore and get a shot, you get high, but it's the same sort of monotony. You are not getting away with anything. The thing is to hide and outslick someone. Drugs is a hell of a game; it gives you a million things to talk about.

This informant was not a newcomer to the use of heroin, but a 30-year-old veteran of fifteen years of heroin use on the street. *Soldiers of fortune* is the way another informant summed up the lives of heroin users.

Not all, but certainly a large majority of, heroin users are in the category, which is the subject of this paper. It is their activities which constitute the social problem which New York City and other urban centers face today. The ultimate solution to the problem, as with all the problems which result from social injustice, lies in the creation of legitimate opportunities for a meaningful life for those who want it. While waiting for the ultimate solution, reparative measures must be taken. There are four major approaches to the treatment and rehabilitation of heroin users: (1) drug treatment (opiate substitutes or antagonists), (2) psychotherapy, (3) existentialist-oriented group self-help (Synanon prototype), (4) educational and vocational training and placement.

To the extent that the observations and conclusions reported in this paper are valid, a treatment and rehabilitation program emphasizing educational and vocational training is indicated for the large majority of heroin users. At the Manhattan State Hospital Drug Addiction Unit, an intensive educational and vocational program, supported by psychological and social treatment methods, has been created in an effort to prepare the patient for a legitimate career which has a future and is rewarding and satisfying. The three-year program is divided into three parts: (1) eight months of education, vocational training, and therapy in the hospital; (2) one month in the night hospital, while working or taking further training in the community during the day; (3) twenty-seven months of aftercare, which includes, where needed, further education and training, vocational placement, and psychological and social counseling. With this opportunity for a comprehensive social reparation, those who have not been too severely damaged by society have a second chance for a legitimate, meaningful life.

References

Chein, Isidor, et al. *The Road to H: Narcotics, Delinquency, and Social Policy*. New York: Basic Books, Inc., 1964.

City of New York, Police Department. Statistical Report: *Narcotics*, 1966.

Cloward, Richard A., and Ohlin, Lloyd E. *Delinquency and Opportunity*. Glencoe, IL: The Free Press, 1960.

Kardiner, Abraham, et al. *The Individual and His Society*. New York: Columbia University Press, 1939.

Malinowski, Bronislaw. *Argonauts of the Western Pacific*. London: Routledge and Kegan Paul Ltd., 1922.

Martin, W. R., Personal Communication, 1967.

Sharoff, Robert, Personal Communication, 1967.

Whyte, W. F. *Street Corner Society*. Chicago: The University of Chicago Press, 1955.

For Discussion

The authors argue that the daily activities in which heroin users are involved create purposeful lives among users, particularly when legitimate educational and work opportunities are limited. However, some heroin users, e.g., physicians, are employed in prestigious careers in which a sense of purpose is derived from their work. How would Preble and Casey explain heroin use among these individuals?

18

Gen-X Junkie

Ethnographic Research With Young White Heroin Users in Washington, D.C.

Todd G. Pierce

In *this next article, Todd Pierce uses ethnographic research to study drug users' social networks. He traces the evolution of networks from their formation to their dissolution. By comparing data on young white heroin users with older African American users, Pierce finds important age/ethnic differences in the areas of networks and risk behaviors. He also documents users' perceptions about their own addictions. Pierce's work and his emphasis on social networks demonstrates the importance of understanding subcultural differences when developing effective harm reduction interventions.*

Introduction: Research Objectives, Design, and Population

Historically, both ethnographic and epidemiologic research conducted with IDUs [intravenous drug users] focuses on people from poor socioeconomic situations. They are easier to access on the streets, monetary incentives for interview participation is very attractive, the ethnographer can be fit within the IDUs world view (often as an HIV counselor, outreach worker, or case manager), and they are at the most risk for HIV because intravenous drug use or sex-for-crack exchanges are overrepresented in poorer populations.

Beyond the possible political implications, maintaining this exclusive and extended focus (fifteen some-odd years of HIV research with these populations) also limits our theoretical understanding of the nature of networks of IDUs and the gambit of risk behaviors. This project focuses on economically well-off white IDUs or those who grew up in that socioeconomic condition. "Studying up" or "sideways," meaning the study of people with either the same or greater levels of mainstream power (than that of the researcher's), allows us to better understand the range of behaviors we are investigating while also allowing us to create a better cultural comparative model. As Murphy (1987) points out, IDUs can be found in every part of our society, not just the inner city.

Ethnographic data for this study were based on a network analysis of the IDUs. These networks of IDUs were extracted from larger complex units of social analysis: metropolitan areas, suburban communities, inner city or downtown club scenes, drug market and use areas, etc. (see Hannerz, 1980: 170–201). The networks were made up of an "extremely complex interlinkage" (Hannerz, 1992: 69) of networks with their own "perspectives" (*ibid.*) or world views on how they structure meaning within their perceived realities. For the purposes of this study, selected network variables (i.e., IDUs, young, white) were sampled for analysis. Network analysis can be a very powerful tool for social sciences (Aldrich, 1982: 293), but to fully understand these networks we must also consider the interlinking networks that make up the sampled networks (i.e., the wider communities from which the network members come, their histories, economies, and so on) and must analyze both the group and individual levels within their social and cultural contexts (Curtis et al., 1995; see also Bolt, 1957; Mitchell, 1969; Barnes, 1972).

The core sample for this study was drawn from a snowball sampling design and consisted of 12 white intravenous drug users (six male/six female) ranging in ages from 19 to 31. The snowball sample was achieved through the ethnographer's networking through the social networks of the IDUs first, and then introduced to the IDUs from their friends and other IDUs. The typical scenario would occur over a game of eight ball (pool) where the ethnographer's opponent would ask what the ethnographer did for a living, and then when told that he studied heroin users, the opponent would say "Oh, I have a friend that you should meet. He's a junkie." Then the ethnographer would give the opponent his business card and tell him to give it to the friend to arrange for a meeting.

In total, 12 egocentric networks were studied. The sample of networks contained two or three core or main members as well as periphery and outer periphery members. Primary analysis for each network was based on dyadic and triadic core relationships within each network (Neaigus et al., 1995). Each network had members that connected one network to the next (a "bridger"). Bridged networks contained white, black, and Hispanic members. Most of the 12 IDUs in the main sample came from a white, suburban, middle- or upper-middle-class background. Several were from very "well-off" families. All had at least a high school education, while some had either a four-year college degree or some college. Other individuals in the study included eight who were either heroin or cocaine snorters, cocaine injectors, or rehabilitated heroin injectors. In addition to these eight, about 25 peripheral network members were included in the study. These members were part of the social environment of the 12 core IDUs and were either cocaine snorters or sexual conjugates (sex partners) of the core. The individuals and the networks studied were part of extremely complex micro- and macro-cultural formations, which in turn influenced their drug-use behaviors (see Grund et al., 1991; Singer et al., 1992; Watters, 1988, 1989).

Through intensive participant observation, the ethnographer accessed drug users within the music and club "scene" of Washington, DC, and created relationships with several heroin IDUs, which led to the meeting of other IDUs (the snowball). Ultimately, he was exposed to a multitude of aspects of the users' lives. These aspects included the activities and rituals of club life, after-hours bars, pool halls, family life and relations, sexual relationships, friendships, and involvement with the drug economy and other users.

All subjects for this project were informed of the ethnographer's research objectives and were guaranteed confidentiality. Almost all of the subjects for the study admitted to wanting to participate because of the money offered for the interviews, but later came to rather enjoy working with the ethnographer. After a time the ethnographer and the subjects became close friends and colleagues, working together in this ethnographer endeavor.

Research Methodology

A variety of ethnographic research methods were employed at different levels throughout the research. All methods were embedded within the context of intensive participant observation. The ethnographer participated in all life activities with most of the research subjects, save for drug use, though he did drink alcohol. An average of 50 hours of participant observation were conducted every week for approximately 104 weeks. The ethnographer often ate, slept, and socialized at the informants' houses, as did the informants at the ethnographer's house. Toward the end of the research project, several subjects divulged their addictions to their families. Because the ethnographer knew the families, the subjects also told them what the ethnographer was up to. This compromised the ethnographer's research status, since the proverbial cat had been let out of the bag. But, in fact, this actually aided the family because they were able to talk to the ethnographer about addiction and were happy their family member was working with him. It aided in creating an open and respectful relationship for all parties concerned.

Life histories (Langness, 1965; see also Langness and Frank, 1981; Kroeber, 1961) were obtained from all of the core sample members. These interviews typically lasted two to three hours and were conducted either at the ethnographer's office, home, or a coffee shop. The respondents were paid $30 to $40 for the interview, depending on how long it took to do. The interviews investigated the respondent's life from birth to the present, covering all aspects of life, and focusing on drug use as it occurred.

Even recall interviews (Agar, 1980) were utilized to elicit data on past injection events to establish a self-report record of injection behaviors, their contexts, and network dynamics. The event recalls attempted to reconstruct specific events or instances within the respondent's recent life history. These interviews were conducted in coordination with the life histories and took place at the same time/place. Directed observations (developed for the Needle Hygiene Project but modified to include network-focused data collection for this project) (see Note 1) of injection events (see Note 2) were conducted with individual and multiperson injection events to record personal and network-based injection rituals. These observations were performed within the natural contexts of the individual's and network's injection locations. The observations aimed at data on network dynamics, needle hygiene practices, and other injection behaviors as they occurred within different times and spaces so as to capture variations on the injection theme in relation to contexts. All observational data were recorded in tables designed specifically for this task (previously utilized for the Needle Hygiene Project) and within field notes for future analysis.

Network plots, or diagrams that illustrate network connections and relations, were created with each informant. These plots depicted network membership, relationships, positions within other cultural and behavioral realms, and relations within socioeconomic structures (including relations within the drug economy and supply of drugs and needles). These plots were updated periodically and when changes occurred within the networks. Informants regularly aided the ethnographer in keeping track of the plots and verified field note data for him during sporadic and periodic follow-up sessions as a means of ensuring data reliability and to check the validity of data. Also, a comparative model was used within the analysis so as to help establish differences and ranges in behaviors and meanings within and between different types of networks. Different young white networks were compared for variations in structure, formation, changes over time, and possible dissolution. Also, the young white networks were compared to older black IDU networks on which data had also been collected during the same years (see Note 3). These black networks offered completely different structural dynamics than the white, which aided in creating a range of possibilities for comparisons. The exact same research methods were used with all networks. These comparisons will be utilized throughout the network descriptions to illustrate distinct differences between certain network characteristics and behaviors.

Network Attributes: Formation, Change, and Dissolution

Network Formation

When studying the creation of an IDU network, you must first ask whether networks formed before or after drug use were put into the mix. In most cases the networks studied in DC turned to injecting drugs after network formation. This point is central for our understanding of risk networks because it helps us better understand the foundations of the network itself (thus a better understanding of the risk relations). In most cases the network members knew each other and had a relationship prior to drug use. Those who did not know their network before "using" acquired them after accessing key roles within their drug environment (i.e., drug running).

What was discovered in DC was that there were two general ways young white IDU networks formed. The first was a network relationship that stemmed from long-term friendships. The second was centered around IDUs that had an ability to cop dope successfully.

Cindy's network is a good example of a long-term friendship network. Her network had three main members who were IDUs, one of which was her boyfriend (her main sex partner). She also had a number of other sexual partners who were part of her network, but they were not IDUs. The main members of the network, Cindy (age 20), her boyfriend Jimmy (age 31), and her best friend Sandy (age 19), had had a relationship before shooting up together. Cindy and Sandy had known each other since the age of 13 or 14. They had literally grown up together and had been hanging out in the rock and roll "scene" since their early teenage years. Cindy had started injecting with one of her boyfriends when she was in her late teens. Sandy had acquired a snorting habit by using with several of her friends, but then asked Cindy to help her in administering her first injection. The ethnographer witnessed her first injection (Pierce, forthcoming: 1), and interviewed Sandy the next day to discuss the event, and why she did it with Cindy:

> She's (Cindy) been an intravenous drug user for years, and she never wanted me to, she wouldn't, we hadn't done heroin together. We never have done heroin together until this [past] weekend, because she doesn't want me to get like her, she doesn't want me to shoot up heroin. She doesn't like this, but she saw that I was going to do it anyway. And she's lonely, really. She's very lonely. She's got her boyfriend, and he's not very nice to her, and she kind of didn't want me to do it, but she really like, I mean that's what she told me afterwards. She said "I really enjoy doing this with you, even though it's very bad." Then she's like "Okay, fine. Let's get the heroin, let's get the needles. We'll do this." She taught me how to do it. I've seen it done before, I just never went that step until this weekend. (Pierce Interview: WX: 14)

This scenario was common for most of the users in the study. In fact, all of the users [were] "turned on" to injection through a friend who was using. In such cases the formation of both young white and black injection networks came from much deeper sociocultural roots, i.e., neighborhood communities or schoolmates, than simply the need to inject. People are generally social beings, and form networks within their lives to satisfy different social needs they have (i.e., feeling accepted, belonging, loved). Different networks fulfill different needs. Some networks, like the family, may fulfill a need for stability or safety, others may be for advancement of knowledge, or adventure. Like many social activities, the first time one does something, it is usually done with somebody else who can experience it with you or show you how to do it.

In order to bring a network analysis to a deeper level here, we ask why and how people associate with each other in different cultural surroundings. Though anthropologists and sociologists alike have tackled this issue in some depth (indeed, historically this has been the mission of both disciplines), the topic cannot be given the proper attention in this discussion. But the bottom line is that most people do not experiment with heroin or start injecting it on their own. They are brought into a risk network of current users or they create a network of experimental users who eventually develop substantial habits (see Note 4). In order to fully understand the creation and the dynamics of a network, one must first understand the nature of its formation.

With experimentation come new experiences and the feelings and knowledge that come with them. The evolution of a person's drug addiction is a learning process that is often learned with their network, but also on their own through trial and error. Sandy explains for us the feelings she had about injecting heroin as opposed to just snorting it:

> I'm used to needles because I have a bad history with asthma, and I'm just used to needles from getting blood drawn, and whatever, and I find it kind of . . . it's hard to explain, it's a lot more sexy, almost. It's a lot more, you're really getting into the whole feel of the high. It's part of . . . the preparation's almost like, it's an anticipation . . . you're not just spreading a few lines out and snorting it this time. You're now cooking it and you're putting a needle in your vein. It's, if you have time to kind of sit there and do it, like have the whole symbolism thing, it's, it makes it a lot more impressive in your mind. It's uh, I don't, it's hard to explain. It's almost a fun thing, but it's not fun. I mean the pain of the needle, or whatever, that's not fun, but it's, you've got these little toys to play with, and you've got all this stuff that you have, that's illegal. And if you get caught, you feel like shit with it, but when you have it, it's almost like it's, it's more . . . almost like a toy . . . drugs. To play with, I don't know, it's not a happy thing, if you really think about it, but it gets you really excited about the whole thing and it's fun.

. . . It's almost like a permanent thing in your mind. You're really going to get high. It's really happening, you're really getting prepared for this whole thing, things like that, it's just the whole anticipation of getting high. You've got to do all [these things], it's part of the whole process. (Pierce Interview: WX: 14)

How these new experiences are discussed and learned within a network and certain socioeconomic contexts are important for understanding the injection processes, the personal nature and the social nature of the drug-using rituals (see Note 5). Also, the behavior that is learned through trial and error as an individual IDU builds a habit is important because it illustrates how some behaviors are not taught or discussed. Many aspects of drug misuse were not discussed by network members, such as morning sickness from withdrawal symptoms. In one discussion with the ethnographer, early on in her addiction, Sandy had described having a headache all day long. The ethnographer asked her how much dope she was using. She replied "three or four bags a night." Essentially, she was binging on heroin, but only at night instead of a constant stream of use throughout the day. And she was unaware of the detox effects occurring in the morning. Nobody from her network had told her! Even though her network members were very experienced users. In fact, it was the ethnographer who had to educate her on her biophysical reactions to the drugs. "Man, you just don't know why you have these headaches all day do you? You're dope sick!" She was horrified upon learning this. It was as if the reality of her level of use had just set in. That's when her long uphill struggle to recovery started, after the fact. A few days after learning this she told the ethnographer her headaches were all better, now she "got off E" (see Note 6) in the morning with that coveted first shot of dope for the day.

This transference of cultural information (or lack of it) is important for understanding risk reduction in injection behaviors because it tells us how people learn (or do not learn) certain behavioral procedures for injecting drugs. And, to make matters more complicated, this transference of information happens differently for all subpopulations or microcultures.

The second type of network formation is centered around copping dope. Young, new, white IDUs generally have a lot of difficulty trying to cop dope off the street. They fall prey to more experienced IDUs who will "take" them for all they are worth. They are literally sitting ducks for a "hard-core" street junkie who knows the ropes. Also, dealers do not trust people whom they do not know well, and so will be reluctant to sell to them. Therefore, the young white user must earn his stripes on the streets by going through a series of rip-offs and takes, gaining access to a runner, and then establishing a steady relationship. Not all young white IDUs can or want to do this. It is a risky endeavor, and the stakes are high when playing the street game. Only a few users from this study were any good at copping their own dope; even fewer held the highly respected runner position.

What this meant was that users who were not very adept at copping for themselves sought out users who could do that for them (for a small fee, usually in the form of money or drugs). In the first type of network formation discussed earlier, the network members were forced to go through trial and error routines in order to cop. In most cases only one of the members would do the copping for the entire network. Some of these successful buyers would find routes to copping other than the streets, like a dealer at a night club or an acquaintance from another network who had access to the drug. If a trusting relationship could be established with that acquaintance, then maybe the buyer and his or her network would join up with the runner's network, thus expanding the network based on the need for drugs (on the seeker's side), the need for money (on the runner's side), and trust. The runner then becomes the bridger of the two networks (the runner's own network and that of the seeker).

A good example of such network formation was Ken's, a 25-year-old white male, with long brown hair and tattoos. He's a musician, works at different clubs as a doorman, and plays a good game of pool. He is the center of his network because he is a drug runner. He was taught how to deal drugs by an older black man (Q) who had been running drugs for about 20 years, and who is also part of Ken's network. Ken has six network members, both male and female; all are white except for Q. His network members are not only customers for drugs, but they are also friends. He has known many of them for several years and socializes with them outside the context of injecting or scoring drugs. Although they pay him either in drugs or money for helping them score, the relationship doesn't stop there. They will often eat meals together, stay at each other's apartments, go out on the town together, etc.

Ken is a bridger to Q's network, which consists of about 30 people from different ethnic and socioeconomic backgrounds. Although Ken has injected with Q at Ken's apartment (which doubles as an exclusive shooting gallery), there is no risk of HIV infection between the two men or the two networks. This is because there is no direct or indirect sharing occurring during injection episodes. In networks that do directly or indirectly share drug-use equipment, bridgers can be a very high-risk agent for the network members because they can spread the virus from one network to the next. But because Ken's network is very safe in their drug-use behaviors, there is no (or extremely low) risk of infection.

There are other ways that networks form as well, most of which happen by the pure chance of being at the same place at the same time. A good example of this might be if one user sees another trying to cop some dope on the street and decides to approach the person to either aid in copping or to maybe ask if the person knows where they can get a good deal. They might even go as far as to pool their money in an attempt to cop a higher quantity of dope. This is rare, but it does happen.

IDUs from the study also reported making contacts at methadone clinics and NA meetings. In these environs it might be more risky to approach somebody because they are all supposed to be cleaning up. But they usually can tell if somebody is high, and so they approach them anyway. DC does not have a needle exchange program, and needles cannot be legally purchased without a prescription (a topic that will be covered later). But IDUs that I have worked with in Hartford, Connecticut, have reported making network connections at needle exchange points (see Note 7). These connections are usually for the purpose of locating "good dope" rather than network expansion per se.

A nice example of how networks are created can be drawn from the ethnographer's own experiences when meeting the respondents for this project. The ethnographer was not familiar with DC nor its drug scene. He did not know anybody when he moved into town, but found in-roads to one or two IDUs located within the alternative punk scene (see Note 8) (from which the ethnographer himself hails). These in-roads occurred within the social networks of the IDUs and through participating in social activities (like pool, as described earlier). The ethnographer then had those IDUs introduce him to other IDUs in their network, or members of other networks. The chain of people made up the sample for the study: it is not much different for an IDU who moves into town and doesn't know anybody, let alone other IDUs. This sort of network begins with a superficial "weak link" or peripheral connection within a network (as opposed to long-term "core" connections like Cindy and Sandy's), but that changes over time as relationships are developed.

The differences found between the way younger white risk networks formed in comparison to older African American networks is revealing. Most of the black IDUs studied had grown up in neighborhoods with a long history of drug economies. Many had relatives working within that economy as drug dealers, hustlers of some sort, and users. Their neighborhoods were inundated with drugs, and they quickly learned what it was all about at a young age. Many of the black IDUs had histories of incarceration because of their dealings with the drug market. Many of the users (almost all of them) had grown up knowing each other, but had entered the drug scene at different points in their lives. Their networks were much larger than the whites, yet they tended to have a small core network in which they created relationships based on either sexual relations or hustling schemes. The number of people they might inject with is much higher and changes more rapidly, but those people appear to be drawn from a limited number of people within their neighborhood.

The young white IDUs, in contrast, tend to come from suburban communities that do not have a visible active drug economy of nearly the scale that is found in poorer urban neighborhoods. They learn about drugs in their teenage years, and in many cases pass through a series of drugs before ending up on heroin (see Note 9). Their networks are small, with only a few people at the core (close sexual relations and best friends), and those networks are usually formed around trying to cop dope. They do not cop in their home neighborhoods (dealers are hard to find in Bethesda, MD), they do not use them frequently, and they have very few run-ins with the law.

In sum, one critical difference between the black low-income (or informal economy incomes only) networks and white middle-class networks was that the black networks were focused on getting money to buy the dope (they knew exactly how to go about getting it, but couldn't afford it), while the whites were focused on purchasing it (they had sufficient economic means to afford it, but were not good at getting it). Exact opposites in that respect, but both working for the same goal: Dope.

Network Changes

Networks were tracked over time to examine changes in size, relationships, risk behavior, and drug-use activities such as copping and connections within the street economy. The core of the networks changed very little. When it did, it was often spurred on by one of the members cleaning up off drugs (rehabilitating) or through changes within relationships, e.g., two or more of the network members might get into a dispute over some topic, maybe over drugs or some other social issue. Over the one year of the study, the IDUs became better at copping for

themselves as well as better at finding sources of new needles.

When rehabilitation of a person occurs, it can cause the network to splinter into two or more separate groups, depending on that person's role within the network. Ken's group is a good example of this sort of splintering. Ken cleaned up about halfway through the study. This caused his network members to form three different networks with other IDUs or primary dyadic relations. As soon as Ken is taken out of the picture, a drastic change occurs as the remaining members scramble for resources. Because Ken was the main drug supply for many of the network members, they now had to find their own way to cop drugs. To lessen this burden, Ken gave several of the network members the information and phone numbers they would need to cop the drugs.

Each of the members still consider Ken a friend, but he "had to do what he had to do," which meant clean up. But they were then stuck for another way to get drugs. Also, the members reverted to their main partners as a core network for support. The network did not actually dissolve completely; it just changed on a drug-use level.

As discussed earlier, networks also change as the members meet other people who can cop for them or offer something the network can use, i.e., money. This brings us back full circle to network formation. Networks also change when members move to other cities. In most cases the original network is kept while members from the new location are added on, thus making the IDU who moved a bridger of two networks. This happened with Cindy's network. She moved with her boyfriend to a beach in Virginia where they created a large network for whom they ran drugs from DC. They would drive back and forth in her sports car every couple of days on drug runs. Cindy hid the 10 packs of dope in a condom that she inserted into her vagina, just in case the police pulled them over. This new "beach" network was abandoned as soon as the summer was over and Cindy moved back to DC.

Network Dissolution

The most drastic change that any network can go through is total dissolution. This can happen through extreme splintering or when all or most of the network members quit using drugs (kick, clean up, rehabilitate, etc.). This happened with Cindy's network. By the end of the study Cindy and Sandy had cleaned up, Cindy had broken up with her boyfriend, and all other members had been dropped, save for a few sex partners (who changed every couple of months). Her boyfriend continued to use, but with a new network. In Cindy's network case, two of the three main or core members had cleaned up, and this caused the network to dissolve completely. Although the network may have been created before any of the members were IDUs (meaning long-term friendship-based nets), upon dissolution those ties were in most cases severed as well. Many of the IDUs had to change their social environments in order to stay clean, which meant getting rid of old friends and the places they socialized at. Cindy's boyfriend was cut out of the picture completely, but Sandy was kept as a friend because they were trying to clean up together. Even though they remained friends, they did not socialize together as much as they used to. They both began to rebuild their lives separately by creating new networks of friends and relationships.

Another network that dissolved was centered around a 25-year-old woman named Carol and her 22-year-old boyfriend Jim. They had three main members to their network and several not so important members. In this network's case the main core people were very different in terms of social status. Carol had a B.A. in philosophy and was very driven toward an upwardly mobile lifestyle, while her boyfriend was an untrained artist who also played the drums and was using drugs at a higher rate than Carol. Jim lived at an apartment that was paid for by his mother's husband (stepfather), but was thrown out after he had attempted suicide. The stepfather thought it was bad for his image to have the stepson around, so he evicted him.

When Jim moved to a homeless shelter, he and Carol (who was living with her parents) decided they should kick their habits. In short, Carol was able to kick and he was not, even though they were both taking methadone. This caused a tremendous strain on their love relationship, and ultimately ended in dissolution of the relationship. During their attempt at kicking they had severed ties with the other network members, at least that is what Carol thought. Jim continued contact with several of them after they had supposedly broken up. She discovered this and eventually left town so that she could be away from the environment completely. In this case the core members of the network changed, the dynamics of the network changed, and a different network was maintained by one of the original core members. This is not a case of splintering, but rather a reorganization.

Drug Use Behaviors: Needle Procurement, Needle Hygiene, and HIV Risk

Unlike most IDU subpopulations, the young white IDUs in this study were extremely safe users. As noted by many researchers, seropositivity levels will vary from population to population based on several factors (Price et al., 1995; see also Allen et al., 1992; Berkelman et al., 1989; Des Jarlais et al., 1988; Quinn et al., 1989; Siegal et al., 1991). Actual seropositivity data for the sample networks were not gathered. Self-report data indicated that only one member of the study was HIV-positive, but he did not directly or indirectly share any of his drug-use paraphernalia. In fact, there was almost no direct or indirect sharing of syringes or drug-use equipment observed within any of the direct observations of injection events of the networks. Most of the IDUs studied have the resources to buy their own bags of dope, which decreases the chance of indirect sharing occurring. And because most come from a well-educated and well-off economic background, they have had access to a wealth of information about HIV, safe sex, safe drug use, and safe cleaning practices. Basic concepts of viral transmission were well known by all of the IDUs studied, which made them very conscious of their behaviors.

The young white subpopulation worked with might be considered sexually liberal due to the high rate of sexual partners they had. Several of the participants had an average of one new partner a month, in many cases they had co-occurring sexual relationships (affairs or multiple partners), and in some cases there were group sexual encounters (two men and one woman, or two women and one man). These cases usually occurred when the participants were intoxicated (drunk), but were reportedly consensual events. New partners or new sexual adventures were always reported to the ethnographer as if they were telling stories of a great hunting expedition. One informant, Cindy, would even run up to the ethnographer with a smile and say, "I have a new one for my network plot!" And 9 times out of 10 she meant a new sexual partner. Although most are aware of and practice safe sex, there were many reports of unsafe sex, usually during sex when drunk.

Syringe procurement was usually done by buying the needles off the street or from a pharmacy. Although the latter is not legal in DC (you must have a prescription), it was easily done by a well-dressed young white person. The typical scenario was that the IDU cleaned themselves up, dressed up in their finest clothes, and came up with a line for why they needed the needles. One informant (Carol) said she needed them to inject vitamin B. In most cases the pharmacist took the line and made them sign a waver, releasing the pharmacy of any legal responsibilities they might have for selling the works to someone without a prescription.

When purchasing on the street, young white IDUs have to trek into some pretty rough areas to find sellers. A large network of black sellers (the network discussed above in the discussion on network formation) sold works as their hustle. Most of the works they sell are new and in sealed packages. But in some cases they will use the needles and then try to sell them as new, without cleaning them first. This is looked down upon by most

sellers, and they will often yell at those who do. It is considered a very bad thing to do, even among other needle sellers. But it does happen, which puts the young white user at risk when purchasing a needle from the street.

Awareness of needle hygiene and hygienic drug use is well known among this population. It is enforced by many of them in conversation and in practice. One of the networks worked with had an HIV-positive member who had contracted HIV from sharing needles in the 1980s. He was an older IDU, but was very aware of his HIV status and so made sure he did not share liquids or syringes with anybody else. He did not disclose his status to anybody besides the ethnographer, but promoted safe use within his network " . . . because it's the right thing to do." As discussed earlier, direct sharing was extremely rare within the white networks that were observed. In fact, the only direct sharing observed was between two core members of a network that had two outer periphery members within it as well. This core is made up of a 31-year-old man named Tim and his 22-year-old girlfriend Lucy. They keep their own sets of works, but they get them mixed up on occasion.

Because they divide their bags of dope in liquid (they are a live-in couple and pool all resources), they do partake in indirect sharing. They also have unprotected sex. This does not create any real risks for them or their network because it is a contained sharing of fluids. They do not indirectly or directly share with anybody else, nor do they routinely have sex with other people (Lucy does have sex with other women on occasion). This would place her at some small risk of HIV transmission, in which case, if infected, she could then infect Tim. This is a possible risk, but slim in comparison to other risky behaviors (such as unprotected vaginal or anal sex and sharing needles). In sum, young white IDUs were found to be at little risk for HIV in comparison to older black IDU networks. This had a lot to do with socioeconomic and educational levels as well as the level of drug use. While indirect sharing (though the sharing of cookers, cottons, or rinse water) is almost nonexistent in this population, it is the norm within the older black population. While direct sharing of syringes/needles is close to nil within the younger white population, it does happen on occasions within the older black networks.

Level of drug use and economic resources are key to understanding the differences between different types of IDU risk networks. The young white users who began to build up substantial heroin habits began to use up more than their economic resources could support. This eventually made them have to rely on street hustles to get by. By that time, when they had used their other resources, they had potentially gained access to dealers for whom they could run drugs. This helped them carry their habits for a while longer. That, too, would only last so long before they exceeded that resource. Then they were left to the streets with virtually no knowledge of the cultures of the street economy, and so they became prey to those who are accustomed to it, i.e., those who are from a poorer socioeconomic condition and who are very familiar with the streets. When this happens to young white middle-class heroin users, it is usually time for them to kick.

Kicking the Dope: Economic Loss, Cultural Stresses, and Transitions

Heroin addiction has taken on many cultural symbols within the larger part of American society, both in the way it is imagined and in the ways we have treated it. These symbols are utilized by the user and the non-user alike when discussing drug use and addiction. A young white heroin user's addiction is commonly couched within a context of personal trauma or depression. It is the saddened "rock star" or the depressed inner turmoil of the teenager. Their pain is imagined as being inner pain, with psychological issues that must be addressed. A poor black user's addiction is often discussed in relation to larger exterior circumstances. He or she is often discussed in terms of systemic poverty and institutionalized racism. The "system" has gone wrong, not the addict. This is a terribly interesting and important fact, and must be kept in mind when studying these sorts of microcultures. The users at both ends of the economic spectrum will often use this discourse. The white users often referred to personal problems in their lives that led them to drug use. The black users often referred to a lack of jobs and opportunities and to poverty as being causes of their drug addictions.

Also, the way in which heroin addiction is discussed and illustrated by the popular media and academia reflects the same discourse used by the addicts themselves (see Note 9). It is common to see writings on heroin addiction (or drug addiction in general) among minorities being represented with statistics and graphical charts. This is a depersonalized way of representing real people. On the other hand, young white addicts are often represented, especially in the media, through documentaries in a journalistic style—very personal, very tragic. Interestingly enough, the users do read these types of reports or are at least familiar with the discourse, and mimic its rhetoric. This is the mimetic process that Taussig describes (1993) that often leads to mimetic excess: copies of copies of copies, for which there is no original. We are left only with creations of perceived realities controlled through specific discourses (e.g., journalism, social or medical sciences, anthropology, etc.).

Understanding how an addict perceives his or her addiction, how and why they became an addict, is important for trying to understand why they want to clean up, and how they do it.

Cleaning up off a heroin habit is an interesting topic because it relates to all the topics discussed above: The reasons why networks form, their changes, their dissolution, their risk behaviors, etc. What was discovered through watching several of the younger white IDUs enlarge their habit size was that they went through the phases of use and economic support discussed above, but they had also undergone stresses as they underwent transitions from the white suburban life they grew up with and knew so well to the urban ghetto and the street-based economies of the drug world. The users were quickly losing parts of their "selves" as the different cultural roles that created them, i.e., the student, the daughter or son, the champion horse rider, the hard worker, the brother or sister, etc., began to slip away as the drugs took over their lives (chemically, socially). They slowly but surely moved closer to the street environment, to the home of "the real junkies," the hardened street addict that researchers of today are so familiar with. They didn't realize that these street junkies were no different than themselves, just better at surviving within their own environment.

Beyond being traumatic to the young white user emotionally, heading to the street life can often be deadly as they do the wrong things in the street because they don't know the proper roles in that environment. Also, they must learn the street way of using, where you do NOT divide bags of dope in powder form because you might end up ripping someone else off of their 0.02 cc of dope or end up with less cut than them. Thus the users now find themselves in a world of higher risk for HIV and no way to get out, except to kick.

In most cases kicking came well before that point, not because they couldn't afford the drugs. Rather, it was also personal stresses that caused the kick. The fear of losing friends, family, and social status was enough stress to force the IDUs to clean up. These cultural and social forces can be a powerful influence in a person's life, more powerful than dope. When these things are slowly being torn away, and the user sees himself or herself changing both physically and culturally, it scares the living daylights out of them. And when the next stop is some street corner or a shooting gallery, it's often enough to help them try to kick. Although many of the white IDUs had visited such locations, it was only because they were trying to cop. But they were not part of that scene, and they didn't know how to act or play the role when there.

Kicking dope happened a lot with the young white IDUs in the study. Many of them had attempted it numerous times with some success. They might stay clean for a few months, half a year, maybe a few years. But then they'd end up using again, building a habit, losing cultural identities, running short of money, and then kicking completely

or ending up on the streets. In most cases kicking was done informally, without knowledge of their habit or cleanup being divulged to anyone outside their drug use and close social networks. This was either done through "chipping" one's way down to detox (meaning they used less and less each day), the straight kick (no drugs to help the pain of withdrawal), or they used drugs purchased on the street to ease the pain of the kick (drugs that help you sleep it off were preferable). The ethnographer aided several IDUs who asked him to help them kick. One stayed at his apartment during the initial kick.

Compared to the older black IDUs, the younger white IDUs attempted kicking much more. The process of using, stresses, and kicking discussed above occurred rapidly and multiple times for most, while the older black IDUs were able to maintain a consistent habit for up to 20 years. This is because they have a limited economic resource that is determined, by and large, by their particular hustle. For instance, a needle seller knows he can sell only so many needles in a day, and so he pretty much knows how much dope he will be able to shoot in a day. This amount may vary on "good" days, but it is pretty constant. The white user, on the other hand, will build a large habit quickly, and thus he or she will "crash and burn" quickly, which leads to the repeated kicks. Many of the older black IDUs talk about wanting to kick, but because they are from the streets they do not feel the cultural stresses that might influence a kick attempt at the same level by the younger whites. Many of the older black IDUs kicked only when forced to do so by the law (either when locked up or forced into a rehab clinic for a 21-day detoxification).

Recommendations: Understanding Variation in Networks and HIV Risk

This research with young white IDUs offers the drug research and HIV intervention fields several insights. For one, through an ethnographic approach to network analysis, one that not only includes risk relations but also socioeconomic and cultural variables, we can better understand the possible range of HIV risk-related behaviors among injection drug users. Also, through an understanding of the different processes IDUs from different socioeconomic backgrounds go through within their histories of drug use, we can better understand the root causes of drug addiction and rehabilitation.

Future ethnographic research with IDUs should attempt to create more culturally comparative research models that analyze networks across different ethnic, gender, and socioeconomic ranges. This will help assist harm reduction and HIV prevention more effectively because it will allow us to better understand the finer points and differences in drug addiction, drug-use behaviors, and HIV risk.

Acknowledgements

Research for this study was conducted in Washington, DC, mainly in the Shaw, Adams Morgan, Dupont Circle, and Mount Pleasant neighborhoods, and the Virginia and Maryland suburbs of DC. This project was inspired through research for the National Opinion Research Center (NORC) in their research project entitled The Networks Project. NORC's project was a multisite epidemiological and ethnographic study of various intravenous drug users (IDU) networks performed in 1995–1996. Access to the white IDU networks was gained during NORC's project, and continued with a more intensive research focus for the Community Epidemiology Work Group (CEWG) project under the direction of Dr. Michael Agar.

Notes

1. The Needle Hygiene Project (NHP) was a seven-city ethnographic study that was conducted in 1993. The methodology for this project demanded that the ethnographers be able to collect comparative data across all sites. To do this, the ethnographers utilized a method they developed called "directed observation" of injection drug use behaviors. Todd Pierce, M.A., Michael Clatts, Ph.D., Steve Koester, Ph.D., and Laurie Price, Ph.D., developed this method and the NIDA Field Manual for this seven-city project.

2. An injection event is defined as the observed time of injection behaviors. The parameters of the event are determined by the ethnographer's presence at the location of the behaviors (i.e., shooting galleries). The event can be brief or several hours long, and may include several actual injection "episodes." Data collected for "events" include the macro- and microlevel environmental situation of the event (i.e., location, time of day, police presence), how the money for drugs and syringe were obtained (the "hustle"), how drugs and injection equipment were actually obtained, how they were used, and by whom, throughout the event, and disposal of equipment, as well as all microcultural dynamics of the users in the event (power relations, etc.).

3. Twenty egocentric black networks (10 male/10 female) were studied for this project, forming four separate clusters of networks. The exact same ethnographic methods used for data collection on the whites were also used for the blacks and Latinos that were part of the study. The Latinos from the study are not discussed in this article. In DC, Latino IDUs are uncommon, and were often bridgers or peripheral members of either black or white networks.

4. I am making a generalization across all types of heroin users and injection networks here—white, black, and Latino. Although there may be cases of individuals using on their own, it is very rare that they started using alone at the start of their injection use. It is also rare that they continue to use alone. Many "older" or seasoned IDUs will report being "loners," but with only a little ethnographic investigating it is found that they indeed have an extensive network of people they use with on occasion.

5. I am not supporting the "gateway" theoretical discussions here. On the contrary, there is an incredible difference between smoking marijuana and injecting heroin. Unfortunately, there is neither the time nor space to debate this topic within this text. One suggestion I can propose for this debate would be to consider gateway networks as a key factor in drug misuse. Social networks, including drug use networks, do not form due to a predetermined or acquired biophysical condition, i.e., drug misuse and the biochemical changes the brain goes through with this "disease." This can be illustrated by my argument that most first-time experiences an individual has usually occur with someone else (smoking, drinking, sex, dancing, eating, and so on). The jury is still out on the genetically prede-

termined drug addict, which is also used in the gateway discourse. To that end of the debate I would have to pose the question: Is it because one or both parents were addicts, or was it growing up in an environment of addicts where the youth is constantly surrounded with their behavioral routines?

6. "Get off E" is to satisfy the "craving" for heroin. The term is allegorical to a car that has an empty gasoline tank.

7. Research in Hartford, Connecticut, was conducted during 1990–1994 under the direction of Merrill Singer, Ph.D., at The Hispanic Health Council of Hartford, Connecticut, funded by HIN for the NIDA Cooperative Agreement and Needle Hygiene Project.

8. The "alternative" punk scene refers to the punk rock microcultures that had developed during the early 1970s and had developed and changed throughout the 80s and 90s. Although these microcultures (Hannerz, 1992) differ in many ways, there are some common links in ideologies and cultural material (i.e., music, clothing style).

9. For popular representations of heroin addiction, see the texts *Junky* by W. S. Burroughs (1977) (which was first published as *Junkie* under the pen name William Lee). Also, see the writings of Jim Carroll [*The Basketball Diaries, Forced Entries* (1987)]. For recent articles in popular magazines, refer to *Details*, April 1996, pp. 68–70, "Love in Vein"; or *Newsweek*, August 1996 lifestyle report, "Rockers, Models, and the *New* Allure of Heroin" (emphasis added). From 1988 to 1997 a slew of major motion pictures were produced that either directly or indirectly illustrated the junky lifestyle. Also, on any given day in America you can see portrayals of junked-out models on the nod in blue jeans and perfume commercials. Heroin chic!

References

Agar, M. (1980) *The Professional Stranger: An Informal Introduction to Ethnography.* New York: Academic Press.

Aldrich, H. (1982) "The origins and persistence of social networks." In Marsden and Man (eds.), *Social Structure and Network Analysis.* Beverly Hills, CA: Sage.

Allen, D. M., Onorato, I. M., Green, T. A.; and the Field Service Branch of the CDC (1992) "HIV infection in intravenous drug users entering drug treatment, United States 1988 to 1989," *Am. J. Public Health* 82: 541–546.

Barnes, J. (1972) *Social Networks.* Reading, MA: Addison-Wesley.

Berkelman, R. L., Heyward, W. L., Stehr-Green, J. K., and Curran, J. W. (1989) "Epidemiology of human immunodeficiency virus infection and acquired immunodeficiency syndrome," *Am. J. Med.* 86: 761–770.

Bolt, E. (1957) *Family and Social Network: Roles, Norms, and External Relationships in Ordinary Urban Families.* London: Tavistock.

Burroughs, W. S. (1953) *Junky.* New York: Penguin Books, Ace Books, 1977.

Carroll, J. (1987) *Forced Entries: The Downtown Diaries: 1971–1973.* New York: Penguin Books.

Curtis, R., Freedman, S., Neaigus, A., Jose, B., Goldstein, M., and Ildefonso, G. (1995) "Street-level drug markets: Network structure and HIV risk," *Soc. Networks* 17: 229–249.

Des Jarlais, D. C., Friedman, S. R., and Stroneburner, R. L. (1988) "HIV infection and intravenous drug use: Critical issues in transmission dynamics, infection outcomes, and prevention," *Rev. Infect. Dis.* 10: 151–158.

Grund, J., Kaplan, C., and Adriaans, N. (1991) "Needle sharing in the Netherlands: An ethnographic analysis," *Am. J. Public Health* 81: 1602–1607.

Hannerz, U. (1980) *Exploring the City: Inquiries Toward an Urban Anthropology.* New York: Columbia University Press.

Hannerz, U. (1992) *Cultural Complexity: Studies in the Social Organization of Meaning.* New York: Columbia University Press.

Katel, P., and Hager, M. (1996) "Rockers, models and the new allure of heroin." *Newsweek*, pp. 50–56, August 26.

Kroeber, A. E. (1961) *Ishi in Two Worlds: A Biography of the Last Wild Indian in North America.* Berkeley, CA: Sage Press.

Langness, L. L. (1965) *The Life History Method in Anthropology.* New York: Holt, Rinehart and Winston.

Langness, L. L., and Frank, G. (1981) *Lives: An Anthropological Approach to Biography.* Navato, CA: Chandler and Sharp.

Mitchell, J. C. (1969) "The concept and use of social networks." In J. C. Mitchell (ed.), *Social Networks in Urban Situations.* Manchester, UK: Manchester University Press.

Murphy, S. (1987) "Intravenous drug use and AIDS: Notes on the social economy of needle sharing," *Contemp. Drug Problem.* pp. 373–395.

Neaigus, A., Friedman, S., Goldstein, M., Ildefonso, G., Curtis, R., and Jose, B. (1995) "Using dyadic data for a network analysis of

HIV infection and risk behaviors among injection drug users." In Needle, Coyle, Genser, and Trotter (eds.), *Social Networks, Drug Abuse, and HIV Transmission* (NIDA Research Monograph 151), Rockville, MD: NIDA.

Pierce, T. G. (forthcoming) *Use Twice and Destroy: An Ethnography of Young White Heroin Users.*

Price, R., Cottler, L., Mager, D., and Murray, K. (1995) "Injection drug use, characteristics of significant others, and HIV-risk behaviors." In Needle, Coyle, Genser, and Trotter (eds.), *Social Networks, Drug Abuse, and HIV Transmission* (NIDA Research Monograph 151), Rockville, MD: NIDA.

Quinn, T. C., Zacarias, F. R. K., and St. John, R. K. (1989) "HIV and HTLV-1 infections in Americans: A regional perspective," *Medicine* 68: 189–209.

Scott, H., and Drake, S. (1996) Love in vein. *Details Magazine* (New York, NY), pp. 68–70.

Siegal, H. A., Carlson, R. G., Falck, R., Li, L., Forney, M. A., Rapp, R. C., Baumgartner, K., Myers, W., and Nelson, M. (1991) "HIV infection and risk behaviors among intravenous drug users in low seroprevalence areas in the Midwest," *Am. J. Public Health* 81: 1642–1644.

Singer, M., Zhongke, J., Schensul, J., Weeks, M., and Page, J. (1992) "AIDS and the IV drug user: The local context in prevention efforts," *Med. Anthropol.* 14: 285–306.

Taussig, M. (1993) *Mimesis and Alternity: A Particular History of the Senses.* New York: Routledge, Chapman and Hall.

Watters, J. (1988) "Meaning and context: The social facts of intravenous drug use and HIV transmission in the inner city," *J. Psychoactive Drugs* 20: 173–177.

Watters, J. (1989) "Observations on the importance of social context in HIV transmission among intravenous drug users," *J. Drug Issues* 19: 9–26.

For Discussion

Given the importance of social networks in the lives of drug users, how might these networks be used to generate more positive outcome for drug users?

19

Termination of an Established Needle Exchange

A Study of Claims and Their Impact*

Robert S. Broadhead

Yaël Van Hulst

Douglas D. Heckathorn

change services. Needle-exchange staff members also continue to risk arrest, prosecution, and imprisonment. Whereas previous studies have focused on the effectiveness of needle-exchange programs, we offer an analysis of a unique event, the closure of a well-established needle-exchange. The study consists of two parts. The first analysis examines the claims-making that succeeded in defining the needle exchange as a public health hazard and a social problem, causing it to be closed after several years of operation. In the second part, based on initial and follow-up interviews with needle-exchange clients, surveys of public drug-using sites, and ethnographic interviews, we present an impact analysis of the exchange's closure. The analysis provides a case study showing how a community's demonstrably effective HIV prevention efforts can be quickly eroded by the termination of a key harm-reduction service.

Unlike several other countries, the United States has generally opposed the implementation of needle-exchange schemes. In this article, Robert Broadhead and his colleagues provide a detailed description of the events that led to the closure in 1997 of a needle-exchange scheme in a small town in Connecticut. Their analysis focuses on the application of two theoretical approaches in their examination of "claims making." The authors also focus on how the closure affected injecting drug users in that area. Using two waves of interview data collected before and after the closure of the needle-exchange program, the authors describe how the closure affected changes in risk behaviors among injecting drug users in the area.

Despite the wealth of scientific findings showing that needle-exchange programs reduce unsafe injection practices, and that these practices are the direct or indirect cause of one third of new HIV infections in the United States, the future of needle exchange in this country remains uncertain. The federal government continues to ban the use of federal funds to support needle-exchange programs. In many cities with large numbers of HIV-positive drug injectors, local and state officials continue to oppose the implementation of ex-

The many scientific studies documenting the effectiveness of needle-exchange programs in reducing HIV transmission among injection drug users (IDUs) have been reviewed over the last five years by several expert panels, including ones organized by the U.S. General Accounting Office (1993), the University of California for the Centers for Disease Control (Lune et al., 1993), the National Research Council and the Institute of Medicine of the National Academy of Sciences (Normand et al., 1995), and the National Institutes of Health (1997). In April 1998, the Secretary of Health and Human Services, Donna Shalala, responded to yet another comprehensive review panel, the 34-member Presidential Advisory Council on HIV/AIDS, by officially acknowledging that "A meticulous scientific review has now proven that needle-exchange programs can reduce the transmission of HIV and save lives without losing ground in the battle against illegal drugs" (HHS Press Release, 1998).

However, despite the preponderance of scientific findings documenting the effectiveness of needle-exchange programs, and the evidence that unsafe injection practices continue to be the direct or indirect cause of one in three AIDS cases reported in the United States (Holmberg, 1996; Morbidity and Mortality Weekly Report, 1998, 1997; *Lancet*, 1998), the future of needle exchange in this country remains uncertain. For political reasons, the federal government continues to ban using federal funds to support needle-exchange programs (Stolberg, 1998). In many cities with large numbers of IDUs and HIV cases, local and state officials continue to oppose implementing exchange services (*DRCNet*, 1997a; Fitzsimon, 1998; Moore, 1996; *Newsbrief*, 1998), and staffs of needle-exchange programs in many cities continue to risk arrest, prosecution and imprisonment (*DRCNet*, 1998, 1997b; *New York Times*, 1997).

In light of the broad and forceful opposition to needle exchange, and the uncertain future of many programs, it is important that studies on the effectiveness of needle-exchange be complemented with studies that examine the impact on IDUs' risk behaviors when needle-exchange and other "harm reduction" (Erickson et al., 1996) services are disrupted and/or terminated. We present the first such study: an empirical investigation of the closure of an established, state-sponsored needle exchange, and the impact on its former clients' HIV-related risk behaviors and on the community at large.

The study consists of two parts, relying on a synthesis of social constructionist and objectivist approaches. The first analyzes the claimsmaking that succeeded over time in defining the Windham, Connecticut, needle exchange as a public health hazard and social problem, sufficient to close it after several years of operation. Like other social constructionist analyses, it details the career of the claimsmaking process, the principal claimants, the specific claims lodged against the exchange, and the reasons why the counter claims of the exchange's defenders were overwhelmed and the exchange was closed, regardless of the preponderance of scientific evidence documenting the effectiveness of needle-exchange programs to combat HIV.

In the second part, we present an objectivist analysis of the impact of the exchange's closure on its clients' drug-related risk behaviors and on the larger community. For three full years prior to the closure of the Windham needle-exchange, the Eastern Connecticut Health Outreach (ECHO) project, directed by Broadhead and Heckathorn, recruited and interviewed active IDUs in several Connecticut towns regarding their injection risk practices and methods of procuring clean syringes. This research has been published elsewhere (Broadhead et al., 1995; Broadhead et al., 1998; Heckathorn et al. in press) and is similar to other community demonstration research projects that targeted IDUs to examine and reduce their risk behaviors related to HIV (Brown and Beschner, 1993).

In Windham, for three years prior to the closure of the needle exchange, the ECHO project interviewed IDU respondents and provided HIV test counseling and education/prevention services. In March 1997, the needle-exchange program, which operated entirely independent of the ECHO project, was closed. Over the next 11 months, the ECHO project re-interviewed 111 ECHO respondents who were still active injectors. Of these, 78 were re-accessed three months later for a "post-closure follow-up" interview. Using the ECHO project's "pre-closure" interviews in Windham as a baseline, the analysis reports on several significant changes in Windham IDUs' drug-related risk behaviors that occurred following the needle exchange's closure. This case study shows how a community's demonstrably effective HIV prevention efforts can be quickly eroded by the termination of a key harm-reduction service.

In addition, following each formal post-closure interview, we conducted an open-ended ethnographic interview, seeking respondents' observations regarding how the closure of the needle exchange affected their peers. Finally, in the fall of 1996, the ECHO project staff began surveying several public outdoor areas within Windham for discarded syringes and other drug paraphernalia.

Basing the research on both constructionist and objectivist approaches generated an analysis that empirically documents the real-world consequences of a successful claimsmaking campaign. This documentation, however, also ironically disproves many of the major claims asserted by the exchange's opponents.

Background

In July 1992, in order to combat the spread of HIV, the Connecticut General Assembly passed legislation authorizing state support for needle-exchange programs and nonprescription sale of syringes in pharmacies (Groseclose et al., 1995). In 1993, a statewide assessment showed that most Connecticut pharmacies sold nonprescription syringes, that fewer IDUs were obtaining syringes from street sources (Valleroy et al., 1995), and that rates of syringe sharing had decreased under the new law (Groseclose et al., 1995). By 1994, six state-sponsored needle exchanges were operating, including one in Windham, a town located in the northeast corner of Connecticut.

According to the 1990 U.S. census, the town of Windham (also referred to by locals as Willimantic, a borough within the town), had a population of approximately 22,000 (81% white, 15% Hispanic [primarily ethnic Puerto Ricans], 2% African-American, and 2% other). As of July, 1998, Windham had accumulated 96 diagnosed AIDS cases of which 40 percent were white, 41 percent Hispanic, and 19 percent African-American (Connecticut State Office of AIDS, 1998). Sixty-three percent of Windham's AIDS cases are linked to injection drug use—a proportion almost twice the national average, and 13 percentage points higher than the state's rate of 50 percent (State of Connecticut, 1996).

The Windham needle exchange originally began as an underground operation in March 1990 through the efforts of two community activists. Over the next two years, local police arrested both of them repeatedly. Although the state's attorney attempted to prosecute the activists on several occasions, the charges against them, in every instance, were eventually dropped or dismissed. When the new Connecticut legislation took effect in 1993, the Windham needle exchange affiliated with a local social-service agency, and received state funding to operate. The exchange operated five days a week,

six hours a day, staffed by several part-time workers, including one of the original activists who came to be referred to as the "senior exchanger." By 1996, the exchange reported it had registered 308 IDUs, of whom some 200 were described as regulars. By all accounts, including ours based on numerous ethnographic visits by ECHO project researchers to the exchange over several years, the exchange enjoyed a far-reaching and positive rapport with Windham-area IDUs. However, in March 1997, following ten months of tumultuous public debate and criticism, the state defunded and closed the Windham needle exchange.

Part I: The Social Construction of a Public Health Hazard

The needle exchange's problems began in May 1996 when it was attacked publicly by the same state's attorney who, years earlier, had tried repeatedly to prosecute the exchange activists. In a speech before the Windham Business Council, the state's attorney claimed that the plethora of social services in Windham was disproportionate to other nearby towns, and that such services created more problems than they solved. He claimed that the growth of services for drug users, and especially the needle exchange, caused the town's drug problem:

> Needles bring addicts. They are the only people that need them. They bring addicts from all over the east, east of the Connecticut river. Addicts bring sellers. . . . When you have addicts, sellers, and needles, you have drug purchases occurring. Where? Any street corner. (State's Attorney, 1996) (C. Jenson, 1996a).

The state's attorney claimed that, because of services for drug users, the town as a whole was being ruined:

> Willimantic provides "one stop shopping" for every possible undesirable within eastern Connecticut radius east of the Connecticut River. Every addict . . . knows that Willimantic has the cheapest good quality heroin within this radius. It has the clean needles to shoot it up with, it has the no-waiting-list HIV program to get your medical treatment, it has a cen-

tral welfare check office, alternative incarceration center, cheap housing, and so on, and so on. These are the realities of your community that are killing your community right now. (State's Attorney, 1996)

The attorney's attack gained appreciable momentum several weeks later when the town's local paper, *The Chronicle*—which would become both a major interactional arena for claimsmaking, as well as a not-so-subtle opponent of the exchange—ran a lead story in bold headlines entitled "A Needle's Prick: How Life Changed In An Instant" (Chase, 1996a). The story reported that a two-and-a-half-year-old girl jabbed herself with a syringe found while playing in her yard. The state's attorney pounced on the incident and staged a dramatic news event (Chase, 1996b). At the town's police headquarters, flanked by the chief of police, officers, and reporters, the attorney unveiled 369 needles spread out over a long table that he claimed had been picked up around town over the last three weeks. When questioned, the state's attorney was vague about where and when the syringes were found. He did, however, emphasize that 72 percent of the syringes were the Terumo brand, the type provided by the needle exchange (Bond, 1996). (Terumo is also a common diabetic syringe sold by pharmacies.) Further, he claimed the 88 percent return rate on the more than 53,000 syringes given out in 1995 should be seen as a failure, rather than a success. He laid the blame for "the dramatic increase in the number of discarded hypodermic needles being found on the playgrounds of Willimantic" squarely on the needle exchange and called for the state to investigate the program (Bond and Kline, 1996).

The needle-stick incident, in conjunction with the state attorney's attack on the town's social services, precipitated a flood of angry letters to *The Chronicle*, as well as heated town council meetings and a public forum at the local high school where Windham residents vented their outrage. Many residents and some local officials made highly inflammatory remarks about the exchange and, following the state attorney's example, found it an easy scapegoat for virtually all of Windham's problems. A member of the city's board of selectmen castigated the state AIDS director, who funded the exchange, by claiming: "Your program is a menace to clean-living people, and you and your kind are the problem, not the solution" (*The Chronicle*, 1996a). In another letter, the selectman wrote: "Our state representatives facilitated the funding for a program, which gives junkies needles. What the heck is next? Condoms for rapists? Bullets for murderers" (*The Chronicle*, 1996b)? A member of the town's Board of Finance asked: "How can you stop the proliferation of drugs if we are funding their addiction [through the needle exchange]" (Faulkner, 1997). Other residents chimed in: "For years, our romantic Willimantic has been declining to a cesspool of drug users, drug pushers, hookers and derelicts" (*The Chronicle*, 1996c). Another resident wrote of "the role the needle exchange played in the problem of the economic deterioration of Willimantic" (*The Chronicle*, 1997a). The editors of *The Chronicle* also joined the fray. In a front-page article on a needle exchange voted down in a nearby Massachusetts town, *The Chronicle* editors highlighted a quote from one of the exchange's opponents in a special box in bold type: "We've been talking about a cockroach for four years. Now we've put it right in the middle of the dining room table. It doesn't belong here. The voters will vote it down" (C. Jensen, 1996a).

Throughout this period, many Windham residents also attempted to defend the needle exchange in letters to the editor of *The Chronicle* and statements in public meetings. One defender wrote:

As [the State's Attorney] knows, needles come from many different sources. Pharmacies, doctors' offices, hospitals, medical clinics, veterinarians, farms, diabetics, and individuals all dispense syringes. Of these, ONLY needle-exchange programs make any effort to collect dirty syringes. (*The Chronicle*, 1996d)

Others pointed out the inflammatory rhetoric of the exchange's opponents. For example, in letters to *The Chronicle*, residents wrote, "I feel the media blitz that followed [the needle-stick] was a sensationalized coverage of a sad incident" (*The Chronicle,* 1996e); and,

> It is such a shame and embarrassment to have someone on the Board of Selectmen who is so ignorant of the problem of addictions and HIV issues. [The Selectman] writes often about the needle exchange, demeaning it and the "liberals" and "junkies." He spews on and on about addicts and unfortunately knows nothing about addictions. (*The Chronicle,* 1996f)

In a town council meeting before two committees, Broadhead discussed the long list of prestigious professional organizations, such as the American Medical Association, and the National Academy of Sciences, that had gone on record endorsing needle-exchange programs, and he also summarized the scientific evidence on the effectiveness of needle exchange, relying on the then-most recent and comprehensive published review organized by the Institute of Medicine of the National Academy of Sciences (Normand et al., 1995). After his presentation, one committee member accused Broadhead of having a vested interest in the exchange because he was a scientist and directed an HIV prevention project for IDUs in Windham. She concluded by directing him to "Take your needles and go back to Willington or any other place you're from" (Faulkner, 1996). When Broadhead objected strongly, the seventy-something committeewoman then screamed, "Well, after this meeting, I'll see you outside and we'll settle this thing once and for all!"

Factors Shaping Claimsmaking Against the Needle-Exchange

Despite the preponderance of scientific evidence on the effectiveness of needle-exchange programs, and the long list of prestigious organizations endorsing them, there were several factors, some structured, others interactional and serendipitous, that shaped the controversy in favor of the exchange's opponents.

First, fueled by the War on Drugs, the opponents of the exchange appealed to a large pool of local public sentiment vehemently against illicit drugs, drug users in general, and especially injectors, who are among the most despised groups in society. In contrast, local public sentiment in favor of combating HIV, or in helping active drug users learn how to protect their health, is vastly weaker. As the National Commission on AIDS (1990) found in its report on small-town and rural Americans, the spread of HIV is fueled "by an epidemic of fear and bigotry" towards drug users, homosexuals, and persons with AIDS. As a result, throughout the controversy, the potential base of public support available for the needle-exchange's defenders to rally was far smaller than the large reservoir of hatred toward drug users that the exchange's opponents were eager to exploit.

Second, both the needle-exchange's staff and its parent agency were caught off-guard by the state attorney's attack, and by the skill with which he proceeded to build his "case" over the next several months. As a seasoned prosecutor, the state's attorney brought considerable experience to bear in construing recent events as "evidence," and in using the news media to "prosecute" the exchange. His efforts reflected strategic thinking, in staging of events and making disclosures, and in playing on the emotions of Windham's residents—the "jury." In contrast, the needle-exchange staff and its parent agency had no strategy, did not know what to do, and were immediately thrown on the defensive, from which they never recovered.

Third, after years of operating illegally, the exchange's underground legacy continued to shape the staff's orientation toward the community and the community's orientation toward the exchange. Although the needle exchange received state approval and funding, and the community had come to tolerate the program, the exchange was housed well out of public view, in a back-alley garage off Main Street. The exchange was neither a service the city pointed to with pride, nor something that enhanced the city's reputation. As a new addition to the city's network of health services, the needle exchange remained a pariah.

Reciprocally, the needle-exchange staff clung to their identities as activists who, through acts of civil disobedience, were proud of having brought the exchange into existence, despite arrests, legal persecution, and considerable hostility and ridicule from some Windham residents. The staff's main reference group was their clients, and they worked hard to be both accepted and respected by the IDU community, rather than the community at large. Thus, after coming aboveground in 1993, until being attacked three years later, the staff of the exchange did little to broaden their public support or develop a rapport with the larger community. The staff did not bother to educate the community about their success in working with drug injectors partly because the community was not particularly interested and partly because the staff continued to see themselves as dissidents, at odds with the community and its hostile, moralistic attitude against drug users. Thus, when the attack on the exchange came from the state's attorney, and then gained in momentum, the exchange became increasingly exposed and isolated, a convenient object for all kinds of rhetorical excesses, as exemplified by one councilman's claim: "The needle exchange is one gear in the big drug addiction machine. By allowing its presence here, we're condoning and enabling drug use" (C. Jensen, 1996b).

Finally, as the needle exchange came under increased scrutiny, its problems snowballed.

Confusion Over Policy. When the news media questioned the senior needle exchanger about the exchange's return rate of 88 percent, he claimed that state policy allowed for such a return rate, and that a one-for-one exchange was not required. When contacted, state officials claimed otherwise and vowed to work with the program to reach a 100 percent return rate. This made the exchange appear to be operating not only in violation of state policy, but also confused about what the policy was in the first place. Shortly thereafter, the parent agency's director admitted publicly that the exchange had "fallen short of the mark," and that "we're making an executive decision to go for a 100 percent exchange rate" (Chase, 1996b). This embarrassment for the needle exchange, and the promise to improve itself, simply fueled the self-righteous indignation of its critics.

Bad Attitude. When questioned in a newspaper interview about the lack of a one-for-one policy, the senior exchanger appeared defiant when he stated: "We are not mandated by the state to have a 1-to-1 exchange. And until we're told we have to do that, we're going to operate the way we do" (C. Jensen, 1996c). Two weeks later, in a letter to *The Chronicle*, the senior exchanger wrote: "It's evident that I have made mistakes regarding these operations. I humbly apologize for any problems that this may have caused" (*The Chronicle*, 1996g). However, the senior exchanger's admission of error and apology did not generate greater sympathy for the exchange, but further emboldened the exchange's opponents and strengthened their resolve to see the program terminated. The editors of *The Chronicle* described the senior exchanger's "attitude" as an example of an outlaw mentality: "a holdover from the needle exchange's days as an underground operation [that] continues to dog the program and has undermined the necessary public confidence for [it] . . ." (*The Chronicle*, 1996h). The director of the exchange's parent agency, during a discussion with Broadhead, also commented on the staff's attitude: "Training was something the [exchange] staff resisted because they didn't think the state had anything to teach them."

Inadequate Staff Regulation. A front-page article in *The Chronicle*, entitled "State Clamps Down on the Needle Exchange," itemized a list of improvements the state had determined the exchange needed to make: commitment to a one-for-one exchange policy; improved record-keeping on clients and needles; stricter inventory controls; better dissemination of information to clients about proper needle disposal; and staff training (Shayer, 1996a). These problems, as they surfaced due to the increased scrutiny of the needle exchange, sent a strong message to Windham residents: the program was far too loose. The following day, an editorial in *The Chronicle*, asked, "How did things get so out of hand?" (*The Chronicle*, 1996i).

Public Relations Blunders. A prominent supporter of the needle exchange observed that one reason the exchange had an 88 percent return rate was because the Windham police had a negative attitude toward addicts, deterring them from bringing their needles back in to exchange: "Willimantic is the only place in the state where law enforcement could be contributing to the problem" (Chase, 1996c). The chief of police immediately disputed this allegation as "ludicrous" (Chase, 1996d). One week later, as reported in *The Chronicle* (Shayer, 1996b), the prominent supporter apologized to the chief by telephone and a formal letter. This failed attempt to deflect some blame away from the exchange further strengthened the case being built against it.

In addition, the parent agency of the needle exchange was asked by the town's First Selectman to organize an action team in response to the discarded needle problem. The team created and posted warning signs informing children of what to do if they found a syringe. The sign showed a hand reaching for a syringe, encircled and bisected with a slash through it, the international symbol for "NO." Above the image in large letters read, "IF YOU FIND A NEEDLE DO NOT TOUCH IT." Below the symbol read, "FIND AN ADULT." The town installed the signs in all parks and recreation areas a week before 3,000 children and their parents from 268 soccer teams converged in Windham for a double-elimination tournament. This "in your face" warning sign directed at children, posted throughout Windham, infuriated many residents. One city councilman exclaimed about the signs, "They're awful. I don't know what kind of perception [the First Selectman's] trying to give about our town. He's killing our town" (C. Jensen, 1996c). An editorial in *The Chronicle* followed with the title, "Get Rid Of Those Unflattering Signs" (*The Chronicle*, 1997b). The defenders' well-intentioned efforts inadvertently besmirched the town's image and provoked a public outcry. Shortly thereafter, in March 1997, the signs were removed, and the exchange was closed.

For these reasons, the attack on the exchange began and grew, overwhelming the claims defending it, regardless of the preponderance of scientific evidence on the effectiveness of needle exchange in combating HIV, or the large number of AIDS cases in Windham caused by unsafe injection practices.

As the claimsmaking intensified during this ten-month period, other prevention efforts also became affected. For example, the seven local pharmacies in town became increasingly unwilling to sell syringes over the counter for fear of being blamed for the needle problem and having their business hurt. Two years before the needle-exchange controversy, the ECHO project had determined that all seven of Windham's local pharmacies were selling syringes over the counter. In early November 1996, in the midst of the controversy, we sent a male graduate student to the same pharmacies to purchase syringes, and four of the seven turned him away. Later in the month we sent a female graduate student, and five of the seven pharmacies turned her away. Moreover, one of the two remaining pharmacies still willing to sell syringes over the counter required that each customer also purchase a $3.00 "sharp safe" container to ensure proper disposal.

Clearly, a trend of growing anxiety and anger about the "needle problem" in Windham affected the city's AIDS prevention efforts and its continuing willingness to work with drug users, resulting in the closing of the needle exchange.

Part II: The Impact of the Windham Needle-Exchange's Closure

From March 1994 through February 1997, the ECHO project conducted 330 initial and 173 first follow-up risk-assessment interviews of Windham IDUs. In March 1997, the needle exchange closed. Over the next eleven months, the ECHO project began rerecruiting former ECHO respondents who had remained in the area and continued as active injectors. This resulted in 111 "post-closure initial" interviews and 78 three-month "post-closure follow-up" interviews. Below we report on several changes in Windham IDUs' drug-related risk behaviors that occurred in the months following the closure of the needle exchange.

In addition, following each post-closure interview, we conducted an open-ended ethnographic interview with respondents bearing on how the closure of the needle exchange affected the local drug scene—i.e., on the flow of drugs into town; changes in the size and composition of the local drug scene and respondents' peer-networks; shifts in drug dealing operations and the drug market; drug users' access to new syringes through local pharmacies, underground needle exchanges, shooting galleries, and "black market" sources.

Also, in the fall of 1996, in the early stages of the controversy, we began conducting periodic surveys of public outdoor areas in Windham where high levels of drug use occur. At four different sites, we recorded the number of discarded syringes. Both as a public service, and to avoid recounting items during subsequent surveys, we collected these syringes. At one of these locations, we also counted and picked up all dope bags, syringe wrappers, and syringe caps. After the needle exchange closed in March 1997, we continued these inspections for another year and a half, through September 1998. These data, combined with the ethnographic interviews of the post-closure respondents, allowed us to assess the impact of the needle exchange's closure on the larger community. Specifically, it allowed us to assess any significant changes in: IDUs' use of various outdoor areas in Windham; the volume of discarded syringes and related paraphernalia around town; and the characteristics of, and seasonal variations in, the town's outdoor injection drug scene.

Changes in IDUs' Risk Behaviors

We asked the post-closure subjects the same sets of questions they had been asked when interviewed as ECHO subjects. These included questions about their primary source of new syringes and about their drug-related risk behaviors, such as rates of re-using or sharing syringes or other drug-related paraphernalia such as cookers/filters and water. Thus the post-closure interviews allowed us to compare subjects' self-reported

Table 19.1

Demographics: Before and After the Closure of the Needle Exchange

Characteristic	Before Closure of the Needle Exchange (n = 330) %	After Closure of the Needle Exchange (n = 111) %	p
Gender			.811[a]
Male	69	68	
Female	31	32	
Race/Ethnicity			.867[a]
African-American	14	14	
Non-Hispanic White	62	59	
Hispanic	22	23	
Other	2	4	
Education			.110[a]
Never graduated high school	46	44	
High school graduate	32	41	
1 yr. college or more	22	15	
HIV Status			.588[a]
–	86	84	
+	14	16	
Age [mean (s.d.)]	35 (7.88)	36 (7.69)	.873[b]

[a]Two-sided; Chi-Square test.
[b]Independent T-Test.

behaviors before and after closure of the needle-exchange program.

As reported in Table 19.1, there were no statistically significant differences in the demographic composition of the pre-closure ECHO and the post-closure sample. The post-closure sample is virtually identical to the ECHO sample with respect to gender, race/ethnicity, education, HIV status and age.

Obtaining Syringes From Safe Sources. As reported in Table 19.2, before the needle exchange closed, 58 percent of the ECHO sample reported at their initial interview that their primary source for new syringes over the last 30 days was the Windham needle exchange, while 28 percent preferred to purchase their syringes in local pharmacies. Taken together, this means that 86 percent of the ECHO sample routinely obtained their syringes from what could be defined as "safe sources"; i.e., sources from which there is no doubt that the syringes were new and unused. Conversely, 14 percent of the ECHO sample reported obtaining their new syringes over the last 30 days from "unsafe sources"; i.e., friends and family, non-IDU diabetics, or "street sources," where some doubt exists as to whether the syringes were new and unused. Among those IDUs who obtained syringes from "unsafe sources," only

4 percent resorted to "street sources"; this is the least safe source, because dealers sometimes repackage used syringes and sell them as new (Friedman et al., 1987).

The needle exchange's closure reduced access to syringes from safe sources. The IDUs who reported receiving syringes from unsafe sources in the "post-closure initial" interview increased to 36 percent, a statistically significant 165 percent increase over the pre-closure baseline of 14 percent. In the subsequent "post-closure follow-up" interview, reliance on unsafe sources of syringes increased further: Those receiving syringes from unsafe sources increased to 51 percent, nearly quadruple the pre-closure baseline. Reliance on syringes from street sources increased even more sharply, from 4 percent before closure to 22 percent at the post-closure initial interview and 38 percent in the post-closure follow-up interview. Thus, reliance on the least safe source of syringes increased almost tenfold.

In the ethnographic interviews, many respondents noted that with the closure of the exchange, and the increased unwillingness of most pharmacies to sell syringes over the counter, a black market in syringes had developed. They reported syringes being sold on the street during regular business hours

Table 19.2

Primary Syringe Source for 30 Days Prior to Interview

Syringe Source	Before Closure of the Needle Exchange	After Closure of the Needle Exchange	
	Initial %	Post-Closure Initial* %	Post-Closure Follow-Up %
Safe	86	64	49
Pharmacy	28	58	44
Needle Exchange	58	6	5
Unsafe	14	36	51
Family/Friends	5	5	5
Diabetic Non-IDU	5	9	8
Street Source/Other	4	22	38
Total	100	100	100
	(n = 302)	(n = 86)	(n = 76)

* Initial interviews by Safe/Unsafe Source: Chi-Square = 22.363, df = 1, p = .000.

Table 19.3

Risk Behaviors: Before and After the Closure of the Needle Exchange

Risk Behaviors	Before Closure of the Needle Exchange		After Closure of the Needle Exchange	
	Initial	First Follow-Up	Post-Closure Initial	Post-Closure Follow-Up
Mean number of times used	5.56	3.52	7.68**	8.18***
syringe before disposal	(n = 322)	(n = 173)	(n = 105)	(n = 78)
Percent who shared syringe	22	16	34++	15
in last 30 days	(n = 278)	(n = 136)	(n = 89)	(n = 66)
Percent who shared cooker/filter	43	36	41	32
in last 30 days	(n = 281)	(n = 140)	(n = 87)	(n = 65)
Percent who shared water	32	28	37	28
in last 30 days	(n = 265)	(n = 134)	(n = 74)	(n = 50)

**p = .018, *** p = .000.
++Chi-Square = 4.669, df = 1, p = .031.

for between $1 and $2 and for $5 to $10 at night. Clearly, the closure of the Windham exchange led to a significant increase in the percentage of IDUs obtaining syringes from unsafe sources, especially "street sources," sharply increasing the possibility that syringes infected with HIV and other blood-borne pathogens would be shared. These data suggest that HIV-prevention efforts in Windham lost significant ground with the closure of the needle exchange.

Changes in Core Risk Behaviors. Table 19.3 reports on Windham IDUs' changes in core risk behaviors before and after closure of the needle exchange. Before the needle exchange closed, the mean number of times a syringe was re-used before disposal was 5.56 times at the initial interview. This fell to 3.52 times at the first follow-up interview. However, after closure of the needle exchange, progress in reducing the syringe re-use rate vanished. At the post-closure initial interview, the mean number of times a syringe was re-used before disposal increased to 7.68 times—a statistically significant 118 percent increase from the first follow-up interview before the exchange closed. Syringe reuse increased further at the post-closure follow-up interview, to 8.18 times per syringe, a 131 percent increase from their first follow-up interview before the exchange

closed. In the ethnographic interviews, IDUs reported that they were holding on to their syringes because they were uncertain where and whether they could obtain new ones. Several IDUs reported they had not discarded any syringes since the exchange closed.

Syringe reuse among IDUs affects HIV transmission because a relationship has been documented between the amount of time syringes remain in circulation and rates of HIV infection and other blood-borne diseases, such as hepatitis B and C. As reported by Kaplan and Heimer (1992, 1994) in their highly respected "needle circulation" study, a needle exchange reduces the circulation of syringes, which reduces the probability that they will become infected. In turn, the fewer infected syringes in circulation proportionately reduces the likelihood that a person will use a syringe infected with HIV and other blood-related diseases. However, after the closure of the Windham needle exchange, there was a sharp increase in the amount of time that used needles remained in circulation, creating a proportional increase in the probability that Windham IDUs were likely to re-use and share infected syringes.

The closure of the exchange also significantly increased self-reported syringe sharing. In the initial pre-closure interview, 22 percent of respondents reported sharing a syringe within the last 30 days. This declined 27 percent to 16 percent in the pre-closure first follow-up interview. After the exchange's closure, syringe sharing significantly increased to 34 percent, a level 51 percent higher than was reported during the pre-closure initial interview, and more than double from the pre-closure first follow-up. Syringe sharing then declined 55 percent from the post-closure initial rate of 34 percent to 15 percent in the post-closure follow-up interviews, for a statistically significant 55 percent decrease. This decrease may be the result of the harm-reduction education provided by the interview staff after the completion of the post-closure initial interview, during which respondents were reminded of the basic steps they needed to follow to reduce their risk of becoming infected with HIV.

The impact of the exchange's closure on sharing injection-related paraphernalia was qualitatively similar, yet weaker (see Table 19.3). The sharing of cookers/filters and rinse water declined between the pre-closure initial and the first follow-up interviews. Incidents of reported sharing then increased after the exchange's closure, and then declined again in the post-closure follow-up interview. None of these changes, however, reached the level of statistical significance.

The Impact on the Larger Community

Windham IDUs made several adjustments in reaction to the closure of the needle exchange, primarily in substantially increasing both their procurement of new syringes from unsafe sources and in their re-use of used syringes. Both adjustments significantly increased their risks of contracting or spreading HIV and other blood-borne pathogens. Further, based on periodic outdoor surveys of the larger community, the closure of the needle exchange appeared to have no significant impact on the larger drug scene.

Discarded Syringes

In the fall of 1996, the ECHO project began surveying four high-use, outdoor community sites for discarded syringes. In addition to the ECHO project survey, the town of Windham maintained a monthly "recovery log" of syringes found by the police department, the department of public works, and an AIDS prevention outreach worker. As reported in Figure 19.1, both the ECHO project survey and the recovery logs maintained by the town of Windham demonstrate that outdoor injection drug activities are highly seasonal in Windham, no doubt due to the harshness of New England winters. In the ECHO survey, the peak before closure (i.e., 22 in fall 1996) is virtually identical to subsequent numbers (23 in summer 1997, 21 in fall 1997, and 23 in summer 1998), suggesting no change in discarded syringes. By contrast, in the town's recovery logs, the syringe recovery rates slightly increased after the closure. The peak before closure (56 in fall 1996) is somewhat lower than the summer and fall rates after closure (98 in summer 1997, 98 in fall 1997, and 91 in summer 1998). The practice continued to occur even though IDUs reported an increase in the number of syringes they hoarded and re-used.

Discarded Drug-Related Paraphernalia

At one of the four outdoor locations where we surveyed and collected syringes, we also picked up all syringe wrappers, needle caps, and dope bags. These paraphernalia are significant because they serve as an indication of the volume of drug use in public areas. We collected this debris at only one site because of the large volume of material found, and the large amount of time and effort collection entailed. As reported in Figure 19.1, the counting and collection of syringe wrappers and needle caps displays a qualitatively similar trend to that of syringe collections, with seasonal variations from low levels of activity during colder months (e.g., 5 in winter 1996–97, and 3 in winter 1997–98) and much higher levels of activity during warmer months (e.g., 48 in fall 1996, 58 in summer 1997, and 46 in summer 1998).

Figure 19.1

Outdoor Survey Results of Drug-Related Debris in Windham

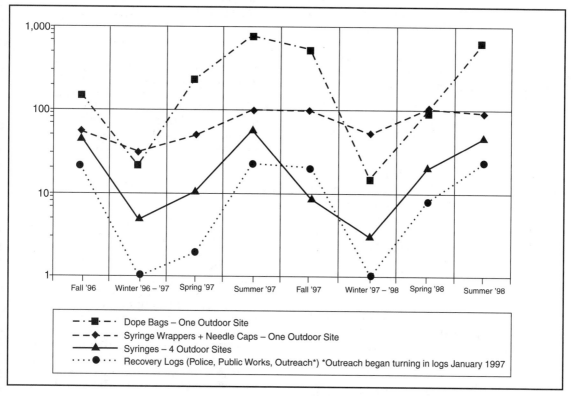

The number of dope bags collected varied from a low of 15 in winter 1997–98, to peaks of 776 in summer 1997, and 643 in the summer 1998, and also exhibiting a seasonal pattern (see Figure 19.1). In Connecticut, heroin is generally sold for $10 to $20 in small bags (folded paper) about the size of a large postage stamp, and the bags are imprinted with a symbol or name, such as Bronco, Black Sunday, Magic Three, F-16, Bad Boy, Crazy Boy, High Power, or Five Star. In surveying any high-use site in town (there are approximately seven such sites), perhaps along a wooded path, within a stand of trees, or among bushes in a park, it is common to come upon small areas littered with scores of dope bags and related debris, where people prepare their "fix" and shoot up. With the loss of foliage in the winter and early spring, which makes such areas visible to passersby, combined with the cold weather, IDUs move their drug use indoors.

Thus, the community survey data regarding publicly discarded syringes, syringe wrappers, needle caps, and dope bags, along with the town's own recovery logs, strongly indicate that, contrary to the claims made by needle exchange's critics, neither Windham's drug scene, nor the amount of discarded syringes and other drug-related paraphernalia, diminished after the closure of the town's needle exchange.

The Stability and Appeal of the Windham Drug Scene

We conducted open-ended ethnographic interviews with 107 post-closure respondents, seeking their observations on the impact of the needle exchange's closure on the community. These interviews provide additional, strong evidence of the stability and continuing appeal of the Windham drug scene after the closure of the needle exchange. For example, very few IDUs reported any change in the availability of drugs in Windham after the needle exchange closed. The few who did described different locations in town where drugs were being purchased, but no change in the availability of drugs or in their cost. Not one respondent ever mentioned purchasing drugs in the vicinity of the needle exchange while it operated. Nor did any respondent describe the needle exchange as in some way a part or extension of Windham's drug scene. Among respondents from out of town (45 percent of the ethnographic interview respondents), not one mentioned the needle exchange as a reason why they would specifically come to Windham. When asked, "Would you ever come to Willimantic to get needles?" a male, out-of-town respondent gave a blunt but typical reply: "No. It's got to be dope."

The Availability of New Syringes in Windham

In describing the Windham drug scene, all the respondents in the ethnographic interviews emphasized that drug users' first concern on a day-to-day basis is obtaining their drugs and then, after that, making do as best they can in consuming them. Thus, with the closure of the exchange, as a male respondent explained:

> That's what the problem is now—not having new needles all the time because of the money. Because you've got to go and buy the dope before you go buy the new needles, and [if you're short] you're gonna use an old needle until the damn thing breaks—until the needle falls off and it disintegrates on you.

This is especially true, as virtually all the respondents emphasized, for IDUs who are "dope sick." Time and again, respondents emphasized that, as described by a male respondent:

> If someone on the street don't have no money, don't have no needle, they gonna use a dirty needle. I mean, this is not an option . . . if he's sick, he needs! He has dope, he's sick—he needs dope and he needs a needle—he'll use [a dirty syringe]! There's no two ways about it!

The biggest change in the community according to virtually all of the respondents was their greatly decreased ability to obtain new syringes. This necessitated adjustments in behavior. The following statement by a female respondent typifies a common response:

> The biggest difference is, now people are using other people's works because they have to, because the pharmacies in Willimantic—you can't buy em. You cannot buy them! If you could buy them here in Willi there would be less people using other people's needles and there would be less headaches.

Another male respondent elaborated further:

> Well, the closing of the needle exchange has been a—and not just for me personally—I can see it's been a problem for every IV drug user in the Willimantic area. That goes right to the people who will now end up sharing needles more often. They'll be using duller needles and wrecking the hell out of their arms now. With the needle exchange, people didn't have to worry about using dull needles and getting abscesses and sharing needles. . . . Now it's a problem, especially with just one pharmacy that I know of that will sell them to you. It's a problem.

In response to the scarcity of new syringes, the respondents spoke of another change in the community that came after the needle exchange's closure: the development of a black market in syringes. Many respondents spoke of turning to "street sources" to obtain new syringes. They did so because most Windham pharmacies will not sell syringes without a physician's prescription, and many respondents reported being treated rudely when they tried to purchase needles. Nonetheless, respondents noted that, while they could purchase syringes from street sources, they did so at considerable risk:

> You don't know what you're buying on the street! Ya know, they can clean em [used syringes] real good where they look new and stick em back in and then put that crazy glue along the plastic. You don't know what you're buying.

As another respondent explained:

A lot of people buy them [from the street]. I mean, if you look at it, and see that it's sharp, they'll think that it's brand new. A lot of people will examine. But if you really examine it you can really tell that it's not new . . . [the dealers] burn em, they burn em. They bum the tips so that the seals go back together.

These comments suggest that dealers repackaging used syringes and selling them as new, a practice observed early in the HIV epidemic in New York City (Friedman et al., 1987), emerged in Windham as a reaction to IDUs' inability to obtain needles from safe sources.

New Injection-Related Risk Behaviors in Windham

Respondents in the ethnographic interviews reported HIV risk behaviors that they had not observed during the years in which the needle exchange operated. Some of these involved forms of sharing behavior not previously documented in the HIV-prevention literature.

Syringe sharing occurs in several different ways. First, sharing in the most usual sense refers to instances in which IDUs borrow used injection equipment from, or lend to, others to use in preparing and injecting drugs. Most respondents reported observing an increase in this type of sharing; as one stated: "Well, yeah, that [i.e., an increase in sharing syringes] is new since the exchange closed. I ain't never seen people take other people's needle right after you're getting high, with the blood still on it, and then stick it." Respondents also reported another form of syringe sharing—scavenging for parts of discarded or broken syringes in order to rebuild worn-out syringes, a practice we came to call "pirating." Though pirating does not involve borrowing equipment from a known person, scavenging syringe parts found around town obviously entails HIV risks. A male injector described pirating:

Well, there's a spot where people between [a local housing project and major drug selling area] and where we live that's like a half-way point. That's where we "give up" and just go in and do it right there.

People will leave cookers, their works. Even if they're broken we'll take 'em home to use the plunger. . . . We can make one needle [i.e., syringe] last through three different needles. . . . And that's where we basically get our stuff—from the outside.

Second, sharing is also commonly understood to be the result of "front-loading" or "back-loading" (Grund et al., 1996). Both processes involve drug users using one syringe to deliver a measured dose of a drug into another syringe, either through the front (by taking the needle off) or the back (by removing the shaft and plunger). Both risks involve sharing drugs contaminated during the preparation and measuring process, rather than sharing contaminated equipment. In Windham, because syringes are now being re-used at far higher rates due to their scarcity, it has become increasingly likely that contaminated drugs, rather than equipment, are being inadvertently shared, but in ways that IDUs do not think of as "sharing." Often groups of users prepare drugs in a common "cooker." Participants then each draw an agreed upon dose into their own syringes, using the numerical calibration on the barrel to measure the correct amount. This form of sharing entails risk, because the contents of the cooker can become progressively contaminated by multiple needles being dipped in it.

However, following the needle exchange's closure, a more hazardous form of sharing was also reported. Through repeatedly re-using syringes, respondents reported that the numbers on the barrel wear off rather quickly, especially on the most popular syringe, the "non-reusable" ½ or 1 cc plastic diabetic syringes. When the syringe a person carries loses its calibrations, other peoples' syringes are then used to measure the drugs, which can result in contamination. The contaminated drugs can be put in another container that a user will then draw from, or distributed through front- or back-loading:

If you get [a syringe] with numbers on it, you end up sharing. If someone's got numbers on it, that syringe goes around the room so everyone can measure up their shot. Everyone likes numbers you know . . . everything that goes into the house has to be split.

Thus, since the closure of the needle exchange in Windham, at least two new forms of sharing behavior were reported. First, the rebuilding of syringes from discarded syringes and parts does not involve direct lending or borrowing of a peer's injection equipment—so it was not thought to be "syringe sharing" by respondents. Second, many users in a group may use a syringe with numbers still on it to measure a fair dose, because the calibrations on their own syringes have rubbed off. Respondents also do not appear to define this new practice as "sharing." Both risk behaviors are examples of IDUs' pragmatic adjustments to the shortage of new syringes since the closing of the Windham needle exchange and the unwillingness of local pharmacies to sell syringes over the counter. They show how IDUs' adaptations under adverse circumstances proliferate the risks for HIV transmission to which they and their peers (including their sexual partners) are exposed.

For Discussion

Given the continuing, broad opposition to needle-exchange programs, it is essential that studies documenting the effectiveness of needle-exchange services be complemented with studies of the impact of needle exchange and other harm-reduction services being disrupted and/or terminated. This analysis suggests that, in pursuing such studies, researchers would benefit from combining social constructionist and objectivist approaches because, pursued in combination, the two perspectives offer a more comprehensive understanding of the evolution of events and their consequences than in studies using only one approach. In addition, in pursuing both approaches, we were able to document empirically the real-world consequences of a successful claims-making campaign. Ironically, this documentation disproved many of the major claims asserted by the exchange's opponents.

Claimsmaking about the Windham needle exchange made the program a scapegoat for virtually all of Windham's drug-related problems, and even the economic decline of the city itself. Although, like a storm, the claimsmaking began, gained in strength, peaked, then blew itself and the needle exchange away, *virtually all of the problems blamed on the exchange still remain in Windham, including a very large and active illicit drug scene.* In fact, Windham now faces even more problems: The progress the town made over the years in reducing drug users' risk behaviors has lost substantial ground. The needle exchange is closed. The ECHO project, a research prevention project that recruited, interviewed, and provided prevention education to 330 IDUs in the Windham area over several years, concluded in March 1998. Almost all of Windham's local pharmacies now refuse to sell syringes over the counter, even though the state legislature in 1992 authorized pharmacies to do so expressly for the purpose of reducing the spread of HIV. In short, because of the success of the claimsmaking campaign—much of it based on assertions now disproved about the relationship between the exchange and the town's drug problem and economic decline—Windham has seriously crippled its ability to protect the community against HIV and other drug-related problems. By studying both the claimsmaking process and the impact of the exchange's closure, we document findings that other communities may wish to consider seriously and that researchers may wish to consider in designing studies of similar events.

Our study demonstrates that claimsmaking can be shaped and influenced by chance events, blunders, and other problematic elements. For example, the initial attack on the Windham exchange by the state's attorney might have ended quickly had the child needle-stick incident not occurred. That event, itself, might have proved less pivotal had the main claimant, the state's attorney, been less skilled at strategically presenting and mobilizing support for his case. As claims about the exchange became public and were dramatized through the local newspaper, scrutiny of the exchange intensified. However, had no further problems with the service been discovered, the claims against it still might have faded away. But the increased scrutiny led to the discovery of more problems in the exchange's operation, the recognition of which further strengthened its critics' position.

Some of the problems that weakened the case for the exchange were potentially avoidable. The recognition of such problems, and the identification of ways they can be avoided or reduced, reinforce the importance of studies of this kind.

One avoidable problem concerned the *attitude* of the needle-exchange staff. Needle-exchanges and other service programs established through acts of defiance and civil disobedience may rightly feel proud of their brave beginnings. But once established, defiant attitudes and staff reputations as "radicals" can work to perpetuate a service's isolation and its status as an outsider. Organizational strength grows with forging alliances and interorganizational relationships. The latter require needle-exchange staff to become more conventional and professional in their orientation toward their work, their clients, and their place in the larger community among other social/health service providers. Needle-exchange staff who continue to revel in their radicalism increase the vulnerability of the programs they operate to community opposition.

Second, the Windham needle exchange neglected to broaden its *purpose*. The exchange was born with the single goal of preventing the spread of HIV and other blood-borne diseases among drug users. All other considerations were deemed secondary or unimportant. It was essential for the staff to assume a nonjudgmental attitude to the fact that their clients were active drug users. The staff's primary concern was providing clients with the knowledge and materials to inject drugs more safely. However, once the needle exchange became established, its sense of purpose did not expand to address additional concerns, particularly those of the larger community, such as encouraging users to reduce or stop their injection practices, promoting drug treatment, teaching users how to dispose properly of syringes and other paraphernalia, promoting self-help groups among drug users, and serving

as a liaison between the larger community and the drug-using community. With respect to the latter, the Windham exchange staff did little to educate the public about their work and their clients, or to educate their clients about the concerns of the larger community. Thus, the Windham experience suggests that, as needle exchanges become established, they must expand their purpose and be seen as accommodating and serving the concerns of the community-at-large as much as they serve the concerns of their drug-using clients.

A third avoidable problem concerned a lack of *accountability* in the exchange's operation. As needle exchanges become more established, the larger community expects them to account for their operating practices, expenditure of funds, and quality of services, as conventional services must do. Accountability requires the establishment and promulgation of standards and policies. The Windham exchange suffered from confusion over its own policies and standards, lack of staff training and quality control, and inadequate record keeping. Thus, the lesson from Windham is that, as needle exchanges become more established, they need to become more traditional in their reporting practices, record-keeping, and staff supervision and training, as well as in making explicit their regulations and policies.

Still, in societies like the United States, where a "War on Drugs" is not only pervasive but dwarfs in budget and propaganda all efforts for drug users to prevent AIDS and related diseases, the fate of such services will always be precarious, vulnerable to scapegoating and community opposition. However, when communities disrupt or terminate disease-prevention programs whose proven efficacy rests on overwhelming scientific findings, they do so at their own peril and folly. For example, while it appears there were only losers in Windham following the closure of the needle exchange, the opponents of the exchange can claim a symbolic victory: over the scientific experts and what a city councilman dismissed as their "charts, graphs, bells and whistles"; over the town's social services that are "a major part of the problem," as charged by the state's attorney;

and over the drug-using community that is "not part of the community anyway," as many residents claimed. As a leading critic of the Windham exchange asserted, "The people at the exchange are the guests of our town. If we don't want them here, we should be able to get them out. This is our home" (C. Jensen, 1996b). Thus, even with Science on their side, as well as Attitude, Purpose and Accountability, there may always be needle exchange and other harm-reduction programs that never square with some communities' constructions of "reality."

References

Bond, Don (1996) "Users stick up for needle exchange." *Norwich Bulletin* (August 20): A1, A2.

Bond, Don, and Greg Kline (1996) "State's attorney seeks needle exchange query." *Norwich Bulletin* (August 19): A1, A2.

Broadhead, Robert S., Douglas D. Heckathorn, Jean-Paul C. Grund, L. Synn Stern, and Denise L. Anthony (1995) "Drug users versus outreach workers in combating AIDS: Preliminary results of a peer-driven intervention." *The Journal of Drug Issues* 25(3):531–564.

Broadhead, Robert S., Douglas D. Heckathorn, David L. Weakliem, Denise L. Anthony, Heather Madray, Robert J. Mills, and James J. Hughes (1998) "Harnessing peer networks as an instrument for AIDS prevention: Results from a peer-driven intervention." *Public Health Reports* 113(1):42–57.

Brown, Barry S., and George M. Beschner (1993) *Handbook on Risk of AIDS: Injection Drug Users and Sexual Partners*. Westport, Conn.: Greenwood Press.

Chase, Philip Wilson (1996a) "A needle's prick: How life changed in an instant." *The Chronicle* (August 1)1:1, 9. (1996b) "Exchange pledges better collection." *The Chronicle* (August 20):1, 9. (1996c) "Needles: A foul ball away." *The Chronicle* (August 15):1, 10. (1996d) "Police chief: Don't blame us for city's needle problems." *The Chronicle* (August 16):3.

The Chronicle (1997a) "I'm very grateful." Letter to the Editor (March 22):6. (1997b) "Get rid of those unflattering signs." Editorial (March 5):6. (1996a) "She's the problem, not the solution." Letter to the Editor (September 13):6. (1996b) "I can't believe it." Letter to the Editor (September 26):6. (1996c) "Public shouldn't have to live in fear." Letter to the Editor (October 14):6. (1996d) "Needle exchange is in accord with law." Letter to the Editor (September 23):6. (1996e) "I offer my opinion on needle exchange." Letter to the Editor (September 30):6. (1996f) "Kiss should expand his knowledge." Letter to the Editor (September 20):6. (1996g) "I humbly apologize." Letter to the Editor (September 7):6. (1996h) "Needle exchange needs a change." Editorial (November 16):6. (1996i) "Follow the law or scrap exchange." Editorial (August 30):6.

Connecticut State Office of AIDS (1998) *Acquired Immunodeficiency Syndrome (AIDS) Surveillance Report*. Hartford, Conn.: State of Connecticut.

DRCNet (1997a) Approval for a needle exchange program in New Bedford, Massachusetts defeated in a ballot measure. (August). (1997b) Santa Cruz needle exchange facing arrests. (May 1). (1998) Cleveland needle exchanger arrested. (April 28).

Erickson, Patricia, Diane M. Riley, Yuet W. Cheung, and Pat A. OHare (eds.) (1996) *Harm Reduction: A New Direction for Drug Policies and Programs*. Toronto: University of Toronto Press.

Faulkner, Dale (1997) "Both sides gear up for needle bill airing." *The Chronicle* (February 15):1, 10. (1996) "Panel wants needle exchange thrown out." *The Chronicle* (November 8):1, 8.

Fitzsimon, Chris (1998) "Needle exchange debate misses point: Political considerations win at expense of facts, science, people's lives." *Triangle Business Journal* (May 11):39.

Friedman, Samuel R., Don C. Des Jarlais, Jo L. Sotheran, Jody Garber, Henry Cohen, and Donald Smith (1987) "AIDS and self-organization among intravenous drug users." *The International Journal of the Addictions* 22:201–219.

Groseclose, Samuel L, Beth Weinstein, T. Stephen Jones, Linda A. Valleroy, Laura J. Fehrs, and William J. Kassler (1995) "Impact of increased legal access to needles and syringes on practices of injecting-drug users and police officers—Connecticut, 1992–1993." *Journal of Acquired Immune Deficiency Syndromes and Human Retrovirology* 10:82–89.

Grund, Jean-Paul C., Samuel R. Friedman, L. Synn Stem, Benny Jose, Alan Neaigus, Richard Curtis, and Don C. Des Jarlais (1996) "Drug sharing among injection drug users: Patterns, social context, and implications for transmission of blood-borne pathogens." *Social Science and Medicine* 42(5):691–703.

HHS Press Release (1998) "Research shows needle exchange programs reduce HIV infections without increasing drug use." Department of Health and Human Services. (April 20).

Heckathorn, Douglas D., Robert S. Broadhead, Denise L. Anthony, and David L. Weakliem in Press "AIDS and social networks: Prevention through network mobilization." *Sociological Focus* 32.

Holmberg, Scott D. (1996) "The estimated prevalence and incidence of HIV in 96 large US metropolitan areas." *American Journal of Public Health* 86:642–654.

Jensen, Cindi (1996a) "Needle exchange faces vote in Massachusetts." *The Chronicle* (October 30):1, 9. (1996b) "Petition seeks ouster of needle exchange." *The Chronicle* (October 4): 1, 8. (1996c) "Selectman exchange words over signs." *The Chronicle* (October 12):1, 8.

Jensen, Steve (1996) "Stronger needle-exchange controls sought." *Hartford Courant* (August 20):A3, A10.

Kaplan, Edward H., and Robert Heimer (1994) "HIV incidence among needle exchange participants: Estimates from syringe tracking and testing." *Journal of Acquired Immune Deficiency Syndromes* 7(2):182–189. (1992) "HIV prevention among intravenous drug users: Model-based estimates from New Haven's legal needle exchange." *Journal of Acquired Immune Deficiency Syndromes* 5(2):163–169.

Lancet (1998) "Needle exchange programmes in the USA: Time to act now." Editorial 351:75.

Lune, Peter, Arthur L. Reingold, Benjamin Bowser, Donna Chen, Jill Foley, Joseph Guydish, James G. Kahn, Sandra Lane, and James L. Sorensen (1993) *The Public Health Impact of Needle Exchange Programs in the United States and Abroad*, Volume I. San Francisco, CA: University of California.

Moore, Elizabeth (1996) "Experts' needle exchange stand rejected by state health chief." *Chief Ledger* (January 25):37.

Morbidity and Mortality Weekly Report (1998) "Update: Syringe-exchange programs— United States, 1997." 47(31):652–655. (1997) "Update: Syringe-exchange programs— United States, 1996." 46(24):565–568.

New York Times (1997) "Guilty verdict for founders of needle exchange program." Metropolitan Desk (August 12):B2.

National Commission on AIDS (1990) *Research, the Workforce and the HIV Epidemic in Rural America.* Report Number Three. Washington, D.C.: U. S. Government Printing Office.

National Institutes of Health Consensus Development Conference Statement, February 11–13 (1997) "Interventions to prevent HIV risk behaviors." NIH Consensus Statement Online No. 104:14(3): 1–24.

Newsbrief (1998) "Colorado needle exchange bill defeated." (March–April):5.

Normand, Jacques, David Vlahov, and Lincoln E. Moses (1995) *Preventing HIV Transmission: The Role of Sterile Needles and Bleach.* Washington, D.C.: National Academy Press.

Shayer, Harold C. (1996) "State clamps down on needle exchange." *The Chronicle* (August 29):1, 4.

State's Attorney (1996) Presentation by State's Attorney at the Willimantic Downtown Business Council's Quarterly Meeting held at the Main Street Cafe. Unpublished audio transcription. Willimantic, Connecticut. (May 15).

State of Connecticut (1996) *AIDS in Connecticut.* Annual Surveillance Report, December 31, 1996. AIDS Epidemiology Program—Infectious Diseases Division. State of Connecticut. Hartford, Conn.: Department of Public Health, Bureau of Community Health.

Stolberg, Sheryl Gay (1998) "Clinton decides not to finance needle program." *New York Times* (April 21):A1, A18.

U.S. General Accounting Office (1993) "Needle exchange programs: Research suggests promise as an AIDS prevention strategy." Report Number GAO/HRD-93-60. Washington, D.C.: U.S. Government Printing Office.

Valleroy, Linda A., Beth Weinstein, T. Stephen Jones, Samuel L. Groseclose, Robert T. Rolfs, and William J. Kassler (1995) "Impact on increased legal access to needles and syringes on community pharmacies' needle and syringe sales—Connecticut, 1992–1993." *Journal of Acquired Immune Deficiency Syndromes and Human Retrovirology* 10:73–81.

*We wish to thank *The National Institute on Drug Abuse* for funding support of this project (RO1 DA 08014). We also are indebted to Michael Carbone, Rob Mills, Jay Hughes and George Barton for their research contributions; to Jean Paul Grund and Robert Heimer for crucial research suggestions; and to Perception Programs, Inc. and its outreach staff in Willimantic, Connecticut, for their efforts.

For Discussion

Why have various localities in the United States been so opposed to needle exchange?

Part V

Cocaine and Other Stimulants

Although chewing coca leaves for their mild stimulant effects had been a part of South America's Andean culture for perhaps a thousand years, for some reason the practice never became popular in either Europe or the United States. During the latter part of the nineteenth century, however, Angelo Mariani of Corsica brought the unobtrusive Peruvian coca shrub to the notice of the rest of the world. After importing tons of coca leaves to his native land, he produced an extract that he mixed with wine and called Vin Coca Mariani. The wine was an immediate success, publicized as a magical beverage that would free the body from fatigue, lift the spirits, and create a lasting sense of well-being. Vin Coca brought Mariani immediate wealth and fame, a situation that did not go unnoticed by John Styth Pemberton of Atlanta, Georgia. In 1885, Pemberton developed a product that he registered as French Wine Coca—Ideal Nerve and Tonic Stimulant. It was originally a medicinal preparation, but the following year he added an additional ingredient, changed it into a soft drink, and renamed it Coca-Cola. Although the extracts of coca may have indeed made Pemberton's cola "the real thing," the actual cocaine content of the leaves was (and remains) quite low—1 percent or less by weight.

The full potency of the coca leaf had remained unknown until 1859, when cocaine was first isolated in its pure form. Yet little use was made of the new alkaloid until 1883,

when Dr. Theodor Aschenbrandt secured a supply of the drug and issued it to Bavarian soldiers during maneuvers. Aschenbrandt, a German military physician, noted the beneficial effects of cocaine, particularly its ability to suppress fatigue. Among those who read Aschenbrandt's account with fascination was a struggling young Viennese neurologist, Sigmund Freud. Suffering from chronic fatigue, depression, and various neurotic symptoms, Freud obtained a measure of cocaine and tried it himself. Finding the initial results to be quite favorable, Freud decided that cocaine was a "magical drug."

In July 1884, less than three months after Freud's initial experiences with cocaine, his first essay on the drug was published. Freud then pressed the drug onto his friends and colleagues, urging that they use it both for themselves and their patients; he gave it to his sisters and his fiancée and continued to use it himself. By the close of the 1880s, however, Freud and the others who had praised cocaine as an all-purpose wonder drug began to withdraw their support for it in light of an increasing number of reports of compulsive use and undesirable side effects. Yet by 1890 the patent-medicine industry in the United States had also discovered the benefits of the unregulated use of cocaine. The industry quickly added the drug to its reservoir of home remedies, touting it as not only helpful for everything from alcoholism to venereal disease but also as a cure for addiction to other patent medicines. Because the new tonics contained substantial amounts of cocaine, they did indeed make users feel better, at least initially, thus spiriting the patent-medicine industry into its golden age of popularity.

By the early years of the twentieth century, however, the steady progress of medical science had provided physicians with an even better understanding of the abuse liability of cocaine. In 1906 the Pure Food and Drug Act was passed, bringing about a significant decline in the use of cocaine. The use of the drug did not entirely disappear, however. The drug moved underground, to the netherworlds of crime, the bizarre, and the avant-garde, where it remained for some 40 years. Its major devotees included prostitutes and poets, artists and writers, jazz musicians, fortune-tellers, and criminals. By the 1950s, cocaine use had spread to such other exotic groups as the "beatniks" of New York's Greenwich Village and San Francisco's North Beach, and the movie colony of Hollywood. It was used to such an extent among the urban "smart set" that coke became known as "the rich man's drug."

During the late 1960s and early 1970s, cocaine use began to move from the underground to mainstream society. At that time, most users viewed cocaine as a relatively "safe" drug. They inhaled it in relatively small quantities, and use typically occurred within a social-recreational context. But as the availability of cocaine increased during the late sixties, so too did the number of users and the mechanisms for ingesting it. Some users began to sprinkle street cocaine on tobacco or marijuana and smoke it as a cigarette or in a pipe, but this method did not produce effects distinctly different from inhalation, or "snorting."

A new alternative—freebasing, or the smoking of "freebase" cocaine—soon became available. Freebase cocaine is actually a different chemical product from cocaine itself. In the process of freebasing, street cocaine—which is usually in the form of a hydrochloride salt—is treated with a liquid base (such as ammonia) or baking soda to remove the hydrochloric acid. The free cocaine, or cocaine base (and hence the name

"freebase"), is then dissolved in a solvent such as ether, from which the purified cocaine is crystallized. These crystals are then crushed and used in a special glass pipe. Smoking freebase cocaine provides a more potent rush and a more powerful high than inhaling regular cocaine. By 1977, it was estimated that there were some four million users of cocaine, with as many as 10 percent of these freebasing the drug exclusively. Yet few outside of the drug-using and drug research and treatment communities were even aware of the existence of the freebase culture. Fewer still had an understanding of the new complications that freebasing had introduced to the cocaine scene.

The complications are several. First, cocaine in any of its forms is highly seductive. With freebasing, the euphoria is more intense than that achieved when the drug is inhaled. Moreover, this intense euphoria subsides into irritable craving after only a few minutes, thus influencing many users to continue freebasing for days at a time until either they or their drug supplies are fully exhausted. Second, the practice of freebasing is expensive. When a user snorts cocaine, a single gram can last the social user an entire weekend or longer. With street cocaine ranging in price anywhere from $50 to $200 a gram depending on availability and purity, even this method of ingestion can be a costly recreational pursuit. With freebasing, the cost factor can undergo a geometric increase. Habitual users have been known to freebase continuously for three or four days without sleep, using up to 150 grams of cocaine in a 72-hour period. Third, one special danger of freebasing is the proximity of highly flammable ether (or rum when it is used instead of water as a coolant in the pipe) to an open flame. This problem is enhanced by the fact that the user is generally suffering from a loss of coordination produced by the cocaine or a combination of cocaine and alcohol. As such, in many freebasing situations the volatile concoction has exploded in the face of the user.

Freebasing is but one variety of cocaine smoking. Common in the drug-using communities of Colombia, Bolivia, Venezuela, Ecuador, Peru, and Brazil is the use of coca paste, known to most South Americans as "basuco," "susuko," and "pasta basica de cocaina." Coca paste is an intermediate product in the processing of the coca leaf into cocaine. In the initial stages of coca processing, the leaves are pulverized, soaked in alcohol mixed with benzol (a petroleum derivative used in the manufacture of motor fuels, detergents, and insecticides), and shaken. The alcohol/benzol mixture is then drained, sulfuric acid is added, and the solution is shaken again. Next, a precipitate is formed when sodium carbonate is added to the solution. When the result is washed with kerosene and chilled, crystals of crude cocaine, or coca paste, are left behind. While the cocaine content of leaves is relatively low—0.5 to 1 percent by weight—paste has a cocaine concentration ranging up to 90 percent, but more commonly about 40 percent. Coca paste is typically smoked straight or in cigarettes mixed with either tobacco or marijuana.

Beyond coca, cocaine, freebase, and basuco, there is also *crack* cocaine. Contrary to popular belief, crack is not a product of the 1980s. Rather, it was first reported in the literature during the early 1970s. At that time, however, knowledge of crack, known then as "garbage freebase," seemed to be restricted to segments of cocaine's freebasing subculture. Crack is processed from cocaine hydrochloride by using ammonia or baking soda and water and heating it to remove the hydrochloride. The result is a pebble-sized crystalline form of cocaine base.

Contrary to another popular belief, crack is neither "freebase cocaine" nor "purified cocaine." Part of the confusion about what crack actually is comes from the various ways the word "freebase" is used in the drug community. "Freebase" (the noun) is a drug, a cocaine product converted to the base state from cocaine hydrochloride after adulterants have been chemically removed. Crack is converted to the base state without removing the adulterants. "Freebasing" (the act) means to inhale vapors of cocaine base, of which crack is but one form. Finally, crack is not purified cocaine; the baking soda remains as a salt after it is processed, which reduces the overall purity of the product. And

interestingly, crack gets its name from the fact that the residue of baking soda often causes a crackling sound when heated.

The rediscovery of crack during the early 1980s seemed to occur simultaneously on the East and West coasts. As a result of the Colombian government's attempts to reduce the amount of illicit cocaine production within its borders, it apparently, at least for a time, had successfully restricted the amount of ether available for transforming coca paste into cocaine hydrochloride. The result was the diversion of coca paste from Colombia, through Central America and the Caribbean, into South Florida for conversion into cocaine. Spillage from shipments through the Caribbean corridor acquainted local island populations with coca paste smoking, which developed into the forerunner of crack cocaine in 1980. Known as "baking-soda base," "base-rock," "gravel," and "roxanne," the prototype was a smokable product composed of coca paste, baking soda, water, and rum. Immigrants from Jamaica, Trinidad, and locations along the Leeward and Windward Islands chain introduced the crack prototype to Caribbean inner-city populations in Miami and New York, where it was ultimately produced from cocaine hydrochloride rather than coca paste.

Apparently at about the same time, a Los Angeles basement chemist rediscovered the rock variety of baking-soda cocaine, and it was initially referred to as "cocaine rock." It was an immediate success, as was the East Coast type, for a variety of reasons. First, it could be smoked rather than snorted. When cocaine is smoked, it is more rapidly absorbed and reportedly crosses the blood-brain barrier within a few seconds. Hence, it creates an almost instantaneous high. Second, it was cheap. While a gram of cocaine for snorting may cost $50 or more, depending on its purity, the same gram can be transformed into any number of "rocks," depending on their size. For the user, this meant that individual "rocks" could be purchased for as little as $2, $5, $10, or $20. For the seller, $50 worth of cocaine hydrochloride (purchased wholesale for $30) could generate as much as $150 when sold as rocks. Third, it was easily hidden and transportable, and when hawked in small glass vials, it could be readily scrutinized by potential buyers.

By the close of 1985, crack had come to the attention of the media and was predicted to be the "wave of the future" among substance abusers, and by mid-1986 national headlines were calling crack a glorified version of cocaine and the major street drug of abuse in the United States. Also, there was the belief that crack was responsible for rising rates of street crime.

As the media blitzed the American people with lurid stories depicting the hazards of crack, Congress and the White House began drawing plans for a more concerted war on crack and other drugs. At the same time, crack use was reported in Canada, England, Finland, Hong Kong, Spain, South Africa, Egypt, India, Mexico, Belize, and Brazil. By the middle of the 1990s, however, the use of crack had begun to decline in many of America's inner-city communities. In other locales, more hard-core users continued to ingest the drug.

Within the context we have outlined, the following chapters examine the history of cocaine, patterns of cocaine use, and the current controversies related to the prosecution of pregnant cocaine users and the sentencing of crack users in the federal courts. Two other stimulants—amphetamine and methamphetamine—are examined as well.

These synthetic drugs were used historically for medicinal purposes, although their misuse and abuse are described in this section. In addition, the drug known as "ice" is examined. A form of methamphetamine, and a stimulant like cocaine and crack, "ice" was expected to be the "new drug epidemic"—an epidemic that never was.

Additional Readings

Belenko, Steven R. (1993). *Crack and the Evolution of Anti-drug Policy.* Westport, CT: Greenwood Press.

Bourgois, Philippe. (2003). "Crack and the Political Economy of Social Suffering." *Addiction Research & Theory, Special Issue: Crack Chronicles,* 11(1): 31–37.

Inciardi, James A., and Hilary L. Surratt. (2001). "Drug Use, Street Crime, and Sex-Trading Among Cocaine-Dependent Women: Implications for Public Health and Criminal Justice Policy." *Journal of Psychoactive Drugs,* 33(4): 379–389.

Inciardi, James A., Hilary L. Surratt, and Christine A. Saum. (1997). *Cocaine-Exposed Infants: Social, Legal and Public Health Issues.* Thousand Oaks, CA: Sage Publications.

Jenkins, Philip. (1999). *Synthetic Panics: The Symbolic Politics of Designer Drugs.* New York: New York University Press.

Sterk, Claire E. (1999). *Fast Lives: Women Who Use Crack Cocaine.* Philadelphia: Temple University Press.

Streatfeild, Dominic. (2001). *Cocaine [An Unauthorized Biography].* New York: Thomas Dunne Books. ✦

20
America's First Cocaine Epidemic

David F. Musto

Widespread public perception would suggest that cocaine emerged initially as a drug of choice in the 1980s. In this essay, this myth is dispelled with a description of the drug's popularity beginning in the late 1800s. Using several illustrations, the author discusses the three phases of this first cocaine epidemic. He describes the four-decade process in which cocaine initially was readily available and endorsed by the medical community but then was prohibited.

Only a decade ago, many prominent Americans tolerated and even touted the use of cocaine. From Capitol Hill to Wall Street, the young and moneyed set made the drug its favorite "leisure pharmaceutical." Some talked of decriminalizing the "harmless" white powder. But that changed after cocaine overdoses killed several celebrities—including Hollywood's John Belushi in 1982 and college basketball star Len Bias in 1986. Last year, the drug claimed 1,582 lives in the United States and was a factor in countless crimes. Crack, a cheap form of cocaine, is now considered a scourge of the nation's ghettos; teenage dealers wage murderous turf battles within blocks of the Capitol dome. Lawmakers clamor for a war on drugs but despair of finding a way to win it. All this has a familiar ring to it, says Yale's David Musto. Here he recalls what happened a century ago, when America entered its first cocaine craze.

"I have tested [the] effect of coca," wrote a youthful Sigmund Freud in his famed essay *On Coca* (1884), "which wards off hunger, sleep, and fatigue and steels one to intellec-tual effort, some dozen times on myself." Like other doctors who had tested the drug, he found that the euphoria it induced was not followed by depression or any other un-pleasant aftereffects. "Furthermore," wrote Freud, "a first dose or even repeated doses of coca produce no compulsive desire to use the stimulant further."

With obvious wonder, Freud described the remarkable experiments of 78-year-old Sir Robert Christison, a world-famous toxi-cologist at the University of Edinburgh: "During the third experiment he chewed two drams of coca leaves and was able to com-plete [a 15-mile] walk without the exhaus-tion experienced on the earlier occasions; when he arrived home, despite the fact that he had been nine hours without food or drink, he experienced no hunger or thirst, and woke the next morning without feeling at all tired."

Freud's "song of praise to this magical substance," as he described it, was only one of many that were sung by various medical authorities before the turn of the century. In-deed, Freud had become interested in coca because American physicians, the drug's earliest and heartiest enthusiasts, had "dis-covered" that it could reduce the cravings of opiate addicts and alcoholics. Freud's inter-est was not academic. He was seeking a cure for the addiction of his colleague, Ernst von Fleischl-Marxow. "At present," Freud ob-served in 1884, "there seems to be some promise of widespread recognition and use of coca preparations in North America, while in Europe doctors scarcely know them by name."

In America, where the cocaine fad would reach greater heights than in Europe, the ability to cure opiate addictions was re-garded as only one of cocaine's marvelous powers. While morphine and other torpor-inducing opiates were beginning to seem positively un-American, cocaine seemed to increase alertness and efficiency, much-prized qualities in the industrializing na-tion. In 1880, Dr. W.H. Bentley, writing in De-troit's *Therapeutic Gazette*, hailed coca as "the desideratum . . . in health and disease." The gazette's editors, quoting another medi-cal journal, cheerily endorsed this view:

"One feels like trying coca, with or without the opium-habit. A harmless remedy for the blues is imperial. And so say we."

Encouraged by the nation's leading medical authorities, and with no laws restricting the sale, consumption, or advertising of cocaine (or any other drugs), entrepreneurs quickly made cocaine an elixir for the masses. Lasting from around 1885 to the 1920s, America's first great cocaine epidemic went through three phases: the introduction during the 1880s, as cocaine rapidly gained acceptance; a middle period, when its use spread and its ill effects came to light; and a final, repressive stage after the turn of the century, when cocaine became the most feared of all illicit drugs.

North Americans, to be sure, were not the first inhabitants of this hemisphere to discover or extol the powers of the "magical leaf." For centuries before (and after) the arrival of the Europeans, the Indians of the Andes had chewed coca leaves to gain relief from hunger and fatigue. The drug spread beyond South America only after 1860, when an Austrian chemist named Albert Niemann learned how to isolate the active ingredient, cocaine. When Freud published his first praise of the elixir, pure cocaine, along with the milder coca, was already available to Americans in drug and grocery stores, saloons, and from mail-order patent-medicine vendors. By 1885, the major U.S. manufacturer, Parke, Davis & Co., of Detroit and New York, was selling cocaine and coca in 15 forms, including coca-leaf cigarettes and cheroots, cocaine inhalant, a Coca Cordial, cocaine crystals, and cocaine in solution for hypodermic injection.

Parke, Davis reported that it had repeatedly stepped up production during 1885 in order to satisfy the public's growing appetite. A Parke, Davis advertisement informed doctors of the drug's uses:

> An enumeration of the diseases in which coca and cocaine have been found of service would include a category of almost all the maladies that flesh is heir to.... Allowing for the exaggeration of enthusiasm, it remains the fact that already cocaine claims a place in medicine and surgery equal to that of opium and qui-

nine, and coca has been held to be better adapted for use as a popular restorative and stimulant than either tea or coffee.

The American craving for cocaine was not satisfied by domestic producers alone. From Paris came a variety of popular cocaine concoctions manufactured by Angelo Mariani. "Vin Mariani," a mixture of wine and coca, arrived on the drugstore shelf with a raft of celebrity endorsements, including those of Pope Leo XIII, Thomas Edison, Sarah Bernhardt, Emile Zola, Henrik Ibsen, and the Prince of Wales. "Since a single bottle of Mariani's extraordinary coca wine guarantees a lifetime of a hundred years," exclaimed novelist Jules Verne, "I shall be obliged to live until the year 2700." Mariani boasted that Ulysses S. Grant took another of his products, "Thé Mariani," once a day during his last illness in 1885, allowing the ex-president to complete his famous *Memoirs*.

For consumers on a budget, the new wonder drug was available in less exalted forms. Coca-Cola, for example, contained a minute amount[1] of cocaine—enough to provide a noticeable lift, if not a "high." The "real thing" began life as a coca wine in 1885. In deference, ironically, to the widespread temperance sentiment of the day, the company replaced the alcohol content of the drink with soda water and flavorings, which allowed it to market Coke as a healthful "soft drink"—a "brain tonic" to relieve headaches and cure "all nervous affections." With the successful marketing of Coca-Cola and similar refreshers, the neighborhood drugstore soda fountain of late-19th-century America came to serve as the poor man's Saratoga Springs. There, the weary citizen could choose from among dozens of soda pop pick-me-ups, including Cola Coke, Rocco Cola, Koca Nola, Nerv Ola, Wise Ola, and one with the simple and direct name, Dope.

Cocaine also was offered as an asthma remedy and an antidote for toothache pain. (Other patent medicines contained opiates, such as morphine and heroin.) Dr. Nathan Tucker's Asthma Specific, a popular catarrh powder, or snuff, considered to be an excellent cure for hay fever and asthma, contained as much as half a gram of pure cocaine per package. Thanks to its remarkable ability to shrink the nasal mucous membranes and drain the sinuses, cocaine became the official remedy of the American Hay Fever Association.

In the six states and innumerable counties that were "dry" during the mid 1890s, workingmen found snuffs, soft drinks, and other cocaine products a cheap substitute for hard liquor. In states where teetotalers had not prevailed, bartenders often put a pinch of cocaine in a shot of whiskey to add punch to the drink. Peddlers sold it door to door. And some employers in the construction and mining industries found practical uses for the drug, reportedly distributing it to their workers to keep them going at a high pitch.

How much cocaine did Americans consume? Judging from its wide legal availability, and given its seductive appeal, it is safe to assume that they were using substantial amounts by the turn of the century. The limited import statistics for the leaf and manufactured cocaine suggest that use peaked shortly after 1900, just as cocaine was being transformed in the public mind from a tonic into a terror.[2] Legal imports of coca leaves during that period averaged about 1.5 million pounds annually and the amount of cocaine averaged 200,000 ounces. (Today, the United States has roughly three times the population it did in 1900 but consumes more than 10 times as much cocaine—perhaps 2.5 million ounces annually.)

At first, there were few reports of chronic cocaine abuse. Confronted with one example in 1887, Dr. William A. Hammond, former Surgeon General of the Army, and one of the most prominent cocaine advocates of the era, dismissed it as a "case of preference, and not a case of irresistible habit." However, by 1890 the *Medical Record* cited some 400 cases of habit mostly among people being treated, as Freud and others had recommended, for addiction to morphine and other opiates.

In fact, Freud himself watched his friend Ernst von Fleischl-Marxow disintegrate into a state of "cocainist" delirium before he died in 1891. Freud claimed that he had not intended for von Fleischl-Marxow to inject the drug, and he withdrew his support for its use

as a treatment for morphine addiction. But he never publicly renounced other uses of the drug.

By the turn of the century, cocaine was becoming more and more suspect. A thorough investigation by a committee of the Connecticut State Medical Society in 1896 concluded that cocaine cures for hay fever and other ailments had been a major cause of drug dependency, and "the danger of addiction outweighs the little efficacy attributed to the remedy." It recommended that cocaine be made available only to physicians, for use as a local anesthetic. Scattered newspaper reports—"Another Physician a Victim To The Baneful Drug"—books such as Annie Meyers' *Eight Years in Cocaine Hell* (1902), word of mouth, and articles in *Ladies' Home Journal, Collier's,* and other popular magazines brought more bad news. The debilitating effects of Sherlock Holmes's cocaine habit were familiar enough to earn a place in an 1899 Broadway play bearing the name of the brilliant British detective.

Once the miracle drug of upper-class professionals, cocaine came to be considered a curse of both the American demimonde and pathetic middle-class victims of patent medicines. The "Report of Committee on the Acquirement of Drug Habits" in the *American Journal of Pharmacy* (1903) declared that most users were "bohemians, gamblers, high- and low-class prostitutes, night porters, bell boys, burglars, racketeers, pimps, and casual laborers." That year, reflecting the public's growing suspicion of cocaine, the Coca-Cola company replaced the stimulant with a milder, more acceptable one, caffeine—the first, one might say, of the "new formula" Cokes.

A 1909 *New York Times* report on "The Growing Menace of the Use of Cocaine"—published even as use was declining—noted that the drug was used at lower-class "sniff parties," destroying "its victims more swiftly and surely than opium." In the *Century Magazine,* Charles B. Towns, a national anti-drug activist, issued a grave warning: "The most harmful of all habit forming drugs is cocaine. Nothing so quickly deteriorates [sic] its victim or provides so short a cut to the insane asylum."

As early as 1887, the states had begun enacting their own (largely ineffective) laws against cocaine and other drugs. In 1913, New York passed the toughest statute to date, completely outlawing cocaine, except for certain medical uses. By the beginning of World War I, all 48 states had anti-cocaine laws on the books. Fourteen states also inaugurated "drug education" programs in the public schools.

And what role did the federal government play? A small one, at first. According to the Constitutional doctrines of the day, Washington had virtually no power to police the drug trade directly. The federal Pure Food and Drug Act of 1906 merely required labelling of any cocaine content in over-the-counter remedies. But official Washington was jolted by the effects of the cocaine "epidemic" in its own backyard, much as it has become alarmed today by hundreds of crack cocaine-related killings in the Federal District. For years, the District of Columbia's chief of police, Major Sylvester, had been warning Congress (which then governed the city directly) of cocaine's horrifying effects. "The cocaine habit is by far the greatest menace to society, because the victims are generally vicious. The use of this drug superinduces jealousy and predisposes [sic] to commit criminal acts," he declared. In 1909, President Theodore Roosevelt's Homes Commission presented the testimony of Sylvester and other officials to an alarmed Congress, which promptly restricted legal drug sales in the nation's capital.

At the same time, the drug problem took on an international dimension. Roosevelt's State Department, under Elihu Root, had assumed the lead in attempting to regulate the free-wheeling international opium trade. Root's motives were mixed. By siding with the Chinese against Britain and other European powers that were reaping large profits in the Chinese opium market, Root hoped to gain trade concessions from the Chinese. Moreover, Root hoped, like some officials in Washington today, that he could solve America's drug problem by stamping out the cultivation of opium poppies and coca bushes abroad. But a nation that led such an international moral crusade, Root realized, would have to have exemplary anti-drug laws of its own.

In 1910, President William Howard Taft presented a State Department report on drugs to Congress. Cocaine officially became Public Enemy No. 1:

> The illicit sale of [cocaine] . . . and the habitual use of it temporarily raises the power of a criminal to a point where in resisting arrest there is no hesitation to murder. It is more appalling in its effects than any other habit-forming drug used in the United States.

The report also stirred racist fears, adding that "it has been authoritatively stated that cocaine is often the direct incentive to the crime of rape by negroes of the South, and other sections of the country." (Likewise, opium was considered to be a special vice of the nation's Chinatowns.) Terrifying rumors told of criminals who gained superhuman strength, cunning, and efficiency under the influence of cocaine. Convinced that black "cocaine fiends" could withstand normal .32 caliber bullets, some police departments in the South reportedly switched to .38 caliber revolvers.

By December 1914, when Congress passed the Harrison Act, tightly regulating the distribution and sale of drugs, the use of cocaine and other drugs was considered so completely beyond the pale that the law itself seemed routine. The *New York Times* did not even note the passage of the Harrison Act until two weeks after the fact. The vote was overshadowed by a popular crusade against a more controversial target, Demon Rum, a crusade which brought thousands of temperance demonstrators to Washington that December. From the gallery of the House of Representatives, temperance advocates hung a Prohibition petition bearing six million signatures.

But the public's adamant anti-cocaine sentiment, which had reduced the drug's appeal after the turn of the century and resulted in legal restrictions, now facilitated operation of the laws. Unlike Prohibition, which was not backed by a public consensus, the Harrison Act—which Congress made more restrictive over the years—was largely successful.

What happened to cocaine? Of course, some Americans continued to acquire and use it, but their numbers eventually shrank. Peer pressure and the threat of punishment combined to drive cocaine underground. Only occasional—and often negative—references to it appeared in movies and popular songs during the 1920s and 1930s. Cole Porter announced, "I get no kick from cocaine" in his 1934 musical, *Anything Goes*, and an impish Charlie Chaplin, in the movie *Modern Times* (1936), gained such superhuman strength from sniffing "nose powder" that he was able to break out of jail.

By the time I was in medical school, during the late 1950s, cocaine was described to medical students as a drug that used to be a problem in the United States. It was news to us.

The people who had lived through the nation's first cocaine epidemic and knew that the euphoria induced by the drug was a dangerous delusion had grown old and passed from the scene. Cocaine's notorious reputation died with them. By the 1960s, America was ready for another fling with this most seductive and dangerous drug.

Notes

1. Coca Cola's cocaine content was .0025 percent in 1900, and may have been greater during the 1880s.

2. It is also difficult to determine how many Americans were addicted to cocaine. Because they can live with their addictions for 20 or 30 years, opium addicts (of whom there were perhaps 250,000 around the turn of the century) are a relatively stable population, and thus easier to count. Cocaine addicts, on the other hand, do not live long if they do not quit, so their ranks are constantly changing.

For Discussion

It is believed that use of cocaine was minimal between 1930 and 1960. Discuss alternative explanations for the drug's alleged lack of popularity during these decades.

Reprinted from: David F. Musto, "America's First Cocaine Epidemic" in *The Wilson Quarterly*, Summer 1989, pp. 59–64. Copyright © 1989 by The Woodrow Wilson International Center for Scholars. Reprinted by permission. ✦

21

African Americans, Crack, and Crime

James A. Inciardi
Hilary L. Surratt

Historically, various anti-drug policies have targeted ethnic minorities. Current federal law allows for more severe penalties for possession of crack-cocaine than for cocaine powder and this sentencing policy has been criticized on the grounds that it discriminates against African Americans.

Media portrayal has contributed to the perception that crack-cocaine is used disproportionately among African Americans and these media portrayals are described briefly in this essay. The authors then report findings from their study of an ethnically diverse sample of cocaine users in Miami. The results show that crack use does not differ substantively across ethnic groups. Moreover, although crack users engage in various criminal activities, the authors observed only a few ethnic differences in relation to the crack-crime connection.

This one provision, the crack statute, has been directly responsible for incarcerating nearly an entire generation of young black American men for very long periods. It has created a situation that reeks with inhumanity and injustice. The scales of justice have been turned topsy-turvy so that those masterminds, the kingpins of drug trafficking, escape detection while those whose role is minimal, even trivial, are hoisted on the spears of an enraged electorate and at the pinnacle of their youth are imprisoned for years while those responsible for the evil of the day remain free.

— (United States District Court Judge Clyde S. Cahill, 1994)

Although Judge Cahill's remarks are both melodramatic and somewhat overstated, his point is well taken. Under the current federal sentencing scheme for cocaine offenses, crimes involving *crack*-cocaine are punished far more severely than those involving *powder*-cocaine (U.S. Sentencing Commission 1993). In fact, the Federal Sentencing Guidelines treat a given amount of crack as equivalent to 100 times the amount of powder-cocaine. Thus, this 100-to-one ratio results in sentences for crack defendants that are considerably more severe than sentences for those whose offenses involve other forms of cocaine (see Figure 21.1).

This oddity in the federal sentencing scheme is best illustrated with the story of Derrick Curry, a 20-year-old African American college student who was also a small-time crack dealer (see Leiby 1994). In 1990, Curry was one of several Washington, D.C.-area men involved in the distribution of crack who were under surveillance in a joint F.B.I./D.E.A. sting operation. At one point in the investigation, undercover agents had supplied Curry—who was no more than a low-level drug courier—with a cellular phone in exchange for crack. All of his telephone conversations about his crack deliveries were recorded, and eventually were used as evidence against him. On the day of Curry's arrest, agents found just over a pound of

Figure 21.1

Minimum Sentences (in Years) for First Offenders Under Federal Sentencing Guidelines

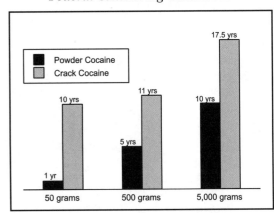

crack in his car, along with a criminal justice textbook (mine as a matter of fact) and a spiral notebook with his name on it. He was eventually convicted by a federal jury of conspiracy and distribution of crack, and sentenced to prison for 19 years and seven months, with no possibility of parole.

Derrick Curry's sentence, by almost any available standard, is incomprehensively severe. It is nearly three times the prison sentence served by most murderers in the United States; it is four times the prison sentence served by most kidnappers; it is five times the prison sentence served by most rapists; and it is ten times the prison sentence served by those who illegally possess guns.

Many African American defendants have argued in the federal courts, unsuccessfully for the most part, that this sentencing scheme discriminates against them on the basis of race. They point to the fact that, at least in the public's perception, crack-cocaine is primarily associated with black sellers and users, whereas powder cocaine is primarily associated with white users and sellers (Cauchon 1993).

To a large extent, this perception of crack as a "black" or "African American" drug can be traced to the mass media. In their many analyses of the crack epidemic, journalists have portrayed crack use and crack-related crime as essentially problems of blacks in inner-city neighborhoods. Magazine photographs show young African American men and women smoking crack in abandoned buildings, minority youths with guns in their jeans holding handfuls of crack, and even the former (and once again current) Washington, D.C. mayor Marion Barry, smoking crack. Headlines proclaim "A Tide of Drug Killings: The Crack Plague Spurs More Inner City Murders" and "Prisoners of Crack: Eight Years of Reagan Politics Corrupted a Generation of Urban Black Americans and Devastated Their Communities." Feature articles highlight "Drugs and the Black Community" and "The New Criminal Recruits of the Inner City, the Children Who Deal Crack." Altogether, journalists have presented a crack/crime/African American interconnection that would appear to be a simple, well established fact of American life.

The problem with these representations is that only part of it all has been clearly and accurately documented in media reports—that crack has had a destructive impact on black inner-city communities. The evidence presented for more specific crack/crime/African American connections is far more tenuous, leaving a series of unanswered questions. Is the crack/crime association mere sensationalism, or are crack users commonly involved in criminal behavior? Is any crack/crime relationship really a more general cocaine/crime association, or are crack users more crime-involved than other cocaine users? Is it really so that most crack users are African Americans, as typically portrayed in media reports? Are users of any and all forms of cocaine predominantly African Americans, or are African American cocaine users more likely than white or Latino/a users to use cocaine in the specific form of crack? Hasn't crack spread well beyond inner-city neighborhoods into working class suburbs, and if so, isn't there a white crack/crime problem? Are any such ethnic differences anything more than socioeconomic differences?

These questions, even without answers, suggest a considerably more complex relationship between crack use, crime by crack users, and race/ethnicity than that implied by mass media reports. Much of the complexity is due to the fact that multiple considerations other than race/ethnicity are at issue. These factors cannot be disentangled with urban war zone reporting techniques, but instead require scientific methods of sample selection and data analysis.

The Crack/Crime Connection

The relationship between crack use and crime has received considerable attention since the late 1980s, but the available studies have rarely examined race/ethnic differences. Nevertheless, at least the crack/crime linkages appear to be rather clear cut, particularly with regard to crack selling and violence (Goldstein et al. 1991; Hamid 1990; Inciardi, Lockwood, and Pottieger 1993, pp. 116–31; Inciardi and Pottieger 1991; Klein and Maxson 1985; McBride and Swartz 1990). The media reports appear to be correct in implying that crack users are commonly involved in criminal behavior.

Prior research is also fairly consistent in its answer to another question about the crack/crime/race connection. Many studies suggest crack users are more often African Americans. For example, a disproportionate amount of crack use among African Americans is indicated in official statistics from the National Institute on Drug Abuse (NIDA) Household Survey. In 1991, 4.3 percent of blacks surveyed had used crack, compared to only 1.5 percent of whites and 2.1 percent of Latinos/as. Race/ethnic differences in lifetime crack use were especially large among people aged 26 to 34 years old: the 9.2 percent of blacks reporting use is some three times that of the 2.8 percent for whites or 3.7 percent for Latinos/as (National Institute on Drug Abuse 1991). However, because whites represent the majority of the U.S. population, these percentage estimates imply that in terms of absolute numbers, most crack users are *not* African Americans, but whites. NIDA's estimates of current crack use—defined as use in the past month—are 0.7 percent for blacks, 0.4 percent for Latinos/as, and 0.2 percent for whites. This translates to population estimates of 172,000 black crack users, 68,000 Latino/a crack users, and 238,000 white crack users. That is, of the 479,000 crack users estimated for the 1991 U.S. household population, 49.9 percent were white, 14.2 percent were Latino/a, and only 35.9 percent were African Americans.

While NIDA's Household Survey provides the *best available* evidence on race/ethnic distributions of crack users, it should also be noted that this does not mean it is necessarily a *good* estimate. Very low percentage estimates in this type of study—such as those given for current crack use—mean less reliable estimates. Further, as a survey of the general household population, the NIDA study does not include populations critical to examining race/ethnic differences in crack use, such as runaways and other homeless people, addicts in residential treatment, incarcerated populations, and those living on the street and in drug subcultures

that are generally inaccessible through standard survey methods. Other official statistics do include some of these populations—notably the National Institute of Justice's Drug Use Forecasting (DUF) program and NIDA's Drug Abuse Warning Network (DAWN)—but they cannot separate crack use from other cocaine use and they do not report statistics in a way that permits extrapolation to population estimates.

Beyond these two points—a strong crack/crime relationship and no more than a weak crack/black association—very little published research exists on ethnic differences specifically among *crack* users, let alone ethnic differences in crimes among crack users. In fact, there is surprisingly little research on ethnic differences concerning any type of illegal drug use or its correlates. Moreover, the work that has been done is suspect for purposes of understanding race-ethnicity/drug-use relationships because it is almost all based on samples of either students or drug treatment patients, and ethnic minorities have both higher rates of school dropout and lower rates of treatment seeking than whites (Collins 1992; Rebach 1992).

The most research attention in this regard has focused on adolescents, primarily students. The findings generally show that ethnic differences in drug use are explained by background variables, particularly income and availability (Adlaf, Smart, and Tan 1989; Kandel, Single, and Kessler 1976; Maddehian, Newcomb, and Bentler 1986; Wallace and Bachman 1991). More importantly, studies indicate that most drug use rates—including those of alcohol, cocaine, pills of all types, cigarettes, hallucinogens, and inhalants—are *lowest* among black adolescents (Bachman et al. 1991; Kandel, Single, and Kessler 1976; National Institute on Drug Abuse 1991; Rebach 1992; Segal 1989). Latino/a males, however, are generally found more likely to have used cocaine than either whites or blacks (Bachman et al. 1991; Marin 1990; National Institute on Drug Abuse 1991; Wallace and Bachman 1991).

Among adult drug users, most research on ethnic differences comes from studies of heroin addicts in treatment in which, usually, only two ethnic categories are compared: black and white, or Latino/a and white Anglo. These studies suggest that minorities, including African Americans, Puerto Ricans, and Mexican Americans, are overrepresented among heroin users (Anglin et al. 1988; Ball and Chambers 1970; Kleinman and Lukoff 1978). Studies of cocaine and crack users also indicate disproportionate use among minorities (Carroll and Rounsaville 1992; Johnson, Elmoghazy, and Dunlap 1990). As in the studies of students, however, ethnicity generally is found to interact with other variables. In particular, an interaction effect between gender and ethnicity has been documented in several studies (Austin and Gilbert 1989; Prendergast et al. 1989), and other researchers have presented their results separately for males and females to clarify the ethnic differences within gender categories and to avoid the complexity of this interaction (Anglin et al. 1988; Wallace and Bachman 1991).

More recently, treatment status also has been recognized as an important confounding factor in the study of ethnic differences in drug use. One recent study, for example, found that 55 percent of 298 cocaine users in treatment were white, whereas among 101 cocaine users *not* in treatment, only 14 percent were white (Carroll and Rounsaville 1992). Treatment status of cocaine users also appears to be entangled with gender and other differences (Boyd and Mieczkowski 1990; Brunswick, Messeri, and Aidala 1990; Chitwood and Morningstar 1985; Griffin et al. 1989; Rounsaville and Kleber 1985).

Altogether, social science research pertinent to the alleged crack/crime/black linkage can be summarized as follows. First, it is limited, particularly on the specific topic of crack. Second, it has documented a *crack/ crime* association. Third, it suggests that any *black/crack* association is a limited one— higher rates of crack use for blacks than for whites and Latinos/as, but fewer black crack users than non-black crack users. Fourth and most importantly, it repeatedly documents the complexity of drug use/race-ethnicity relationships and the consequent requirement for a large, demographically diverse sample in order to study this subject adequately. Drug users who differ in ethnic-

ity invariably also differ in ways that have nothing to do with ethnicity, such as gender, and in additional ways that are correlated with ethnicity, such as income levels and residence patterns, and in still other ways such as treatment status for which relationships to ethnicity are still not well understood. These other differences tend to either explain the drug/ethnicity differences or to make the sample size too small for the kind of analysis that would even permit study of this possibility. For the specific problem of the crack/crime/black association alleged in media reports, many of these methodological difficulties are overcome in a recent study of a large, demographically diverse sample of cocaine users.

Studying Crack/Crime Connections

Drug use patterns and criminal behavior were the focus of a study conducted between September 1987 and August 1991 in the Miami, Florida, metropolitan area. A total of 699 cocaine users were interviewed, 349 of them in residential treatment at the time and 350 on the street. Eligible participants were those who reported any cocaine use during the "last 90 days on the street." For the street sample, this was the 90 days prior to interview. For the treatment sample, it was the most recent continuous 90 days on the street prior to treatment entry. This 90-day period was required to be within the two years prior to interview. The total time period referenced by all respondents' "last 90 days on the street" was November 1986 through December 1989.

Questions about drug use and criminal behavior were asked during an interview lasting 30 to 60 minutes, and respondents were paid $10 for their time. Legal protection for subjects was assured by anonymity and a Certificate of Confidentiality from the National Institute on Drug Abuse. This guaranteed that project employees could not be compelled by any court or law enforcement agency to reveal information sources or questionnaire data. Treatment program clients were assured that neither participation nor nonparticipation would affect their program status and that their answers would not be seen by counselors or other program personnel.

Selection of both street and treatment respondents was guided by subsample targets for gender, age, and ethnicity in order to ensure a demographically diverse sample. In the treatment programs, this generally meant returning repeatedly to interview every new client in the hard-to-fill subsamples (younger and white or Latino/a). On the street, subsample targets meant pushing the interview process into a variety of neighborhoods to get the required race-ethnic diversity. Street respondents were located through standard multiple starting-point "snowball sampling" techniques in neighborhoods with high rates of cocaine use by a street interviewer familiar with and well known in the target areas. The details of how this kind of street data collection is done are described elsewhere (Inciardi, Horowitz, and Pottieger 1993, pp. 64–67; Inciardi, Lockwood, and Pottieger 1993, pp. 147–51).

The final sample was 66 percent male and 34 percent female. The 285 black respondents comprised 34 percent of the males and 54 percent of the females; the 273 white respondents were 36 percent of the males and 46 percent of the females; and the 141 Latino/a respondents (108 of them Cuban) made up the remaining 30 percent of the male respondents. Forty-six percent of the respondents were ages 20 to 29, while 28 percent were ages 13 to 19, and 26 percent were 30 to 49 years old.

Questions about cocaine use in the last 90 days on the street were asked separately for six types of cocaine use: snorting, intravenous (IV) use, crack smoking, other (pure, ether-based) freebasing, coca paste smoking, and any other (new) form of cocaine. For each cocaine type, respondents were asked how many days cocaine was used and the usual number of doses per day. "Amount of cocaine use" was then calculated by multiplying "number of usual doses per day" by "number of days that dosage was used," to arrive at an estimated total quantity for each cocaine type used in the respondent's last 90 days on the street. These figures permitted calculation of each cocaine user's "primary cocaine type"—the one cocaine form, if any,

which accounted for 75 percent or more of all cocaine used by each respondent. The resulting estimated totals for each cocaine type were recoded into variables ranging from zero (none) to six (1350+ doses).

Measures for illegal activities were constructed in a similar fashion. For each of 23 crime types, respondents were asked on how many days the offense was committed and the usual number of offenses per day. Total crimes for the 90 days were then computed for each specific offense type. These numbers were combined into totals for six general crime types—violence-related, major property crime, petty property crime, prostitution and procuring, drug trafficking or manufacture, and street-level drug sales.

The Nature of the Connection

This analysis focuses on two issues: (1) the primary type of cocaine used; and, (2) the crack/crime connection, in general and by race-ethnicity, and specifically among African Americans.

The first question addressed is that of whether black cocaine users were more likely than their white and Latino/a counterparts to have crack as their "primary cocaine type." A breakdown by ethnicity alone suggests no black/crack association: the only apparent differences in primary cocaine type by ethnicity are (1) a preference for snorting among Latinos/as (31.9 percent, compared to 12.3–13.2 percent of blacks and whites) and thus *less* preference for crack (58.2 percent, compared to 74.5 percent for both blacks and whites), and (2) more injection use among blacks (8.4 percent, compared to 1.4 percent–1.8 percent of Latinos/as and whites).

Because prior research suggests that gender, age, and treatment status might all be related to race-ethnic differences in cocaine-type preference, these three factors were held constant so that a clearer picture of the relationship between race-ethnicity and primary cocaine type could be examined. The results indicate that among users ages 13 to 29 years who were interviewed on the street, there were very few differences in cocaine use by either ethnicity or gender. Crack was the primary cocaine type for every single street respondent under age 20, and for over 90 percent of street respondents ages 20 to 29, with the sole exception of Latino/a males. For the older cocaine users interviewed on the street, in contrast, both ethnic and gender differences appear. Among whites ages 30 to 49 years, all of the women and most of the men had crack as their primary cocaine type; Latino/a men ages 30 to 49 were split exactly 50-50 between crack and snorting; and black cocaine users ages 30 to 49 were clearly *least* likely to have crack as their primary cocaine type. In fact, among cocaine users ages 30–49 interviewed on the street, it was not crack but injection cocaine that was the primary cocaine type much more likely among blacks than among whites and Latinos/as.

The treatment groups present an even more complicated picture. Over 40 percent of the adolescent respondents used cocaine primarily by snorting, as did more than 20 percent of all women and all Latinos/as. Further, a significant minority of respondents in an apparently random selection of gender, age, and ethnicity subgroups used such a variety of cocaine forms that no one type accounted for 75 percent of their total use. This pattern of "No Primary Cocaine Type" was not seen for even one street respondent. Thus, crack use was clearly less common among the cocaine users in treatment than among their counterparts interviewed on the street, with a particularly strong contrast between users under age 30.

In a follow-up analysis, correlates of having crack as a primary cocaine type were computed. The results indicate that in this sample of 699 cocaine users, the only significant crack/ethnicity correlation indicates that Latino/a males are less likely to prefer crack. That is, being black (or white, for that matter) was unrelated to having crack as a primary cocaine type. Being younger or female, in contrast, was related to a preference for crack use. Street respondents were also much more likely than treatment respondents to have crack as a primary cocaine type.

For still another way of looking at the crack/black connection, correlates were computed for amount of crack used in the last 90 days by only the 499 respondents who were primary crack users. The prior analyses suggest *among cocaine users*, being black is *not* associated with being a crack user. This analysis asked whether *among crack users*, blacks use *more* crack than whites and Latinos/as. The results showed no relationship between amount of crack used and ethnicity or gender. Amount of crack used by primary crack users was significantly, although weakly, correlated with being in treatment, and was clearly related to being older.

The second question of interest is that of whether the crack/crime relationship documented in prior studies is indicative of a more general cocaine/crime association, or whether crack users are actually more crime-involved than other cocaine users. Analysis of only the 298 primary crack users interviewed on the street indicated that the crack/crime correlation among this subgroup is stronger than the general cocaine/crime correlation for all 699 cocaine users. These results suggest that the crack/crime association reported by other researchers is more than just a part of some general correlation between cocaine use and crime.

Given a definite crack/crime connection but only a very weak crack/black connection, the question for analysis necessarily shifts to that of whether there are differences in the crack/crime relationship for crack users of different ethnicities. Far too many crack users are *not* black for the crack/crime association to be a black phenomenon. Thus, is the white or Latino/a crack/crime connection different in degree or type from that for blacks?

This more detailed analysis of the crack/crime relationship was done for only the 298 primary crack users ages 13 to 49 years who were interviewed on the street. As seen in Table 21.1, respondents on the street—regardless of gender or ethnicity—were much more consistent than any other subgroup of cocaine users in preferring crack as their primary cocaine type. Confining further analysis to this subsample thus permits the clearest view of the crack/crime/race-ethnicity relationship because complications of treatment status can be ignored. Further, youth and adult crack users who are not in treatment are also the crack users who present the most obvious problem to policy makers and the criminal justice system, as well as to their families and neighborhoods. Thus, the "street crack user" subsample is arguably also the most appropriate and important one in which to more closely examine the crack/crime relationship.

The criminal involvement of this subsample is extensive, as shown in Table 21.1. Over 96 percent of each gender/race-ethnic category is involved in dealing drugs, most respondents committed petty property crimes, and some also committed major property crimes (burglary or motor vehicle theft) or violent offenses (robbery, assault, or weapons use). However, gender and race-ethnic differences also appear—more prostitution and procuring for women, and especially black women; more major property crimes for men, and especially Latino/a men; more petty property crimes among women; and more violent offenses among black women.

The extent to which these gender and ethnic variations in level of criminal involvement are related to amount of crack used varies greatly by crime type. In fact, strong correlations were found between amount of crack used and involvement with drug sales in most gender and ethnic subgroups. Prostitution was also correlated with amount of crack used for both black and white women. Violence-related offenses, in contrast, were related to the amount of crack used only among white females. Major property crimes, petty property crimes, and drug trafficking were not significantly related to amount of crack used for any of the subgroups.

A final question is why this apparent pattern of ethnic differences in the crack/crime relationship exists. While no differences are apparent among male respondents, the contrast between white and black female respondents seen in Table 21.1 is what would be expected in a sample if the difference were primarily one of differing socioeconomic status. In Miami, as in many other cities across the country, general socioeconomic indicators, such as income, education, and residential patterns, show markedly greater poverty among blacks than among whites.

One aspect of ethnic socioeconomic differences is the availability of economic resources. When respondents in this study were asked about sources of legal income or support, results indicated that job income was highly unusual. In the female street crack user subsample, current job income was reported by only one of the women ages 13–49. Welfare, disability, or other assistance were also rare; such income was reported by four of the 124 women ages 13 to 49 (3.2 percent of this subgroup). Unexpectedly, some kind of investment income was actually more common—15 of the respondents in this subsample reported this type of income. Unlike job income or government assistance, furthermore, reports of invest-

Table 21.1

Type of Crime Committed in the Last 90 Days by 298 Primary Crack Users Interviewed

Crime Type Committed	Male			Female	
	Black (n = 59)	White (n = 65)	Hispanic (n = 50)	Black (n = 56)	White (n = 68)
Violence-Related	19	16	12	22**	12
Major Property	8	13	16	2	0
Petty Property	39	43	41	50	56
Prostitution/Procuring	1	0	0	39**	29
Drug Trafficking	0	0	0	1	0
Drug Dealing	59	65	50	54	65

**Chi-square significant at p = .05.

ment income were significantly more likely among white than black women. Thus, total numbers of female respondents with employment, assistance, and investment income indicate that whites were more likely to have such conventional economic resources than were blacks.

Most respondents, however, did have some legal source of support—most commonly, parents, spouse, or other people. Thus, only one in four of the female street crack user subsample reported obtaining over half of their living expenses from crime. However, economic support from parents, spouse, or other people may have a very different kind of crack/crime relevance—some persons who help pay for a crack user's living expenses may also help support a crack/crime lifestyle. Respondents were asked three questions about living circumstances: (1) Persons lived with last week, including (a) parents (with or without siblings), (b) spouse/opposite-sex partner, and (c) other people; (2) Do any of these people use crack or other cocaine?; and (3) Do any deal it? All co-residents reported as dealers were also reported as users. Results in the female street crack user subsample indicated that *every* respondent living with a spouse or person other than a parent reported living with another cocaine user. In contrast, only 47.8 percent of those living with their parents reported living with other cocaine users.

For the total 124 female street crack users, co-residence with a cocaine user was significantly related to race-ethnicity: 92.9 percent of black respondents reported co-resident cocaine involvement while only 45.6 percent of white respondents did so. In fact, black women were over 15 times more likely than white women to reside with a cocaine user. The relevance of greater cocaine involvement of co-residents is demonstrated by its marked correlations with other crack/crime indicators. Female respondents who reported greater cocaine involvement of co-residents were also significantly more likely to report obtaining more living expenses from crime and more overall crime.

Although no causal inferences can be made from this analysis, it does suggest that crime and crack use are part of a more gen-eral lifestyle that includes such everyday elements as persons with whom one lives and ways of meeting living expenses. The results also indicate that ethnic differences—particularly black/white differences—exist both in elements of that lifestyle and influences upon it. White respondents had less apparent need to commit crimes in order to pay for living expenses, and were also less likely to reside with other cocaine involved persons. Black respondents tended to show the opposite pattern—more living expenses paid for by crime, and more cocaine involvement among co-residents. These results suggest that differences which appear to be ethnic are in fact socioeconomic in nature. That is, it is socioeconomic factors such as: (1) the degree of access to income sources other than crime, and (2) the likelihood of living in a high drug/crime-rate environment which are important for understanding the crack/crime connection.

Discussion

In the 1991 case of *State v. Russell* (477 N.W.2d 886 [Minn. 1991]), the Minnesota Supreme Court invalidated a state law that punished the possession of crack-cocaine more harshly than that of powder-cocaine. The court invalidated the differential punishment largely on the grounds that it constituted an "illicit racial discrimination"—most people convicted of possessing powder-cocaine were white, while most of those convicted of possessing crack were black.

More specifically, under Minnesota Statute 152.023(2), a person is guilty of a "third degree" offense if he or she possesses three or more grams of cocaine base ("crack-cocaine"). Under the same statute, a person must possess ten or more grams of cocaine powder to be guilty of the same offense. A person who possesses less than ten grams of powder is guilty of a fifth degree offense (Section 152.025). Pursuant to these statutes, possession of three grams of crack carries a penalty of up to 20 years in prison, while possession of an equal amount of powder-cocaine carries a penalty of up to five years in prison.

In *State v. Russell*, five African American men who were charged with violating Section 152.023(2) jointly moved the trial court to dismiss the charges on the grounds that the statute had a discriminatory effect on black persons and violated the equal protection guarantees of both the Minnesota and U.S. constitutions. The trial court noted that crack was indeed used primarily by African Americans, and powder-cocaine primarily by whites. Among the many statistics provided to the trial court were those showing that of all people charged with possession of cocaine base in 1988, 97 percent were black; of those charged with possession of powder-cocaine, 80 percent were white. The trial court agreed with the defendants and invalidated the sentencing scheme.

On an appeal brought by the state, it was contended that the state legislature had a permissible and legitimate interest in regulating the possession and sale of both crack- and powder-cocaine, and that it was reasonable for lawmakers to believe that the three grams of crack/ten grams of powder classification would regulate the possession of those drugs by the "street level" dealers at whom the statute was primarily aimed. The Minnesota Supreme Court was not persuaded, however, and affirmed that the sentencing scheme was in violation of the state constitution on equal protection grounds.

On the basis of the analysis in this chapter, is it possible that the Minnesota Supreme Court's holding in *Russell* was wrongly decided? Harvard law professor Randall Kennedy has argued that the Minnesota Case was erroneously decided, and on several grounds (Kennedy 1994). Primarily:

> The portrayal of Minnesota's sentencing statute as a "burden" to blacks as a class is simplistic. Assuming that one believes in criminalizing the distribution of crack cocaine, punishing the conduct is a public good. It is a "burden" on those who are convicted of engaging in this conduct. But it is presumably a benefit for the great mass of law-abiding people (pp. 1266–7).

And Professor Kennedy added:

The Minnesota Supreme Court condemned the statute as imposing a racially discriminatory burden. But what is "racial" about punishment? Justice Wahl [writing the opinion for the court] writes as though the punishment falls upon blacks as a class. But to the extent that the heavier punishment for possession of crack falls upon blacks, it falls not upon blacks as a class but rather upon a subset of the black population—those in violation of the law who are apprehended (p. 1269).

Whether or not one agrees with Professor Kennedy's contentions, the analysis in this chapter suggests that crack may not be an "African American drug" and powder-cocaine a white American drug. The difference is not a race-ethnic matter, but one of socioeconomic status. However, one could argue that the research data presented here are from but one study and from one community, collected in a manner that may not be representative of the crack and cocaine using populations. Indeed, this would be a legitimate criticism, for drug users in Miami are certainly not representative of the nation as a whole. But nevertheless, other data are accumulating which tend to corroborate the Miami findings. Recently, a reanalysis of data from NIDA's 1988 National Household Survey compared race-ethnic group differences in crack smoking (Lillie-Blanton, Anthony, and Schuster 1993). The findings provided evidence that given similar social and environmental conditions (neighborhood, education, income, age, and gender), crack use does not depend on race-specific factors. This would clearly suggest that race-specific explanations of crack use likely obscure the role that social and environmental factors play in the overall epidemiology of crack use.

References

Adlaf, Edward M., Reginald G. Smart, and S. H. Tan (1989) "Ethnicity and Drug Use: A Critical Look," *International Journal of the Addictions* 24:1–18.

Anglin, M. Douglas, Mary W. Booth, Timothy M. Ryan, and Yih-Ing Hser (1988) "Ethnic Differences in Narcotics Addiction. II. Chicano and

Anglo Addiction Career Patterns," *International Journal of the Addictions* 23:1011–27.

Austin, Gregory A. and M. Jean Gilbert (1989) "Substance Abuse Among Latino Youth," *Prevention Update* 3:1–26.

Bachman, Jerald G., John M. Wallace, Patrick M. O'Malley, Lloyd D. Johnston, Candace L. Kurth, and Harold W. Neighbors (1991) "Racial/Ethnic Differences in Smoking, Drinking, and Illicit Drug Use Among American High School Seniors, 1976–89," *American Journal of Public Health* 81:372–77.

Ball, John C. and Carl D. Chambers (1970) "Overview of the Problem," pp. 5–21 in John C. Ball and Carl D. Chambers (eds.), *The Epidemiology of Opiate Addiction in the United States* (Springfield, IL: Charles C Thomas).

Boyd, Carol J. and Thomas Mieczkowski (1990) "Drug Use, Health, Family and Social Support in 'Crack' Cocaine Users," *Addictive Behaviors* 15:481–85.

Brunswick, Ann, Peter A. Messeri, and Angela A. Aidala (1990) "Changing Drug Use Patterns and Treatment Behavior: A Longitudinal Study of Urban Black Youth," pp. 263–311 in R. R. Watson (ed.), *Drug and Alcohol Abuse Prevention* (Clifton, NJ: Humana Press).

Carroll, Kathleen and Bruce J. Rounsaville (1992) "Contrast of Treatment-Seeking and Untreated Cocaine Abusers," *Archives of General Psychiatry* 49:646–71.

Cauchon, Dennis (1993) "Crack Sentencing Disparities Weighed," *USA Today*, November 10, p. 10A.

Chitwood, Dale D. and Patricia C. Morningstar (1985) "Factors Which Differentiate Cocaine Users in Treatment From Nontreatment Users," *International Journal of the Addictions* 20:449–59.

Collins, R. Lorraine (1992) "Methodological Issues in Conducting Substance Abuse Research in Ethnic Minority Populations," *Drugs and Society* 6:59–77.

Goldstein, Paul J., Patricia A. Belluci, Barry J. Spunt, and Thomas Miller (1991) "Volume of Cocaine Use and Violence: A Comparison Between Men and Women," *Journal of Drug Issues* 21:345–67.

Griffin, Margaret L., Roger D. Weiss, Steven M. Mirin, and Ulrike Lange (1989) "A Comparison of Male and Female Cocaine Abusers," *Archives of General Psychiatry* 46:122–26.

Hamid, Ansley (1990) "The Political Economy of Crack Related Violence," *Contemporary Drug Problems* 17:31–78.

Inciardi, James A., Ruth Horowitz, and Anne E. Pottieger (1993) *Street Kids, Street Drugs, Street Crime* (Belmont, CA: Wadsworth).

Inciardi, James A., Dorothy Lockwood, and Anne E. Pottieger (1993) *Women and Crack-Cocaine* (New York: Macmillan).

Inciardi, James A. and Anne E. Pottieger (1991) "Kids, Crack and Crime," *Journal of Drug Issues* 21:257–70.

Johnson, Bruce D., Elsayed Elmoghazy, and Eloise Dunlap (1990) "Crack Abusers and Noncrack Drug Abusers: A Comparison of Drug Use, Drug Sales, and Nondrug Criminality," paper presented at the Annual Meeting of the American Society of Criminology, Baltimore, MD, November 8.

Kandel, Denise B., Eric Single, and Ronald Kessler (1976) "The Epidemiology of Drug Use Among New York State High School Students: Distribution, Trends and Changes in Use," *American Journal of Public Health* 66:43–53.

Kennedy, Randall (1994) "The State, Criminal Law, and Racial Discrimination: A Comment," *Harvard Law Review* 107:1255–1278.

Klein, Malcolm W. and Cheryl Maxson (1985) "'Rock' Sales in South Los Angeles," *Sociology and Social Research* 69:561–65.

Kleinman, Paula Holzman and Irving Faber Lukoff (1978) "Ethnic Differences in Factors Related to Drug Use," *Journal of Health and Social Behavior* 19:190–99.

Leiby, Richard (1994) "A Crack in the System," *Washington Post*, February 20, pp. F1, F4–F5.

Lillie-Blanton, Marsha, James C. Anthony, and Charles R. Schuster (1993) "Probing the Meaning of Racial/Ethnic Group Comparisons in Crack Cocaine Smoking," *Journal of the American Medical Association* 269:993–997.

Maddehian, Ebrahim, Michael D. Newcomb, and Peter M. Bentler (1986) "Adolescents' Substance Use: Impact of Ethnicity, Income and Availability," *Advances in Alcohol and Substance Abuse* 5:63–78.

Marin, Barbara V. (1990) "Latino/a Drug Abuse: Culturally Appropriate Prevention and Treatment," pp. 151–65 in R. R. Watson (ed.), *Drug and Alcohol Abuse Prevention* (Clifton, NJ: Humana Press).

McBride, Duane C. and James A. Swartz (1990) "Drugs and Violence in the Age of Crack Cocaine," pp. 141–69 in Ralph Weisheit (ed.), *Drugs, Crime and the Criminal Justice System* (Cincinnati: Anderson).

National Institute on Drug Abuse (1991) *National Household Survey on Drug Abuse: Popu-*

lation Estimates (Rockville, MD: National Institute on Drug Abuse).

Prendergast, Michael L., Gregory A. Austin, Kenneth I. Maton, and Ralph Baker (1989) "Substance Abuse Among Black Youth," *Prevention Research Update* 4:1–27.

Rebach, Howard (1992) "Alcohol and Drug Use Among American Minorities," *Drugs and Society* 6:23–57.

Rounsaville, Bruce J. and Herbert D. Kleber (1985) "Untreated Opiate Addicts: How Do They Differ from Those Seeking Treatment?" *Archives of General Psychiatry* 42:1072–77.

Segal, Bernard (1989) "Drug-Taking Behavior Among School-Aged Youth: The Alaska Experience and Comparisons with Lower 48 States," *Drugs and Society* 4:1–17.

United States Sentencing Commission (1993) *Hearing on Crack Cocaine* (Washington, DC: November 9).

Wallace, John M. and Jerald G. Bachman (1991) "Explaining Racial/Ethnic Differences in Adolescent Drug Use: The Impact of Background and Lifestyle," *Social Problems* 38:333–57.

For Discussion

Would we expect to find similar results from studies conducted in other communities? Why or why not?

22
Cocaine-Exposed Infants and the Criminalization of Pregnancy

Hilary L. Surratt
James A. Inciardi

Pregnant substance abusers represent a special population whose needs have been ignored. For example, drug treatment admission criteria often exclude pregnant users. In the 1980s, considerable media attention focused on "cocaine babies." In this essay, Surratt and Inciardi describe research findings and dispel myths that relate to cocaine-exposed infants. Pregnant cocaine users are at risk for legal intervention and the authors describe several legal cases whereby pregnant substance users have been prosecuted. The authors claim that the criminal justice response to this population has been punitive and perhaps counterproductive.

The use of cocaine in the United States has a history spanning well over one hundred years, but it was not until the late 1970s that its use had become significantly visible in both rural and urban America. Then, with the appearance of crack in the 1980s and its apparent epidemic use in numerous inner city communities, reports of child abuse and neglect by crack-addicted mothers were publicized in the national media. At the same time, the news media dispensed graphic descriptions of an allegedly growing population of impaired "crack-addicted" infants born (and sometimes abandoned) in the nation's hospitals. And as research programs and studies on the effects of fetal exposure to cocaine increased, legislation was passed in a variety of jurisdictions which served to criminalize cocaine and other drug use during pregnancy.

Without question, cocaine is a seductive and dangerous drug, and any form of cocaine use can have an impact on the developing fetus. Yet scientific proof of a cause and effect relationship between cocaine use and adverse pre- and post-natal consequences has been difficult to establish. Part of the problem is that many cocaine-using mothers abuse other illegal drugs, and many consume alcohol and tobacco as well. Another difficulty lies with much of the early research on prenatal cocaine exposure. Many studies had numerous methodological problems, resulting in either tentative or problematic conclusions. Within this context, it is the intention of this paper to briefly describe what is known about cocaine-exposed infants, and to examine the continuing efforts to criminalize drug use by pregnant women.

'Cocaine Babies'

In 1987, Dr. Ira J. Chasnoff of Northwestern University Medical School estimated that 375,000 infants were drug-exposed each year, and that much of the exposure was from cocaine (Besharov 1990). The existing research on the effects of prenatal substance abuse at that time characterized cocaine-exposed children as moody, often inconsolable, less socially interactive, and less able to bond than other children (Fackelmann 1991; Lester et al. 1991; Rothman 1991). Many researchers also found drug-exposed children to be less attentive and less able to focus on specific tasks than non-exposed children (Chasnoff et al. 1985; Chasnoff et al. 1989; Pinkney 1989; Colen 1990). Other harmful effects attributed to prenatal cocaine exposure included high rates of placental abruption (detachment of the placenta from the uterine wall), growth retardation *in utero*, Sudden Infant Death Syndrome (SIDS), withdrawal symptoms, low birth weight, and physical malformations.

Disturbances of feeding, sleep, and vision were also reported (Chasnoff and Griffith 1989; Chasnoff et al. 1988; Bingol et al. 1987). Many studies, furthermore, characterized these effects as irreversible and suggested that no amount of special attention or educational programs would ever be able to turn these cocaine-exposed infants into well-functioning or adjusted children (Colen 1990; Public Health Foundation 1990).

Such dramatic findings sparked a wave of media reports lamenting the fate of a new generation of "crack babies." Numerous media stories documented the epidemic numbers of cocaine-addicted infants being born in large, urban hospitals across the United States (McNamara 1989; Kerr 1986). More often than not, the media publicized case studies of a few children who had been profoundly affected by prenatal exposure to multiple drugs, not exclusively cocaine. However, headlines which read "The Crack Children," "Crack Babies Born to Life of Suffering," "A Desperate Crack Legacy," and "Crack in the Cradle," focused much of the public's attention on the dangers of cocaine and created the image that "crack babies" were severely damaged human beings (Stone 1989; Kantrowitz and Wingert 1990; Langone 1988; Hopkins 1990). Take, for example, the following excerpts from a story which appeared in the *New York Times* in 1989:

> Babies born to mothers using crack have serious difficulty relating to their world, making friends, playing like normal children, and feeling love for their mother or primary caretakers. Prenatal exposure to illegal drugs, particularly powdered cocaine and crack, seems to be "interfering with the central core of what it is to be human," said Coryl Jones, a research psychologist at the National Institute on Drug Abuse. New research indicates that most babies exposed to illegal drugs appear to be able to develop normal, if low-range intelligence, despite their subnormal emotional development. But the studies suggest that children of addicted mothers may be unable to develop into adults with basic employment skills and unable to form close human relationships (Blakeslee 1989).

Accounts of behavioral disturbances among cocaine-exposed children were particularly commonplace. As frightening reports from weary, disconcerted family members and teachers grew more frequent, public concern over this "lost generation" increased. In the *Miami Herald*, for example:

> The tiny angelic looking boy is only 4 but he has long had a reputation around his day care center. For tantrums. He would hurl himself on the floor and bang his head against the concrete. The boy is a cocaine child—his fragile system damaged by the drug while he was still in the womb. . . . "They're like little jekylls and hydes" said a Fort Lauderdale school principal, "all of a sudden, something will set them off. They start throwing tantrums. They start yelling. They can't control their emotions" (Marks 1990).

Portrayals of cocaine-exposed infants as children out of control, prone to hyperactivity, overstimulation, distractibility, seizures, fits of rage, and violent behavior certainly hampered efforts at finding caretakers for these children in need. By the late 1980s, many jurisdictions required physician reporting of drug use in pregnancy or positive drug tests from infants. Infants who tested positive for cocaine were automatically kept in the hospital and because they were often born prematurely, they frequently required long hospital stays until they were declared medically fit to leave. Many times, however, even when the children became eligible to leave the mother was either unavailable or deemed unfit to care for them. The long search for adequate foster care then began, giving rise to large numbers of "boarder babies" in many urban hospitals (McNamara 1989; Thornton 1988/1989).

Children labeled as "crack babies" have been characterized as having little potential for successful outcomes and as such, prospective adoptive parents have been unwilling to care for them and school teachers have been prepared for the worst. Too often, the media's stereotypic portrayal of "crack babies" has obscured the fact that most children who are exposed to cocaine *in utero* are also exposed to other substances (Griffith et al. 1994; Gonzalez and Campbell 1994). Cocaine using women are much more likely than non-users to smoke cigarettes and use alcohol during pregnancy (Shiono et al. 1995). In fact, researchers estimate that the number of children exposed to alcohol in utero is almost ten times greater than the number exposed to cocaine, affecting approximately 73 percent of all pregnancies (Scherling 1994).

Indeed, by the mid-1990s the National Institute on Drug Abuse (NIDA) suggested that predictions of a "lost generation" of cocaine-exposed children were overstated. NIDA also reported that approximately one half of all infants born to drug-using mothers have no drug-related health effects and suggested that previous estimates of epidemic numbers of cocaine-affected infants resulted from the lack of representative samples and reliable data in early studies (National Institute on Drug Abuse 1994). In fact, many early research studies of prenatal cocaine exposure suffered from a variety of methodological flaws which may call their findings into question. For example, the initial reports which suggested that cocaine use caused a dramatic increase in the likelihood of Sudden Infant Death Syndrome were based on very small, non-representative samples, making the generalizability of the findings questionable (Ward et al. 1989; National Institute on Drug Abuse 1989; Greider 1995; Shiono et al. 1995).

In fact, although the effects of cocaine use in pregnancy are still being debated, the effects of prenatal exposure to alcohol and nicotine are well-documented. A leading cause of mental retardation and birth defects in the United States is Fetal Alcohol Syndrome (Scherling 1994). Alcohol's effects include dysmorphogenesis (the development of ill-shaped or otherwise malformed body structures), growth abnormalities, and cognitive and language deficits. Several studies have found alcohol use and cigarette smoking during pregnancy to be associated with lower IQ scores and poorer language development and cognitive functioning (Streissguth et al. 1989; Fried and Watkinson 1990). Cigarette smoking has also been associated with prenatal complications, low birth weight, and impairment in language and cognitive

development (Fried and O'Connell 1987; Gonzalez and Campbell 1994). In fact, exposure to alcohol and cigarettes has been suggested to have an equal or greater detrimental impact on the infant than exposure to cocaine (Richardson et al. 1993).

In the final analysis, it may be virtually impossible to fully understand the effects of cocaine on the developing fetus. A recent study conducted at Case Western Reserve University, for example, was able to separate the effects of cocaine from those of such factors as alcohol use and poor prenatal care (Singer et al. 2002). The findings suggested that children born to poor, urban women who used cocaine throughout pregnancy were nearly twice as likely as children with similar backgrounds but no prenatal cocaine exposure to have significant cognitive defects during their first two years of life. However, even these findings must be interpreted with caution, since the researchers were unable to control for the effects of other drug use during pregnancy, because it was virtually impossible to find children who were exposed *only* to cocaine.

The Criminalization of Pregnancy

The campaign to combat prenatal drug use in the United States has focused on punitive, rather than rehabilitative intervention, and the public policy battle has occurred under the auspices of the criminal justice system rather than through social welfare and public health programs. Jurisdictions have initiated both criminal and civil actions, and in many cases, a combination of the two. In general, criminal prosecutions are a phenomenon of the post-Reagan era of the late 1980s, which have continued into the twenty-first century. Almost without exception, criminal prosecutions of women who engaged in prenatal substance use have not stood up in the face of legal challenges (Paltrow 1992; Center for Reproductive Law and Policy 1993). Unfortunately, however, many of the women charged under various criminal statutes have lacked the resources to pursue court challenges and have received sentences as an outgrowth of court actions that were (and are), for all intents and purposes, unconstitutional and largely inapplicable in the face of state legislative guidelines.

During the last few years, some of these cases have proceeded to state appellate courts, although none has yet reached the United States Supreme Court. While most actions taken by the state have not survived legal challenge, the courts have been hesitant to dismantle the state's apparent interest in protecting the fetus and holding the mother accountable for prenatal conduct that potentially causes harm. Instead, most appellate courts have overturned convictions on the basis that state action violated the initial intent of the legislature.

One of the most striking aspects of the public concern over the issue of prenatal substance abuse was the speed with which states sought to make prenatal drug ingestion a *criminal*, as opposed to a *public health* or *social welfare*, issue. Instead of attempting to provide pregnant addicts with treatment alternatives, state and city attorneys pursued the prosecutorial route with extreme vigor. Since there were no statutes which specifically criminalized drug use during pregnancy (nor were there any that established criminal liability for maternal conduct resulting in prenatal injuries), prosecutors were forced to use existing laws in creative and often unprecedented ways (Garrity-Rokous 1994; Center for Reproductive Law and Policy 1993). Popular prosecutorial strategies included filing criminal charges for: child abuse and neglect, involuntary manslaughter and homicide, and use of controlled substances. By the mid-1990s, the American Civil Liberties Union (ACLU) estimated that 200–300 women had been prosecuted, generally under abuse and neglect statutes (American Civil Liberties Union Foundation 1995).

The first known prosecution using this approach was the 1977 case of *Reyes v. California*, wherein the defendant gave birth to twins—both of whom were addicted to heroin. The state attempted to prosecute Ms. Reyes under child endangerment laws, but the conviction was later overturned at the appellate level on grounds that the endangerment statute was never intended by the legislature to apply to fetuses.

In another significant case, *People v. Stewart* in 1987, the defendant, Pamela Stewart of San Diego, was charged with criminal conduct following her inability to follow her doctor's advice regarding her pregnancy. Ms. Stewart was suffering from *placenta previa* (a condition where the placenta is implanted in the lower portion of the uterus) and was ordered by her physician to avoid sexual intercourse and to immediately report for medical care in the event of any hemorrhaging. She engaged in vaginal intercourse, ingested amphetamines, and waited 12 hours before seeking medical care for her hemorrhaging. When her newborn was born brain damaged, tested positive for amphetamines, and died six weeks later, Ms. Stewart was charged and convicted of violating a California law that made it a misdemeanor for parents to "willfully omit, without legal excuse, to furnish necessary clothing, food, shelter or medical attendance, or other remedial care for his or her child" (*Cal. Penal Code* 270 1988). Ultimately, Ms. Stewart's conviction was overturned on the basis that the statute was never intended to apply to maternal conduct causing prenatal injury.

In both *Reyes* and *Stewart*, as well as in the vast majority of subsequent abuse and neglect prosecutions, the central issues were typically: (1) whether the fetus could be considered a "child" in the tradition of state child abuse/neglect laws; and, (2) whether prenatal conduct could be considered appropriate criteria for the determination of abuse and neglect sanctions. Additionally, in some jurisdictions, prosecutors must also demonstrate that abuse/neglect laws are intended to apply to maternal, as well as third party, behavior. In addition to California, prosecutors in Colorado, Connecticut, Florida, Indiana, Michigan, Ohio, South Carolina, Texas, and Wyoming have used abuse/neglect laws to convict women who used drugs during their pregnancies (Garrity-Rokous 1994). Most of these convictions have been successfully appealed, generally on the basis that child abuse laws are not intended to apply to fetuses and/or prenatal conduct. Nonetheless, written decisions in several cases which overturned the original convictions did not discourage states from pursuing such prosecutions (see *Welch v. Kentucky* 1993; *Ohio v. Gray* 1992). Instead, the high courts suggested that states pass legislation specifying that prenatal conduct is salient for abuse and neglect prosecutions, and/or legislation that establishes the legal personhood of the fetus.

In a few state jurisdictions, prosecutors have charged mothers with homicide or manslaughter on grounds that the death of their newborn(s) was caused by prenatal drug use. In *Alaska v. Grubbs* (1989), for example, the defendant was charged with manslaughter after her newborn suffered a fatal heart attack believed to have been caused by prenatal cocaine exposure. Ms. Grubbs plead *nolo contendere* (no contest) to a lesser charge and was sentenced to six months in jail followed by probation. Similarly, in the case of *Illinois v. Green* (1989), prosecutors tried to charge a woman with manslaughter following the drug-related death of her newborn son. However, the grand jury refused to indict the defendant due to the inapplicability of the manslaughter statute and the prosecution's violation of the defendant's constitutional right to privacy.

Perhaps the most creative prosecutions of pregnant, drug using women have been those engineered along the lines of specific drug statutes, particularly laws against trafficking and delivery of drugs to minors. Florida was the first state to successfully prosecute under this strategy in the well-known case of *Florida v. Johnson* (1987). Ms. Johnson was turned over to state prosecutors after hospital officials discovered that both of her children had positive toxicologies for cocaine following birth. She was subsequently convicted under a drug delivery statute on the basis that she had "delivered" cocaine to her newborn via the umbilical cord during the 60-second period after birth before the cord was cut. The infant's positive toxicology served as "proof" that she had delivered the drug. Prosecutors argued that the child could be considered a "minor" immediately following its birth (since Florida law does not recognize the legal personhood of a fetus). Ms. Johnson was

subsequently sentenced to 15 years probation. In 1992, the Florida Supreme Court overturned her conviction on grounds that the statute was not intended to apply to cocaine delivery through the umbilical cord.

Other criminal charges that have been launched against pregnant drug users include: contributing to the delinquency of a minor, causing the drug dependency of a child, drug possession, assault with a deadly weapon, vehicular homicide, and drug use. In the case of "pure use" statutes, for example, prosecutors convict pregnant women of using an illegal substance based on the infant's positive toxicology screen. In so doing, prosecutors avoid having to demonstrate negligible harm to the fetus. Additionally, a number of judges have used their discretionary privilege to sanction women whom they suspect of prenatal substance use. Brenda Vaughn of Washington, D.C., for example, was sentenced by the court to nearly four months in jail—an unusually long time for a first offender convicted of check forgery. Indeed, the typical sentence for this offense is probation, but Ms. Vaughn was a known cocaine user and the judge felt that he had to protect her unborn child (*United States v. Vaughn* 1989).

In a more recent case, an Illinois trial judge sentenced a woman to seven years in prison after charging her with violation of probation for failure to report to her probation officer and for using cocaine. The judge admitted to using this long sentence in an attempt to prevent the woman from becoming pregnant and giving birth to a cocaine-addicted child. The woman had recently given birth to a cocaine-addicted infant, and had three other children in foster care with allegedly drug-related disabilities. An Illinois appellate court vacated this sentence indicating that the defendant's due process rights had been violated (*Illinois v. Bedenkop* 1993).

Still other cases have targeted the prenatal ingestion of legal substances. In *Wyoming v. Pfannestiel* (1990), for example, officials charged a woman with child endangerment on grounds that her drinking might harm her unborn child. The case was ultimately dismissed on the basis that causality between alcohol consumption and harm had not been adequately established.

In general, these types of prosecutions have not withstood appellate review, largely because of the ambiguous legal status of the fetus and the departure of such prosecutions from the original intent of state legislatures. Nonetheless, criminal prosecutions have had profound consequences in the lives of many women, particularly those who lack the resources to challenge such claims. In 1992, the Reproductive Freedom Project of the American Civil Liberties Union initiated a study to track the cases of 167 women who had been arrested because of their allegedly "criminal" prenatal conduct. The study found that criminal prosecutions were launched in 24 states and the District of Columbia, although the vast majority were from South Carolina and Florida (Paltrow 1992). In most instances, women plead guilty or negotiated a plea to a lesser charge; in those cases where the defendant challenged the charge, it was nearly always dismissed. With the exception of California, the criminal prosecution of pregnant drug users ended upon a successful legal challenge.

More recently, the popularity of criminal prosecutions appears to have waned. During September 1994, for example, the Medical University of South Carolina announced that it would temporarily end its policy of forwarding names of pregnant women who test positive for cocaine to state prosecutors. The hospital was under pressure from the U.S. Department of Health and Human Services after the DHHS threatened to withdraw $18 million in federal research funding if the hospital continued to violate doctor/patient confidentiality and women's right to privacy. The old policy, known as the Interagency Policy on Management of Substance Abuse During Pregnancy or popularly referred to as the "crack baby program," required that doctors order drug tests if they suspected drug use (Jos, Marshall, and Perlmutter 1995). If the test result was positive, the woman was ordered to enter drug treatment or be arrested. Forty-two pregnant women were arrested under the policy and charged with distributing cocaine to a minor. The new policy requires the hospital to petition the courts to have pregnant drug users committed (involuntarily) to drug treatment (*Associated Press*, September 8, 1994, p. A18).

But in spite of these changes, some criminal prosecutions still occur. In Racine, Wisconsin, during early 1996, 35-year-old Deborah Zimmerman was charged with attempted murder after giving birth to a girl whose blood alcohol level was .199, more than twice the threshold for a legal finding of intoxication. Moreover, the infant was smaller than normal, and her forehead was somewhat flattened—a clear sign of fetal alcohol syndrome (Terry 1996). Going further, in *Whitner v. State* (1996), decided on July 15, 1996, the South Carolina Supreme Court ruled that a defendant who ingested crack during the third trimester of her pregnancy was properly prosecuted under the state's child abuse and endangerment statute. The appellate court emphasized that the statute's protection of persons under the age of 18 extended to a viable fetus.

Most recently, a sharply divided South Carolina Supreme Court upheld the conviction of a woman charged with killing her unborn child by using crack cocaine. In a 3-to-2 ruling handed down on 27 January 2003, the state's highest court held that there was sufficient evidence to convict Regina McKnight of "homicide by child abuse" (*State v. McKnight* 2003). The case began when Ms. McKnight give birth to a stillborn five-pound girl. The baby's gestational age was estimated at between 34 and 37 weeks. An autopsy of the infant revealed the presence of benzoylecgonine, an indicator of cocaine. McKnight was indicted for homicide by child abuse. Although her first trial ended in a mistrial, she was ultimately convicted and received a sentence of 20 years in prison, with eight years suspended. It was the opinion of the South Carolina Supreme Court that Ms. McKnight had "acted with extreme indifference to her child's life."

Cocaine Use and 'Fetal Rights'

An issue often linked to discussions of drug use during pregnancy is the intensifying debate over "fetal rights." Although the notion of "fetal rights" has received considerable attention in recent years, the movement has a history spanning more than four decades (Lieb and Sterk-Elifson 1995; Watkins and Watkins 1992). The emergence of "fetal rights" as a topic for social and legal debate has been attributed to the civil rights movement of the 1960s. Civil rights activists were able to secure legal recognition for people who had traditionally been denied their rights under the law, and some segments of society wished to extend this protection to fetuses, whom they considered to be among the most dispossessed of groups (Watkins and Watkins 1992).

Since its inception, the "fetal rights" movement has maintained that the fetus is a person, that the fetus possesses an existence which is separate from that of its mother, and that this existence should be legally acknowledged. Protective statutes for full-term, viable fetuses have been in existence since the 1961 court decision in *Hoener v. Bertinato* (Bowes and Selgestad 1981). However, the 1960s saw no successful prosecutions with respect to fetal rights violations, perhaps because the benefits of parenthood were thought to outweigh any damages (Weinstein 1983).

The "fetal rights" movement began to gain a stronger foothold throughout the nation during the early 1970s. The 1973 decision rendered in *Roe v. Wade* included language which asserted the state's compelling interest in the life of an unborn fetus (Dal Pazzo and Marsh 1987). Many interested parties viewed this judgment as recognition of the *separate* interest of the fetus, which heretofore had not been acknowledged. Conventional medical opinion had regarded the mother and fetus as a unit, with no existence of the fetus apart from that of the mother. Subsequent to *Roe v. Wade*, a 1977 Rhode Island court ruled that a child was legally entitled to begin life with a sound mind and body, thus validating the right of a fetus to sue for damages (Weinstein 1983).

Going further, some proponents of fetal rights argue that once abortion is no longer an option in the pregnancy (either as a result of statutory prohibitions or a woman's choice not to abort), the court should favor the interests of the fetus over those of its mother (Tomkins and Kepfield 1992). Fetal rights proponents argue that fetuses have a "fundamental right" to be born with a sound mind and body. This latter point served as the basis for decisions favoring the fetus in *In re Baby X* (1980), *Grodin v. Grodin* (1980), and *In re Ruiz* (1986). Tomkins and Kepfield (1992) argue that even in *Roe*, the Court recognized the state's interests in upholding the rights of the fetus at the point of viability. In this case, the Court noted that the woman and her fetus have separate and distinct rights that must be balanced throughout the duration of the pregnancy. During the first trimester, the woman's rights to reproductive privacy take precedence over any interests of the fetus. At the point of viability, however, the balance shifts in favor of the fetus and legitimates the state's protection of fetal rights (through the regulation of abortion) unless the mother's life or health is in jeopardy.

The decision in *Roe* among others (see *Webster v. Reproductive Health Services* 1989) establishes the legitimacy of the state's interest in protecting the rights of the fetus. As such, interventions in the form of criminal prosecution or civil proceedings are entirely justified particularly in cases of prenatal drug use that occurs after the point of viability. However, those who favor this type of state intervention often fail to address the issue of harm beyond citing early studies attesting to the damaging effects of cocaine or alcohol on fetal development, nor do they mention the inequity that has characterized the vast majority of criminal prosecutions and termination of custody proceedings. Rather, they take "harm" as a given and argue that child abuse statutes are particularly suited to state intervention since drug use is constitutive of "abuse" which places a child in imminent harm (Tomkins and Kepfield 1992).

The decisions in *Roe* and *Webster* laid the foundation for court-mandated obstetrical interventions to be sanctioned in many areas of the country. Court-ordered non-therapeutic cesarean sections, hospital detentions, and intrauterine transfusions have been imposed on substance abusing women, terminally ill women, and still others with strong religious objections to medical intervention (Rosner et al. 1989). Although the American College of Obstetricians and Gynecologists issued a statement in 1987 that court-mandated treatment is inadvisable and may eventually result in the criminalization of noncompliance with medical regimens (Justin and Rosner 1989), state courts and legislatures continue to grant rights to fetuses which have heretofore been reserved for persons (Rosner et al. 1989).

As noted earlier, in response to the barrage of "crack baby" stories which appeared in the media throughout the late 1980s and early 1990s, several states tried to adapt existing criminal child neglect and abuse legislation to include the unborn (Peak and Del Papa 1993), thus allowing for the prosecution of the mothers. Several cases were unsuccessfully prosecuted (*People v. Morabito* 1992; *Ohio v. Gray* 1989; *State v. Andrews* 1989) when the courts concluded that a fetus did not constitute a "child" within the child-endangerment statutes (Peak and Del Papa 1993). The decision in *People v. Morabito* further emphasized that it was the responsibility of the legislature to "criminalize the ingestion of cocaine during pregnancy when such ingestion results in harm to the subsequently born child" (Peak and Del Papa 1993). So far, no state has created legislation to impose additional criminal penalties on pregnant drug users (Lieb and Sterk-Elifson 1995).

Postscript

There have been a number of critiques raised against punitive intervention by a variety of individuals and interest groups. Among those who generally oppose criminal sanctions are physicians (and pediatricians in particular), child welfare and social service workers, social science researchers, feminists, liberal politicians, addictions counselors, and many legal advocates (Center for Reproductive Law and Policy 1993). One of the most oft-cited criticisms of punitive intervention is that it will serve to deter pregnant women from seeking treatment for fear they will be prosecuted or will have their babies taken away from them (Hawk 1994;

Keyes 1992). While it does not appear that any rigorous empirical investigations have been undertaken to support this claim, there is an increasing body of anecdotal evidence which indicates that drug using mothers are avoiding treatment and prenatal programs (Larson 1991). Also, critics fear that punitive sanctions will prevent pregnant women from revealing to health care workers their drug use and other information that would be vital to tailoring prenatal treatment to meet the special needs of the woman and her baby (Watkins and Watkins 1992).

Additionally, negative sanctions such as incarceration or fines do little to prevent or even inhibit drug use during or after pregnancy. It has been established empirically that illegal drugs are generally available in prisons (Inciardi 1996), and that prisons often lack the resources to provide drug treatment, obstetric care, and adequate dietary requirements for pregnant women. In this scenario, punitive sanctions may do more harm to the fetus than good (Keyes 1992). Further, incarceration serves to disrupt families and contributes to the problem of "boarder babies," that is, newborns who are forced to remain in hospitals for months because of criminal or civil litigation pending against their mothers (Farr 1995).

Another anticipated consequence of punitive intervention is the "slippery slope" hypothesis. Here, critics argue that criminalizing drug use during pregnancy will necessarily lead to criminalization of "legal" behaviors such as alcohol or tobacco use that also appear to have negative effects on fetal development (Paltrow 1992). Further, since no woman can provide "the perfect womb," prosecution for prenatal drug use may open the door to prosecuting women for any variety of activities during their pregnancies and may subject pregnant women to any number of regulations that deprive them of basic constitutional rights (Paltrow 1992; King 1992). The Nevada Supreme Court illustrates this dilemma in its ruling that Nevada's child endangerment statute does not apply to a pregnant woman's ingestion of illegal drugs:

> To hold otherwise would ascribe to the legislature the intent to criminalize the

conduct of women who ingest any substance that has the potential to harm a fetus. This would open the floodgates to prosecution of pregnant women who ingest such things as alcohol, nicotine, and a range of miscellaneous, otherwise legal, toxins (*Nevada v. Encoe* 1994).

The United States Supreme Court offered its point of view on aspects of the overall dilemma with its ruling in *Ferguson v. City of Charleston*, decided on March 21, 2001. The activities which brought the case to the High Court dated back to 1988, when staff members at a public hospital operated by the Medical University of South Carolina became concerned about an apparent increase in the use of cocaine by patients receiving prenatal treatment. The hospital ordered drug screens on urine samples of patients who were suspected of using cocaine. Those who tested positive were referred to the county drug commission for counseling and treatment.

The police became involved some months later, when hospital officials met with police and instituted a program which added the threat of arrest and prosecution as leverage to force pregnant cocaine users into treatment. And under the new policy, women who tested positive for drugs and had already given birth were arrested. Those who tested positive during pregnancy were to undergo treatment, and would be arrested only if they tested positive a second time or missed an appointment with a drug counselor.

At issue before the Supreme Court was whether the drug testing amounted to unconstitutional searches in violation of the Fourth Amendment. In a 6-to-3 decision, the Court held that police may not work the hospitals to arrange for the drug testing of pregnant women without their consent in order to arrest and prosecute those who test positive. Writing for the majority, Justice John Paul Stevens emphasized:

While the ultimate goal of the program may well have been to get the women in question into substance abuse treatment and off of drugs, the immediate objective of the searches was to generate evidence for law enforcement purposes in order to reach that goal.

Cases Cited

Alaska v. Grubbs, No. 4FA S89 415 Criminal (Sup. Ct. August 25, 1989).

Florida v. Johnson, No. 89-1765 [Cir. Ct., July 13, 1989].

Grodin v. Grodin, 102 Mich. 396, 301 N.W.2d 869 (1980).

Ferguson v. City of Charleston, US SupCt. No. 99-936 (2001).

Hoener v. Bertinato, 67 N.J. Sup. 517 171 A. 2d 140 (1961).

Illinois v. Bedenkop, Ill AppCt, 1stDist, No. 1-92-0604 (8/13/93).

Illinois v. Green, No. 88-CM-8256 (Cir. Ct. filed May 8, 1989).

In re Baby X, 97 Mich. App. 111, 293 N.W.2d 736 (1980).

In re Ruiz, 27 Ohio Misc. 2d 31, 32 (Ct. of Common Pleas 1986).

Ohio v. Gray, 584 N.E. 2d 710 (Ohio 1992).

People v. Morabito, 580 N.Y.S.2d 843 (1992).

People v. Stewart, No. M 508197 (San Diego Mun. Ct., Feb. 23, 1987).

Reyes v. California, 75 Cal. App3d 214 (1977).

Roe v. Wade, 410 U.S. 113 (1973).

State v. Andrews, Family Court of Stark County, Ohio (19 June 1989).

State v. McKnight, SC SupCt, No. 25585 (2003).

United States v. Vaughn, No. F-2172-88B (D.C. Super. Ct. August 23, 1988).

Webster v. Reproductive Health Services, 492 U.S. 490 (1989).

Welch v. Kentucky, No 90-CA-1189-MR (Ky. Ct. App. Feb. 7, 1992).

Whitner v. State, 59 CrL 1377 (1996).

Wyoming v. Pfannestiel, No. 1-90-8CR (Co. Ct. of Laramie, Wyoming, Feb. 1, 1990).

References

American Civil Liberties Union Foundation. (1995). *Criminal prosecutions against pregnant women*. New York: Center for Reproductive Law and Policy.

Associated Press. Hospital gives up notifying police of cocain abusers. *New York Times* (1994, September 8). pp. A18.

Besharov, D. J. (1990). Crack children in foster care. *Children Today*, 19, 21–25, 35.

Bingol, N., Fuchs, M., Diaz, V., Stone, R., and Gromisch, D. (1987). Teratogenicity of cocaine in humans. *Journal of Pediatrics*, 110, 93–96.

Blakeslee, S. (1989, September 17). Crack's toll among babies: A joyless view, even of toys. *New York Times*, p. A1.

Bowes, W. A., and Selgestad, B. (1981). Fetal versus maternal rights: Medical and legal perspectives. *Obstetrics and Gynecology*, 58, 209–214.

Center for Reproductive Law and Policy. (1993). Punishing women for their behavior during pregnancy: A public health disaster. *Reproductive Freedom in Focus*, 1–13.

Chasnoff, I., Chisum, G. M., and Kaplan, W. E. (1988). Maternal cocaine use and genitourinary tract malformations. *Teratology*, 37, 201–204.

Chasnoff, I., Burns, W. J., Schnoll, S. H., and Burns, K. A. (1985). Cocaine use in pregnancy. *The New England Journal of Medicine*, 313, 666–669.

Chasnoff, I. J., and Griffith, D. R. (1989). Cocaine-exposed infants: Two year follow-up. *Pediatric Research*, 25, 249A.

———. (1989). Cocaine: Clinical studies of pregnancy and the newborn. In D. E. Hutchings (Ed.), *Prenatal abuse of licit and illicit drugs*. New York: New York Academy of Sciences.

Chasnoff, I. J., Griffith, D. R., MacGregor, S., Dirkes, K., and Burns, K. A. (1989). Temporal Patterns of Cocaine Use in Pregnancy. *Journal of the American Medical Association*, 261: 1741–1744.

Colen, B. D. (1990, April 23). Cocaine babies: Doctors are becoming increasingly alarmed about the long-term prospects for a growing army of damaged children. *News Monitor: Selected Articles of Interest in the Public Press*, 17–19.

Dal Pazzo, E. E., and Marsh, F. H. (1987). Psychosis and pregnancy: Some new ethical and legal dilemmas for the physician. *American Journal of Obstetrics and Gynecology*, 156 (2), 425–427.

Fackelman, K. (1991). The maternal cocaine connection: A tiny unwitting victim may bear the brunt of drug abuse. *Science News*, 140, 152.

Farr, K. A. (1995). Fetal abuse and the criminalization of behavior during pregnancy. *Crime and Delinquency*, 41 (2), 235–245.

Fried, P. A., and O'Connell, C. M. (1987). A comparison of the effects of prenatal exposure to tobacco, alcohol, cannabis, and caffeine on birth size and subsequent growth. *Neurobehavioral Toxicology and Teratology*, 9, 79–85.

Fried, P. A., and Watkinson, B. (1990). 36 and 48 Month Neurobehavioral Follow-up of Children Prenatally Exposed to Marijuana, Cigarettes, and Alcohol. *Journal of Developmental and Behavioral Pediatrics*, 11, 49–58.

Garrity-Rokous, F. E. (1994). Punitive legal approaches to the problem of prenatal drug exposure. *Infant Mental Health Journal*, 15 (2), 218–237.

Gonzalez, N., and Campbell, M. (1994). Cocaine babies: Does prenatal exposure to cocaine affect development? *Journal of the American Academy of Child and Adolescent Psychiatry*, 33, 16–19.

Greider, K. (1995). Crackpot ideas. *Mother Jones*, July/August, 53–56.

Griffith, D. R., Azuma, S. D., and Chasnoff, I. (1994). Three-year outcome of children exposed prenatally to drugs. *Journal of the American Academy of Child and Adolescent Psychiatry*, 33, 20–27.

Hawk, M. Norton. (1994). How social policies make matters worse: The case of maternal substance abuse. *The Journal of Drug Issues*, 24 (3), 517–526.

Hopkins, E. (1990). Childhood's end. *Rolling Stone*, October 18, 66.

Inciardi, J. A. (1996). Alcohol and drug use in prison. In *Encyclopedia of American Prisons* (pp. 168–170). New York: Macmillan.

Jos, P. H., Marshall, M. F., and Perlmutter, M. (1995). The Charleston policy on cocaine use during pregnancy: A cautionary tale. *Journal of Law, Medicine, and Ethics*, 23, 120–128.

Justin, R. G., and Rosner, F. (1989). Maternal/fetal rights: Two views. *Journal of the American Medical Women's Association*, 44 (3), 90–95.

Kantrowitz, B., and Wingert, P. (1990). The crack children. *Newsweek*, February 12, 62–63.

Kerr, P. (1986). Babies of crack users fill hospital nurseries. *New York Times*, August 25, B1.

Keyes, L. J. (1992). Rethinking the aim of the "War on Drugs": States' roles in preventing substance abuse by pregnant women. *Wisconsin Law Review*, 1, 197–232.

King, P. (1992). Helping women helping children: Drug policy and future generations. *The Milbank Quarterly*, 69 (4), 595–621.

Langone, J. (1988, September 19). Crack comes to the nursery. *Time*, 85.

Larson, C. (1991, Spring). Overview of state legislative and judicial responses. *Future of Children*, a publication of the Center for the Future of Children, The David and Lucile Packard Foundation, 72–83.

Lester, B. M., Corwin, M. J., Sepkowski, C., Seifer, R., Peuker, M., McLaughlin, S., and Golub, H. L. (1991). Neurobehavioral syndromes in cocaine-exposed newborn infants. *Child Development*, 62, 694–705.

Lieb, J. L., and Sterk-Elifson, C. (1995). Crack in the cradle: Social policy and reproductive rights among crack-using females. *Contemporary Drug Problems,* 22, 687–705.

Marks, M. (1990). Kindergarten: Crack's next stop. *The Miami Herald,* April 16, A1.

McNamara, D. (1989). New York City's crack babies. *The New York Doctor,* 2 (7), 1.

National Institute on Drug Abuse. (1989). High risk of cocaine, other drugs: Babies and mothers. *ADAMHA News,* November/December, 3, 12.

———. (1994). New NIDA research suggests crack baby epidemic overblown. *Substance Abuse Letter,* October 17, 3.

New York Times. (1994, September 8). p. A18.

Paltrow, L. (1992). *Criminal prosecutions against pregnant women: National update and overview.* Reproductive Freedom Project, American Civil Liberties Union Foundation.

Peak, K., and Del Papa, F. S. (1993). Criminal justice enters the womb: Enforcing the "right" to be born drug-free. *Journal of Criminal Justice,* 21, 245–263.

Pinkney, D. S. (1989, October 6). Cocaine babies: Lifetime of challenge. *American Medical News.*

Public Health Foundation. (1990). Cocaine-exposed babies may face impaired development. *Public Health Macroview,* January/February, 2.

Richardson, G., Day, N., and McGauhey, P. (1993). The impact of perinatal marijuana and cocaine use on the infant and child. *Clinical Obstetrics and Gynecology,* 36, 302–318.

Rosner, F., Bennett, A. J., Cassell, E. J., Farnsworth, P. B., Landolt, A. B., Loeb, L., Numann, P. J., Ona, F. V., Risemberg, H. M., Sechzer, P. H., and Sordillo, P. P. (1989). Fetal therapy and surgery: Fetal rights versus maternal obligations. *New York State Journal of Medicine,* February, 80–84.

Rothman, S. (1991). New techniques may help cocaine babies. *U.S. Journal.*

Scherling, D. (1994). Prenatal cocaine exposure and childhood psychopathology: A developmental analysis. *American Journal of Orthopsychiatry,* 64 (1), 9–19.

Shiono, P. H., Klebanoff, M. A., Nugent, R. P., Cotch, M. F., Wilkins, D. G., Rollins, D. E., Carey, J. C., and Behrman, R. E. (1995). The impact of cocaine and marijuana use on low birth weight and preterm birth: A multicenter study. *American Journal of Obstetrics and Gynecology,* 172 (1), 19–20.

Singer, L. T., Arendt, R., Minnes, S., Farkas, K., Salvator, A., Kirchner, H. L., and Kleigman, R. (2002). Cognitive and motor outcomes of cocaine-exposed infants. *Journal of the American Medical Association,* 287 (15), 1952–1960.

Stone, A. (1989). Crack babies born to life of suffering. *USA Today,* June 8, 3A.

Streissguth, A. P., Barr, H. M., Sampson, P. D., Darby, B. L., and Martin, D. C. (1989). IQ at age 4 in relation to maternal alcohol use and smoking during pregnancy. *Developmental Psychology,* 25, 3–11.

Terry, D. (1996). In Wisconsin, a rarity of a fetal-harm case. *New York Times,* August 17, p. 6.

Thornton, J. (1988/1989). "Ministering to the 'Boarder Babies,'" U.S. News and World Report, December 26–January 2, 42–45.

Tomkins, A., and Kepfield, S. (1992). Policy responses when women use drugs during pregnancy: Using child abuse laws to combat substance abuse. In T. B. Sondregger (Ed.), *Perinaltal substance abuse: Research findings and clinical implications.* Baltimore: Johns Hopkins University Press.

Ward, S. L., Bautista, D. B., Schuetz, S., Wachsman, L., Bean, X., and Keens, T. G. (1989). Abnormal hypoxic arousal responses in infants of cocaine-abusing mothers. In D. E. Hutchings (Ed.), *Prenatal abuse of licit and illicit drugs: Annals of the New York Academy of Sciences.* New York: New York Academy of Sciences.

Watkins, J., and Watkins, S. (1992). Prenatal drug exposure: The pro and con arguments for criminalizing fetal harm. *Journal of Crime and Justice,* 15 (1), 157–172.

Weinstein, L. (1983). Reproductive and fetal rights: A philosophical ideal or practical necessity? *American Journal of Obstetrics and Gynecology,* 147 (7), 848–849.

For Discussion

1. What explanations might be offered for the "moral panic" surrounding cocaine babies?

2. Is doctor/patient confidentiality violated when physicians report to prosecutors those positive drug screens from either infants or pregnant women?

23

History and Epidemiology of Amphetamine Abuse in the United States

Marissa A. Miller

In *this article, Marissa Miller traces the history of amphetamine use in the United States. Amphetamines were once perceived as safe drugs for treating various medical problems, but, the author notes, more stringent controls on their production were introduced in 1971. Subsequently, the illegal manufacture of methamphetamine, in particular, began to develop. Miller uses data from various sources to describe recent patterns of use. She notes that regional variations in use have emerged and suggests that amphetamine and methamphetamine are likely to represent major drugs of abuse in the future.*

Trends in drug abuse are influenced by many factors, including properties of the drug, characteristics of the abusing population, and the environment within which the abuse occurs, as well as broader issues related to drug manufacturing, marketing, and distribution. Many complex and interrelated elements have converged in promulgating past and present epidemics of amphetamine abuse. This chapter will chronicle the unique history of the development of amphetamine and methamphetamine, the medical and nonmedical use of

these drugs, and subsequent epidemics of abuse in the United States; describe current patterns and trends of abuse and factors influencing these trends; explain how legal control of the manufacture and distribution has influenced the availability and propelled the patterns of abuse; and consider the potential for future abuse of methamphetamine and related substances.

Background

Amphetamines are a class of synthetic stimulants that include several specific chemical agents the most common of which are amphetamine (Benzedrine), methamphetamine (Desoxyn), dextroamphetamine (Dexadrine), and benzphetamine (Didrex), plus the combination amphetamine and dextroamphetamine (Biphetamine) (King and Coleman, 1987). Amphetamines were first manufactured in 1887 (Caldwell, 1980). Methamphetamine was first synthesized in 1919 and closely resembles amphetamine in chemical structure and pharmacologic action. Today the term amphetamine refers generally to popular pharmaceutical pills and capsules used licitly and illicitly. Methamphetamine is a related compound that generally is more sought after due to its long-lasting high. Methamphetamine is the only compound in this class of stimulants that is manufactured to any significant extent in clandestine laboratories in the United States and currently is a more prevalent drug of abuse than amphetamine.

Speed is a term used to describe all the synthetic stimulants including amphetamine and methamphetamine. Illicit methamphetamine is known by names such as 'meth,' 'crystal,' and 'crank.' Amphetamine pills and capsules that have found their way onto the streets are commonly referred to as 'denies,' 'dexies,' 'bennies,' and 'uppers.' Street drug terminology is very location specific and not standardized, so wherever possible any new term will be defined in the text.

History of Early Use

Historically, use of the synthetically manufactured amphetamines and methamphetamine can be traced back to the early 1930s, when medicinally useful attributes of these compounds were discovered. Amphetamine and the closely related methamphetamine exhibited bronchodilator and hypertensive properties: They reversed barbiturate anesthesia and treated lung congestion. Between 1932 and 1946, the pharmaceutical industry developed a list of 39 generally accepted clinical uses for these drugs, including the treatment of schizophrenia, morphine and codeine addiction, tobacco smoking, heart block, head injuries, radiation sickness, low blood pressure, and persistent hiccups (Lukas, 1985). They were promoted as being safe without risks (Grinspoon and Hedblom, 1975). From the time of early use the existence of psychoactive properties was also identified in association with these substances. Extensive use, combined with the inherent properties of the drugs, set the stage for later widespread abuse.

Amphetamines rapidly became popular in the United States. Amphetamine tablets could be obtained without prescription until 1951, and amphetamine inhalers were available until 1959. Amphetamines and methamphetamine were widely marketed during the 1950s and 1960s for obesity, narcolepsy, hyperkinesis, and depression. Housewives were prescribed amphetamines for weight loss; others, including students, businessmen, and truck drivers, used them for their anti-fatigue effects (Ellinwood, 1974). Their popularity was bolstered by low cost and long duration of effect (Fischman, 1990). During World War II amphetamines were used extensively by the American, British, German, and Japanese military as stimulants and insomniacs. An estimated 200 million tablets and pills were supplied to American troops during World War II (Grinspoon and Hedblom, 1975). Some of the American soldiers returned home following the war and continued to use stimulants.

The popularity of amphetamines drove production, and production levels served ultimately to drive popularity. Legal production soared from approximately 3.5 billion tablets in 1958 to 10 billion tablets by 1970 (Grinspoon and Hedblom, 1975). During the 1960s, 20 million prescriptions were written

each year, predominantly for weight reduction purposes (Ellinwood, 1979; Spotts and Spotts, 1980). Prescribing practices escalated until 1967, when 31 million scripts were written. The prevalence of use was much higher among younger adults and in certain areas of the country such as San Francisco (Mellinger et al., 1971).

In the late 1950s some physicians began prescribing intravenously administered methamphetamine as a treatment for heroin addiction. Other doctors and pharmacists became involved in writing illegal prescriptions for liquid amphetamine ampoules (Lake and Quirk, 1984). These practices contributed to the origination of new abuse patterns involving intravenous injection of methamphetamine. The most popular of the injectable ampoules were made by Abbott (Desoxyn) and Burroughs Wellcome (Methedrine). During the first half of 1962 over 500,000 ampules were prescribed (Brecher, 1972; Smith, 1969).

During the 1960s speed use spread to a variety of groups throughout the San Francisco Bay area. Haight-Ashbury, a neighborhood of the Bay area, epitomized the 1960s drug subculture. In Haight-Ashbury speed began to replace hallucinogenic drugs such as LSD in popularity (Pittel and Hofer, 1970). Speed use escalated, and a shift from oral preparations to intravenous abuse occurred. By the early 1960s the San Francisco Bay area was home to a large and increasing number of intravenous methamphetamine users. Intravenous use combined with the development of tolerance, led to escalating use. Serial intravenous speed users became known as 'speed freaks.' A public campaign in response to this trend warned that 'speed kills' (Lukas, 1985). As a result of law enforcement targeting activities, the public health campaign, user demographic changes, and other factors, the prevalence of methamphetamine and amphetamine use dropped after 1972 (Newmeyer, 1988).

Manufacture, Distribution, and Diversion

During the 1960s pharmaceutical amphetamine production soared with the demand from widespread use. However, production levels grew at a rate that far exceeded medical use. One consequence of excessive production combined with widespread popularity was diversion of pharmaceutical grade drugs to illegal traffic and use. The black market in amphetamines involved diversions from pharmaceutical companies, wholesalers, pharmacists, and physicians. It is estimated that up until 1971 between one-half to two-thirds of the 100,000 pounds of pharmaceutical amphetamine produced each year was diverted to black market channels (Grinspoon and Hedblom, 1975). In 1971 the Justice Department began imposing quotas on legal amphetamine production.

The Department of Justice (DOJ) became aware of the magnitude of dispensation of intravenous methamphetamine through illegal prescription writing. The DOJ intervened, and pharmaceutical manufacturers voluntarily removed methamphetamine ampoules from the outpatient prescription marketplace (Spotts and Spotts, 1980). Abbott withdrew Desoxyn in 1962 and Burroughs Wellcome withdrew Methedrine in 1963. This action left intravenous methamphetamine users without a product that could be readily injected. Demand was created for an inexpensive water-soluble powder product.

What resulted was the emergence of the first illicit 'bathtub' methamphetamine laboratories in late 1962 in San Francisco to satisfy the demand for a user-friendly product (Morgan et al., 1994). The early illicit methamphetamine was synthesized from phenyl-2-propanone (P-2-P) and methylamine by a process referred to as the amalgam method, resulting in a racemic mixture of *d*- (the more pharmacologically active form) and *l*-isomer methamphetamine. A few legitimate chemists are believed to have helped several groups develop this manufacturing process (Morgan et al., 1994). The illicit product was less potent and less pure than the pharmaceutical product which is all *d*-isomer methamphetamine. The newly manufactured product became known by a number of street names such as: 'crank,' 'bathtub crank,' 'biker crank,' 'peanut butter,' 'prope-dope,' and 'wire.'

Whereas prior to 1962 the quality and purity of methamphetamine was defined by pharmaceutical supplies, after 1962 the availability and quality of the illicit product was unpredictable. Up until 1974 only 30% of street samples purported to be methamphetamine truly were methamphetamine. 'Look-alike' speed, a combination of phenylpropanolamine, ephedrine, and caffeine, sometimes with other constituents, flooded the street market (Lake and Quirk, 1984). From 1975 to 1983 the meth content of street samples increased from 60% to over 90%. Over time, clandestinely manufactured methamphetamine came to dominate the street speed market (Puder et al., 1988).

With the escalation of use during the 1960s came an increase in violence and a diffusion of clandestine manufacturing and distribution of speed outward from Haight-Ashbury to other areas along the West Coast (Smith, 1970). By 1965, outlaw motorcycle gangs, notorious for their depraved and unlawful activities and realizing there was profit to be made, began manufacturing and distributing speed (National Narcotics Intelligence Consumers Committee, 1993). Crank became regarded as the best speed for the biker lifestyle, which emphasized fast high-risk motorcycling, fighting, heavy drinking, partying, and barbiturate use (Thompson, 1967). The combination of the affinity of bikers and their lifestyle for the drug, and the sizeable profits to be made from its manufacture and distribution, led to increasing involvement and dominance over distribution by mid-1960. Biker distribution of crank diffused north to Oregon and Washington State and into Southern California. The laboratories were located primarily in rural areas.

The Department of Justice recognized the involvement of outlaw biker groups, in particular the Hell's Angels, in methamphetamine manufacture and distribution and began targeting these groups. During the 1980s, the law enforcement pressure combined with the dissemination of a new method of synthesis led to significant changes in methamphetamine distribution networks. The shift was to smaller producers and groups of friends or family who cooperated to produce small amounts of methamphetamine in low-tech tabs (NNICC, 1993). Beginning around 1980, methamphetamine laboratories began to proliferate around San Diego and use in that area escalated.

The illicit manufacture of methamphetamine is relatively simple and can be carried out by individuals without special knowledge or expertise provided a detailed recipe is available (Irvine and Chin, 1991; Bureau of Justice Statistics, 1992). Laboratory operators include high school dropouts and highly educated chemists. Clandestine laboratories are commonly operated on an irregular basis. Frequently a batch of product is produced and the laboratory is disassembled, stored, or moved to a new location. Sites for laboratories vary from sophisticated underground hideaways to motel rooms, kitchens, or garages (NNICC, 1993). Laboratories tend to be located in more secluded rural sites, initially to avoid discovery due to fumes and odors vented during the production process (Irvine and Chin, 1991). The precursors and methods used in methamphetamine synthesis can vary from laboratory to laboratory. In many cases the producers possess insufficient knowledge and skill to carry out the synthesis appropriately and completely. In these cases the purity and quality of the end product suffer, with the output containing large levels of contaminants and unreacted precursors.

The Drug Enforcement Administration reports that methamphetamine is the most prevalent clandestinely manufactured controlled substance in the United States (DEA, 1993). The number of clandestine methamphetamine laboratories seized rose dramatically during the 1980s, from 88 in 1981 to 652 in 1989. This dramatic increase reflects both increased law enforcement pursuit of clandestine laboratories and the expansion of clandestine production. Since 1989, there has been a decrease in laboratory seizures to 429 in 1990, 315 in 1991, and 288 in 1992. Consistent with previous years, the clandestine manufacture of methamphetamine was located primarily in the West and Southwest United States. During 1992, 78% of the laboratories seized were located in the Denver, Los Angeles, Phoenix, San Diego, San Francisco, and Seattle DEA field areas (NNICC, 1993). Methamphetamine laboratories accounted for more than 87% of all clandestine laboratory seizures during 1992. The decrease in the number of methamphetamine laboratories seized in the United States during the 1990s as compared to the large number of laboratory seizures during 1989, is believed to be largely a result of the enactment and enforcement of the Chemical Diversion and Trafficking Act of 1988, which placed the distribution of 12 precursor and eight essential chemicals used in the production of illicit drugs under federal control (DEA, 1993).

Currently the ephedrine reduction method is the principal means employed in the manufacture of methamphetamine. This relatively simple process originated in Southern California and now is widespread throughout the United States (NNICC, 1993). The resulting product is the *d*-isomer of methamphetamine. Reportedly, new and altered chemical processes for clandestine manufacturing of methamphetamine are emerging on the West Coast, including the tetrahydrofuran (THF) synthesis (Wrede and Murphy, 1994) and a relatively simple synthesis procedure that is a variation of the ephedrine reduction method that is called 'cold cook' because no external heat source is required for the synthesis to proceed (Dode and Dye, 1994; DEA, 1993).

During 1992 the individuals and groups involved in manufacture and distribution of methamphetamine were diverse and numerous and included independent entrepreneurs, outlaw motorcycle gangs, and Hispanic polydrug trafficking organizations (NNICC, 1993). Independent entrepreneur involvement was broad and distributed nationally. Motorcycle gangs influenced production in select areas, and Mexican traffickers dominated the large-scale production and distribution in San Diego, Riverside, San Bernardino, and Fresno areas of California (NNICC, 1993; DEA, 1993). The Mexican traffickers typically manufacture large quantities of methamphetamine in Mexico and smuggle the finished product into California through heroin and marijuana trafficking routes, with the potential for distribution throughout the United States. Mexican smuggling of precursor chemicals such as ephedrine into California also provides evidence of their domination of methamphetamine production in the West (DEA, 1993). The emergence of this new trafficking and distribution scheme involving large quantities of methamphetamine may serve to drive a new widespread epidemic of use in endemic regions and new areas. Increases in methamphetamine use in Phoenix are attributed to a newly forged trafficking relationship between Mexican nationals and local Hispanics (Dode and Dye, 1994).

This brief but significant history of use and abuse of amphetamine and methamphetamine (decades rather than centuries) has laid the foundation for continued abuse of methamphetamine, the arrival of new dosage forms, and the emergence of new chemically related analogues.

Current Trends of Methamphetamine Abuse

Due to its illicit and illegal nature, the direct, reliable, and consistent measurement of substance abuse is difficult, if not impossible. As a result, the description of patterns and trends of drug abuse are derived from a variety of data sources, some more scientifically rigorous than others. These sources of information are interpreted as available and patterns and trends inferred from them. Data sources include national probability surveys such as the Monitoring the Future study (MTF), nationally representative surveillance systems akin to the Drug Abuse Warning Network (DAWN) and the Drug Use Forecasting system (DUF), state-based treatment data, small-scale field studies, and ethnographic observational research.

DAWN Data

The first measured surge in methamphetamine use following what has been described historically in Haight-Ashbury during the 1960s and early 1970s, occurred during the mid-1980s among metropolitan areas primarily along the West Coast. These increases were first picked up through ethnographic research and field studies (NIDA, 1986; NIDA, 1989), and later recognized through the Drug Abuse Warning Network (DAWN) system and reported through the Community Epidemiology Work Group, a network of researchers from major metropolitan areas of the United States who provide ongoing community level surveillance of drug abuse.

The DAWN is a national surveillance system that monitors hospital emergencies and deaths associated with drug abuse. The DAWN system was begun in the early 1970s as a random sample of hospital emergency departments; over time the number and type of participating hospitals changed, and the representativeness of the sample was compromised. The current system was revitalized, and a new sample drawn in 1986 to represent all hospital emergency departments in the coterminous United States. Nonfederal, short-stay, general hospitals with a 24-hour emergency department are eligible for inclusion in DAWN. Twenty-one Metropolitan Statistical Areas (MSAs) are designated for oversampling. Hospitals outside of these 21 areas are assigned to a national panel and sampled. A total of 685 hospitals were selected for the sample and 508 hospitals (74%) participated in the survey in 1993 (Office of Applied Studies, 1994a). Participation in DAWN is voluntary and involves a designated reporter within each facility reviewing hospital emergency department (ED) admission records.

An episode report is submitted each time a patient visits a DAWN hospital with problems relating to their own drug use. The case definition involves four criteria, all of which must be met: the patient must be treated in the hospital's ED, the presenting complaint must have been induced by or related to drug use at any time preceding the episode, the case must involve the nonmedical use of a legal drug or any use of an illegal drug, and the patient's reason for taking the drug/drugs must include dependence, suicide attempt, or psychic effect. If all the above criteria are met, then the ED visit is deemed a drug episode. For each drug episode, in addition to alcohol in combination, up to four substances may be recorded as drug mentions. Drug episodes are not synonymous with the number of individuals involved in the reported episodes. One person may make repeated visits to one or several EDs with each episode recorded independently.

The limitations of this system are that the data are only as good as the information recorded by the hospital ED staff and reflect only self-reported drug use by the patient without laboratory confirmation. DAWN does not provide a complete image of problems associated with drug use but only reflects the impact of drug use on hospital EDs in the United States and the sort of drug-related problems that bring patients into emergency departments.

The DAWN emergency department data showed statistically significant increases in mentions of methamphetamine/speed in Atlanta, Dallas, Los Angeles, Phoenix, San Diego, and Seattle between 1986 and 1988

(NIDA, 1989). During 1988 and 1989 the national level of methamphetamine/speed emergency room mentions held steady, a drop was experienced in 1990 with a steady increase from 1990 through 1993 (Figure 23.1). In 1993 10,052 episodes (preliminary estimates) involving the use of methamphetamine/speed were reported in the coterminous United States up from a low of 4,887 reported in 1991, a 106% increase (OAS, 1994b). A total of 466,897 drug-related emergency room episodes were recorded for 1993, cocaine accounted for 123,317 (26.4%) and heroin accounted for 62,965 (13.5%), with meth/speed involved in just over 2% of the episodes, ranking 12th among all drug-related episodes. From 1990 through 1993 national estimates of total drug-related ED episodes increased 26% from 371,208 to 466,897 respectively, and increased 8% between 1992 and 1993. Approximately 10% of the 1992 to 1993 increase is attributable to increases in meth/speed mentions (OAS, 1994b).

Figure 23.1

Estimated Number of Methamphetamine/Speed Emergency Room Mentions in the Coterminous United States by Year: 1988–1993

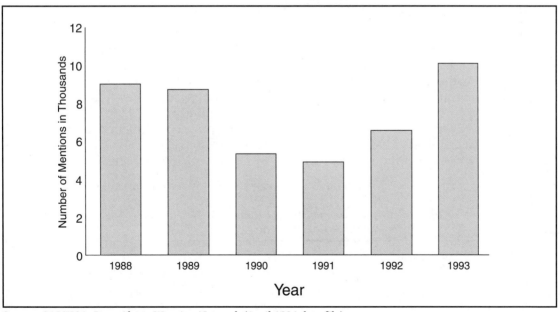

Source: SAMHSA, Drug Abuse Warning Network (April 1994 data file).
Note: The 1993 estimates are preliminary.

Figure 23.2

Estimated Number of Methamphetamine/Speed Emergency Room Mentions in
Selected U.S. Metropolitan Areas by Year: 1988–1993

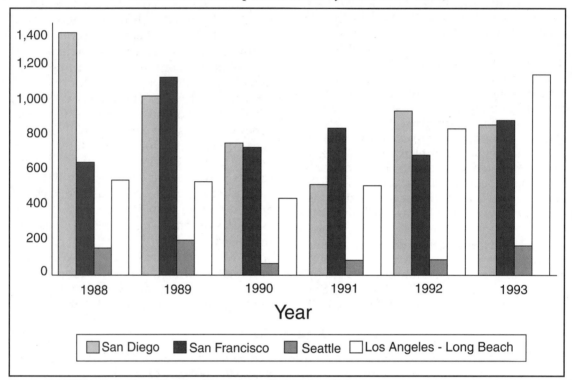

Source: SAMHSA, Drug Abuse Warning Network (April 1994 data file).
Note: The 1993 estimates are preliminary.

West Coast U.S. cities including San Diego, San Francisco, Seattle, and Los Angeles-Long Beach accounted for over 30% of the total 1993 methamphetamine/speed ED mentions (1993 preliminary estimates). Over the six-year period from 1988 through 1993, San Diego exhibited consistently high numbers of methamphetamine/speed ED mentions, leading all other cities during three years of this time period (Figure 23.2). Los Angeles led all MSAs in number of methamphetamine/speed mentions in 1993 with 1,140 accounting for 11% of total U.S. methamphetamine/speed mentions, followed by San Francisco, San Diego and Seattle with 879, 850, and 161 respectively (Table 23.1).

Table 23.1

Estimated Number of Methamphetamine/Speed Emergency Room Mentions in Selected U.S.
Metropolitan Areas by Year: 1988–1993

U.S.	8992	8722	5236	4887	6563	10052
San Diego	1372	1021	758	515	931	850
San Francisco	639	1125	740	839	688	879
Seattle	142	201	59	90	99	161
Los Angeles–Long Beach	536	536	442	506	828	1140
Year	1988	1989	1990	1991	1992	1993

The profile of a typical methamphetamine user in 1993 is someone in the middle-age range, male, and white (Source: SAMHSA, weighted preliminary 1993 estimates from the April 1994 data file). During 1993, 35% of meth/speed mentions occurred in the 18–25 year age range and 37% in the 26–34 age range. The ratio of males to females using meth/speed ranged from 5:1 in San Francisco to 1.7:1 in San Diego. The predominant motivation for use was dependence (34%), followed by recreational use (27%), followed by unknown (25%). The reason for ED contact for meth/speed mentions was unexpected reaction (37%), overdose (29%), and chronic effects (13%), with withdrawal, seeking detoxification, accident/injury, other, and unknown together comprising the remaining percentage. The route of administration reported for the DAWN mentions was 31% unknown, 27% sniffed or snorted, 22% injected, and 11% oral.

State Treatment Admission Data

Several large nationally based treatment data systems exist. The emphasis within these data systems is on admission data concerning the most prevalent drugs of abuse, namely alcohol, marijuana, cocaine, and heroin. Data singular to methamphetamine were not readily available from these sources. State and city level admissions trends are reported for areas that have a significant methamphetamine problem.

In San Diego during 1993 amphetamine and methamphetamine primary admissions to publicly funded treatment programs totaled 2,376, a 37% increase from 1992 (Haight, 1994). Methamphetamine was the most frequently reported nonalcohol primary drug of abuse among those entering drug treatment programs during 1993, accounting for 41% of all nonalcohol treatment admissions. Numbers of methamphetamine admissions are rivaling alcohol admissions, which historically have been most prevalent. The median age of methamphetamine users entering treatment was 28 in 1993, tending to be younger than cocaine or heroin users. The racial distribution of methamphetamine users entering treatment was 71% white, 5% African American, and 17% Hispanic. An increase was seen in the number of methamphetamine treatment admissions reporting smoking as the preferred route of administration. In 1989, 4% reported smoking as compared to 23% in 1993.

In San Francisco primary admissions for amphetamine abuse totaled 1,357 increasing 17% from 1992 levels (Newmeyer, 1994). Amphetamine admissions accounted for just over 5% of the total non-alcohol admissions, behind heroin (67%), and cocaine (23%). The number and percent of amphetamine admissions has increased steadily each year since 1988 with 534 admissions (3.3%) reported in 1988, and 1,357 (5.2%) reported in 1993.

Statewide methamphetamine treatment admissions in Hawaii have increased from 152 in 1991, to 268 in 1992, to an all-time high of 495 in 1993 (Wood, 1995). These data represent about 90% of the state-supported treatment facilities and do not include two large private facilities. In 1993, methamphetamine admissions accounted for 28% of the total admissions, second only to marijuana admissions (excluding alcohol). The trend of treatment admissions continued to increase into the first half of 1994.

Several drug use indicators including treatment admissions point to escalations of methamphetamine use in Phoenix, Arizona (Dode and Dye, 1994). The number of detoxification admissions for methamphetamine increased by 114% between 1992 and 1993 and ranked second behind heroin among non-alcohol admissions. Admissions of methamphetamine users to treatment through criminal justice programs rose from zero prior to 1992 to 30% in one program and 15% in another program during 1993.

Amphetamine and methamphetamine admissions account for a small proportion of overall admissions in most other cities and States (NIDA, 1994). In Colorado amphetamine admissions comprised 5.6% of the total, a slight increase over 1992. In Texas, Seattle, and Los Angeles amphetamine and methamphetamine admissions account for 3%, and in Minneapolis 2%, of nonalcohol admissions.

DUF Data

The Drug Use Forecasting (DUF) system is a monitoring system collaboratively administered by the National Institute of Justice and 24 booking facility sites across the nation. Interviews and urine drug tests for 10 illicit compounds are conducted at the time of booking of adult male, adult female, and juvenile arrestees, and represent drug use among those involved with the criminal justice system. For approximately 14 consecutive evenings each quarter, local staff interview and obtain voluntary urine specimens from a sample of newly booked arrestees. At each site approximately 225 males are sampled, and in some sites female arrestees and juvenile arrestees/detainees are also sampled. Response rates are 90% for the interview portion and 80% for the urine specimen portion of the system (NIJ, 1994a).

The DUF sample attempts to represent a sufficient distribution of arrest charges by limiting the number of male booked arrestees who are charged with the sale or possession of drugs (otherwise a majority of the sample would be made up of drug charge arrestees). Persons charged with drug charges are more likely to be using drugs at the time of arrest, so this limitation tends to underestimate drug use in the male arrestee population. The DUF sample also generally excludes driving offenses, emphasizing more serious crimes. In contrast, in order to obtain sufficient numbers of arrestees, all adult female and juvenile arrestees brought to the booking center or detention facility during the data collection period are included in the DUF sample, regardless of the charge.

Urine specimens are tested for cocaine, opiates, marijuana, PCP, methadone, benzodiazepines, methaqualone, propoxyphene, barbiturates, and amphetamines. All amphetamine positive results are further tested to eliminate exposure to over-the-counter products. The testing detects drug use that occurred in the previous two to three days for most compounds. PCP and

marijuana use may be detected as long as several weeks prior to the testing date.

In 1993 the DUF system collected data from 20,550 adult male booked arrestees in 23 sites (NIJ, 1994a). Data from 8,070 adult female booked arrestees were collected at 20 of these sites. Twelve DUF sites collected male juvenile arrestee/detainee data (NIJ, 1994b). At most sites during 1993 cocaine was the most prevalent drug among male arrestees, followed by marijuana (seven sites reported a rate of marijuana use higher than cocaine). Cocaine use among male adult arrestees ranged from a low of 19% in Omaha, Nebraska, to a high of 66% in Manhattan, New York, with a median percentage of 43. Marijuana use ranged from 21% in Manhattan to 42% in Omaha, with a median value of 28%. Opiate use ranged from a low of 1% in Fort Lauderdale, Florida to a high of 28% in Chicago, Illinois. Data from 20 sites revealed female arrestees to have marijuana in their urine a median of 16.5% of the time (range of 9% to 25%); and a range of opiate use from 3% to 23%. Results for juvenile arrestees/detainees nearly exclusively showed marijuana and cocaine use.

Overall, during 1993 in the majority of sites amphetamine use was very low or nonexistent. The predominant portion of amphetamine use was clustered in Western cities, including San Diego, California; San Jose, California; Los Angeles, California; Phoenix, Arizona; and Portland, Oregon. The level of amphetamine abuse among adult male arrestees within these sites ranged from 36% in San Diego to 8% in Los Angeles, and 53% in San Diego to 10% in Los Angeles among female arrestees (NIJ, 1994a [Source: DUF 1993 data file]). San Diego had the largest prevalence of amphetamine use for all three user groups during 1993; males (36%), females (53%), and juvenile males (14%) were positive for amphetamine abuse. In San Diego, among male arrestees, amphetamine abuse followed marijuana and cocaine abuse at 36% compared to 40% and 37% respectively. Amphetamine abuse led all other drugs for females in San Diego. Phoenix had the second highest prevalence of amphetamine abuse, with 16% of males and 26% of females testing positive. In all five Western cities the percentage of female arrestees testing positive for amphetamines was higher than the male arrestee counterpart at the same site.

Emergence of Ice

During the mid and late 1980s, ice, a high-potency, high-purity, and smokable methamphetamine hydrochloride was identified as a problem initially by Hawaiian law enforcement sources and later, through Hawaiian drug treatment programs. At the time of the emergence of ice the resident Hawaiian population had limited experience with mainland forms of methamphetamine. Hawaiian users widely believed ice to be a 'new drug,' and not related to other forms of speed. On the street this product, which resembles rock candy in appearance, was most commonly referred to as 'ice,' 'crystal,' 'shabu' (Japanese), or 'batu' (Filipino). In Hawaii the drug is almost exclusively smoked in a glass pipe. The inhalation of vapors leads to rapid absorption into the bloodstream and dissemination to the brain, resulting in the immediate onset of effects, similar to what is experienced by intravenous administration (Chiang and Hawks, 1989).

The unique combination of characteristics of ice—namely, high potency, high purity, and rapid onset of effects by smoking—resulted in an escalation of use among many abusers on the Island of Oahu (Miller and Tomas, 1989). The use pattern that emerged was one of bingeing and crashing, or continuous smoking in runs of three to eight days followed by complete exhaustion, usually characterized by deep prolonged sleep. Many adverse social, psychological, and medical consequences, including rapid addiction were experienced by binge users (Miller, 1991).

The presence of ice in Hawaii dates back to the late 1970s. During the early to mid-1980s ice use was limited to small ethnic gangs, but the outbreak beginning in mid-1980s and peaking in the late 1980s found use spreading to numerous ethnic minorities, the Pacific-Asian majority, Caucasians, both genders, people of all ages, and all socioeconomic classes (Miller, 1991).

Prior to 1990, all the ice entering Hawaii originated from Asian sources, namely Korea, Taiwan, and the Philippines (DEA, 1989). Ice distribution in Hawaii was an economic enterprise developed by organized crime networks in Japan and Korea with large corporate investors (Adamski, 1992; Schoenberger, 1992). Availability of ice in Hawaii was widespread through 1990. By 1991 the availability had decreased, price had skyrocketed, and use indicators were declining (Wood, 1995). Large seizures of ice made by Chinese authorities in 1991 and 1992 confirm that illicit methamphetamine manufacture was also occurring in China. It is believed the Chinese contraband was smuggled into Japan, the Philippines, Hawaii, and the mainland United States during the early 1990s (NNICC, 1993). Current data are not available on the location and extent of ice manufacture within the United States.

Chemical Analogues

Synthesis of designer drugs or chemically related analogues to methamphetamine and amphetamine are emerging as new public health problems. Reports from ethnographers of a sharp increase of use of methylene deoxymethamphetamine (MDMA, XTC, Ecstasy) in association with the 'rave' scene have been received from San Francisco, Dallas, Houston, Miami, and Denver (NIDA, 1994; Kotarba, 1993; and Harrison, 1994). The rave scene is an increasingly popular form of dance and recreation predominantly frequented by young whites, but open to people of all ages, at clandestine locations (frequently abandoned warehouses), where high volume music and high tech entertainment is available. The use of hallucinogens, methamphetamine, or MDMA is often incorporated into the overall experience of the rave (Office of National Drug Control Policy, 1995). MDMA is most commonly swallowed or snorted but can be smoked or injected. In addition to methamphetamine-like effects, MDMA may cause sensory enhancements and distortions and mild visual hallucinations.

To date, MDMA use has not been detected to any large degree on a national level through drug use indicator systems based on drug associated emergency room mentions, medical examiner reports, or within treatment data. Case reports and ethnographic information provide a glimpse of the problem but cannot be relied upon to represent the full scope and extent of this drug problem.

N-methylcathinone hydrochloride (methcathinone, 'cat,' 'goob,' 'sniff,' 'star,' 'wonder star'), a structural and pharmacological analogue of methamphetamine, is a potent and easily manufactured stimulant gaining popularity in the Midwest (Goldstone, 1993; DEA, 1994; Pinkert and Harwood, 1993). Cathinones occur naturally in the leaves of the khat shrub (*catha edulis*), which are chewed in East Africa and southern Arabia for the mild stimulant effects. Methcathinone is typically snorted but can be smoked and injected. Symptoms and adverse effects similar to methamphetamine are reported for methcathinone.

Michigan treatment programs report increasing numbers of methcathinone admissions; as many as 60 treatment admissions were reported statewide between October 1993 and March 1994 (Calkins and Hussain, 1994). Laboratories producing methcathinone were first identified in 1991, when five laboratory sites were seized in the Michigan Upper Peninsula. Methcathinone manufacturing is relatively simple from easily obtained materials; the technology is spreading to other nearby states throughout the Midwest and West (DEA, 1994).

Patterns of Youth Drug Abuse

The Monitoring the Future Study, also known widely as the National High School Senior Survey, has been conducted each year since 1975 under a National Institute on Drug Abuse grant to the University of Michigan Institute for Social Research (Johnston et al., 1991). The 1994 survey represents the 20th annual survey of high school seniors; data on 8th and 10th grade students have been collected since 1991. In 1994 a national

Figure 23.3
Estimated Prevalence of Lifetime, Past Year, and Past Month Use of Stimulants Among High School Seniors: 1982–1994

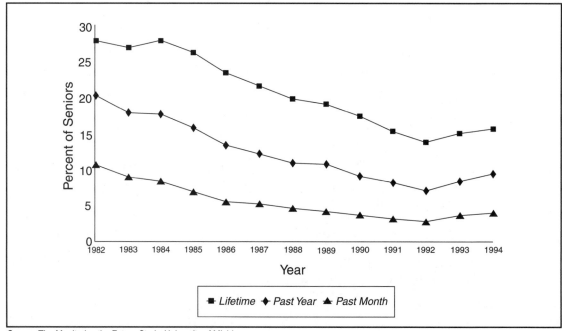

Source: The Monitoring the Future Study. University of Michigan.

Figure 23.4

Estimated Prevalence of Lifetime, Past Year, and Past Month Use of Stimulants Among High School Seniors (1982–1994) and Eighth and Tenth Graders (1991–1994)

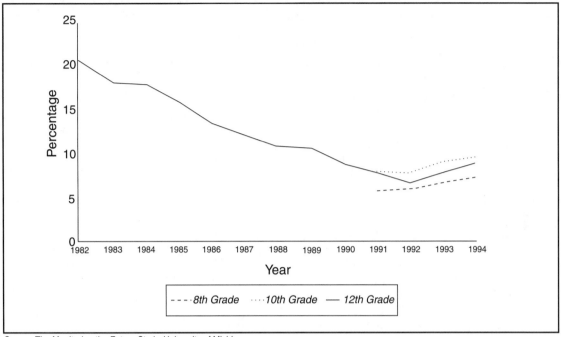

Source: The Monitoring the Future Study. University of Michigan.

probability sample of 15,929 high school seniors in 139 public and private schools nationwide was selected to be representative of all seniors in the continental United States. The students completed self-administered questionnaires during the spring of the year. Questions from the MTF Study solicit responses on use of amphetamines referred to as 'uppers,' 'ups,' 'speed,' 'bennies,' 'decries,' 'pep pills,' and 'diet Pills' (HITS, 1994).

From 1982 to 1992, lifetime, past year, and past month use of stimulants (amphetamines) by high school seniors declined (Figure 23.3). This decline was consistent with an increase in anti-drug attitudes and beliefs in the harmfulness of drug use. Since 1992 there have been significant increases in lifetime, past year, and past month use of stimulants by high school seniors during both 1993 and 1994 (Figure 23.3). During 1991 through 1994 the study also showed a dramatic upturn in past year use of stimulants among 8th and 10th graders, parallel-

ing the increase seen among seniors (Figure 23.4). Among senior students, lifetime use increased for amphetamines from 13.9% to 15.7%, and increased for crystal methamphetamine (ice) from 2.9% to 3.4% over the 1992 to 1994 period (HHS, 1994). These estimates of drug use prevalence by the MTF study may be underestimates due to the fact that the survey is conducted in secondary school classrooms and does not represent drug use by dropouts. Dropouts have been shown to have much higher drug use than seniors in the MTF study (Gfroerer, 1993).

Since 1991 there has been a steady and accelerating decline in perceived risk of drug use, with only 65% in 1994 reporting a great risk associated with regular marijuana use as compared to 79% of seniors in 1991. Perceived risk of use of other drugs such as cocaine and LSD also declined. This decline in perceived risk of drug use is consistent with the increases in drug use demonstrated during the same time period. Perceived dangers and attitudes of peers toward drug use have been shown to predict future drug use.

Conclusion

In conclusion, methamphetamine abuse is endemic in West Coast U.S. cities and Hawaii. From early use by housewives, students, businessmen, and truck drivers, methamphetamine continues to be a significant drug of abuse in the U.S. Morgan et al. (1994) in their study described current methamphetamine use to be firmly entrenched in disenfranchised communities, among troubled individuals and dysfunctional families, and spreading to new user groups. The favorable side-effects such as euphoria, increased energy levels, sexual enhancement, and weight loss makes methamphetamine appealing to diverse population subgroups. With the potential for widespread dissemination, factors such as easy availability, low cost, long duration of effect, and multiple methods of administration may also serve to increase its acceptance in new groups and areas.

The potential for expanded methamphetamine use is particularly significant in light of increasing youth use of drugs (including amphetamines), changing attitudes toward drug use in general, the availability of new dosage forms, and new venues for use. Rave scenes, where both methamphetamine and its analogue MDMA are sold and experimented with, serve as sites for spread into younger age cohorts and higher socioeconomic groups than have historically abused methamphetamine. Ice, a smokable form of methamphetamine, continues to wreak havoc and devastation within low socioeconomic status and working-class Hawaiian neighborhoods. Cat, an analogue, is gaining acceptance and use in the Midwest, and the potential for new analogues presenting new threats to the public health is significant.

Methamphetamine poses current challenges to our public health and future legacies for our youth and promises to remain problematic in American society for years to come.

Acknowledgement

A special acknowledgment to Arthur Hughes, National Institute on Drug Abuse, for his valued assistance.

References

Adamski, M. (1992) "Yakuza Investors Sink Roots in Isles," *Honolulu Star Bulletin*, October 16.

Brecher, E. M. (1972) *Licit and Illicit Drugs.* Boston: Little Brown.

Bureau of Justice Statistics (BJS). (1992) *Drugs, Crime and the Justice System—A National Report.* Washington, D.C.: U.S. Department of Justice, U.S. Government Printing Office (NJS–133652).

Caldwell, J. (1980) *Amphetamines and Related Stimulants: Chemical, Biological, Clinical, and Sociological Aspects.* Boca Raton, Florida: CRC Press, Inc.

Calkins, R. F., and Hussain K. L. (1994) "Drug Abuse Trends in Detroit/Wayne County, Michigan." In: *Epidemiologic Trends in Drug Abuse. Volume II: Proceedings of the Community Epidemiology Work Group June 1994.* Rockville, Maryland: National Institute on Drug Abuse (NIH Pub. No. 94–3854).

Chiang, N., and Hawks, R. (1989) *Pyrolysis Studies: Cocaine, Phencyclidine, Heroin and Methamphetamine.* Technical Review Brief. Rockville, Maryland: National Institute on Drug Abuse.

Dode, I. L., and Dye, C. (1994) "Drug Abuse Trends in Phoenix and Arizona." In *Epidemiologic Trends in Drug Abuse. Volume II: Proceedings of the Community Epidemiology Work Group June 1994.* Rockville, Maryland: National Institute on Drug Abuse (NIH Pub. No. 94–3854).

Drug Enforcement Administration. (1993) *Methcathinone (CAT) Drug Fact Sheet.* Washington, D.C.: U.S. Department of Justice, Intelligence Division (DEA–94007).

Drug Enforcement Administration. (1994) *U.S. Drug Threat Assessment: 1993. Drug Intelligence Report.* Washington, D.C.: U.S. Department of Justice (DEA–93042).

Drug Enforcement Administration. (1989) "A Special Report on 'Ice'." In *Epidemiologic Trends in Drug Abuse.* (Proceedings of the Community Epidemiology Work Group December 1989.) Supt. of Docs., U.S. Govt. Print. Off., Washington, DC (DHHS Pub. No. 721–757:20058).

Ellinwood, E. H. (1974) "Epidemiology of Stimulant Abuse." In E. Josephson and E. Carroll (eds.), *Drug Use*. Washington D.C.: Hemisphere Publishing Corporation.

Ellinwood, E. H. (1979) "Amphetamines/Anorectics." In R. DuPont, A. Goldstein, and J. O'Donnell (eds.), *Handbook on Drug Abuse*. Washington, D.C.: National Institute on Drug Abuse.

Fischman, M. W. (1990) "History and Current Use of Methamphetamine in the United States." In: *Cocaine and Methamphetamine: Behavioral Toxicology, Clinical Psychiatry and Epidemiology*. Proceedings from Japan-U.S. Scientific Symposium '90' on Drug Dependence and Abuse. Tokyo, Japan.

Gfroerer, J. (1993) "An Overview of the National Household Survey on Drug Abuse and Related Methodological Research." Proceedings of the Survey Research Section of the American Statistical Association, Joint Statistical Meetings, August 1992. Boston, Massachusetts.

Grinspoon, L., and Hedblom, P. (1975) *The Speed Culture, Amphetamine Use and Abuse in America*. Cambridge, Mass.: Harvard University Press.

Goldstone, M. S. (1993) "Cat: Methcathinone—a New Drug of Abuse." *JAMA* 269, p. 2508.

Haight, M. A. (1994) "Drug Abuse Trends in San Diego County." In *Epidemiologic Trends in Drug Abuse. Volume II: Proceedings of the Community Epidemiology Work Group June 1994*. Rockville, Maryland: National Institute on Drug Abuse (NIH Pub. No. 94–3854).

Harrison, L. (1994) "Raving in Colorado: An Amateur's Field Notes." In *Epidemiologic Trends in Drug Abuse. Volume II: Proceedings of the Community Epidemiology Work Group June 1994*. Rockville, Maryland: National Institute on Drug Abuse (NIH Pub. No. 94–3854).

Health and Human Services. (1994) *HHS Releases High School Drug Abuse and "DAWN" Surveys*. U.S. Department of Health and Human Services Press Release, Monday, December 12.

Irvine, G., and Chin, L. (1991) "The Environmental Impact and Adverse Health Effects of the Clandestine Manufacture of Methamphetamine." In M. A. Miller and N. J. Kozel (eds.), *Methamphetamine Abuse: Epidemiologic Issues and Implications*. NIDA Research Monograph 115. Rockville, Maryland: U.S. Dept. of Health and Human Services.

Johnston, L. D., O'Malley, P. M., and Bachman, J. G. (1991) *Drug Use Among American High School Seniors, College Students and Young Adults, 1975-1990, Volume I—High School Seniors*. Rockville, Maryland: National Institute on Drug Abuse (DHHS Pub. No. [ADM] 91–1813).

King, P. K., and Coleman, J. H. (1987) "Stimulants and Narcotic Drugs." *Pediatric Clinics of North America*, 34 (2): 349–362.

Kotarba, J. A. (1993) *The Rave Scene in Houston, Texas: An Ethnographic Analysis*. Austin, Texas: Texas Commission on Alcohol and Drug Abuse.

Lake, C., and Quirk, R. (1984) "Stimulants and Look-Alike Drugs." *Psychiatric Clinics North America* 7: 689–701.

Lukas, S. E. (1985) *The Encyclopaedia of Psychoactive Drugs. Amphetamines. Danger in the Fast Lane*. New York: Chelsea House.

Mellinger, G. D., Balter, M. B., and Manheimer, D. I. (1971) "Patterns of Psychotherapeutic Drug Use Among Adults in San Francisco." *Archives of General Psychiatry*, November, pp. 385–395.

Miller, M. A. (1991) "Trends and Patterns of Methamphetamine Smoking in Hawaii." In M. A. Miller and N. J. Kozel (eds.), *National Institute on Drug Abuse Research Monograph Series No. 115: Methamphetamine Abuse: Epidemiologic Issues and Implications*. Washington, D.C.: Supt. of Docs., U.S. Govt. Print. Off. (DHHS Pub. No. [ADM]91–1836).

Miller, M. A., and Tomas, J. M. (1989) "Past and Current Methamphetamine Epidemics." *In Epidemiologic Trends in Drug Abuse: Proceedings of the Community Epidemiology Work Group December 1989*. Washington, D.C.: Supt. of Docs., U.S. Govt. Print. Off. (DHHS Pub. No. 721–757:20058).

Morgan, P., Beck, J., Joe, K., McDonnell, D., and Gutierrez, R. (1994) *Ice and Other Methamphetamine Use*. Final Report to the National Institute on Drug Abuse. National Institute of Health. U.S. Government Printing Office.

Morgan, J. P., and Kagan, D. X. (1978) "The Impact on Street Amphetamine Quality of the 1970 Controlled Substances Act." *Journal of Psychedelic Drugs* 10: 303–317.

National Institute of Justice (NIJ). (1994a) *Drug Use Forecasting 1993 Annual Report on Adult Arrestees: Drugs and Crime in America's Cities*. Washington, D.C.: U.S. Department of Justice, National Institute of Justice.

National Institute of Justice (NIJ). (1994b) *Drug Use Forecasting 1993 Annual Report Juvenile Arrestee/Detainees: Drugs and Crime in America's Cities*. Washington, D.C.: U.S. Department of Justice, National Institute of justice.

National Institute on Drug Abuse. (1986) *Drug Abuse Trends and Research Issues. Proceedings of the Community Epidemiology Work Group December 1986*. Washington, D.C.: U.S. Govt. Print. Off. (DHHS Pub. No. 181–332:60315).

National Institute on Drug Abuse. (1989) *Methamphetamine Abuse in the United States*. Washington, D.C.: Supt. of Docs., U.S. Govt. Print. Off. (DHHS Pub. No. [ADM]89–1608).

National Institute on Drug Abuse. (1994) *Epidemiologic Trends in Drug Abuse. Volume 1: Highlights and Executive Summary. Community Epidemiology Work Group (June 1994)*. Rockville, Maryland: National Institute on Drug Abuse (NIH Pub. No. 94–3853).

National Narcotics Intelligence Consumers Committee. (1993) *The NNICC Report 1992*. Washington, D.C.: Department of Justice, Drug Enforcement Administration.

Newmeyer, J. A. (1994) "Drug Use in the San Francisco Bay Area." In *Epidemiologic Trends in Drug Abuse. Volume II: Proceedings of the Community Epidemiology Work Group June 1994*. Rockville, Maryland: National Institute on Drug Abuse (NIH Pub. No. 94–3854).

Newmeyer, J. A. (1988) "The Prevalence of Drug Use in San Francisco in 1987." *Journal of Psychoactive Drugs* 20 (2): 185–189.

Newmeyer, J. A. (1978) "The Epidemiology of the Use of Amphetamine and Related Substances." *Journal of Psychedelic Drugs* 10 (4): 293–302.

Office of Applied Studies. (1994a) *Statistical Series: Annual Emergency Room Data 1992 Data from the Drug Abuse Warning Network (DAWN)*. Series 1, No. 12 A. Rockville, Maryland: Substance Abuse and Mental Health Services Administration (DHHS Pub. No. [SMA]94–2080).

Office of Applied Studies. (1994b) *Preliminary Estimates from the Drug Abuse Warning Network 1993, Preliminary Estimates of Drug-Related Emergency Department Episodes. Advance Report Number 8, December 1994*. Rockville, Maryland: Substance Abuse and Mental Health Services Administration.

Office of National Drug Control Policy. (1995) *Pulse Check—National Trends in Drug Abuse*. Washington, D.C.: Executive Office of the President.

Pinkert, D., and Harwood, H. J. (1993) *"Khat, (Cathaedulis): Background and Policy Questions."* Prepared for National Institute on Drug Abuse (in draft). Rockville, Maryland: Drug Abuse Policy Center.

Pittel, S. M., and Hofer, R. (1970) "The Transition to Amphetamine Abuse." In E. H. Ellinwood and S. Cohen (eds.), *Current Concepts on Amphetamine Abuse*. National Institute of Mental Health, Washington, D.C.: Supt. of Docs., U.S. Govt. Print. Off. (DHEW Pub. No. [HSM]72–9085).

Puder, K. S., Kagan, D. V., and Morgan, J. P. (1988) "Illicit Methamphetamine: Analysis, Synthesis, and Availability." *American Journal Drug Alcohol Abuse* 14: 463–473.

Schoenberger, K. (1992) "Yakuza Expand on Mainland." *Honolulu Advertiser*, January 5.

Smith, R. (1969) "The World of the Haight-Ashbury Speed Freak." *Journal of Psychoactive Drugs* 2 (2): 77–83.

Smith, R. C. (1970) "Compulsive Methamphetamine Abuse and Violence in the Haight-Ashbury District." In E. H. Ellinwood and S. Cohen (eds.), *Current Concepts on Amphetamine Abuse*. National Institute of Mental Health. Washington, D.C.: Supt. of Docs., U.S. Govt. Print. Off. (DHEW Pub. No. [HSM]72–908).

Spotts, J. V., and Spotts, C. A. (1980) *Use and Abuse of Amphetamine and Its Substitutes*. NIDA Research Issues 25. Washington, D.C.: National Institute on Drug Abuse.

Thompson, H. S. (1967) *The Hell's Angels*. New York: Ballantine.

Wood, D. W. (1995) "Illicit Drug Use in Honolulu and the State of Hawaii." In *Epidemiologic Trends in Drug Abuse. Volume II: Proceedings of the Community Epidemiology Work Group*.

Wrede, A. F., and Murphy, L. D. (1994) "Recent Drug Abuse Trends in the Seattle King County Area." In *Epidemiologic Trends in Drug Abuse. Volume II: Community Epidemiology Work Group June 1994*. Rockville, Maryland: National Institute on Drug Abuse (NIH Pub. No. 94–3854).

For Discussion

1. Compare Miller's perspective on methamphetamine with that described by Jenkins in this section.

2. Discuss whether recent patterns of amphetamine and methamphetamine use might have been different if production controls had not been developed in 1971.

Reprinted from: Marissa Miller, "History and Epidemiology of Amphetamine Abuse in the United States" in *Amphetamine Misuse: International Perspectives on Current Trends*, pp. 113–133, edited by Hilary Klee. Copyright © 1997 Overseas Publishers Association, Amsterdam B.V. published in the Netherlands by Harwood Academic Publishers. Reprinted with permission of Gordon and Breach Publishers. ✦

24

'The Ice Age'

The Social Construction of a Drug Panic

Philip Jenkins

This article focuses on methamphetamine ("Ice"). Philip Jenkins traces the brief history, the manufacture, and contemporary usage of the drug. The article's major focus, however, is on the media (and government) response to methamphetamine. Jenkins discusses the powerful labels (e.g., epidemic) and media symbolism that emerged during the moral panic over methamphetamine. He also provides an important comparison between the media response to methamphetamine and to cocaine. The author notes that the panic over methamphetamine was not substantiated by drug use indicators, and he provides possible explanations for the moral panic.

In 1989 and 1990 there was much media and political concern about use of the drug "ice," or smokable crystal methamphetamine, which was believed to pose a social threat potentially as great as that of crack cocaine. This concern was not sustained, however, and references to the topic diminished sharply within a few months. The incident thus offers a valuable opportunity to trace the history of a drug panic from its origins to its eclipse. Particular emphasis is placed on the role of domestic political divisions, especially in Hawaii, in citing the panic. It is suggested that this incident illustrates both the manner in which local problems come to be projected on the national political arena and the limitations inherent in such a process. The paper explores the rhetorical devices used to create a sense of impending menace around the supposed danger, and the rea-sons why such an apparently plausible danger failed to gain more public attention or credence.

Research in illicit drugs has often empha-sized the disparity between the perceived threat of a substance and the actual social harm involved. A distinguished literature deals with successive drug "panics," which have focused on marijuana in the 1930s, am-phetamines in the 1950s, glue sniffing in the 1960s, and crack cocaine in the last decade (Brecher, 1972; Musto, 1973; Reinarman and Levine, 1989; Goode, 1984:310–34). This is not to argue that any of these substances is harmless or (necessarily) socially accept-able, but in each case, the extravagant claims permit us to employ the term *panic*.

Drug scares generally follow broadly sim-ilar patterns in which it is suggested, for ex-ample, that the drug in question is currently enjoying an explosive growth in popularity; that it is extremely addictive, and that even occasional use can cause severe physical ad-diction; and that it is destructive to the user or to others, threatening health or encourag-ing bizarre and violent behavior. Such claims are buttressed in a number of ways, including the use of exemplary cases and the parading of what appear to be objective sta-tistics and scientific studies; the latter often turn out to be rather questionable on further examination. In addition, claims makers usually demonstrate a certain historical am-nesia, often rediscovering problems that in fact are well-established while failing to note how thoroughly earlier panics were discredited.

Social scientists have explained such peri-odic waves of concern in various ways. Many emphasize the role of political or bureau-cratic interest groups seeking to enhance their claims on resources and status. Others stress the role of factors in the broader soci-ety, such as ethnic or generational tension and hostility, which come to be symbolized by the drug in question. In this sense it is al-most irrelevant whether the claims pre-sented by the rhetoric of a "panic" are well-founded or wholly spurious: The panic itself is valuable in itself for what it suggests about the perceptions of a society as a whole, and specifically of policymakers and legislators.

The incident thus has great significance for understanding the social construction of crime and deviance.

Some claims are widely accepted and have the effect of remolding law and public policy: the crack issue has done so in the last decade (Reinarman and Levine, 1989). Other issues, however, are more ephemeral, and the claims appear to enjoy far less success. In recent years we have witnessed a dramatic example of such a short-lived panic in the public reaction to the alleged boom in the use of the drug "ice," or smokable methamphetamine. During 1989 and early 1990, it was widely claimed that this substance was becoming enormously popular in certain regions, and that it had the potential to "sweep the nation" in a few months or years. Dramatic statistics were offered to support these claims; it was suggested that ice was uniquely dangerous in combining extremely addictive qualities with the advantages of cheapness, easy access, and domestic manufacture. The media panic about ice found its focus in Congressional hearings during October 1989 and January 1990. The stage seemed to be set for a repetition of the crack "explosion" of 1986.

This concern about ice was not sustained, however, and media references to the topic diminished sharply within a few months. Outside a few cities and regions, the issue either has ceased to exist or is dormant. The incident thus offers an unusual opportunity to trace the creation of a drug panic from its inception to its eclipse. In understanding the phenomenon, we must emphasize that "ice" originated as a very localized event, confined largely to Hawaii, and that the words *epidemic* and *explosion* arose from partisan and bureaucratic rivalries within that state. The projection of this local concern onto the national stage was made possible by a number of factors, including the existence of specialized agencies and investigative bodies focusing on drug issues, and the intensification of public expectations and fears following the crack scare. I suggest that all these elements still exist and are likely to lead in future to other ephemeral drug panics. The "ice" incident is likely to be repeated in various forms.

The Methamphetamine Industry

Methamphetamine is a stimulant of the central nervous system which, as a street drug, is often known as "speed" or "crank" (Graham, 1976; Grinspoon, 1975; *Methamphetamine Abuse*, 1989; Miller and Kozel 1991). The illegal manufacture of methamphetamines began in the early 1960s, and networks of clandestine laboratories emerged to produce several synthetic drugs. During the 1970s, such laboratories tended increasingly to shift their production towards methamphetamine and away from other synthetics such as PCP (Jenkins, 1992b). Between 1981 and 1984, methamphetamine producers represented half of all laboratory seizures; by 1988 they exceeded 80 percent (*U.S. Congress: Laboratories*, 1980; *U.S. Congress: Re-emergence*, 1990:25, 90–91).

The attractions of the industry were obvious. The manufacturing process required little expertise; several cheap "hands-on" manuals were available to provide detailed instruction. A laboratory could make as much as five to 10 pounds of methamphetamine in a week, and the pure substance usually was "cut" repeatedly for street sale. The annual production of a laboratory thus might be worth several million dollars (Jenkins, 1992b). In 1989 a Dallas police officer remarked, "We think the profit is much greater when we look at methamphetamine production, as compared to heroin or cocaine. We know that an investment of $3000 to $4000 in chemicals, in glassware, can turn a profit of $25,000 to $30,000." (*U.S. Congress: Re-Emergence*, 1990:39).

One appeal of methamphetamine was that the substance was manufactured in the United States and did not need the sophisticated importation and distribution networks required for heroin or cocaine. Laboratories needed no elaborate facilities or natural resources beyond an ample supply of electricity, and distribution demanded little more than convenient access to the interstate highway network (Skeers, 1992; Weingarten, 1989; Witkin, 1989).

During the 1980s, methamphetamine manufacture tended to become strongly regionalized. In the late 1970s and early 1980s, the Philadelphia area was said to be "the speed capital of the world," with networks of hundreds of laboratories in the southern and eastern parts of the state (Jenkins, 1992b; *U.S. Congress: Profile*, 1983). By the mid-1980s, the city of Eugene, Oregon, was believed to enjoy a similar role in manufacturing; other law enforcement sources emphasized the importance of San Diego and the San Francisco Bay area (*Organized Crime in California*, 1989:55; Wiedrich 1987). In 1987 and 1988 more than 300 methamphetamine laboratories were seized in the San Diego area alone. Centers of methamphetamine use included Denver, Portland (Oregon), Dallas, and Phoenix; some problems also were observed in Los Angeles, San Francisco, and Seattle (*Arrestee Drug Use*, 1990:6; *U.S. Congress: Re-Emergence*, 1990:37, 46). Though it is hard to assess the extent of methamphetamine use, there appears to be substantial demand in many parts of the nation (Isikoff, 1989; Miller and Kozel, 1991; Morgan, 1992; *Methamphetamine Abuse in the United States*, 1989).

The Emergence of Ice

Like other drugs, methamphetamine can be taken in various ways: either injected, smoked, or ingested orally. The dominant mode of use tends to reflect the tastes and traditions of local subcultures. In view of the highly regional nature of manufacture and distribution, suppliers do not find it difficult to accommodate these local tastes, and it is natural to find wide disparities in patterns of use. Fashions that emerge in one city or region can become dominant in that area without making much impact elsewhere. In short, there is no such thing as a national market in methamphetamines.

During the 1980s, a vogue for smokable crystal methamphetamine developed in Hawaii and some Western states under the common nickname *ice* (Cho, 1990; Pennell, 1990). A similar, though somewhat less pure, product called *glass* also made its appearance in California. The manufacturing process has been described as follows:

Two basic methods are used to produce crystal meth. The first and most common method is the reaction of phenyl-2-propanone (P2P or phenylacetone) and methylamine. The second method uses ephedrine as a precursor. The second method uses a simple formula and does not require the use of controlled precursors. It is known as the ephedrine/red phosphorus method and requires the use of a hydrogenator. It takes two to four days to make a batch of ice. . . .

In Honolulu, crystal meth is most commonly smoked with a glass pipe, the bowl of which becomes coated with a milky white, brownish or black residue, depending on the form of crystal meth used. A gram of ice sells for $250 to $400 in Honolulu right now, with a $\frac{1}{10}$ gram paper going for $50 to $75. It is inexpensive to produce, so the profit margin is tremendous (*U.S. Congress: Re-Emergence*, 1990:74–75).

The drug itself had long been known and used in this crystal form, but apparently the specific process used to make the extremely pure ice was not yet in use in the United States itself. Instead the substance, like the fashion for its use, had been imported from the Pacific Rim. Amphetamines, specifically methamphetamines, had long been popular in Japan and other east Asian countries. In that region, illicit markets were supplied by sizable narcotic networks with roots in organized crime among both Chinese triads and Japanese *yakuza's* (Delfs, 1991). During the 1970s and 1980s, such networks had collaborated in a variety of activities, including product counterfeiting and trafficking in guns and prostitutes in addition to narcotics; we have much evidence of cooperative endeavors, based (for example) in Taiwan or South Korea (Buruma and McBeth, 1984–85; Posner, 1988). For methamphetamines the *yakuza* had developed manufacturing facilities in South Korea; these supplied much of East Asia, though the triads also were active in Hong Kong (Kaplan and Dubro, 1986:198–200; *U.S. Congress: Re-Emergence*, 1990:11, 99). Entrepreneurs and distributors might be nationals of any of a dozen Asian countries.

Though illegal, the amphetamine drug "family" was stigmatized far less severely than opiates, cocaine, or even marijuana. Most estimates place the number of regular amphetamine (*shabu*) users in Japan at more than half a million. In the 1980s, smokable methamphetamine became the drug of choice among upwardly mobile urban dwellers in several Pacific Rim nations, especially Taiwan, South Korea, and the Philippines (Delfs, 1991; McBeth, 1989; Savadove, 1991).

Therefore, it is not surprising to find a similar habit developing in Hawaii, which has so many cultural and economic affinities with the Pacific Rim, and in which Japanese organized crime had developed a strong foothold. In fact, Kaplan and Dubro's (1986) study of the *yakuza* calls Hawaii the "forty-eighth Prefecture," an annex to the 47 administrative units of the Japanese home islands. *Yakuza*-supplied amphetamines were identified in the state during the 1970s, and Korean-manufactured methamphetamines appeared in the following decade (Shoenberger, 1989). Beginning in 1987, island authorities had described an "ice problem," linked in part to Filipino youth gangs and Korean groups (*US. Congress: Re-Emergence*, 1990:5).

Discovering a Problem

By 1989, law enforcement agencies were finding evidence of localized use of smokable methamphetamine originally in Hawaii and subsequently in and around San Diego. The perceived "wave" of new activity was epitomized by a series of federal drug raids on 20 laboratories in southern California during March, and by a series of smaller raids over the next year (Ford, 1990; Reza, 1989). Concern about the drug in Hawaii was given a new focus in March 1989 by the arrest of a substantial ice-importation ring headed by one Paciano Guerrero (*U.S. Congress: Drug Crisis*, 1990:74–75; *U.S. Congress: Re-Emergence*, 1990:70–72).

It might be thought that the perceived boom in the smokable drug reflected strictly local conditions, unlikely to be replicated in other areas. Even in Hawaii, the problem

was confined largely to Oahu (*U.S. Congress: Drug Crisis*, 1990:56, 205, 215). Now, however, there began a media campaign to emphasize the perils of the "new" drug, and the danger that this would soon be reflected across the nation. A headline in the *Los Angeles Times*, for example, read "Potent Form of Speed Could Be Drug of 90s" (Corwin, 1989). *The Economist* noted that ice could make crack seem almost benign ("Drugs: Ice Overdose," 1989). Rep. Charles Rangel coined the alliterative description "the narcotics nemesis of the nineties" (*U.S. Congress: Re-Emergence*, 1990:59).

The theme was taken up by all the major regional newspapers and national newsmagazines, as well as more specialized publications serving the medical and pharmaceutical communities (Cho, 1990; "Illicit Methamphetamine," 1991; Zurer, 1989). Between September and December 1989, major stories appeared in the *New York Times* (Bishop, 1989), *The Washington Post* (Thompson, 1989), *The Atlanta Constitution* (Curriden, 1989), *The Economist* ("Drugs; Ice Overdose," 1989), *The Boston Globe* (Howe, 1989; Tabor, 1989), *The Chicago Tribune* (Weingarten, 1989), *The Christian Science Monitor* (Larmer, 1989), and *Newsweek* (Lerner, 1989). The tone of the coverage was epitomized by the *New York Times* headline "Fear Grows Over Effects of a New Smokable Drug" (Bishop, 1989). This story was printed on the front page; equal prominence was given to ice-related stories on the front pages of the *Los Angeles Times* (Corwin, 1989) and *The Chicago Tribune* (Weingarten, 1989). In October the *Los Angeles Times* presented a series of four stories on ice within a nine-day period (Corwin, 1989; Essoyan, 1989; Shoenberger, 1989; Zamichow, 1989). Clearly, pronouncements about the new drug were finding a ready and enthusiastic market in the mass media.

The jeremiads about ice were heard most frequently in the last quarter of 1989, though a few stories appeared in early 1990, and television news shows such as *60 Minutes* sustained the focus on methamphetamines in general for a few months more ("Meth," 1990). The height of the panic, however, can be identified clearly between about September 1989 and February 1990. (See Table 24.1 for a chronology of media accounts.)

The peak of public concern can be associated with Congressional hearings on this topic; Rep. Rangel's Subcommittee on Narcotics Abuse and Control held a session titled "The Re-Emergence of Methamphetamine" in October. A follow-up session, the "Drug Crisis in Hawaii," was held in Honolulu the following January (*U.S. Congress: Re-Emergence*, 1990; *U.S. Congress: Drug Crisis*, 1990). For criticisms of the latter session as a Congressional junket, see Anderson and Van Atta, 1990). Taken together with the media accounts, the hearings became the chief vehicle for the burgeoning panic about ice. Here it will be useful to analyze the language and rhetoric employed to present the new phenomenon as a major problem.

The Rhetoric of Ice

Certain themes and expressions recur with striking regularity. Ice was new, potent, and dangerous, and had acquired high prestige as the new "in" drug. Taken together, these features meant that the use of ice apparently was about to expand rapidly and to create a national menace at least comparable to crack cocaine.

The experience of Hawaii was recounted often, as in a *Boston Globe* story titled "Ice in an Island Paradise" (Tabor, 1989). The use of ice, in the words of a Congressional report, "has escalated in such leaps and bounds that we have not been able to keep pace" (*U.S. Congress: Re-Emergence*, 1990:2). Generally such accounts suggested that what such areas were experiencing today would be the fate of the whole country in a few months or years. Honolulu police chief Douglas Gibb told the story of a New York City Korean gang that had flown some members to Honolulu to attack some local Samoans. "The whole purpose . . . was to come into town to establish a connection for ice, a line for ice to take back to New York" (*U.S. Congress: Re-Emergence*, 1990:8). "It is probably only a matter of time until other parts of the country start to see crystal meth and its attendant problems . . . we fully expect the Ice Age to spread east from Hawaii" (p. 77).

The idea that ice was gradually penetrating areas of the mainland gave a local angle to media reporting of the drug in cities such as Atlanta (Curriden, 1989), Boston (Howe, 1989), and Philadelphia (Durso, 1992). In the Congressional hearings, this was a frequent theme. One subcommittee member noted, "We have got ice in Virginia . . . it is for sure coming our way and we had better get ready for it" (*U.S. Congress: Re-Emergence*, 1990:19). Another member stated, "Reports are already filtering in of ice use in New York and Washington DC" (*U.S. Congress: Drug Crisis*, 1990:3). A lengthy investigative account in *Rolling Stone* quoted law enforcement officials, who believed that the Hawaii "epidemic" soon would sweep the mainland and that the drug would surpass both heroin and cocaine, marking a new and still more deadly era in drug abuse (Sager, 1990).

One paradox was that ice, by its nature, negated some of the obvious advantages of methamphetamine: as an imported drug, for example, it encountered the obstacles and expense involved in crossing national borders. The witnesses at the hearings, however, emphasized repeatedly that it would only be a matter of time before domestic manufacturers learned to reproduce Asian techniques; at that point, ice would begin to conquer the American "speed" market. In the words of a Dallas police official, "We have cooks, we have numerous cooks scattered throughout the country, literally thousands of persons who are qualified to make methamphetamine. So, we have the processes in place to make ice. I think we also have a ready consumer market out there, individuals who want the drug. I have no doubt that ice will come to the United States" (*U.S. Congress: Re-Emergence*, 1990:39–40).

Particularly evocative was the word *epidemic*, which was employed in most of the accounts, with its implications of plague, disease, and uncontrollable spread (compare Reinarman and Levine, 1989). During the Congressional hearings, U.S. Attorney Daniel Bent described Hawaii ice use as already an "epidemic" (*U.S. Congress: Re-Emergence*, 1990:5). When a DEA spokesman was quoted as having denied the validity of the "epidemic," he was taken to task by

Table 24.1

Chronology of Media Accounts, 1989–1991

1989

September		
First ice-related stories in mainland newspapers		
Sept. 16	*New York Times*	(Bishop 1989)
October		
Oct. 1	*Boston Globe*	(Howe 1989)
Oct. 8	*Los Angeles Times*	(Shoenberger 1989)
Oct.14	*Los Angeles Times*	(Essoyan 1989)
Oct. 16	*Los Angeles Times*	(Essoyan 1989)
Oct. 16	*Los Angeles Times*	(Zamichow 1989)
Oct. 24	Congressional hearings, *The Re-Emergence of Methamphetamine*	
November		
Nov. 6	*Chemical and Engineering News*	(Zurer 1989)
Nov. 21	*Washington Post*	(Thompson 1989)
Nov. 27	*Newsweek*	(Lerner 1989)
Nov. 30	*Atlanta Constitution*	(Curriden 1989)
December		
Dec. 2	*The Economist*	("Drugs: Ice Overdose" 1989)
Dec. 8	*Boston Globe*	(Tabor 1989)
Dec. 8	*Christian Science Monitor*	(Larmer 1989)
Dec. 18	*Jet*	(Carthane 1989)

1990

January		
Jan. 13	Congressional hearings on *The Drug Crisis in Hawaii*	
February		
Feb. 8	*Rolling Stone*	(Sager 1990)
February	*Good Housekeeping*	(Holland 1990)
April		
April 22	CBS news program *60 Minutes* broadcasts story on methamphetamine trafficking ("Meth" 1990)	
May		
May 23	*Journal of the American Medical Association*	(Cotton 1989)
August		
Aug. 10	*Science*	(Cho 1990)

1991

March		
March 6	*Journal of the American Medical Association*	(Hong, Matzuyama, and Nur 1991)
May		
May 9	*Washington Post*	(Holley, Venant, and Essoyan 1991)
June		
June 30	*Emergency Medicine*	("Illicit Methamphetamine" 1991)

members of the committee, especially Florida Rep. Tom Lewis, who described the opinion as "irresponsible" and "lackadaisi-cal" (p. 17). "Epidemic" was a politically

valuable concept that would not be abandoned easily.

Other significant terms included *deluge, plague,* and *crisis.* Congressman Rangel remarked that Honolulu police were "deluged" by ice (*U.S. Congress: Re-Emergence*, 1990:1). Sociologist Elliott Currie spoke of "this hidden methamphetamine plague" (p. 44). The word *crisis* was much used, generally in the context of an "emerging" crisis, to suggest that what had gone before was trivial compared to what would come in future (p. 61). As has been noted, the January hearings of the Narcotics Subcommittee were devoted explicitly to the drug crisis in Hawaii.

The term ice offered great potential for writers, suggesting as it did the phrase *ice age* and thus implying that the drug somehow could dominate American society so strongly that it could give its name to an era. The phrase *The Ice Age* was employed both by Douglas Gibb and Hawaii Rep. Daniel Akaka in the Congressional hearings (*U.S. Congress: Re-Emergence*, 1990:3, 77). It was used subsequently for major investigative accounts in *Rolling Stone* in 1990 and in the *Washington Post* in 1991 (Holley, Venant, and Essoyan, 1991; Sager, 1990; compare LaBianca, 1992). "Ice" also suggested "chilling" in the metaphorical sense of "extremely frightening"; it was used in this sense by several journalists. In late 1989, for example, the *Atlanta Constitution* carried the headline "Police Chilled by New In-Drug: Ice" (Curriden, 1989). Within two weeks, the *Christian Science Monitor* warned similarly, "Ice Chills U.S. Anti-Drug Officials" (Larmer, 1989).

In addition, these arguments were stated by individuals and agencies with great expertise in the field. Every news story was buttressed by the opinions of prominent and credible law enforcement officials, police, and prosecutors from California and Hawaii, together with academics and other experts. In the Congressional hearings, major witnesses included Daniel Bent, the U.S. attorney for Hawaii; Douglas Gibb, the police chief of Honolulu; and David Westrate of the DEA; all were prestigious and experienced officials. Other presentations were made by reputable doctors and academics. The potential "ice epidemic" thus appeared both plausible and threatening.

Ice and Cocaine

One potent element of the attack on ice involved the analogy with cocaine. In seeking to portray a new problem as serious or dangerous, one well-known rhetorical device is to stigmatize that problem by associating it with another, already familiar issue, thus placing it into an existing context. Problem construction is a cumulative or incremental process in which each issue is built, to some extent, on its predecessors. As Best remarks,

> As an acknowledged subject for concern, a well established social problem becomes a resource, a foundation upon which other claims may be built. Rather than struggling to bring recognition to a new problem, claimants may find it easier to expand an existing problem's domain. These new claims take the form (new problem) X is really a type of (established problem) Y (1990:65–66).

Issue (X) therefore demands the array of responses and reactions that already have been judged appropriate for Problem (Y). This is the process described by Hall et al. (1978:223) as "convergence."

> [C]onvergence occurs when two or more activities are linked in the process of signification so as to implicitly or explicitly draw parallels between them. Thus the image of "student hooliganism" links student protest to the separate problem of hooliganism—whose stereotypical characteristics are already part of socially available knowledge. . . . In both cases, the net effect is amplification, not in the real events being described but in their threat potential for society (1978:223).

By 1989 cocaine, especially crack cocaine, had been invested with an enormous amount of "threat potential," suggested, for example, by the "drug war" rhetoric, which was then at its height. President George Bush had made the "drug war" a major part of his domestic policy; his commitment to drug eradication was symbolized by the appointment of William Bennett as "drug czar." During 1989, American activism against international drug traffickers contributed to the near-civil war in Colombia, beginning in August, and to the invasion of

Panama in December. Media coverage in the latter part of the year featured almost daily news of violence and conflict associated with these incidents. In September, President Bush made a nationally televised address on drug control strategy, in which he stated, "All of us agree that the gravest domestic threat facing our nation today is drugs . . . our most serious problem today is cocaine and in particular crack." Producing a sample of crack, which he said had been purchased close to the White House, the president continued, "It's as innocent looking as candy, but it is turning our cities into battle zones, and it is murdering our children. Let there be no mistake, this stuff is poison" ("Text," 1989). President Bush argued that the drug control budget for the coming year should be raised by more than one-third from the 1989 figure, to $8 billion.

If crack was indeed "the gravest domestic threat," then it was a highly effective strategy to suggest that ice was associated somehow with the better-known drug. Superficial parallels also existed. It could be suggested, for example, that crack was an especially virulent and addictive form of powder cocaine, while ice bore a similar relationship to "regular" methamphetamine. Also, the two substances were similar in general appearance and means of ingestion. The ice threat was amplified by its association with crack, an association pursued most vigorously on the Narcotics Subcommittee by Rep. Akaka. From the viewpoint of the media, the analogy with crack made ice an attractive subject because its dangers and thus its social significance could be comprehended easily; thus the drug would be likely to excite public concern and fear.

Ice was said to cause as much social damage as cocaine, in terms of overdoses and emergency room admissions (Gross, 1988; "Illicit Methamphetamine," 1991). Rep. Akaka stated that in Hawaii, ice contributed to the problems that elsewhere were linked to crack: "ice-addicted babies, gang activities, turf battles and hospital emergency cases of overdoses . . . this drug has the capacity to drag our country even deeper into the dark abyss created by crack" (*U.S. Congress: Re-Emergence*, 1990:3). "It doesn't make any difference whether it is ice, crack, crank, cocaine. We are losing kids. We are corrupting our police departments. We are corrupting our political arena. We are breaking up families" (p. 17).

U.S. Attorney Daniel Bent stated that ice was "presenting the same problems to Hawaii as crack cocaine has in areas of the Continental United States in terms of its popularity, availability, addiction potential and destructiveness" (*U.S. Congress: Re-Emergence*, 1990:64). It was alleged to stimulate violent behavior even more sharply than did crack; Hawaii, it was said, was seeing the birth of a generation of "crystal meth babies" (*U.S. Congress: Drug Crisis*, 1990:2, 226–33; *U.S. Congress: Re-Emergence*, 1990:66, 76; for the idea of the "crack baby," however, see Jacobs, 1991). Such remarks made the two drugs appear all but indistinguishable; in fact, Rep. Akaka even asked a witness, "Can you explain to me the differences between crack, crank, ice and croak . . . ?" (*U.S. Congress: Re-Emergence*, 1990:54).

In some ways, ice could be made to appear even more dangerous than crack. First, it was superior to crack because of its lower cost and its longer-lasting high. The effects were reported to last from four to 14 hours, as opposed to a few minutes for crack (Carthane, 1989; Holley et al., 1991). Also, ice did not necessarily have to be imported from overseas (though it was imported currently); therefore it did not encounter the stringent restrictions imposed by Customs and the Coast Guard as part of the current "war on drugs." In addition, ice lacked the features that might safeguard individuals from experimenting with other sustances. It did not require injection, as did heroin, and did not yet have the destructive associations of crack cocaine. By 1989, crack had acquired undesirable connotations that deterred many people from using it: It was associated with cultures of violence and extreme urban poverty, and was linked especially with racial minorities.

In contrast, methamphetamine generally was linked to hard work. Insofar as it had any racial overtones, it tended to be favored by white users (*Methamphetamine Abuse in the United States*, 1989; Miller and Kozal,

1991). Nationally, said the congressional account, "the typical methamphetamine user is a white male 22 to 26 years of age, who is employed in a blue-collar job. The most frequently cited occupations are in construction trades and the trucking industry" (*U.S. Congress: Re-Emergence*, 1990:87). In the San Diego region, "abusing populations are predominantly white, lower middle income, high school educated, young adults ranging in age from 18–35 years" (p. 111). A Texas police officer stated, "The persons who we most often encounter in Dallas, the users we most often enocounter are primarily Caucasian, primarily lower income" (p. 39).

Ice users tend to fit a similar profile. In Hawaii, ice was "popular in the workplace, particularly among blue collar workers, people who do mechanical tasks, and it has also spread into office workplaces as well . . . (it is) the drug of choice for on the job use in Honolulu. . . . It is generally in the blue collar community and the service community" (*U.S. Congress: Re-Emergence*, 1990:6–9). In short, ice could appeal to white or Asian middle-class people; teenagers especially were at risk. The title of a *Good Housekeeping* article described ice as "A New Drug Nice Kids Can Get Hooked On" (Holland, 1990). Women also were believed to be particularly vulnerable: "In Honolulu, most ice users range in age from the late teens to the early thirties. The drug is popular with young women, perhaps because users tend to lose weight" (*U.S. Congress: Re-Emergence*, 1990:75).

It was suggested that ice might be able to wreak havoc in all sections of society, not merely in the inner cities. Rep. Rangel thus was tapping into potent fears when he wrote, "[W]e shudder to think of what would happen in this country if the devastation of the crack crisis were doubled or even tripled by adding on a whole new layer of illicit drug abuse" (*U.S. Congress: Re-Emergence*, 1990:59). This rhetoric was even more powerful in the context of current developments in the "drug war" at home and overseas.

Whatever Became of Ice?

"Ice" thus was attracting quite fervent interest. One might suggest that it had the potential to attract the same kind of fear as crack. The recent precedent of crack cocaine provided a set of stereotyped images and rhetoric on which ice could build readily, with the added "bonus" that ice threatened to reproduce these disturbing images outside the African-American urban community. Ice (it appeared) could cause the same kind of havoc as crack in geographical, social, and ethnic settings still untouched by ice or any other "hard" drug. It would not be difficult to imagine that the new problem could thrive through the use of ethnic and xenophobic stereotypes: the substance was imported from Asia, and had Japanese connotations. *Yakuza* drug dealers might easily acquire the stigma that had adhered earlier to gangsters from immigrant ethnic groups such as Jews and Italians.

In addition, it has been argued that intense media attention to a particular drug might tend to incite interest in the substance, and to lead to experimentation. Prophecies of an "epidemic" thus might be self-fulfilling in that they could unwittingly generate the problem that activists were seeking to avoid (MacDonald and Estep, 1985; compare Young, 1971). In the 1960s this kind of imitation caused glue sniffing to spread at "incredible speed . . . the enemies of glue-sniffing popularized the custom all by themselves" (Brecher, 1972:326, 332). In the 1980s it was suggested that media portrayals of the effects of crack cocaine might have excited interest among users of powdered cocaine. With these precedents in mind, observers of ice warned that ice was being "beautifully advertised by the media" to cocaine users (Cotton, 1990). *The Journal of the American Medical Association* warned, "News articles describing (ice) as like 'ten orgasms pronto' are working like paid ads. . . . If the media says it's an epidemic, drug adventurers say everybody's using it so I've got to try it" (Cotton, 1990).

The ice danger, however, did not materialize as a national crisis, and the prospective "plague" faded rapidly in early 1990. Media accounts became far less frequent from February onwards, and virtually none appeared between August 1990 and spring 1991 (see Table 24.1). In part this silence reflected the new concern of the media with political affairs in Iraq and the Persian Gulf, but the ice panic had been declining sharply for several months before the August invasion of Kuwait. The rather sudden eclipse of the ice problem requires explanation.

Some observers had been skeptical even during the height of the panic, and witnesses at the October hearings faced criticism for their use of the term *epidemic*. The evidence presented also contained clear contradictions—for example, in the damage caused by ice. Early reports of the testimony quoted Chief Gibb's statements that "since 1985, there have been 32 deaths in Honolulu attributed to ice," including eight homicides and seven suicides. (*U.S. Congress: Re-Emergence*, 1990:76). Gibb, however, also stated that "32 people were confirmed to have crystal methamphetamine in their system at the time of deaths," which does not necessarily establish a causal link between the drug and the fatality (pp. 7–8). Hawaii's Governor Waihee placed the number of deaths at 36, of whom "three died as a direct result, and 32 had traces of the drug in their systems" (p. 80). It was embarrassing when Gibb was publicly challenged on his statistics; as a result, the early claims about the impact of the drug, even in Hawaii, were reduced substantially. Thus it was even more difficult to claim that ice presented a potential national menace.

During the October hearings, one DEA spokesman commented, "I can confirm there is a drug out there called ice, which is certainly bad news. But D.E.A. agents are not looking for it yet. . . . It will take a while for ice to proliferate. When we get reports from police departments that ice has gotten to be at the epidemic state, such as crack did in 1985, then we will move in" (*U.S. Congress: Re-Emergence*, 1990:17). Such a drug "explosion" seemed remote, however. In early 1990, testing of arrestees confirmed considerable amphetamine use in San Diego, Portland, Phoenix, and San Jose, but the figures did not appear to be growing.

Moreover, ice as such had made few inroads among the arrestees, though a substantial majority knew the substance by reputation: the media were cited overwhelmingly as the main source. Even in San Diego, almost 70 percent of those who knew about ice based their knowledge on media accounts rather than on information provided by friends or dealers. Nationwide the proportion who admitted ever having used ice nowhere exceeded 3 percent (though no community in Hawaii was included in the survey) (*Arrestee Drug Use*, 1990:6; Pennell, 1990). This picture was confirmed by other survey data. Among male hustlers and sex workers in San Francisco, for example, ice had made very limited inroads, even among heavy users of methamphetamine. Moreover, the number of habitual ice users in such groups remained negligible (Lauderback and Waldorf, 1992).

Largely on the basis of such data and of the reexamination of the drug's impact in Hawaii itself, law enforcement and DEA officials soon were saying that the danger of ice had been substantially overstated. Media rhetoric subsided within a few months of the Congressional hearings. Ice continues to be popular in some regions, but the language of epidemic no longer seems realistic—if it ever did.

The Construction of the Ice Danger

In retrospect it seems certain that the menace of ice was considerably overstated, and we might well ask how such a misperception could emerge. A considerable literature exists on the origins of such scares and perceived social problems; some of the explanations suggested by that literature seem relevant here. Many researchers, for example, follow some form of what is generally known as the "moral entrepreneur" theory. The classic discussion of this term comes from Becker, who emphasized the role of a particular individual in the formulation of American narcotics policy in the 1930s:

Wherever rules are created and applied we should be alive to the possible presence of an enterprising individual or group. Their activities can properly be called "moral enterprise" for what they are enterprising about is the creation of a new fragment of the moral constitution of society, its code of right and wrong (1963:145).

Such entrepreneurs might have diverse motives. In the case of a drug panic, for example, we might find activism by an interest group or a bureaucratic agency that was seeking to portray a serious social danger in order to focus public attention on issues falling within its scope of activity. This effort would permit the agency to expand its influence and resources, and might allow local authorities and law enforcement agencies to justify and request for federal funding and other support. In such circumstances, we often find a cyclical pattern in which greater concern causes more resources to be devoted to a problem; the result is more detection and more vigorous prosecution of the activity in question. This process in turn generates statistical evidence that can be used to intensify public concern, and thus to argue for still more resources. "Epidemics" thus can be self-sustaining.

Such bureaucratic concerns may have played some role in the case of ice. One recurrent theme of the hearings was the need to strengthen still further the numbers and resources of the DEA (*U.S. Congress: Re-Emergence*, 1990:8–9). This agency had grown in numbers from 1,900 in 1980 to 2,900 in 1989. Currently it was requesting 160 new agents, chiefly for international enforcement in Latin America and the Pacific Rim (34–35). An ice panic therefore served the interests of the DEA, but it certainly cannot serve as a full explanation. As we have seen, the DEA was strongly critical of the exaggerated claims made for ice, and during 1990 was instrumental in damping down the nascent panic. In January, for example, the head of the Honolulu office wrote that ice was still confined largely to Hawaii and "very limited West Coast areas"; otherwise, he reported, "we know of no ice samples (having) been analyzed elsewhere in the United States" (*U.S. Congress: Drug Crisis*, 1990:76).

Instead of examining national groups and controversies, it would be more profitable to consider the needs of the political and bureaucratic interests in Hawaii that sponsored most of the extravagant claims about ice and first identified an "epidemic." For example, the major claims makers heard by the Congressional committees included two of the leading figures in the state's law enforcement bureaucracy, police chief Douglas Gibb and U.S. attorney Daniel Bent. The evidence offered by these two witnesses accounted for more than one-third of the total testimony presented during the October hearings, and both men emphasized the "epidemic" quality of the ice threat. As in the case of the DEA, an ice panic would enhance the reputation of local police agencies as well as increasing their access to resources. In addition, the powerful office of U.S. attorney often provides any incumbent with the opportunity to win prestige and visibility that can be translated subsequently into a wider political career. This is not to suggest that either individual was insincere in his claims about the ice problem, but both had clear bureaucratic interests in formulating the issue in a particular way.

Electoral politics also played a role in shaping official claims and statements. At the opening of the 1989 hearings, which did so much to put ice on the map of American social problems, Congressman Rangel emphasized that the impetus for concern came chiefly from the Hawaii Congressional delegation of Representatives Daniel Akaka and Patricia Saiki. Both in fact had a strong vested interest in appearing to be active and interested in drug issues, and in adopting hard-line antidrug stances. Therefore they stood to benefit from making ice seem as perilous and as threatening as possible; both can be viewed as classical moral entrepreneurs.

This political context can be observed if we describe recent developments in Hawaii, traditionally one of the most loyally Democratic states in the nation (Smith and Pratt, 1992). In the 1980s, for example, both of the Democratic U.S. senators could count regularly on receiving 70 to 80 percent of the votes cast, and the powerful governor's office remained firmly in Democratic hands throughout these years (Benenson, 1991).

Republicans were placed extremely poorly; they won offices chiefly when Democratic factions were split, as when Republican Patricia Saiki won the First Congressional District. By 1989 she had retained this position in two elections, but with progressively slimmer majorities. Democrat Daniel Akaka had remained firmly in control of the Second District in every contest since 1976.

Saiki's presence as a Republican representative therefore might appear anomalous, but the Republicans had one major point of potential strength, namely in the general area of law and order. Throughout the decade, Democratic authorities had been involved in a series of scandals; these had exposed alleged links between organized crime and the labor unions, which play so crucial a role in Hawaii Democratic politics. These incidents reached a climax in 1984 with the investigation by Charles F. Marsland, the Republican Honolulu city/county prosecutor, into a series of gangland murders that included the killing of Marsland's own son. Marsland targeted a prominent political ally of Democratic Governor George Ariyoshi as the alleged "godfather" of organized crime in the state (Turner, 1984a, 1984b). The ensuing scandals and lawsuits did not destroy Democratic power. In fact, the next governor, elected in 1986, was a close associate of Ariyoshi, but the incident suggested one area in which Democrats were politically vulnerable: Daniel Akaka himself had been an Ariyoshi protégé. In addition, he is of native Hawaiian descent, and thus could potentially be associated with Larry Mehau, the ethnically Hawaiian "godfather."

In the following years, Saiki and Akaka emerged as powerful figures in Hawaii politics, and they clashed on crime-related issues. In the U.S. Congress, Saiki voted for a measure to extend the death penalty to major drug dealers, which Akaka opposed. The rivalry between the two was especially significant in 1989, when it became increasingly likely that soon they would be vying for a U.S. Senate seat in Hawaii. The junior senator's position currently was held by Spark Matsunaga, a very popular figure first elected in 1972, but a series of health crises beginning in 1984 made it unlikely that Matsunaga would run again in 1990, even if he completed his current term.

Therefore it was likely that within a year, Saiki would challenge Akaka for the hitherto solidly Democratic Senate seat, but the balance in this apparently unequal match could be tipped in a number of ways. One would be the ethnic factor. As noted above, Akaka is a native Hawaiian. The strongest faction in his Democratic party, however, is Japanese-American, a group to which Saiki could be expected to appeal. In addition, it would be natural to portray the relatively liberal Akaka as soft on crime and drugs, and possibly not sufficiently vigorous in the war on local organized crime. As a result, it was important for Akaka to rebut such charges; his membership on the House Subcommittee on Narcotic Abuse provided an ideal opportunity.

Both representatives therefore needed to appear strong on drug issues, and ideally both needed national media credentials as antidrug crusaders. Local ethnic and partisan alignments, however, circumscribed the kinds of rhetoric that would be appropriate in such a campaign. Although organized crime in general could be denounced, it is significant that none of the ice rhetoric focused on the specifically Japanese component of drug manufacture and distribution or on the role of the *yakuza* described so frequently by other law enforcement agencies and investigators. One might suggest that the nature of the forthcoming Hawaii elections made such accusations too sensitive to be presented at that time, for fear of perpetrating ethnic slurs against one of the most influential communities in the islands.

In fact, both Akaka and Saiki succeeded in gaining significant political capital from the ice issue. Saiki earned credit for having brought the problem to national attention and for requesting increased resources, but Akaka also shared the credit, and was not portrayed as soft on the crime issue in any sense. Akaka first used the term *ice age* in the hearings, and drew some of the starkest analogies between ice and crack. Both confirmed their role as standard-bearers of their respective parties. When Senator Matsunaga died a few months later, in April 1990, Akaka was the natural choice to fill the unexpired portion of his term. Both he and Saiki easily won their parties' nominations for the November election ("Hawaiian Politics," 1990). That contest normally would have been a Democratic walkover, but Saiki had established her prestige so firmly that she made it a close race, and lost only narrowly to Akaka. He thereby became the first native Hawaiian to be represented in the U.S. Senate (Saiki went on to head the federal Small Business Administration) (Reinhold, 1990; Richburg, 1990).

Domestic politics in Hawaii thus made it likely that the state representatives would seek to focus on a crime or drug problem of local significance. It was by no means apparent, however, that these issues would come to wider attention, especially when conditions and controversies in Hawaii so rarely attract the attention of the national media. The opportunity was provided by Akaka's service on the House Narcotics Subcommittee, where he was aided by another representative with a strong record in drug issues and a long career as a "moral entrepreneur." This was a Pennsylvania representative named Lawrence Coughlin, from the thirteenth district in suburban Montgomery County, outside Philadelphia. Coughlin, the ranking Republican on the Narcotics Subcommittee, was instrumental in bringing Akaka's views to Rangel's attention. His advocacy was significant in showing that ice was causing concern far outside Hawaii, and legitimately could be presented as a national issue.

Other agendas, however, may have been at work here as well. Coughlin's interest in methamphetamine issues dated back at least to the late 1970s, when he had been one of the most active supporters of the theory that Philadelphia was the "speed capital of the world" (Jenkins, 1992a, b). To illustrate this questionable assertion, Coughlin had publicized stories from local Montgomery County newspapers as if they represented conditions throughout the state or the nation, and in effect had generated a mythology about the prevalence of speed in southeastern Pennsylvania. In 1980, largely at Coughlin's behest, the Narcotics Select

Committee had been persuaded to hold special hearings in Philadelphia, where local issues and investigations received national attention (*U.S. Congress: Laboratories*, 1980). The campaign to link Philadelphia with speed was so successful that it became the focus of the popular 1985 film *Witness*, whose plot concerns a huge shipment of the precursor chemical P2P. Coughlin thus emerges as a long-standing protagonist of a "speed menace." As a result, it is scarcely surprising to see the limited experience of Hawaii extrapolated to the entire nation in the 1989–1990 hearings, just as had happened with conditions in Philadelphia in 1980.

Transforming Local Issues Into National Problems

In studying social problems, one critical theme is the relationship between local and national perceptions, and the way in which some (but by no means all) local phenomena come to be regarded as issues of far wider significance. The panic about ice serves to remind us that drug problems are extremely localized, and that in crime, as in so much else, it is difficult to generalize about the American experience. Drug problems rarely strike the nation in a regular or homogeneous way. Much has been written about the "crack epidemic" that swept the United States in the mid-1980s, but we must always remember that this phenomenon was highly localized. The "epidemic" initially was centered in the major cities of the east and west coasts, but scarcely penetrated large sections of the midwest until the early 1990s. This situation has many possible explanations—the strength of local traditions and subcultures, patterns of law enforcement vagaries of manufacture and supply, the interests of criminal groups—but the point is that a "panic" might be well under way in one area years before it is felt elsewhere, and it is by no means inevitable that it ever will move beyond the original region (for the localized nature of drug cultures, see, for example, Weisheit, 1992).

On the other hand, certain extraneous factors demand that a local problem should be viewed in a national context, and that policy responses should be developed accordingly. One important element in this regard is the mass media, which had come, during the 1980s, to treat drug-related stories as events of major significance. Newspapers assigned journalists to cover such stories as their sole or major responsibility; thus the papers had a vested interest in the constant generation of newsworthy items in this area.[1] One way to achieve this goal was to focus on local concerns or incidents, but to project them as if they were of wider, even national significance. A notorious example appeared in 1986 in the CBS television documentary *48 Hours on Crack Street*. This program presented the (then) essentially New York City problem of crack cocaine as if it were already a national epidemic, with vials littering the streets and parks of virtually every community across the country (Reinarman and Levine, 1989). Though largely spurious, this account had enormous influence in generating fears of a national crack epidemic.

In the early 1980s, before the advent of crack, the media often presented the localized PCP problem in Washington, D.C., in such a way as to suggest that it soon would become a national crisis. (Such "extrapolations" are not confined to drug issues: Witness the suggestions, at about that time, that Los Angeles's distinctive gang problems were spreading to cities throughout the nation.) Once the media present a problem in this way, Congressional hearings permit the issue to be discussed in another national forum, with the certainty that national news coverage will reinforce perceptions of a widespread crisis.

This process of "nationalization" gives rich opportunities to local activists, moral entrepreneurs, or claims makers who wish to draw attention to a particular issue, and who do so by presenting it as more dangerous or more important than it may be in fact. One natural way to do this is to suggest that a local issue either is national in scope or has a strong potential to become so in the very near future: in short, that it is about to "sweep the nation." This process enhances the importance of local campaigns; it also of-

fers the local moral entrepreneurs the opportunity to acquire the status of national leaders and experts, should their analysis be accepted. This enhancement, in turn, can reinforce the position of local figures in their home areas.

The panic about ice is a model example of this process. The use of the drug was a local phenomenon; the national concern about the drug in 1989 derived chiefly from Hawaii's elected officials and law enforcement agencies with a definite political agenda. For two specific reasons, they were relatively successful in projecting their concerns. First, the recent experience of crack made it easy for them to represent ice, in effect, as part of the same problem; this process is known by the rhetorical term *convergence*. The ice phenomenon occurred at precisely the right time, when the rhetoric about crack was still fresh in the public mind and when the "drug war" was reaching a crescendo. It is difficult to imagine that the ice issue would have arisen at all if public expectations had not been conditioned by these recent precedents.

Second, the intense public focus on drug issues during the 1980s had created bureaucracies and political frameworks able to publicize information and opinion about drugs. These groups, such as the DEA, the NIDA, and the Narcotics Subcommittee itself, had excellent media ties and could be relied on to provide newsworthy stories about crime and drug abuse. In the case of the Congressional committee, it is inevitable that members of any political organization charged with investigating drug problems will attempt to attract as much publicity as possible by presenting themselves as concerned, active, well-informed guardians of the public good. There are few better opportunities to do so than by recognizing a problem at an early stage to prevent it reaching crisis proportions. The case of Hawaii offered the committee members the chance to investigate and combat a drug problem in a proactive, farsighted way.

No significant risk was involved in this strategy. If an "ice epidemic" occurred, the committee earned credit for having predicted it and for urging preemptive action; if it faded away, the committee could claim that its forethought had prevented a drug crisis. Conversely, there was much to be lost by cautious or skeptical reactions to an incipient crisis. If the predicted menace actually materialized, an agency or an administration stood to attract most of the blame for the ensuing problems.

None of the factors that produced the ice panic has changed significantly since 1989, or is likely to change significantly in the near future. Therefore it is probable that local drug fads will be presented once again as potential crises, likely to spread rapidly across the entire country. Social scientists must recognize and publicize the social and political factors that generate such misleading expectations.

Note

1. I am indebted to one of the anonymous reviewers for raising this point when I originally submitted this article to *Justice Quarterly*.

References

Anderson, J., and D. Van Atta (1990) "Big Plane Junket for Hill Spouses." *Washington Post*, January 10, p. 3.

Arrestee Drug Use (1990) National Institute of Justice, Research in Action. Washington, DC: U.S. Government Printing Office.

Becker, H. (1963) *Outsiders*. New York: Free Press.

Benenson, B. (1991) "Democrats Reassert Primacy in Hawaii Politics." *Congressional Quarterly*, October 12.

Best, J. (1990) *Threatened Children*. Chicago: University of Chicago Press.

Bishop, K. (1989) "Fear Grows Over Effects of a New Smokable Drug." *New York Times*, September 16, p. 4A.

Brecher, E.M. (1972) *Licit and Illicit Drugs*. Boston: Little, Brown.

Buruma, I., and J. McBeth (1984–85) "An East Side Story . . . ." *Far Eastern Economic Review*, 27 December/3 January, p. 15.

Carthane, A. (1989) "Will New Drug 'Ice' Freeze Hope in Black Communities?" *Jet*, December 18.

Cho, A.K. (1990) "Ice: A New Dosage Form of an Old Drug." *Science* (249):831–34.

Corwin, M. (1989) "Potent Form of Speed Could Be Drug of 90s." *Los Angeles Times*, October 8, p. 1A.

Cotton, P. (1990) "Medium Isn't Accurate Ice Age Message." *Journal of the American Medical Association* (263):2717.

Curriden, M. (1989) "Police Chilled by New In Drug: Ice." *Atlanta Constitution*, November 30, p. 1.

Delfs, R. (1991) "Cocaine Surge." *Far Eastern Economic Review*, November 21, p. 7.

"Drugs: Ice Overdose" (1989) *Economist*, December 2, pp. 29–30.

Durso, C. (1992) "Powerful Drug 'Ice' Is Found at Lab." *Philadelphia Inquirer*, August 14, p. 1B.

Essoyan, S. (1989) "Use of Highly Addictive 'Ice' Growing in Hawaii." *Los Angeles Times*, October 16, p. 3A.

Ford, A. (1990) "Federal, Local Police Raid House in San Diego." *Los Angeles Times*, July 26, p. 7A.

Goode, E. (1984) *Drugs in American Society*. 2nd ed. New York: Knopf.

Graham, J.M. (1976) "Amphetamine Politics on Capital Hill." In W.J. Chambliss and M. Mankoff (eds.), *Whose Law? What Order?*, pp. 107–22. New York: Wiley.

Grinspoon, L. (1975) *The Speed Culture: Amphetamine Use and Abuse in America*. Cambridge, MA: Harvard University Press.

Gross, J. (1988) "Speed's Gain in Use Could Rival Crack." *New York Times*, November 27, p. A9.

Hall, S., Critcher, C., Jefferson, T., Clarke, J., and Roberta, B. (1978) *Policing the Crisis*. London: Macmillan.

"Hawaiian Politics: Ethnic Pineapple Salad" (1990) *Economist*, October 20, p. 32.

Holland, L. (1990) "All about Ice: New Drug Nice Kids Can Get Hooked On." *Good Housekeeping*, February, pp. 215–16.

Holley, D., E. Vernant, and S. Essoyan (1991) "The Ice Age." *Washington Post*, May 9, p. 1A.

Hong, R., E. Matsuyama, and K. Nur (1991) "Cardiomyopathy Associated with the Smoking of Crystal Methamphetamine." *Journal of the American Medical Association* (265):1152–54.

Howe, P.J. (1989) "Ice Worse Than Crack, Officials Warn." *Boston Globe*, October 1, p. 2.

"Illicit Methamphetamine: Street Drug on the Rise." (1991) *Emergency Medicine*, June 30, pp. 13–17.

Isikoff, M. (1989) "Rural Drug Users Spur Comeback of Crank." *Washington Post*, February 20, p. 3A.

Jacobs, J. (1991) "Debunking the Crack Baby Myths." *Centre Daily Times*, State College, PA, August 11, p. 6k.

Jenkins, Philip (1992a) "Narcotics Trafficking and the American Mafia: The Myth of Internal Prohibition." *Crime, Law, and Social Change* 18:303–318.

Jenkins, Philip (1992b) "The Speed Capital of the World: Organizing the Methamphetamine Industry in Philadelphia 1970–1990." *Criminal Justice Policy Review* 6(1):17–39.

Kaplan, D.E., and A. Dubro (1986) *Yakuza*. Reading, MA: Addison-Wesley.

LaBianca, D.A. (1992) "The Drug Scene's New Ice Age." *USA Today*, January, pp. 54–56.

Larmer, B. (1989) "Ice Chills U.S. Anti-Drug Officials." *Christian Science Monitor*, December 8, p. 7.

Lauderback, D., and D. Waldorf (1992) "Whatever Happened to Ice?" Paper presented at meetings of the American Society of Criminology, New Orleans.

Lerner, M. L. (1989) "The Fire of Ice." *Newsweek*, November 27, p. 26.

MacDonald, P. T., and R. Estep (1985) "Prime Time Drug Depictions." *Contemporary Drug Problems* 12(3):419–38.

McBeth, J. (1989) "The Junkie Culture: Supercharged Speed Is Scourge of Manila's Smart Set." *Far Eastern Economic Review*, November 23, pp. 23–25.

"Meth" (1990) Report broadcast on "*60 Minutes,*" April 22.

Methamphetamine Abuse in the United States (1989) Rockville, MD: U.S. Department of Health and Human Services.

Miller, M.A., and N.J. Kozel (1991) *Methamphetamine Abuse: Epidemiological Issues and Implications*. Rockville, MD: U.S. Department of Health and Human Services.

Morgan, J.P. (1992) "Amphetamine and Methamphetamine During the 1990s." *Pediatrics in Review* 13(9):330–336.

Musto, D. (1973) *The American Disease: Origins of Narcotic Control*. New Haven: Yale University Press.

Organized Crime in California: Annual Report to the California Legislature (1989) State of California: Department of Justice.

Pennell, S. (1990) "Ice: DUF Interview Results from San Diego." *NIJ Reports* 221:12–13.

Posner, G.L. (1988) *Warlords of Crime*. New York: McGraw-Hill.

Reinarman, C., and H.G. Levine (1989) "The Crack Attack: Politics and Media in America's Latest Drug Scare." In Joel Best (ed.), *Images of Issues*, pp. 115–37. Hawthorne, NY: Aldine.

Reinhold, R. (1990) "Hawaii Race Tests Democratic Hold." *New York Times*, November 1, p. 9B.

Reza, H.G. (1989) "Raids Shut 23 Drug Labs." *Los Angeles Times*, March 20.

Richburg, K.B. (1990) "For Hawaii Democrats, Anxiety Over Safe Seats." *Washington Post*, November 1, p. 7A.

Sager, M. (1990) "The Ice Age." *Rolling Stone*, February 8, pp. 53–57.

Savadove, B. (1991) "High Society: Growing Drug Abuse Reflects Economic Changes." *Far Eastern Economic Review*, September 12, pp. 45–46.

Shoenberger, K. (1989) "South Korea Seen as Major Source of Ice Narcotic." *Los Angeles Times*, October 14, p. 9A.

Skeers, V.M. (1992) "Illegal Methamphetamine Drug Laboratories." *Journal of Environmental Health* 55(3):6–9.

Smith, Z.A., and R.C. Pratt, eds. (1992) *Politics and Public Policy in Hawaii*. Albany: SUNY Press.

Tabor, M. (1989) "Ice in an Island Paradise." *Boston Globe*, December 8, p. 7.

"Text of President's Speech on Drug Control Strategy" (1989) *New York Times*, September 6, p. 4A.

Thompson, L. (1989) "Ice: New Smokable Form of Speed." *Washington Post*, November 21, p. 2.

Turner, W. (1984a) "Hawaii Criminal's Pledge to Talk Seen as Door to Underworld." *New York Times*, July 24, p. 11A.

——. (1984b) "Inquiry on Murders in Hawaii Brings Governor and Prosecutor into Conflict." *New York Times*, August 28, p. 7A.

U.S. Congress: Drug Crisis (1990) *Drug Crisis in Hawaii: Hearing before the Select Committee on Narcotics Abuse and Control House of Representatives 101st Congress, Second Session. January 13. 1990*. Washington, DC: U.S. Government Printing Office.

U.S. Congress: Laboratories (1980) *Illicit Methamphetamine Laboratories in the Pennsylvania/New Jersey/Delaware Area: Hearing before the Select Committee on Narcotics Abuse and Control, U.S. House of Representatives, 96th Congress, Second Session, July 7, 1980*. Washington, DC: U.S. Government Printing Office.

U.S. Congress: Profile (1983) *Profile of Organized Crime: Mid-Atlantic Region: Hearings before the Permanent Subcommittee on Investigations of the Committee on Governmental Affairs, United States Senate, 98th Congress. First Ses-*

sion. February 15, 23, and 24, 1983. Washington, DC: U.S. Government Printing Office.

U.S. Congress: Re-Emergence (1990) *The Re-Emergence of Methamphetamine: Hearings before the Subcommittee on Narcotics Abuse and Control. U.S. House of Representatives, 101st Congress, First Session. October 24, 1989.* Washington, DC: U.S. Government Printing Office.

U.S. Congress: Small Business (1988) *Impact of Clandestine Drug Laboratories on Small Business: Hearings before the Subcommittee on Regulation and Business Opportunities of the Committee on Small Business, U.S. House of Representatives, 100th Congress, Second Session. Eugene, Oregon. May 13, 1988.* Washington, DC: U.S. Government Printing Office.

Weingarten, P. (1989) "Profits, Perils, Higher for Today's Bootleggers." *Chicago Tribune*, September 14, p. 16.

Weisheit, R.A. (1992) *Domestic Marijuana: A Neglected Industry.* Westport, CT: Greenwood.

Wiedrich, B. (1987) "San Diego Has Become National Center for Manufacture of Methamphetamine." *Chicago Tribune*, April 20, p. 11.

Witkin, G. (1989) "The New Midnight Dumpers." *U.S. News and World Report*, January 9, p. 23.

Young, J. (1971) "Drugs and the Media." *Drugs and Society* 2(1):14–18.

Zamichow, N. (1989) "Navy Hopes Drug Test Will Detect, Deter Meth Users." *Los Angeles Times*, October 16, p. 6A.

Zurer, P.S. (1989) "Federal Officials Plot Strategy to Stop Methamphetamine Spread." *Chemical and Engineering News*, November 6, pp. 13–16.

For Discussion

1. Discuss the possibility of whether drug panics can be productive for society.

2. Who, if anyone, benefits from drug panics?

Part VI

Hallucinogens and Other Psychoactive Drugs

During the 1960s, the use of drugs seemed to have leaped from the more marginal zones of society to the very mainstream of community life. No longer were drugs limited to the inner cities and the half-worlds of the jazz scene and the underground bohemian subcultures. Rather, their use had become suddenly and dramatically apparent among members of the adolescent and young adult populations of rural and urban middle-class America. By the close of the decade, commentators were maintaining that ours was "the addicted society," that through drugs millions had become "seekers" of "instant enlightenment," that drug taking and drug seeking would persist as continuing facts of American social life, and that there was a "drug revolution" in which the United States had entered a "new chemical age."

Whatever the ultimate causes of the drug revolution of the sixties, America's younger generations—or at least noticeable segments of them—had embraced drugs. The drug scene had become the arena of "happening" America; "turning on" to drugs to relax and to share friendship and love seemed to have become commonplace. And the prophet—the high priest, as he called himself—of the new chemical age was a psychology instructor at Harvard University's Center for Research in Human Personality, the late Dr. Timothy Leary.

Leary had been an advocate of the use of LSD, and his messages on the idea had been numerous and shocking both to the political establishment and to hundreds of thousands of mothers and fathers across the nation. In *The Realist*, a radical periodical of the 1960s, Leary hypothesized,

> I predict that psychedelic drugs will be used in all schools in the near future as educational devices—not only marijuana and LSD, to teach kids how to use their sense organs and other cellular equipment effectively—but new and more powerful psychochemicals. . . .

Perhaps most frightening of all to the older generation were Leary's comments to some 15,000 cheering San Francisco youths on the afternoon of March 26, 1967. As a modern-day Pied Piper, Leary addressed his audience:

> *Turn on* to the scene, *tune in* to what's happening; and *drop out* of high school, college, grad school . . . follow me, the hard way.

The hysteria over Leary, LSD, and other psychedelic substances had been threefold. First, the drug scene was especially frightening to mainstream society because it reflected a willful rejection of rationality, order, and predictability. Second, there was the stigmatized association of drug use with antiwar protests and anti-establishment, long-haired, unwashed, radical "hippie" LSD users. And third, there were the drug's negative effects, the reported "bad trips" that seemed to border on mental illness. Particularly in the case of LSD, the rumors of how it could "blow one's mind" became legion. One story told of a youth, high on the drug, who took a swan dive in front of a truck moving at 70 mph. Another spoke of two "tripping" teenagers who stared directly into the sun until they were permanently blinded. A third described how LSD's effects on the chromosomes resulted in fetal abnormalities. The stories were never documented and were probably untrue. What were true, however, were the reports of LSD "flashbacks." Occurring with only a small percentage of the users, individuals would re-experience the LSD-induced state, days, weeks, and sometimes months after the original "trip," without having taken the drug again.

Despite the lurid reports, as it turned out LSD was not in fact widely used on a regular basis beyond a few social groups that were fully dedicated to drug experiences. In fact, the psychedelic substances had quickly earned reputations as being dangerous and unpredictable, and most people avoided them. By the close of the 1960s, all hallucinogenic drugs had been placed under strict legal control, and the number of users was minimal.

In the years since, interest in LSD and other hallucinogens periodically re-emerges for short periods of time, and every few years a new "psychedelic" is introduced to the American drug scene.

During the 1990s and on into the twenty-first century, the "fad drugs" have been the "club drugs" or "dance drugs"—all of which have become associated with clubs, electronic music festivals, "circuit parties," and "raves." Raves are all-night dance parties, many of which occur without the appropriate licenses or permits required for holding public events. They are typically held in abandoned warehouses, airplane hangers, open fields, and other venues where large numbers of participants (up to 20,000) can be accommodated. Circuit parties, which have roots in both the rave subculture and

AIDS fundraising efforts by the gay community, are annual events (with corporate sponsors) that can attract several thousand men (upward of 15,000 to 25,000) with the allure of music, laser shows, and dancing. Although many circuit parties are one-night AIDS charity events, they often bloom into weeklong "unofficial" parties at local clubs and venues as well.

At many raves, clubs, and parties, some form of drug use is the norm. The most notable of the "club drugs" are MDMA, Ritalin, amphetamines and methamphetamine, ketamine, Rohypnol, GHB, "whippits," LSD, and a range of other hallucinogens. The attraction of these drugs is the seemingly increased stamina that they engender, enabling partygoers to dance all night, as well as the intoxicating highs that are said to deepen the overall experience. Many users tend to experiment with a variety of club drugs in combination, often with alcohol, which can lead to unexpected adverse reactions.

MDMA (Ecstasy). The most popular of the club drugs, and a drug of choice among many youths and adults well beyond the dance subcultures, is MDMA (3,4-methylenedioxymethamphetamine). Better known as "Ecstasy," and sometimes referred to as "X," "N," "XTC," "E," "Adam," "Clarity," and "Lover's Speed," it is a synthetic compound related to both mescaline and the amphetamines and is commonly (however incorrectly) labeled as a hallucinogen.

Ritalin. The trade name for methylphenidate, Ritalin is a medication prescribed for children with attention-deficit hyperactivity disorder (ADHD), an abnormally high level of activity. It is also occasionally prescribed for treating narcolepsy, a condition characterized by sudden attacks of deep sleep. Because of its stimulant properties, the abuse of the drug has become widespread. Adolescents and young adults reportedly use Ritalin for appetite suppression, wakefulness, increased attentiveness, and euphoria—effects that make it ideal for long nights of dancing (or in the case of some students, studying).

Ketamine. Ketamine, also known as "K," "Special K," "Vitamin K," and "Cat," is an injectable anesthetic that has been approved for both human and animal use in medical settings since 1970. Some 90 percent of the Ketamine legally sold today, however, is intended for veterinary use. The drug gained popularity for abuse in the 1980s, when it was realized that large doses caused reactions similar to those of phencyclidine (PCP), such as dreamlike states and hallucinations.

Gamma-Hydroxybutyrate (GHB). Known on the street as "G," "Grievous Bodily Harm," "Liquid Ecstasy," and "Georgia Home Boy," GHB can be produced as a clear liquid, white powder, tablet, or in capsule form, and it is often used in combination with alcohol, making it extremely dangerous. GHB is often manufactured in homes with recipes and ingredients found and purchased on the Internet. The drug is typically abused either for its intoxicating/sedative/euphoriant properties or for its growth hormone-releasing effects for muscle development.

Whippits. Whippits are small containers of nitrous oxide (also known as "laughing gas" for dental anesthesia) intended for home use in whipped cream charging bottles. The "whippits" used in the nightlife scene are somewhat different from those used for whipping cream. Generally they are balloons or plastic bags of nitrous oxide, filled and sold by a supplier in or near the rave. The euphoria resulting from "huffing" (inhaling) nitrous oxide, which lasts from 2 to 10 minutes, is considered by some to enhance the dance party experience.

Rohypnol. Sometimes referred to as "roofies," "rophies," "Roche," and the "forget-me pill," Rohypnol belongs to the class of drugs known as benzodiazepines (such as Valium, Halcion, Xanax). Rohypnol is tasteless and odorless, and it dissolves easily in carbonated beverages. The sedative and toxic effects of Rohypnol are aggravated by the use of alcohol. Even without alcohol, a dose of Rohypnol as small as one milligram can impair the user for 8 to 12 hours. Rohypnol is usually taken orally, although there are reports that it can be ground up and snorted. The drug can cause profound "anterograde amnesia"; that is, individuals may not remember events they experienced while under the effects of the drug. It is for this reason that Rohypnol has been referred to as the "date rape" drug.

In the five articles in this section, LSD is discussed at length, as are the various "club drugs" that have become known as "date rape" drugs. High-risk behavior linked to club drug use is also explored: The nexus of circuit parties, drug use, and unsafe sex among gay men is detailed, as is the practice of Ketamine injection among youth in New York City. This part concludes with a "healthy settings" approach to nightclubs. Given that clubbing and drug use are popular activities among young people around the world, harm minimization initiatives are perhaps the best way to protect the health and lives of these individuals.

Additional Readings

Cohen, Richard S. (1998). *The Love Drug: Marching to the Beat of Ecstasy*. Binghamton, NY: The Hawthorn Press.

Henderson, Leigh A., and William J. Glass. (1998). *LSD: Still With Us After All These Years*. San Francisco: Jossey-Bass.

Holland, J. (Ed.). (2001). *Ecstasy: The Complete Guide. A Comprehensive Look at the Risks and Benefits of MDMA*. Rochester, VT: Park Street Press.

Leary, Timothy W. (1964). "Introduction." In David Soloman (Ed.), *LSD: The Consciousness-Expanding Drug* (pp. 1–21). New York: G. P. Putnam.

Owen, Frank. (2003). *Clubland: The Fabulous Rise and Murderous Fall of Club Culture*. New York: St. Martin's Press. ✦

25
Rise of Hallucinogen Use

Dana Hunt

Dana Hunt traces the history and "re-emergence" of hallucinogens, e.g., LSD, in the United States. Drawing from basic survey data, Hunt notes that users of LSD tend to be white and from higher income groups. These data also show interesting trends. For example, Hunt notes that the percentage of persons who continue to use LSD (as opposed to using one time only for experimental purposes) is higher than in years past. The author also reviews other data and describes how patterns of LSD consumption differ across geographic regions in the United States and across various university and college settings.

In the public imagination, few periods in history have been so linked to a type of drug as the 1960s were to psychedelics, or hallucinogens. Widespread experimentation with drugs such as LSD, peyote, and psilocybin ("magic mushrooms") influenced many aspects of American pop culture—clothing, music, art, and language. Many people discussed but few followed Timothy Leary's advice to "tune in and turn on." Americans nevertheless tried psychedelic drugs at an unprecedented rate. According to the first National Household Survey on Drug Abuse (NHSDA) in 1972, 5 percent of Americans, almost all of them under the age of 18, had used psychedelics at least once; by 1979 lifetime prevalence was reported as 25 percent among young adults ages 18–25.

In the mid-1980s the use of psychedelics dramatically declined as cocaine became the drug of choice. Law enforcement seizures of LSD and other hallucinogens dropped pre-

Issues and Findings

Discussed in this Brief: The history of hallucinogen use in the United States, a comparison of past and present user groups, and the impact of today's use and distribution patterns on law enforcement and public health and safety.

Key issues: Psychedelic drugs figured prominently in the hippie culture of the 1960s and 1970s, but their popularity declined during the 1980s. Recent studies reveal that hallucinogen use is on the rise in the 1990s, particularly among young adults of the same socioeconomic class as those who embraced these substances in previous decades. While current hallucinogen users seem to have little involvement in criminal activities, their drug-taking behavior places them at risk of harming themselves or others.

Key findings: Five sources were used to study the resurgence of hallucinogen use in this country. Data from these sources indicate that:

- Hallucinogens are relatively inexpensive, domestically produced, and not part of a network of distributors battling over markets or territory.

- Between 1991 and 1996, the percentage of Americans who had used psychedelics at least once in their lives grew from 6 to 14 percent.

- The percentage of high school seniors who believe that trying LSD or using it regularly is a "great risk" has declined significantly. Between 1991 and 1996, the percentage of seniors who said they disapproved of LSD use even once or twice fell from 90 to 80 percent.

- Thirty-four percent of college and university officials reported that hallucinogen use, particularly of LSD and psilocybin, is increasing on their campuses. Campus sources identified hallucinogen users today as mainstream students, not the more marginal or "hippie" students of the 1960s. Private and public campuses are equally likely to report hallucinogen use; religious schools are most likely to report little or no use. Larger campuses and institutions in urban areas report the widest range of drug use.

- The rise in hallucinogen use coincided with the growth of "raves," underground dance parties that cater to those under age 21.

- Systemic violence associated with the trafficking of heroin and cocaine has not been found with hallucinogen trafficking. The Drug Enforcement Administration reports that a relatively small number of producers and distributors located in Northern California have controlled the LSD market for a number of years.

- Repeated doses of hallucinogens or ingestion of multiple substances can produce highly adverse effects, including death. In addition, the auditory and visual distortion resulting from hallucinogen ingestion can last for 10 to 12 hours, thus endangering a user who drives, his or her passengers, pedestrians, and the occupants of other cars in proximity.

Target audience: Drug enforcement and drug treatment practitioners, college and university officials, high school administrators, public health officials, drug policy coordinators, and researchers. ✦

cipitously, as did emergency room reports of adverse effects of hallucinogen use. However, by the early 1990s, interest in hallucinogens seemed to resurface among users whose demographic profile was similar to that of users in the 1960s—young men and women, often middle class, who typically declined to use heroin or cocaine. Reports of LSD use and distribution at places as surprising as the U.S. Naval Academy[1] highlight the return of these drugs among student populations. In addition to familiar hallucinogens, newer compounds have surfaced (see "Drugs Classified as Hallucinogens or Psychedelics").

This research in brief traces the historical use of hallucinogens in the United States and discusses the implications—in terms of law enforcement and public safety—of their current popularity among youths and young adults. To conduct the analysis for the study summarized here, researchers from Abt Associates Inc. relied on national survey data and two telephone surveys conducted specifically for this report (see "Data Sources").

Recent History of Hallucinogen Use

Hallucinogens are not new. Many naturally occurring substances such as peyote, psilocybin, or mescaline have long been used in cultural and religious contexts, and LSD was synthesized in Europe in the late 1930s. However, until the 1950s, when psychiatric researchers investigated the possible therapeutic value of LSD, recognition that certain drugs had hallucinogenic properties was very limited.

LSD did not receive popular attention until the early 1960s, when the late Timothy Leary and Richard Alpert, his colleague at Harvard University, began experimenting with the drug on themselves, other academics, local artists, and students. Leary was dismissed from Harvard for promoting LSD, but he continued to advocate its use as a positive mind-altering experience and identified psychedelics as part of a counter cultural or lifestyle choice. Although nonmedical use of LSD continued to rise throughout the 1960s, scientific interest declined. In 1974 the National Institute of Mental Health concluded that LSD had no therapeutic use.[2]

The interest in LSD during the 1960s also prompted users to seek out naturally occurring substances that produced the same experiential effects. In fact, a variety of substances in nature produce transitory visual or auditory distortion, e.g., cannabis, thornapple, peyote, and jimsonweed. One of the oldest hallucinogens known to Western scientists is mescaline, a derivative of the peyote cactus, used for centuries in natural medicines and religious ceremonies. Substances such as peyote, mescaline, and a variety of exotic fungi (e.g., psilocybin mushrooms) can be smoked, brewed in tea, chewed, and incorporated into food. In the 1960s users exchanged and published recipes for preparation of hallucinogens through popular publications of the era.

How many people actually used hallucinogens during the 1960s and 1970s? In 1974, 17 percent of all Americans reported they

Figure 25.1

Use of Hallucinogens by High School Seniors

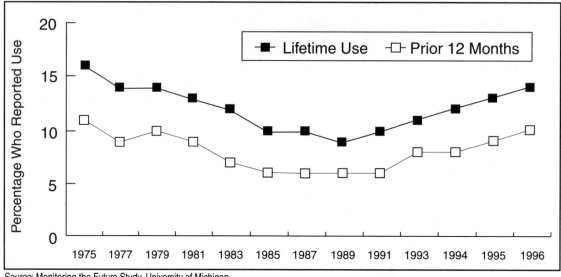

Source: Monitoring the Future Study, University of Michigan

had used a hallucinogen in their lifetime. According to NHSDA, lifetime prevalence among the young adult population rose to 20 percent in 1977 and 25 percent by 1979.

During the same period, other surveys made similar findings. In 1975 the Monitoring the Future (MTF) Study reported that 16 percent of high school seniors across the country had used hallucinogens at some point. A 1980 survey of New York State high school students showed that, by age 18, 25 percent had used hallucinogens.[3] These figures represented a remarkable rise in the use of drugs that less than 15 years earlier had been virtually unknown.

Who Is Using Hallucinogens Now?

Until the late 1980s and early 1990s, hallucinogens appeared to be out of vogue as the generation of original users aged. By 1982, 6 percent of adults over 26 years old reported that they had used hallucinogens at least once, but fewer than 1 percent reported use in the prior year.[4] In 1992, however, drug ethnographers reporting to *Pulse Check* began noticing increased availability of hallucinogens in many areas of the country. At the

same time, researchers studying the emerging music and dance phenomena known as "raves" found LSD, MDMA, ketamine, and 2C–B playing a significant part in these activities.[5]

National survey data supported this observation. Figure 25.1 shows high school seniors' self-reported hallucinogen use for selected years of the MTF study. As these data indicate, the first year (1975) of the survey produced the highest lifetime use (16 percent), followed by a gradual decline that continued until the end of the 1980s. In 1991 the percentage reporting lifetime use again began to rise, reaching 11 percent in 1993, 13 percent in 1995, and 14 percent in 1996. Use in the prior 12-month period also declined throughout the 1980s, reached a low of 6 percent in 1985, then rose to 8 percent in 1993 and 1994, 9 percent in 1995, and 10 percent in 1996. Figure 25.2 indicates that LSD has typically been the most commonly used hallucinogen, although a similar but smaller rise in the use of any hallucinogens is also apparent.

Data from a 1992 Dade County, Florida, survey showed an even higher level of use among high school and college students. The

Dade County student survey indicated that 17 percent of high school seniors reported using LSD at least once, a figure almost five times the 1991 level and considerably higher than the level reported in the national MTF study.[6]

In recent years, increased hallucinogen use has been concentrated primarily among white students, a group that has the highest rates of use (both lifetime and annual) for hallucinogens, inhalants, and tranquilizers. According to the 1994 national survey of high school students, 8 percent of white se-

niors reported using LSD in the prior 12 months compared with less than 1 percent of African-American and 5 percent of Hispanic seniors. Use also appears to be related to socioeconomic status (SES). Data indicate that as the overall use level of LSD began to increase in the late 1980s and early 1990s, a positive relationship between socioeconomic status and use emerged. Students from the highest income groups are now twice as likely as those from the lowest SES group to have used LSD in the previous 12 months. This relationship, however, has

Drugs Classified as Hallucinogens or Psychedelics

The terms "hallucinogen" and "psychedelic" refer to both synthetic and organic substances that can produce visual, auditory, and tactile distortions in users. The group of drugs so designated generally includes:[7]

- LSD (d-lysergic acid diethylamide) and Nexus (4-bromo-2, 5 dimethoxyphenethylamine)—synthetic or laboratory-derived substances that at varying dosages produce degrees of perceptual distortion. LSD is most often soaked into patterned paper, though it may also be distributed in tablet, crystalline, or liquid forms. Nexus is structurally related to mescaline and produces sensory distortion lasting 4 to 8 hours.

- Mescaline, peyote, bufotenine, belladonna, and various fungi—substances derived from plants or other sources in nature that, when smoked, eaten, or otherwise ingested, quickly produce altered perceptual states.

- PCP (phencyclidine) and ketamine hydrochloride (Special K)—central nervous system agents that produce anesthetic, analgesic, and hallucinogenic effects.[8] These substances were originally tested in humans for their anesthetic use during minor surgery, but use was eventually restricted to the tranquilization of large animals in veterinary medicine. PCP and ketamine appear most often in powder form ("dust"), but they can also be found as liquids.

- MDMA (methylene dioxymethamphetamine), or Ecstasy—a synthetic methamphetamine compound that produces both psychedelic and

stimulant effects. MDMA was used clinically until 1988, when the Food and Drug Administration reclassified it as a Schedule I controlled substance (i.e., one with no approved use) because of its abuse potential. MDMA is most often found in the form of tablets or capsules.

Hallucinogens are defined more by the effects they produce than by any common chemical structure. In part the term "hallucinogen" refers to a drug's ability to distort reality. Although persons with psychotic disturbances may hallucinate without an external stimulus, normal individuals can induce the same (but temporary) effect using hallucinogenic drugs.[9] Hallucinogens as a group produce varying levels of visual, auditory, and tactile distortions and/or "out of body" sensations. As with all drugs, the intensity of effect depends not only on ingestion of a specific drug and dose but also on the user's perception or expectation of the experience.[10]

Hallucinogens differ in several ways from other commonly abused drugs such as heroin or cocaine. Although their reality-distorting effects may make them attractive and reinforce repeated usage, most hallucinogens are not physiologically addictive in the same way that opiates or even sedatives are, that is, if tolerance is established, hallucinogens do not produce long-term physiological craving after their effects have worn off.[11] They also differ in the duration of drug action. Unlike the effects of cocaine, which last for only minutes, and those of heroin, which last for a couple hours, the active effects of hallucinogens can continue for several hours. Only methamphetamine can produce a similar long-lasting effect from a single ingestion. ✦

Figure 25.2

Prior-Year Use of Hallucinogens by High School Seniors

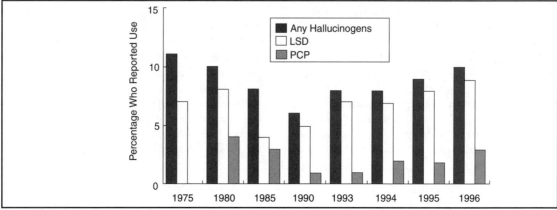

Source: Monitoring the Future Study, University of Michigan.

Data Sources

Data for this report came from the following five sources:

- **National Household Survey on Drug Abuse**. First conducted in 1971, NHSDA is supported by the Substance Abuse and Mental Health Services Administration and is a national probability sample of household members 12 years and older. Respondents are interviewed about their current and past use of a wide range of illegal and legal drugs, including alcohol.

- **Monitoring the Future Study**. Supported by the National Institute on Drug Abuse (NIDA) and conducted annually since 1975, this survey administers questionnaires to a national probability sample of high school seniors in the United States. Questionnaires are also mailed to a sample from each of the previous senior class samples for up to 10 years after high school. Since 1991 the survey has also included samples of 8th- and 10th-grade students.

- *Pulse Check*. Conducted quarterly since 1992 and semiannually since spring 1996 by the Office of National Drug Control Policy (ONDCP), *Pulse Check* gathers information from telephone interviews with 15–20 ethnographic sources, 10–15 police agencies, and 50–60 drug treatment providers from across the country. While not a probability

sample, it is nevertheless a timely report from persons working "on the front lines" of law enforcement and drug abuse research and treatment.

- **Survey of colleges and universities**. A random sample of 4-year colleges and universities was developed for this analysis. The sampling was distributed evenly between public and private institutions in all geographic areas. Sources knowledgeable about student drug use (on-campus drug program officers or counselors, student health directors, student affairs officers) were interviewed by telephone in October 1995. Questions were asked about which drugs were used most often on campus and what types of students were using them; if applicable, more detailed information was sought on hallucinogen use. Of the 100 institutions sampled, approximately 60 were determined to be eligible for inclusion in this report.[12]

- **Survey of drug treatment programs for adolescents**. The 1992 NIDA National Drug Abuse Treatment Unit Survey was also used as a framework to develop a random sample of adolescent drug treatment programs from across the United States. Twenty-five program or clinical directors were interviewed by telephone using the same guidelines described above for college sources. ✦

Figure 25.3

Prior-Year Use of Hallucinogens, Cocaine and Marijuana by High School Seniors

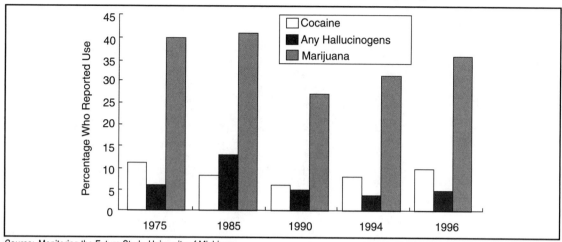

Source: Monitoring the Future Study, University of Michigan.

nothing to do with price; the cost of hallucinogens is lower than that of both cocaine and heroin.[13]

Although interest in hallucinogens is resurgent, it is difficult to quantify use that continues beyond initial experimentation or to determine whether the rise in hallucinogen use is part of a general upswing in the use of all illegal drugs. Figure 25.3 shows trends in hallucinogen, cocaine, and marijuana use among high school seniors in the year prior to the survey.

The overall increase in illicit drug use by teens and young adults is driven by significant growth in the use by high school students of marijuana, hallucinogens, and, to a lesser degree, crack cocaine. From 1993 to 1996, the percentage of 8th, 10th, and 12th graders who reported using marijuana in the previous year rose steadily, reaching 18 percent, 34 percent, and 36 percent respectively. Daily use of marijuana also rose in all high school grades surveyed. As is true for marijuana, the figure in 1996 for prior-year use of hallucinogens continued to rise to levels statistically and significantly higher than 1995 levels among all grades.

The high school senior survey provides data on noncontinuation rates of drug use.[14] Unfortunately, data show that many of these teens persist as users beyond experimentation. Since 1992 noncontinuation rates for LSD have been the lowest reported in 10 years;[15] that is, more students are starting to use hallucinogens and fewer are stopping.

Not surprisingly, data on juveniles involved with the criminal justice system show even higher rates of illicit drug consumption. Figure 25.4, which reports data from 12th graders who have been arrested and tested for drugs as part of the juvenile Drug Use Forecasting (DUF) program and from the MTF study, shows that use of all illicit drugs has increased in the 1990s, but use of LSD and stimulants has doubled. Renewed interest in hallucinogens coincides with a perception of reduced risk and greater peer support for use. The high school survey data indicate a significant decline in the percentage of seniors who feel that trying LSD or using it regularly is a "great risk." In 1991, 90 percent of high school seniors reported that they disapproved of LSD use even once or twice. That number had dropped to 83 percent in 1994 and to 80 percent in 1996. The percentage of high school seniors who said none of their friends used MDMA decreased significantly from 88 percent in 1990 to 76 percent in 1996.

Figure 25.4

Thirty-Day Prevalence for Twelfth Graders, by Drug and Year

Percentage Reporting Past 30-Day Use	1991	1992	1993	1994	1995
Any illicit drug?					
DUF	37.0	44.3	53.7	58.2	62.7
MTF	16.4	14.4	18.3	21.9	23.8
Any illicit drug other than marijuana?					
DUF	12.1	14.5	16.9	19.1	22.3
MTF	7.1	6.3	7.9	8.8	10.0
Marijuana					
DUF	34.9	41.4	51.0	55.2	59.5
MTF	13.8	11.9	15.5	19.0	21.2
LSD					
DUF	3.3	4.3	5.1	5.0	7.2
MTF	1.9	2.0	2.4	2.6	4.0
PCP					
DUF	2.0	1.8	1.9	1.8	3.7
MTF	0.5	0.6	1.0	0.7	0.6
Cocaine					
DUF	4.5	5.3	5.9	5.7	4.9
MTF	1.4	1.3	1.3	1.5	1.8
Crack					
DUF	3.5	2.6	2.5	4.0	5.5
MTF	0.7	0.6	0.7	0.8	1.0
Heroin					
DUF	0.2	0.3	0.4	0.5	1.1
MTF	0.2	0.3	0.2	0.3	0.6
Amphetamine/Stimulants					
DUF	2.9	4.0	6.2	10.2	7.9
MTF	3.2	2.8	3.7	4.0	4.0
Methamphetamine/Ice					
DUF	2.3	3.0	4.6	8.1	7.8
MTF	0.6	0.5	0.6	0.7	1.1

Sources: Drug Use Forecasting Program and Monitoring the Future Study.

The report also indicates that hallucinogens are increasingly accessible to high school students. In 1992, 45 percent of high school seniors described LSD as "easy or fairly easy to get"; in 1996 that percentage had risen to 51 percent. The survey authors speculate that although attention has been focused on cocaine and crack for many years, little media coverage has been devoted to hallucinogens and fewer opportunities have existed to observe their adverse effects. This situation may have added to "generational forgetting"[16]— today's teens knowing less than teens from the previous generation—to the point that hallucinogens surpass cocaine in popularity for all groups except Hispanics.

NHSDA data (see Figure 25.5) depict a similar, although less dramatic, time trend than that reported in the MTF studies. In the first year of this survey (1972), 5 percent of youths under 18 said they had used a hallucinogen one or more times. That figure peaked by 1979 (7 percent of respondents under age 17 and 25 percent between the ages of 18 [and] 25), began to decline, and dropped dramatically for those under 25 in 1985. In

Figure 25.5

Lifetime Prevalence of Hallucinogen Use by Age

Age	1972	1977	1979	1982	1985	1991	1992	1993	1994	1995
12–17 Any Use (Hallucinogens)	4.8%	4.6%	7.1%	5.2%	3.2%	3.3%	2.6%	2.9%	4.0%	5.4%
18–25 Any Use (Hallucinogens)	–	19.8%	25.1%	21.1%	11.6%	13.2%	13.4%	12.5%	14.5%	14.1%
26–34 Any Use (Hallucinogens)	–	2.6%	4.5%	6.4%*	16.7%	15.5%	15.6%	15.9%	15.5%	15.2%
35+ Any Use (Hallucinogens)	–	–	–	–	2.2%	5.2%	5.2%	6.6%	6.2%	7.6%

* Includes all users over 26 years old.
Source: National Household Survey on Drug Abuse (1972–1994).

the late 1980s and early 1990s, however, the trend began to change somewhat. Among young adults (ages 18–25), lifetime prevalence began to rise from 12 percent in 1985 to 15 percent in 1994. In the most recently published survey, 14 percent of respondents between the ages of 18 and 25 and 5 percent between the ages of 12 and 17 reported using a hallucinogen at least once. As is true for the high school survey data, NHSDA data indicate that much of this increase has been among whites and Hispanics (see Figure 25.6). The greatest concentration of reported lifetime use is found among two groups: white youths ages 18–25 (19 percent) and Hispanics ages 18–25 (9 percent).

Although the NHSDA and MTF surveys show increases in hallucinogen use, particularly among the young, data from emergency rooms (ERs) across the country do not. The percentages of ER mentions for LSD or PCP in the Drug Abuse Warning Network (DAWN) are low (fewer than 0.01 percent); this has been the case throughout the past two decades. However, notable increases in ER mentions have been seen in four cities: Atlanta, Washington, D.C., Chicago, and Seattle. Although hallucinogens have long been known to produce some adverse reactions in users, particularly over time, the

lower potency of today's hallucinogens may not produce acute incidents requiring emergency medical attention. There is increasing anecdotal evidence, however, that the lower dosage drug is simply being consumed more frequently than in the past.[17]

Variations Across the United States

National probability samples have limited ability to reflect recent changes in drug use because of the time needed to conduct the survey, analyze the results, and report the findings. Therefore, the following sources were used to examine hallucinogen use across the United States in 1996: the ONDCP *Pulse Check* series, Community Epidemiology Work Group (CEWG) at NIDA, and two telephone surveys conducted for this report. Although these sources reveal that a renewed interest in hallucinogens is national in scope, they also show regional variation. Epidemiologists reporting to CEWG from New York, Atlanta, San Francisco, Seattle, Miami, and cities in Texas noted increased hallucinogen use.[18] Other areas, such as New Orleans and Denver, report that LSD is widely available for purchase, but indicator data do not reflect any changes in use.

LSD is produced in domestic labs concentrated in Northern California and shipped by mail or couriers through what law enforcement officials describe as a well-established network of distributors.[19] *Pulse Check* and Drug Enforcement Administration (DEA) sources report that LSD is sold primarily in paper or blotter form, with each sheet divided into squares of single dose units containing approximately 25–60 micrograms of the substance. It may also be sold as "microdots" (small tablets) or in gelatin squares ("window panes"). A dose (approximately 55 micrograms) sells for $1–$10.

The unit dosages consumed by users in the 1990s are less concentrated than those taken in the 1960s—the heyday of LSD consumption—when dosages were typically 100–200 micrograms. In the San Francisco area, *Pulse Check* ethnographers report that users experience shorter "trips," lasting only a few hours, and milder hallucinogenic effects than was true of LSD trips 20 years ago. Interviews with rave-goers also indicate a milder and shorter effect from today's LSD.[20] However, Miami CEWG data show that users may increase the number of doses to make up for reduced potency, thus producing new patterns of use. LSD may also be combined or sequenced with other drugs to enhance or extend its effect. For example, one study describes young users who practice "candy-flipping," or combining in sequence MDMA or methamphetamine with LSD.[21]

Both *Pulse Check* and CEWG sources report user interest in naturally occurring hallucinogens such as peyote or mescaline. In the October 1994 *Pulse Check*, three sources reported that youths had come into emergency rooms exhibiting symptoms brought on by ingesting jimsonweed, a plant in the deadly nightshade family whose active ingredient, belladonna, has hallucinogenic properties. Even in relatively small quantities, however, it is generally toxic. Other drugs that have been mentioned in both sources include peyote, mescaline, psilocybin, and bufotenine, all of which have been relatively absent from the drug culture for many years.

New synthetic drugs have generated renewed interest in hallucinogen use. MDMA is one of the most popular of these newer drugs; other drugs that have surfaced in recent years include Nexus and ketamine. Ketamine use has been reported in New York for more than 2 years, and it is increasingly being used as a "club drug" in New Jersey, Delaware, Washington, D.C., Florida, and Georgia. Ketamine is packaged in bag-

Figure 25.6

Lifetime Prevalence of Hallucinogen Use by Ethnicity

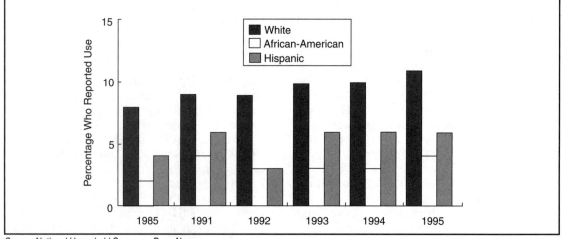

Source: National Household Survey on Drug Abuse.

gies or capsules and sells for approximately $10–$20 per dose.

Hallucinogen Use on College Campuses

In October 1995 telephone surveys conducted with 59 college and university officials knowledgeable about student drug use indicated that hallucinogens, particularly LSD and psilocybin, are popular in many areas of the country. Of the campuses surveyed, 34 percent reported increasing hallucinogen use, 7 percent reported decreasing use, and 39 percent reported no change. Figure 25.7 shows the drugs used most frequently on campuses across the country. Alcohol and marijuana are the most commonly cited (83 and 78 percent, respectively). However, 44 percent of campuses reported student use of hallucinogens; all cited LSD and 57 percent cited psilocybin and MDMA as the specific hallucinogens students use. Officials at one large Midwestern university claimed that their own campus

survey revealed that 10 percent of students had tried hallucinogens at some time, but only 2 percent had used one of these drugs in the prior 30 days. Similar figures from other campus surveys were reported, ranging from 3 percent to 19 percent lifetime prevalence. Many officials stressed that although hallucinogen use was appearing on campus, it was still confined to a small segment of students and dwarfed by marijuana and alcohol consumption. In several instances campus officials also believe that, although hallucinogen use has only recently resurfaced, it may already have peaked.

Campus sources reported that individuals of both genders and all ethnic groups in the student body are hallucinogen users, although the greatest interest seems to be concentrated among younger students. Unlike the 1960s, when hallucinogens were identified with the more marginal or "hippie" culture, today hallucinogens are used among mainstream students.

Private campuses were as likely as public ones to report hallucinogen use, and reli-

Figure 25.7

"What Types of Drugs Are Used Most Often by Students on your Campus?"

Drug	Region I[a] N = 15	Region II[b] N = 17	Region III[c] N = 11	Region IV[d] N = 16	Total N = 59
Opiates	0	0	1	1	2
Cocaine	1	4	7	4	16
Crack	1	5	1	1	8
Marijuana	12	12	11	11	46
Hallucinogens	2	8	6	10	26
Inhalants	2	0	2	1	5
Tranquilizers	2	0	0	1	3
Methamphetamine	3	0	3	6	12
Alcohol	15	12	11	11	49
Other	1	0	0	1	2
No drug use	1	4	0	4	9

[a]Region I: Connecticut, Maine, Massachusetts, New Hampshire, New Jersey, New York, Pennsylvania, Rhode Island, and Vermont
[b]Region II: Alabama, Arkansas, Delaware, Florida, Georgia, Kentucky, Louisiana, Maryland, Mississippi, North Carolina, Oklahoma, South Carolina, Tennessee, Texas, Virginia, Washington, D.C., and West Virginia
[c]Region III: Illinois, Indiana, Iowa, Kansas, Michigan, Minnesota, Missouri, Nebraska, North Dakota, Ohio, South Dakota, and Wisconsin
[d]Region IV: Arizona, California, Colorado, Idaho, Montana, Nevada, New Mexico, Oregon, Utah, Washington, and Wyoming
Source: Survey of Colleges and Universities.

gious schools were least likely to do so. Because of student accessibility to the off-campus urban club scene, larger campuses and institutions in urban areas reported the widest range of drug use.

Young Users and Treatment

Drug treatment programs across the United States that specialize in treating substance abusers under 18 years old were surveyed about their current population of patients. These sources said their clients use a variety of drugs, although alcohol, marijuana, and hallucinogens (particularly LSD) are the most frequently abused substances. For most youths in treatment, hallucinogen consumption is part of an extensive drug use history; rarely do counselors see adolescents who abuse only hallucinogens. Anecdotal reports from some counselors indicate as many as 80 percent of clients have used hallucinogens; others report diagnosing as many as three or four cases per week of adolescents with hallucinogen-related perceptual disorders. The anecdotal reports attribute the visual system damage to the number of "trips" (including consecutive multiple doses of LSD) that teens often take. The media have reported similar patterns of abuse among young party-goers who ingest large amounts of Ecstasy (seven or eight doses) that may result in long-term, harmful effects on mood, sleep, appetite, and impulse control.[22]

What Are 'Club Drugs'?

Hallucinogens are often reported as part of the "club drug scene"—a term that refers to the use of particular drugs by teens and young adults who frequent music or dance clubs geared to their age group. In general, these are the same youths found in the campus survey: young, often fairly affluent men and women who have limited histories of using drugs such as heroin or cocaine. Urban-area ethnographic sources for *Pulse Check* report hallucinogen use among patrons of the many nightclubs that cater to persons under 21 years of age. Many such clubs serve no alcohol and can attract clientele as young

as 13 or 14 years old. In New York City, heroin or cocaine may also be part of the club drug scene, although this seems to be the exception. The most frequently reported club drugs are LSD, MDMA, Nexus, and ketamine. In fact, young club participants in Miami actively scorn "harder" drugs but embrace LSD, MDMA, and other hallucinogens as "safe."

A study conducted by Abt Associates Inc. in 1994 examined "raves," phenomena closely tied to the club culture, and the drugs that may be used there.[23] A rave is a large party where participants often dance all night to "house music," technically synthesized rhythms of 120–180 beats per minute played at earsplitting decibel levels. Raves were fashionable in Europe during the late 1980s and have become popular in the United States in recent years. They attract a predominantly middle-income audience, often high school and college students. Whereas they were once "underground"[24]—the whereabouts of the events passed by word of mouth—raves are now openly advertised and discussed on electronic mail services.

Although the music and frenetic activity of raves have little in common with the almost dreamy pace of the hallucinogen culture of the 1960s, other aspects of the phenomena indicate an active nostalgia for that era: its fashions, emphasis on the "spirituality" of attending raves, promotion of nonviolence, and the use of marijuana and a variety of hallucinogens.

Abt Associates Inc. researchers examined rave activity in New York and San Francisco, informally interviewing participants as well as organizers about various aspects of rave activity, including drug use.[25] They found that the drugs most commonly associated with raves are marijuana and hallucinogens, although methamphetamines and alcohol were evident. Among the hallucinogens, MDMA and LSD were the most popular drugs—the ones some participants associated with the spiritual ethos attached to the events. As was true in the earlier era of hallucinogen use, some rave participants associated a range of benefits, including personal enlightenment, with the use of these drugs. The researchers also found that participants were unaware of the possible harm that repeated or uncontrolled use could produce.

Implications for Law Enforcement and Public Safety

The nature of different drugs (e.g., physical effects produced, costs) is often directly linked to the problems they present for law enforcement. Stimulants (e.g., methamphetamines) and depressants (e.g., alcohol) produce unique psychopharmacological effects (such as agitation, paranoia, or irritability) in users that may make them more difficult for law enforcement officers to restrain. The expense of a drug may also predict users' involvement with income-generating crimes. One researcher characterizes three types of violence or crime associated with drugs:[26]

- Pharmacologic: crime related to a drug's pharmacological effects on the user

- Economic: crime associated with a drug's costs to the user

- Systemic: crime associated with trafficking of a drug

Hallucinogens have not been linked to pharmacologic crime primarily because of their sedative effects. They cost relatively little ($1–$5 per unit dose) for the long-lasting results they produce, and their use is concentrated among middle- to upper-income youths with greater access to funds, a fact that reduces the likelihood that economically driven crime would be associated with their use.

The systemic violence connected to heroin and cocaine trafficking has not been found with hallucinogen trafficking. DEA reports that a relatively small number of producers and distributors located in Northern California have controlled the LSD market for a number of years.[27] A handful of chemists, some of whom have been working since the 1960s and 1970s, synthesize the bulk of the drugs produced and distribute them throughout the country. Quantities are shipped from suppliers to known contacts (often on a prepaid basis) and distributed through established user networks. Although some local production of hallucino-

gens exists, the chemists or producers involved in such enterprises generally confine their products to local markets and therefore pose little threat to established traffickers. LSD may also be distributed at concerts, although ethnographic research indicates that much of the hallucinogen use associated with raves occurs prior to attendance.

Threats to the safety of users and those with whom they come in contact are major problems associated with hallucinogen use. Health risks for drugs such as MDMA include dehydration, appetite suppression, and heartbeat disruption. Adverse psychological reactions, which some users experience with high and/or repeated doses of hallucinogens, are well documented; they include psychotic episodes, panic disorder, and long-term sensory distortion.

In addition to health risks, concerns for public safety are related to hallucinogen use. The use of multiple substances is troubling. Any of the club drugs taken alone can impair motor skills; in combination they can produce deadly synergistic effects. The enduring effects of drugs such as LSD or MDMA can pose special problems. For example, ingestion of a drug with the potential to cause visual and auditory distortion lasting 10–12 hours may mean that the user will drive home from a party while still under its influence. The opinion of one experienced State police source quoted in the October 1994 *Pulse Check* reflects a concern shared by several respondents: "Kids think they're fine to drive, but their reaction time is all off, and they get into trouble."

Summary

As crack has been the drug of the inner city for a decade, hallucinogens appear to be a popular drug among today's young, more affluent users. All sources reported their popularity among nonminority high school and college users who often reside outside the inner cities. The drugs are relatively inexpensive, domestically produced, and part of a stable, noncompetitive distribution network. Despite law enforcement efforts to disrupt the production and distribution of hallucinogens, a small number of manufacturers have provided a relatively steady supply, distributed through local user networks, for more than 20 years. Although rising use may not pose severe threats to law enforcement, it does present problems for public health officials in terms of the health and safety of young users who are rediscovering this family of drugs.

Author's Note

This study was conducted under cooperative agreement 94-IJ-CX-C007, awarded to Abt Associates Inc. by the National Institute of Justice.

Findings and conclusions of the research reported here are those of the author and do not necessarily reflect the official position or policies of the U.S. Department of Justice.

Notes

1. Bradsher, K. (1995) "All midshipmen drug tested after two caught with LSD." *New York Times*, October 18, A18.

2. Henderson, L., and W. Glass (eds.) (1994) *LSD: Still With Us After All These Years*. Lexington, MA: Lexington Books.

3. Kandel, D. (1982) "Epidemiology and psychological perspectives in adolescent drug use," *Journal of the American Academy of Child Psychology* 21(4):328–347.

4. Miller, J., et al. (1982) *National Survey on Drug Abuse: Main Findings*. Washington, D.C.: National Institute on Drug Abuse.

5. Harlow, D. (1994) "Raves and drug use: An exploratory study." A Research Application Review working paper for internal distribution prepared by Abt Associates Inc.

6. Community Epidemiology Work Group (1995) *Epidemiologic Trends in Drug Abuse*. Rockville, MD: National Institute on Drug Abuse.

7. There has long been debate whether marijuana and hashish should be included in the hallucinogen category because the active ingredient in both (tetrahydrocannabinol, or THC) produces some hallucinogenic effects. They were not included in this report.

8. Because PCP is often included in data sets with hallucinogens, it is included in this analysis even though PCP users are demographically different from other hallucinogen users. Its use is more geographically limited, and PCP use constitutes a small portion of reports in the hallucinogen category.

9. Szara, S. (1994) "Are hallucinogens psychoheuristic?" In G. Lin and R. Glennon (eds.), *Hallucinogens: An Update*. NIDA Research Monograph Series 146, Rockville, MD: National Institute on Drug Abuse, pp. 33–52.

   Some users report experiencing "flashbacks" of distorted perception long after the drug is taken, and these often long-delayed reactions are not well understood.

   Strassman, R. (1984) "Adverse reactions to psychedelic drugs: A review of the literature," *Journal of Nervous and Mental Disorder* 172:577–595.

10. Zinberg, N. (1984) *Drug, Set and Setting*. New Haven, CT: Yale University Press. Zinberg called this the impact of "set and setting" on drug use. The set is the expectation the user brings to the experience, e.g., the user is expecting to get high. The setting is the context in which the drug is taken—at a party, while alone, in the hospital. Both have a direct influence on the perception of its effect.

11. Glennon, R. (1994) "Classical hallucinogens: An introductory overview." In C. Lin and R. Glennon (eds.), *Hallucinogens: An Update*. NIDA Research Monograph Series 146, Rockville, MD: National Institute on Drug Abuse, pp. 4–33.

12. Institutions that offered almost exclusively graduate or continuing education programs were eliminated from the analysis in this report because they served a different, older student population than were found in 4-year institutions.

13. Johnston, L., P. O'Malley, and J. Bachman (1995) *National Survey Results on Drug Abuse from the Monitoring the Future Study (1975–1993)*. Rockville, MD: National Institute on Drug Abuse.

14. *Ibid.*, 54. Noncontinuation rates are calculated as the percentage of those who report that they have used a drug at least once in their lives but not in the 12 months prior to the survey.

15. *Ibid.*, 54.

16. *Ibid.*, 12.

17. Community Epidemiology Work Group, *Epidemiologic Trends in Drug Abuse*.

18. *Ibid.*

19. Drug Enforcement Administration (1995) "LSD in the Unites States." Drug Intelligence Report, Washington, D.C.: U.S. Department of Justice.

20. Harlow, "Raves and drug use: An exploratory study."

21. *Ibid.*

22. Blakeslee, S. (1995) "Popular drug may damage brain," *New York Times*, August 15, C5.

23. Harlow, "Raves and drug use: An exploratory study."

24. The underground nature of the initial raves had less to do with drug use and more to do with the fact that initial promoters, often not professional promoters or club owners, did not have permits to hold large gatherings.

25. Harlow, "Raves and drug use: An exploratory study."

26. Goldstein, P. (1985) "The drugs/violence nexus: A tripartite conceptualized framework," *Journal of Drug Issues* 15:493–506.

27. Drug Enforcement Administration, "LSD in the United States."

For Discussion

Legally, should hallucinogenic drugs be treated the same as cocaine and heroin? Why or why not?

Reprinted from: Dana Hunt, "Rise of Hallucinogen Use" in *National Institute of Justice Research Brief*, October 1997. ✦

26
Rohypnol, GHB, and Ketamine

New Trends in Date-Rape Drugs

Christine A. Saum
Nicole L. Mott
Erik F. Dietz

Christine Saum and her colleagues examine three drugs that have recently gained popularity and come to the forefront: Rohypnol, GHB, and Ketamine, known collectively as "date-rape drugs." The authors describe the history of these drugs, legal and illegal usage, as well as the legal issues pertaining to changes in classification, and the creation of new crime categories. Each of these drugs has been associated with sexual assault. Rohypnol, for example, can produce memory and psychomotor impairment, effects that contribute to sexual assault victimization.

"Date-rape drugs" and the controversy surrounding their use have become a part of the popular culture of the United States. References to these types of psychoactive substances may invoke images of youths partying on the club scene with dangerous illegal substances. But they are more likely to depict victims who are sexually assaulted under the influence of Rohypnol, GHB, or Ketamine. Indeed, it is not uncommon to learn about tragic events involving one or more date-rape drugs in daily news reports (see, for example, "3 Guilty of Manslaughter in Date-Rape Drug Case," *New York Times*, March 15, 2000). Moreover, college students, bar-goers, and others are repeatedly advised

to keep a close watch on their beverages. They are warned that they could be unknowingly drugged by offenders wishing to take advantage of them in a helpless state. The National Institute on Drug Abuse (NIDA, 1999) is currently distributing a Community Drug Alert Bulletin in an attempt to combat the increasing use of Rohypnol, GHB, and Ketamine. Alan Leshner, the director of NIDA, reports that the harm caused by date-rape and other club drugs is "not yet a national crisis," but that his agency's efforts are focusing on trying to prevent one by "getting into the path of the plague" (ADAW, 1999a).

Along with the escalating public awareness and media attention surrounding these drugs, there has been an increase in the number of substances being placed in the date-rape drug category. Rohypnol was the first to gain this notorious distinction, and was referred to as "the date-rape pill." Now, rather than battling one dangerous pill, we are contending with several date-rape drugs. Of late, GHB, sometimes referred to as "Grievous Bodily Harm," has surpassed Rohypnol as the most feared date-rape drug. This distinction has been spawned by GHB's easy-to-access Internet recipes and a nationally publicized murder trial. Likewise, Ketamine, or "Special K," which is stolen from veterinarians' offices and used to place its consumers in a sometimes helpless, LSD-like state, has gained notoriety. Other drugs like MDMA (Ecstasy) and methamphetamine, which are more often termed "club drugs" due to their popularity on the dance club and "rave"[1] party scene, have also been referred to as date-rape drugs. This label likely refers to the potential that these substances have to induce extreme disinhibition and physical incapacitation.

It is interesting to note that other substances that have many of the same qualities of the date-rape drugs are rarely thought of for inclusion under this category. In particular, alcohol, which is more closely associated with sexual assault than any other drug (CASA, 1999), could easily be depicted as *the* date-rape drug. Perhaps it is true that many drugs produce unconsciousness, especially when combined with alcohol. But some substances such as Rohypnol, GHB, and Ketamine are fast-acting and extremely potent, which has gained them their particular notoriety (ONDCP, 1998). In addition, the fact that these drugs may be used to facilitate a crime in an unsuspecting or completely disabled victim differentiates them from a more typical substance abuse and sexual violence scenario. Moreover, Rohypnol, GHB, and Ketamine have all recently undergone scheduling changes requiring more severe penalties for illegal use—an additional indicator of their unique standing among more conventional drugs.

This paper describes the three drugs most commonly included under the category of date-rape drugs: Rohypnol, GHB, and Ketamine. Each drug will be discussed in terms of the drug's effects, its current popularity as a party or recreational drug, its use as a tool in rape or other sexual assault, and political and legal issues surrounding drug classification and criminal sanctioning.

Rohypnol

Rohypnol is a powerful sedative-hypnotic drug prescribed extensively throughout the world, but it is illegal in the United States. The drug has become popular among American youths as a party or club drug, providing a cheap means of extended, yet intense, intoxication. Moreover, aside from its emergence as a recreational drug, it has generated the most contention as a date-rape drug. Indeed, individuals have been alleged to slip Rohypnol tablets (better known as "roofies"[2]) into beverages and then sexually abuse their sedated victims. A potent, contemporary version of the Mickey Finn,[3] Rohypnol has the ability to render its users extremely disinhibited, helpless, and otherwise vulnerable. Even small doses of Rohypnol combined with alcohol can induce amnesia, earning the nickname "the mind eraser" and, more notoriously, "the date-rape pill of choice."

A Rohypnol tablet, once placed in a liquid, is colorless, tasteless, and dissolves easily—adding to the deceitful nature of its use in criminal activities. To counteract this potentially dangerous quality of Rohypnol, the drug's manufacturer has formulated a new version of the drug that fizzes and turns blue when placed in a liquid (Hoffman-LaRoche, 1999). However, this formulation has not yet been approved for manufacture in all locations.

Rohypnol (generic name, flunitrazepam) belongs to the benzodiazepine family of central nervous system depressants, as does the well-known tranquilizer Valium (diazepam).[4] Manufactured and marketed by the Swiss-based Hoffman-La Roche Inc. pharmaceutical company, Rohypnol is, perhaps surprisingly, the most widely prescribed sedative-hypnotic in Western Europe (NIDA, 1995). More than 2.3 million doses of Rohypnol are sold worldwide each day (Friend, 1996).

Although not available by prescription in the United States, Rohypnol is nonetheless obtainable on the streets, particularly in the Southeastern and Southwestern states. Typically, the greatest quantities of Rohypnol have arrived in the United States from Mexico and Colombia. One investigation estimated that 1.4 million pills were being moved through the Laredo, Texas–Mexico border crossing each year, and further, that 43% of the people declaring prescription drugs over a one-year period at this border were importing Rohypnol (Shephard and McKeithan, 1995). Until only recently, Rohypnol was "legally" imported into the United States from among the more than 80 nations that permit its legitimate use. Although Rohypnol has always been a controlled substance, a three-month supply for personal use was generally permitted to be brought into the United States if accompanied by a medical prescription.[5]

Rohypnol first came to the attention of law enforcement officials in the late 1980s and early 1990s. Reports of misuse of the drug increased steadily from 1993 through 1996 (DEA, 1995a; ONDCP, 1998a). The Office of National Drug Control Policy listed Rohypnol as an "emerging drug" in the 1996 edition of *The National Drug Control Strategy* (ONDCP, 1996). However, in 1997 police encounters, seizures, and emergency department admissions related to Rohypnol were fewer than in recent years (ONDCP, 1998a). Possible reasons for the decrease in use include increased law enforcement efforts and stricter sanctions for illegal possession. At the same time, newer data examining Rohypnol use in 1998 indicate that there has been a resurgence in Rohypnol use (Woodworth, 1999).

Popularity as a Recreational Drug

Rohypnol misuse in the United States has been reported primarily by adolescents and young adults (Saum and Inciardi, 1997).[6] Drug researchers term Rohypnol a "lunch money drug," referring to its affordability by even very young consumers. Once in the United States, Rohypnol is sold at a street price ranging from $.50 to over $10.00 per pill, averaging about $5.00 or less per tablet (DEA, 1995b; Up Front Drug Information Center 1994; DEA, 2000a). Moreover, because the effects of Rohypnol remain strong for several hours, it has gained a reputation among teens and college students as a very inexpensive, yet intense "high." As one university's police Victim Advocate Program coordinator explained:

> Kids see it as a cheap way to get intoxi-cated faster. Instead of a six-pack, it only takes one beer (and a Rohypnol tablet) to get drunk. (Grudman, 1995)

The popularity of Rohypnol is enhanced by its rapid onset and long-lasting effects, pro-viding the user with a prolonged period of intoxication. Accordingly, Rohypnol has also been referred to as the "alcohol or buzz extender." One Rohypnol user and former dealer at the University of Texas spoke about the drug:

> It makes you forget everything that is going on in your world. There's no hang-over, and it only costs $5. For $5, nothing could do for you what Rohypnol could do. (Bonnin, 1997)

An additional explanation for Rohypnol's acceptance among youths may be due to commonly held misperceptions about the drug (DEA, 1995a; Woodward, 1999). First, many erroneously believe that Rohypnol tablets are unadulterated and therefore safe because they come in presealed bubble packs. Pills are generally viewed as safer than

such drugs as cocaine or heroin or other loose (unpackaged/unregulated) substances pur-chased on the "street." And, second, it is mis-takenly believed that the presence of Rohypnol cannot be detected by urine test-ing. However, although a specific test for Ro-hypnol is available, routine urine screens or breathalizer tests fail to detect its presence.

The National Institute on Drug Abuse's Community Epidemiology Work Group (CEWG) has addressed the misuse of Rohypnol. In 1995, they reported that the use of Rohypnol was one of the fastest grow-ing drug problems among adolescents and young adults in South Florida and Texas, and that it appeared to be spreading rapidly across the United States (CEWG, 1995). The DEA seized over half a million Rohypnol tab-lets between January 1985 and February 1999, with most of the seizures occurring be-tween 1994 and 1996 (Woodworth, 1999). In 1998 the number of tablets seized increased over the previous year, indicating that de-spite the rescheduling efforts, there is still significant diversion of Rohypnol products. In the most recent CEWG (1999) report, there is evidence that clonazepam (brand name, Rivotril), an anticonvulsant drug in the same family as Rohypnol, is also increasing in popularity (CEWG, 1999).

National data on emergency department visits indicates that clonazepam mentions have increased 277% from 1990–1997 (CEWG, 1999). Moreover, the most recent CEWG report specifically mentions that Rivotril, which can be legally imported from Mexico, is replacing Rohypnol as a drug of abuse. Finally, the DEA reports that counter-feit Rohypnol tablets containing a benzo-diazepine other than Rohypnol were first encountered in 1997 and that Texas officials reported that other Mexican drug products were being imported and sold as a substitute for the drug (ONDCP, 1998a).

As a result of new, stricter sanctions for possession of the drug, and increasing diffi-culties in terms of accessibility, former Rohypnol users are now both knowingly and unknowingly thought to be using prescrip-tion drugs that have similar properties as Rohypnol (ONDCP, 1998a; CEWG, 1999). One danger of using a substitute or "look-alike" pharmaceutical product sold in place of Rohypnol is that the drug quality may vary significantly. In addition, the lack of knowledge regarding what drug was ingested can complicate the task of emergency response personnel (DEA, 2000a).

Two Texas studies have examined the voluntary use of Rohypnol. Field interviews of 66 persons who identified themselves as Rohypnol users found that many were actually using other benzodiazepines instead of or in addition to Rohypnol. Reported adverse effects of these drugs included amnesia, overdose, injuries, auto accidents, and death. A few male subjects acknowledged having given women a Rohypnol pill (both with and without their knowledge) to increase the subjects' chances of having sex and one woman subject reported knowing of several instances of females being drugged with Rohypnol (Calhoun et al., 1996).

The prevalence, patterns, and correlates of voluntary Rohypnol use were examined in a sample of adolescent women entering reproductive health clinics. Of the 904 women surveyed, lifetime use of Rohypnol was reported by 6%. Ten percent of these users reported experiencing physical or sexual victimization after Rohypnol use (Rickert, Wiemann, and Berenson, 1999). This study underscores the risk associated between Rohypnol use and serious health and victimization concerns among women.

Political and Legal Issues

In response to Rohypnol's reported use as a tool to facilitate sex crimes, in March of 1996 the U.S. government launched a strict prohibition on the importation of Rohypnol (see "Import of 'Date-Rape' Pill Banned," *Washington Post*, March 3, 1996, p. A3). Senator Joseph R. Biden hailed this decision as significant progress in the "war on drugs," ("Biden Blasts Rohypnol," *Wilmington News Journal*, March 10, 1996, p. B6), and President Bill Clinton maintained that the prohibition of Rohypnol was a step in protecting our children's futures (*News Release*, Office of the Press Secretary, March 6, 1996).

Issues relating to the reclassification and criminal sanctioning of Rohypnol were debated in the U.S. Congress in October of 1996. The Drug-Induced Rape-Prevention and Punishment Act was signed into law, which increased the penalties up to 20 years in prison for the use of Rohypnol or any controlled substance in a sexual assault or other violent crime. This act also increased penalties for the possession, manufacture, or distribution of an illegal drug with the intent to use it in the commission of a violent crime. Interestingly, in implementing these new penalty provisions, the U.S. Sentencing Commission established sentencing guidelines for Rohypnol that were above those generally applicable to Schedule I and Schedule II depressant drugs—drugs more tightly controlled than Rohypnol (Woodworth, 1999). Yet, at that time, Congress agreed not to reschedule Rohypnol until further research had been effected.

In 1996, the Drug Enforcement Administration proceeded with an attempt to reclassify Rohypnol from its current status as a Schedule IV drug (indicating low potential for abuse) to a Schedule I drug, which would designate Rohypnol as having a high potential for abuse as well as no accepted medical use. As a Schedule I drug, Rohypnol would carry the same penalties for possession as do LSD and heroin. According to the Controlled Substances Act (CSA), the Department of Health and Human Services (DHHS) is required to study the abuse and trafficking of Rohypnol and make a recommendation for reclassification. In January of 1997, after scientific and medical review, the DHHS recommended that Rohypnol remain a Schedule IV drug because its abuse potential was no different than other benzodiazepines (Woodworth, 1999). The DEA acted in accordance with this recommendation.

Individual states are not required to follow the Federal CSA guidelines if they believe that existing controls are inadequate to address the needs in their jurisdiction. Reacting primarily to escalating reports of Rohypnol's use in rape cases, the state of Florida temporarily declared Rohypnol a Schedule I drug in June of 1996. Florida's attorney general Robert A. Butterworth felt so strongly about the dangers of Rohypnol that he exercised his emergency powers to reschedule the drug (Weikel, 1996). More recently, several other states including Idaho, Minnesota, New Mexico, North Dakota, Oklahoma, and Pennsylvania have placed Rohypnol under Schedule I control (ONDCP, 1998a; Woodward, 1999).

The manufacturer of Rohypnol has not supported the attempt to reschedule the drug in the United States. Hoffman-La Roche fears that such a move would negatively affect the standing of Rohypnol worldwide. Indeed, despite its problematic status in the United States, Rohypnol is said to have a respectable reputation throughout the rest of the world (Friend, 1996). In addition, since many countries follow the United States' drug classification schedule, if reclassified, Rohypnol could become illegal in countries where it is currently used widely. These changes would subsequently lead to a considerable decrease in annual revenues for Hoffman-La Roche.

Although the emergence of Rohypnol has garnered much controversy in the United States, all problems associated with the drug have not been limited to the U.S. Rohypnol is commonly misused in Europe and elsewhere by persons who have developed an addiction to the substance. And in Mexico and South America, where it is sold over the counter for the treatment of insomnia, levels of misuse may be even higher (Bond et al., 1994). Consequently, in 1995 the World Health Organization moved Rohypnol from a more loosely regulated Schedule IV drug to a more strictly regulated Schedule III drug on an international drug classification system (DEA, 1995a). Along with more restrictive controls, Schedule III drugs incorporate harsher penalties for possession and distribution. Rohypnol has the designation of being the first benzodiazepine to require these stricter regulations. Misuse of Rohypnol throughout the world typically refers to individuals who develop physical dependence on the drug. Interestingly, however, the alarm surrounding the use of Rohypnol to facilitate sexual assault appears to be a phenomenon that occurs largely in the United States.

The 'Date-Rape Pill'

The pharmacological properties of Rohypnol make it a suitable candidate for its designation as a "date-rape drug." Rohypnol intoxication is characterized by marked sedative and such other potentially dangerous effects as extreme disinhibition, severe memory impairment or amnesia, muscle relaxation, visual impediment, and slowing of psychomotor performance. Most of these effects, specifically the amnesia and disinhibition, demonstrate that a person who unknowingly (or even knowingly) ingested this drug would be an easy target for sexual or other criminal victimization. Hoffman-La Roche includes its own warning about the risky properties of Rohypnol and its side effects in the drug's package insert, which reads:

> Some patients may have no recollection of any awakenings occurring in the six to eight hours during which the drug exerts its action.[7]

Moreover, when Rohypnol is combined with other sedatives, antidepressants, or analgesics, its effects are greatly intensified.

Rohypnol is occasionally used as a primary intoxicant, but investigations reveal that when it is misused, it is more often ingested along with alcohol (DEA, 1995a; Woodworth, 1999). Alcohol and Rohypnol have a mutually potentiating effect—ingestion of one drug strengthens the effects of the other. Rohypnol is unlikely to produce death when taken alone, even in cases of overdose (Smith, Wesson, and Calhoun, 1996). However, in combination with alcohol, Rohypnol can be lethal due to enhanced nervous system depression—a person can become so sedated that he or she may completely stop breathing. Extreme disinhibition and blackouts lasting several hours have been reported after ingestion of Rohypnol in combination with alcohol.

As for Rohypnol's reputation as a "date-rape drug," there is no evidence of an epidemic problem, although there exist several documented cases and many anecdotal reports of the drug's use in sexual crimes.[8] Unfortunately, there are currently no statewide or national databases available to gauge this problem. Additionally, since Rohypnol-related sex crimes are virtually impossible to detect, it is unlikely that we can appraise the true extent of the problem.

The account of one victim, a 25-year-old student at the University of California at San Diego, appears to be typical of rape cases where Rohypnol misuse is suspected. The woman believed that Rohypnol had been put into a glass of wine she was consuming at a concert. She later woke up naked, and could not remember that she had been raped until sometime after its occurrence (Laboy, 1995). Since a victim may not remember details until days later, if at all, it is too late to test for Rohypnol in a urine or blood sample or to examine a victim for evidence of rape.

The crime of rape is highly unreported for many reasons, including fear, embarrassment, and distrust of the criminal justice system. Thus, prosecuting cases where women claim to have been drugged with Rohypnol is especially troublesome. In addition to the usual reasons why victims are reluctant to report rapes, these women may have been drinking alcohol or using other drugs, adding to their apprehension about reporting the crime. And, due to the amnesiac effects of Rohypnol, historical clues of the rape event are difficult to obtain (Anglin, Spears, and Hutson, 1997).

An attorney had described Rohypnol as a "crime in a pill" (Pazdera, 1995), referring to the several sexual assault cases he had been involved with where the drug was used to intentionally incapacitate victims. This attorney also commented:

> It's very difficult making these cases. Usually these victims don't remember a thing. It's almost like the perfect crime. Because they (the offenders) don't have to worry about a witness testifying against them. (Kidwell and Piloto, 1996)

Nevertheless, there have been successful prosecutions of individuals who have used Rohypnol during the commission of a crime. A Florida man who bragged to his friends that he had drugged over a dozen women with Rohypnol and then raped them, pled no contest to sexually battering an incapaci-

tated person, a first-degree felony, and was subsequently sentenced to eight years in prison (Seligmann and King, 1996). Since 1994, the DEA is aware of at least nine individuals who have been convicted of sexual assault in five state court cases in which there was evidence that Rohypnol was used to incapacitate the victim (Woodworth, 1999). Moreover, the DEA reports that 17 other sexual assault cases between 1994 and 1998 contain evidence to suggest that Rohypnol was used to facilitate the crime (Woodworth, 1999).

Former Broward County (Florida) assistant state attorney Bob Nichols has prosecuted Rohypnol-related sexual assault cases over the past few years. He believes that the use of Rohypnol for recreation and for criminal activity in the Miami area has reached a plateau due to the media coverage of date-rape drugs, education of potential victims, and law enforcement awareness of this drug (Nichols, 2000). Nichols handled several recent cases where Rohypnol was suspected, but drug tests were found to be positive for Valium or Xanax. Nichols describes this recent trend where individuals are believed to have been sedated with Rohypnol, but are returned positive screens for drugs other than Rohypnol, as "Roofie copycat crimes" (Nichols, 1997).

The manufacturer of Rohypnol offers free drug testing for individuals who believe that they have been a victim of a crime of sexual abuse facilitated with Rohypnol. This testing is offered in conjunction with law enforcement centers and rape crisis clinics, as most of these facilities do not have the resources to perform the specific test for Rohypnol. To ensure the most accurate results, a urine test must be obtained within 60–72 hours of the drug's ingestion.

A recent study reported on the results of urine samples sent in from rape crisis centers, law enforcement agencies, and hospital emergency rooms from persons in 49 states who believed that they were drugged and then sexually assaulted (ElSohly and Salamone, 1999). Over eleven hundred samples sent in between May 1996 and June 1998 were screened for the presence of Rohypnol and other substances. Only six tested positive for Rohypnol, and most of these positive tests were found to indicate use of other drugs as well. Caution is advised in interpreting these results. The authors indicate that there were 50 additional samples that found traces of Rohypnol, in the first testing procedure, but were not confirmed with a second test and thus were not counted as official positive tests. In addition, over 700 of the remaining urine samples tested positive for other substances, including alcohol, cocaine, marijuana, and other benzodiazepines. Perhaps the most important finding of this study is that over 20 different substances were found to be associated with the crime of sexual assault.

Rohypnol's manufacturer is concerned about the misuse of its product. Hoffman-La Roche has generated an ad campaign promoted on the radio, television, and in print public service announcements cautioning women about the potential dangers of this drug. One ad shows a photograph of a man's hand holding a drink beneath the words "WOMEN BEWARE!" and a television spot shows a man slipping a tablet into a woman's drink while she is distracted by friends (Fields, 1996). In addition, the company is funding the distribution of educational fliers on Rohypnol to members of the health care industry and law enforcement agencies, and has initiated studies to learn more about the patterns of misuse surrounding the drug (Hopper, 1995; Laboy, 1995). Hoffman-La Roche is now working with the DC Rape Crisis Center to prepare additional educational tools and to operate a date-rape drug information line (Hoffman-La Roche, 1999).

Physical modifications of the Rohypnol tablet have been effected in an attempt to curtail unauthorized use. The two-milligram Rohypnol pill, the most widely abused form of the drug, was phased out beginning in 1996, and a less potent version is currently being marketed (Day, 1996; DEA, 2000a). As mentioned earlier, Rohypnol tablets have also been reformulated so that they will fizz and turn blue when placed into liquids. Finally, a miniaturized kit may soon be made available so that individuals can conduct a personalized test for the presence of Rohypnol if they suspect the drug has been slipped into their beverage (Guterman 1998).

GHB

There has been much public and political interest surrounding GHB and its notoriety as a date-rape drug. Law enforcement agencies, drug policy groups, and the media have considered GHB to be an imminent problem, but little is actually known about patterns of misuse of this drug. Like Rohypnol, GHB is not approved for medical use in the United States, but became popular with high school and college students for its inexpensive, yet long-lasting intoxicating effects. Currently, insufficient information exists as to the extent of GHB use as a recreational drug, and even less is understood about the use of this drug by sexual predators.

GHB, known on the street as Grievous Bodily Harm, Liquid Ecstasy, and Easy Lay, has recently received greater national attention since the conviction of three Detroit teens for slipping the drug into the drinks of three girls at a party. The young men were convicted of involuntary manslaughter on March 15, 2000, after supplying the women beverages laced with GHB. One of the girls died, and [another] remained in a coma for 12 hours before fully recovering. The third woman was not injured, as she did not consume her drink (Bradsher, 2000).

GHB (gamma-hydroxybutyrate) is a naturally occurring substance found, in minute quantities, in the human brain. Although it has been hypothesized that GHB acts as a neurotransmitter due to its structural similarity to other such neurochemicals, its actual physiological use remains unknown (Galloway et al., 1997). GHB was first synthesized in 1960—prior to the 1963 discovery that it existed as a natural substance in the brain. Its properties, the ability to induce a sleep-like state and depressive function on the central nervous system, spurred interest in its use as an anesthetic. However, as clinical trials uncovered an association between the use of GHB and both petite and grand mal seizures, its popularity faded (Marwick, 1997). Although GHB's popularity as an anesthetic diminished, the use of this drug increased in other areas. For example, it has been examined since 1970 for the treatment of sleep disorders such as narcolepsy. GHB has been experimented with as a sedative to replace L-Tryptophan, which was taken off the market by the FDA in 1989 (Marwick, 1997). In addition, experiments have been conducted in Europe to examine GHB's use as a surgical anesthetic and to determine whether or not GHB is effective in treating alcohol and opiate dependence (Galloway et al., 1997; Rosen et al., 1997).

In the late 1970's, GHB was determined to have steroid-like properties. Since then, its use as a "natural" muscle growth agent became popular among body builders (Marwick, 1997). In fact, until the late 1980's, GHB was a popular over-the-counter supplement used to reduce body fat and increase muscle growth. However, increasing reports of GHB-induced comas, illnesses, and seizures prompted the FDA to issue a warning about its toxic effects in 1991. And by 1992, it was ordered to be completely removed from the shelves (Nightingale, 1991). Today, despite FDA advisories declaring the drug unsafe, GHB is promoted and sold on the Internet and on the steroid black market as an alternative to anabolic steroids (ONDCP, 1999).

Interestingly, one of the main ingredients in GHB, GBL (gamma butyrolactone), was until very recently sold over the counter in diet supplements and other weight-loss aids. When ingested, GBL converts into GHB within the body. GBL can also be used to manufacture GHB by adding it to either lye or a common drain cleaner. GBL is a commonly found chemical and is normally used as an industrial floor stripper (DEA, 2000). In January 1999, the Food and Drug Administration (FDA) called for a voluntary recall of GBL, warning consumers not to use the drug (FDA, 1999). As of that date, the FDA reported at least 55 cases of GBL-associated adverse health effects, including one death (FDA, 1999).

Currently, there are formal restrictions as to the buying or selling of GBL, due to its potential for easy conversion into GHB, as well as the related adverse health effects. The Hilary Farias and Samantha Reid Date-Rape Prohibition Act of 1999 was signed in February 2000. At that time, GBL became a List 1 chemical, subject to the criminal, civil, and administrative sanctions of the Controlled Substances Act (DEA, 2000b). List 1 chemicals are chemicals that are regulated due to their use in manufacturing a controlled substance.

Typically, GHB is consumed in a liquid form. It may be ingested as a solution comprised of distilled water and pure drug, or its powdered form may be mixed with another liquid to mask its salty taste. It is generally sold in small vials the size of hotel shampoo bottles or eyedrop containers. The DEA has also confiscated samples in spring water and mouthwash bottles; some have been disguised by adding food coloring or flavorings (DEA, 2000b). The average size of a dose can range from approximately 1 to 5 grams. On the streets, a dose is normally considered a capful or teaspoon full and sells for $5 to $10 per "hit" (ONDCP, 1999).

The effects from ingestion of GHB vary greatly, depending on the size of the dose as well as the strength of chemicals used in formulating the mixture. The onset of effects occurs within 15–20 minutes and last 3–6 hours (DEA, 2000b). Consumption of less than one gram of GHB generally contributes to a feeling of relaxation and a reduction in inhibitions. Consuming one to two grams may intensify the feeling of relaxation while slowing the heart rate and respiration. In higher doses, such as those above two grams, individuals may experience a compromised ability to control motor and speech functions (ONDCP, 1999). Further, a coma-like sleep frequently occurs after consuming large doses, and may require intubation to awaken the user. Other side effects of a dose this size include, nausea, vomiting, seizures, hallucinations, and amnesia.

As with Rohypnol, GHB is often added to alcoholic beverages. This combination potentiates the psychoactive and depressant effects of GHB (Woodworth, 1999). Indeed, although GHB is dangerous enough by itself, when mixed with alcohol, respiratory depression, coma, and death are more likely to occur (DEA, 2000b). Indeed, many of the deaths associated with GHB have involved the use of this drug along with alcohol or other drugs (Woodworth, 1999).

Due to the fact that GHB is produced by amateurs, samples vary greatly in terms of strength and purity. Indeed, the unauthorized production of the drug by "home chemists" often results in a GHB solution with a dangerously high acidity level. Consumption of this mixture over time may result in the pronounced erosion of the esophagus (ONDCP, 1999). Moreover, since users simply cannot know how much GHB they are getting, unintentional overdoses are common (Zickler, 2000).

Because the widespread use of GHB is relatively recent, the long-term health effects of prolonged use cannot be definitively stated. However, it does appear that addiction and dependency may result for those who chronically use GHB (Zukin, 1999). Users of this drug have reported that they need higher and higher doses to get the effects they want, and further that they cannot stop using GHB when they have attempted to do so (Zickler, 2000).

Although there are many documented negative side effects associated with GHB, it remains a popular drug on the club scene. In Atlanta, GHB is one of the most popular manufactured drugs on the market and is reported to be widely available from local gyms and at gay male clubs (CEWG, 1999). GHB is reportedly taken as a pleasure enhancer that depresses the central nervous system, inducing an intoxicated state (ONDCP, 1999). The use of GHB in the club scenes is likely due in part to the effects that it shares with Rohypnol, namely that of euphoria and lowered inhibitions. GHB has also been reportedly used as a sedative to both reduce the effects of stimulants such as cocaine and methamphetamine, or hallucinogenics such as LSD, and to prevent physical withdrawal symptoms (ONDCP, 1999).

The use of GHB among youth can be seen in the escalating number of emergency-related admissions for GHB-associated symptoms. Table 26.1 shows the greatest increase among those ages 18 to 25, followed closely by those ages 26 to 34. Further, the use of GHB is divided most greatly by gender in the years 1994 through 1997. It is only in 1998 that we see the number of womens' emergency room visits related to GHB symptoms surpass the number of visits for men.

There are other indicators of GHB's emergence across the country. Poison Control Centers in Miami have reported a drastic increase in the number of calls for GHB-induced unconsciousness (NIDA, 1998). Further, GHB was cited as the cause of several overdose deaths in New Orleans in 1998, and is the reported drug of choice among gay white males in the French Quarter. Also in 1998, Denver's Poison Control Center reported 33 calls involving the use of GHB,

Table 26.1

Emergency Room Visits Related to GHB in the United States and Selected Metropolitan Areas: By Age/Gender

Age	1992	1993	1994	1995	1996	1997	1998* Midyear
6–17	–	–	–	–	14	27	10
18–25	–	22	26	80	427	475	223
26–34	–	12	25	60	163	201	126
35+	–	–	–	–	30	58	25
Gender							
Male	–	15	29	94	506	530	190
Female	14	21	20	51	125	228	195

Table adapted from ONDCP 1999
* Numbers are based on data through June of 1998.

about half of which were considered life threatening (CEWG, 1999). Along these lines, as of mid-1998, GHB has been implicated in at least 26 deaths nationwide (Zickler, 2000). Finally, the DEA has documented 63 deaths attributed to GHB since 1995 (DEA, 2000b).

The above statistics do not account for the actual extent of GHB use across the country. One of the problems with obtaining accurate statistics regarding the use of GHB is the relative difficulty associated with detecting it. Similar to Rohypnol, GHB is a clear liquid that can be readily combined with numerous other liquids such as juice or alcohol without significantly altering the taste. The detection of GHB is further hampered as the body processes the drug very quickly. It can be excreted completely in four to five hours, depending on how it was ingested. Moreover, unless ingestion of GHB is suspected, routine toxicology screenings will not detect it. Currently, the only way to determine the presence of the drug is with a specialized blood or urine test (Asa, 1999).

The use of GHB as a recreational drug is somewhat easier to document than is its use to facilitate a sexual assault. One of the street names associated with GHB, "Easy Lay," speaks to its potential usage to facilitate a sex crime. The potential to use GHB as a date-rape drug is great, since it is relatively undetectable, easy to access, and simple to administer. And, depending on the size of the individual and the dosage, the resulting unconsciousness could leave the victim defenseless. This is what happened to the young woman mentioned in the introduction, Samantha Reid, after drinking a Mountain Dew soft drink laced with the drug at a suburban Detroit party. She never regained consciousness, dying later [the] next day. Although there was no indication that a sexual assault occurred, prosecutors told police that the men had put GHB in the drinks to make the party more "lively" (Bradsher, 2000).

GHB is more commonly appearing in date-rape cases in certain parts of the country (Haworth, 1998). National statistics from the Drug Enforcement Agency indicate that since 1990 there have been 15 sexual assault cases involving 30 victims under the influence of GHB (DEA, 2000b). And, in Seattle,

emergency rooms are reporting increasing numbers of GHB-related cases of rape. Finally, local observations indicate that GHB is involved in an increasing number of sexual assault cases in Los Angeles (CEWG, 1999).

The FBI has described a case of GHB-associated sexual assault (ASA, 1999). A former disc jockey slipped GHB into young women's drinks, took them home after [they became] intoxicated, and then raped them. In this case the offender also took pornographic photographs of the women while they were in a state of unconsciousness.

The study that was mentioned earlier examined urine samples from persons who believed that they were drugged and then sexually assaulted. Samples were tested for the presence of GHB (ElSohly and Salamone, 1999). Results indicate that of the 1,179 samples sent in between May of 1996 and June of 1998, 48 tested positive for GHB. This number is likely underestimated due to the fact that GHB is cleared from the body so rapidly.

As the frequency of date-rape cases involving the use of GHB has increased, a number of state and federal lawmakers have proposed legislation banning the possession and manufacture of the drug. For example, Representative Sheila Jackson-Lee (D.-Texas) introduced legislation making it easier to prosecute individuals who alter the manufacturing of GHB so much that it no longer fits the drug's legal definition. Further, Governor Paul Cellucci of Massachusetts signed a law that created a new category of crime: drug-induced kidnaping. This law sets a maximum of life imprisonment for an individual convicted of using drugs in the commission of a crime where the victim is held against her will. It also increases the maximum sentence for a person convicted of drugging someone with the intent to rape from three years to life (ADAW, 1998). The increased usage of GHB in date-rape cases prompted the passage of the *Drug Induced Rape Prevention and Punishment Act of 1996*, mentioned earlier in this chapter (ONDCP, 1999).

The federal classification of GHB has only recently changed. President Bill Clinton signed a bill into legislation making it illegal under federal law to possess or manufacture GHB. The bill was passed by a vote of 339 to 2 and accepted with only minor revisions, such as an exception for the study of GHB's effectiveness in treating sleeping disorders. In March of 2000, GHB was added to the Schedule I category of controlled substances that includes heroin and LSD, which have severe penalties for possession or manufacture (DEA, 2000b).

Prior to the passage of this legislation, GHB had been under federal review for some time. During this period, numerous states had already passed bills scheduling the drug into all four levels of control. States such as Alabama, Nebraska, and Rhode Island all listed GHB as a schedule I substance. California, Florida, Indiana, Louisiana, and New Hampshire listed GHB as a Schedule II drug. Finally, Minnesota, New Jersey, and South Dakota listed it as Schedule III while GHB was placed under Schedule IV control by Alaska, Connecticut, North Carolina, and Tennessee (ONDCP, 1999).

Despite these legislative efforts and the action by the FDA, the underground manufacture of GHB appears to be continuing. This is due in part to the ready availability and inexpensive nature of the ingredients needed for its formulation. Additionally, it is easy to retrieve instructions or recipes for making the drug directly from the Internet. The convenience of making GHB is further enhanced by numerous illicit websites that offer "kits" containing all the ingredients necessary to make "home-brewed" batches of the drug in clandestine laboratories.

Ketamine

Virtually unknown five to 10 years ago, the popularity of illicit Ketamine has risen dramatically (ONDCP, 1998b). In the 1990s the social-recreational use of Ketamine emerged in the context of a subcultural music phenomenon called "acid house music," a large part of the rave party culture (Dotson, Ackerman, and West, 1995). Ketamine, the only drug discussed here that is approved for medical use in the U. S., is included in the date-rape category due to its ability to pro-

duce amnesia and to disassociate the user from reality.

Ketamine Hydrochloride is a synthetic drug that was produced in 1965 by the University of Michigan in their search for a safe general anesthetic agent. Ketamine was mass produced by Parke-Davis as a "battlefield medicine" during the Vietnam War, as it works quickly to relieve pain but does not depress respiratory and circulatory functions (Farrell, 1998). Today Ketamine which, is also known by its brand names Ketalar or Ketaset, is marketed in the U. S. and in a number of foreign countries as an anesthetic for both human and veterinary medical use (Zukin, 1999). However, approximately 90% of all Ketamine sold legally is for veterinary use (NIDA, 1999). Ketamine is most often used for surgical procedures on animals rather than on humans due to the many adverse side effects associated with this drug, such as visual hallucinations.

Interestingly, the side effects that made Ketamine unpopular as an anesthetic have made it popular as a recreational drug (Farrell, 1998). Ketamine has been described as a "dissociative" anesthetic having hallucinogenic properties similar to PCP and LSD, although these effects do not last as long. Ketamine users interviewed by ethnographers examining local drug abuse situations across the country described the effects of the drug as feeling as though the mind is separate from the body (ONDCP, 1998b). Users in a website discussion have describe the effects of this drug as feeling as close to dying as you can get while still alive. Many Ketamine users report that they feel paralyzed and have a complete break with reality; often the user does not perceive his or her immediate surroundings, including other people.

The popularity of Ketamine is evident in popular culture. Ketamine has been featured on television in an episode of "X-Files" and has been a subject of popular song lyrics (Cloud, 1997). One song by The Chemical Brothers called "Lost in the K-Hole" uses the term "K-Hole" as jargon for a bad trip or a massive sensory deprivation experience detaching the user from reality. Often the bad

Ketamine trip is equated with a "near-death experience" (Cloud, 1997; Fenwick, 1997).

The hallucinogenic effects of Ketamine are typically produced in five to twenty minutes and last approximately one to two hours. Yet, prolonged effects on an individual's senses, judgment, and coordination may be hindered for as long as 18-24 hours (DEA, 1997). A dose-related progression of effects move from a state of dreamy intoxication to delirium accompanied by the inability to move, feel pain, or remember what has occurred while the user was under the drug's influence (ADAW, 1999b). Since the incapacitating effects of Ketamine are similar to the effects of Rohypnol and GHB, it too has the potential for use as a "date rape" drug.

Serious consequences have been reported from illegal use of Ketamine. For instance, in 1999 reports of three deaths due to Ketamine were reported in New Orleans (CEWG, 1999). Similarly, in Detroit, six calls for help as a result of Ketamine overdoses were made to the Poison Control Center between January and June of 1999 (CEWG, 1999). In addition, over 207 Ketamine related hospital emergency room visits have been reported by the DEA (1999). Heart disease, liver disease, seizures, long-term cognitive problems, and fatal respiratory arrest may result from Ketamine use (Wetzstein, 2000). Since Ketamine lowers the heart rate, oxygen starvation to the brain and muscles is possible. Some of the less severe side effects of the drug include nausea, dizziness, and a difficult and unpleasant recovery period.

Despite these potentially dangerous effects of Ketamine, it is increasingly becoming a popular street drug. Generally, youth have experimented with this drug at rave parties or club scenes (Cloud, 1997; Dotson, Ackerman, and West, 1995). The DEA has reported over 500 incidents of sale or use of Ketamine at such parties or college campuses nationwide (DEA, 1999). Reports generated from law enforcement agencies, medical facilities, emergency room visits, and poison control centers have also documented the increased use and abuse of Ketamine (CEWG, 1999).

On the street, Ketamine has been nicknamed Special K, KitKat, Cat Valium, Super Acid, or just "K" (Wetzstein, 2000). It is often found in liquid form, but it has also been baked into a powder or found in the form of pills (Farrell, 1998). In liquid form, the drug is applied to marijuana or tobacco products. Ketamine has also reportedly been used as an alternative to cocaine (CEWG, 1999). The drug can be injected intravenously or intramuscularly, taken orally or nasally (Wetzstein, 2000). Depending on the dosage and the method used for ingesting the drug, the effects can differ widely. As we have seen with Rohypnol and GHB, combining Ketamine with other drugs, including alcohol, can be deadly. The Drug Abuse Warning Network (DAWN) reports that Ketamine is often combined with drugs such as GHB, heroin, cocaine, ecstasy, or marijuana (DEA, 1999).

Ketamine appears to be relatively inexpensive to use, much like Rohypnol and GHB. Depending on the purity of the drug, the market value is approximately $40 to $100 per gram of powder or $50 to $70 per cubic centimeter of liquid—usually sold in vials (DEA, 1997). A "bump" or single dose is sold for approximately $10 to $20 (DEA, 1997; CEWG, 1999).

There has been no documented evidence of a clandestine manufacturer of Ketamine (Woodworth, 1999). The most likely reason for this is that the synthesis of the drug is a very complex process. Thus, all of the Ketamine encountered by law enforcement to date has been diverted or stolen from legitimate sources (Woodworth, 1999). Typically, Ketamine is obtained from burglarized veterinary clinics or illegally obtained through shipments intended for other countries (CEWG, 1999).

The recent upsurge of Ketamine use among youth has spawned legislative action. On August 12, 1999, the Justice Department adopted the recommendation of the Department of Health and Human Services that Ketamine should be classified as a Schedule III drug under the Controlled Substance Act (ADAW, 1999a). Since drug scheduling depends on a drug's potential accepted medical use, Ketamine carries a lower penalty, according to the federal scheduling criteria, than other hallucinogenic drugs without any accepted medical use, such as PCP or LSD (Woodworth, 1999). Thus, possession or sale of PCP and LSD at the state level is generally prosecuted as a more serious, felony crime.

Currently fifteen states (including California, Florida, and Delaware) have followed federal scheduling recommendations and have classified Ketamine into Schedule III at the state level. Missouri and Tennessee have placed Ketamine in Schedule IV, and Massachusetts has placed this drug under the same category as LSD and PCP (Woodworth, 1999). However, in most other states, possession of Ketamine remains a misdemeanor offense. Indeed, since Ketamine, like Rohypnol, does have accepted medical uses, it is difficult to impose strict punishments on offenders for simple possession of the drug.

There have been a few prosecutions involving illegal use of Ketamine. Two men were charged in 1995 with illegal use and alteration of the prescription drug Ketamine (Farley, 1996). Offenders in Minneapolis, New Orleans, and Wayne County, Michigan, have been charged with burglary of veterinary clinics in addition to drug possession charges (CEWG, 1999). As a result of animal hospital burglaries, a variety of medical and veterinary groups are supporting legislation that will increase penalties for such offenses.

There has been only one official report of Ketamine used to facilitate a sexual assault (DEA, 1999). Nevertheless, Ketamine does have the potential for incapacitating unknowing and even voluntary users. It is interesting, however, that this drug has fallen into the "date-rape drug" category despite little evidence thus far that it has been used in that capacity.

Emerging research has begun to inform the paucity of existing knowledge about this drug and its effects. Interestingly, this research has explored some additional medical uses of Ketamine. For instance, studies have been conducted on the use of Ketamine as an aid to psychotherapy (Jansen, 1999). Psychiatrists and researchers at the National Institutes of Mental Health in Maryland believe that the symptoms of schizophrenia are similar to those experienced under the influence of Ketamine. Thus, human subject research with this drug may provide new insights into a treatment for this elusive illness. However valuable this research may prove to be, it can only increase our knowledge about the drug in a controlled setting. It is not likely to address problems associated with recreational use of Ketamine where, for example, it may be used in a club setting and is likely to be combined with alcohol or other drugs.

Thirty-five years after its development, the potential uses and effects of Ketamine are still not well understood. However, with the increase in acceptance among youth, and the link with other date-rape drugs, Ketamine has now entered into the realm of public awareness. This is perhaps the first significant step in furthering our knowledge of the patterns of Ketamine misuse, including recreational usage as well as the potential for use as a date-rape drug.

Conclusion

As the number of drugs that are associated with date-rape scenarios has increased, federal and state lawmakers are becoming more inclined to use tough legislation (ADAW, 1999a). These measures, which have been adopted, target the distributors of the drugs as well as those who use them recreationally or to commit crimes. As mentioned earlier, the Drug-Induced Rape Prevention and Punishment Act and the recent Massachusetts law establishing a new category of crime, "drug-induced kidnaping," intend to more severely punish offenders using a date-rape drug to commit a crime (ADAW, 1998; 1999a).

States have also taken steps to combat the influx of Rohypnol-related problems. For example, in Florida impaired drivers are now screened for Rohypnol intoxication when they appear drunk but register low blood-alcohol levels (CEWG, 1995). And police in Los Angeles County have added a test for the presence of GHB drug to their already routine screening for Rohypnol (Rosenberg and Katel, 1997). In Seattle, emergency rooms are now testing for GHB, and some medical examiners now test for the presence of Rohypnol in drug-related deaths (CEWG,

1999). Similar actions may soon be implemented for other date-rape or club drugs.

It is difficult to speculate as to whether the misuse of Rohypnol, GHB, and Ketamine in the United States is a transient fad or a potential epidemic. Researchers have warned the nation not to underestimate the harm of date-rape and other club drugs, indicating the potential for a new national tragedy (Zickler, 2000). The affordability and extended period of intoxication associated with these drugs may continue to make them attractive to even very young users. Indeed, most accounts point towards increasing use of date-rape drugs in areas where they have already been prevalent and suggest that their popularity is spreading elsewhere (ONDCP, 1998b; NIDA, 1999). And, further, while the specific use of Rohypnol, GHB, and Ketamine for the purpose of rape may not be pervasive, it is a cause for concern.

The increasing knowledge of date-rape drugs brought about through word of mouth, personal experience, or the media may have led others to falsely suspect either Rohypnol, GHB, or Ketamine as the reason for their extreme intoxication or memory impairment. It is important to remember that use of many substances can cause effects similar to those produced by date-rape drugs and that alcohol remains the drug most commonly utilized by sexual predators. In addition, victims of rape (and of most violent crimes) are themselves frequently under the influence of alcohol or other drugs at the time of assault. Moreover, because rape is among the most underreported of all crimes, and testing for Rohypnol, GHB, and Ketamine must be completed shortly after ingestion, it is unlikely that we will ever know the actual extent of the use of these drugs in sexual crimes.

Though the popularity of Rohypnol, GHB, and Ketamine by recreational users appears to be on the rise, it is becoming evident that other drugs with similar psychoactive properties are now being used as substitutes for these drugs. This is most apparent with Rohypnol, due to the drug's increasingly notorious reputation and the stricter penalties associated with its use. A similar phenomenon may occur with GHB, since this drug is currently undergoing much scrutiny. However, because GHB can be easily made by its users, the potential for regulation is not as great. It is more difficult to speculate on Ketamine, since it is the most recent to emerge on the club scene, although like Rohypnol, it is now closely regulated.

The date-rape drugs, Rohypnol, GHB, and Ketamine, have gained the attention of legislators, medical personnel, law enforcement officers, researchers, and parents. We need to continue to collect data on the use and abuse of these drugs and track these patterns throughout the country. We need to express caution to recreational users that they may be using deadly combinations of what they consider to be relatively safe "party" drugs. In addition, we need to stress that these drugs can be addictive, a fact [of] which many young people are unaware (ADAW, 1999a). We need to determine the extent to which these drugs are used to intoxicate, sedate, and incapacitate others. And more specifically, when they are used as a tool by sexual predators. Along these lines, we need to continue to warn people of a potentially dangerous plight in our society: crime facilitated by drugs. And, although drug-related sexual assaults are nothing new, we need to continue to monitor these contemporary trends in age-old problems. At the same time, we should remember that although Rohypnol, GHB, and Ketamine have become known for their use as date-rape drugs, they are abused more frequently for other reasons.

Notes

1. Raves are parties that revolve around music, dancing, and socializing, typically lasting all night. The use of various illicit drugs in nightclub and rave settings have become increasingly popular (ONDCP, 1998). While raves were not originally intended to serve as a nexus for illicit drug sales, the culture surrounding the events has created a favorable environment for these activities (DEA, 2000a).

2. Although correctly pronounced ro-HIP-nol, the drug is commonly mispronounced RU-finol, perhaps lending explanation to the origin of its most popular street name, "roofies." An alternative derivation of the street name credits roof repairers. Many roofers who

moved to Southern Florida after the Hurricane Andrew disaster (often from Mexico) were said to have brought Rohypnol with them and thus may have popularized its use. Additional slang names for Rohypnol include ruffies, rope, roche, rib, and R-2, among others.

3. The use of Rohypnol to facilitate a criminal act can be equated to "slipping someone a Mickey." The Mickey Finn has traditionally been known as "knockout drops"—a powder slipped into liquor to render a bar patron unconscious for the purpose of theft or other criminal intent. A Mickey was formulated with chloral hydrate, also a sedative-hypnotic drug. For a history of the Mickey Finn, see Inciardi, 1977.

4. Rohypnol is often described as "10 times more potent than Valium"; however, this is not a pharmacologically correct comparison. It is unacceptable to compare the two drugs in terms of strength because Rohypnol is a sleeping pill, while Valium is an anti-anxiety drug.

5. A DEA spokesperson explained that U.S. Customs officials were not strict about the prescription requirement and that prescriptions, if evident, were often illegal. Much of the reason for the leniency about prescription drug importation has been related to informal policies adopted by the DEA, U.S. Customs, and the FDA (Federal Drug Administration) allowing anti-viral and cancer drugs that are not available for sale in the U.S. to be brought into the country for treatment of HIV and other illnesses.

6. Although Rohypnol use is most common among youths, other populations are reported to use the drug for varying reasons (see Bond et al., 1994). Heroin users are said to take Rohypnol to enhance the effects of low-quality heroin or methadone and to relieve withdrawal symptoms. Use of Rohypnol for this purpose has been reported by drug users in Spain, Malaysia, and worldwide (DEA, 1995a). Similarly, cocaine users have been found to use Rohypnol to ease the intensity of the "crash" following cocaine and crack binges (Up Front Drug Information Center, 1995; ONDCP, 1998).

7. Package insert for Rohypnol, provided by Hoffman-La Roche & Co. Ltd., Basel, Switzerland.

8. The employment of Rohypnol as a tool in the enactment of crimes other than those of a sexual nature is reported to occur as well. For example, a person may use a Rohypnol tablet to drug a victim prior to a robbery or theft. In Europe, prostitutes have been using Rohypnol to their advantage for years; it is said to be common for sex workers to drop Rohypnol tablets into their clients' drinks and proceed to steal their wallets and other valuables after sedation occurs. (Personal communication with Dr. Zuzana Panisova, General Secretariat of the Board of Ministries for Drug Dependencies and Drug Control, Office of the Government of the Slovak Republic, June 4, 1996.)

References

Alcoholism and Drug Abuse Weekly. (1998) "Federal, state leaders take closer look at date-rape drugs," August 17, 10(32), p. 6.

Alcoholism and Drug Abuse Weekly. (1999a) "NIDA will spearhead club drug prevention effort," December 13, 11(47), p. 3.

Alcoholism and Drug Abuse Weekly. (1999b) "Feds classify Ketamine as controlled substance," August 2, 11(30), p. 7.

Anglin, D., Spears K. L., and Hutson, H. R. (1997) "Flunitrazepam and its involvement in date or acquaintance rape." *Academy of Emergency Medicine* 4(4):323–326.

Asa, J. (1999) "GHB: Grievous Bodily Harm." *The FBI Law Enforcement Bulletin* 68(4):21–25.

Bond, A., Seijas, D., Dawling, S., and Lader, M., (1994) "Systemic absorption and abuse liability of snorted flunitrazepam." *Addiction* 89:821–30.

Bonnin, J. (1997) "Two illegal party drugs leave young Central Texas users vulnerable." *American-Statesman*, February 2, p. E1.

Bradsher, K. (2000) "3 Guilty of manslaughter in date-rape drug case." *The New York Times*, March 15, p. A14.

Calhoun, S., Wesson, D., Galloway, G., and Smith, D. (1996) "Abuse of Flunitrazepam (Rohypnol) and other Benzodiazepines in Austin and South Texas." *Journal of Psychoactive Drugs* 28(2):183–189.

Center on Addiction and Substance Abuse. (1999) *Dangerous Liaisons: Substance Abuse and Sex*. New York: National Center on Addiction and Substance Abuse.

Cloud, John. (1997) "Is your kid on K?" *Time*, 150(16):90–91.

Community Epidemiology Work Group. (1995) *Epidemiological Trends in Drug Abuse: Advance Report*. Rockville, MD: National Institute on Drug Abuse.

——. (1999) *Epidemiological Trends in Drug Abuse: Advance Report*. Rockville, MD: National Institute on Drug Abuse.

Day, K. (1996) "Countering ill effects of an abused drug." *The Washington Post*. p. H1 (2), November 2.

Dotson, J. W., Ackerman, D. L., and West, L. J. (1995) "Ketamine abuse." *Journal of Drug Issues* 25(4):751–757.

Drug Enforcement Administration. (1995a) Flunitrazepam (Rohypnol). *DEA Highlights*. Washington, D.C.: U.S. Department of Justice.

——. (1995b) *National Narcotics Intelligence Consumers Committee 1994: The Supply of Illicit Drugs in the U.S.* Washington, D.C.: U.S. Department of Justice.

——. (1997) *Ketamine Abuse Increasing*. Washington, D.C.: U.S. Department of Justice.

——. (1999) *DEA Press Release: DEA to control "Special K" for the first time*. July 13. Washington, D.C.: U.S. Department of Justice.

——. (2000a) An overview of club drugs. *Drug Intelligence Brief*. February. Washington, D.C.: U.S. Department of Justice.

——. (2000b) *Gamma Hydroxybutyric Acid*. March 23. Washington, D.C.: Office of Diversion Control.

ElSohly, M., and Salamone, S. (1999) "Prevalence of drugs used in cases of alleged sexual assault." *Journal of Analytic Toxicology*, 23(3):141–146.

Farley, D. (1996) "Illegal use of vet drug results in fines, probation." *FDA Consumer* 30(3):28.

Farrell, John S. (1998) "An overview of Ketamine abuse." *The Police Chief* 65(2):47.

Fenwick, P. (1997) "Is the near-death experience only N-Methyl-D-Aspartate blocking? Comments on 'The Ketamine model of the near-death experience' by Dr. K. L. R. Jansen." *Journal of Near-Death Studies* 16(1):43–55.

Fields, T. (1996) "Maker of 'Date Rape Pill' announces plans to fight abuse." *Associated Press*, June 14.

Friend, T. (1996) "Monster drug soon to be on same list as LSD, heroin." *USA Today*, June 20, p. 1A.

Food and Drug Administration. (1999) "FDA warns about products containing Gamma Butyrolactone or GBL and asks companies to issue a recall." *FDA Talk Paper*. Washington, D.C.: FDA.

Galloway, G., Frederick, S., Staggers, F., Gonzales, M., Stalcup, S., and Smith, D. (1997) "Gamma-hydroxybuterate: An emerging drug of abuse that causes physical dependence." *Addiction* 92(1):89–96.

Grudman, N. (1995) "A rise in roofies." *The Independent Florida Alligator*. Gainesville, FL: University of Florida. November 29, p. 3.

Guterman, L. (1998) "Nailing the drug rapists." *New Scientist* 160(2164):4.

Haworth, Karla. (1998) "The growing popularity of a new drug alarms health educators: GHB has been linked to deaths and date-rapes on campuses." *The Chronicle of Higher Education*, p. A31.

Hoffman-La Roche. (1999) Letter from Gail R. Safian, Public Affairs. September 27.

Hopper, L. (1995) "Cheap, strong and easy to get, illegal drug gains popularity." *Austin-American Statesman*, December 18, p. A1.

Inciardi, J. A. (1977) "The changing life of Mickey Finn: Some notes on chloral hydrate down through the ages." *The Journal of Popular Culture* 11(3):591–596.

Jansen, K. L. R. (1999) "Ketamine and quantum psychiatry." *Asylum: Psychedelics and Psychiatry*, 11(3):19–21.

Kidwell, D., and Piloto, C. (1996) "Colorless, odorless pills (roofies) send rape rate soaring." *The Miami Herald*, February 15, p. A7.

Laboy, J. (1995) "'Date rape drug' raises fear in O.C." *The Orange County Register*, p. B1, November 26.

Marwick, C. (1997) "Coma-inducing drug may be reclassified." *Journal of the American Medical Association* 277(19):1505–1506.

National Institute on Drug Abuse. (1995) International research on the epidemiology of drug abuse. *National Institutes of Health Guide*. Vol. 24(2). June 16. Rockville, MD: Department of Health and Human Services.

——. (1999) Club Drugs. *Community Drug Alert Bulletin*. Rockville, MD: Department of Health and Human Services.

——. (1998) Rohypnol and GHB. *NIDA INFOFAX*, Rockville, MD: Department of Health and Human Services.

News Release. (1996). *Remarks by the President at Swearing-in Ceremony for General Barry McCaffrey as Director of the Office of National Drug Control Policy*. Washington, D.C.: Office of the Press Secretary. March 6.

Nichols, Bob. (1997) Personal Communication. Broward County, Florida Prosecutor's Office. February 26.

——. (2000) Personal Communication. Broward County, Florida. April 6.

Nightingale, S. (1991) "Warning about GHB." *Journal of the American Medical Association* 265(14):1802.

Office of National Drug Control Policy. (1996) *The National Drug Strategy: 1996.* Washington, D.C.: Executive Office of the President.

——. (1998a) *Fact Sheet: Rohypnol.* June. Washington, D.C.: Executive Office of the President.

——. (1998b) *Pulse Check: Trends in Drug Abuse—January–June 1998.* Winter. Washington, D.C.: Executive Office of the President.

——. (1999) *Fact Sheet: Gamma Hydrohybutyrate (GHB).* November. Washington, D.C.: Executive Office of the President.

Pazdera, D. (1995) "Official: Drug used in rapes—victims passing out under 'roofies' spell." *Sun-Sentinel,* July 10, p. 1B.

Rickert, V., Wiemann, C., and Berenson, A. (1999) "Prevalence, patterns, and correlates of voluntary Flunitrazepam use." *Pediatrics* 103(1): p. e6.

Rosen, M., Pearsall, H. R. Woods, S., and Kosten, T. (1997) "Effects of GHB in opiod-dependent patients." *Journal of Substance Abuse Treatment,* 14(2):149–154.

Rosenberg, D., and Katel, P. (1997) "Death of the Party." *Newsweek,* October 27, p. 55.

Saum, C. A., and Inciardi, J. A. (1997) "Rohypnol misuse in the United States." *Substance Use and Misuse* 32(6):723–731.

Seligmann, J., and King, P. (1996) "Roofies: The date-rape drug." *Newsweek,* 127(9): February 26, p. 54.

Shephard, M. D., and McKeithan, K. (1995) Examination of the type and amount of pharmaceutical products being declared by U.S. residents upon returning to the U.S. from Mexico at the Laredo-Texas Border Crossing. *Final Paper submitted to the National Association of Chain Drug Stores and the Texas Pharmacological Foundation.* February.

Smith, D. E., Wesson, D. R., and Calhoun, S. (1996) *Rohypnol (Flunitrazepam).* San Francisco, CA: Haight-Ashbury Free Clinic, Inc.

Up Front Drug Information Center. (1994) Information for action: Drug surveillance news. *Dade/Monroe Drug Fax.* Miami, FL: Up Front Drug Information Center. February 28.

Washington Post. (1996) "Import of 'date-rape' pill banned," March 3, p. A2.

Weikel, D. (1996) "'Rape drug' battle rages." *Los Angeles Times,* p. A1, August 19.

Wetzstein, Cheryl. (2000) "Club drugs K.O. the young." *Insight on the news* 16(1):29.

Wilmington News Journal. (1996) "Biden blasts Rohypnol," March 10, p. B6.

Woodworth, Terrance. (1999) *Drug Enforcement Administration: Congressional Testimony.* March 11. Washington, D.C.: U.S. Department of Justice.

Zickler, P. (2000) NIDA launches initiative to combat club drugs. *NIDA NOTES,* 14(6): p. 1.

Zukin, S. (1999). Statement before the Subcommittee on Oversight and Investigations, Committee on Commerce, U.S. House of Representatives, March 11.

For Discussion

Would the number of sexual assaults decline if "date-rape" drugs were no longer available? Why or why not?

27

Circuit Party Attendance, Club Drug Use, and Unsafe Sex in Gay Men

Andrew M. Mattison[a]
Michael W. Ross[b]
Tanya Wolfson[a]
Donald Franklin
HNRC Group[a,1]

Several drugs of choice are associated with particular venues and settings. In this article, Andrew Mattison and his colleagues examine the relationship between drug use and unsafe sex among gay males who attended selected circuit parties. The findings suggest that frequent use of alcohol, MDMA, Ketamine, and other drugs is associated with unsafe sex at circuit parties. However, only one substance—poppers—was associated with unsafe sexual behavior during the 12-month period prior to the study.

Introduction

In most large metropolitan areas, there are several gay clubs (some of which may function primarily on weekends) characterized by dancing, light shows, and live or recorded music played by disk jockeys. In addition, across the US and Canada, circuit parties, events that are usually annual in any location, may attract from 15,000 to 25,000 men

and be characterized by spectacular laser shows, music designed to enhance the effect of the shows, and the drugs commonly taken to enhance the whole experience (Lewis & Ross, 1995). It has been estimated (Electric Dreams Foundation, personal communication) that there are 75 such events per year in the US and Canada. Several years ago, an estimated 150,000 to 200,000 gay men in the US paid for tickets to attend these parties, and ticket sales continue to rise. Since the inception of the parties, a regular "circuit" of the most famous ones has developed. Despite differences in regularity, location, and size, clubs and circuit parties are common venues for the use of "club drugs." The most common of these are methylenedioxymethamphetamine (Ecstasy), ketamine (Special K), methamphetamine (crystal meth), and most recently y-hydroxybutyrate (GHB) (Li et al., 1998), along with more common drugs of abuse such as cocaine, marijuana, and alcohol. In April 2000, the President of the Gay and Lesbian Medical Association called for urgent research on the "devastating results in our emergency rooms" of club drugs, specifically GHB, and noted their "severe increase" (Frontiers Newsmagazine, 2000).

Ostrow (2000) argues that drugs may facilitate HIV-unsafe sexual behaviors by decreasing both anxiety and self-observation, which may otherwise inhibit pleasurable sexual experiences. They may also provide a "scripted" release from internal, social, and peer group norms, thus resulting in more automatic behaviors that are more rewarding because awareness of their consequences is diminished. Using a case-control approach to HIV seroconversion, nitrite and cocaine use were the significant independent risk factors for infection once receptive anal exposures and condom use were controlled for (Ostrow, DiFranceisco, Chmiel, Wagstaff, & Welsch, 1995). Ostrow and McKirnan (1997) argue that taken together, these observations suggest that the association between drug use and unprotected anal sex could account for a significant proportion of new HIV seroconversions taking place in this population of drug-using homosexual men. They also note that the patterns of sexual risk and drug use in this population are clearly *epi-*

sodic rather than *consistent*. Such episodes include circuit parties.

A factor adding to their risk of adverse effects is that drugs are rarely used singly. McNall and Remafedi (1999) conducted an analysis of data derived from nine annual cross-sectional surveys on 877 young (< 21) homosexual and bisexual men in Minneapolis-St. Paul. Clustering study subjects into groups by drug use revealed three distinct clusters of drug users: those who primarily used alcohol; those who used mostly alcohol and marijuana; and those who used cocaine, alcohol, marijuana, and a variety of other substances. These data are consistent with those of Chesney, Barrett, and Stall (1998) on homosexual male HIV seroconverters in San Francisco. They followed a sample of 337 baseline HIV-negative men for 6 years, controlling for needle use, and reported that men who have sex with men (MSM) who seroconverted were consistently likely to report use of marijuana, volatile nitrites ("poppers"), amphetamines, and cocaine than were matched MSM who did not seroconvert. Chesney et al. suggest that the mechanisms leading to seroconversion may include (1) stimulants and inhalants increasing arousal and delaying ejaculation, (2) the disinhibitory effects of substance use, and (3) substance abuse and high-risk sexual behavior occurring within long-standing social networks, so that sexual mixing in such networks results in increased seroconversion if unprotected anal intercourse is a norm and there is a high background prevalence of HIV (Chesney et al., 1998).

Apart from the largely qualitative work of Lewis and Ross (1995) on drug use and HIV risk behavior in circuit parties, there are no research data on the prevalence of use of club drugs, the demographics of men who attend circuit parties, or the association of club drugs with unsafe sex. We present a preliminary report on these questions.

Methods

The first author collected data at three major circuit parties in North America in 1998–1999 in diverse geographical areas of the country. The estimated attendance of the three parties, all of which were held over holiday weekends, were 25,000, 15,000 and 10,000, respectively. All data collection was undertaken with the active support of the party producers and based on a two-page, 16-item questionnaire derived from 24 preliminary interviews with party patrons and previous research. It took on average 3 min to complete and was distributed by patron volunteers approaching patrons with the questionnaire on a clipboard at several occasions over the 3-day circuit party events. These occasions were included at Party 1: in the line to the coat-check (the party was in the north during winter) on the first night, in a booth in the exhibition hall between 11 pm and 2 am on the second night, and at the "morning after" party. At Party 2, patrons were approached during the beach party (this party was in the south) in daytime, at the hotel party ticket pick-up line, and from a table at the entrance to the late night party. At Party 3, patrons were approached in the line at the party hotel for ticket pick-up, and at poolside (this party was in the west) during the 3 days of the event. It was estimated that the refusal rate was between 1% and 5%; 15 uncompleted, discarded questionnaires were from the 11 pm–2 am data collection at Party 1, where some patrons were apparently chemically incapacitated. There was no incentive provided and if respondents were approached more than once, they indicated previous completion of the instrument. A total of 1169 usable questionnaires were obtained, which were entered into SPSSx (SPSS, Chicago, IL) and S-PLUS (Statistical Sciences, Seattle, WA) for statistical analysis. The anonymous questionnaire sought information on demographics, reasons for party attendance, number of circuit parties attended, number of sexual partners, and drug use and unsafe sex both during and outside of circuit parties.

Analyses

The data were subject to calculation of simple frequencies and percentages. A binary measure of unsafe sex was computed from the questions asking for number of instances of unprotected anal insertive and receptive sex in the past 12 months. Levels of unsafe sex in the past 12 months were also cross-tabulated with drugs individually, and Pearson χ^2 Tests were used to evaluate the relationship between the two variables. A multivariate logistic regression was also performed, predicting unsafe sex from binary measures (yes/no) of reported use of eight club drugs: alcohol, Ecstasy, Special K, cocaine, crystal meth, GHB, marijuana, and poppers. Odds ratios were computed for each of the predictor drugs. We also obtained another measure for unprotected anal sex. This new measure targeted behavior at parties (rather than in the past 12 months overall) and was in conjunction with the use of specific drugs. Party patrons were dichotomized based on this measure, and we used Pearson χ^2 Tests to evaluate the relationship between patrons who did and did not have unsafe sex and their levels of reported drug use at the parties (occasional vs. frequent). Since patrons were not asked about unsafe sexual behavior at the party if they did not use a particular drug, for this analysis, a comparison with nonusers was not possible. Similar analyses (Pearson χ^2 Test) were performed to evaluate the relationship between unsafe sex in the past 12 months and reasons reported for attending the circuit party. Bonferroni correction for multiple testing was applied in all χ^2 analyses.

Results

The demographic summary of party patrons is presented in Table 27.1. It shows that, on average, one is dealing with a relatively wealthy and well-educated cohort at circuit parties. Looking at HIV serostatus,

80% of those interviewed were HIV-negative, 13% HIV-positive, 4% had been tested but did not know, and 3% had never been tested.

Over half of the party patrons reported use of alcohol (79%), Ecstasy (72%), and Special K (60%) at parties in the past 12 months. Over a third reported using cocaine (39%), crystal meth (36%), poppers (39%), and marijuana (45%) in the same time period. Over a quarter had used GHB (28%). Reasons reported for circuit party attendance were (strongly agree) (1) to celebrate, have fun (97%); (2) to dance, enjoy music (97%); (3) to be with friends (95%); (4) to escape from usual day-to-day routines (84%); (5) to look and feel good (86%); (6) to have an intense gay experience (73%); (7) to be wild and uninhibited (68%); (8) to party, use drugs (58%); (9) to have sex (43%); and (10) to forget about HIV/AIDS (14%).

The relationship between each of the party drugs and unsafe sexual behavior at the party while under the influence of these drugs was evaluated by a set of χ^2 tests. After the Bonferroni correction was applied, only P-values lower than .0125 were considered significant. Our data show that *at the party,* unsafe sexual behavior was significantly associated with frequent (as opposed to occasional) use of Ecstasy (χ^2 = 6.37, *df* = 1, P-value = .01), Special K (χ^2 = 6.66, *df* = 1, P-value = .01), and poppers (χ^2 = 7.30, *df* = 1, P-value = .01). There was no significant association between unsafe sexual behavior and frequent use of any of the other party drugs (Table 27.2).

When levels of unsafe sex in the past 12 months were univariately cross-tabulated with drug use at circuit parties (no use vs.

Table 27.1

Demographic Summary of Circuit Party Patrons

Mean age (S.D.)	33.5 years (6.5)
% with Bachelor's degree or higher	68
% Caucasian	76
% with annual income of US$50,000 or more	50
% with boyfriend or partner	49
Median length of relationship (where exists)	2 years

Table 27.2

Drugs Used and Unsafe Sex While Using

Substance	Unsafe sex		χ^2	P-value
	No	Yes		
Alcohol			5.75	0.02
Sometimes	290	44		
Often	239	62		
Ecstasy			6.37	0.01
Sometimes	250	26		
Often	245	50		
Special K			6.66	0.01
Sometimes	199	16		
Often	192	36		
Cocaine			0.10	0.75
Sometimes	194	23		
Often	53	8		
Crystal meth			4.67	0.03
Sometimes	146	24		
Often	73	25		
GHB/GLB			0.31	0.58
Sometimes	107	20		
Often	56	14		
Marijuana			2.64	0.11
Sometimes	185	17		
Often	76	14		
Poppers			7.30	0.01
Sometimes	159	30		
Often	52	24		

any amount of use), only poppers showed a significant association (χ^2 = 8.33, df = 1, P-value = .004). Recall that this is now a different measure of unsafe sex, which covers the entire 12 months, including but not limited to behavior at parties. The logistic regression summary in Table 27.3 presents coefficients and odds ratios (exponentials of the coefficients) for predicting unsafe sex by the use of party drugs. Only poppers show a statistically significant association with unsafe sexual activity in the past 12 months. The P-values for GHB and crystal meth show a trend, although the odds ratios are not high and their confidence intervals straddle one, suggesting that the increase in odds is not noteworthy.

We also looked at the relationship between reasons for attending circuit parties and unsafe sex in the past 12 months. Participants were asked to strongly agree, agree, disagree, or strongly disagree with 10 possible reasons for attending. We dichotomized the answers into agree/strongly agree and disagree/strongly disagree groups. After the Bonferroni correction, three reasons showed a significant association with unsafe sex in the past 12 months: to Have Sex (χ^2 = 7.82, df = 1, P-value = .005), to be Uninhibited and Wild (χ^2 = 19.76, df = 1, P-value < .0000), and to Look and Feel Good: χ^2 = 6.39, df = 1, P-value = .012). Since party patrons overwhelmingly agreed that they attended parties "to celebrate," "to be with friends," and "to dance and enjoy music," it was difficult to determine unsafe sex patterns specific to these reasons.

Discussion

These data offer a closer look at the relationship between substance use and unsafe sex in a group of circuit party patrons who are well educated and economically com-

Table 27.3

Logistic Regression Summary: Unsafe Sex Predicted by Club Drug Use

	Coefficient	P-value	Odds ratio	95% CI
Alcohol	0.122	0.307	1.13	(0.70, 1.81)
Ecstasy	−0.380	0.075	0.68	(0.41, 1.15)
Special K	−0.270	0.157	0.76	(0.45, 1.29)
Cocaine	0.241	0.145	1.27	(0.82, 1.99)
Crystal Meth	0.333	0.085	1.40	(0.87, 2.24)
GHB/GLB	0.368	0.064	1.45	(0.90, 2.32)
Marijuana	0.097	0.317	1.10	(0.74, 1.64)
Poppers	0.540	0.004	1.72	(1.16, 2.55)

fortable. These patrons are part of a "party circuit," with multiple party attendance and drug use being the norm. It is interesting that the reasons for party attendance appeared to also predict unsafe sexual behavior, with attending "to have sex," to be "uninhibited and wild," and "to look and feel good" all predicting higher levels of unsafe sexual behavior. However, the reasons for party attendance were overwhelmingly related to nonsexual and nondrug desires of community, enjoyment, and celebration. These data show a remarkably similar picture to the work of Lewis and Ross (1995) on Sydney circuit parties but in addition provide some quantitative assessment of the prevalence of drug use and the risks associated with particular drugs.

It is apparent that reported unsafe sexual behavior in this sample is relatively low, at 15% in the past 12 months including at circuit parties. Drug use prevalence in the past 12 months was high, with over half of the sample using alcohol, Ecstasy, or ketamine at circuit parties. However, between a quarter and a third of participants surveyed used other potentially dangerous drugs (GHB, crystal methamphetamine, and cocaine). Of particular concern was the fact that for multiple drug use (including alcohol), the modal number was four drugs used (not necessarily concurrently) at circuit parties in the past year. The data suggest a dose-response relationship between number of drugs used and unsafe sex, with 10% of those using just one drug reporting unsafe sex in the past 12 months compared with 26% of those who had used seven or eight drugs. It is probably a reasonable conjecture that not only is it likely that users of multiple drugs are less likely to be able to predict or control drug interactions but also that as the number of drugs used simultaneously increases, disinhibition and amnesia may increase. From the data, poppers appear to be most closely associated with unsafe sex in the past year: these data are consistent with previous data on poppers, which are used specifically in association with sex.

These data should be interpreted with several cautions in mind. This was a nonrandom sample of convenience and it was not possible to discern an association between drug use and unsafe sex *at the party*, because data were not available for unsafe sex *at circuit parties* in nondrug users. However, these data *were* available for unsafe sex in the past 12 months and provide a crude index of risk. Our conservative measure of unsafe sex may underestimate risk, but because we were not able to separate out risky behavior in mutually monogamous and HIV-seroconcordant relationships, this may conversely bias toward overestimation. Nonresponse data were excluded from the computation of percentages, possibly biasing the results. We are not able to estimate whether the voluntary nonrandom nature of this survey may have led to any bias toward (or against) drug use in the sample. Nevertheless, there are no published data available on the circuit party phenomenon and its patrons in the US. These data indicate that patrons tend to be well educated and financially secure.

It is apparent that some drugs are associated with elevated risk of unsafe sex in addition to the morbidity and possibly mortality associated with the drugs. Multiple drug use is a particular concern and we believe from these preliminary data that a case can be made for increased research, including a focus on interventions to reduce both drug and sexual risk, in the circuit party subpopulation of gay men.

Acknowledgements

The HIV Neurobehavioral Research Center (HNRC) is supported by Center award P50-MH 45294 from NIMH.

Notes

a. HIV Neurobehavioral Research Center, University of California at San Diego, 150 W. Washington, San Diego, CA 92103, USA

b. WHO Center for Health Promotion and Prevention Research, School of Public Health, University of Texas-Houston Health Science Center, PO Box 20036, Houston, TX 77225, USA

1. The San Diego HIV Neurobehavioral Research Center [HNRC] group is affiliated with the University of California–San Diego, the Naval Hospital San Diego, and the San Diego Veterans Affairs Healthcare System and includes: Igor Grant, MD (Director); J. Hampton Atkinson, MD and J. Allen McCutchan, MD (Co-Directors); Thomas D. Marcotte, PhD (Center Manager); Naval Hospital San Diego: Mark R. Wallace, MD (P.I.); Neuromedical Component: J. Allen McCutchan, MD (P.I.), Ronald J. Ellis, MD, Scott Letendre, MD, Rachel Schrier, PhD; Neurobehavioral Component: Robert K. Heaton, PhD (P.I.), Mariana Cherner, PhD, Julie Rippeth, PhD; Imaging Component: Terry Jernigan, PhD (P.I.), John Hesselink, MD; Neuropathology Component: Eliezer Masliah, MD (P.I.); Clinical Trials Component: J. Allen McCutchan, MD, J. Hampton Atkinson, MD, Ronald J. Ellis, MD, PhD, Scott Letendre, MD; Data Management Unit: Daniel R. Masys, MD (P.I.), Michelle Frybarger, BA (Data Systems Manager); Statistics Unit: Ian Abramson, PhD (P.I.), Reena Deutsch, PhD, Tanya Wolfson, MA.

References

Chesney, M. A., Barrett, D. C., & Stall, R. (1998). Histories of substance abuse and risk behavior: precursors to HIV seroconversion in homosexual men. *American Journal of Public Health 88*, 113–116.

———. Dying to party. *Frontiers Newsmagazine 18* (25), p. 30.

Lewis, L. A., & Ross, M. W. (1995). *A select body: the gay dance party subculture and the HIV/AIDS pandemic.* London: Cassell.

Li, J., Stokes, S. A., & Woeckener, A. (1998). A tale of novel intoxication: seven cases of y-hydroxybutyric acid overdose. *Annals of Emergency Medicine 31*, 723–728.

McNall, M., & Remafedi, G. (1999). Relationship between amphetamine and other substance use to unprotected intercourse among young men who have sex with men. *Archives of Pediatrics and Adolescent Medicine 153*, 1130–1135.

Ostrow, D. G. (2000). The role of drugs in the sexual lives of men who have sex with men: continuing barriers to researching this question. *AIDS and Behavior 4*, 205–219.

Ostrow, D. G., DiFranceisco, W. J., Chmiel, J. S., Wagstaff, D. A., & Wesch, J. (1995). A case-control study of human immunodeficiency virus type 1 seroconversion and risk-related behaviors in the Chicago MACS/CCS Cohort, 1984–1992. *American Journal of Epidemiology 142*, 875–883.

Ostrow, D. G., & McKirnan, D. (1997). Prevention of substance-related high-risk sexual behavior among gay men: critical review of the literature and proposed harm reduction approach. *Journal of the Gay and Lesbian Medical Association 1*, 97–110.

For Discussion

Could this study be applicable outside of the gay community? Are any of the motivations for attending circuit parties the same reasons that individuals attend clubs and bars on any given weekend?

28

Ketamine Injection Among High Risk Youth

Preliminary Findings From New York City

Stephen E. Lankenau
Michael C. Clatts

Most studies of injecting drug users are based primarily on heroin users. However, as this article shows, injecting drug users do not represent a homogeneous group. Stephen E. Lankenau and Michael C. Clatts conduct research into Ketamine injectors and find that members of this group differ from what is known about heroin injectors. For example, Ketamine users often inject several times during the same episode, and the social setting in which Ketamine users inject often includes several other injectors. The authors also observe that a number of Ketamine injectors frequently lend or borrow drug paraphernalia from other IDUs. All of these behaviors can increase the possibility of the transmission of infectious disease, including HIV.

Introduction

Ketamine, also known as Special K, or K, is among the several illicit substances recently classified as "club drugs." Ketamine and other so-called club drugs, such as MDMA and GHB, are synthetic substances that are consumed to alter a user's experience within a recreational setting (Curran & Morgan, 2000; Reynolds, 1997). Among these drugs, ketamine is particularly noteworthy because it is commonly administered in multiple

ways. Ketamine is sold illicitly in pill, powder, and liquid form, and it may be swallowed, drunk, smoked, sniffed, and injected (Jansen, 2001). In this article, we describe a small sample of young ketamine injectors living in New York City to highlight the current social and behavioral practices associated with ketamine injection—practices that may place ketamine injectors at risk for infectious diseases.

Ethnographic research that specifically examines injection drug using practices can lead to important discoveries about viral transmission and harm reduction strategies. While the sharing of syringes has been long identified as a primary means of transmitting HIV (Des Jarlais, Friedman, & Stoneburner, 1988), more recently, ancillary injection paraphernalia, such as "cookers," water, heat sources, and filters, have been found to be additional sources of risk for bloodborne pathogens. For instance, based upon ethnographic interviews and observations of heroin injectors preparing both tar and powder heroin in cookers, Clatts et al. (1999) found that tar heroin required longer exposure to a heat source before dissolving in water. Subsequent laboratory studies modeling these findings revealed that heating heroin solutions in a cooker for 15 seconds or more reduced HIV-1 viability below detectable levels.

Similarly, this article uses qualitative interviews to understand infectious disease risk associated with ketamine injection by focusing on specific injection events among a sample of young drug injectors. As this study demonstrates, ketamine injectors utilize a different series of injection practices and different types of paraphernalia compared to other types of injection drug use, such as heroin. Consequently, ketamine injection practices may pose new or different kinds of injection risks.

Ketamine: A Brief History

Ketamine was developed in the United States in 1962 and later patented by Parke-Davis in 1966. Marketed under trade names such as Ketaset and Ketaject, ketamine was promoted as a fast-acting general anesthetic. Ketamine became the most widely used battlefield anesthetic during the Vietnam War (Siegel, 1978) and was approved by the Food and Drug Administration (FDA) for use among children and elderly in 1970. Gradually, ketamine became used less in medical settings after clinical administrations revealed certain complications in some patients, such as vivid dreaming, hallucinations, and confused states (Fine, Weissman, & Finestone, 1974; Perel & Davidson, 1976). Currently, ketamine is dispensed primarily by veterinarians as an animal sedative (Curran & Morgan, 2000). It is also administered to humans by physicians under certain medical circumstances, such as treating postoperative (Nikolajsen, Hansen, & Jensen, 1997) and chronic pain (Fine, 1997) and sedating pediatric patients (Green et al., 1999). In both veterinary and hospital settings, ketamine is administered via injection and is purchased from pharmaceutical companies where it is manufactured as a liquid.

While recreational ketamine use became increasingly popular in the United States and Europe in the last decade, the non-medical use of ketamine extends back to the mid-1960s. Ketamine was dispensed by underground "medicinal chemists" from Michigan as early as 1967 (Jansen, 2001), while solutions of ketamine were sold on the streets in Los Angeles and San Francisco in 1971 (Siegel, 1978). By the late 1970s, the FDA released a report on ketamine abuse, and the National Institutes on Drug Abuse (NIDA) published a monograph on phencyclidine that included an article on ketamine intoxication (Jansen, 2001). Recreational ketamine use—sniffing in particular—became more widespread during the late 1980s and early 1990s in combination with new types of dance music played at house parties and raves (Dotson, Ackerman, & West, 1995). In 1997, New York State passed a law criminalizing the sale or possession of ketamine. Following reports of the sale, theft, and abuse of ketamine, the Drug Enforcement Administration (DEA) placed ketamine into schedule III of the Controlled Substance Act (CSA) in August 1999. Upon being listed as a Schedule III

drug, it became illegal in the United States to possess ketamine for recreational or nonmedical purposes. In New York State, for instance, the possession of ketamine is a misdemeanor offense, which can carry penalties of six months in jail and a $1,000 fine.

There has been some confusion in classifying ketamine in relation to more common illicit drugs, such as MDMA and LSD, since ketamine can produce a range of experiences depending upon dosage. Ketamine can be a stimulant in low doses and can also cause potent psychedelic experiences in moderate and high doses. It has been described as a "dissociative anesthetic," meaning the drug causes users to feel both sedated and separated from their bodies (Jansen, 2001), yet the drug is not a depressant. Rather, ketamine is a derivative of phencyclidine, or PCP, and both are chemical compounds known as arylcyclohexylamines. Like PCP, ketamine stimulates the vital functions of heartbeat and respiration, though ketamine is less toxic and shorter acting than PCP (Weil & Rosen, 1983).

While no epidemiological studies currently exist detailing the extent of the nonmedical use of ketamine or the modes of administering it, a 1999 report on drug use in 21 U.S. cities and metropolitan areas reported ketamine use in eight cities while intramuscular injections of ketamine were reported in three of those cities—Boston, New Orleans, and Minneapolis/St. Paul (CEWG, 1999). In an updated 2000 report, eight additional cities or metropolitan areas reported ketamine use, including two cities—New York and Seattle—that reported ketamine injection, though intramuscular versus intravenous injections were not specified (CEWG, 2000). Additionally, intravenous injections of ketamine have been reported among small samples of users (Jansen, 2001; Siegal, 1977) and single individuals (Lilly, 1978). Collectively, these recent reports and older accounts suggest that ketamine use—injection in particular—is occurring in cities across the United States. In particular, as we report in this article, injecting ketamine is an emerging practice among youth that carries certain risks for viral transmission. However, these risks have not been described or examined in previous studies.

Methods and Sample

We first learned that youths were injecting ketamine in New York City while conducting ethnographic research on two other at-risk populations—young men who have sex with men (YMSM) and injection drug users who shoot crack cocaine. In the course of interviewing injection drug users from these two populations, and during conversations with outreach workers who served these populations, we learned that ketamine injection was occurring among street-involved youth. Upon realizing the potential risks associated with ketamine injection practices, we initiated an exploratory study focused on high risk youth who injected ketamine.

Our data was gathered by the lead author who recruited 25 ketamine injectors (n = 25) from street and park settings in Manhattan's East and West Villages. To qualify for an interview, a youth had to meet two criteria: aged between 18 and 25 years old and had ever injected ketamine. Upon meeting the criteria, each youth agreed to a 30-minute, semi-structured interview focusing on the details of their most recent ketamine injection, the effects of injecting ketamine, and their history of ketamine and other injection drug use. Hence, our sample constitutes an active drug using, out-of-treatment, youth population.

Table 28.1 presents the sample demographics of the 25 ketamine injectors recruited into the study. The youths were typically in their early 20s, white, and male. We use the term "street involvement" to describe a particular relationship between youths and informal economic generating activities, such as drug dealing, sex work, and panhandling, or structural housing circumstances, such as homelessness. However, these categories are not mutually exclusive. Nearly all of the youth interviewed were connected to the street economy in some manner, which ultimately had implications for their ketamine use.

Findings

Polydrug Use

The majority of the youth in the sample were injection drug users, or had experimented with injection drug use, prior to injecting ketamine for the first time. The median age at injection initiation of any drug was 17 years old. Over half of the sample (56%) initiated injection drug use with a substance other than ketamine, such as heroin, cocaine, or methamphetamine. However, a relatively large proportion (44%) of the youth began their drug injection career with ketamine. The median age at ketamine injection initiation was 18 years old. Hence, youths were slightly older when they began injecting ketamine compared to other injection drugs.

As the sample's history of injection drug use suggests, these ketamine injectors were polydrug users. Heroin, cocaine, crack, PCP, MDMA, LSD, methamphetamine, and marijuana were drugs commonly used by these young injectors in the months prior to being interviewed. In fact, 56% of the sample used one or more of these drugs before, during, or after their most recent injection of ketamine. However, equally significant is that 44% of

Table 28.1

Sample Demographics

Age	Median	N
Range 18–25	21	25
Race/Ethnicity	**%**	**N**
African-American/Black	8	2
Caucasian/White	64	16
Latino/Hispanic	24	6
Native American	4	1
Gender	**%**	**N**
Male	92	23
Female	8	2
Street Involvement	**%**	**N**
Homeless	44	11
Sex Work	36	9
Drug Dealing	32	8
Panhandling	20	5

the sample did not use any other drugs in addition to ketamine during their most recent injection. In other words, ketamine was the drug of choice for a number of users during a specific drug injection event.

In addition to injecting ketamine, 80% of the youth had sniffed ketamine during their drug-using careers. Youths reported several advantages of injecting ketamine over sniffing the drug: some found that sniffing aggravated their nasal passages and that injecting produced a "cleaner" high; others who developed a tolerance to ketamine from sniffing found that injecting was a more potent and reliable mode of administering the drug. It is noteworthy that 20% (or five youth) had never sniffed ketamine—a more common mode of administering the drug—and had only injected ketamine. In fact, these five youth had all initiated their injection drug use career with either heroin or cocaine prior to their first time injecting ketamine. Additionally, all five injected ketamine intravenously during their last ketamine injection event. This finding indicates that a user's preferred mode of administering certain drugs, like heroin or cocaine, is often transferred to administering a new drug, such as ketamine.

K-Hole

Many injectors reported that a primary reason for injecting ketamine was to "fall into" or achieve a "k-hole." A k-hole is a general term that injectors applied to the intense psychological and somatic state experienced while under the influence of ketamine. K-holes were more reliably achieved—and more intensely experienced—by injecting the drug. After injecting ketamine, users reported feeling a momentary rush of energy followed by physical immobilization and social detachment for the duration of the experience, which could last from 10 to 60 minutes, depending upon the dosage. A k-hole is characterized by a distorted sense of space, such as a small room appearing the size of a football field, and an indistinct awareness of time, such as a few minutes seeming like an hour. As a user's body slowed and disengaged from everyday conceptions of time and space, his or her mind tuned into

often pleasant—though sometimes bizarre—experiential realms, such as spiritual journeys, interactions with famous or fictitious persons, and hallucinatory visions. Once the drug was processed by the body, however, users reported that the k-hole ended rather abruptly but could be quickly reentered following another injection of ketamine.

Injection Risk Factors

Figure 28.1 displays several factors present during the youths' last ketamine injection episode that placed them at risk for viral transmission. First, ketamine was almost always injected in a group setting among other injectors. Youths reported that these injection groups were as large as 10 people. Large injection groups pose risks (particularly when paraphernalia is shared) since greater numbers of injectors increase the odds that someone in the group is infected with HIV or hepatitis. Second, multiple injections of ketamine were typical, such as 8 to 10 injections over a period of several hours. Multiple injections increase the likelihood that injection paraphernalia will be shared—particularly when the drug injected is one that produces feelings of disorientation. Third, over half of the injectors reported some form of paraphernalia sharing, such as syringes or bottles of ketamine, but most commonly a bottle of ketamine. Liquid ketamine is typically packaged in a sealed 10 cc bottle with a flat rubber lid that is designed to be pierced by a needle point. Youths reported that two or more injectors would pull shots of ketamine from the same common bottle over the course of administering multiple injections of ketamine. Fourth, a relatively large proportion (though less than half) of injectors obtained their syringe from an indirect source, such as a friend who received needles from a needle exchange, a person on the street selling syringes, or an unfamiliar member of the injection group. Injectors who obtain syringes from such indirect sources increase the possibility of obtaining a used or tainted syringe. Fifth, ketamine was frequently obtained for free—a fact suggesting that ketamine is a social or "party drug." Youths who reported receiving ketamine for free indicated that the injection

Figure 28.1

Risk Factors During Last Ketamine Injection Episode (N = 25)

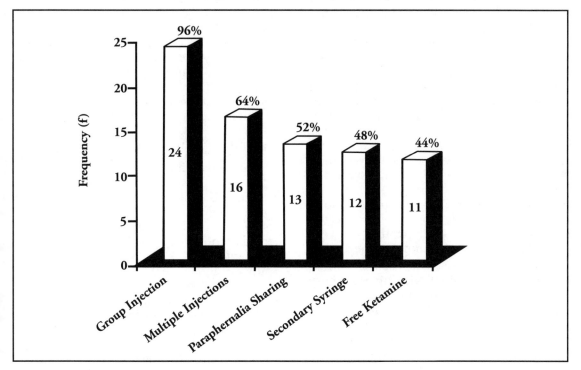

that followed was often spontaneous. During these unplanned drug injection events, youths reported forgoing certain precautions, such as bringing their own injection paraphernalia to the injection setting.

At the time of the youths' most recent injection, the drug was injected both intramuscularly (68%) and intravenously (32%). As noted earlier, intravenous injectors typically had injected other drugs previous to ketamine, such as heroin or cocaine, and were accustomed to intravenous drug injections. The intramuscular ketamine injectors were either new injection drug users who did not want to inject the drug intravenously or were intravenous drug users who were initiated into ketamine injection by an injection group who administered the drug intramuscularly. Shooting ketamine intramuscularly produced a slower-acting, longer high, whereas administering ketamine intravenously led to a quicker, shorter high. Intravenous injections pose a greater risk for viral

transmission than intramuscular injections since intramuscular injections typically do not pull blood into the needle or syringe.

Patterns of Ketamine Use

The frequency of injecting ketamine within the past year varied widely among the youth. For instance, 20% had injected ketamine only one time within the past year, while another 12% had injected ketamine 100 times or more (n = 4 cases or 16% were missing). Although, 10 was the median number of injections within the past year, or less than once per month. This variability in the number of ketamine injections within the past year reveals two primary facts about ketamine injection and ketamine use.

First, the dynamics surrounding injecting ketamine along with the pharmacological effects of the drug produced a range of experiences that some users found disturbing and impacted upon levels of use. Among youth who injected ketamine only one time in the past year were those who were reluctant to become regular users of drug injection paraphernalia, while others found the effects of ketamine unpleasant, which included vomiting. However, the great majority injected the drug multiple times in the past year—suggesting that most found the experience pleasurable and intriguing. Second, the number of ketamine injections in the past year was also impacted by the availability of the drug. Most reported that the supply of ketamine—particularly liquid ketamine—was variable so that a month or two might pass when the drug was very difficult to obtain. During these dry periods, youths reported injecting ketamine less frequently. In contrast, youths who had a steady supply of ketamine as a result of dealing the drug injected ketamine more frequently in the past year than those youth that did not deal the drug.

During the youths' most recent injection, ketamine was obtained via three primary ways: received from friends for free, obtained as a result of dealing ketamine themselves, or bought from a drug dealer. Dealers obtained ketamine from two main sources: veterinarian offices, where it was stolen or diverted, or Mexico, where it was manufactured and packaged into 10 cc bottles, and could be purchased without a prescription. After obtaining bottles or cases of bottles, dealers sold bottles of liquid ketamine, known as a "lick," or converted it into powder by heating the liquid until it became crystallized. In New York City, bottles of ketamine sold for between $60 and $80, while one bottle could be converted into powder valued at $200 or more.

The majority of youths (72%) reported that their most recent injection of ketamine occurred in New York City (80% when including suburban New Jersey). Other cities where the most recent injection occurred included Portland, Oregon; San Francisco; and rural locations in West Virginia and Montana during outdoor raves. However, this sample population is more mobile than these findings suggest. Including these five sites outside of New York City, youths reported injecting ketamine on other occasions in more than 35 cities and locations across the United State—large cities like Los Angeles and Seattle, but also smaller cities, such as Asheville, North Carolina and Grand Rapids, Michigan. These reports indicate that ketamine is injected across a much broader area than indicated by the current epidemiological data (CEWG, 1999; CEWG, 2000). Additionally, these findings point to the mobility of the youth population under study. Many youth traveled from city to city as a result of homelessness, while others traveled to visit friends or attend raves in other cities.

Ketamine: A Club Drug?

The convention of labeling ketamine as "club drug," while capturing the fact that ketamine is commonly consumed in a social environment, does not accurately locate the settings where ketamine was most often injected among these youth. In fact, only 16% of the injections occurred at raves (more typically outdoor raves), and another 8% happened at indoor house parties. Instead, the most common setting was a street or park (36%), and another 8% injected ketamine inside a public bathroom. The remaining 32% injected inside an apartment or house among groups of injectors numbering between two and six persons. Additionally, after injecting ketamine in these typical settings, none of the youths reported attending a club or rave. (It should be noted that all of the youths had attended raves or clubs on other occasions.) Rather, the youths reported that injecting ketamine often created an experience in its own right that did not require a specialized setting, such as a rave. Interestingly, relatively mundane activities typically followed the injection or injections of ketamine, such as listening to music, watching television, walking the streets, talking about the high, consuming other drugs, or sleeping. Hence, these findings suggest that ketamine is injected recreationally in a variety of settings and is typically injected and experienced apart from the club or rave environs.

Discussion

Our findings indicate that ketamine injectors are an important population of young injection drug users worthy of further study.

For as we report, the injection practices, injection groups, and use norms surrounding ketamine differ from heroin, cocaine, crack, and methamphetamine injection drug use: intramuscular injections were more common than intravenous injections; injection groups were often large; multiple injections within a single episode were common; bottles rather than cookers were shared; and the drug was often obtained for free. These findings suggest that the drug injection practices among ketamine injectors place themselves at risk for bloodborne pathogens, such as HIV, HBV, and HCV.

Additional research is necessary to follow young ketamine injectors longitudinally to learn whether, and under what circumstances, they transition to injecting other drugs. The majority of the youths in this sample had injected other drugs prior to ketamine injection initiation, but a large proportion began their injection drug use career with ketamine. The availability and supply of ketamine, which varies over the course of a year, may be an important factor in explaining the transition from ketamine injection to other injection drug use. Additionally, the type of ketamine available to users, such as powder versus liquid, may affect the transition from sniffing to injecting ketamine.

More research is needed to examine how the injection practices and injection groups among young ketamine injectors compare in different cities and locations. For as we indicated, New York City is only one of many cities where youth reported injecting ketamine. We anticipate variability in risk practices across settings since ketamine injection is a relatively new phenomenon and information about how to inject ketamine is diffuse among users.

We also indicated that involvement in the street economy—homelessness, drug dealing, and sex work—was common among this sample of young ketamine injectors. Future studies need to examine how the contingencies surrounding marginalized street existences, such as relationships with sex work partners and within drug dealing networks, affect trajectories into ketamine injection. Additionally, focusing on street-involved

youth populations, such as ketamine injectors, is likely to yield information on emerging drug trends since youth are frequently enmeshed in varied drug-using and drug-selling networks.

We reported that a large proportion of users did not combine ketamine with other drugs. Rather, they injected only ketamine during their most recent ketamine injection event. This finding should temper certain assumptions about club drug use—that drugs, such as ketamine, are always or frequently used in combination with other drugs, such as MDMA and GHB, to create a synergistic drug experience. In particular, ketamine injection should not be viewed as synonymous with other club drug use, nor viewed as presenting the same health risks as other club drugs.

Likewise, calling ketamine a "club drug" may be a misnomer. The youths in this study largely reported injecting ketamine in settings other than clubs or raves. Whether due to the disorienting effects of injecting ketamine, the stigma often attached to injection drug use, or the pressure from law enforcement to police and sometimes close clubs, ketamine is most often injected in private dwellings. In other words, ketamine use—at least ketamine injection—has moved outside of the club environs and has become a recreational practice similar to (though not nearly as widespread) smoking marijuana or ingesting LSD.

One limitation to this data, in addition to the small sample size, is the relatively homogenous demographic profile of the ketamine injectors interviewed: young, male, and white. While this profile may reflect the larger population of ketamine injectors, future research should continue to target street-involved youth but with a greater emphasis on obtaining a sample that includes more women and more members of racial and sexual minorities. Collecting a more diverse sample could reveal different injection practices and injection groups that may have further implications for infectious disease risk.

Lastly, ketamine injectors represent an emerging, though often hidden, population of injection drug users. As these findings indicate, ketamine injectors frequently obtained syringes from sources other than needle exchanges. This lack of direct contact with needle exchanges, while problematic in that ketamine injectors are not using a verifiable distributor of clean syringes, means that ketamine injection practices and related problems are less likely to be reported in syringe exchange data. Similarly, ketamine injectors, particularly those who only inject ketamine, are likely to be missed by studies focusing on heroin, cocaine, or methamphetamine injection. Hence, more studies focusing on ketamine injection are needed to gain additional understanding into the risks and experiences connected to injecting ketamine.

Acknowledgements

This research was conducted under the auspices of a grant from the National Institute on Drug Abuse (DA13893).

References

Clatts, M. C., Heimer R., Abdala, N., Goldsamt, L., Sotheran, J. L., Anderson, K. T., Gallo, T. M., Hoffer, L. D., Luciano, P. A., & Kyriakides, T. 1999. HIV-1 transmission in injection paraphernalia: Heating drug solutions may inactive HIV-1. *JAIDS, 22,* 194–199.

Community Epidemiological Working Group (CEWG). 1999. *Epidemiological trends in drug abuse. Volume 1: Proceedings of the Community Epidemiological Work Group.* Bethesda, MD: National Institutes of Health, Division of Epidemiology and Prevention Research, National Institute of Drug Abuse.

——. 2000. *Epidemiological trends in drug abuse. Volume 1: Proceedings of the Community Epidemiological Work Group.* Bethesda, MD: National Institutes of Health, Division of Epidemiology and Prevention Research, National Institute of Drug Abuse.

Curran, V. & Morgan, C. 2000. Cognitive, dissociative and psychotogenic effects of ketamine in recreational users on the night of drug use and 3 days later. *Addiction, 95,* 575–590.

Des Jarlais, D. C., Friedman, S. R., & Stoneburner, R. 1988. HIV infection and intravenous drug use: Critical issues in transmission dynamics, infection outcomes, and prevention. *Review of Infectious Disease, 10,* 151–158.

Dotson, J. W., Ackerman, D. L., & West, L. J. 1995. Ketamine abuse. *Journal of Drug Issues, 25,* 751–757.

Fine, J., Weissman, J., & Finestone, E. C. 1974. Side effects after ketamine anesthesia: Transient blindness. *Anesthesia and Analgesia, 53,* 72–74.

Fine, P. G. 1999. Low-dose ketamine in the management of opioid nonresponsive terminal cancer pain. *Journal of Pain Symptom Management, 17,* 296–300.

Green, S. M., C. B. Hummel, W. A. Wittlake, S. G. Rothrock, G. A. Hopkins, & Garrett, W. 1999. What is the optimal dose of intramuscular Ketamine for pediatric sedation? *Academy of Emergency Medicine, January 6,* 21–26.

Jansen, K. 2001. *Ketamine: Dreams and realities.* Sarasota, FL: Multidisciplinary Association for Psychedelic Studies.

Lilly, J. 1978. *The scientist: A novel autobiography.* Philadelphia: Lippincott.

Nikolajsen, L., Hansen, P. O., & Jensen, T. S. 1997. Oral ketamine therapy in the treatment of postamputation stump pain. *Acta Anaesthesiol Scandinavia, 41,* 427–429.

Perel, A. & Davidson, J. T. 1976. Recurrent hallucinations following ketamine. *Anaesthesia, 31,* 1081–1083.

Reynolds, S. 1997. Rave culture: Living dream or living death? In Redhead, S. (Ed), *The clubcultures reader* (pp. 84–93). Malden, MA: Blackwell Publishers.

Siegel, R. K. 1978. Phenylcyclidine and ketamine intoxication: A study of four populations of recreational users. In Peterson, R. C. & Stillman, R. C. (Eds.), *Phencyclidine abuse: An appraisal* (pp. 119–147). NIDA research monograph 21. Rockville, MD: National Institutes on Drug Abuse (NIDA).

Weil, A. & Rosen, W. 1983. *Chocolate to morphine: Understanding mind-active drugs.* Boston: Houghton Mifflin Company.

For Discussion

How accurate is it to describe ketamine as a "club drug"? Does the setting in which the drug is used have an effect on the intended experience? How, if at all, does the user's route of administration influence the perception of ketamine as a "club drug"?

29

Healthy Nightclubs and Recreational Substance Use

From a Harm Minimisation to a Healthy Settings Approach

Mark A. Bellis[a]
Karen Hughes[b]
Helen Lowey[b]

Mark Bellis and his colleagues suggest that reducing the harm associated with drug use is best understood from a "healthy settings" approach. Characteristics of the venues in which some drugs are consumed often contribute to injury, ill health, and risk taking among drug users. A "healthy settings" approach offers solutions for minimizing these negative implications of drug taking.

Introduction

In the UK alone, approximately 3.5 million individuals go to nightclubs each week (Mintel International Group, 2000). Most of these are younger people and a large proportion of them consume illegal drugs often in combination with alcohol (Measham, Aldridge, & Parker, 2001). The relationship between recreational drug use and dance music events is now well established (Release and Winstock). In the UK, for instance, estimates of ecstasy, amphetamine, and cocaine use in regular clubbers (i.e. attendees at nightclubs) or those travelling abroad to visit international nightclub resorts (e.g.

Ibiza) far exceed average levels of consumption by individuals in the general population (Bellis, Hale, Bennett, Chaudry, & Kilfoyle, 2000) (Table 29.1).

The acute and long-term problems relating to *recreational* (i.e. ecstasy, amphetamine, and cocaine) drug use are the subject of a wide range of studies (Parrott and Reneman) and form the rationale for a variety of health interventions (Niesnk and Page). Thus, ecstasy use has been linked to short-term health effects such as hyperthermia (Henry, Jeffreys, & Dawling, 1992) as well as long-term effects such as memory problems (Reneman et al., 2001). Interventions addressing recreational drug use have often been outreach based (Crew 2000, 2001) and focused on disseminating information on adverse effects of drugs and how to avoid them, problems around combining substances (often drugs and alcohol), and courses of action necessary when acute adverse effects are experienced. However, there is now a growing recognition that the adverse effects of club drugs are strongly related to the environment in which they are used rather than resulting solely from the toxic properties of substances themselves (Calafat et al., 2001). Often, reports of ecstasy-related deaths refer to the temperature of the environment—The most likely cause of death is heatstroke. The temperature inside the club had reached 40°C (Burke, 2001) or in other instances the lack of basic facilities to redress the effects of dancing and substance use—A number of people complained about lack of water (Bowcott, 2001).

In this paper, we argue that the relationship between the health effects of substance use and the environment in which they are used is much wider than temperature control and access to water and extends across the entire nightlife setting. We explore the wide range of factors that contribute to risk in nighttime environments and describe initiatives that effectively address these issues without curtailing fun. Consequently, we argue that by adopting a broad settings approach (World Health Organisation, 1997) to nightclubs, inclusive solutions to reducing harm in clubs (including that caused by

Table 29.1

Levels of Drug Use in Three UK Surveys

	British Crime Survey[a] (%)	Ibiza Uncovered Survey[b] (%)	Dancing on Drugs Survey[c] (%)
Cannabis	22	51	69.5
Ecstasy	5	39	51.4
Amphetamine	5	27	53.5
Cocaine	5	26	27.1

[a] 16–29-year-olds in the general population; drugs used in last 12 months (Ramsay, Baker, Goulden, Sharp, & Sondhi, 2001).
[b] 6–29-year-olds who visited Ibiza during Summer 2000; drugs used in last 6 months (Bellis et al., 2000).
[c] 5–57-year-olds attending dance events; drugs used in last 3 months (Measham et al., 2000).

drugs) can be better developed and disseminated. Furthermore, the same approach can also facilitate multidisciplinary involvement in nightlife health, taking health issues solely from health departments and placing the responsibility also in the hands of organisations such as local authorities, police, voluntary organisations, club owners and managers, door staff, and clubbers themselves. Finally, we suggest that with worldwide growth in dance music tourism, this multidisciplinary approach needs to be extended to include travel and tourism organisations and requires collaboration on an international level.

Healthy Settings and Nightclubs

A healthy settings approach (World Health Organisation, 1997) recognises that the effects of any particular setting on an individual's health are related to the general conditions within that setting, perhaps more than they are to provision of health or other care facilities. The nightclub setting at its most basic is a building that provides loud music, often with a repetitive beat, a dance area that usually has low background light and intermittent bright lighting effects and a licensed bar. Developing this environment as a healthy setting must recognise that large numbers of clubbers regularly consume substances such as alcohol, drugs, and tobacco (often in combination) and consequently experience a variety of psychological and physiological effects. Furthermore, the criminal nature of some drug use and environmental

factors such as poor ventilation mean substance consumption can directly affect staff, for example, pressure on door staff to allow drugs into clubs (Morris, 1998) and passive smoking affecting bar staff, respectively (Jones, Love, Thomson, Green, & Howden-Chapman, 2001).

Some settings approaches to club health are well established. Harm minimisation messages advising sipping water, avoiding mixing alcohol with ecstasy, and taking periods of rest provide the essential information for individuals to protect their health (London Drugs Policy Forum, 1996). However, without cool areas within the club, often referred to as chill out areas (London Drug Policy Forum, 1996) and access to free cold water, such advice cannot be implemented. Equally, when adverse reactions to drugs are experienced, a separate appropriately stocked first-aid room, trained staff, and access for emergency services are all required to allow the best chance of recovery. However, other often more deleterious effects on health are also related to nightlife and substance use. In the UK in 1999, 19% of all violent acts (n = 3,246,000) occurred outside a pub or club. Overall, 40% of violent incidents were related to alcohol use and 18% to drugs (Kershaw et al., 2000). The paraphernalia of alcohol use also contributes to harm, with 5000 people being attacked with pint glasses every year of whom many are scarred for life (Deehan, 1999). Thus, both the promotion of aggression by, for instance, alcohol (Institute of Alcohol Studies, 2001) and the paraphernalia of substance use play parts in the harm caused by violence.

Less frequently addressed issues, which are important to a settings approach to club health, include the risk of smoking and in particular fire. Large amounts of electrical equipment, the use of old converted premises, low lighting, and a high proportion of smokers (Measham et al., 2001) all contribute to making nightclubs high-risk environments. Additionally, substance use can mean that patrons can be disorientated, leading to further implications particularly if an emergency evacuation of the building is required. A healthy setting should promote well-marked fire exits (some have been known to be camouflaged to fit in with club décor), crowd control training (Newcombe, 1994), and strict compliance with fire limits on the building's capacity (Ministry of Health, 1999). The effects of fires in clubs can be horrific, as graphically illustrated by the loss of life associated with recent incidents (BBC News, 2000; CNN, 2000; and The Guardian, 2001). However, the effects of smoking alone may also be significant. Dancing while holding a cigarette can result in damage to eyes of those nearby (Luke, 1999), whilst non-smoking bar staff are subject to heavy exposure to environmental tobacco smoke while at work (Jarvis, Foulds, & Feyerabend, 1992).

Noise levels in clubs can also pose a substantial risk to health. UK guidance on protection at work suggests earplugs are used when levels regularly exceed 90 dB (Health and Safety Executive, 1999). However, noise levels in many nightclubs reach 120 dB (Royal National Institute for Deaf People, 1999) and at some points noise can approach the pain threshold (140 dB) (Walsh, 2000). However, those utilising the nighttime environment are unlikely to recognise the effects on their hearing. The clubbing experience, especially in conjunction with substance use, distracts from concerns about health effects and in the case of some drugs (e.g. ketamine or cocaine) may even anaesthetise the user against pain (European Monitoring Centre for Drugs and Drug Addiction, 2000). As increasing numbers of young people are exposed to loud music in dance clubs, it would be expected that more young people would develop hearing problems. In fact, a survey by the Medical Research Council Institute of Hearing Research found that 66% of club goers reported temporary hearing problems after attending a nightclub (Smith & Davis, 1999). Policies about maximum noise levels in clubs can address some of these issues. However, noise is not just a concern within the club but may also affect the surrounding environment, either through loud music contaminating nearby residential areas or through the noise of inebriated clubbers appearing on the street when clubs finally close (BBC Devon, 2001). Such noise may also be associated with violence (often related to alcohol and drug use), lack of appropriate access to public transport (leaving long waits or drink/drug driving as the only alternatives), and difficulties in coordinating an adequate police presence when clubs close (Calafat et al., 2001).

Furthermore, any comprehensive approach to a healthy club setting should recognise the close relationship between substance use and sexual health. A variety of studies identify the relaxation of safe sex measures (particularly condom use) associated with alcohol and drug-taking (e.g. Poulin & Graham, 2001). One study has identified individuals using drugs, particularly GHB, specifically in order to temporarily forget safe sex messages they have previously heard (Clark, Cook, Syed, Ashton, & Bellis, 2001). Addressing such issues means providing safe sex information within the club setting and combining this with easy access to condoms. Fire, noise, sex, and other areas for health promotion and protection in the nighttime environment as well as their relationship with substance use are summarised in Table 29.2.

Disseminating Knowledge and Developing Solutions

The use of substances often contributes to the dangers presented within the nighttime environment. Previously, harm minimisation has tended to focus on direct effects of drug use. However, basic measures to alter

Table 29.2

Some Wider Club Health Issues, Their Relationship With Substance Use, and Developing a Setting Response

Health risk	Relationship to substance use	Setting response	Groups involved
Dehydration and hyperthermia	Ecstasy alters thermoregulation (McCann, Slate, & Ricaurte, 1996) Increased energetic dancing Alcohol consumption causes dehydration	Prevent overcrowding Well ventilation and temperature control Cool and quieter chill outs areas or ability to leave and reenter Access to cool, free water Information on effects of taking drugs Pill testing First-aid room and staff training	Club owners/staff Drug outreach workers Health promotion groups Licensing authority Club goers Local A&E
Fire	High levels of smoking among club goers Intoxication leads to disorientation when exiting clubs Flammable clubbing clothes (e.g. PVC)	Prevent overcrowding High visibility and accessible emergency exits Availability and maintenance of all fire equipment Ensure electrical equipment is safe Encourage use of noncombustible material	Club owners/staff Fire authorities Building inspectors Licensing authority Club goers
Damage to hearing	Alcohol and drugs reduce awareness of potential hearing damage Greater exposure to noise due to prolonged dancing	Set maximum levels on systems Restricted areas around speakers Make earplugs available Information on the effects of excessive noise Information on signs of hearing damage	Club owners/staff Club goers Environmental inspectors Licensing authority Health promotion Club goers
STIs and unwanted pregnancies	Alcohol and drugs reduce inhibitions (Calafat, 2000) Substances help forget safe sex message (Clark et al., 2001)	Easy availability of condoms Information on safer sex	Health promotion Public health department Contraception services Club owners Club goers
Accident Glass Burns Falls General	Disorentation Anaesthetising effect of substances (European Monitoring Centre for Drugs and Drug Addiction, 2000) Lack of fear and increased confidence Increased risk-taking	Toughened glass or plastic bottles No drinking/smoking on dance floor Provide places to dispose of cigarettes Well-lit and clear stairwells Restricted access to potentially dangerous areas Secure fixtures and fittings are secure On-site first-aid	Club owners/staff Public health departments Health promotion groups Licensing authority Club goers
Violence	Alcohol and drugs increase aggression Drug dealing (Morris, 1998) Steroid and cocaine use by door staff (Lenehan & McVeigh, 1998) Increased risk-taking, lower inhibitions	Stagger closing times Increase public transport availability throughout night Plastic/toughened glass Registration and training of door staff Complaints procedures and Policing	Club owners/staff Police Licensing authority Club goers Transport authority

Table 29.2 *(continued)*

Health risk	Relationship to substance use	Setting response	Groups involved
Drink/drug driving	Increased confidence Lack of coordination Increased risk-taking, lower inhibitions (Crowley & Courney, 2000)	Provide cheap soft drinks Public transport: taxis, buses, and trains available Information of safety issues Special club buses provided by clubs	Club owners/staff Health promotion group Club goers PoliceTransport authority
Passive smoking	Increased smoking when out Many "occasional" smokers Link between smoking and other substance use (Lewinsohn, Rohde, & Brown, 1999)	Adequate ventilation (especially behind the bar) Adequate "break areas" for staff No smoking areas Information on dangers of smoking	Club owners Outreach workers Smoking prevention groups Health promotion groups Licensing authority Club goers

the environment can substantially reduce substance-related harm. Measures to reduce violence in and around clubs include training and registration of door staff, good lighting around the main entrance, and public transport integrated into the nighttime environment so that individuals can quickly and easily leave city centres (London and Calafat). Specific measures to reduce spillage of bottles from bars and clubs onto streets can also reduce the risk of glass-related injuries (The Kirklees Partnership, 1999). Inside, club design should anticipate and acknowledge the exuberant behaviour and intoxicated state of patrons by restricting access to any areas where falls are likely and ensuring exits are well lit and distinctive (London Drug Policy Forum, 1996).

Importantly, the process of tackling harm reduction across the entire nightlife setting legitimises the inclusion of a wide variety of organisations and individuals who may have felt that they could not engage in dialogue solely on a drug use agenda. These groups may include club and bar owners, club goers and club staff, event promoters, local authorities and politicians, environmental health officials, and travel and tour operators as well as youth services, health services, police, and other emergency services. Furthermore, sometimes, this mix of individuals produces novel solutions. For example, to reduce night crime and increase public safety, the owners of a number of neighbour-

ing venues have supported the employment [of] a uniformed police officer dedicated to patrolling outside their premises (Greater Manchester Police, 2001). Also, in North Devon, a police initiative involved handing out free lollipops as clubbers left nightclubs in order to reduce noise in the surrounding areas (BBC Devon, 2001).

International Considerations

The recent clubbing phenomenon probably has its routes in Ibiza where the mix of music (known as the Balearic Beat) and concurrent use of ecstasy rose to popularity (Calafat et al., 1998). Today, travelling in the form of dance music tourism (individuals specifically travelling abroad to attend dance events or choosing to holiday in destinations renowned for their nightlife) is more popular than ever. Major international clubbing resorts include Ibiza in Spain, Rimini in Italy, and Ayia Napa in Cyprus. Clubbing has additional elements of risk when undertaken in an unfamiliar country. Thus, geography abroad is often unfamiliar, and combined with a different language, this can mean health services or other forms of help are difficult to locate and access. Furthermore, accessing items such as condoms or emergency contraception may also prove more difficult. Legislation can be different and poorly understood, leading to unexpected confrontations with judicial services. If drugs are purchased, the supplier will often be untested, raising the possibility of counterfeits. Equally, alcohol measures may vary in size and purity from standard measures within individuals' home countries. When alcohol and drugs are consumed, a combination of hotter climates, longer periods of dancing, and possible gastrointestinal infections increase the risk of severe dehydration. Importantly, however, along with environmental change, individuals abroad are often free from the social constraints of work and family that restrict their substance use and sexual behaviour (Ryan and Kinder, 1996). Thus, an individual may go clubbing one night per week while at home, whereas during a 2-week trip abroad the same individual may visit a club every night. This in turn can significantly alter an individual's exposure to substances. For instance, around a third of all young people from the UK who visited Ibiza in 1999 used ecstasy while on the island. The vast majority of these also used ecstasy in the UK (Bellis et al., 2000). However, the way in which people used ecstasy while abroad was significantly different. Of ecstasy users, only 3% used the drug 5 or more days a week in the UK while 45% of the same group used the drug 5 or more days a week while in Ibiza. Similar trends in increased frequency of use were also seen for alcohol, amphetamine, and cocaine.

Little is currently known about the health effects of such periods of intense substance use. Clearly, the opportunities for adverse reactions are substantially increased where multiple drugs are being regularly consumed along with alcohol on a nightly basis. Furthermore, intense periods of consumption provide at least the possibility that more frequent drug use could continue when individuals return home, potentially moving individuals' habits further towards problematic use.

In order to address the health needs of the increasingly large numbers of young people who regularly travel to experience international nightlife, new approaches to health promotion and protection are required. New literature and campaigns are needed that provide international information on substance use and nightlife health for those travelling abroad. They should tackle the broad range of risks to health, including environmental considerations, but should also address the changes in substance use that occur while abroad (Bellis et al., 2000). Access to such information can utilise new technologies affiliated with club culture (e.g. the Internet) and popular with the major clubbing age groups (Hughes & Bellis, in press). Good examples of such sites are already available (*www.dancesafe.org* and *www.ravesafe.org*).

Conclusions

Around the world, clubbing is now well established as a major feature of the nighttime environment. It provides a social outlet for millions of individuals every week and developing a popular club scene has reinvigorated many cities bringing money and employment. Substance use in clubs is strongly affiliated with relaxation, exercise (Gaule, Dugdill, Peiser, & Guppy, 2001), and meeting new sexual partners. Whether these pastimes lead to increased well-being or ill health depends on the environment and the specific behaviour of individuals. Developing clubs as a healthy setting requires interventions that protect and promote health while retaining fun as a central feature. Where interventions or regulations substantially reduce fun young people may look elsewhere for their entertainment (e.g. illegal parties). Consequently, organisations need to recognise the importance of involving young people in the development of nighttime health interventions.

Substance use is one of the major risks to health in the nighttime environment both through its direct effects on individuals' health and through the alterations in behaviour and perception that it causes. However, many organisations and individuals do not feel either comfortable or equipped to engage in drug-specific interventions or even discussions. By developing a healthy settings approach to clubs, the emphasis of health interventions can be diverted away from solely drug use to include a wider range of issues. This means key individuals and organisations (including club owners, staff, promoters, and major industries) can be engaged in a harm minimisation agenda that includes drug use along with alcohol, tobacco, transport, security, and other environmental issues. Furthermore, tackling a broad range of issues in the nighttime environment reaches groups that are difficult to reach through education or occupational settings, such as those who play truant or are unemployed.

Some countries have already engaged in this more holistic approach to nighttime health by generating broader guidelines on safer clubs and clubbing (e.g. London; Ministry and Newcombe). However, with cheaper air travel and young people having greater expendable income (Calafat et al., 2001) combined with the international nature of the clubbing phenomenon, a significant proportion of an individual's annual clubbing nights can be spent in nightclubs abroad where risks to health may be even greater. As a result, guidelines are required to provide basic standards for nightclubs on an international basis and different interventions need to be developed to address local and international needs. Efforts to develop international guidelines on club health are already underway *(www.clubhealth.org.uk)*. However, empirical evidence on changes in individuals' behaviour when abroad (Bellis et al., 2001) and the resultant effects on health are both rare and urgently needed. Without such intelligence, the appropriate structure of health interventions to minimise harm for millions of dance music tourists remains unclear and the burden of ill health carried especially by younger people may unnecessarily be increasing.

Acknowledgements

This paper draws on original research measuring levels of substance use by individuals holidaying abroad. That work would not have been possible without the support of the Health Authorities of the North West Region. In particular, we would like to thank Mr. Rod Thomson and Professor John Ashton whose interest and support for developing a healthy nightlife has been fundamental to this work.

Notes

a. Birkenhead and Wallasey Primary Care Trust, St. Catherine's Hospital, Church Road, Birkenhead, CH42 0LQ, UK.

b. Centre for Public Health, Liverpool John Moores University, 70 Great Crosshall Street, Liverpool, L3 2AB, UK.

References

BBC Devon News (2001). Lollipops gag late-night revellers. *BBC News* (online).

BBC News (2000). Mexico club blaze kills 19. *BBC News*, Friday, 20 October 2000.

Bellis, M. A., Hale, G., Bennett, A., Chaudry, M., & Kilfoyle, M. (2000). Ibiza uncovered: changes in substance use and sexual behaviour amongst young people visiting an international night-life resort. *International Journal on Drug Policy 11*, pp. 235–244.

Bellis, M. A., Hughes, K., Bennett, A., & Chaudri, M. (2001). *Three years of research on risk behaviour in Ibiza* (in preparation).

Bowcott, O. (2001). Ecstasy deaths may have been caused by heat, not a bad batch. *The Guardian*, Saturday, 30 June 2001.

Burke, J. (2001). Ecstasy's death toll "set to go on rising". *The Guardian*, Sunday, 1 July 2001.

Calafat, A., Fernandez, C., Juan, M., Bellis, M. A., Bohrn, K., Hakkarainen, P., Kilfoyle-Carrington, M., Kokkevi, A., Maalste, N., Mendes, F., Siamou, I., Simojn, J., Stocco, P., & Zavatti, P. (2001). *Risk and control in the recreational drug culture: SONAR project*. Spain: IREFREA.

Calafat, A., Stocco, P., Mendes, F., Simon, J., van de Wijngaart, G., Sureda, M., Palmer, A., Maalste, N., & Zapatti, P. (1998). *Characteristics and social representation of ecstasy in Europe*. Valencia: IREFREA and European Commission.

Clark, P., Cook, P. A., Syed, Q., Ashton, J. R., & Bellis, M. A. (2001). *Re-emerging syphilis in the North West: lessons from the Manchester outbreak*. Liverpool: Public Health Sector, Liverpool John Moores University.

CNN (2000). Christmas fire kills at least 309 at China shopping centre. *CNN*, 27 December 2000.

Crew 2000 (2001). Development of strategies for secondary prevention in drug use. Patterns of drug use amongst young people at clubs and pre-club bars in Edinburgh. *Project Report*. Edinburgh: Crew 2000.

Crowley, J., & Courney, R. (2000). The relation between drug use, impaired driving and traffic accidents. *The results of an investigation* carried out for the European Monitoring Centre on Drugs and Drug Addictions (EMCDDA), Lisbon. Proceedings of Road Traffic and Drugs, Strasbourg, 19–21 April 1999. Council of Europe Publishing.

Deehan, A. (1999). *Alcohol and crime: taking stock.* Policing and Reducing Crime Unit, Crime Reduction Research Series Paper 3. London: Home Office.

European Monitoring Centre for Drugs and Drug Addiction (2000). *Report on the risk assessment of ketamine in the framework of the joint action on new synthetic drugs.* Portugal: EMCDDA.

Gaule, S., Dugdill, L., Peiser, B., & Guppy, A. (2001). *Moving beyond the drugs and deviance issues: rave dancing as a health promoting alternative to conventional physical activity.* In: Proceedings of club health 2002. Liverpool John Moores University and Trimbos Institute. Available at: *www.clubhealth.org.uk.*

Greater Manchester Police (2001). *Manchester City Centre venues team up with police to reduce night crime.* Press release.

Health and Safety Executive (1999). *Introducing the noise at work guidelines: a brief guide to the guidelines controlling noise at work.* INDG75 (rev) C150 11/99. Suffolk: HSE Books.

Henry, J. A., Jeffreys, K. J., & Dawling, S. (1992). Toxicity and deaths from 3,4-methylenedioxymethamphetamine ("Ecstasy"). *Lancet, 340,* pp. 384–387.

Hughes, K., & Bellis, M. A. (1992). *Disseminating public health information and the public health evidence base: assessing the current and future potential for the Internet and e-mail.* Health Development Agency and North West Public Health Observatory (in press).

Institute of Alcohol Studies (2001). *Alcohol and crime. IAS factsheet.* Cambridgeshire: Institute of Alcohol Studies.

Jarvis, M. J., Foulds, J., & Feyerabend, C. (1992). Exposure to passive smoking among bar staff. *British Journal of Addiction, 87,* 111–113.

Jones, S., Love, C., Thomson, G., Green, R., & Howden-Chapman, P. (2001). Second-hand smoke at work: the exposure, perceptions and attitudes of bar and restaurant workers to environmental tobacco smoke. *Australian and New Zealand Journal of Public Health 25,* 90–93.

Kershaw, C., Budd, T., Kinshott, G., Mattinson, J., Mayhew, P., & Myhill, A. (2000). *The 2000 British crime survey.* Home Office Statistical Bulletin 18/00. London: Home Office.

Lenehan, P., & McVeigh, J. (1998). *Anabolic steroids: a guide for professionals.* The Drugs and Sport Information Service, University of Liverpool.

Lewinsohn, P. M., Rohde, P., & Brown, R. A. (1999). Level of current and past adolescent cigarette smoking as predictors of future substance use disorders in young adulthood. *Addiction 94,* 913–921.

London Drug Policy Forum (1996). *Dance till dawn safely: a code of practice on health and safety at dance venues.* London: Drug Policy Forum.

Luke, C. (1999). A little nightclub medicine. In M. Kilfoyle, & M. A. Bellis (Eds.), 1999. *Club health: the health of the clubbing nation.* Liverpool: Department of Public Health, Liverpool John Moores University.

McCann, U. D., Slate, S. O., & Ricaurte, G. A. (1996). Adverse reactions with 3,4-methylenedioxymethamphetamine (MDMA: "ecstasy"). *Drug Safety 15,* 107.

Measham, F., Aldridge, J., & Parker, H. (2001). *Dancing on drugs: risk, health and hedonism in the British club scene.* London: Free Association Books.

Ministry of Health (1999). *Guidelines for SAFE dance parties: the big book.* New Zealand: Ministry of Health.

Mintel International Group (2000). *Nightclubs and discotechques: market size and trends.* Report Code 11/2000, London.

Morris, S. (1998). *Clubs, drugs and doormen.* Crime Detection and Prevention Series Paper 86, Police Research Group, London: Home Office.

Newcombe, R. (1994). *Safer dancing: guidelines for good practice at dance parties and nightclubs.* Liverpool: 3D Pub.

Niesnk, R., Nikken, G., Jansen, F., & Spruit, I. (2000). *The drug information and monitoring service (DIMS) in the Netherlands: a unique tool for monitoring party drugs.* Proceedings of club health 2002. Liverpool John Moores University and Trimbos Institute. Available at: *www.clubhealth.org.uk.*

Page, S. (2000). *Death on the dancefloor.* Proceedings of club health 2002. Liverpool John Moores University and Trimbos Institute. Available at: *www.clubhealth.org.uk.*

Parrott, A. C., Milani, R. M., Parmar, R., & Turner, J. D. (2001). Recreational ecstasy/MDMA and other drug users from the UK and Italy: psychiatric problems and psychobiological problems. *Psychopharmacology 159,* 77–82.

Poulin, C., & Graham, L. (2001). The association between substance use, unplanned sexual intercourse and other sexual behaviours among adolescent students. *Addiction 96,* 607–621.

Ramsay, M., Baker, P., Goulden, C., Sharp, C., & Sondhi, A. (2001). *Drug misuse declared in 2000: results from the British crime survey.* Home Office Research Study 224. London: Home Office.

Release (1997). *Drugs and dance survey: an insight into the culture.* London: Release.

Reneman, L., Lavalaye, J., Schmand, B., de Wolff, F. A., van den Brink, W., den Heeten, G. J., & Booij, J. (2001). Cortical serotonin transporter density and verbal memory in individuals who stopped using methylenedioxy-methamphetamine (MDMA or "ecstasy"): preliminary findings.

Royal National Institute for Deaf People (1999). *Safer sound: an analysis of musical noise and hearing damage.* London: RNID.

Ryan, C., & Kinder, R. (1996). Sex, tourism and sex tourism: fulfilling similar needs? *Tourist Management, 17,* 507–518.

Smith, P., & Davis, A. (1999). Social noise and hearing loss. *Lancet, 353,* 1185.

The Guardian (2001). Dutch fire toll climbs to 10 with 17 fighting for life. *The Guardian,* Wednesday, 3 January 2001.

The Kirklees Partnership (1999). *Boiling point preventer: a code of practice for dealing with drugs and violence in pubs and clubs.* Yorkshire: The Kirklees Partnership.

Walsh, E. (2000). *Dangerous decibels: dancing until deaf.* San Francisco: The Bay Area Reporter, Hearing Education and Awareness for Rockers.

Winstock, A. R., Griffiths, P., & Stewart, D. (2001). Drugs and the dance music scene: a survey of current drug use patterns among a sample of dance music enthusiasts in the UK. *Drug and Alcohol Dependence, 64,* 9–17.

World Health Organisation (1997). *The Jakarta declaration on leading health promotion into the 21st century.* Fourth international conference on health promotion, Jakarta, 21–25 July 1997.

For Discussion

How beneficial would it be to establish international guidelines for healthy nightclubs? What are the most important issues to address, and how would specific recommendations be enforced?

Part VII

Drugs and Crime

For generations, while commentators on the American drug scene have been sensationalizing the crimes committed by users of heroin, cocaine, and other drugs, researchers and clinicians have argued a related series of questions. Is criminal behavior antecedent to addiction, or does criminality emerge subsequent to addiction? More specifically, is crime the result of or a response to a special set of life circumstances brought about by the addiction to narcotic drugs? Or conversely, is addiction per se a deviant tendency characteristic of individuals already prone to offensive behavior? Moreover, and assuming that criminality may indeed be a pre-addiction phenomenon, does the onset of the chronic use of narcotics bring about a change in the nature, intensity, and frequency of deviant and criminal acts? Does criminal involvement tend to increase or decrease subsequent to addiction? Furthermore, there are related questions: What kinds of criminal offenses do addicts engage in? Do they tend toward violent acts of aggression? Or are their crimes strictly profit oriented and geared toward the violation of the sanctity of private property? Or is it both?

As early as the 1920s, researchers conducted studies seeking to unravel these very questions. Particularly, Edouard Sandoz at the Municipal Court of Boston and Lawrence Kolb at the U.S. Public Health Service examined the backgrounds of hundreds of heroin users, focusing on the drugs-crime

relationship. What they found within criminal justice and treatment populations were several different types of cases. Some drug users were habitual criminals and likely always had been; others were simply violators of the Harrison Act, having been arrested for no more than the illegal possession of narcotics. Moreover, among both types a record of violent crimes was absent.

The analyses provided by Sandoz, Kolb, and others established the parameters of several points of view:

- Addicts ought to be the object of vigorous law-enforcement activity, since the majority are members of a criminal element and drug addiction is simply one of the later phases of their deviant careers.

- Addicts prey upon legitimate society, and the effects of their drug use do indeed predispose them to serious criminal transgressions.

- Addicts are essentially law-abiding citizens who are forced to steal to adequately support their drug habits.

- Addicts are not necessarily criminals but are forced to associate with an underworld element that tend to maintain control over the distribution of illicit drugs.

The notion that addicts ought to be the objects of vigorous police activity, a posture that might be called the *criminal model of*

343

drug abuse, was actively and relentlessly pursued by the Federal Bureau of Narcotics and other law enforcement groups. Their argument was fixed on the notion of criminality, for, on the basis of their own observations, the vast majority of heroin users were members of criminal groups. To support this view, the Bureau of Narcotics pointed to several studies that demonstrated that most addicts were already criminals before they began using heroin. Addicts, the bureau emphasized, represent a destructive force confronting the people of America. Whatever the sources of their addiction, they are members of a highly subversive and antisocial group. For the bureau, this position did indeed have some basis in reality. Having been charged with the enforcement of a law that prohibited the possession, sale, and distribution of narcotics, bureau agents were confronted with *criminal* addicts, often under the most dangerous of circumstances. It was not uncommon for agents to be wounded or even killed in arrest situations, and analyses of the careers of many addicts demonstrated that their criminal records were lengthy. But the bureau was incorrect in its belief that all drug users were from the same mold. Studies of drug-using populations have noted the existence of numerous and alternative patterns of narcotic addiction.

During the years between 1900 and 1960, for example, there was a pattern of addiction characteristic of a core of middle-aged, white Southerners. Identified through patient records at federal drug-treatment facilities, these users were usually addicted to morphine or paregoric, and their drugs had been obtained from physicians through legal or quasi-legal means. As "patients" under treatment for some illness, these addicts were not members of any deviant subculture and did not have contacts with other addicts.

There were also groups of *hidden addicts* who, because of sufficient income or access to a legitimate source of drugs, had no need to make contacts with visibly criminal cultures to obtain drugs. Among these were musicians, physicians, and members of other segments of the health professions.

Finally, there was the stereotyped heroin street addict—the narcotics user of the American inner cities depicted in the mass media. Heroin street addicts were typically from the socially and economically deprived segments of the urban population. They began their careers with drug experimentation as adolescents for the sake of excitement or thrills, to conform with peer-group activities and expectations, or to strike back at the authority structures that they opposed. The use of alcohol, marijuana, codeine, or pills generally initiated them into substance abuse, and later drug intake focused primarily on heroin. Their status of addiction was often said to have emerged as a result of an addiction-prone personality, and they supported their habits through illegal means. Also among this group were polydrug users— those who concurrently abused a variety of drugs.

By mid-century, most law-enforcement agencies focused their attention and commentary on those who manifested the pattern of heroin street addiction. Their judgments and assertions were often a response to the clinicians and social scientists of the time who had put forth the notion of what might be called a medical model of drug abuse, as opposed to the *criminal* view held by law enforcement. The medical model, which physicians first proposed in the late nineteenth century, held that addiction is a chronic and relapsing disease. The addict, it was argued, should be dealt with as any patient suffering from some physiological or medical disorder. At the same time, numerous proponents of the view sought to mitigate addict criminality by putting forth the "enslavement theory of addiction." The idea here was that the monopolistic controls over the heroin black market forced "sick" and otherwise "law-abiding" drug users into lives of crime to support their habits.

In retrospect, from the 1920s through the close of the 1960s, hundreds of studies of the relationship between crime and addiction were conducted. Invariably, when one analysis supported the medical model of addiction, the next would affirm the criminal model. Given these repeated contradictions, something had to be wrong—and indeed something was. The theories, hypotheses, conclusions, and other findings generated by almost the entire spectrum of research were actually of little value, for major biases and deficiencies were built into the very nature of their designs. Data-gathering enterprises on criminal activity had usually restricted themselves to drug-users' arrest histories, and there can be little argument about the inadequacy of official criminal statistics as measures of the incidence and prevalence of offense behavior. Those studies that did manage to go beyond arrest figures to probe self-reported criminal activity were invariably limited to either incarcerated heroin users or addicts in treatment settings. The few efforts that did manage to locate active heroin users in the street community typically examined the samples' drug-taking behaviors to the exclusion of their drug-seeking behaviors. Given the many methodological difficulties, it was impossible to draw many reliable conclusions about the nature of drug-related crime—about its magnitude, shape, scope, or direction. Moreover, and perhaps most important, the conclusions being drawn from the generations of studies were not taking a number of important features of the drug scene into account: that there were many different kinds of drugs and drug users; that the nature and patterns of drug use were constantly shifting and changing; that the purity, potency, and availability of drugs were dynamic, rather than static; and that both drug-related crime and drug-using criminals were undergoing continuous metamorphosis. It was not until the 1970s that research began to reliably address these issues in order to generate a better understanding of the drugs-crime connection in the American drug scene. In the following chapters, aspects of this research are presented.

Additional Readings

Bean, Philip. (2001). *Drugs and Crime*. Portland, OR: Willan Publishing.

Kurtz, Steven P., and James A. Inciardi. (2003). "Crystal Meth, Gay Men, and Circuit Parties." *Law Enforcement Executive Forum*, 3(4): 97–114.

Menard, Scott, Sharon Mihalic, and David Huizinga. (2001). "Drugs and Crime Revisited." *Justice Quarterly*, 18(2): 269–299.

Newcomb, Michael D., Elisha R. Galaif, and Jennifer Vargas Carmona. (2001). "The Drug-Crime Nexus in a Community Sample of Adults." *Psychology of Addictive Behaviors*, 15(3): 185–193.

Walters, Glenn D. (1994). *Drugs and Crime in Lifestyle Perspective*. Thousand Oaks, CA: Sage Publications. ✦

30

The Drugs-Crime Connection

David N. Nurco
Timothy W. Kinlock
Thomas E. Hanlon

The nature of the drug-crime relationship is not altogether clear. Is addiction another expression of a criminal lifestyle? Or do addicts commit crime to support their addictions? In the opening essay of this section, David N. Nurco and his colleagues address these important questions, while discussing a number of problems associated with previous studies. Addicts, they argue, should not be classified as a homogeneous group. Some drug users do not commit crime except for drug possession and sale. For others, criminal activity occurs before the onset of addiction, while some commit crimes to support their addictions. The authors conclude with suggestions for improving our knowledge of the drug-crime connection.

The first recorded speculation regarding a link between narcotic drugs and crime appeared more than a hundred years ago.[1]

Since that time, there has been a long and continuing controversy in the United States about the relationship between narcotic addiction and crime. On one side were those advocating the "criminal model of addiction,"[2] who regarded addicts as confirmed criminals who endanger society by their anti-social behavior. This viewpoint was epitomized by the late Harry J. Anslinger, the first head of the Federal Bureau of Narcotics, who served in this capacity from 1930 to 1962. Similar viewpoints were publicly expressed as early as 1924.

As David Musto noted in his comprehensive historical account, *The American Disease*, it was stated in testimony before Congress that heroin was a stimulus to the commission of crime.[3] In this testimony, Dr. Alexander Lambert, the head of the Mayor's Committee on Drug Addiction for New York City, expressed the view that heroin tended to destroy the sense of responsibility to the herd. The commissioner of health of Chicago, Dr. Herman Bundesen, went even further, stating that "the root of the social evil is essentially in our dope, our habit-forming drugs [the] main cause of prostitution and crime."[4] Although there were differences in emphasis and interpretation among those who held that heroin use promoted crime, it was generally agreed that heroin was destructive and criminogenic.

The other side in this historical controversy took the position that narcotic addicts were not criminals, but deprived or mentally ill individuals who were "forced" into the commission of petty theft in order to support their habit. This viewpoint was emphatically presented by Harry Barnes and Negley Teeters of Temple University in their 1945 textbook, *New Horizons in Criminology*:

> It is now definitely demonstrated that most serious cases of drug addiction are the result of neurotic conditions, namely, mental and nervous disorders growing out of deep-seated mental conflicts in the individual . . . It is not likely, however, that a normal person will become an addict . . . Alarmist literature and the propaganda of the crusaders against drug addiction have created a grotesquely exaggerated impression of the danger to society from the drug addict.[5]

This notion has been frequently referred to as the "enslavement theory of addiction."[6] It was based on a medical model, and the proponents of this view advocated the treatment of narcotic addiction by psychiatrists or other physicians. Those who supported this idea included many clinicians and social scientists of the 1950s and 1960s.

Regardless of which side one took in this controversy, it was often assumed that all narcotic addicts were alike. This concept of uniformity was tacitly assumed by most researchers of the drugs-crime connection before the 1970s.

As researchers from the National Institute of Justice summarized in a comprehensive literature review published in 1980, the majority of studies concentrated on how certain factors affect most addicts, largely ignoring the fact that "these factors all affect addicts differently" and that addicts "should not be viewed as a homogeneous group that follow the same career paths."[7] This appears to be one of the major flaws inherent in earlier research.

Research on the Drugs-Crime Connection

Literature reviews have documented that hundreds of studies of the relationship between addiction and crime were performed from the 1920s to the late 1970s.[8] Several reviewers have commented that these studies contained numerous flaws. As James A. Inciardi has summarized elsewhere,[9] the theories, hypotheses, conclusions, and other findings generated by these studies were of little value, since there were considerable biases and deficiencies in their designs. Given the many methodological difficulties, it was impossible to draw reliable conclusions about the magnitude, shape, scope, or direction of drug-related crime.

In their 1987 review article, "Characterizing Criminal Careers," Alfred Blumstein and Jacqueline Cohen maintained that "even though the subjects of crime and crime control have been major issues of public debate, and despite their regular appearance as one of the nation's most serious problems, significant advances in empirical research related to these issues are relatively recent. . . ." They also emphasized that "more effectively disentangling the apparent drug-crime nexus is of particular concern."[10]

Not until the 1970s and 1980s were more sophisticated studies of the relationship between drug use and crime finally undertaken. In their book, *Taking Care of Business*,[11] published in 1985, Bruce D. Johnson and his associates at the New York

State Division of Substance Abuse Services noted that earlier literature reviews had concluded that little was known about the crime rates of heroin abusers and emphasized the need for improved information about the criminal behavior of drug users. They cited the 1967 report of the President's Commission on Law Enforcement and the Administration of Justice: "Only minimal comprehensive data are available relative to the issue of the drugs/crime relationship";[12] and the 1976 Panel on Drug Use and Criminal Behavior: "Convincing empirical data on drug abuse and crime . . . are generally unavailable—the principal reason being the lack of a long-term, research program in the area."[13]

While there were some notable exceptions, the results of studies revealing differential characteristics among narcotic addicts were usually ignored by policy makers. Examples of these exceptions were the works of Edward Sandoz at the Municipal Court of Boston and Lawrence Holt from the U.S. Public Health Service.[14] Both series of studies suggested that there were different types of addicts. Some were habitual criminals and were so before becoming addicted. On the other hand, others were simply violators of the Harrison Act, having been arrested for illegal possession of narcotics. Unfortunately, the notion of heterogeneity of addicts did not become evident until much later.

Methodological Deficiencies of Early Studies

Evidence of criminal activity among narcotic users is longstanding and abundant; however, it is apparent that relationships among the important variables involved are much more complex than were initially believed. As mentioned, literature reviews of studies conducted on the relationship between narcotic addiction and crime found that these investigations contained several important methodological deficiencies. Among the most commonly mentioned problems were the following:

1. The employment of seriously deficient measures of criminality.

2. The preoccupation with the single-cause issue or the "chicken-egg" question of which came first, crime or drugs.

3. The use of "captive" samples of narcotic addicts.

4. The failure to apply measures of criminal activity over time.

5. The failure to correctly identify the empirical precursors, correlates, possible determinants, and patterns of criminality, and the ignoring of the co-variation of such factors within an addict population.

Measurement of Crime Among Narcotic Addicts

Probably the most serious methodological problem contained in early studies of the relationship between drug use and crime has been the use of official arrest records, or "rap sheets," as indicators of criminal activity. In a review of sixty-five studies to determine the methods of measuring individual criminal behavior, James J. Collins and his co-workers concluded that "arrest data are a seriously deficient indicator of criminal involvement—in fact, it is more accurate to view arrest data as an indicator of criminal justice *system* involvement."[15] In other words, arrest data more properly measure how often one *gets caught* for committing crime, and there is far from a one-to-one relationship between how often someone is caught and how much crime he or she commits.[16]

Several studies employing confidential self-report interview methods have shown that the use of arrest data as an indicator of the amounts and types of crimes actually committed results in gross underestimates.[17] These investigations have found that less than 1 percent of all offenses reported by addicts resulted in arrest. Typical of findings emphasizing the inadequacy of official statistics as measures of the incidence and prevalence of criminal behavior are those of Inciardi.[18] In one of his studies, Inciardi noted that his sample of 573 Miami narcotic abusers had engaged in criminal activity for an average of two years before their first arrest. Also, he

indicated that subsequent arrest rates were extremely low. Of 215,105 offenses reported by the respondents over a one-year period, only 609, or one arrest for every 353 crimes committed (0.3 percent), resulted in arrest.[19]

A common finding of the research of Jan M. Chaiken and Marcia R. Chaiken has been that number of arrests is a poor predictor of who the most dangerous criminals are. Analyzing arrest data and self-reported crime in a Rand Corporation study of over two thousand offenders in three states, these investigators concluded that it was impossible to identify serious and frequent offenders from official records, since "the vast majority of those who do commit all of these crimes (robbery, assault, and drug sales) have not been convicted of them."[20] Although all respondents had been arrested, it was found that arrests were so infrequent and the official records so inadequate that it was impossible to distinguish the serious and persistent offenders from the less serious ones. Chaiken and Chaiken found that only about 10 percent of self-reported violent predators could be so identified by arrest records.[21]

In our studies of narcotic addicts in Baltimore, we have obtained similar results.[22] In one of these studies, we analyzed the self-reports and arrest data of a sample of 243 addicts. While these addicts had a total of 2,869 arrests over an eleven-year period, they also had accumulated 473,738 days of crime, resulting in a ratio of arrests to crime days of .006. Not only were arrests an extreme underestimate of how much crime was committed, but also the arrests were biased with regard to both the type of offense committed and the frequency of offenses. Violent crimes were more likely than other crimes to result in arrest, and the probability of arrest decreased for addicts with high crime rates.[23]

The Validity of Self-Reported Crime

Any study relying primarily on informant self-disclosure must eventually come to grips with the issue of the accuracy, or veridicality, of such information.[24] In this context, the self-reports of drug addicts are particularly suspect because of the deviant and illegal nature of their lifestyles. In addition to possible distortions introduced in order to conceal unsavory aspects of their lives, genuine errors in recalling information about events that occurred years earlier can further affect the accuracy of the information obtained. However, evidence in the literature indicates that addicts, as a group, tend to be surprisingly truthful and accurate in their replies to a wide range of questions when interviewed under non-threatening conditions.[25] Validation studies that have been conducted have used the following methods: comparing self-reports of arrests with official records, comparing information on drug use with urinalysis results, and using repeat-interview procedures.

It is, of course, clear that the social context and the conditions under which interviews are conducted may affect the addicts' motivation to be candid, equivocal, or deceitful. Thus, even though interview information is obtained in the context of research, it would be just as unwarranted to maintain that addicts' responses are invariably valid as it would be to assume that they are invalid. Research procedures that appear to be particularly important to the securing of valid interview data include the following: the addict's recognition of the availability of an official record (that allows corroboration of self-report information); the interviewer's thorough knowledge of the addict subculture, as well as his or her competence, experience, and training in interviewing procedures; the absence of an authoritarian or retribution function in the interview; the assurance of confidentiality; and the use of a structured instrument that enables internal consistency checks and the offering of meaningful time-reference points to assist in the recall of information. (The "addict career" interview, which will be discussed in more detail later, is especially useful in this respect.)

The Crime-Days per Year-at-Risk Concept

Several investigators of the drugs-crime connection have been striving to develop a meaningful application of what has been termed "lambda"—the rate of offending per unit of time (usually a year) for a given population at risk. Our own calculations involving a variation of this index have used self-reported information from narcotic addicts, covering varying periods, while addicted and not addicted to narcotics over a lifetime of narcotic drug use. Because narcotic addicts may engage in hundreds of offenses per year, it has proved useful to express the magnitude of their criminal behavior in terms of the number of crime-days per year-at-risk (while at large in the community), rather than in terms of the total number of offenses committed per year. A *crime-day* is conceptually defined as a twenty-four-hour period, during which one or more crimes are committed by a given individual. Thus, crime-days per year-at-risk is a rate of occurrence that varies from 0 to 365.

Our use of the crime-days per year-at-risk measure has served to document the continuity of high crime rates among narcotic addicts over extended periods. Although there are differences in the types of crimes that individual addicts engage in, their overall high rates of criminality characteristically persist throughout their periods of addiction. The continuity of these high crime rates is remarkable. An analysis of crime-days per year-at-risk for 354 addicts interviewed between 1973 and 1978 revealed that the crime-day means for the first seven addiction periods were 255, 244, 259, 257, 254, 336, and 236, respectively. Thus, the high rate of criminality reported not only was persistent on a day-to-day basis, but also tended to continue over an extended number of years and periods of addiction.[26]

Use of the crime-days per year-at-risk approach has also enabled us to document a reduction in crime when individuals are not actively addicted. Inasmuch as the life course of narcotic addiction or "addict career," while in the community, is characterized by numerous periods of addiction and nonaddiction, it is feasible to compare the amounts of crime committed by individuals when they are addicted and when they are not.[27] When crime rates were compared in this manner, it was found that the number of crime-days per year-at-risk averaged 255 during periods of active addiction and only 65 during periods of nonaddiction.[28] There was, then, a 75-percent decrease in criminality from addiction to nonaddiction. Further analysis showed that there was a decline in annualized crime rates during successive nonaddiction periods as well. Conversely, crime rates during successive addiction periods remained high.

A subsequent study of 250 addicts in Baltimore and New York whom our staff interviewed between 1983 and 1984 provided similar results. It was found that the number of overall crime-days per year-at-risk during periods of addiction averaged 259, while the rate for periods of nonaddiction was 108.[29]

Narcotic Addict Types

There has long been a nagging concern about the order of first occurrence of drug abuse and crime, and about the directional nature of the relationship between the two. Many early studies of the drugs-crime connection were preoccupied with this question. The inquiry was typically stated as an either-or, mutually exclusive one. Addicts either committed crimes to support their habits or were criminals to begin with, addiction merely being one more manifestation of a deviant lifestyle. As mentioned, regardless of whatever side one took, there was general consensus that addicts basically comprised a homogeneous group. Only recently (since the 1970s) have researchers begun to systematically evaluate the differential characteristics of narcotic addicts. A major outgrowth of research, based on an assumption of heterogeneity, has been the derivation of narcotic addict types. Such information is just beginning to be available for consideration by policy makers.

Our own work in this area of research has determined that addicts vary along a host of dimensions, including the degree to which they engage in crime.[30] Some individuals are extremely criminal before they become addicted, while others turn to criminal behavior only as a result of their addiction. There are addicts who do not commit any crime, except for possession of illegal drugs, while others commit several crimes per day and carry weapons while doing so. Certain addicts may maintain rather stable levels of crime, while the criminal behavior of others

may trend upward or downward, as addiction careers extend over time. Also, many addicts undergo treatment for their addictions, while others remain addicted for long periods of time, with no intention of being treated for their drug problems. Only by carefully examining the various kinds of narcotic addicts will more effective use be made of treatment facilities and correctional resources.

In one of our studies of addicts, we classified a sample of 460 individuals, according to criminality, employment, and adequacy of income to meet needs.[31] Two of the types generated by this classification were so different from one another that they suggested two distinct ways of dealing with drug activities. The first type, the "successful criminal," is accustomed to having more than enough money from illicit sources to meet his needs. The second type, the "working addict," is employed at least eight hours a day and is only involved minimally in criminal activities. The successful criminal would appear to be a poor candidate for treatment that counsels him to seek a legitimate job, paying far less than his illegal income. For such a strategy to succeed, this type of addict would have to be monitored closely to ascertain whether or not he was returning to drug abuse and crime. Should reinvolvement occur, he should be promptly referred back to the court for disposition. In contrast, the working addict attempts to live in two worlds, the "straight world" and the drug subculture; his struggle to maintain this precarious balance makes him a prime candidate for receiving help in planning for a more legitimate lifestyle. It is believed that such meaningful, pragmatic typologies will ultimately serve to increase the effectiveness of prevention, rehabilitation, and correctional efforts with respect to the individual at risk.

Use of 'Captive' Samples

Several literature reviews have reported that most investigations of the criminal behavior of narcotic addicts have ignored the problem of population representativeness.[32] Many researchers have studied only "captive" addicts (those in jail or in treatment) who may possess characteristics quite different from those of addicts at large in the community. This fact obviously compromises the generalizability of results.

While a truly random sample of narcotic addicts is apparently impossible to achieve, since the activity is illegal and therefore often unseen, making the population incapable of complete enumeration, in the 1970s, attempts were begun to minimize these difficulties. One example was our own study, which employed a "community-wide" population, consisting of all individuals identified as narcotic addicts by the Baltimore City Police over a twenty-year period.[33] Another approach to the representativeness problem has been the use of samples of narcotic abusers "on the street." In this type of research, ethnographic methods have been used. Often researchers employ ex-addicts or become familiar themselves with the addict subculture in various ways. An example of the latter, the setting up of "storefronts," is exemplified by the work in New York City of Edward A. Preble and John J. Casey[34] in the 1960s and of Bruce Johnson, Paul Goldstein, and others in the 1970s and 1980s.[35]

Ethnographic research may provide a means of obtaining valuable insights into the procurement of information regarding the drugs-crime connection that has not been possible through traditional research. As Goldstein summarized in 1981:

> Careful and probing research is needed to explicate the dynamics underlying both drugs and crime, and the multi-faceted relationship between the two phenomena. Ethnographic techniques may well hold the most promise in this regard. Interviewing subjects in institutional settings, or perusing official statistics, is a poor substitute for being with subjects on a daily basis.[36]

Measures of Criminal Activity Over Time

Career patterns of criminal behavior and drug use were typically ignored in earlier research,[37] most studies having dealt with single-event, pre- and post-intervention comparisons of criminal behavior.[38] Systematically measuring criminal activity over time is a relatively new development. As William H. McGlothlin[39] and other reviewers have noted, however, unless suitable adjustments are made, the age of the addict may become a confounding variable. Since research has shown that many individuals tend to "mature out" of both crime and addiction over time, the decreased prevalence of illicit behavior among older (more experienced) addicts may be a phenomenon associated with age. One way of dealing with this methodologically, as Blumstein and Cohen have suggested, is by "tracking carefully the patterns of offending by individual criminals in order to collect reliable data," which "involves the characterization of the longitudinal pattern of crime events for offenders and assessment of factors that affect that pattern."[40]

A way of applying this method to the joint study of crime and addiction over time has centered around the notion of "addict careers." As mentioned earlier, the addict career, or the time from the first regular narcotic use to the present, is divided into periods of addiction and nonaddiction. Using this longitudinal method, crime rates can be compared between different addiction status periods, as well as over successive periods of addiction and nonaddiction.[41] This form of interview schedule has also been successfully used by McGlothlin, and later by Douglas Anglin, at UCLA in their follow-up studies of addicts.[42]

Types and Extent of Drug-Related Crime

Many researchers have concluded that the prevalence and diversity of criminal involvement by narcotic addicts are high, and that this involvement is primarily for the purpose of supporting the use of drugs. Further, it has been a consistent finding that initiation into both substance abuse and criminal activity occurs at an early age. In particular, several investigators have found that, among samples of drug-using offenders, those who reported the most crime as adults, including the most violent crime, were characteristically precocious in their drug use and illegal activity.[43]

It has also been a uniform finding that frequency of narcotic use is generally associated with higher crime rates. Johnson and his associates[44] found that the heaviest heroin users were more likely to be classified as serious offenders. In their research, such individuals were found to be disproportionately represented in the highest categories of criminal involvement and had the highest incomes from major crime. Examining a broader range of drug abusers, the Research Triangle Institute group[45] reported that "expensive" drug use was at least a partial explanation for income-generating crime. These investigators found that more-than-once-a-day heroin and cocaine use predicted comparatively high levels of illegal income. Further examination of the drug-use-frequency/income-from-crime relationship suggested that, whereas low-use levels are supportable without resort to illegal activity, frequent daily use rarely is. And Chaiken and Chaiken,[46] classifying prison and jail inmates as addicted heroin users, nonaddicted heroin users, nonheroin drug users, and nondrug users, found that addicted heroin users had markedly higher levels of criminal activity than did nonheroin drug users.

In explanation of the above results, one might argue that those individuals prone to be heavy drug users are also innately prone to become involved in criminal activity. Evidence of a more direct relationship between narcotic drug-use frequency and crime requires longitudinal, intra-subject information on narcotic-abusing individuals over periods varying with respect to frequency of narcotic drug use. In our own studies of addict careers, the consistently high rates of criminality associated with addiction periods and the markedly lower rates found in the nonaddiction periods provide substantial support for a causal component in the relationship of drug use to crime. The most parsimonious explanation of these within-group changes in crime rates with varying amounts of narcotic use is that narcotic addiction contributes to an increase in crime. Without engaging in a discussion of causal analysis, it seems evident from the totality of the data that heroin addiction is criminogenic in the same sense that cigarette smoking or air pollutants are carcinogenic—they can, and often do, lead to increased inci-

dence, although they are not the only causal agents.

Although individual addicts vary with respect to the crime they engage in, narcotic addicts as a group engage in many different types of criminal activity. Examining a sample of male and female narcotic users in Miami between 1978 and 1981, Inciardi found that over a preceding twelve-month period, the 573 individuals in this sample were responsible for over 82,000 drug sales, nearly 6,000 robberies and assaults, 6,700 burglaries, and 900 car thefts, as well as for more than 25,000 instances of shoplifting and 46,000 other types of larceny and fraud. Overall, they were responsible for a total of 215,105 criminal offenses of all types during the twelve-month reporting period, or an average of 375 offenses per narcotic user.[47]

Drug-Distribution Crimes

Drug-distribution crimes (e.g., dealing, copping, tasting) appear to account for a sizable proportion of all crimes performed by narcotic abusers. For Inciardi's sample, drug sales was by far the most frequent crime, accounting for 38 percent of all offenses. The respondents averaged 144 drug sales per year.[48] A sample of 201 heroin abusers studied by Johnson reported committing, on the average, 828 crimes per year per user. The most frequent crime was drug sales, or dealing, which accounted for 34 percent of all crimes. The second most frequent crime was copping (buying for others), which constituted 28 percent of all crimes. Taken together, these and other drug-distribution offenses accounted for 65 percent of all crimes reported.[49]

Our recent studies of addicts interviewed in Baltimore and New York, during 1983 and 1984, also documented the dominance of drug-distribution crimes. This sample of 250 male addicts reported performing drug-distribution crimes on nearly 48,000 days while addicted, the average time spent addicted being nearly eight years. On average, the addicts were involved in drug-distribution crimes 191 days per year. For the entire sample, drug-distribution crimes accounted for 48.3 percent of all crime-days. Comparisons of crime-days frequencies with those reported by an earlier sample of addicts interviewed, during 1973–1978, revealed a higher proportion of drug-distribution crimes and a lower proportion of theft crimes in the more recent sample. In the earlier sample, drug-distribution crimes accounted for only 27 percent of the crime-days, while theft crimes made up 38 percent of the crime-days.[50]

The 100 subjects interviewed in Baltimore were also examined in a separate series of analyses, comparing crime-days results with those for an earlier sample of Baltimore addicts.[51] It was found that, for both black and white addicts, crime increased overall, with the greatest area of increase in drug-distribution crimes. This was true of crimes committed during both addiction periods and nonaddiction periods. Minor differences in study procedures, however, render these findings tentative rather than conclusive.

Violent Crimes

Obviously, because of their severe consequences to victims, policy makers and the media have emphasized violent drug-related crimes. While investigations by us and others have reported that violent crimes make up a small proportion of all crimes committed by addicts, the actual number of such offenses is still large, since addicts commit so many crimes. For example, in Inciardi's sample of 573 narcotic users, the proportion of violent crimes committed in the year before the interview constituted only 2.8 percent of all offenses, but this amounted to nearly six thousand offenses, since a total of 215,105 crimes were committed.[52]

Paul Goldstein[53] has recorded many ethnographic accounts of violent drug-related acts from both perpetrators and victims in New York City. Resulting from this research is his theory that violent crime and drugs can be related in three different ways. The psychopharmacological model of violence implies that individuals act violently because of the short- or long-term effects of the ingestion of certain substances. Crimes resulting from withdrawal effects of heroin or directly related to barbiturate or PCP use are examples of this. The economically com-

pulsive model suggests that violent crime is committed to obtain money to purchase drugs. This applies primarily to expensive drugs, such as heroin and cocaine. The systemic model purports that violence results from the traditionally aggressive patterns of interaction within the drug-distribution system. Killing or assaulting someone for distributing "bad" drugs is an example of this.

A study of 578 homicides in Manhattan in 1981 found that 38 percent of the male victims and 14 percent of the female victims were murdered as result of drug-related activity.[54] This report, published in 1986, stated that the observed proportion of homicides related to drug and other criminal activities was higher than had been reported previously in the United States. The authors concluded that rather than being related to pharmacological actions producing aggressive and homicidal behavior, the effects of drugs were probably indirect and related to drug-seeking activities. They concluded that "the fact that over one-third of male homicide victims in Manhattan in 1981 died in drug-related homicides attests to the magnitude and the impact of the drug problem, particularly with narcotics."[55]

Non-Narcotic Drug Use and Crime

While it has been acknowledged that a substantial relationship exists between narcotic addiction and crime, the situation has been somewhat less clear with regard to non-narcotic drugs. In a comprehensive review of the literature published in 1980, Robert P. Gandossy and his associates found the evidence connecting the use of various non-narcotic drugs to crime to be inconclusive.[56] A further problem concerning this issue is that narcotic and non-narcotic drugs are often used in combination. Thus, disentangling their joint relationship to criminal behavior, let alone resolving the issue of cause and effect, is problematical. Research endeavors in the past decade, however, have made several advances in addressing these difficulties.

One method of approaching the issue has been to study the crime rates of individuals, during a particular period in which they were strictly non-narcotic users and had never become addicted to narcotics. Inciardi interviewed a sample of 429 such individuals in the years 1978–1981.[57] Reporting both a high prevalence and a diversity of crimes, these individuals admitted to committing a total of 137,076 offenses, for an average of 320 crimes per user, over a one-year period. This rate was slightly lower and the diversity of crimes somewhat less than those found for a sample of narcotic users interviewed during the same period. Of the crimes committed by the non-narcotic users, drug sales accounted for 28 percent, prostitution for 18 percent, and shoplifting for 16 percent.[58]

Another way of studying the non-narcotic, drug-crime relationship has been to correlate rates of various types of crime with the use of non-narcotic drugs during periods of addiction and nonaddiction to narcotics. Our own findings from this type of approach have consistently indicated that the use of certain non-narcotic drugs by narcotic addicts is associated with the commission of certain types of crime, although this varied somewhat by ethnic group and narcotic addiction status.[59] Cocaine use was found to have a particularly high association with several different types of crime, including theft, violent crimes, drug dealing, and confidence games. This association appeared to be stronger in black and Hispanic addicts than in white addicts.[60]

Treatment and Rehabilitation

Most of the addicts we have studied in over twenty years of research have been arrested a number of times and have spent considerable time in prison. Many addicts have also had at least one treatment experience for narcotic drug abuse. However, these arrests, periods of incarceration, and treatment experiences appear to have had little deterrent effect on subsequent criminal behavior in the community for a good many addicts. As we have indicated elsewhere,[61] the finding of continuity and persistence of criminal behavior among narcotic addicts stands out as a major conclusion of our research.

Some encouraging findings concerning rehabilitation efforts have involved the use of legal pressures accompanied by a moni-toring or surveillance component. Studies of the California Civil Addict Program by McGlothlin and Anglin[62] found that court-ordered, drug-free outpatient treatment accompanied by supervision, including urine testing and weekly visits to a parole officer, was associated with reduced criminal activity. Other studies, conducted by investigators at the Research Triangle Institute (RTI) in North Carolina, found that legal pressure was positively related to retention in treatment programs, and that time in treatment was a significant factor in the reduction of criminal behavior following treatment.[63] And, encouraged by their findings in a recently reported study of legal pressure and methadone-maintenance outcome, Anglin and his colleagues[64] argue for greater utilization of community drug treatment by pretrial, probation, and parole agencies.

By far the most ambitious series of studies of the influence of treatment on the behavior of the narcotic addict has been that conducted by the Institute of Behavioral Research at Texas Christian University in Ft. Worth.[65] Based on a client reporting system for community-based drug abuse programs, titled Drug Abuse Reporting Program (DARP), this treatment-outcome evaluation research involved a comparison of the effectiveness of methadone-maintenance programs (therapeutic communities, outpatient drug-free treatments, outpatient detoxification clinics, and no treatment). Major criteria of effectiveness included illicit drug use and criminality, along with alcohol use, employment, and need for further treatment. Post-treatment results over a three-year follow-up period were available for four to five thousand clients, with many individuals being followed for as long as six years after treatment admission.

Findings of the DARP revealed a clear-cut superiority of methadone maintenance, therapeutic community, and outpatient drug-free treatment over outpatient detoxification and no treatment. No further differentiation was made among the three effective treatment approaches, all of which produced a marked reduction in self-reported narcotic drug use and criminal behavior. Regardless of treatment type, outcomes associated with treatments of less than ninety days tended to be poor. Persons with less criminal involvement before treatment and persons employed before treatment were more likely to demonstrate favorable outcomes. As apparent in our own research, criminal activity during follow-up was related to daily drug use. And, consistent with the results of other studies, there was no obvious interaction between client and treatment types in terms of outcome.[66]

For DARP clients, during-treatment performance, including longer program involvement and completion of the program, was also positively related to outcome. As in the RTI studies, the marked improvement that tended to occur after the first few months of treatment, particularly with methadone maintenance, suggested a compliance factor associated with coercive entry and program surveillance. After this marked change, there was continued improvement over time in treatment, which suggested a therapeutic effect, due to the development of motivation that was also instrumental in the clients' remaining in treatment.[67]

Policy Implications

Although narcotic addicts as a group extensively engage in crime, the amounts and types of crimes committed vary considerably across individuals. The criminal activity of most addicts is strongly influenced by current addiction status. Narcotic addicts commit millions of crimes per year in the United States, and many of these offenses are of a serious nature. In a very real sense, it can be said that illicit narcotic drugs "drive" crime. Therefore, there is a pressing need to address the problem by continuing to inform the public and its leaders concerning the magnitude and perseverance of criminal behavior among heroin addicts.

As several recent writers have suggested,[68] one approach to a solution involves the early identification of those individuals prone to commit large numbers of serious crimes. Our studies, as well as those by Chaiken and Chaiken, have indicated that, among offenders, those who are precocious in crime and poly-drug use will most likely become the most dangerous, long-term criminals.[69] In addition, we are currently studying the etiology of drug abuse, with the goal of determining the distinguishing characteristics of those individuals who later become addicts, as opposed to their peers who do not. Such information will eventually be useful in planning prevention and intervention strategies.

Another policy with regard to drug abuse and crime centers on the targeted reduction of the amounts of illicit drugs, especially heroin and cocaine, consumed by daily users. Implementation of this policy would involve identifying criminally active, daily heroin and cocaine users and ensuring that they are treated and closely monitored in order to alter their drug-abuse patterns. Our studies suggest that this particular strategy may work best with addicts minimally involved in crime before becoming addicted and during periods of nonaddiction (i.e., those whose criminal activity is more exclusively related to supporting a habit).[70]

In determining an appropriate disposition of a narcotic drug abuser after arrest, it should again be emphasized that there is not a one-to-one relationship between official arrest records and extent of criminal activity. For a more accurate estimate of the latter, it is important that frequency of narcotic abuse also be determined. From our experiences and those of Johnson and his associates, it appears that the more criminally prone, heaviest narcotic abusers are "slipping through the cracks of the criminal justice system."[71] These individuals are committing more crimes per arrest and are managing to avoid involvement in drug-abuse treatment efforts.

Identifying the "heavy" drug abuser is, however, problematic. While individuals tend to be truthful in reporting drug use in research situations, where confidentiality and immunity from prosecution are ordinarily guaranteed, there is evidence that, on arrest, they are likely to conceal their recent drug use.[72] As a result of this finding, urine testing of arrestees has been recommended as an additional means of identifying those who are habitual drug users. Urine testing has, therefore, been utilized in many jurisdictions as an additional means of identifying arrestees who are drug users. It has recently been estimated that approximately 70 percent of those arrested for serious crimes in major U.S. cities test positive for at least one illicit drug.[73] However, while a single positive urinalysis result is a valid indicator of recent drug use, it is not sufficient to identify an individual as a frequent and persistent drug user. As several researchers have indicated, a series of positive results over a long period of time tends to be a more accurate indicator.[74]

At the very least, it would be advisable for criminal justice authorities to give more concerted attention to evidence concerning the drug activity of individuals who are arrested. One useful approach to this task would be to develop a triage/liaison service within the criminal justice system that would deal exclusively with the disposition of drug-abusing offenders. This service would provide a much-needed link between the criminal justice system and a variety of drug-abuse treatment programs available for rehabilitation. Major functions of the service would include participation in decisions regarding sentencing, parole, and probation, as well as in implementation of procedures for the appropriate placement, monitoring, and evaluation of outcome for all narcotic addict arrestees. Thus, this service would be an important resource to clinicians who treat drug abusers, as well as to judges and other criminal justice system officials who are involved in the disposition of individual cases.

It is important to reiterate that all narcotic addicts are not alike. What works with one type of addict may not work with another. Some addicts commit a considerable amount of crime, regardless of whether they are addicted, and they may engage in crime several years before becoming addicted to narcotics. On the other hand, other addicts may not commit much crime and may only commit crimes directly related to their use of drugs; during periods of nonaddiction, their criminal activities may drop to trivial levels. As we have emphasized, there are clearly different types of addicts and different pathways to addiction. Effective strate-

gies for dealing with the drugs-crime problem will depend, to a significant extent, on recognizing this diversity among addicts and on tailoring counter-measures, both therapeutic and judicial, to individual requirements.

Legalizing Drug Use

Some policy makers have proposed that drug-related crime be curtailed by legalizing the use of illicit drugs, making them openly available at little or no cost. This is offered as an admittedly simplistic solution that requires the development of strategies aimed at preserving the smooth functioning of society and mitigating damage to addiction-prone individuals. Outlandish as it may seem, this is an intriguing notion, the ramifications of which bear consideration, in view of the lack of effectiveness of current methods of controlling drug use that largely involve attempts at cutting off the sources of drug supply.

A look at history is particularly helpful in conceptualizing the polarity of this issue. During the era of prohibition of alcohol use in this country, emphasis was placed on eliminating sources of supply. As a consequence, alcoholism became less of a national problem, but organized crime flourished in its nearly exclusive role as distributor of alcoholic products. The subsequent repeal of the prohibition, while dealing a significant blow to the underworld, undeniably increased the number of alcoholics and problematic drinkers in our society.[75]

We are now faced with an analogous situation. Unless innovative strategies are developed, the alternative to the high level of drug-related crime associated with strict drug control appears to be an inevitable rise in the number of drug-dependent individuals in society. Ignoring ethical and moral issues for the moment, from a purely pragmatic standpoint, there is the question of how many drug-dependent individuals society can tolerate.

Basic unresolved questions make any position taken, with regard to the impact of the legalization of drugs, a matter of educated opinion, at best. No one knows for certain the extent to which legalization of drugs in this country would increase the number of addicts, nor whether such a strategy would eventually undermine the integrity of our society. Few would deny, however, that the greater availability of, and easier access to, drugs would increase drug use (and addiction) beyond current levels. Whether this nation can be adequately prepared to deal with the consequences of this increase is, again, a matter of conjecture that is beyond the scope of this chapter. More pertinent is this question: What would be the impact of open drug availability on drug-related crime?

To a large extent, the amount of drug-related crime committed is proportional to the costs of drugs, and the latter depend to a large extent on supply and demand. On the supply side, there are two important considerations with regard to legalization, both of which have to do with the effects of a vigorously enforced policy of interdiction. When it is most effective, a policy of interdiction reduces the supply of drugs and, as a consequence, raises the prices people have to pay for them. It also increases the risks associated with drug production and distribution and thus increases the compensation demanded by drug suppliers for their services. Again, the end result is higher drug prices. Assuming that interdiction will never entirely eliminate the supply of drugs, the ironic conclusion is that vigorously enforced interdiction may very well be instrumental in increasing drug-related crime.

In view of the above, some would argue that legalizing drugs would lead to substantial reductions in drug costs and a corresponding reduction in drug-related crime. Such an argument, however, assumes exclusive, trouble-free governmental regulation of the drug supply. Such an assumption would appear to be untenable. The possibility of providing a more desirable drug price and/or purity, unrestricted quantity, personal anonymity, lack of restrictions with regard to age, and other similar inducements could readily lead to black-market competition in drug sales and thus continue the involvement of illegitimate sources of drug supply. Also, the argument ignores the impulsivity and lack of control associated with the use of certain drugs and the crime-linked effects of such drugs as PCP (which produces both self-destructive and assaultive behavior) and cocaine (the excessive use of which has been associated with violence stemming from affective disturbance and paranoid ideation).

This leads us to a consideration of the demand side of the equation, relating supply and demand to drug cost and attendant crime. In view of the above, and the fact that greater demand is associated with increased cost, adoption of intervention strategies aimed at diminishing demand for illicit drugs appears to be the most suitable approach to dealing with the issue of drugs and crime. Consequently, an appropriate policy recommendation would be that concerted attempts be made to dissuade individuals from becoming involved with drugs, along with persistent efforts to wean them off drugs when and if they do become involved. Drug-prevention and treatment programs employing both novel and already proven approaches should, therefore, be targeted for increased support on a national level by both governmental agencies and private funding sources. To the extent that it is drug-related, criminal activity in this country should show discernible signs of abatement with any subsequent decrease in drug demand that can thus be effected.

Notes

1. James A. Inciardi, ed., *The Drugs-Crime Connection* (Beverly Hills, CA: Sage, 1981), 7.

2. James A. Inciardi, *The War on Drugs: Heroin, Cocaine, and Public Policy* (Palo Alto, CA: Mayfield, 1986), 106.

3. David F. Musto, *The American Disease: Origins of Narcotic Control* (New Haven, CT: Yale University Press, 1973).

4. *Ibid.*, 326.

5. Harry E. Barnes and Negley K. Teeters, *New Horizons in Criminology* (New York: Prentice-Hall, 1945), 877.

6. Inciardi, *The War on Drugs*, 148.

7. Robert P. Gandossy, Jay R. Williams, Jo Cohen, and Henrick J. Harwood, *Drugs and Crime: A Survey and Analysis of the Literature* (Washington, DC: U.S. Department of Justice, National Institute of Justice, 1980), 67.

8. See Harold Finestone, "Narcotics and Criminality," *Law and Contemporary Problems* 22 (Winter 1957):72–85; Gregory A. Austin and Dan J. Lettieri, *Drugs and Crime: The Relationship of Drug Use and Concomitant Criminal Behavior* (Rockville, MD: National Institute on Drug Abuse, 1976); Inciardi, *The Drugs-Crime Connection;* David N. Nurco, John C. Ball, John W. Shaffer, and Thomas E. Hanlon, "The Criminality of Narcotic Addicts," *Journal of Nervous and Mental Disease* 173 (1985):94–102; Inciardi, *The War on Drugs.*

9. Inciardi, *The War on Drugs.*

10. Alfred Blumstein and Jacqueline Cohen, "Characterizing Criminal Careers," *Science* 237 (1987):985–91.

11. Bruce D. Johnson, Paul J. Goldstein, Edward Preble, James Schmeidler, Douglas S. Lipton, Barry Spunt, and Thomas Miller, *Taking Care of Business: The Economics of Crime by Heroin Abusers* (Lexington, MA: Lexington, 1985).

12. President's Commission on Law Enforcement and the Administration of Justice, *The Challenge of Crime in a Free Society* (Washington, DC: U.S. Government Printing Office, 1967), 229.

13. Robert Shellow, ed., *Drug Use and Crime: Report of the Panel on Drug Use and Criminal Behavior* (Washington, DC: National Technical Information Service, 1976), 5.

14. Inciardi, *The War on Drugs.*

15. James J. Collins, J. Valley Rachal, Robert L. Hubbard, Elizabeth R. Cavanaugh, S. Gail Craddock, and Patricia L. Kristiansen, *Criminality in a Drug Treatment Sample: Measurement Issues and Initial Findings* (Research Triangle Park, NC: Research Triangle Institute, 1982), 27.

16. Jan M. Chaiken and Marcia R. Chaiken, *Who Gets Caught Doing Crime?* (Los Angeles: Hamilton, Rabinovitz, Szanton, and Alschuler, Inc., 1985).

17. See James A. Inciardi and Carl D. Chambers, "Unreported Criminal Involvement of Narcotic Addicts," *Journal of Drug Issues* 2 (1972):57–64; William H. McGlothlin, M. Douglas Anglin, and Bruce D. Wilson, "Narcotic Addiction and Crime," *Criminology* 16 (1978):293–316; John C. Ball, Lawrence Rosen, John A. Flueck, and David N. Nurco, "Lifetime Criminality of Heroin Addicts in the United States," *Journal of Drug Issues* 12 (1982):225–39.

18. Inciardi, *The War on Drugs.*

19. *Ibid.,* 127.

20. Jan M. Chaiken and Marcia R. Chaiken, *Varieties of Criminal Behavior: Summary and Policy Implications* (Santa Monica, CA: Rand, 1982), 18.

21. Chaiken and Chaiken, *Who Gets Caught Doing Crime?*

22. Ball, Rosen, Flueck, and Nurco, "Lifetime Criminality of Heroin Addicts."

23. *Ibid.*

24. Richard C. Stephens, "The Truthfulness of Addict Respondents in Research Projects," *International Journal of the Addictions* 7 (1972):549–58.

25. See John C. Ball, "The Reliability and Validity of Interview Data Obtained from Narcotic Drug Addicts," *American Journal of Sociology* 72 (1972):549–58; Stephens, "The Truthfulness"; Arthur J. Bonito, David N. Nurco, and John W. Shaffer, "The Veridicality of Addicts' Self-Reports in Social Research," *International Journal of the Addictions* 11 (1976):719–24.

26. John C. Ball, John W. Shaffer, and David N. Nurco, "The Day-to-Day Criminality of Heroin Addicts in Baltimore—A Study in the Continuity of Offense Rates," *Drug and Alcohol Dependence* 12 (1983):119–42.

27. See Ball, Rosen, Flueck, and Nurco, "Lifetime Criminality of Heroin Addicts"; Hall, Shaffer, and Nurco, "The Day-to-Day Criminality"; John W. Shaffer, David N. Nurco, and Timothy W. Kinlock, "A New Classification of Narcotic Addicts," *Comprehensive Psychiatry* 25 (1984):315–28; David N. Nurco, John W. Shaffer, John C. Ball, Timothy W. Kinlock, and John Langrod, "A Comparison by Ethnic Group and City of the Criminal Activities of Narcotic Addicts," *Journal of Nervous and Mental Disease* 174 (1986):112–116.

28. Ball, Shaffer, and Nurco, "The Day-to-Day Criminality," 123.

29. *Ibid.*

30. See David N. Nurco, Ira H. Cisin, and Mitchell B. Balter, "Addict Careers I: A New Typology," *International Journal of the Addictions* 8 (1981):1305–25; "Addict Careers II: The First Ten Years," *International Journal of the Addictions* 8 (1981):1327–56; "Addict Careers III: Trends Across Time," *International Journal of the Addictions* 8 (1981):1357–72; David N. Nurco and John W. Shaffer, "Types and Characteristics of Addicts in the Community," *Drug and Alcohol Dependence* 9 (1982):43–78; Shaffer, Nurco, and Kinlock,

"A New Classification"; David N. Nurco, Thomas E. Hanlon, Mitchell B. Balter, Timothy W. Kinlock, and Evelyn Slaght, "A Classification of Narcotic Addicts Based on Type, Amount, and Severity of Crime," *Journal of Drug Issues* (in press).

31. Nurco and Shaffer, "Types and Characteristics."

32. See Gandossy, Williams, Cohen, and Harwood, *Drugs and Crime*; Anne E. Pottieger, "Sample Bias in Drugs/Crime Research: An Empirical Study," in *The Drugs-Crime Connection*, ed. James A. Inciardi (Beverly Hills, CA: Sage, 1981), 207–38; George Speckart and M. Douglas Anglin, "Narcotics and Crime: An Analysis of Existing Evidence for a Causal Relationship," *Behavioral Sciences and the Law* 3 (1985):259–82.

33. David N. Nurco and Robert L. DuPont, "A Preliminary Report on Crime and Addiction Within a Community-Wide Population of Narcotic Addicts," *Drug and Alcohol Dependence* 2 (1977):109–21.

34. Edward A. Preble and John J. Casey, Jr., "Taking Care of Business: The Heroin User's Life on the Street," *International Journal of the Addictions* 4 (1969):1–24.

35. See Paul J. Goldstein, "Getting Over: Economic Alternatives to Predating Crime Among Street Drug Users," in *The Drugs-Crime Connection*, ed. James A. Inciardi (Beverly Hills, CA: Sage, 1981), 67–84; Johnson et al., *Taking Care of Business*.

36. Goldstein, "Getting Over," 82–83.

37. Gandossy, Williams, Cohen, and Harwood, *Drugs and Crime*, 67.

38. See William H. McGlothlin, "Drugs and Crime," in *Handbook on Drug Abuse*, ed. Robert L. DuPont, Avram Goldstein, and John O'Donnell (Washington, DC: National Institute on Drug Abuse and Office of Drug Policy, 1979), 357–64; Gandossy, Williams, Cohen, and Harwood, *Drugs and Crime*, 110.

39. McGlothlin, "Drugs and Crime."

40. Blumstein and Cohen, "Characterizing Criminal Careers," 985.

41. See David N. Nurco, "A Discussion of Validity," in *Self-Reporting Methods in Estimating Drug Abuse*, ed. Beatrice A. Rouse, Nicholas J. Kozel, and Louise G. Richards (Rockville, MD: National Institute on Drug Abuse, 1985), 4–11.

42. See McGlothlin, Anglin, and Wilson, "Narcotic Addiction and Crime"; M. Douglas Anglin and George Speckart, "Narcotics Use, Property Crime, and Dealing: Structural Dynamics Across the Addiction Career," *Journal of Quantitative Criminology* 2 (1986):355–75.

43. See Chaiken and Chaiken, *Varieties of Criminal Behavior*; Shaffer, Nurco, and Kinlock, "A New Classification."

44. Johnson et al., *Taking Care of Business*.

45. James J. Collins, Robert L. Hubbard, and J. Valley Rachal, *Heroin and Cocaine Use and Illegal Income* (Research Triangle Park, NC: Research Triangle Institute, 1984).

46. Chaiken and Chaiken, *Varieties of Criminal Behavior*.

47. *Ibid.*

48. *Ibid.*

49. Johnson et al., *Taking Care of Business*, 77.

50. Nurco, Shaffer, Ball, Kinlock, and Langrod, "A Comparison by Ethnic Group and City."

51. *Ibid.*

52. Chaiken and Chaiken, *Varieties of Criminal Behavior*.

53. Paul J. Goldstein, "Drugs and Violent Behavior" (Paper presented at the annual meeting of the Academy of Criminal Justice Sciences, Louisville, KY, 28 April 1982).

54. Kenneth Tardiff, Elliot M. Gross, and Steven F. Messner, "A Study of Homicide in Manhattan, 1981," *American Journal of Public Health* 76 (1986):139–43.

55. *Ibid.*, 143.

56. Gandossy, Williams, Cohen, and Harwood, *Drugs and Crime*.

57. Inciardi, *The War on Drugs*, 128–30.

58. *Ibid.*

59. See John W. Shaffer, David N. Nurco, John C. Ball, and Timothy W. Kinlock, "The Frequency of Nonnarcotic Drug Use and Its Relationship to Criminal Activity Among Narcotic Addicts," *Comprehensive Psychiatry* 26 (1985):558–66; David N. Nurco, Timothy W. Kinlock, Thomas E. Hanlon, and John C. Ball, "Nonnarcotic Drug Use Over an Addiction Career—A Study of Heroin Addicts in Baltimore and New York City," *Comprehensive Psychiatry* 29 (1988):450–59.

60. *Ibid.*

61. Nurco, Ball, Shaffer, and Hanlon, "The Criminality of Narcotic Addicts."

62. See William H. McGlothlin, M. Douglas Anglin, and Bruce D. Wilson, *An Evaluation of the California Civil Addict Program* (Washington, DC: U.S. Government Printing Office, 1977); M. Douglas Anglin and William H.

McGlothlin, "Outcome of Narcotic Addict Treatment in California," in *Drug Abuse Treatment Evaluation: Strategies, Progress, and Prospects*, ed. Frank Tims and Jacqueline P. Ludford (Washington, DC: U.S. Government Printing Office, 1984), 106–28.

63. See James J. Collins and Margaret Allison, "Legal Coercion and Retention in Drug Abuse Treatment," *Hospital and Community Psychiatry* 34 (1983):1145–49; Robert L. Hubbard, J. Valley Rachal, S. Gail Craddock, and Elizabeth R. Cavanaugh, "Treatment Outcome Prospective Study (TOPS): Client Characteristics and Behaviors Before, During, and After Treatment," in *Drug Abuse Treatment Evaluation: Strategies, Progress, and Prospects*, ed. Frank Tims and Jacqueline P. Ludford (Washington, DC: U.S. Government Printing Office, 1984), 42–68.

64. M. Douglas Anglin, Mary-Lynn Brecht, and Ebrahim Maddahian, "Pretreatment Characteristics and Treatment Performance of Legally Coerced Versus Voluntary Methadone-Maintenance Admissions," *Criminology* 27 (1989):537–57.

65. D. Dwayne Simpson and Saul B. Sells, *Highlights of the DARP Follow-Up Research on the Evaluation of Drug Abuse Treatment Effectiveness* (Ft. Worth: Institute of Behavioral Research, Texas Christian University, 1981).

66. Shaffer, Nurco, Ball, and Kinlock, "The Frequency of Nonnarcotic Drug Use and Its Relationship to Criminal Activity Among Narcotics Addicts."

67. Simpson and Sells, *Highlights of the DARP.*

68. See Chaiken and Chaiken, *Varieties of Criminal Behavior;* Peter W. Greenwood, *Selective Incapacitation* (Santa Monica, CA: Rand, 1982); Nurco, Ball, Shaffer, and Hanlon, "The Criminality of Narcotic Addicts."

69. *Ibid.*

70. See David N. Nurco, Thomas E. Hanlon, Timothy W. Kinlock, and Karen R. Duszynski, "Differential Patterns of Criminal Activity Over an Addiction Career," *Criminology* (in press).

71. Bruce D. Johnson, Paul Goldstein, Edward Preble, James Schneidler, Douglas S. Lipton, Barry Spunt, Nina Duchaine, Reuben Norman, Thomas Miller, Nancy Meggett, Andrea Kale, and Deborah Hand, *Economic Behavior of Street Opiate Users: Final Report* (New York: Narcotic and Drug Research, Inc., 1983), 232.

72. Eric Wish, "Drug-Use Forecasting: New York 1984 to 1986," *National Institute of Justice Research in Action*, February 1987.

73. James R. Stewart (director, National Institute of Justice), *NIJ Reports*, no. 213 (Washington: U.S. Department of Justice, March–April 1989), 1–3.

74. See Chaiken and Chaiken, *Varieties of Criminal Behavior;* Eric D. Wish, Mary A. Toborg, and John P. Bellasai, *Identifying Drug Users and Monitoring Them During Conditional Release* (Washington, DC: U.S. Department of Justice, 1987); Marcia R. Chaiken and Bruce D. Johnson, *Characteristics of Different Types of Drug-Involved Offenders* (Washington: U.S. Department of Justice, 1988).

75. Mark Moore and Dean Gerston, eds., *Alcohol and Public Policy: Beyond the Shadow of Prohibition* (Washington, DC: National Academy Press, 1981).

For Discussion

How might the drugs-crime relationship differ by gender, and what are the implications for drug treatment and policy?

31

Drug Use and Street Crime in Miami

An (Almost) Twenty-Year Retrospective

James A. Inciardi
Anne E. Pottieger

Researchers at the University of Delaware have been conducting field studies of drug use and crime in Miami, Florida, since 1977. This article reviews this research and its contributions to understanding drugs-crime relationships. Early studies tested mechanisms for accessing street populations of heroin users and assessing the nature and extent of their drug use and criminality. Subsequent studies targeted a variety of crime-involved heroin and cocaine users, including women as well as men, serious delinquents, adolescent and adult crack users, and cocaine users in treatment as well as on the street. Major findings include the low risk of arrest for income-generating crimes committed by heroin users, and the prevalence of HIV-risk behaviors among both serious delinquents and women crack users. Analyses consistently show the critical importance of sample characteristics in research on drug use, including age, cohort, and street-versus-treatment status.

Beginnings

When the first author started as a research assistant at the New York State Narcotic Addiction Control Commission in 1968, one of his first assignments was to summarize existing research on the relationship between drug use and crime. So he looked at the literature all the way back to the 1920s, when the first empirical studies were done. The most common theoretical framework throughout this research seemed to be the "chicken-egg" question: which came first in an opiate addict's career, addiction or criminal behavior? (For summaries, see Austin and Lettieri, 1976; Chambers, 1974; Gandossey et al., 1980; Greenberg and Adler, 1974; Inciardi, 1974; Weissman, 1978.) About half of the studies concluded that opiate addiction came first. This finding was usually explained by some form of "enslavement theory"—the argument that opiate addiction enslaves people to such a degree that otherwise law-abiding citizens are forced to commit crimes to support their drug habits. The other half of the drugs and crime studies found that addicts were criminals first, and that opiate addiction was just a later stage in an already established deviant lifestyle.

The sample selection and analytic methods in these studies were striking demonstrations of how research on the drugs-crime relationship can be limited by methodological shortcomings. We all still live with this problem today, of course. This explains why a review committee can always find something wrong with the methodology discussion in any grant application. But, in the early drugs-crime literature, the problems were truly blatant. Most notably, the great majority of the studies looked exclusively at addicts in treatment—forgetting about drug users in the criminal justice system, and forgetting about that great number of street addicts with no interest in treatment and no history of treatment. The few studies that did not have treatment samples were done with addicts in jails and prisons—additional biased samples and in particular other kinds of institutionalized samples. Moreover, most samples were very small; the exception was studies in which the data were confined to the contents of official records. The measures employed in these early studies were also totally inadequate. Onset of criminality, for example, was most commonly indicated by date of first arrest (see Chambers, 1974; Greenberg and Adler, 1974).

At the Narcotic Commission, the first author and the Research Director decided to try conducting a self-report study of crime among addicts. Self-report crime studies, of course, had been around a long time. They were first conducted in the 1940s with college students, and a study of self-reported crime in the 1950s done with ordinary high school students (Short and Nye, 1958) revolutionized the study of juvenile delinquency. But even by the late 1960s, scarcely any specific information was available about crimes committed by heroin addicts: What offense types did they commit? How many? The Narcotic Commission study, designed by the first author and the late Carl D. Chambers, who was the Narcotic Commission's Director of Research at the time, was published in 1972 (Inciardi and Chambers, 1972). As in most prior research on heroin users, the sample had been identified from treatment records and it was a small sample (38 men and 22 women certified to the Commission for treatment). But as far as we know, it was the first published study of addicts' self-reported criminal behavior—not just arrest charges, but what kinds of offenses addicts were committing, and in what numbers. The study was limited in many ways, but it planted the seeds for what became almost twenty years of street research on drug use and crime in Miami.

In 1971 the first author left New York and relocated to Miami, Florida. He took research positions with both the Metropolitan Dade County Comprehensive Drug Program and the Division of Addiction Sciences at the University of Miami School of Medicine. Over the next five years he made many contacts with Miami treatment agency staff members and criminal justice system personnel. But some of the research he did during this time also brought him in contact with various and sundry users, dealers, traffickers, arms merchants, and mercenaries—both active and retired—and many others who inhabit the netherworlds and underworlds of crime and vice in Miami. The street studies included observations and tracking of the emergence of the cocaine freebase culture, the diversion of illegal methadone, the diffusion of such new drugs as PCP and methaqualone, and the beginnings of cocaine as a major drug of choice. Many of the street contacts developed in this research were very helpful later in starting multiple snowball-contact chains to locate street sample respondents in our own studies.

In 1973 he helped to design a study that was one of the first projects ever funded by a new federal agency—the one we now call the National Institute on Drug Abuse (NIDA); he later took over as director of the project. This was a study of acute drug reactions that included interviews in hospital emergency rooms with patients admitted for acute drug reactions, as well as analysis of the medical records for the 11,287 drug emergencies seen at Miami's Jackson Memorial Hospital from 1972 through 1976 (see Inciardi et al., 1978, 1979). While completing this study he submitted a new grant application to NIDA to test a methodology for doing street studies of drugs and crime, with Miami as the proposed field site. By the time the grant was funded, he was no longer in Miami. Or, more accurately, in 1976 he officially left. But in virtual reality, he has lived in two places ever since, which is how he manages to hold faculty positions at both the University of Delaware and the University of Miami School of Medicine.

The Unapprehended Crime Study

The first grant was awarded in 1977 to the first author as the Principal Investigator at his new location at the University of Delaware. The second author has just completed her Ph.D. and was hired as the only full-time employee on the study. The project was entitled "Exploratory Study of Unapprehended Criminality Among Heroin Users and Non-Drug Offenders." By contemporary standards, it was a very small grant—direct costs under $95,000 a year, for 2 years. When we extended the study with a second 2-year grant, the budget was even smaller. Our project officer at the time, Dan J. Lettieri, said it was always easier to get a grant through NIDA if the costs were under $100,000—so we used that as a guideline, and it seemed to work. We were able to operate with such low costs because the project was really just the two of us plus a part-time secretary and some part-time interviewers—ex-addicts the first author had worked with in Miami. For most of our studies, the lead interviewer was the late Brian R. Russe, a former addict, a wonderful interviewer, and one of the few people living in Miami in the 1970s who was actually born there.

In this first study we developed the methods and many of the interests that we continued and expanded in our later work. Similar ways of locating and interviewing respondents, as it turned out, were being developed in other places at the same time. These methods shared some characteristics with ethnography, in that ethnographers had been doing in-depth interviews with small samples for a long time. But what we were doing was pseudostructured, rapport-dependent street studies with large samples—so it wasn't ethnography and it wasn't survey research either.

Between July 1977 and August 1978 we did 1,002 interviews in Miami for the Unapprehended Crime Study. It was basically a multiple-starting-point snowball sample street study. Some 270 interviews were done in treatment programs and jails, but the main data source was 732 street interviews. This approach was possible because of the skills and contacts of the interviewers. They had extensive experience in talking to drug-involved criminals, knowledge of the local drug scene, and thorough training in use of a highly structured interview instrument. The questions focused on past and current use of 21 drug types and committing—and being arrested for—22 crime types during the last 12 months; a few additional questions concerned demographic characteristics, arrest history, earliest crimes, and drug treatment history. Interviewers used their street connections to begin finding criminal offenders to interview and then asked each respondent for referrals to other offenders. Refusal rates were below 5%, probably because interviewers met potential respondents through personal introductions, the interview was short (about 40 minutes at most), respondents were paid a small fee in consideration of their time ($5), and people doing drugs and

crime tend to enjoy talking about drugs and crime.

The street interviews included 476 active male and female heroin users, who were not that easy to find because Miami has never really been much of a heroin city. Folklore had it that since the 1930s and the early days of Al Capone, Lucky Luciano, and Meyer Lansky, Miami was a vacation spot and family playground for the members of organized crime. Because of this, narcotics were considered verboten in Miami, and the trafficking and local distribution of dangerous drugs were dealt with quite harshly. In fact, a 78-year-old former heroin addict interviewed by the first author at the Miami Rescue Mission during the mid-1980s recalled:

> I remember it all very clear. Back in those days Al Capone had a place on on of those islands between Miami and Miami Beach. He'd have a lot of guests come down, and there were other racketeers from New York and Chicago that would vacation here with their families. They had places on Miami Beach, and they didn't want no drugs down here. They wanted Miami to be a family-like place. So word had it that if you wanted to bring in drugs, you went to Tampa, not Miami. Drugs in Miami were taboo.

In spite of that history, Miami ultimately became one of the drug import capitals of the Americas. But at least since the late 1960s, the big drugs in Miami have been cocaine and Dilaudid rather than heroin. In fact, when we were first doing these studies, periodically we would get phone calls from the Drug Enforcement Administration (DEA) asking: "Our agents just came off the street in Miami and they said there's no heroin in the White community, is this true?" As the resident pseudoethnographer, the first author would be able to give them that kind of information and tell them that "Yeah, it's true, it's not a heroin area."

The study respondents also included criminal offenders who were not heroin users, recruited in the same Miami neighborhoods, jails, and prisons. In addition, we did street, treatment, and jail/prison interviews with 743 heroin users and other offenders in San Antonio during 1977 and 1978. In 1979 and 1980, we extended the Unapprehended Crime Study into Delaware, New York City, and Dayton, Ohio. These were smaller samples (under 200 respondents) of more limited scope—prison interviews in Delaware, street interviews in New York, and treatment-centered interviews in Dayton.

We had numerous problems getting these studies going. Our first difficulties were with research administration. The University of Delaware had a lot of experience with chemical engineering research, but they had never seen anything like a street study of drug use and crime. They never even had a full-time social science research employee before the second author was hired. The personnel plan in the grant application had to be completely rewritten—salary amounts, methods for paying interviewers, everything. Then, when we started interviewing, we paid our respondents $5 for the time they spent participating in our 40 minute interview. The University had no problem with the payment, but they wanted a signed, dated, standard receipt. They couldn't understand why we couldn't give them the respondent's name, address, Social Security Number, and signature for an interview in which someone admitted committing a certain number of illegal acts of a particular sort in the prior 12 months. Chemical engineers don't have to worry about confidentiality and gaining respondent trust. We eventually worked out a system in which interviewers signed certifications that they did the interviews and paid the respondents, and we signed certifications that we were in possession of the interviews. The University reluctantly accepted these as enough signatures. But the next year, the University hired a high-powered Philadelphia auditing firm to come to look at project expenditures, the signature sheets, and the general financial procedures for the grant. But we got through the audit, and they've accepted this type of arrangement ever since, however begrudgingly.

In the field, the biggest problem was respondent difficulties with recall. We asked about age at first use and first regular use of 21 specific drugs and drug types, as well as age at five other events; we asked for a complete listing of offense types and ages for all arrests; and we asked for an estimated number of offenses done in the last 12 months, and the number of those offenses resulting in arrest, for 22 different categories of crime. These details all required interviewers to help respondents reconstruct histories by breaking events down into smaller, more manageable periods of time. For example, one man interviewed by the first author, when asked how many burglaries he had done in the last 12 months, said "thousands." This provoked an assurance that, while interesting, this number was useless. What did "thousands" mean? So the two of them looked at a calendar and figured out how many of those months the respondent was on the street, when his birthday occurred, the date that he overdosed, the day his mother died, the date he was arrested, where he was for Christmas, which day he was stabbed in a fight with a connection, and other dates. Then they could work with the smaller time periods between these memorable dates. When the whole puzzle was put together, it turned out that those "thousands" of burglaries were actually only 40 to 50 (see Inciardi, 1986, pp. 120–122).

In contrast to respondent recall, getting respondents to trust us really wasn't much of a problem. They didn't feel particularly threatened in talking to us about their illegal behavior. We approached most of them with an introduction from someone they knew, and we also had a Confidentiality Certificate from NIDA. This is a signed document that guarantees that researchers cannot be forced to divulge the identity of their informants to any law enforcement authority, court, or grand jury. Respondents were made aware of the Certificate and were given copies if they requested it. In addition, we asked questions in such a way that from the point of view of a court of law, the answers were hearsay evidence. That is, an interviewer's information about the respondent's illegal behavior would come not from personal knowledge but only from what someone else said; such information is not admissible as testimony in an American court. Most of our respondents had been arrested, so they understood what hearsay evidence is. Further, our interviews were anonymous—we didn't ask for names or any other information that would let particular respondents be identified. If we had done so, we could have had nice respondent-payment receipts for the University of Delaware—but confidentiality is a critical protection that we could offer to respondents to encourage their trust and cooperation.

The most important findings in this first study are shown fairly well in Tables 31.1 and 31.2, taken from one of the first publications out of this research (Inciardi, 1979). First, we found that the amount of crime committed by heroin addicts was far beyond what most people imagined. For example, combining the male and female subsamples reported in the tables, the first 356 active

heroin users in the sample reported a total of 118,134 offenses in the prior 12 months. The majority of these crimes were victimless offenses such as drug sales and prostitution, but this still leaves a large number of major felonies—3,901 robberies, 4,278 burglaries, 14,856 shoplifting offenses, and several thousand other larcenies. The tables also indicate that very few of these heroin users did no crime, and the great majority were involved in multiple types of crime. Of the men, for example, 92% sold drugs, 69% committed burglaries, 59% shoplifted, and 59% sold or traded stolen goods. Of the women, 81% sold drugs, 73% were prostitutes, 70% shoplifted, and 51% did prostitutes' thefts

Table 31.1

Criminal Activity in the Prior 12 Months, 239 Active Male Heroin Users, 1977–1978 [a]

Crime type	Total offenses	Percentage of total offenses	Percentage of sample involved	Percentage of offenses resulting in arrest	
Robbery	3,328	4.1	46.9	0.3	(n = 11)
Assault	170	0.2	20.9	0.6	(n = 1)
Burglary	4,093	5.1	69.0	0.7	(n = 30)
Vehicle theft	398	0.5	22.6	0.5	(n = 2)
Theft from vehicle	877	1.1	29.3	0.7	(n = 6)
Shoplifting	9,685	12.0	59.4	0.2	(n = 15)
Pickpocketing	11	<0.1	0.8	0.0	(n = 0)
Prostitute's theft	62	<0.1	1.3	1.6	(n = 1)
Confidence games	1,267	1.6	30.1	0.0	(n = 0)
Forgery, counterfeiting	1,711	2.1	40.2	0.4	(n = 6)
Fraud	185	0.2	12.1	1.1	(n = 2)
Extortion	648	0.8	10.0	0.0	(n = 0)
Loan sharking	463	0.5	13.0	0.0	(n = 0)
Stolen goods offenses	6,527	8.1	59.4	<0.1	(n = 3)
Other theft	1,009	1.3	35.1	0.5	(n = 5)
Arson	65	<0.1	2.9	0.0	(n = 0)
Vandalism	58	<0.1	8.8	1.7	(n = 1)
Prostitution	2	<0.1	0.4	0.0	(n = 0)
Procuring (pimping)	2,819	3.5	30.5	<0.1	(n = 1)
Drug sales	40,897	51.0	91.6	0.2	(n = 93)
Gambling	6,306	7.8	38.5	<0.1	(n = 3)
Alcohol offenses	58	<0.1	6.3	10.3	(n = 6)
All other	5	<0.1	2.1	60.0	(n = 3)
TOTAL	80,644	100.0	97.4	0.2	(n = 189)
Mean per respondent	337				

[a]*Source:* Inciardi (1979), Table 4.

(i.e., as prostitutes, they stole from their own customers).

A second major finding, also reflected in these tables, is the minuscule arrest clearance rate for the crimes of these heroin users. Under three-tenths of one percent of the total crimes ended up in arrest. That's one arrest for every 413 offenses committed. We found this kind of extremely low rate for not only the grand totals but also for the most common offense types—drug sales, shoplifting, prostitution, stolen goods offenses. This finding shows very clearly just how inaccurate arrest data are as indicators of the nature or extent of criminal behavior.

A third significance of the Unapprehended Crime Study was the detailed age data it collected. Most notably, this information shows

that the chicken-egg question about drug use and crime—which came first?—can result in completely contradictory answers, depending on the measures used. For this same sample of 356 heroin users (Inciardi 1979), for example, we found the following median ages:

		Males	Females
1.	First alcohol use	12.8	13.8
2.	First marijuana use	15.5	15.4
3.	First crime	15.1	15.9
4.	First heroin use	18.7	18.2

Lines 3 and 4 indicate that crime precedes heroin use. But if one looks not at heroin use but at marijuana, which is almost always the first drug requiring contact with

Table 31.2

Criminal Activity in the Prior 12 Months, 117 Active Female Heroin Users, 1977–1978[a]

Crime type	Total offenses	Percentage of total offenses	Percentage of sample involved	Percentage of offenses resulting in arrest	
Robbery	573	1.5	17.1	0.5	(n = 3)
Assault	26	<0.1	7.7	11.5	(n = 3)
Burglary	185	0.5	20.5	1.1	(n = 2)
Vehicle theft	5	<0.1	1.7	0.0	(n = 0)
Theft from vehicle	182	0.5	18.8	0.5	(n = 1)
Shoplifting	5,171	13.8	70.1	0.3	(n = 13)
Pickpocketing	162	0.4	4.3	0.0	(n = 0)
Prostitute's theft	1,345	3.6	51.3	0.0	(n = 0)
Confidence games	251	0.7	17.1	0.0	(n = 0)
Forgery, counterfeiting	888	2.4	29.9	0.3	(n = 3)
Fraud	34	<0.1	6.0	0.0	(n = 0)
Extortion	41	0.1	4.3	0.0	(n = 0)
Loan sharking	1	<0.1	0.9	0.0	(n = 0)
Stolen goods offenses	1,006	2.7	36.8	<0.1	(n = 4)
Other theft	182	0.5	20.5	0.5	(n = 1)
Arson	88	0.2	3.4	0.0	(n = 0)
Vandalism	3	<0.1	1.7	0.0	(n = 0)
Prostitution	14,307	38.2	72.6	0.3	(n = 37)
Procuring (pimping)	1,153	3.1	23.1	0.0	(n = 0)
Drug sales	11,289	30.1	81.2	0.2	(n = 23)
Gambling	574	1.5	22.2	0.0	(n = 0)
Alcohol offenses	22	<0.1	6.8	22.7	(n = 5)
All other	2	<0.1	2.1	100.0	(n = 2)
TOTAL	37,490	100.0	94.9	0.3	(n = 97)
Mean per respondent	320				

[a]*Source:* Inciardi (1979), Table 5.

the illegal drug market, Lines 2 and 3 suggest that street crime and street drug use tend to begin within less than a year of each other. Then again, if the drug use indicator is further broadened to consider alcohol use, Lines 1 and 3 suggest that use of at least one drug—alcohol—precedes crime by several years. This example shows that even with the same kind of indicator (median age at first occurrence), in the same data set, it is possible to get three different answers to the chicken-egg question: crime first, crime and drugs at about the same time, and drug use first. This question doubtless remained so controversial for so long in the early drugs-crime literature because different investigators were using the same theoretical referents, but counting completely different things.

A fourth major finding from the Unapprehended Crime Study is the importance of sample characteristics in drug research, a subject area made possible by the large number of cross-cutting subsamples in this data set—city, drug use type, gender, ethnicity, age group, and street/treatment/prison status. A comparison of drug type, for example, showed that compared to other criminal offenders, heroin users commit more crimes, are involved in a greater variety of offenses, and commit significantly more of such serious crimes as robbery and burglary (Inciardi, 1986, pp. 126–131). Similarly, a comparison of three pairs of subsamples in which city, gender, race/ethnicity, and age were all controlled showed significant differences between active and institutionalized respondents in regard to drug use and drugs-crime history; further, the existence or even the direction of the differences was not always the same in different cities (Pottieger, 1981). And in an analysis of the 697 Miami interviews with male street criminals, we found significant differences by age group in demographic characteristics, drug use history, current drug use, and crime types committed in the last 12 months (Pottieger and Inciardi, 1981). A corollary of these cross-cutting subgroup differences is that any effort to get a useful sample of drug users is going to end up with many different "types" of drug users, which has implications for what

the data will look like in a real versus fictional—i.e., fraudulent—sample. Two papers based on the Unapprehended Crime Study data describe this phenomenon (Inciardi, 1981, 1982).

Finally, the Unapprehended Crime Study also resulted in three publications about the crime and heroin connection specifically among women (Datesman and Inciardi, 1979; Inciardi, 1980; Inciardi et al., 1982). The articles themselves were not particularly noteworthy. They used somewhat different approaches for data analysis, but they all pointed out the exaggerated importance of prostitution in the (small) literature on drug use and crime among women, showing a variety of data to indicate that most crime by female heroin users in Miami was not prostitution. This is also apparent from Tables 31.1 and 31.2 for example. Relatedly, these articles showed that a significant number of the crimes committed by female heroin users were shoplifting and other property offenses, and that most female heroin users in Miami (like their male counterparts) were engaged in multiple crime types rather than specializing. What is significant about these articles is not their relatively simple findings, but their publication dates. By 1982 a century's worth of literature contained fewer than 30 reports that did anything more than mention the combined topic of women, crime, and drugs, and in the majority of even these, at least one of the three areas—most often crime or the small subsample of women—was of clearly secondary interest. These three articles from the Unapprehended Crime Study, then, represented probably 10% of the total existing literature on women, drugs, and crime.

Our next grant application took off from this work in two ways. One was that we recognized how few studies had looked at crime among female heroin users. This was a major gap in the research literature, and we could fill it. The other connection to the Unapprehended Crime project was that we knew we couldn't publish much more on women, drug use, and crime with the data we had. We didn't have enough variables or enough female respondents. Our Miami street sample included only 153 female heroin users, and there were really too few women in the other Miami subsamples or in the other city samples for comparisons. So our next grant application was for a study to focus entirely on women.

The Women Drug Users' Study

The title of the next project was "Criminal Patterns among Women Drug Users." This was a 3-year study that, like the other grants, had a small budget and was a deliberately multiple subsample study. From March 1983 to June 1984 we interviewed 481 women in Miami and, through arrangements with Narcotic and Drug Research Inc. (NDRI, now known as National Development and Research Institute), 459 women in New York. The first author did 230 of the Miami street interviews himself. Again, we did interviews in treatment programs and jails/prisons as well as on the street, and we also talked to both heroin users and other offenders in the same neighborhoods and institutions, although this time we set separate targets for the comparison groups that would permit large enough subsamples for separate analyses. Similarly, to get a better handle on ethnic differences, we restricted eligibility to White, Black, and Cuban women in Miami, and White, Black, and Puerto Rican women in New York. We kept most of the interview questions from the Unapprehended Crime Study so that that the newer and older data would remain comparable. But our six-page instrument grew to ten pages in order to cover subject matter of particular interest to the study of female heroin users. We added more questions about income sources and other demographic characteristics, treatment history, early crime history, and crime partnerships. Part of the space was made up by reducing the 21 drug categories to 12 by combining types (for example, barbiturates and nonbarbiturate sedatives were put into a single prescription "sedatives" [category]); we also tried a more efficient way of asking how the drugs were obtained. This interview required about 60 minutes at most, still within a realistic limit for interviewing active drug users.

When we compared the 1977–1978 and 1983–1984 street interviews with female heroin users, we found differences in both drug use and criminal patterns (Inciardi and Pottieger, 1986). Adding to the 6-year time difference between interview phases was a 3.4 year difference in median age for these two samples, with the earlier group being the older one. So they were actually different drug-use cohorts. The women interviewed in 1977–1978 had experimented with a broader range of drugs, but the 1983–1984 cohort was more deeply involved with heroin and cocaine use—they started regular use at an earlier age and they were using more frequently in the 90 days before interview. The differences in crime were even larger, as seen in the differences between Table 31.1, discussed earlier, and Table 31.3 for the 1983–1984 interviews. (In the published article a slightly larger subsample from the Unapprehended Crime Study data was used, but Table 31.1 is close enough for present purposes.)

The 1977–1979 respondents reported committing a mean of 320 offenses in the prior 12 months, but the 1983–1984 sample reported a mean of 461 crimes for the last 6 months, a time period only half as long. In the latter group, only about 10% of the total offenses were property crimes, markedly smaller than the corresponding percentage for the older cohort. The younger cohort also committed fewer crimes of violence, although this was a small category for both samples. Drug sales made up some of the difference, even though a smaller percentage of the 1983–1984 cohort sold drugs. But the greatest change was accounted for by prostitution, which represented 38% of the first cohort's crimes but 54% of the second cohort's.

It is possible that the more numerous crimes of the second cohort were a consequence of their heavier use of heroin and cocaine. But we argued that it was more likely that the cohort differences in both drug use and crime were effects of differences between the two time periods in drug fads and, especially, law enforcement patterns. By 1983–1984 the prescription drugs used more

Table 31.3

Criminal Activity in the Prior 6 Months, 133 Active Female Heroin Users, 1983–1984 [a]

Crime type	Total offenses	Percentage of total offenses	Percentage of sample involved	Percentage of offenses resulting in arrest	
Robbery	77	0.1	16.5	3.9	(n = 3)
Assault	183	0.3	16.5	0.0	(n = 0)
Burglary	792	1.3	33.8	0.5	(n = 4)
Vehicle theft	22	<0.1	0.9	0.0	(n = 0)
Theft from vehicle	107	0.2	17.3	0.0	(n = 0)
Shoplifting	1,885	3.1	30.8	0.2	(n = 3)
Pickpocketing	53	0.1	9.8	0.0	(n = 0)
Prostitute's theft	1,359	2.2	33.8	0.0	(n = 0)
Confidence games	463	0.8	13.5	0.0	(n = 0)
Extortion	20	<0.1	3.0	0.0	(n = 0)
Loan sharking	20	<0.1	.8	0.0	(n = 0)
Stolen goods offenses	967	1.6	15.0	0.2	(n = 2)
All other theft [b]	500	0.8	19.5	0.5	(n = 1)
Arson-vandalism	0	0.0	.0	NA	
Prostitution	33,044	53.9	54.1	0.1	(n = 27)
Procuring (pimping)	726	1.2	19.5	0.1	(n = 1)
Drug sales	21,067	34.4	55.6	<0.1	(n = 7)
TOTAL	61,285	100.0		0.1	(n = 47)
Mean per respondent	461				

[a]*Source:* Inciardi and Pottieger (1986), Table 6.

[b]"All other theft": Forgery (checks, credit cards, prescriptions, other), other check and credit card offenses, other sneak theft, embezzlement, welfare/foodstamp fraud, other fraud, thefts from vending machines, other thefts.

frequently by the earlier cohorts were more tightly controlled; LSD and speed were less popular than—and largely replaced by—PCP; heroin and cocaine were much easier to obtain; and there was a general crackdown on violence, theft, and drug users involving not just police and courts but also public opinion, homeowner and business installation of protection devices, and the formation of neighborhood crime watch groups. Eventually, heroin users themselves recognized that burglary, robbery, and larceny were much more dangerous occupations than they used to be. The response of women, in particular, to the increased danger was to decrease their involvement in such offenses and instead shift to prostitution or selling drugs.

A different kind of shift in crime types for female heroin users is discussed in our analysis of women who moved from drug business to the sex trade (Inciardi, 1986, pp. 163–167). The reason for this transition is often changes in the heroin market. It is not uncommon for drug supplies to dry up for short periods of time because of either increased police activity or general interruptions in drug-supply networks. When this happens, small-scale dealers simply have no heroin to sell and addict-dealers are doing well to find heroin for their own needs. At the same time, heroin prices typically escalate because of the scarcity. This leaves a dealer who is shut out of the market with no choice but to find another way of getting money. For women, prostitution is an available alternative. The women themselves generally define it as dirtier, harder, and more dangerous than selling heroin—but it paid better and was a more stable source of income. For this reason, many women who shifted from dealing to prostitution during a heroin shortage continued even after the shortage was over.

Other findings from the Women Drug Users' Study are further elaborations on subject matter we originally explored in the Unapprehended Crime Study. Table 31.3, for example, shows as clearly as Tables 31.1 and 31.2 that heroin users commit very high numbers of crimes and that extremely few of those crimes result in arrest. Similarly, the comparisons of crime among opiate and nonopiate using prostitutes in the Women Drug Users' Study (Inciardi, 1986, pp. 167–169) lead to the same conclusions as those previously discussed for the primarily male samples of heroin and nonheroin offenders: opiate users commit more crimes, are involved in a greater variety of offenses, and are more often involved in violent offenses (Inciardi, 1986, pp. 126–131).

The Serious Delinquency Study

The origins of the next project date to a request from Mike Backenheimer, our NIDA project officer at the time, for the first author to be a discussant at a conference on juvenile delinquency in April 1984. The "paper" he was supposed to discuss turned out to be a massive report on a very large, complex delinquency study directed by Delbert Elliott. The first author did his critique, and he listened to other presentations on delinquency and drug use, and he heard some interesting ideas. But it struck him as odd that the research all seemed to use questionnaires administered in schools, or interviews with teenagers in the general household population—that is, only random sample survey procedures. He talked to the assorted delinquency experts at the conference, and looked at their literature reviews and, sure enough, it appeared that there hadn't been a street study of hardcore delinquents for almost 20 years.

After the conference the two of us talked about this strange finding. It looked like a perfect opportunity to put together a proposal to continue our work in Miami, looking at crime and drug use among serious delinquents on the street. And that's basically what we did. Technically, "Drug Use and Serious Delinquency" was Years 8 through 10 of what began as a little 2-year study in 1977. The budget was still just barely over that magic number of $100,000 a year. We defined a "serious delinquent" as a person 12 to 17 years of age who, in the prior 12 months, committed at least 10 of what the Federal Bureau of Investigation refers to as "Index Crimes" (criminal homicide, forcible rape, aggravated assault, robbery, burglary, larceny/theft, and motor vehicle theft) or 100 lesser offenses. All 611 of the interviews were done on the street in Miami between December 1985 and November 1987, using the same recruitment techniques as described above for our adult interview respondents. No interviews were done in institutions; no names were drawn from institutional records. Demographic targets put tight controls over gender, race/ethnicity, and age intersects for the sample to ensure a demographically diverse sample while at the same time obtaining enough interviews in any given category to permit comparisons. Thus, the age 12 to 13 category included only Black and White boys, not Hispanics and not girls; and Hispanic girls were not included in the sample design, simply because they were known to be "invisible" to both police and researchers, or virtually nonexistent. The first author did 60 of the interviews himself.

The first major contribution of the Serious Delinquency Study to drugs-crime research was the information it collected on crack use and distribution. Even though the media hadn't discovered it yet, we knew that crack-cocaine had been in Miami for quite some time. The first author had observed Miami's cocaine freebase culture during the early 1970s, and the "rock" cocaine (later called "crack") culture by 1981. Because we knew that crack was in Miami, we included it as a drug type on the interview schedule for the study. Still, we were surprised when it turned out that 96% of the first 308 youths interviewed had tried crack and, during the prior 90 days, 87% used it three or more times a week (Inciardi, 1987). Given these high rates, additional funds were secured from NIDA to further study crack use in the remainder of the project. We constructed some supplementary questions about crack that we were able to get into the field for use with the final 254 interviews. We asked how respondents first heard of crack, their opinions of its effects, how they obtained it, whether its use changed their other drug use or crime, and even what it looked like. This gave us some of the first detailed information on crack collected by social scientists rather than journalists or law enforcement officials (Inciardi, 1988). Furthermore, the paper about the preliminary findings on the first 308 respondents (Inciardi, 1987) was likely the first published study on crack in the scientific literature.

The crack distribution data came primarily from the last supplementary question on crack. The item was open-ended and asked, "Do you deal in crack or help a crack dealer or anything like that? What?" The write-in answers reduced to four levels of involvement in the crack business: None, Minor, Dealer, and Dealer+. In the "None" category were the 50 youths (19.7%) with no involvement at all in the crack business. Another 20 youths (7.9%) had only "Minor" involvement—either they sold crack only to their friends or they worked in the crack business only in nonsales positions such as being a lookout for a dealer or steering customers to a crack house. The "Dealer" category was the largest; these 138 youths (54.3%) were involved directly in the retail sale of crack. Finally, 46 respondents were designated as "Dealer+" because they not only sold crack but also manufactured, smuggled, or wholesaled it.

The relationships between Crack Business Involvement Level and the other drug and crime indicators in the study are amazingly consistent. As shown in Table 31.4, the greater the involvement in the crack business, the more other drug and crime entanglement of all kinds—more drinking, more marijuana use, more pills, more crack, greater frequency of earning crack by being paid in it, more cash spent on crack for personal use, more robberies and assaults in the prior 12 months, more burglaries and motor vehicle thefts, and, of course, more drug sales (Inciardi et al., 1993a, pp. 97–116; Inciardi and Pottieger, 1991).

Further, the greater the involvement in the crack business, the younger the median age at which these youths had started using alcohol, marijuana, pills, and cocaine, and the younger they were when they first sold drugs. Youths in the "Dealer" and "Dealer+" categories were also more likely to have experimented with using heroin and doing robbery, and their median age at first theft and first robbery was generally some 2 years younger than for their counterparts in the "None" and "Minor" categories. Altogether, these findings suggested to us that crack distribution attracted those teenagers who were already the most involved with drug use and crime, but at the same time, that crack distribution is highly criminogenic in that it leads serious delinquents to become even more seriously involved in crime.

We also found that crack dealing was important in the careers of female as well as male delinquents. Prostitution is not included in Table 31.4 because it does not show the same progression over the four Crack Business Involvement levels as is seen for the other crime types. However, the reason for this apparent lack of relationship is that there were too few girls in the "Minor" and "Dealer+" categories (1 and 2, respectively). When only the female respondents to the supplemental crack questions were considered, results similar to Table 31.4 were obtained for a two category "Crack Dealer?" yes/no dichotomy. That is, even with only 37 cases, crack dealing by seriously delinquent girls had strong, significant correlations with their other drug and crime involvement. Table 31.5 shows the specifics for current crime.

A second contribution of the Serious Delinquency Study was another finding with real-life relevance: the considerable frequency of high HIV-risk activities among serious delinquents. We found strikingly high levels of involvement in prostitution, intravenous (IV) drug use, and sex-for-crack exchanges, especially in some subgroups (Inciardi, 1989; Inciardi et al., 1993a, pp. 180–189; Inciardi et al., 1991). Perhaps most at risk were female delinquents: of the 100 young women ages 14 to 17 in the sample, 87% engaged in prostitution in the 12

Table 31.4

Drug Use and Crime by Crack Business Involvement Level, 254 Serious Delinquents, 1985–1987[a]

Drug use and crime type	None (N = 50)	Minor (N = 20)	Dealer (N = 138)	Dealer+ (N = 46)
Use, last 90 days (% "yes"):				
Alcohol, 3+ days/week	18.0	20.0	47.1	65.2
Marijuana, every day	66.0	80.0	91.3	100.0
Pills (depressants), 3+ days/week	2.0	5.0	32.6	50.0
Crack, every day	2.0	5.0	70.3	87.0
Was paid in crack for dealing, 6+ times last 12 months (% "yes")	15.8	35.0	84.8	91.3
Money spent on crack for own use, last 90 days (median $)	75	225	2,000	2,500
Did, last 12 months (% "yes"):				
Robbery	12.0	40.0	66.7	95.7
Assault	4.0	0.0	8.0	17.4
Burglary	24.0	25.0	70.3	91.3
Motor vehicle theft	30.0	35.0	57.2	73.9
Thefts from vehicle	34.0	30.0	75.4	84.8
Shoplifting	90.0	95.0	100.0	100.0
Confidence games	6.0	5.0	53.6	63.0
Bad paper[b]	10.5	5.0	60.1	73.9
Stolen goods offenses	76.0	85.0	94.9	97.8
Drug business (any)	86.0	100.0	100.0	100.0
Number of crimes done last 12 months (mean):				
Major felonies[c]	9	8	42	64
Petty property crime	110	197	234	222
Drug business	196	332	510	1082

[a]Source: Adapted from Inciardi and Pottieger (1991), Tables 3, 5, 7, and 8.
[b]"Bad paper": Forged/fraudulent checks, credit card use, prescriptions.
[c]"Major felonies": Robbery, assault, burglary, motor vehicle thefts.

months before interview and 38% used drugs intravenously in the prior 90 days. Similarly, of the 30 female crack users responding to the supplemental interview questions about crack, 90% sometimes exchanged sexual services for crack and 53% did so frequently (six or more times in the prior year). Black youths were also a high HIV-risk group in that IV drug use was reported by over half of Black respondents ages 16 and 17, both male and female, as well as 40% of girls and 31% of boys ages 14 and 15. Of all 611 youths interviewed, 56% had at least tried heroin and 40% had tried IV use of heroin or speed. Further, these high HIV-risk activities were associated with each other and with increased drug involvement of all types—not only heroin and cocaine but also alcohol, marijuana, and pills. This suggests that drug use of any type is at least an indirect HIV-risk behavior for serious delinquents. In addition, the notorious tendency of cocaine addicts to neglect food, sleep, and other requirements of good health means that use of crack and other cocaine increases the susceptibility to any and all kinds of infection, including with HIV.

A third contribution of the Serious Delinquency Study to drugs-crime research is the book-length treatment given to the role of drug use in serious delinquency (Inciardi et al., 1993a). Even the basic descriptive materials included in this book are of value because they concern a sample type that had

Table 31.5

Crime During the Last 12 Months by Crack Dealing, 37 Serious Delinquent Females,
1985–1987[a]

| Crime type | Number done | Crack dealer (%) | | ρ[b] |
		No (N = 13)	Yes (N = 24)	
Major felonies	None	61.5	8.3	+.54
	1–12	30.8	50.0	
	13–24	0.0	16.7	
	25–47	7.7	8.3	
	50+	0.0	16.7	
Petty property	0–12	15.4	0.0	+.79
	13–74	53.8	4.2	
	75–145	23.1	0.0	
	150–298	7.7	45.8	
	300+	0.0	50.0	
Prostitution and procuring	None	30.8	0.0	+.69
	1–72	23.1	0.0	
	100–160	7.7	4.2	
	175–320	30.8	29.2	
	350+	7.7	66.7	
Drug business	0–20	38.5	0.0	+.57
	25–120	7.7	4.2	
	125–225	23.1	12.5	
	250–475	23.1	37.5	
	500+	7.7	45.8	

[a]*Source:* Adapted from Inciardi et al. (1993b), Table 6.6.
[b]ρ = Spearman (rank-order) correlation coefficient significant at $p < .001$ between crack dealer (no = 0, yes = 1) and the crime type (1–5 for the five ranked categories listed). "Major felony": Robbery, assault, burglary, motor vehicle theft. The one female included in the "Minor" column of Table 31.4 was excluded from this analysis; the two "Dealer+" females are included here with other dealers.

not been studied in several decades—a street sample of hard-core delinquents, and in particular a large, demographically diverse, nongang sample. Deep involvement in drug use was just as obvious a characteristic of this sample as extensive criminal behavior. The traditional way of handling this dual involvement was to treat drug use as just one more type of delinquent behavior. But our study results suggested that for serious delinquents, drug use may be much more than this. In our sample, drug sales were a very common first crime; drug use and other illegal behaviors tended to appear at about the same time in the histories of these serious delinquents; and regular drug use tended to *precede* regular profit-making crime. Further, crack-market participation, as dis-

cussed above, was consistently associated with earlier and more serious involvement of these teenagers in both drug use and crime, including violent crime.

Fourth, we were able to look at gender and race/ethnicity differences among serious delinquents in drug use, crime, and drugs-crime relationships (Horowitz and Pottieger, 1991; Inciardi et al., 1993a; Soriano and De La Rosa, 1990). We found surprisingly little variation by gender, except for the prominence of prostitution in female crime patterns. This finding stands in sharp contrast to decades of delinquency theory and research suggesting that serious delinquency is a male phenomenon. Similarly, we also found minimal drug and crime variations by race or ethnicity, contradicting the implication of prior theory and research that Black males are likely to be the most serious of serious delinquents. When sociodemographic background does make a difference among serious delinquents, it is most likely to be at the entry point. That is, gender and social class tend to present sociocultural situations—rules, expectations, social enforcement efforts—that result in different entry routes into serious delinquency for males versus females and for youths from poor versus better-off families. But once youth from these varied backgrounds are enmeshed in street life, differences in current drug and crime behaviors are minimal.

The Crack and Crime Study

In part because of our findings in the Serious Delinquency Study, we decided to apply for a larger grant to look at patterns of crack use and criminality among adults as well as teenagers. The project title was "Crack Abuse Patterns and Crime Linkages." Interviews were conducted between April 1988 and March 1990 in the Miami metropolitan area with 699 cocaine users, 349 of them interviewed in residential treatment and 350 on the street. Street recruitment techniques remained the same as those used in all our previous studies, except that we had only one interviewer—Brian Russe, our best interviewer. Treatment interviews with adults were done on weekends by three interviewers, all of whom had full-time jobs during weekdays, at one of the largest residential treatment centers in the metropolitan area. By arrangement with the program, one or more interviewers (depending on their personal schedules) went to the treatment center on weekends, recruited volunteers from among new enrollees, and conducted one to three interviews each. Similar arrangements were worked out at a residential treatment program for adolescent boys.

Even though crime was one focus of study, sample eligibility did not require criminal involvement. This made recruitment easier than in the prior studies. Other than demographic subsample restrictions, the only sample eligibility criterion was use of any cocaine form during the last 90 days

on the street. Subsample targets were set as combinations of gender, age-group, and race/ethnicity categories in order to ensure demographic diversity and to enhance comparability between the street and treatment samples. The targets were met in the street sample by an even split between five groups: Black, White, and Hispanic males, and Black and White females with about 100 respondents each in the 13–17 and 18–24 age-groups and the remainder ages 25 to 49. We spent more time and effort trying to meet the same goal for the treatment sample, but with less success. Actual treatment admissions were more heavily overbalanced toward older cocaine users. In addition, no residential treatment facility for adolescent females existed in the metro area. Our treatment sample thus ended up older and more male than the design (and the street sample). Overall, about a third of the respondents were women, about a fifth were ages 12 to 17, and the overall age range was 13 to 49.

The principal examination of the drugs-crime relationship from the Crack and Crime Study (Inciardi and Pottieger, 1994) was patterned after the drugs and crime analysis from the Unapprehended Crime Study (Inciardi, 1979) and also includes comparisons of the results to that earlier study. To enhance the comparability of the samples, only the 387 adult "primary-crack users" were included—persons at least 18 years old for whom crack represented at least 75% of all cocaine used during the last 90 days on the street. This excluded other cocaine users in order to focus on the crack-crime relationship, and it excluded younger crack users because so few heroin users in prior studies, including our own, have been under 18 years of age. Comparison of the street samples of 1977–1978 heroin users and the 1988–1990 primary crack users shows both differences and similarities.

The drug use and crime histories of the two samples were very similar: experience with multiple drugs, some degree of crime involvement, and a sequence of median ages in which alcohol use came first, then both crime and the use of an illegal drug (almost always marijuana), and only after another 2 or more years, first cocaine use by the crack users and first heroin use among the heroin users. The histories of the two samples were different in that the crack users began both drug use and crime at markedly younger ages, had used fewer different drug types, and were much less likely to have been in any kind of drug-user treatment program. In contrast to the heroin users, furthermore, very few gender differences in drugs-crime histories were apparent for the crack users.

Another difference in crime histories was also reflected in current crimes, namely, the prominence of drug sales. Dealing was reported as the first criminal offense by only 10% of the male heroin users, compared to 71% of the male crack users; among women, the contrast was 13% for heroin users compared to 64% for crack users. Similarly, while Tables 31.1 and 31.2 indicate that for heroin users, drug sales were 51% of male

crimes and 30% of female crimes in the last 12 months, Table 31.6 shows that for both male and female crack users in the street sample, retail drug sales accounted for over 97% of all crimes committed in the last 90 days. Further, some drug sale involvement was reported by even more of the crack users than of the heroin users, and the crack users averaged many more sales per member of the sample—thousands of sales in the last 90 days, compared to under 200 in the last 12 months for the heroin users.

These differences in drug sales reflect differences in both drug characteristics and drug purchasing practices. Heroin users typically use three to five doses a day to satisfy an opiate addiction (see, e.g., Johnson et al., 1985). Even considering how diluted heroin is by the time it reaches the average user, there are severe limits on how many times

Table 31.6

Criminal Activity in the Prior 3 Months, 198 Active Adult Crack Users, 1988–1990 [a]

Crime type	Men (N = 114)		Women (N = 84)	
	Total offenses	Percentage of sample involved	Total offenses	Percentage of sample involved
Robberies	19	3.5	3	1.2
Assaults	0	0.0	3	3.6
Other weapon show/use	9,743	36.8	119	29.8
Burglaries	89	19.3	3	1.2
Vehicle thefts	27	9.6	0	0.0
Thefts from vehicle	104	36.0	43	32.1
Shoplifting	723	59.6	989	83.3
Pickpocketing	0	0.0	0	0.2
Prostitute's thefts	0	0.0	52	29.8
Confidence games	25	9.6	12	7.1
Bad paper[b]	415	64.0	252	69.0
Drug thefts	12	6.1	106	3.6
Other sneak thefts	4	1.8	0	0.0
Stolen goods offenses	483	36.8	195	15.5
Wholesale drug sales	0	0.0	0	0.0
Make or smuggle drugs	0	0.0	0	0.0
Retail drug sales	683,595	100.0	258,849	94.0
Prostitution	0	0.0	3,228	65.5
Procuring	2	0.9	2,241	65.5
TOTAL	695,241	100.0	266,095	100.0
Mean number per subject	6,099		3,168	

[a]*Source:* Inciardi and Pottieger (1994), Table 4.
[b]"Bad paper": Kited and forged checks, fraudulent credit card use, forged prescriptions.

per day heroin can be injected before the user would pass out and perhaps die of an overdose. Ten injections per day, for example, is a heroin dosing schedule that is virtually unheard of—a heroin high will normally last 3 to 5 hours. But crack users can easily manage 10 doses per day, or even dozens per day, because the high lasts only 5 to 10 minutes. Further, it is not uncommon for crack users to purchase only enough crack for one use. If each user buys crack many times a day, then retail crack dealers make many sales per user each day—and their total sales per year or per quarter then will average thousands rather than hundreds.

Crack users interviewed in treatment, however, reported a more varied list of offenses. As shown in Table 31.7, fewer than 40% of the treatment respondents did any retail drug sales, and these offenses ac-

counted for about two-thirds of all crimes reported by treatment respondents for their last 90 days on the street. These respondents also reported significantly fewer total crimes per offender than were reported by the street sample—only a tenth as many for the men and a fifth as many for the women.

Even though the crack users interviewed in treatment reported many fewer crimes than their counterparts from the street sample, their average for the last 90 days on the street (642 for men, 647 for women) was still about twice that of the 1977–1978 heroin user street sample for the last 12 months (337 for men, 320 for women). Similarly, only three offenses by the crack street sample resulted in arrest (two for men, one for women), compared to 51 in the crack treatment sample (23 for men, 28 for women)—but this is still significantly fewer per offense or even per

Table 31.7

Criminal Activity in the Last 3 Months on the Street, 189 Adult Crack Users in Treatment, 1988–1990 [a]

	Men (N = 116)		Women (N = 73)	
Crime type	Total offenses	Percentage of sample involved	Total offenses	Percentage of sample involved
Robberies	883	9.5	107	8.2
Assaults	371	18.1	48	6.8
Other weapon show/use	366	12.1	21	8.2
Burglaries	997	19.0	176	11.0
Vehicle thefts	35	6.0	40	4.1
Thefts from vehicle	1,111	17.2	15	6.8
Shoplifting	1,949	26.7	344	13.7
Pickpocketing	2	0.9	1	1.4
Prostitute's thefts	10	1.7	573	17.8
Confidence games	5,446	31.0	1,610	19.2
Bad paper[b]	1,455	19.8	637	21.9
Drug thefts	1,222	12.1	221	12.3
Other sneak thefts	778	31.9	443	23.3
Stolen goods offenses	6,098	53.4	1,273	37.0
Wholesale drug sales	3,652	15.5	1,470	8.2
Make or smuggle drugs	424	8.6	261	8.2
Retail drug sales	46,338	34.5	31,624	38.4
Prostitution	1,561	4.3	8,253	43.8
Procuring	1,737	8.6	86	4.1
TOTAL	74,435	83.6	47,203	78.1
Mean number per subject	642		647	

[a]Source: Inciardi and Pottieger (1994), Table 5.
[b]"Bad paper": Kited and forged checks, fraudulent credit card use, forged prescriptions.

offender than the 286 crimes resulting in arrests for the heroin users shown in Tables 31.1 and 31.2.

This analysis (Inciardi and Pottieger, 1994) showed numerous differences in crime and drugs—crime characteristics between the street and treatment samples for the Crack and Crime Study. We concluded in this article that the street sample was actually a special kind of crack user subsample—specifically, a user-dealer group with fairly well controlled crack habits, fairly steady criminal incomes, and a commitment to the user-dealer-street lifestyle. These respondents had been using drugs, including cocaine, for longer than their counterparts in treatment, and yet only one street respondent had ever been in treatment. The treatment sample may be more characteristic of the general population of crack users—more likely to use crack in a binge pattern, less uniformly crime involved, less street-oriented in general, and a population that got in trouble as the result of crack use. Differences in the drug use characteristics of the street and treatment samples are described in other analyses of the adult primary crack users (Pottieger et al., 1992, 1995).

In addition, we looked at the issue of race/ethnicity differences in the crack-crime relationship (Lockwood et al., 1993, 1995; Inciardi et al., 1996). This subject is of particular interest because mass media reports have consistently implied that crack and crack-related crimes are predominantly African-American problems. The Crack and Crime Study provides no confirmation of this hypothesized crack/Black association. Among the total 699 cocaine users interviewed, Blacks were no more likely than Whites to have crack as their primary cocaine type. Similarly, among the 499 primary crack users, there was no association between using more crack and being Black (or White). However, in a detailed analysis of drugs-crime relationships between the 257 youth and young adult primary crack users interviewed on the street, we did find that race was significantly associated with economic and ecological factors. Being White was correlated with less crime, but also less apparent need for crime to pay for living expenses, plus less cocaine involvement among the people living with the respondents. Correlations with being Black showed the opposite pattern—more crime, less legal income, more living expenses paid for by crime, and more cocaine use by people the respondents lived with. We concluded that the difference suggests that race in these analyses had a socioeconomic meaning: degree of access to income sources other than crime, and likelihood of living in an environment with both a high drug use rate and a high street crime rate.

The Sex-For-Crack Study

The Sex-for-Crack project was the outgrowth of the Miami component of an eight-city study of sex-for-crack exchanges. The research was initiated and funded by the National Institute on Drug Abuse to accomplish four goals: 1) to develop some preliminary insights into the attributes and patterns of "sex-for-crack" exchanges, particularly those that were occurring in crack houses; 2) to determine the general characteristics of individuals who exchanged sex for crack, or sex for money to purchase crack; 3) to assess the potential impact of sex-for-crack exchange behaviors on the spread of HIV infection; and 4) to target significant areas for further study. The other cities in the project were Philadelphia, Newark, San Francisco, New York, Los Angeles, Chicago, and Denver (see Ratner, 1993). Although the first author never had had any formal training in ethnography, he was chosen for the Miami part of the study because of his many years of street research and the contacts he had developed in the local drug community. It was through these associations that he communicated with the members of the various drug organizations and subcultures and gained entry into crack houses.

In Miami, systematic interviews were conducted with 17 men and 35 women who were heavy crack users and who had exchanged sex for either crack or money to buy crack during the prior 30 days (see Inciardi et al., 1993b; Inciardi, 1995). These interviews were structured by a list of questions that focused on current and past drug use and sexual behaviors, crack house activities, other HIV risk behaviors, and knowledge and concerns about AIDS. The interviews were conducted between November 1989 and February 1990 by two employees of an AIDS intervention project who had extensive experience in interviewing on such sensitive topics as drug use, crime, and sexual practices. Some respondents were recruited from the street by seasoned outreach workers; 60% were drawn from a pool of recent admissions (within the previous 48 hours) to local drug treatment programs. In addition, from January 1988 through February 1992, the first author personally visited 11 different crack houses in the Miami area, several more than once. He also conducted scores of unstructured interviews with "key informants," including crack users (some in crack houses, others on the street), crack and/or cocaine dealers, and police officers familiar with the greater Miami drug scene. Additional insights were obtained from conversations with numerous other players in the local street cultures. The 52 structured interviews were recorded and transcribed, yielding more than 4,000 printed pages; this material was also subjected to two different kinds of computer-assisted analysis. The first author's own observations and interviews resulted in a lengthy collection of field notes, added to as often as opportunity and memory permitted.

All of the 52 respondents for the structured interviews had long histories of illicit drug use. As shown in Table 31.8, they began with marijuana at a mean age of 14 or 15 years. Many experimented with inhalants, hallucinogens, or speed pills, and two out of three tried depressant pills. Injection drug use was not uncommon: 38.5% tried intravenous (IV) cocaine and 15% to 30% experimented with IV speed, heroin, or *speedball* (heroin and cocaine in combination). All of the men and all but one of the women had snorted cocaine; 75% did so "regularly"— three or more days a week—at some time in their lives. They first tried crack at a mean age of 24 years, moving on to regular use very soon thereafter. Some 31% of the sample began daily crack use immediately after first trying crack; an additional 27% used it

daily by the end of their first month, and almost 80% of the 52 respondents used it daily within 6 months after their first use.

In the 30 days prior to interview, many respondents used alcohol, marijuana, or cocaine powder (by snorting), as shown in Table 31.8. A few also used pills or IV drugs. But crack clearly predominated current drug-use patterns. Some 58% of these informants used crack every single day, 73% used it on at least 20 days, and 92% used it at least 15 of the prior 30 days. None used crack fewer than 10 days out of the last 30. A common pattern among those using less than daily was to smoke crack continuously for several days in a row, skipping sleep and meals, and then to sleep for a day or two. The binge lasted as long as crack was available to them and they had any means to purchase it, be that money, sex, stolen goods, other drugs, or household furniture. The binging pattern made it difficult for some informants to calculate how many crack rocks they consumed on a day they used crack. Thus, 23% could only report that they were high on crack all day long. Another 23% reported using 20 and 50 rocks per day of use— which translates to $100 to $250 a day on crack.

The sex-for-crack informants also had long active sexual histories. Their mean age at first sexual intercourse was 14 years; the first exchange of sex for money or drugs tended to occur in their late teens or early twenties, as shown in Table 31.8. Among the 17 male crack users, more than half had 25 or more male sex partners in the last 30 days; 5 of the 17 had 100 or more male partners. Almost three-fourths of these men had more than 25 female sex partners during the same period. Moreover, 42% participated in vaginal sex more than 25 times; 88% participated in oral sex more than 25 times, with a fourth engaging in oral sex 100 or more times; just under half participated in anal insertive sex at least once; and 30% engaged in anal receptive sex during this 30-day period. Finally, 30% of these men masturbated other men, with one individual providing this service more than 25 times. The women appeared to be even more sexually active than the men. Almost 90% of the women had 100 or more

Table 31.8

Drug Use and Sexual Behavior, 52 Sex-for-Crack Offenders, 1989–1990[a]

Drug or sex behavior		Women (N = 35)	Men (N = 17)
% Ever used	Marijuana	100.0	100.0
	Inhalant	37.1	52.9
	Hallucinogen	42.9	47.1
	Uppers	42.9	47.1
	Downers	65.7	70.6
	Cocaine	97.1	100.0
	IV cocaine	37.1	41.2
% Ever sex for	Money	100.0	94.1
	Drugs	100.0	70.5
Mean age at first	Marijuana	14.8	13.6
	Cocaine	18.8	17.7
	Crack	24.0	24.2
	Regular crack	24.4	24.5
	Sex	13.8	14.4
	Sex for money	20.4	19.1
	Sex for drugs	23.2	22.3
% Used in last 30 days	Alcohol	100.0	88.2
	Daily alcohol	51.4	47.1
	Marijuana	100.0	64.7
	Cocaine	48.6	29.4
	Regular crack	100.0	94.1
	Daily crack	57.1	58.8
Rocks per day on crack (%)	"All day"	20.0	29.4
	20 or more	48.6	41.2
	10 or more	62.9	76.5

[a] "Daily": all 30 of the last 30 days. "Regular": 3 or more days a week, or 12+ days in the last 30. All respondents were heavy crack users who had traded sex for either crack or the money to buy crack.

male sex partners, and 11% had as many as 25 female partners. Some 39% of these women participated in vaginal sex more than 50 times, 57% engaged in oral sex more than 50 times, 20% participated in anal sex, and 29% reported masturbating men, with one woman doing so on more than 50 occasions.

These data suggest that both men and women who exchange sex for crack are at significant risk for HIV infection. In addition to engaging in frequent high risk sexual activities with multiple partners, these informants had many sexual exchanges that were unprotected. For example, only 23% of the women always insisted that their partners use condoms during vaginal sex. During oral sex, even fewer (14%) of these women always did so. Only 7 of the 35 women engaged in anal sex during the 30 days prior to interview, but of those 7 only 2 *always* insisted that their partners use condoms.

Effective AIDS-related prevention and intervention efforts will be difficult to implement for sex-for-crack offenders. We believe that because of the compulsive nature of crack use, anything less than intensive residential drug treatment is likely to fail. Moreover, although long-term follow-up studies of crack users in treatment have yet to be conducted, anecdotal reports from clinicians suggest that patient attrition and relapse rates are high. Crack users in general, and those who exchange sex for crack in particular, appear to represent a problem population for which specially focused prevention and outreach initiatives must be designed.

Discussion

Much was realized from the Miami studies. We learned that for most street drug users, drug use per se was not the root cause of criminality. The great majority had already embarked on criminal careers prior to the onset of expensive drug use. This timing contradicts the basic argument of the "enslavement theory of addiction"—that otherwise law-abiding heroin and cocaine users are forced into lives of crime in order to support their drug habits. But at the same time, it is clear to us that drugs are driving crime. That is, although drug use does not necessarily initiate criminal careers among users, it freezes users into patterns of criminality that are more intense and unremitting than they would have been without drugs.

Through the course of these studies we often asked ourselves, "so what?" We wanted to generate more than knowledge for knowledge's sake, more than longer publication lists on our résumés! Our findings and experiences indicated clearly that much human suffering is associated with drug use. We wanted our research to be useful in efforts to reduce this misery. This led us to two further activities.

One was that the first author began writing more and more policy analyses. All might be considered examinations of "the war on drugs"—federal drug policy, criminal justice system reactions to drug users, current and potential intersects between the justice system and drug treatment, national drug problems and policy in other nations, the overlap between the drug problem and the AIDS problem, and the drug-legalization campaign (e.g., Inciardi, 1986, 1990, 1991, 1992).

The research findings from the studies described in this article, for example, directly contradict the argument that legalizing drugs would reduce the crime associated with drug use (Chambliss, 1988; Nadelmann, 1988a, 1988b, 1988c; Trebach, 1989, 1990). This simplistic idea has great appeal to people seeking control and predictability, but in reality heroin and cocaine addiction are only one symptom in a complex of problems experienced by drug users and their families, especially in urban poverty areas. Legalizing drugs not only fails to address this chaos and complexity, it would add to it by making drugs even more available (see, e.g., Inciardi and McBride, 1989). A large literature now suggests that drug addiction is *overdetermined behavior*. That is, physical dependence is secondary to the wide range of influences that instigate and regulate drug-taking and drug-seeking behaviors. Drug addiction is a disorder of the whole person, affecting some or all areas of functioning. Most drug-involved criminal offenders have cognitive problems, many have psychological dysfunctions, their thinking may be unrealistic or disorganized, their values are misshapen, and many have deficits in educational and employment skills. Their families and schools often do not have the resources with which to resolve these problems. On the other hand, an apparent resolution—drug involvement as a psychological refuge—is offered by the local drug users that exist today in virtually any American community. At the same time, the larger society—by means of government law and policy, corporate policies and values, popular culture, and the personal greed of political and financial elites—not only fails to address these problems but appears to aggravate them in that the poor get poorer and their children see even less hope for the future. In essence, drug dependence is a response to a series of social, cultural, and psychological disturbances.

This view led to the second addition to our drugs-crime research: a strong focus on treatment. The view of drug addiction as a disorder of the whole person implies that what street addicts need is not freely available drugs, but access to treatment. Further, we believe that for most drug-involved criminal offenders, treatment must be long-term, intensive, residential, and oriented toward "habilitation" rather than "rehabilitation." *Rehabilitation* means return to a way of life previously known and perhaps forgotten or rejected, whereas *habilitation* involves the client's initial socialization into a productive and responsible way of life.

Our current study in Miami looks specifically at treatment entry. This is a 4-year project entitled "Barriers to Treatment for Cocaine-Dependent Women." Interviewing began in late 1994 and will go through 1996—20 years from our first Miami interviews for NIDA in 1977. The plan is for 900 interviews with crime-involved, cocaine-dependent women; 450 on the street and 450 in treatment. The lengthy interviewing phase is necessary because of the sluggish flow of women into drug treatment even though our treatment interviewers are now recruiting respondents in nine residential programs and four outpatient programs. The impetus for this project is the widely recognized lack of attention paid to the special problems of chemically dependent women, and the consequent difficulties that treatment programs have in attracting and retaining female clients (see Reed's definitive 1985 article; also, Mondanaro, 1989). Miami treatment agencies have been aware of these problems and they have made special efforts to attract women. Notwithstanding these efforts, Miami is suitable for this research project not only because of our contacts, but also because of the fairly large population of cocaine-dependent women. We are interviewing women with prior treatment experience and no prior treatment, women who voluntarily entered and those who were coerced into it, women who want to enter treatment but haven't, and women who have no interest in treatment.

In addition to the Miami study, we are also involved in other research on drug use, crime, and treatment. The largest project entails a system of three therapeutic communities (TCs) in correctional settings in Delaware—one in a men's prison, one in the women's prison, and one in a work release program that the graduates of the two prison TCs enter before they are permitted to leave the state correctional system. This is both a drugs-crime study and a treatment evaluation; it is also an HIV seroprevalence study (Inciardi et al., 1994). The treatment results to date are very encouraging. The great majority of program graduates are arrest-free and drug-free at follow-up. Our integrated treatment system—prison TC, then work-release TC, then release to the community plus TC aftercare—seems to be intersecting the drugs-crime connection (Martin et al., 1995).

For the future, we are working on several proposals to expand treatment opportunities for Delaware offenders. In addition, we received a grant from NIDA to do a long term follow-up study of the TC graduates and dropouts, and a comparison group. In fact, that study is funded through the year 2005, so in a few years we should have pretty good data on prisoners with and without TC treatment.

Acknowledgements

The Miami research described in this paper was supported by Health and Human Services grants 1-R01-DA01827, 1-R01-DA04862, and 1-R01-DA08615 from the National Institute on Drug Abuse.

References

Austin, G. A., and Lettieri, D. J. (Eds.) (1976). *Drugs and Crime*. Rockville, MD: National Institute on Drug Abuse.

Chambers, C. D. (1974). Narcotic addiction and crime: An empirical review. In J. A. Inciardi and C. D. Chambers (Eds.), *Drugs and the Criminal Justice System* (pp. 125–142). Beverly Hills, CA: Sage.

Chambliss, W. J. (1988). Testimony, *Legalization of Illicit Drugs: Impact and Feasibility*. Hearing Before the Select Committee on Narcotics Abuse and Control, House of Representatives, One Hundredth Congress, Second Session, September 29, Washington, DC.

Datesman, S. K., and Inciardi, J. A. (1979). Female heroin use, criminality, and prostitution. *Contemp. Drug Probl.* 8: 445–473.

Gandossey, R. P., Williams, J. R., Cohen, J., and Harwood, H. J. (1980). *Drugs and Crime: A Survey and Analysis of the Literature*. Washington, DC: National Institute of Justice.

Greenberg, S. W., and Adler, F. (1974). Crime and addiction: An empirical analysis of the literature, 1920–1973. *Contemp. Drug Probl.* 3: 221–270.

Horowitz, R., and Pottieger, A. E. (1991). Gender bias in juvenile justice system handling of seriously crime-involved youths. *J. Res. Crime Delinq.* 28: 75–100.

Inciardi, J. A. (1974). The vilification of euphoria: Some perspectives on an illusive issue. *Addict. Dis.* 1: 241–267.

——. (1979). Heroin use and street crime. *Crime Delinq.* 25: 335–346.

——. (1980). Women, heroin, and property crime. In F. R. Scarpitti and S. K. Datesman (Eds.), *Women, Crime, and Criminal Justice* (pp. 214–222). New York, NY: Oxford University Press.

——. (1981). Fictitious data in drug abuse research. *Int. J. Addict.* 16: 377–380.

——. (1982). The production and detection of fraud in street studies of crime and drugs. *J. Drug Issues* 12: 285–291.

——. (1986). *The War on Drugs: Heroin, Cocaine, Crime, and Public Policy*. Palo Alto, CA: Mayfield.

——. (1987). Beyond cocaine: Basuco, crack, and other coca products. *Contemp. Drug Probl.* 14: 461–492.

——. (1988). *Crack-cocaine in Miami*. Paper presented at the NIDA Technical Review Meeting, May 3–4. Published in S. Schober and C. Schade (Eds.), *The Epidemiology of Cocaine Use and Abuse* (pp. 263–274). Rockville, MD: National Institute on Drug Abuse, 1991.

——. (1989). Trading sex for crack among juvenile drug users: A research note. *Contemp. Drug Probl.* 16: 689–700.

——. (Ed.) (1990). *Handbook of Drug Control in the United States*. Westport, CT: Greenwood.

——. (Ed.) (1991). *The Drug Legalization Debate*. Newbury Park, CA: Sage.

——. (1992). *The War on Drugs II: The Continuing Epic of Heroin, Cocaine, Crack, Crime, AIDS, and Public Policy*. Mountain View, CA: Mayfield.

——. (1995). Crack, crack house sex, and HIV risk. *Arch. Sex. Behav.* 24: 249–269.

Inciardi, J. A., and Chambers, C. D. (1972). Unreported criminal involvement of narcotic addicts. *J. Drug Issues* 2: 57–64.

Inciardi, J. A., Horowitz, R., and Pottieger, A. E. (1993a). *Street Kids, Street Drugs, Street Crime: An Examination of Drug Use and Serious Delinquency in Miami*. Belmont, CA: Wadsworth.

Inciardi, J. A., Lockwood, D., Martin, S. S., Pottieger, A. E., and Scarpitti, F. R. (1994). HIV infection among Delaware prison releases. *The Prison Journal*. New York, NY: Macmillan.

Inciardi, J. A., Lockwood, D., and Pottieger, A. E. (1993b). *Women and Crack-Cocaine*. New York, NY: Macmillan.

Inciardi, J. A., and McBride, D. C. (1989). Legalization: A high-risk alternative in the war on drugs. *Am. Behav. Sci.* 32(3): 259–289.

Inciardi, J. A., McBride, D. C., Pottieger, A. E., Russe, B. R., Wells, K. S., and Siegal, H. A. (1979). *Acute Drug Reactions in a Hospital Emergency Room* (Services Research Report Series). Rockville, MD: National Institute on Drug Abuse.

Inciardi, J. A., and Pottieger, A. E. (1986). Drug use and crime among two cohorts of women narcotics users: An empirical assessment. *J. Drug Issues* 16: 91–106.

——. (1991). Kids, crack, and crime. *J. Drug Issues* 21: 257–270.

——. (1994). Crack cocaine use and street crime. *J. Drug Issues* 24: 273–292.

Inciardi, J. A., Pottieger, A. E., and Faupel, C. E. (1982). Black women, heroin, and property crime: Some empirical notes. *J. Drug Issues* 12: 241–250.

Inciardi, J. A., Pottieger, A. E., Forney, M. A., Chitwood, D. D., and McBride, D. C. (1991). Prostitution, IV drug use, and sex-for-crack exchanges among serious delinquents: Risks for HIV infection. *Criminology* 29: 221–235.

Inciardi, J. A., Pottieger, A. E., and Surratt, H. L. (1996). African Americans and the crack-crime connection. In D. D. Chitwood, J. E. Rivers, and J. A. Inciardi, and the South Florida AIDS Research Consortium, *The American Pipe Dream: Crack Cocaine and the Inner City*. Fort Worth, TX: Harcourt Brace.

Inciardi, J. A., Russe, B. R., Pottieger, A. E., McBride, D. C., and Siegal, H. A. (1978). *Legal and Illicit Drug Use: Acute Reactions of Emergency Room Populations*. New York, NY: Praeger.

Johnson, B. D., Goldstein, P. J., Preble, E., Schmeilder, J., Lipton, D. S., Spunt, B., and Miller, T. (1985). *Taking Care of Business: The Economics of Crime by Heroin Abusers*. Lexington, MA: Lexington Books.

Lockwood, D., Pottieger, A. E., and Inciardi, J. A. (1993). *Cocaine and Street Crime: The Relevance of Cocaine Type, Demographics, and Street/Treatment Sample*. Paper presented at the Annual Meeting of the Academy of Criminal Justice Sciences, Kansas City, March.

——. (1995). Crack use, crime by crack users, and ethnicity. In D. F. Hawkins (Ed.), *Ethnicity, Race and Crime* (pp. 212–234). Albany, NY: SUNY Press.

Martin, S. S., Butzin, C. A., and Inciardi, J. A. (1995). Assessment of a multistage therapeutic community for drug-involved offenders. *J. Psychoactive Drugs* 27: 109–116.

Mondanaro, J. (1989). *Chemically Dependent Women: Assessment and Treatment.* Lexington, MA: Lexington Books.

Nadelmann, E. A. (1988a). The case for legalization. *Public Interest* 92: 3–31.

——. (1988b). U.S. drug policy: A bad export. *Foreign Policy* 70: 83–108.

——. (1988c). Testimony, *Legalization of Illicit Drugs: Impact and Feasibility.* Hearing Before the Select Committee on Narcotics Abuse and Control, House of Representatives, One Hundredth Congress, Second Session, September 29, Washington, DC.

Pottieger, A. E. (1981). Sample bias in drugs/crime research: An empirical study. In J. A. Inciardi (Ed.), *The Drugs/Crime Connection* (pp. 207–237). Beverly Hills, CA: Sage.

Pottieger, A. E., and Inciardi, J. A. (1981). Aging on the street: Drug use and crime among older men. *J. Psychedelic Drugs* 13: 199–211.

Pottieger, A. E., Tressell, P. A., Inciardi, J. A., and Rosales, T. A. (1992). Cocaine use patterns and overdose. *J. Psychoactive Drugs* 24: 399–410.

Pottieger, A. E., Tressell, P. A., Surratt, H. L., Inciardi, J. A., and Chitwood, D. D. (1995). Drug use patterns of adult crack users in street versus residential treatment samples. *J. Psychoactive Drugs* 27: 27–38.

Ratner, M. S. (1993). *Crack Pipe as Pimp.* New York, NY: Lexington Books.

Reed, B. G. (1985). Drug misuse and dependency in women: The meaning and implications of being considered a special population or minority group. *Int. J. Addict.* 20: 13–62.

Short, J. F., and Nye, F. I. (1958). Extent of unrecorded juvenile delinquency: Tentative conclusions. *J. Crim. Law Criminal.* 49: 296–312.

Soriano, F. I., and De La Rosa, M. R. (1990). Cocaine use and criminal activities among Hispanic juvenile delinquents in Florida. In R. Glick and J. Moore (Eds.), *Drugs in Hispanic Communities* (pp. 55–73). New Brunswick, NJ: Rutgers University Press.

Trebach, A. S. (1989). Tough choices: The practical politics of drug policy reform. *Am. Behav. Sci.* 32: 249–258.

——. (1990). A bundle of peaceful compromises. *J. Drug Issues* 20: 515–531.

Weissman, J. C. (1978). Understanding the drugs and crime connection: A systematic examination of drugs and crime relationships. *J. Psychedelic Drugs* 10: 171–192.

For Discussion

1. What can be concluded about the relationship between drug use and crime in Miami?

2. What appears to be the relationship between crimes committed and arrests?

3. Has the nature and extent of crime changed over time?

Reprinted from: James A. Inciardi and Anne E. Pottieger, "Drug Use and Street Crime in Miami: An (Almost) Twenty-Year Retrospective." In *Substance Use and Misuse* 33(9), pp. 1839–1870. Copyright © 1998 by Marcel Dekker. Reprinted with permission. ✦

32

The Drugs/ Violence Nexus

A Tripartite Conceptual Framework

Paul J. Goldstein

Most of the research that addresses linkages between drug use and crime focuses on property crime. Less understood is the relationship between drugs and violence. In this regard, Paul J. Goldstein draws from existing research to propose a framework for considering the drugs/violence nexus. One linkage is psychopharmacological—drugs alter behavior by reducing inhibitions or instigating aggression. By contrast, economically compulsive violence occurs when individuals commit violent crimes in their efforts to secure funds to purchase drugs for self-use. Systemic violence is associated with the turf battles and struggles for control in the drug dealing and trafficking industries.

Drug use, as well as the social context in which that use occurs, are etiological factors in a wide range of other social phenomena. Drug use is known to be causally related to a variety of physical and mental health problems, crime, poor school performance, family disruption, and the like. Previous research has also consistently found strong connections between drugs and violence.

For example, Zahn and Bencivengo (1974) reported that in Philadelphia, in 1972, homicide was the leading cause of death among drug users, higher even than deaths due to adverse effects of drugs; and drugs accounted for approximately 31 percent of the homicides in Philadelphia.

Monforte and Spitz (1975), after studying autopsy and police reports in Michigan, suggested that drug use and distribution may be more strongly related to homicide than to property crime. Preble (1980) conducted an ethnographic study of heroin addicts in East Harlem between 1965 and 1967. About fifteen years later, in 1979 and 1980, he followed up the 78 participants and obtained detailed information about what had happened to them. He found that 28 had died. Eleven, 40 percent of the deaths, were the victims of homicide. The New York City Police Department (1983) classified about 24 percent of known homicides in 1981 as drug-related.

The drugs/violence nexus also appears consistently in newspaper headlines. For example, a seventeen-year-old boy who committed suicide by hanging himself in his jail cell had earlier confessed to committing a ritual stabbing and mutilation killing of another youth, because he believed the boy had stolen ten bags of PCP from him (*New York Times*, July 12, 1984). A New York City transit policeman was beaten with his own nightstick and his chin was nearly bitten off by a fare-beater who was high on angel dust (*New York Post*, September 19, 1984). A thirty-nine-year-old mother of three was killed by a stray bullet fired during a fight between drug dealers on the lower east side of Manhattan (*New York Post*, October 10, 1984). A front-page headline in the *New York Times* (October 29, 1984) claimed that "Increase in Gang Killings on Coast Is Traced to Narcotics Trafficking." Less than a month later, another *New York Times* front-page headline announced that "Cocaine Traffickers Kill 17 in Peru Raid on Anti-Drug Team" (November 19, 1984). A Miami police official was quoted on television as saying that one-third of the homicides in Miami in 1984 were cocaine-related.

Even though the relationship between drugs and violence has been consistently documented in both the popular press and in social scientific research, it is only recently that attempts have been made to assess this problem on a national level. One such effort estimated that 10 percent of the homicides and assaults nationwide are the result of drug use (Harwood et al. 1984). Another recent report estimated that, in the United States in 1980, over 2,000 homicides were drug-related and, assuming an average life span of 65 years, resulted in the loss of about 70,000 years of life. This report further estimated that, in 1980, over 460,000 assaults were drug-related, and that, in about 140,000 of these assaults, the victims sustained physical injury, leading to about 50,000 days of hospitalization (Goldstein and Hunt 1984).

While the association between drugs and violence appears strong, and drug use and trafficking appear to be important etiological factors in the incidence of violence, there has been little effort to place this relationship into a conceptual framework to guide further empirical research. The purpose of this paper is to introduce such a framework.

Information for this report was gathered during the course of three separate empirical investigations. Sixty women were interviewed in 1976 and 1977 for a study of the relationship between prostitution and drugs (Goldstein 1979). Between 1978 and 1982, an ethnographic study was undertaken of the economic behavior of 201 street opiate users in Harlem.[1] Finally, in 1984, I began a study of the relationship between drugs and violence on the lower east side of Manhattan.[2] That study is guided by the conceptual framework presented below.

Drugs and violence are seen as being related in three possible ways: the psychopharmacological, the economically compulsive, and the systemic. Each of these models must be viewed, in a theoretical sense, as "ideal types," i.e., as hypothetically concrete ". . . devices intended to institute comparisons as precise as the stage of one's theory and the precision of one's instruments allow" (Martindale 1959:58–59). In fact, it will be shown below that there can be overlap between the three models. However, this overlap does not detract from the heuristic value of the tripartite conceptual framework.

Psychopharmacological Violence

The psychopharmacological model suggests that some individuals, as a result of short- or long-term ingestion of specific substances, may become excitable, irrational, and may exhibit violent behavior. The most relevant substances in this regard are probably alcohol, stimulants, barbiturates, and PCP. A lengthy literature exists, examining the relationship between these substances and violence (Tinklenberg 1973; Virkunnen 1974; Glaser 1974; Gerson et al. 1979; Ellinswood 1971; Smith 1972; Asnis and Smith 1978; d'Orban 1976; Feldman et al. 1979). Early reports which sought to employ a psychopharmacological model to attribute violent behavior to the use of opiates and marijuana have now been largely discredited (Finestone 1967; Inciardi and Chambers 1972; Kozel et al. 1972; Greenberg and Adler 1974; Schatzman 1975; Kramer 1976). In a classic statement of this point, Kolb argued the following.

> There is probably no more absurd fallacy prevalent than the notion that murders are committed and daylight robberies and holdups are carried out by men stimulated by large doses of cocaine or heroin which have temporarily distorted them into self-imagined heroes incapable of fear . . . violent crime would be much less prevalent if all habitual criminals were addicts who could obtain sufficient morphine or heroin to keep themselves fully charged with one of these drugs at all times. (Kolb 1925:78)

Kolb's point must be modified in one very important way. He is correct in claiming that ingestion of opiates is unlikely to lead to violence. However, the irritability associated with the withdrawal syndrome from opiates may indeed lead to violence. For example, in previous research on the relationship between drugs and prostitution, I found that heroin-using prostitutes often linked robbing and/or assaulting clients with the withdrawal experience (Goldstein 1979). These women reported that they preferred to talk a "trick" out of his money, but if they were feeling "sick," i.e., experiencing withdrawal symptoms, that they would be too irritable to engage in gentle conning. In such cases, they might attack the client, take his money, purchase sufficient heroin to "get straight," and then go back on the street. In a more relaxed physical and mental state, these women claimed that they could then behave like prostitutes rather than robbers.

Drug use may also have a reverse psychopharmacological effect and ameliorate violent tendencies. In such cases, persons who are prone to acting violently may engage in self-medication, in order to control their violent impulses. Several subjects have reported doing this. The drugs chosen for this function are typically heroin or tranquilizers.

Psychopharmacological violence may involve drug use by either offender or victim. In other words, drug use may contribute to a person behaving violently, or it may alter a person's behavior, in such a manner as to bring about that person's violent victimization. Previous research indicates relatively high frequencies of alcohol consumption in rape (Amir 1971; Rada 1975) and homicide victims (Shupe 1954; Wolfgang 1958). Public intoxication may invite a robbery or mugging. One study found that, in rapes where only the victim was intoxicated, she was significantly more likely to be physically injured (Johnson et al. 1978).

It is difficult to estimate the true rate of victim-precipitated psychopharmacological violence, because many such instances go unreported and, hence, unrecorded in official records. My own research in New York over the last decade indicated that many intoxicated victims do not report their victimization. Such victims say that they do not wish to talk to the police while drunk or "stoned." Further, since they are frequently confused about details of the event and, perhaps, unable to remember what their assailant looked like, they argue that reporting the event would be futile.

Assuming that the psychopharmacological violence is not precipitated by the victim, the victim can then be just about anybody. Psychopharmacological violence can erupt in the home and lead to spouse or child abuse. Psychopharmacological violence can occur in the workplace, on the streets, in bars, and so on. The incidence of psycho-pharmacological violence is impossible to assess at the present time, both because many instances go unreported and because when cases are reported, the psychopharmacological state of the offender is seldom recorded in official records.

Economic-Compulsive Violence

The economically compulsive model suggests that some drug users engage in economically-oriented violent crime, e.g., robbery, in order to support costly drug use. Heroin and cocaine, because they are expensive drugs typified by compulsive patterns of use, are the most relevant substances in this category. Economically compulsive actors are not primarily motivated by impulses to act out violently. Rather, their primary motivation is to obtain money to purchase drugs. Violence generally results from some factor in the social context in which the economic crime is perpetrated. Such factors include the perpetrator's own nervousness, the victim's reaction, weaponry (or the lack of it) carried by either offender or victim, the intercession of bystanders, and so on.

Research indicates that most heroin users avoid violent acquisitive crime, if viable nonviolent alternatives exist (Preble and Casey 1969; Swezey 1973; Cushman 1974; Gould 1974; Goldstein and Duchaine 1980; Goldstein 1979; Johnson et al. 1985). This is because violent crime is more dangerous, embodies a greater threat of prison if one is apprehended, and because perpetrators may lack a basic orientation toward violent behavior. Bingham Dai reported similar findings nearly fifty years ago. His study of the criminal records of over one thousand opiate addicts in Chicago revealed that the most common offenses for which they were arrested were violations of the narcotics laws, followed by offenses against property.

> . . . it is interesting to note that comparatively few of them resorted to violence in their criminal activities. The small percentage of addicts, committing such crimes as robbery, assault and battery, homicide, and others that involve the use of force, seems to discredit the view shared by many that the use of drugs has

the effect of causing an individual to be a heartless criminal. On the contrary, our figures suggest that most of the crimes committed by addicts were of a peaceful nature that involve more the use of wit than that of force. (Dai 1937:69)

Victims of economic-compulsive violence, like those of psychopharmacological violence, can be anybody. Previous research (Goldstein and Johnson 1983; Johnson et al. 1985) indicates that the most common victims of this form of drug-related violence are people residing in the same neighborhoods as the offender. Frequently, the victims are engaged in illicit activities themselves. Other drug users, strangers coming into the neighborhood to buy drugs, numbers runners, and prostitutes are all common targets of economic-compulsive violence.

While research does indicate that most of the crimes committed by most of the drug users are of the non-violent variety, e.g., shoplifting, prostitution, drug selling, there are little data that indicate what proportion of violent economic crimes are committed for drug-related reasons. No national criminal justice data bases contain information on the motivations or drug-use pattern of offenders as they relate to specific crimes.

Systemic Violence

In the systemic model, violence is intrinsic to involvement with any illicit substance. Systemic violence refers to the traditionally aggressive patterns of interaction within the system of drug distribution and use. Some examples of systemic violence follow below:

1. disputes over territory between rival drug dealers.

2. assaults and homicides committed within dealing hierarchies as a means of enforcing normative codes.

3. robberies of drug dealers and the usually violent retaliation by the dealer or his/her bosses.

4. elimination of informers.

5. punishment for selling adulterated or phony drugs.

6. punishment for failing to pay one's debts.

7. disputes over drugs or drug paraphernalia.

8. robbery violence related to the social ecology of copping areas.

Substantial numbers of users of any drug become involved in drug distribution as their drug-using careers progress and, hence, increase their risk of becoming a victim or perpetrator of systemic violence. Examples of each type of systemic violence mentioned above are readily available.

We recently reported that much of the heroin in New York City is being distinctively packaged and sold under "brand names" (Goldstein et al. 1984). These labeling practices are frequently abused, and this abuse has led to violence. Among the more common abuses are the following: dealers mark an inferior-quality heroin with a currently popular brand name; users purchase the good heroin, use it, then repackage the bag with milk sugar for resale; the popular brand is purchased, the bag is "tapped," and further diluted for resale.

These practices get the real dealers of the popular brand very upset. Their heroin starts to get a bad reputation on the streets, and they lose sales. Purchasers of the phony bags may accost the real dealers, complaining about the poor quality and demanding their money back. The real dealers then seek out the purveyors of the phony bags. Threats, assaults, and/or homicides may ensue.

A common form of norm violation in the drug trade is known as "messing up the money." Basically, this involves a subordinate returning less money to his superior than is expected. For example, a street dealer is given a consignment of drugs to sell and is expected to return to his supplier or lieutenant with a specific amount of money. However, for any of a variety of reasons, he returns with too little money or fails to return at all. Some of the reasons why he might be short on his money are that he used some or all of the drugs himself; he sold all of the drugs, but then spent some or all of the money; he gave out too many "shorts," i.e., he sold the drugs for less than he should have; he was robbed, either of his drugs or of the money that he obtained from selling them.

When a street dealer fails to return sufficient money, his superior has several options. If only a small amount of money is involved, and the street dealer has few prior transgressions and a convincing justification for the current shortage, his superior is likely to give him another consignment and allow him to make up the shortage from his share of the new consignment. Other options include firing the street dealer, having him beaten up, or having him killed.

In a recent study, a lieutenant in a heroin dealing operation had been rather lax in supervising the six street dealers working under him. Just about everybody was "messing up the money," including himself. One day, the supplier and two "soldiers" picked up the lieutenant and took him for a ride in their car. The lieutenant was afraid that he was going to be killed. However, after cruising for a while, they spotted one of the street dealers who had been "messing up the money." The two soldiers jumped from the car and beat him with iron pipes. They positioned him in the street and drove the car over his legs, crippling him for life. The supplier then suggested to the lieutenant that he would be well-advised to run the operation more tightly in the future.

An interesting addendum to this discussion is that the "code of the streets" dictates that "blood cancels all debts." In other words, if a street dealer has "messed up the money" and is subsequently beaten up or wounded, then he no longer owes the money. The shedding of blood has canceled the debt.

The above account illustrates a direct punishment for a norm violation. Violence may also arise in the course of a dispute that stems from a norm violation. I was recently told of such an incident. A drug dealer operated out of an apartment in New York City. Prospective purchasers would line up in the hallway of the apartment house and give their money to a young Hispanic woman who worked for the dealer. The woman would then get the drugs from the dealer and give them to the buyers. Dealers seldom allow customers into the space where the drugs are actually kept.

One day, the line was long and three black men waited patiently to make their purchase. Finally, it was their turn. However, the woman bypassed them in favor of two Hispanic men who were at the back of the line. The Hispanic men made a large purchase, and the woman announced that the dealer had sold out for the day. The blacks were furious. An argument ensued, shots were fired, and one of the Hispanic men was killed. The norm violator in this case, the woman, was fired by the dealer.

A common precipitator of violence in the drug scene is the robbery of a dealer. No dealer who wishes to stay in business can allow himself or his associates to be robbed. Most dealers maintain an arsenal of weapons and a staff that knows how to use them. A subject in a recent study reported going with two friends to "take off" a neighborhood social club that was a narcotics distribution center. In the course of the hold-up, they shot one of the employees and beat up several other men and women. In retrospect, the subject admitted that they had probably used excessive force, but that at the time it had seemed justified because they were outnumbered about fifteen to three. One of the victims recognized one of the robbers. This robber was later shot to death in the street.

The Pulitzer Prize-winning study of narcotics trafficking, *The Heroin Trail*, documents many instances of systemic violence. One concerns Joseph Fucillo, a Brooklyn drug dealer who became a police informant in 1972.

> One day, as his wife watched from the window of their home in the Bensonhurst section of Brooklyn, Fucillo backed his car out of the driveway, and two men in ski masks walked up to it. Two guns fired rapidly and seven bullets went into Fucillo's head. He died. (*Newsday* Staff and Editors, 1974:226)

A pimp stated that he would never allow a "junkie broad" to work for him. One of his reasons was that an addicted woman might be easily turned into an informant by the police. When asked what he would do if one of his women did start to use narcotics, he replied that, if she didn't know too much about his activities, he would just fire her. However, if she did know too much, he would kill her (Goldstein 1979:107).

New York Magazine reported an event that was tragic both in its consequence and in the fact that it is so typical of the current drug scene.

> Sylvester, a sixteen-year-old boy, is stabbed in the chest . . . in the Crown Heights section of Brooklyn. He is taken to St. Mary's Hospital and dies a short time later. According to a witness, Sylvester sold marijuana to a group of adolescents a few days before the incident. His customers were apparently dissatisfied with its quality. Tonight, the teenagers, a group of about eight or ten, find Sylvester on the street and complain about the bad grass. The leader of the group, John Green, demands their money back. Sylvester then picks up a couple of bottles and throws them at the group, running away down the block. The teenagers chase Sylvester down Lincoln Place, where he picks up a stick and starts swinging. Knocking the stick out of his hand, John Green plunges a four-inch knife into Sylvester's chest. Green and the others escape from the scene. At one p.m. Sunday afternoon, in apparent retaliation for the Sylvester murder, John Green is shot once in the left rear side of the body. He too is taken to St. Mary's, where he too dies. (Goro 1977:31)

Violence associated with disputes over drugs has long been endemic in the drug world. Friends come to blows, because one refuses to give the other a "taste." A husband beats his wife, because she raided his "stash."

The current AIDS scare has led to an increasing amount of violence because of intravenous drug users' fear of contracting this fatal disease from contaminated "works." Some sellers of needles and syringes claim that the used works that they are trying to sell are actually new and unused. If discovered by would-be purchasers, violence may ensue. I was recently told of one incident that allegedly led to the death of two men. A heroin user kept a set of works in a "shooting gallery" that were for his exclusive use. One day, another man used these works. The owner of the works discovered what had happened and stabbed this man to death. He later stabbed a friend to death who was present when the stranger had used the works, had done nothing to stop him, and had failed to inform the owner of what had happened.

The social ecology of copping areas is generally well-suited for the perpetration of robbery violence. Most major copping areas in New York City are located in poor ghetto neighborhoods, such as Harlem. In these neighborhoods, drug users and dealers are frequent targets for robberies because they are known to be carrying something of value, and because they are unlikely to report their victimization. Dealers are sometimes forced to police their own blocks, so that customers may come and go in safety.

A subject in a current study earns money by copping drugs for other people. He stated that he was recently forced to protect one of his clients by fighting off two would-be robbers with a garbage-can lid. Interestingly, he knew the two attackers from the street, but he claimed to harbor no ill will towards them. He stated that they did what they had to do, and he did what he had to do.

Victims of systemic violence are usually those involved in drug use or trafficking. Occasionally, non-involved individuals become innocent victims. The case of a woman being killed by a stray bullet fired in a dispute between rival drug dealers was cited earlier. Several cases have been reported where whole families of drug dealers, including wives and young children, have perished in narcotics gang wars. However, the vast majority of victims of systemic violence are those who use drugs, who sell drugs, or are otherwise engaged in some aspect of the drug business.

Various sources have stressed the importance of what I have termed the systemic model in explaining drugs/violence relationships. Blumm (1970) points out that, with the exception of alcohol, most drug users are not violent, but that this point does not apply to the typical dealer for whom there is strong evidence linking drugs and violence. Smith (1972), in his discussion of amphetamines and violence in San Francisco's Haight-Ashbury district, stated that the primary cause of violence on the streets was "burning," i.e., selling phony or adulterated drugs. Several sources suggest that studying the area of systemic violence may be more important than the study of the relationship of drug use to crime on the level of the individual user.

Racket-associated violence, a result of the intense competition for enormous profits involved in drugs, is flourishing. This is not the "crime in the streets" which is often associated with drugs, but an underworld in which ordinarily those people suffer from violence who in one way or another have become related to the traffic. (Fitzpatrick 1974:360)

Because these criminal entrepreneurs operate outside the law in their drug transactions, they are not bound by business etiquette in their competition with each other, in their collection of debts, or in their non-drug investments. Terror, violence, extortion, bribery, or any other expedient strategy is relied upon by these criminals. . . . (Glaser 1974:53)

Where a commodity is scarce and highly in demand (as may be the case with drugs), extreme measures of control, i.e., homicide, may be involved. Further, in areas of high scarcity and inelastic demand, bitter arguments centering on the commodity are likely to ensue. When such arguments take place in a subculture where violence is the modus operandi, and where implements of violence, e.g., guns, are readily available, homicide is likely to be the result. (Zahn 1975:409)

Zahn pointed out the importance of systemic violence in her recent study of homicide in twentieth-century United States. She showed that homicide rates peaked in the 1920s and early 1930s, declined and leveled off thereafter, began to rise in 1965, and peaked again in 1974. This analysis led to the following conclusion:

In terms of research directions, this historical review would suggest that closer attention be paid to the connection between markets for illegal goods and the overall rate of homicide violence. It seems possible, if not likely, that establishing and maintaining a market for illegal goods (booze in the 1920s and early 1930s; heroin and cocaine in the late 1960s and early 1970s) may involve controlling and/or reducing the competition, solving disputes between alternate suppliers or eliminating dissatisfied customers. . . . The use of guns in illegal markets may also be triggered by the constant fear of being caught either by a rival or by the police. Such fear may increase the perceived need for protection, i.e., a gun, thus may increase the arming of these populations and a resulting increased likelihood of use. For the overall society, this may mean a higher homicide rate. (Zahn 1980:128)

It was stated above that the three models of the drugs/violence nexus contained in the tripartite conceptual framework should be viewed as ideal types, and that overlap could occur between them. For example, a heroin user preparing to commit an act of economic-compulsive violence, e.g., a robbery, might ingest some alcohol or stimulants to give himself the courage to do the crime. This event now contains elements of both economic-compulsive and psychopharmacological violence. If the target of his robbery attempt was a drug dealer, the event would contain elements of all three types of drug-related violence.

The conceptual framework allows the event to be effectively analyzed and broken down into constituent parts and processes. The roles played in the event by different sorts of drugs can be explicated. In the above example, the need for money to purchase heroin was the primary motivation for the act. Alcohol and stimulants were ingested after the act was decided upon because of the robber's need for courage, and, presumably, because prior experience with these substances led the perpetrator to believe that they would serve that psychopharmacological function.

The choice of target, a drug dealer, is open for empirical investigation. It may turn out that the reason the heroin user needed to commit the robbery was because that dealer had cheated him earlier in the day on a drug purchase, perhaps selling him "dummy" bags. Our robber, needing to "get straight" and not having any more money, decides that robbing this unscrupulous dealer would be an appropriate revenge.

Several subjects in our studies reported committing economic-compulsive acts out of fear of becoming a victim of systemic violence. These were street dealers who had "messed up the money" and who were terrified of what their superiors might do to them. Some had already been threatened. This motivated them to do robberies as a quick way to obtain the money that they owed.

Thus, as the concepts are employed, a fuller understanding of the event emerges. The roles played by specific drugs become clearer. The actor's motivations and the process by which he undertakes to commit a robbery are elaborated upon.

If the above events were to be examined in official crime records, assuming they were reported, they would be listed as robberies. Victim-perpetrator relationships would probably be unknown, though they might be listed as "acquaintance" or "stranger." No mention of drugs would be made.

Victims of systemic violence frequently lie to the police about the circumstances of their victimization. Not a single research subject whom I have interviewed who was the victim of systemic violence and who was forced to give an account of his or her victimization to the police admitted that he or she had been assaulted because of owing a drug supplier money or selling somebody phony or adulterated drugs. All such victims simply claimed to have been robbed.

It would make little difference if the robbery were to develop into a homicide. The classification of the event would change from robbery to homicide, but victim-perpetrator relationship and nature of the homicide would remain unknown or be coded in such a broad fashion that the information would not be very useful. No mention of drugs would be made. Attention will now be focused on the quality of data available on the national level to elaborate on the drugs/violence nexus.

Quality of Data Available on Drugs/Violence Nexus

The drugs/violence nexus is one of the most important criminological and health issues, for which rigorously collected data is currently unavailable. While a variety of ethnographic studies focus on violent behavior of drug users, most of this material is not quantitative and does not allow national projections to be made. Official statistics collected in the criminal justice and health care systems do not link acts of criminal violence and resultant injuries or death to antecedent drug activity of victims or perpetrators. Broad recording categories make it virtually impossible to determine whether the offender or victim was a drug user or distributor, or whether the pharmacological status of either victim or offender was related to the specific event.

Uniform Crime Reports (UCR), collected by the Federal Bureau of Investigation, is the most visible source of crime data in the country. However, it is not very useful for an elaboration of the relationship between drugs and violence. UCR is a measure of crimes known to the police. Many crimes are not reported. The 1980 National Crime Survey found that the following proportions of violent victimizations were not reported to the police: 57 percent of the rapes; 41 percent of the robberies; 52 percent of the assaults (BJS 1982:71). UCR data on homicide, due to the presence of a body, is the most reliable crime-incidence category.

Reporting schedules, to which local law-enforcement agencies must adhere, frequently result in data being submitted to UCR before investigative work has been completed; and, hence, large numbers of unknowns usually appear in relevant categories. The New York City Police Department has addressed this issue by holding an annual debriefing of detective-squad commanders about all homicides that occurred in their precincts during the preceding year. It was in the context of these debriefings that the significance of drug-related homicides first emerged and became an important analytic category for the NYPD Crime Analysis Unit. The new data gathered during these debriefings have never been included in UCR, because no structure exists for their transmission. This has led to such curious statistical phenomena as New York City reporting more drug-related homicides for a given year than UCR reports for the nation as a whole, including New York City.

The major difficulty in using UCR to estimate drug-related violent crime is the lack of a descriptive component to supplement the quantitative presentation. The drug-relatedness of violent events is simply not coded. Therefore, it is not possible to link specific violent acts to antecedent drug activities of either victim or perpetrator.

An alternative data source is the National Crime Survey (NCS). This annual report issued by the Bureau of Justice Statistics (BJS) is based on data obtained from a stratified, multi-stage cluster sample. The basic sampling unit is the household. Respondents within households are asked for all instances of victimization in the past year. Projections are then made to the nation as a whole.

As was the case with UCR, the NCS is not very useful for elaborating on the drugs/violence nexus. Street drug users frequently are not part of a household, i.e., they may sleep in abandoned buildings, in subways, on park benches. Thus, a population that is posited to be at especially high risk for drug-related violence is likely to be underrepresented in this data. Also, victims may have difficulty recalling specific events or be reluctant to describe them to an interviewer.

> Research on the capacity of victims to recall specific kinds of crime . . . indicates that assault is the least well-recalled of the crimes measured by the NCS. This may stem in part from the observed tendency of victims not to report crimes committed by offenders known to them, especially if they are relatives. In addition, it is suspected that, among certain groups, crimes that contain the elements of assault are a part of everyday life and, thus, are simply forgotten or are not considered worth mentioning to a survey interviewer. Taken together, these recall problems may result in a substantial understatement of the "true" rate of victimization from assault. (Bureau of Justice Statistics 1982:94)

A major problem with the NCS is that victims seldom know the motivation of offenders for committing acts of violence. Of course, this is less the case with systemic vio-

lence than it is with either psychopharmacological or economic-compulsive violence. With regard to psychopharmacological violence, victims may not be able to discern that assailants are "high" and, even if they could, it would be difficult to ascertain what substances are involved. Similarly, victims of economic-compulsive violence may not know that they are being robbed in order to finance a drug habit.

Summary and Conclusions

Drugs and violence were shown to be related in three possible ways: psychopharmacologically, economic-compulsively, and systemically. These different forms of drug-related violence were shown to be related to different types of substance use, different motivations of violent perpetrators, different types of victims, and differential influence by social context. Current methods of collecting national-crime data were shown to be insensitive to the etiological role played by drug use and trafficking in creating violent crime.

No evidence currently exists as to the proportions of violence engaged in by drug users and traffickers that may be attributed to each of the three posited models. We need such data. My own impression, arising from research in New York, is that the area of systemic violence accounts for most of the violence perpetrated by, and directed at, drug users.

Systemic violence is normatively embedded in the social and economic networks of drug users and sellers. Drug use, the drug business, and the violence connected to both of these phenomena, are all aspects of the same general lifestyle. Individuals caught in this lifestyle value the experience of substance use, recognize the risks involved, and struggle for survival on a daily basis. That struggle is clearly a major contributor to the total volume of crime and violence in American society.

Notes

1. This research was supported by the New York State Division of Substance Abuse Services; by a Public Health Service Award from the

National Institute on Drug Abuse (RO1-DA 01926); and by an interagency agreement between NIDA (RO1-DA 02355) and the Law Enforcement Assistance Administration (LEAA-J-IAA-005-8).

2. This research is being supported by the New York State Division of Substance Abuse Services and by a Public Health Service Award from the National Institute on Drug Abuse (RO1-DA 03182).

References

Amir, M. 1971. *Patterns in Forcible Rape*. Chicago: University of Chicago Press.

Asnis, S., and R. Smith. 1978. Amphetamine Abuse and Violence, *Journal of Psychedelic Drugs*, 10:317–377.

Biernacki, P. 1979. Junkie Work, Hustles, and Social Status Among Heroin Addicts, *Journal of Drug Issues*, 9:535–550.

Blumm, Richard and Associates. 1970. *Students and Drugs*. San Francisco, CA: Jossey-Bass.

Bureau of Justice Statistics. 1982. *Criminal Victimization in the United States*, 1980. Washington, DC: United States Department of Justice.

Cushman, P. 1974. Relationship between Narcotic Addiction and Crime, *Federal Probation*, 38:38–43.

Dai, B. 1937. *Opium Addiction in Chicago*. Montclair: Patterson Smith.

d'Orban, P. T. 1976. Barbiturate Abuse, *Journal of Medical Ethics*, 2:63–67.

Eckerman, W., J. Bates, J. Rachall, and W. Poole. 1971. *Drug Usage and Arrest Charges: A Study of Drug Usage and Arrest Charges among Arrestees in Six Metropolitan Areas of the United States*. Washington, DC: United States Department of Justice.

Ellinswood, E. 1971. Assault and Homicide Associated with Amphetamine Abuse, *American Journal of Psychiatry*, 127:1170–1175.

Feldman, H., M. H. Agar, and G. M. Beschner (eds.) 1979. *Angel Dust: An Ethnographic Study of PCP Users*. Lexington: Lexington Books.

Finestone, H. 1967. Narcotics and Criminality, *Law and Contemporary Problems*, 22:60–85.

Fink, L., and M. Hyatt. 1978. Drug Use and Violent Behavior, *Journal of Drug Education*, 8:139–149.

Fitzpatrick, J. P. 1974. Drugs, Alcohol, and Violent Crime, *Addictive Diseases*, 1:353–367.

Gerson, L. W., and D. A. Preston. 1979. Alcohol Consumption and the Incidence of Violent Crime, *Journal of Studies on Alcohol*, 40:307–312.

Glaser, D. 1974. Interlocking Dualities in Drug Use, Drug Control, and Crime, in Inciardi, J. A., and C. Chambers (eds.), *Drugs and the Criminal Justice System*. Beverly Hills: Sage Publications.

Goldstein, P. J. 1979. *Prostitution and Drugs*. Lexington: Lexington Books.

——. 1981. Getting Over: Economic Alternatives to Predatory Crime Among Street Drug Users, in Inciardi, J. A. (ed.), *The Drugs/Crime Connection*. Beverly Hills: Sage Publications.

Goldstein, P. J., and N. Duchaine. 1980. Daily Criminal Activities of Street Drug Users, paper presented at annual meetings of the American Society of Criminology.

Goldstein, P. J., and B. D. Johnson. 1983. Robbery Among Heroin Users, presented at annual meetings of the Society for the Study of Social Problems.

Goldstein, P. J., and D. Hunt. 1984. Health Consequences of Drug Use, report to the Carter Center of Emory University and The Centers for Disease Control.

Goldstein, P. J., D. S. Lipton, E. Preble, I. Sobel, T. Miller, W. Abbott, W. Paige, and F. Soto. 1984. The Marketing of Street Heroin in New York City, *Journal of Drug Issues*, 14:553–566.

Goro, H. 1977. Saturday Night Dead, *New York Magazine*, 10:31.

Gould, L. 1974. Crime and the Addict: Beyond Common Sense, in Inciardi, J. A., and C. Chambers (eds.), *Drugs and the Criminal Justice System*. Beverly Hills: Sage Publications.

Greenberg, S., and F. Adler. 1974. Crime and Addiction: An Empirical Analysis of the Literature, 1920-1973, *Contemporary Drug Problems*, 3:221–270.

Harwood, H., D. Napolitano, P. Kristiansen, and J. Collins. 1984. *Economic Costs to Society of Alcohol and Drug Abuse and Mental Illness*. Final Report to the Alcohol, Drug Abuse and Mental Health Administration.

Inciardi, J. A., and C. Chambers. 1972. Unreported Criminal Involvement of Narcotic Addicts, *Journal of Drug Issues*, 2:57–64.

Johnson, B. D., P. J. Goldstein, E. Preble, J. Schmeidler, D. S. Lipton, B. Spunt, and T. Mille. 1985. *Taking Care of Business: The Economics of Crime by Heroin Abusers*. Lexington: Lexington Books.

Johnson, S., L. Gibson, and R. Linden. 1978. Alcohol and Rape in Winnepeg: 1966–1975, *Journal of Studies on Alcohol*, 39:1887–1894.

Klepfisz, A., and J. Racy. 1973. Homicide and LSD, *JAMA* 223:429–430.

Kolb, L. 1925. Drug Addiction and its Relation to Crime, *Mental Hygiene*, 9:74–89.

Kozel, N., R. Dupont, and B. Brown. 1972. A Study of Narcotic Involvement in an Offender Population, *International Journal of the Addictions,* 7:443–450.

Kramer, J. C. 1976. From Demon to Ally—How Mythology Has and May Yet Alter National Drug Policy, *Journal of Drug Issues,* 6:390–406.

McBride, D. 1981. Drugs and Violence, in Inciardi, J. A. (ed.), *The Drugs/Crime Connection.* Beverly Hills: Sage Publications.

Martindale, D. 1959. Sociological Theory and the Ideal Type, in Gross, L. (ed.), *Symposium on Sociological Theory.* New York: Harper and Row.

Monforte, J. R., and W. U. Spitz. 1975. Narcotic Abuse Among Homicides in Detroit, *Journal of Forensic Sciences,* 20:186–190.

Newsday Staff and Editors. 1974. *The Heroin Trail.* New York: Holt, Rinehart, and Winston.

New York City Police Department. 1983. *Homicide Analysis: 1981.*

Petersen, R., and R. Stillman (eds.). 1978. *Phencyclidine Abuse: An Appraisal.* Rockville, MD: National Institute on Drug Abuse.

Preble, E. 1980. El Barrio Revisited, paper presented at annual meetings of the Society for Applied Anthropology.

Preble, E., and J. Casey. 1969. Taking Care of Business: The Heroin User's Life on the Street, *International Journal of the Addictions,* 4:1–24.

Rada, R. 1975. Alcoholism and Forcible Rape, *American Journal of Psychiatry,* 132:444–446.

Schatzman, M. 1975. Cocaine and the Drug Problem, *Journal of Psychedelic Drugs,* 77–81.

Shupe, L. M. 1954. Alcohol and Crime: A Study of the Urine Alcohol Concentration Found in 882 Persons Arrested During or Immediately After the Commission of a Felony, *Journal of Criminal Law, Criminology, and Police Science,* 44:661–664.

Smith, R. 1972. Speed and Violence: Compulsive Methamphetamine Abuse and Criminality in the Haight-Ashbury District, in C. Zarsfonetis (ed.), *Drug Abuse: Proceedings of the International Conference.* Philadelphia: Lea and Febiger.

Swezey, R. 1973. Estimating Drug-Crime Relationships, *International Journal of the Addictions,* 8:701–721.

Tinklenberg, J. 1973. Drugs and Crime, in National Commission on Marijuana and Drug Abuse, Drug Use in America: Problems in Perspective. Appendix, Volume 1, Patterns and Consequences of Drug Use. Washington, DC: United States Government Printing Office.

Virkunnen, M. 1974. Alcohol as a Factor Precipitating Aggression and Conflict Behavior Leading to Homicide, *British Journal of the Addictions,* 69:149–154.

Wolfgang, M. E. 1958. *Patterns in Criminal Homicide.* Philadelphia: University of Philadelphia Press.

Zahn, M. A. 1975. The Female Homicide Victim, *Criminology,* 13:409.

——. 1980. Homicide in the Twentieth Century United States, in Inciardi, J. A., and C. E. Faupel (eds.), *History and Crime.* Beverly Hills: Sage Publications.

Zahn, M. A., and M. Bencivengo. 1974. Violent Death: A Comparison between Drug Users and Non-Drug Users, *Addictive Diseases,* 1:283–296.

For Discussion

The psychopharmacological linkage between drug use and violence assumes that some drug users have little control over their actions. Is it fair to punish these offenders in the same manner that we punish those users who engage in systemic violence?

Reprinted from: Paul J. Goldstein, "The Drugs/Violence Nexus: A Tripartite Conceptual Framework." In *Journal of Drug Issues* (Fall 1985), pp. 493–506. Copyright © 1985 by *Journal of Drug Issues.* All rights reserved. Reprinted with permission. ✦

33

Women in the Street-Level Drug Economy

Continuity or Change?*

Lisa Maher
Kathleen Daly

In this article, Lisa Maher and Kathleen Daly use ethnographic research to examine women's roles in the informal drug economy. The authors find that the drug labor market is stratified by gender within which women are more likely than men to occupy lower-level positions. Women are viewed as untrustworthy and unable to engage in and respond appropriately to drug-related violence. Moreover, the authors find that opportunities for sex-for-drug exchanges have declined, and potential earnings from these exchanges are limited.

Images of women in the contemporary drug economy are highly mixed. Most scholars emphasize *change* in women's roles in U.S. drug markets of 1960–1985, organized primarily around heroin, compared to women's roles in more recent drug markets with the advent of crack cocaine (e.g., Baskin et al., 1993; Bourgois, 1989; Dunlap and Johnson, 1992; Inciardi et al., 1993; Mieczkowski, 1994; C. Taylor, 1993). Some emphasize *continuity* from previous decades (Adler, 1985; Koester and Schwartz, 1993; Maher and Curtis, 1992). Others suggest that both change and continuity are evident, with women inhabiting "two social worlds" (Fagan, 1994:212): one of increased participation in, and the other of continued

restriction by, male-dominated street and drug networks.

One should expect, on the one hand, to see variation in women's positions in the drug economy. Research on drug markets in New York City (Bourgois, 1995; Curtis and Sviridoff, 1994; Hamid, 1990, 1992; Johnson et al., 1985, 1992; Williams, 1989), Miami (Inciardi et al., 1993), Washington, D.C. (Reuter et al., 1990), Detroit (Mieczkowski, 1986, 1990; C. Taylor, 1990), Chicago (Padilla, 1992), Milwaukee (Hagedorn, 1994), Los Angeles and the West Coast (Adler, 1985; Morgan and Joe, 1994; Skolnick, 1989; Waldorf et al., 1991) reveals differences in the racial and ethnic composition of participants and who controls markets, the kinds of drugs sold, how markets are organized, and participants' responses to law enforcement. Such differences are likely to affect women's positions and specific roles.

At the same time, the varied characterizations of women's roles reflect differences in the theoretical assumptions and methodological approaches taken by scholars. For example, women's increasing presence in the drug economies of the late 1980s and early 1990s is said to reflect (1) emancipation from their traditional household responsibilities (Bourgois, 1989; Bourgois and Dunlap, 1993), (2) an extension of their traditional household responsibilities (Wilson, 1993), and (3) the existence of "new opportunities" in street-level drug markets (Mieczkowski, 1994), especially with increased rates of incarceration of minority group men (Baskin et al., 1993). These explanations reveal different assumptions about changes (or not) in the gendered structure of drug markets and about the links (or not) between women's participation in crime and their domestic responsibilities.

Data sources and methods also affect the quality and content of the inferences drawn. Some have analyzed Uniform Crime Report (UCR) arrest data (e.g., Wilson, 1993), others have interviewed women arrested on drug charges or through snowball samples (e.g., Baskin et al., 1993; Fagan, 1994; Inciardi et al., 1993; C. Taylor, 1993), and a handful have conducted ethnographies of particular neighborhoods (e.g., Bourgois, 1989; Maher and Curtis, 1992). While interview-based studies may offer an empirical advantage over the inferences that can be drawn from UCR arrest data, the one-time interview may not elicit complete or reliable information about the changing contexts of women's income generation in the informal economy.

This article presents the results of an ethnographic study of women drug users conducted during 1989–1992 in a New York City neighborhood. We assess whether women's involvement in U.S. drug markets of the mid-1980s onward reflects change, continuity, or a combination of change and continuity from patterns in previous decades. We find that contrary to the conclusions of Baskin et al. (1993), Fagan (1994), Inciardi et al. (1993), Mieczkowski (1994), and C. Taylor (1993), crack cocaine markets have not necessarily provided "new opportunities" for women, nor should such markets be viewed as "equal opportunity employers" (Bourgois, 1989; Wilson, 1993). Our study suggests that recent drug markets continue to be monopolized by men and to offer few opportunities for stable income generation for women. While women's *presence* on the street and in low-level auxiliary roles may have increased, we find that their *participation* as substantive labor in the drug-selling marketplace has not.

Women in the Drug Economy

Drug Markets of the 1960s to the Mid-1980s

Prior to the advent of crack cocaine in the mid-1980s, research on women in the drug economy used one or more of four elements to explain women's restricted roles in selling and distributing drugs:[1] intimate relationships with men, the availability of alternative options for income generation, restrictions on discretionary time, and institutionalized sexism in the underworld.

Female heroin users were often characterized as needing a man to support their consumption (e.g., File, 1976; File et al., 1974; Hser et al., 1987; Smithberg and Westermeyer, 1985; Sutter, 1966). They were also described as being "led" into crime by individual men (Covington, 1985; Pettiway, 1987), although this may apply more to white than minority group women (Anglin and Hser, 1987; Pettiway, 1987). The typical pattern was of low-status roles in which participation was short-lived, sporadic, and mediated by intimate relationships with men (Adler, 1985; Rosenbaum, 1981). Alternative sources of income generation, such as prostitution and shoplifting, may have been preferable to female drug users, especially heroin users (File, 1976; Goldstein, 1979; Hunt, 1990; Inciardi and Pottieger, 1986; James, 1976; Rosenbaum, 1981). Some suggest, in addition, that women's household and childcare responsibilities may have limited their full participation in the drug economy (e.g., Rosenbaum, 1981; A. Taylor, 1993; see also Wilson, 1993).

Women's peripheral roles in male-dominated drug selling networks (Auld et al., 1986; Goldstein, 1979; Rosenbaum, 1981) can also be explained by "institutionalized sexism" in the "underworld" (Steffensmeier, 1983; Steffensmeier and Terry, 1986; see also Box, 1983). Steffensmeier (1983:1013–1015) argues that male lawbreakers prefer to "work, associate, and do business with other men" (homosocial reproduction); they view women as lacking the physical and mental attributes considered essential to working in an uncertain and violent context (sex-typing and task environment of crime). In the drug economy, in particular, women are thought to be unsuitable for higher-level distribution roles because of an inability to manage male workers through threatened violence (Waterston, 1993:114).

Crack Cocaine Markets of the Mid-1980s Onward

Women have been depicted as more active participants in selling and distributing drugs in the crack cocaine economy of the late 1980s compared to previous drug eras. While some find that women's roles continue to be mediated by relationships with men (Koester and Schwartz, 1993; Murphy et al., 1991) and that women remain at the bottom of the drug market hierarchy (Maher and Curtis, 1992), others suggest that there has been decisive change. Specifically, it is argued that "drug business" crimes (that is, street-level drug sales) generate a higher share of women's income than in the past, with a concomitant decrease in prostitution-generated income (Inciardi et al., 1993). More generally, it is argued that the crack-propelled expansion of drug markets has provided "new opportunities" for women.

The "new opportunities" argument is made by the majority of those in the field (see, e.g., Baskin et al., 1993; Bourgois, 1989; Bourgois and Dunlap, 1993; Fagan, 1994; Inciardi et al., 1993; Mieczkowski, 1994). It takes two forms: a general claim that women's emancipation in the wider society is evident in "all aspects of inner-city street life" (Bourgois, 1989:643–644) and a more restricted claim that the weakening of male-dominated street networks and market processes has made it possible for women to enter the drug economy. For example, in his study of New York City women, Fagan (1994:210) concludes that

> while women were consigned secondary, gender-specific roles in . . . [drug] businesses in the past, the size and seemingly frantic activity of the current drug markets has made possible for women new ways to participate in street networks. Their involvement in drug selling at high income levels defies the gendered norms and roles of the past, where drug dealing was an incidental income source often mediated by domestic partnerships . . . the expansion of drug markets in the cocaine economy has provided new ways for women to escape their limited roles, statuses and incomes in previous eras.

While two-thirds of the women in Fagan's (1994) sample did not sell drugs and while most who sold drugs acted alone (p. 197), Fagan was struck by "the emergence of women sellers earning high incomes and avoiding prostitution" (p. 211). He concluded that "two social worlds" of continuity and change characterized women's participation in drug markets. One difficulty in assessing this claim is that no estimate is given of the proportion of women who were earning high incomes from drug business,

avoiding prostitution, and "def[ying] the gendered norms and roles of the past."

Fagan's research offers a good comparison to our study. He draws from interviews with 311 women, the majority of whom were drug users or sellers, in two New York City neighborhoods (Washington Heights and Central Harlem in northern Manhattan). The interviews were conducted during the late 1980s; the sample included women with police arrest records, in residential treatment programs, and those who had not been arrested. The women in our sample lived just a few miles away in Bushwick, a Brooklyn neighborhood. Very few of the Bushwick women were active dealers, and virtually all supported themselves by prostitution. Whereas Fagan sees two worlds of continuity and change, we see just one of continuity. Before describing that social world, we sketch the study site and the methods used in gathering the data.

Research Site and Methods

Research Site

Bushwick, the principal study site, has been described as hosting "the most notorious drug bazaar in Brooklyn and one of the toughest in New York City" (*New York Times*, October 1, 1992:A1). Historically home to large numbers of European Jews, by the 1960s Bushwick was dominated by working-class Italians. Since the late 1960s, the area has become the home of low-income Latino populations, predominantly Puerto Ricans, although Dominicans and Colombians have begun to move in. In 1960 the population was 89% white, 6% black, and 5% Hispanic. By 1990 it was 5% white, 25% black, and 65% Hispanic (Bureau of the Census, 1990). In 1990 Bushwick was Brooklyn's poorest neighborhood with a median household income of $16,287; unemployment was twice the citywide rate; and more than half of all families and two-thirds of all children lived under the official poverty line (Bureau of the Census, 1990).

Between 1988 and 1992 drug distribution in Bushwick was intensely competitive; there were constant confrontations over "turf" as organizations strove to establish control over markets. Like many drug markets in New York City (see, e.g., Curtis and Sviridoff, 1994; Waterston, 1993), Bushwick was highly structured and ethnically segmented. The market, largely closed to outsiders, was dominated by Dominicans with networks organized by kin and pseudo-kin relations.[2]

Fieldwork Methods

Preliminary fieldwork began in the fall of 1989, when the senior author established a field presence in several Brooklyn neighborhoods (Williamsburg, East Flatbush, and Bushwick). By fall 1990 observations and interviews were intensified in Bushwick because it hosted the busiest street-level drug market in Brooklyn and had an active prostitution stroll. As fieldwork progressed, it became apparent that the initial plan of conducting interviews with a large number of women crack users was not, by itself, going to yield a complete picture. For example, few women initially admitted that they performed oral sex for less than $20, and none admitted to participating in sex-for-crack trades.

By the end of December 1991, interviews had been conducted with 211 active women crack users in Williamsburg, East Flatbush, and Bushwick. These were tape recorded and ranged from 20 minutes to 3 hours; they took place in a variety of settings, including private or semiprivate locations (e.g., apartments, shooting galleries, abandoned buildings, cars) and public locales (e.g., restaurants, parks, subways, and public toilets).[3] From January to March 1992, a preliminary data sort was made of the interview and observational material. From that process, 45 women were identified for whom there were repeated observations and interview material. Contact with these women was intimate and extensive; the number of tape-recorded interviews for each woman ranged from 3 to 15. Unless otherwise noted, the research findings reported here are based on this smaller group of 45 Bushwick women.

Profile of the Bushwick Women

The Bushwick women consisted of 20 Latinas (18 Puerto Ricans and 2 Dominicans), 16 African-Americans, and 9 European-Americans; their ages ranged from 19 to 41 years, with a mean of 28 years. At the time of the first interview, all the women used smokable cocaine (or crack), although only 31% used it exclusively; most (69%) had used heroin or powder cocaine prior to using crack. The women's average drug use history was 10.5 years (using the mean as the measure); heroin and powder cocaine initiates had a mean of about 12 years and the smokable cocaine initiates, about 6 years.

Most women (84%) were born in the New York City area, and more than half were born in Brooklyn. About one-quarter were raised in households with both parents present, and over one-third (38%) grew up in a household in which they were subjected to physical abuse. Most (84%) had not completed high school, and 55% had no experience of formal-sector work. A high proportion were homeless (91%), alternating between the street and short-term accommodations in shelters, apartments of friends, and homes of elderly men (see also Maher et al., 1996). Most women were mothers (80%); the 36 mothers had given birth to 96 children, whose ages ranged from newborns to 26 years. Few of the mothers (9%) had their children living with them during the study period. Fourteen women (31%) had tested positive for HIV, and an additional five women believed that they were HIV positive; but most women said they did not know their serostatus. By the end of the study period, two women had stopped using illicit drugs, and five had died: two from HIV-related illnesses and three from homicide.

These 45 women represent the range of ages, racial-ethnic backgrounds, life experiences, and histories of crack-using women among the larger group of Brooklyn women interviewed. We are cognizant, however, of the limits of using ethnographic research in one area to generalize to other areas. For example, there is a somewhat higher proportion of Latinas (44%) in our sample than in Fagan's (1994:225) sample in Central Harlem (23%) and Washington Heights (33%). A higher share of the Bushwick women had not completed high school, had no experience in the formal labor force, and were homeless.

Structure of New York City Crack Markets

Street-level crack markets have frequently been characterized as unregulated markets of freelancers engaged in individual entrepreneurial activity (Hunt, 1990; Reuter et al., 1990). Some evidence suggests, however, that once demand has been established, the freelance model may be superseded by a more structured system of distribution. When the crack epidemic was at its peak in New York City during the late 1980s, Bushwick (like other neighborhoods) hosted highly structured street-level drug markets with pooled interdependence, vertical differentiation, and a formal, multitiered system of organization and control with defined employer-employee relationships (Curtis and Maher, in press; Johnson et al., 1990, 1992). This model is similar to the "runner system" used in heroin distribution (see Mieczkowski, 1986).

In selling crack cocaine, drug business "owners" employ several "crew bosses," "lieutenants," or "managers," who work shifts to ensure an efficient organization of street-level distribution. Managers (as they were known in Brooklyn) act as conduits between owners and lower-level employees. They are responsible for organizing and delivering supplies and collecting revenues. Managers exercise considerable autonomy in the hiring, firing, and payment of workers; they are responsible for labor force discipline and the resolution of workplace grievances and disputes. Next down the hierarchy are the street-level sellers, who perform retailing tasks having little discretion. Sellers are located in a fixed space or "spot" and are assisted by those below them in the hierarchy: lower-level operatives acting as "runners," "look-outs," "steerers," "touts," "holders," and "enforcers." Runners "continuously supply the sellers," look-outs "warn of impending dangers," steerers and touts "advertise and solicit customers," holders "handle drugs or money but not both," and

enforcers "maintain order and intervene in case of trouble" (Johnson et al., 1992:61–64).

In New York City in the early 1990s, it was estimated that 150,000 people were involved in selling or helping to sell crack cocaine on any given day (Williams, 1992:10). Crack sales and distribution became a major source of income for the city's drug users (Hamid, 1990, 1991; Johnson et al., 1994). How, then, did the Bushwick women fit into this drug market structure? We examine women's involvement in a range of drug business activities.

Selling and Distributing Drugs

During the entire three years of fieldwork, including the interviews with the larger group of over 200 women, we did not discover any woman who was a business owner, and just one worked as a manager. The highly structured nature of the market in Bushwick, coupled with its kin-based organization, militated against personal or intimate sexual relationships between female drug users and higher-level male operatives. To the limited extent that they participated in drug selling, women were overwhelmingly concentrated at the lowest levels. They were almost always used as temporary workers when men were arrested or refused to work, or when it was "hot" because of police presence. Table 33.1 shows how the 45 women were involved in Bushwick's drug economy.

Of the 19 women (42%) who had some involvement, the most common role was that of informal steerer or tout. This meant that they recommended a particular brand of heroin to newcomers to the neighborhood in return for "change," usually a dollar or so. These newcomers were usually white men, who may have felt more comfortable approaching women with requests for such information. In turn, the women's perceptions of "white boyz" enabled them to use the situation to their advantage. Although they used only crack, Yolanda, a 38-year-old Latina, and Boy, a 26-year-old African-American woman, engaged in this practice of "tipping" heroin consumers.

Table 33.1

Bushwick Women's Roles in the Drug Economy, 1989–92

	N	%
No Role	26	58
Had Some Role	19	42
	45	100

Of the 19 women with roles in the drug economy during the three-year study period, the following shows what they did. Because most women (N = 13) had more than one role, the total sums to greater than 19.

Selling and Distributing Roles	
Owner	0
Manager	0
Regular Seller	0
Irregular Seller	7
Runner	0
Look-out	0
Steerer or Tout	9
Holder	0
Enforcer	0
Selling/Renting Paraphernalia	
Works Sellers	4
Stem Renters	6
Running a Gallery	3
Copping Drugs for Others	14
Other Drug Business Hustles	
Street Doc	1

NOTE: While we have tried to be precise, we should note that it can be difficult to characterize women's roles—not only because drug markets are fluid and shifting but also because some women had varied mixes of roles over time.

They come up to me. Before they come and buy dope and anything, they ask me what dope is good. I ain't done no dope, but I'm a professional player. . . . They would come to me, they would pay me, they would come "What's good out here?" I would tell them, "Where's a dollar," and that's how I use to make my money. Everyday somebody would come, "Here's a dollar, here's two dollars." (Yolanda) [What other kinds of things?] Bumming up change. [There ain't many people down here with change.] Just the white guys. They give you more faster than your own kind. [You go cop for them?] No, just for change. You tell them what's good on [the] dope side. Tell them anything, I

don't do dope, but I'll tell them anything. Yeah, it's kicking live man. They buy it. Boom! I got my dollar, bye. (Boy)

Within the local drug economy, the availability of labor strongly determines women's participation in street-level distribution roles. Labor supply fluctuates with extra-market forces, such as product availability and police intervention. One consequence of police activity in Bushwick during the study period was a recurring, if temporary, shortage of male workers. Such labor market gaps promoted instability: The replacement of "trusted" sellers (i.e., Latinos) with "untrustworthy" drug users (i.e., women and non-Latinos) eroded the social and kinship ties that had previously served to reduce violence in drug-related disputes (see also Curtis and Sviridoff, 1994).

Early in the fieldwork period (during 1989 and early 1990), both men and women perceived that more women were being offered opportunities to work as street-level sellers than in the past. Such opportunities, it turned out, were often part of a calculated risk-minimization strategy on the part of owners and managers. As Princess, a 32-year-old African-American woman observed, some owners thought that women were less likely to be noticed, searched, or arrested by police:

> Nine times out of ten when the po-leece roll up it's gonna [be] men. And they're not allowed to search a woman, but they have some that will. But if they don' do it, they'll call for a female officer. By the time she gets there, (laughs) if you know how to move around, you better get it off you, unless you jus' want to go to jail. [So you think it works out better for the owners to have women working for them?] Yeah, to use women all the time.

As the fieldwork progressed and the neighborhood became more intensively policed, this view became less tenable. Latisha, a 32-year-old African-American woman, reported that the police became more aggressive in searching women:

> [You see some women dealing a little bit you know.] Yeah, but they starting to go. Now these cop around here starting to

unzip girls' pants and go in their panties. It was, it's not like it was before. You could stick the drugs in your panties 'cause you're a female. Now that's garbage.

Thus, when initially faced with a shortage of regular male labor and large numbers of women seeking low-level selling positions, some managers appear to have adopted the opportunistic use of women to avoid detection and disruption of their businesses. How frequent this practice was is uncertain; we do know that it was short-lived (see also Curtis and Sviridoff, 1994:164).

In previous years (the late 1970s and early 1980s), several Bushwick women had sold drugs in their roles as wives or girlfriends of distributors, but this was no longer the case. During the three-year study period only 12 women (27%) were involved in selling and distributing roles. Of this group of 12, only 7 were able to secure low-level selling positions on an irregular basis. Connie, a 25-year-old Latina, was typical of this small group, and in the following quotation she describes her unstable position within the organization she worked for:

I'm currently working for White Top [crack]. They have a five bundle limit. It might take me an hour or two to sell that, or sometimes as quick as half an hour. I got to ask if I can work. They say yes or no.

Typically the managers said no to women's requests to work. Unlike many male street-level sellers who worked on a regular basis for this organization and were given "shifts" (generally lasting eight hours), Connie had to work off-hours (during daylight hours), which were often riskier and less financially rewarding. Temporary workers were usually given a "bundle limit" (one bundle contains 24 vials), which ensured that they could work only for short periods of time. As Cherrie, a 22-year-old Latina, said,

The last time I sold it was Blue Tops [crack]. That was a week ago. [What, they asked you or you asked them to work?] Oh, they ask me, I say I want to work. [How come they asked you?] I don't

know. They didn't have nobody to work because it was too hot out there. They was too full of cops.

Similarly, although Princess was well-known to the owners and managers of White Top crack, had worked for them many times in the past year, and had "proved" herself by having never once "stepped off" with either drugs or money, she was only given sporadic employment. She reported,

Sometime you can't [sell]. Sometime you can. That's why it's good to save money also. So when you don't get work. [How come they wouldn't give you work on some days?] Because of some favor that someone might've done or y'know, jus'. . . [It's not like they're trying to punish you?] No, but they will do that y'know. Somebody go and tell them something, "Oh, this one's doin' this to the bags or this one's doin' this to the bottles." OK, well they check the bags and they don' see nothin' wrong, but they came to look at it so they're pissed off so they'll take it away from you, y'know.

Violence and Relationships

In addition to being vulnerable to arrest and street robbery, street-level sellers who use drugs constantly grapple with the urge to consume the product and to abscond with the drugs and/or the money. Retaliation by employers toward users who "mess up the money" (Johnson et al., 1985:174) was widely perceived to be swift and certain. Rachel, a 35-year-old European-American woman, said,

Those Dominicans, if you step off with one piece of it, you're gonna get hurt. They don't play. They are sick people.

The prospect of violent retaliation may deter women from selling drugs. Boy, a 26-year-old African-American woman, put it this way:

I don' like their [the managers'] attitude, like if you come up short, dey take it out on you . . . I don' sell no crack or dope for dese niggers. Because dey is crazy. Say for instance you short ten dollars, niggers come across you wit bats and shit. It's not worth it, you could lose your life. If dey say you are short, you could lose you life.

> Even if you were not short and dey say you is short, whatever dey say is gonna go, so you are flicked all the way around.

However, considerable uncertainty surrounds the likelihood that physical punishment will be meted out. This uncertainty can be seen in the comments by Princess, who had a long but sporadic history of street-level sales before and after the advent of crack:

> It's not worth it. Number one, it's not enough. Come on, run away, and then *maybe* then these people want to heavily beat the shit out of you. And then they *may* hit you in the wrong place with the bat and *maybe* kill you (emphasis added).

Such disciplinary practices resemble a complex interplay between "patronage" and "mercy," which features in relations of dependence (Hay, 1975). The unpredictability of punishment may work as a more effective form of control than actual punishment itself. In Bushwick, the actuality of violent retaliation for sellers who "messed up" was further mediated by gender and ethnicity. In this Latino- (mainly Dominican) controlled market, the common perception was that men, and black men especially, were more likely than Latinas to be punished for "stepping off." Rachel described what happened after an African-American man had been badly beaten:

> [What happened to him. I mean he stepped off with a package, right?] Yeah, but everybody has at one time or another. But it's also because he's a black and not a Puerto Rican, and he can't, you know, smooze his way back in like, you know, Mildred steps off with every other package, and so does, you know, Yolanda, they all do. But they're Spanish. And they're girls. So, you know, they can smooze their way back in. You know, a guy who's black and ugly, you know, so they don't want to hear about it.

Relationships in the drug economy are fueled by contradictory expectations. On the one hand, attributes such as trust and reliability are frequently espoused as important to drug-selling organizations. On the other hand, ethnographic informants often refer to the lack of trust and solidarity among organization members. This lack of trust is evident in the constant "scams" sellers and managers pull on each other and the ever-present threat of violence in owner-manager-seller relations.

Strategies of Protection and 'Being Bad'

Women who work the streets to sell or buy drugs are subject to constant harassment and are regularly victimized. The Bushwick women employed several strategies to protect themselves. One of the most important was the adoption of a "badass" (Katz, 1988), "crazy," or "gangsta bitch" stance or attitude, of which having a "bad mouth" was an integral part. As Latisha was fond of saying, "My heart pumps no Kool Aid. I don't even drink the shit." Or as Boy put it,

> Ac' petite, dey treat you petite. I mean you ac' soft, like when you dress dainty and shit ta come over here an' sit onna fuckin' corner. Onna corner an' smoke an you dressed to da teeth, you know, you soft. Right then and there you the center of the crowd, y'know what I'm sayin'? Now put a dainty one and put me, she looks soft. Dey look at me like "don't fuck wid dat bitch, she looks hard." Don' mess wit me caus I look hard y'know . . . Dey don't fuck wit me out here. Dey think I'm crazy.

Acting bad and "being bad" are not the same. Although many Bushwick women presented themselves as "bad" or "crazy," this projection was a street persona and a necessary survival strategy (see also Spalter-Roth, 1988). Despite the external manifestation of aggression, a posture and rhetoric of toughness, and the preemptive use of aggression (Campbell, 1993), women were widely perceived (by men and women alike) as less likely to have the attributes associated with successful managers and street-level sellers. These included the requisite "street cred" and a "rep" for having "heart" or "juice"—masculine qualities associated with toughness and the capacity for violence (Bourgois, 1989; Steffensmeier, 1983; Waterston, 1993). Women's abilities to "talk tough" or "act bad" were apparently not enough to inspire employer confidence. Prospective drug business employers wanted those capable of actually "being bad" (Bourgois, 1989:632). Because female drug users were perceived as unreliable, untrustworthy, and unable to deploy violence and terror effectively, would-be female sellers were at a disadvantage.

Selling Drug Paraphernalia

In Bushwick the sale of drug paraphernalia such as crack stems and pipes was controlled by the bodegas, or corner stores, whereas syringes or "works" were the province of the street. Men dominated both markets, although women were sometimes employed as part-time "works" sellers. Men who regularly sold "sealed" (i.e., new) works had suppliers (typically men who worked in local hospitals) from whom they purchased units called "ten packs" (10 syringes). The benefits of selling syringes were twofold: The penalties were less severe than those for selling drugs, and the rate of return was higher compared to the street-level sale of heroin or crack.[4]

The women who sold works were less likely than their male counterparts to have procured them "commercially." More often they "happened across" a supply of works through a family member or social contact who was a diabetic. Women were also more likely to sell works for others or to sell "used works." Rosa, a 31-year-old Latina, described in detail the dangerous practice of collecting used works strewn around the neighborhood. While she often stored them and later exchanged them for new works from the volunteer needle exchange (which was illegal at the time), Rosa would sometimes select the works she deemed in good condition, "clean" them with bleach and water, and resell them.

Although crack stems and pipes were available from neighborhood bodegas at minimal cost, some smokers chose not to carry stems. These users, almost exclusively men, were from outside the neighborhood. Their reluctance to carry drug paraphernalia provided the women with an additional source of income, usually in the form of a "hit," in exchange for the use of their stem. Sometimes these men were "dates," but more often they were "men on a mission" in the neighborhood or the "working men" who came to the area on Friday and Saturday nights to get high. As Boy put it,

> I be there on the block an' I got my stem and my lighter. I see them cop and I be askin' "yo, you need a stem, you need a light?" People say "yeah man," so they give me a piece.

An additional benefit for those women who rented their stems was the buildup of crack residues in the stems. Many users savored this resin, which they allowed to accumulate before periodically digging it out with "scrapers" fashioned from the metal ribs of discarded umbrellas.

Some women also sold condoms, another form of drug-related paraphernalia in Bushwick. Although condoms were sold at bodegas, usually for $1 each, many of the women obtained free condoms from outreach health workers. Sometimes they sold them at a reduced price (usually 25 cents) to other sex workers, "white boyz," and young men from the neighborhood. Ironically, these same women would then have to purchase condoms at the bodegas when they had "smoked up" all their condoms.

Running Shooting Galleries

A wide range of physical locations were used for drug consumption in Bushwick. Although these sites were referred to generically as "galleries" by drug users and others in the neighborhood, they differed from the traditional heroin shooting gallery in several respects.[5] Bushwick's "galleries" were dominated by men because they had the economic resources or physical prowess to maintain control. Control was also achieved by exploiting women drug users with housing leases. Such women were particularly vulnerable, as the following quotation from Carol, a 40-year-old African-American woman, shows:

> I had my own apartment, myself and my daughter. I started selling crack. From my house. [For who?] Some Jamaican. [How did you get hooked up with that?] Through my boyfriend. They wanted to sell from my apartment. They were supposed to pay me something like $150 a week rent, and then something off the

profits. They used to, you know, flick up the money, like not give me the money. Eventually I went through a whole lot of different dealers. Eventually I stopped payin' my rent because I wanted to get a transfer out of there to get away from everything 'cause soon as one group of crack dealers would get out, another group would come along. [So how long did that go on for?] About four years. Then I lost my apartment, and I sat out in the street.

The few women who were able to maintain successful galleries operated with or under the control of a man or group of men. Cherrie's short-lived effort to set up a gallery in an abandoned burned-out building on "Crack Row" is illustrative. Within two weeks of establishing the gallery (the principal patrons of which were women), Cherrie was forced out of business by the police. The two weeks were marked by constant harassment, confiscation of drugs and property, damage to an already fragile physical plant, physical assaults, and the repeated forced dispersal of gallery occupants. Within a month, two men had established a new gallery on the same site, which, more than a year later, was thriving.

Such differential policing toward male- and female-operated galleries is explicable in light of the larger picture of law enforcement in low-income urban communities, where the primary function is not so much to enforce the law but rather to regulate illegal activities (Whyte, 1943:138). Field observations suggest that the reason the police did not interfere as much with activities in the men's gallery was that they assumed that men were better able than women to control the gallery and to minimize problems of violence and disorder.

Other factors contributed to women's disadvantage in operating galleries, crack houses, and other consumption sites. Male drug users were better placed economically than the women in the sample, most of whom were homeless and without a means of legitimate economic support. When women did have an apartment or physical site, this made them a vulnerable target either for exploitation by male users or dealers (as in

Carol's case) or for harassment by the police (as in Cherrie's). Even when a woman claimed to be in control of a physical location, field observations confirmed that she was not. Thus, in Bushwick, the presence of a man was a prerequisite to the successful operation of drug-consumption sites. The only choice for those women in a position to operate galleries or crack houses was between the "devils they knew" and those they did not.

Copping Drugs

Many Bushwick women supplemented their income by "copping" drugs for others. They almost always copped for men, typically white men. At times these men were dates, but often they were users who feared being caught and wanted someone else to take that risk. As Rachel explained,

> I charge them, just what they want to buy they have to pay me. If they want twenty dollars they have to give me twenty dollars worth on the top because I'm risking my free time. I could get busted copping. They have to pay me the same way, if not, they can go cop. Most of them can't because they don't know the people.

Those who cop drugs for others perform an important service for the drug market because as Biernacki (1979:539) suggests in connection with heroin, "they help to minimize the possibility of infiltration by undercover agents and decrease the chance of a dealer's arrest." In Bushwick the copping role attracted few men; it was regarded by both men and women as a low-status peripheral hustle. Most women saw the female-dominated nature of the job to be part of the parallel sex market in the neighborhood. Outsiders could readily approach women to buy drugs under the guise of buying sex. As Rosa recounted,

> You would [be] surprise. They'd be ahm, be people very important, white people like lawyer, doctors that comes and get off, you'd be surprised. Iss like I got two lawyer, they give me money to go, to go and cop. And they stay down over there parking. . . . [How do you meet them?] Well down the stroll one time they stop

and say you know, "You look like a nice girl though, you know, you wanna make some money fast?" I say, how? So they say you know, "Look out for me." First time they give me like you know, twenty dollars, you know. They see I came back, next time they give me thirty. Like that you know. I have been copping for them like over six months already.

Sometimes this function was performed in conjunction with sex work, as Latisha's comment illustrates:

> He's a cop. He's takin' a chance. He is petrified. Will not get out his car . . . But he never gets less than nine bags [of powder cocaine]. [And he sends you to get it?] And he wants a blow job, right, okay. You know what he's givin' you, a half a bag of blue (blue bag cocaine). That's for you goin' to cop, and for the blow job. That's [worth] two dollars and fifty . . . I can go to jail [for him]. I'm a piece of shit.

Women also felt that, given the reputation of the neighborhood as very "thirsty" (that is, as having a "thirst" or craving for crack), male outsiders were more likely to trust women, especially white women, to purchase drugs on their behalf. Often this trust was misplaced. The combination of naive, inexperienced "white boyz" and experienced "street smart" women produced opportunities for additional income by, for example, simply taking the "cop" money. This was a calculated risk and sometimes things went wrong. A safer practice was to inflate the purchase price of the drugs and to pocket the difference. Rosa explained this particular scam,

> He think it a ten dollar bag, but issa five dollar. But at least I don't be rippin' him off there completely. [But you're taking the risk for him.] Exactly. Sometime he give me a hunert dollars, so I making fifty, right? But sometime he don't get paid, he got no second money, eh. I cop then when I come back the car, he say, "Dear I cannot give you nothin' today," you know. But I still like I say, I gettin' something from him because he think it a ten dollar bag.

Similar scams involved the woman's returning to the client with neither drugs nor money, claiming that she had been ripped off or, less often, shortchanging the client by tapping the vials (removing some crack) or adulterating the drugs (cutting powder cocaine or heroin with other substances). These scams reveal the diversity of women's roles as copping agents and their ingenuity in making the most of limited opportunities.[6]

Other Drug Business Hustles

The practice of injecting intravenous drug users (IDUs) who are unable to inject themselves, because they are inexperienced or have deep or collapsed veins, has been documented by others (e.g., Johnson et al., 1985; Murphy and Waldorf, 1991). Those performing this role are sometimes referred to as "street docs" (Murphy and Waldorf, 1991:16–17). In Bushwick, men typically specialized in this practice. For example, Sam, a Latino injector in his late thirties, lived in one of the makeshift huts or "condos" on a busy street near the main heroin copping area. Those who were in a hurry to consume or who had nowhere else to go would use Sam's place to "get off." Sam had a reputation as a good "hitter" and injected several women in the sample on a regular basis. He provided this service for a few dollars or, more often, a "taste" of whatever substance was being injected.

Only one woman in the sample, Latisha, capitalized on her reputation as a good "hitter" by playing the street doc role. Latisha had a regular arrangement with a young street thug named Crime, notorious for victimizing the women, who had only recently commenced intravenous heroin use and was unable to "hit" himself. While women IDUs were likely to have the requisite level of skill, they were less likely than men to be able to capitalize on it because they did not control an established consumption setting.

Discussion

A major dimension of drug economies, both past and present, is the "human qualities" believed necessary for the performance of various roles. Opportunities for income generation are defined, in part, by who has the necessary qualities or traits and who does not. These traits, whether grounded in cultural perceptions of biology and physiology (e.g., strength and capacity for violence), mental states (e.g., courage and aggressiveness), or kinship (e.g., loyalty and trustworthiness), are primarily differentiated along the lines of gender and race-ethnicity. In this study, we found that women were thought to be not as "strong" as men and that men, particularly black men and Latinos, were thought to be more "bad" and capable of "being bad." The gendered displays of violence that men incorporate into their work routines not only cement their solidarity as men, but also reinscribe these traits as masculine (Messerschmidt, 1993). As a consequence, men are able to justify the exclusion of women from more lucrative "men's work" in the informal economy. All the elements of underworld sexism identified by Steffensmeier (1983)—homosocial reproduction, sex-typing, and the qualities required in a violent task environment—featured prominently in Bushwick's street-level drug economy.

The significance of gender-based capacities and the symbolism used to convey them was evident in the women's use of instrumental aggression. Boy's discussion of how to "dress for success" on the streets reveals that power dressing is "dressing like a man" or "dressing down." It is anything but "dressing dainty." Both on the street and in the boardroom, it appears that a combination of clothing and attitude makes the woman (Kanter, 1981, citing Hennig, 1970). In the drug business, conveying the message "don't mess with me" is integral to maintaining a reputation for "craziness," which the women perceived as affording them some measure of protection.

The Bushwick women's experiences within a highly gender-stratified labor market provide a counter to the romantic notion of the informal drug economy as an "equal opportunity employer" (Bourgois, 1989:630). Their experiences contradict the conventional wisdom, shaped by studies of the labor market experiences of minority group men (e.g., Anderson, 1990; Bourgois, 1989, 1995; Hagedorn, 1994; Padilla, 1992; C. Taylor, 1990; Williams, 1989), that the drug economy acts as a compensatory mechanism, offering paid employment that is not available in the formal labor force. While in theory the built-in supervision and task differentiation of the business model, which characterized drug distribution in Bushwick, should have provided opportunities to both men and women (Johnson et al., 1992), our findings suggest that sellers were overwhelmingly men. Thus, the "new opportunities" said to have emerged with the crack-propelled expansion of drug markets from the mid-1980s onward were not "empty slots" waiting to be filled by those with the requisite skill. Rather, they were slots requiring certain masculine qualities and capacities.

Continuity or Change?

Those scholars who emphasize change in women's roles in the drug economy with the advent of crack cocaine are correct to point out the *possibilities* that an expanded drug economy might have offered women. Where they err, we think, is in claiming that such "new opportunities" were in fact made available to a significant proportion of women. Granted, there were temporary opportunities for women to participate in street-level drug distribution, but they were irregular and short-lived and did not alter male employers' perceptions of women as unreliable, untrustworthy, and incapable of demonstrating an effective capacity for violence.

The only consistently available option for women's income generation was sex work. However, the conditions of street-level sex work have been adversely affected by shifts in social and economic relations produced by widespread crack consumption in low-income neighborhoods like Bushwick. The market became flooded with novice sex workers, the going rates for sexual transactions decreased, and "deviant" sexual expectations by dates increased, as did the levels of violence and victimization (Maher and Curtis, 1992). Ironically, the sting in the tail of the recent crack-fueled expansion of street-level drug markets has been a substantial reduction in the earning capacities of street-level sex workers.

Of the four elements that have been used to explain women's restricted involvement in drug economies of the past, we see evidence of change in two: a diminishing of women's access to drug-selling roles through boyfriends or husbands, especially when drug markets are highly structured and kin based, and decreased economic returns for street-level sex work. Because few Bushwick women had stable households or cared for children, we cannot comment on changes (if any) in discretionary time. Underworld institutionalized sexism was the most powerful element shaping the Bushwick women's experiences in the drug economy; it inhibited their access to drug business work roles and effectively foreclosed their ability to participate as higher-level distributors. For that most crucial element, we find no change from previous decades.

How can we reconcile our findings with those of researchers who say that the crack cocaine economy has facilitated "new opportunities" for women or "new ways for women to escape their limited roles, statuses, and incomes [compared to] previous eras" (Fagan, 1994:210)? One answer is that study samples differ: Compared to Fagan's sample, for example, our sample of Bushwick women contained a somewhat higher share of Latinas, whose economic circumstances were more marginal than those of the women in Central Harlem and Washington Heights. It is also possible that Latino-controlled drug markets are more restrictive of women's participation than, say, those controlled by African-Americans. Those who have studied drug use and dealing in Puerto Rican (Glick, 1990) and Chicano (Moore, 1990) communities suggest that "deviant women" may be less tolerated and more ostracized than their male counterparts. For Bushwick, it would be difficult to disentangle the joint influences of a male-dominated and Dominican-controlled drug market on women's participation. While seven women (16%) engaged in street-level sales during the study period, all women—whether Latina, African-American, or European-American—were denied access to higher levels of the drug business.

We lack research on how racial-ethnic relations structure women's participation in drug markets. Fagan's (1994:200–202) comparison of Central Harlem and Washington Heights indicates that a lower proportion of women in Central Harlem (28%) than in Washington Heights (44%) reported being involved in drug selling; similar proportions (about 16%) were involved in group selling, however. While Fagan noted that drug markets in Washington Heights were Latino-controlled, he did not discuss the organization or ethnic composition of drug markets in Central Harlem. His study would appear to challenge any clear links between "Latino culture"—or the Latina share of women studied—and greater restrictions on women's roles compared to other racial-ethnic groups.

While disparate images of women in the drug economy may result from differences in study samples (including racial-ethnic variation in drug market organization, neighborhood-level variation, and when the study was conducted), a researcher's methods and theories are also crucial. For methods, virtually all U.S. studies of women drug users have employed one-time interviews. The ethnographic approach used in this study reveals that in the absence of a temporal frame and observational data, interviews may provide an incomplete and inaccurate picture. For example, in initial interviews with the larger group of Brooklyn women, we found that when women were asked about sources of income, it was more socially desirable for them to say that it came from drug selling or other kinds of crime than from crack-related prostitution (Maher, in press). The one-time interview also misses the changing and fluid nature of relations in the informal economy. For example, for a short period there was a perception in Bushwick that "new opportunities" existed for women to sell crack. That perception faded as it became clear that managers and owners were "using" women to evade the constraints imposed on them by law enforcement and police search practices. Ethnographic approaches can offer a more dynamic contexualized picture of women's lawbreaking. While such approaches are relatively numerous in the study of adolescent and adult men in the United States (e.g., Anderson, 1990; Bourgois, 1989; Sullivan, 1989), they are rarely utilized in the study of women and girls.

For theory, women lawbreakers are rarely studied as members of social networks or as participants in collective or group-based activity (see also Steffensmeier and Terry, 1986). Nor have women been viewed as economic actors in illegal markets governed by occupational norms and workplace cultures (Maher, 1996). Those making a general claim about "women's emancipation" in the current drug economy ignore the obdurateness of a gender-stratified labor market and associated beliefs and practices that maintain it. Those making the more restricted claim that male-dominated street networks and market processes have weakened, thus allowing entry points for women, need to offer proof for that claim. We would expect to see variation in women's roles, and we would not say that Bushwick represents the general case. However, assertions of women's changing and improved position in the drug economy have not been well proved. Nor are they grounded in theories of how work, including illegal work, is conditioned by relations of gender, race-ethnicity, and sexuality (see, e.g., Daly, 1993; Game and Pringle, 1983; Kanter, 1977; Messerschmidt, 1993; Simpson and Elis, 1995).

Our findings suggest that the advent of crack cocaine and the concomitant expansion of the drug economy cannot be viewed as emancipatory for women drug users. To the extent that "new opportunities" in drug distribution and sales were realized in Bushwick and the wider Brooklyn sample, they were realized by men. Women were confined to an increasingly harsh economic periphery. Not only did the promised opportunities fail to materialize, but the expanding crack market served to deteriorate the conditions of street-level sex work, a labor market that has historically provided a relatively stable source of income for women drug users.

*The research on which this article is based was supported by the award of a Dissertation Fellowship from the Harry Frank Guggen-heim Foundation. We are indebted to the women who participated in the study, to Richard Curtis and Ansley Hamid for their many contributions to the research, and to the reviewers for helpful comments on earlier drafts of this manuscript.

Notes

1. *Selling* refers to the direct exchange of drugs for cash; *distributing* refers to low-level distribution roles that do not involve direct sales but provide assistance to sellers.

2. At one level, language served as a marker of identity; "outsiders" were those who were not "Spanish," with country of origin often less salient than an ability to speak Spanish or "Spanglish." However, the distribution of opportunities for income generation also involved finely calibrated notions of ethnicity.

3. Each woman was given $10 or the equivalent (e.g., cash, food, clothing, cigarettes, makeup, subway tokens, or a combination) for the initial tape-recorded interview. However, field observations and many of the repeat interviews were conducted on the basis of relations of reciprocity that did not involve direct or immediate benefit to those interviewed. While this research focused on women's lives, interviews and observations were also undertaken with the women's female kin, male partners, and children.

4. Street-level drug sellers typically made $1 on a $10 bag of heroin and 50 cents on a $5 vial of crack. Syringe sellers made at least $1.50 per unit, depending on the purchase price and the sale price.

5. While consumption settings in Bushwick more closely resembled heroin shooting galleries (see, e.g., Des Jarlais et al., 1986; Murphy and Waldorf, 1991) than crack houses (see, e.g., Inciardi et al., 1993; Williams, 1992), many sites combined elements of both and most provided for polydrug (heroin and crack) consumption (for further details see Maher, in press).

6. By their own accounts, women took greater risks in order to generate income than they had in the past. More generally, the incidence of risky behavior increased as conditions in the neighborhood and the adjacent street-level sex market deteriorated (Maher and Curtis, 1992; see also Curtis et al., 1995).

References

Adler, Patricia A., 1985. *Wheeling and Dealing: An Ethnography of an Upper-Level Drug Dealing and Smuggling Community*. New York: Columbia University Press.

Anderson, Elijah, 1990. *Streetwise: Race, Class and Change in an Urban Community*. Chicago: University of Chicago Press.

Anglin, M. Douglas and Yih-Ing Hser, 1987. Addicted women and crime. *Criminology* 25:359–397.

Auld, John, Nicholas Dorn, and Nigel South, 1986. Irregular work, irregular pleasures: Heroin in the 1980s. In Roger Matthews and Jock Young (eds.), *Confronting Crime*. London: Sage.

Baskin, Deborah, Ira Sommers, and Jeffrey Pagan, 1993. The political economy of violent female street crime. *Fordham Urban Law Journal* 20:401–407.

Biernacki, Patrick, 1979. Junkie work, hustles, and social status among heroin addicts. *Journal of Drug Issues* 9:535–549.

Bourgois, Philippe, 1989. In search of Horatio Alger: Culture and ideology in the crack economy. *Contemporary Drug Problems* 16:619–649.

——, 1995. *In Search of Respect: Selling Crack in El Barrio*. New York: Cambridge University Press.

Bourgois, Philippe and Eloise Dunlap, 1993. Exorcising sex-for-crack: An ethnographic perspective from Harlem. In Mitchell S. Rawer (ed.), *Crack Pipe as Pimp: An Ethnographic Investigation of Sex-for-Crack Exchanges*. New York: Lexington Books.

Box, Steven, 1983. *Power, Crime and Mystification*. London: Tavistock.

Bureau of the Census, 1990. *Brooklyn in Touch*. Washington, D.C.: U.S. Government Printing Office.

Campbell, Anne, 1993. *Out of Control: Men, Women, and Aggression*. London: Pandora.

Covington, Jeanette, 1985. Gender differences in criminality among heroin users. *Journal of Research in Crime and Delinquency* 22:329–354.

Curtis, Richard and Lisa Maher, (N.D.) Highly structured crack markets in the southside of Williamsburg, Brooklyn. In Jeffrey Fagan (ed.), *The Ecology of Crime and Drug Use in Inner Cities*. New York: Social Science Research Council.

Curtis, Richard and Michelle Sviridoff, 1994. The social organization of street-level drug markets and its impact on the displacement effect. In Robert P. McNamara (ed.), *Crime Displacement: The Other Side of Prevention*. East Rockaway, N.Y.: Cummings and Hathaway.

Curtis, Richard, Samuel R. Friedman, Alan Neaigus, Benny Jose, Marjorie Goldstein, and Gilbert Ildefonso, 1995. Street-level drug markets: Network structure and HIV risk. *Social Networks* 17:229–249.

Daly, Kathleen, 1993. Class-race-gender: Sloganeering in search of meaning. *Social Justice* 20:56–71.

Des Jarlais, Don C., Samuel R. Friedman, and David Strug, 1986. AIDS and needle sharing within the IV drug use subculture. In Douglas A. Feldman and Thomas M. Johnson (eds.), *The Social Dimensions of AIDS: Methods and Theory*. New York: Praeger.

Dunlap, Eloise and Bruce D. Johnson, 1992. Who they are and what they do: Female crack dealers in New York City. Paper presented at the Annual Meeting of the American Society of Criminology, New Orleans, November.

Fagan, Jeffrey, 1994. Women and drugs revisited: Female participation in the cocaine economy. *Journal of Drug Issues* 24:179–225.

File, Karen N., 1976. Sex roles and street roles. *International Journal of the Addictions* 11:263–268.

File, Karen N., Thomas W. McCahill, and Leonard D. Savitz, 1974. Narcotics involvement and female criminality. *Addictive Diseases: An International Journal* 1:177–188.

Game, Ann and Rosemary Pringle, 1983. *Gender at Work*. Sydney: George Allen and Unwin.

Goldstein, Paul J, 1979. *Prostitution and Drugs*. Lexington, Mass.: Lexington Books.

Glick, Ronald, 1990. Survival, income, and status: Drug dealing in the Chicago Puerto Rican community. In Ronald Glick and Joan Moore (eds.), *Drugs in Hispanic Communities*. New Brunswick, N.J.: Rutgers University Press.

Hagedorn, John M., 1994. Homeboys, dope fiends, legits, and new jacks. *Criminology* 32:197–219.

Hamid, Ansley, 1990. The political economy of crack-related violence. *Contemporary Drug Problems* 17:31–78.

——, 1991. From ganja to crack: Caribbean participation in the underground economy in Brooklyn, 1976–1986. Part 2, Establishment of the cocaine (and crack) economy. *International Journal of the Addictions* 26:729–738.

——, 1992. The developmental cycle of a drug epidemic: The cocaine smoking epidemic of 1981–1991. *Journal of Psychoactive Drugs* 24:337–348.

Hay, Douglas, 1975. Property, authority, and the criminal law. In Douglas Hay, Peter Linebaugh, John G. Rule, Edward Palmer Thompson, and Cal Winslow (eds.), *Albion's Fatal Flee.* London: Allen Lane.

Hennig, Margaret, 1970. Career Development for Women Executives. Ph.D. dissertation, Harvard University, Cambridge, Mass.

Hser, Yih-Ing, M. Douglas Anglin, and Mary W. Booth, 1987. Sex differences in addict careers, Part 3, Addiction. *American Journal of Drug and Alcohol Abuse* 13:231–251.

Hunt, Dana, 1990. Drugs and consensual crimes: Drug dealing and prostitution. In Michael Tonry and James Q. Wilson (eds.), *Drugs and Crime. Crime and Justice*, Vol. 13. Chicago: University of Chicago Press.

Inciardi, James A. and Anne E. Pottieger, 1986. Drug use and crime among two cohorts of women narcotics users: An empirical assessment. *Journal of Drug Issues* 16:91–106.

Inciardi, James A., Dorothy Lockwood, and Anne E. Pottieger, 1993. *Women and Crack Cocaine.* New York: Macmillan.

James, Jennifer, 1976. Prostitution and addiction: An interdisciplinary approach. *Addictive Diseases: An International Journal* 2:601–618.

Johnson, Bruce D., Paul J. Goldstein, Edward Preble, James Schmeidler, Douglas S. Lipton, Barry Spunt, and Thomas Miller, 1985. *Taking Care of Business: The Economics of Crime by Heroin Abusers.* Lexington, Mass.: Lexington Books.

Johnson, Bruce D., Terry Williams, Kojo Dei, and Harry Sanabria, 1990. Drug abuse and the inner city: Impact on hard drug users and the community. In Michael Tonry and James Q. Wilson (eds.), *Drugs and Crime. Crime and Justice*, Vol. 13. Chicago: University of Chicago Press.

Johnson, Bruce D., Ansley Hamid, and Harry Sanabria, 1992. Emerging models of crack distribution. In Thomas M. Mieczkowski (ed.), *Drugs and Crime: A Reader.* Boston: Allyn & Bacon.

Johnson, Bruce D., Mangai Natarajan, Eloise Dunlap, and Elsayed Elmoghazy, 1994. Crack abusers and noncrack abusers: Profiles of drug use, drug sales, and nondrug criminality. *Journal of Drug Issues* 24:117–141.

Kanter, Rosabeth Moss, 1977. *Men and Women of the Corporation.* New York: Basic Books.

——, 1981. Women and the structure of organizations: Explorations in theory and behavior. In Oscar Grusky and George A. Miller (eds.), *The Sociology of Organizations: Basic Studies.* 2d ed. New York: The Free Press.

Katz, Jack, 1988. *Seductions of Crime: Moral and Sensual Attractions of Doing Evil.* New York: Basic Books.

Koester, Stephen and Judith Schwartz, 1993. Crack, gangs, sex, and powerlessness: A view from Denver. In Mitchell S. Ratner (ed.), *Crack Pipe as Pimp: An Ethnographic Investigation of Sex-for-Crack Exchanges.* New York: Lexington Books.

Maher, Lisa, (N.D.) *Making It at the Margins: Gender, Race and Work in a Street-Level Drug Economy.* Oxford: Oxford University Press.

——, 1996. Hidden in the light: Discrimination and occupational norms among crack using street-level sexworkers. *Journal of Drug Issues* 26(1):145–175.

Maher, Lisa and Richard Curtis, 1992. Women on the edge of crime: Crack cocaine and the changing contexts of street-level sex work in New York City. *Crime, Law, and Social Change* 18:221–258.

Maher, Lisa, Eloise Dunlap, Bruce D. Johnson, and Ansley Hamid, 1996. Gender, power and alternative living arrangements in the inner-city crack culture. *Journal of Research in Crime and Delinquency* 33:181–205.

Messerschmidt, James D., 1993. *Masculinities and Crime.* Lanham, M.d.: Rowman and Littlefield.

Mieczkowski, Thomas, 1986. Geeking up and throwing down: Heroin street life in Detroit. *Criminology* 24:645–666.

——, 1990. Crack dealing on the street: An exploration of the FBI hypothesis and the Detroit crack trade. Paper presented at the Annual Meeting of the American Society of Criminology, Baltimore, November.

——, 1994. The experiences of women who sell crack: Some descriptive data from the Detroit crack ethnography project. *Journal of Drug Issues* 24:227–248.

Moore, Joan W., 1990. Mexican American women addicts: The influence of family background. In Ronald Glick and Joan Moore (eds.), *Drugs in Hispanic Communities.* New Brunswick, N.J.: Rutgers University Press.

Morgan, Patricia and Karen Joe, 1994. Uncharted terrains: Contexts of experience among women in the illicit drug economy. Paper presented at the Women and Drugs National Conference, Sydney, November.

Murphy, Sheigla and Dan Waldorf, 1991. Kickin' down to the street doc: Shooting galleries in the San Francisco Bay area. *Contemporary Drug Problems* 18:9–29.

Murphy, Sheigla, Dan Waldorf, and Craig Reinarman, 1991. Drifting into dealing: Becoming a cocaine seller. *Qualitative Sociology* 13:321–343.

Padilla, Felix M., 1992. *The Gang as an American Enterprise.* New Brunswick, N.J.: Rutgers University Press.

Pettiway, Leon E., 1987. Participation in crime partnerships by female drug users: The effects of domestic arrangements, drug use, and criminal involvement. *Criminology* 25:741–766.

Reuter, Peter, Robert MacCoun, and Patrick Murphy, 1990. *Money from Crime: A Study of the Economics of Drug Dealing in Washington, D.C.* Santa Monica, Calif.: Rand Corporation.

Rosenbaum, Marsha, 1981. *Women on Heroin.* New Brunswick, N.J.: Rutgers University Press.

Simpson, Sally S. and Lori Elis, 1995. Doing gender: Sorting out the caste and crime conundrum. *Criminology* 33:47–81.

Skolnick, Jerome H. 1989. *The Social Structure of Street Drug Dealing.* Report to the State of California Bureau of Criminal Statistics and Special Services. Sacramento: State of California Executive Office.

Smithberg, Nathan and Joseph Westermeyer, 1985. White dragon pearl syndrome: A female pattern of drug dependence. *American Journal of Drug and Alcohol Abuse* 11:199–207.

Spalter-Roth, Roberta M., 1988. The sexual political economy of street vending in Washington, D.C. In Gracia Clark (ed.), *Traders Versus the State: Anthropological Approaches to Unofficial Economies.* Boulder, Colo.: Westview Press.

Steffensmeier, Darrell, 1983. Organization properties and sex-segregation in the underworld: Building a sociological theory of sex differences in crime. *Social Forces* 61:1010–1032.

Steffensmeier, Darrell J. and Robert M. Terry, 1986. Institutional sexism in the underworld: A view from the inside. *Sociological Inquiry* 56:304–323.

Sullivan, Mercer L., 1989. *Getting Paid: Youth Crime and Work in the Inner City.* Ithaca, N.Y.: Cornell University Press.

Sutter, A. G., 1966. The world of the righteous dope fiend. *Issues in Criminology* 2:177–222.

Taylor. Avril, 1993. *Women Drug Users: An Ethnography of a Female Injecting Community.* Oxford: Clarendon Press.

Taylor, Carl S., 1990. *Dangerous Society.* East Lansing: Michigan State University Press.

——, 1993. *Girls, Gangs, Women and Drugs.* East Lansing: Michigan State University Press.

Waldorf, Dan, Craig Reinarman, and Sheigla Murphy, 1991. *Cocaine Changes: The Experience of Using and Quitting.* Philadelphia, Pa.: Temple University Press.

Waterston, Alisse, 1993. *Street Addicts in the Political Economy.* Philadelphia, P.a.: Temple University Press.

Whyte, William Foote, 1943. *Street Corner Society.* Chicago: University of Chicago Press.

Williams, Terry, 1989. *The Cocaine Kids.* Reading, Mass.: Addison-Wesley.

——, 1992. *Crackhouse: Notes from the End of the Line.* New York: Addison-Wesley.

For Discussion

1. Discuss the ways in which gender roles within the illegal drug economy reflect gender roles in greater society.

2. Relate the findings reported by Maher and Daly to Keire's perspective about the gendering of addiction in Part I of this reader.

Part VIII

Prevention, Intervention, and Treatment

Historically, two major approaches for eliminating the drug problem in the United States have been "prevention" and "treatment."

Looking first at prevention, it would appear that there are many factors that put young people at risk for drug abuse, as well as protective factors that decrease the likelihood that they will use or abuse drugs. Research has shown that the most crucial risk factors for drug abuse are those that influence a child's early development within the family. These factors include parents who abuse drugs or suffer from mental illness, lack of strong parent-child attachments in a nurturing environment, poor parental monitoring, and ineffective parenting, particularly with children who suffer from conduct disorders or have difficult temperaments. Other risk factors involve a child's interaction in environments outside the family—in school, among peers, or in the community at large. These risk factors include inappropriate classroom behavior or failing school performance, poor social skills or affiliation with deviant peers, and a perception that drug use is acceptable within peer, school, or community environments.

The most important protective factors, like risks, come from within the family, but include factors that influence a child in other environments. Among the more important protective factors are strong bonds and clear rules of conduct within a family, involvement of parents in a child's life, suc-cessful school performance, strong bonds with positive institutions such as school and religious organizations, and a child's agreement with the social norm that drug use is not acceptable.

In the area of treatment, a considerable body of literature describes and documents the effectiveness of five major modalities of substance abuse/addiction treatment: chemical detoxification, methadone maintenance, drug-free outpatient treatment, self-help groups, and residential therapeutic communities. Each has its own particular view of substance abuse/addiction, and each affects the client in different ways.

Chemical Detoxification. Designed for persons dependent on narcotic drugs, chemical detoxification programs are typically situated in inpatient settings and endure for 7 to 21 days. The rationale for detoxification as a treatment approach is grounded in two basic principles. The first is a conception of "addiction" as drug craving, accompanied by physical dependence that motivates continued usage, resulting in a tolerance to the drug's effects and a syndrome of identifiable physical and psychological symptoms when the drug is abruptly withdrawn. The second is that the negative aspects of the abstinence syndrome discourage many addicts from attempting withdrawal and hence influence them to continue using drugs. Given this situation, the aim of chemical detoxification is elimination of physiological dependence through a medically supervised procedure.

Methadone, a synthetic narcotic, is the drug of choice for detoxification. Generally, a starting dose of the drug is gradually reduced in small increments until the body adjusts to the drug-free state. While many detoxification programs address only the addict's physical dependence, some provide individual or group counseling in an attempt to address the problems associated with drug abuse, while a few refer clients to other, longer-term treatments.

Almost all narcotics addicts have been in a chemical detoxification program at least once. Studies document, however, that virtually all relapse. Nevertheless, detoxification is temporary treatment that provides addicts with the opportunity for reducing their drug intake; for many, this means that the criminal activity associated with their drug taking and drug seeking is interrupted. Finally, given the association between injection drug use and HIV/AIDS, detoxification programs also provide counseling to reduce AIDS-related risk behaviors.

Methadone Maintenance. Methadone was synthesized during World War II by German chemists when supply lines for morphine were interrupted. Although chemically unlike morphine or heroin, it produces many of the same effects. Methadone was introduced in the United States in 1947, and since the 1960s the drug has been in common use for the treatment of heroin addiction. Known as "methadone maintenance," the treatment program takes advantage of methadone's unique properties as a narcotic. Like all narcotics, methadone is cross-dependent with heroin. As such, it is a substitute narcotic that prevents withdrawal. More important, however, methadone is orally effective, making intravenous use unnecessary. In addition, it is longer acting than heroin, with one oral dose lasting up to 24 hours. These properties have made methadone useful in the management of chronic narcotic addiction.

During the first phase of methadone treatment, the patient is detoxified from heroin on dosages of methadone sufficient to prevent withdrawal without either euphoria or sedation. During the maintenance phase, the patient is stabilized on a dose of methadone high enough to eliminate the craving for heroin. Although this process would appear to substitute one narcotic for another, the rationale behind methadone maintenance is to stabilize the patient on a less debilitating drug and make counseling and other treatment services available.

Studies have demonstrated that while few methadone maintenance patients have remained drug free after treatment, those who remain on methadone have highly favorable outcomes in terms of employment and no arrests. As such, methadone maintenance is effective for blocking heroin dependency.

Drug-Free Outpatient Treatment. Drug-free outpatient treatment encompasses a variety of nonresidential programs that do not use methadone or other pharmacotherapeutic agents. Most are based on a mental health perspective, and the primary services include individual and group therapy, while some offer family therapy and relapse-prevention support. An increasing number of drug-free outpatient programs are including case management services as adjuncts to counseling. The basic case management approach is to assist clients in obtaining needed services in a timely and coordinated manner. The key components of the approach are assessing, planning, linking, monitoring, and advocating for clients within the existing nexus of treatment and social services.

Evaluating the effectiveness of drug-free outpatient treatment is difficult, since programs vary widely—from drop-in "rap" centers to highly structured arrangements that offer counseling or psychotherapy as the treatment mainstay. A number of studies have found that outpatient treatment has been moderately successful in reducing daily drug use and criminal activity. However, the approach appears to be inappropriate for the most troubled and antisocial users.

Self-Help Groups. Self-help groups, also known as 12-step programs, are composed of individuals who meet regularly to stabilize and facilitate their recovery from substance abuse. The best known is Alcoholics Anonymous (AA), in which sobriety is based on fellowship and adhering to the "12 Steps" of recovery. The 12 steps stress faith, confession of wrongdoing, and passivity in the hands of a "higher power" and move group members from a statement of powerlessness over drugs and alcohol to a resolution that they will carry the message of help to others and will practice the principles learned in all affairs.

In addition to AA, other popular self-help groups are Narcotics Anonymous (NA), Cocaine Anonymous (CA), and Drugs Anonymous (DA), and all follow the 12-step model. All of these organizations operate as stand-alone fellowship programs but are used as well as adjuncts to other modalities. Although few evaluation studies of self-help groups have been carried out, the weight of clinical and observational data suggest that they are crucial to facilitating recovery.

Residential Therapeutic Communities. The therapeutic community, or TC, is a total treatment environment in which the primary clinical staff are typically former substance abusers—"recovering addicts"—who themselves were rehabilitated in therapeutic communities. The treatment perspective of the TC is that drug abuse is a disorder of the whole person—that the problem is the *person* and not the drug, that addiction is a *symptom* and not the essence of the disorder. In the TC's view of recovery, the primary goal is to change the negative patterns of behavior, thinking, and feeling that predispose drug use. As such, the overall goal is a responsible drug-free lifestyle. Recovery through the TC process depends on positive and negative pressures to change, and this change is brought about through a self-help process in which relationships of mutual responsibility to every resident in the program are built.

In addition to individual and group counseling, the TC process has a system of explicit rewards that reinforce the value of achievement. As such, privileges are *earned*. In addition, TCs have their own specific rules and regulations that guide the behavior of residents and the management of their facilities. Their purposes are to maintain the safety and health of the community and to train and teach residents through the use of discipline. TC rules and regulations are numerous, with the most conspicuous being total prohibitions against violence, theft, and drug use. Violation of these cardinal rules typically results in immediate expulsion from a TC. Therapeutic communities have been in existence for decades, and their successes have been well documented.

In the chapters that follow, some thoughts on drug education are discussed, followed by an examination of two common treatment modalities—the therapeutic community and methadone maintenance. The final chapter in Part VIII explores the characteristics of middle-class alcoholics and drug addicts who recover from their addictions without the benefit of formal treatment or self-help groups, often called a "natural recovery" process.

Additional Readings

Leukefeld, Carl G., Frank Tims, and David Farabee (Eds.). (2002). *Treatment of Drug Offenders: Policies and Issues*. New York: Springer Publishing Company.

Rawlings, Barbara, and Rowdy Yates. (2001). *Therapeutic Communities for the Treatment of Drug Users*. Philadelphia: Jessica Kingsley Publishers.

Rosenberg, Harold, and Kristina T. Phillips. (2003). "Acceptability and Availability of Harm-Reduction Interventions for Drug Abuse in American Substance Abuse Treatment Agencies." *Psychology of Addictive Behaviors*, 17(3): 203–210.

White, William L. (1998). *Slaying the Dragon: The History of Addiction Treatment and Recovery in America*. Bloomington, IL: Chestnut Health Systems. ✦

34
Safety First

A Reality-Based Approach to Teens, Drugs, and Drug Education

Marsha Rosenbaum

Marsha Rosenbaum begins this essay by describing the historical and contemporary nature of drug education, most of which has been based solely on the philosophy of abstinence. She reviews the findings from evaluation studies of drug prevention programs such as Drug Abuse Resistance Education (D.A.R.E.), and discusses the problems associated with these programs. Rosenbaum proposes an alternative strategy that focuses on a "safety first" approach to drug education.

Although often championed as a new form of weaponry in the War on Drugs, drug education in the United States was first conceived over a century ago by the Women's Christian Temperance Union (WCTU), a leading organization of the anti-alcohol crusade.[1] Early programs claimed to be based on scientific research. Standard textbooks, however, were filled with misinformation: Alcohol would cause permanent damage to the liver, lungs, kidneys, heart and brain; and marijuana could drive users insane and cause homicidal rages. All drugs were portrayed as equally dangerous and addicting. Only total abstinence could save an individual from inevitable destruction.

Post–World War II drug education portrayed *alcohol* in a way more consistent with the beliefs and practices of most Americans, making distinctions between use and *abuse*, and characterizing the majority of users as moderate.[2] *Marijuana*, however, continued to be described as causing crime and insanity, leaving its users exceedingly vulnerable to heroin addiction.[3] The purpose of these programs was to frighten young people out of using *illegal* drugs, utilizing scare tactics reminiscent of the movie *Reefer Madness*, a 1936 propaganda film now universally regarded as factually incorrect.[4]

By the late 1960s and early 1970s, it was clear that exaggerations of danger had failed to prevent a generation of young people (the Baby Boomers) from experimenting with marijuana and other drugs. In response, there was an effort by some educators to take a different tack. Whereas abstinence continued to be promoted as the wisest choice, the idea was to give students all available information about drugs so they might use their education to make responsible decisions.[5]

In the early 1980s, America's new First Lady instituted "Just Say No" as official policy, with the simple goal of prevention of drug use.[6] Anti-drug budgets climbed and "abstinence-only" school-based programs proliferated, with federal funding requiring a firm "zero-tolerance" stance.[7] Materials construed as neutral were prohibited.[8] These new programs were considered sophisticated because they utilized psycho-social innovations. Students were given information about the dangers of drugs as well as techniques for countering "peer pressure." Mrs. Reagan instructed inner city children on how to say "no" to drugs, while "feel good" drug education programs gave them a heavy dose of self-esteem and self-control exercises to fill the alleged void that rendered them "at risk" to the lure of mind-altering drugs.[9]

Today's drug education is *extremely* variable in content as well as quality and price. Classes are sometimes offered as early as kindergarten, and in later grades drug education is often taught in courses such as "family life," or "health education." First, a particular program is adopted by a school and then the school's own teachers or outside "experts" teach the program's curriculum. Some offer video presentations, others stickers, posters, and activity books. Some are designed to stand alone, others to be integrated into health or science curricula.

Some hand out T-shirts and certificates when students complete the program; others have graduation ceremonies at which students are encouraged to take a pledge to remain drug-free. All programs provide information about the negative consequences of drug use and teach resistance/refusal skills. The majority teach students that *most* people do not use drugs, that *abstinence* is the societal norm, and that it is acceptable not to use drugs.[10]

Does Drug Education 'Work'?

Increased governmental funding for "prevention" in the 1980s resulted in a plethora of "approved" drug-education programs, but it is very difficult to know which, if any, drug education programs really "work." We do know that despite prevention education a majority of students experiment with drugs by the time they reach their senior year of high school. Somewhere there is a "disconnect."

Of 49 programs reviewed in *Making the Grade: A Guide to School Drug Prevention Programs,*[11] *only 10 had been subjected to rigorous evaluations. Of these, a handful of programs developed in university settings have shown favorable results in delaying or reducing some drug use. Yet they tend to be rather expensive, hence less available than those programs that are cheaper to administer, aggressively marketed, and of questionable value.*[12]

Some researchers question our ability to determine the effectiveness of drug education programs because the evaluations themselves are too simplistic. They tend to measure student *attitudes* about drugs rather than drug use itself. Unfortunately, attitudes formed about drugs during childhood or early adolescence seem to have little bearing on later decisions, and high school students may rhetorically state reasons for avoiding drugs, yet use them anyway.[13] Furthermore, such evaluations tend to report positive findings, while ignoring or even covering up those that show no effectiveness. In a comprehensive evaluation of several of the most popular programs, D. M. Gorman of Rutgers University's Center of Alcohol Studies argues:

The evidence presented . . . from both national surveys and program evaluations, shows that we have yet to develop successful techniques of school-based drug prevention. The claims made on behalf of this aspect of the nation's drug control policy are largely unsupported by empirical data. Evidence is cited selectively to support the use of certain programs, and there is virtually no systematic testing of interventions developed in line with competing theoretical models of adolescent drug use.[14]

Education researcher Joel Brown and his colleagues conclude that flaws in the way programs are evaluated lead us to believe that drug education is effective, although in reality it is an enormous taxpayer drain with precious few positive effects.[15]

Perhaps no program has been evaluated more than D.A.R.E., which has been tested for its impact on drug use, both immediately after the program's completion and several years later. A study tracking D.A.R.E. students over five years found that the program had "no long-term effects . . . in preventing or reducing adolescent drug use."[16] Another study, funded by the National Institute of Justice, found that "expectations concerning the effectiveness of any school-based curriculum, including D.A.R.E., in changing adolescent drug use behavior should not be overstated."[17] Based on a ten-year follow-up study conducted when D.A.R.E. graduates were twenty years old, a team of researchers led by Donald Lynam at the University of Kentucky concluded that D.A.R.E. created no lasting changes in the outcomes evaluated, including not only legal and illegal drug use, but self-esteem and peer pressure resistance.[18] Other long-term studies have found little or no difference in drug use between D.A.R.E. graduates and non-graduates.[19]

What do students themselves say? A common complaint about the D.A.R.E. program, according to researchers Wysong, Aniskiewicz, and Wright, was from students who did not believe their opinions were taken into account:

It's like nobody cares what we think . . . The D.A.R.E. cops just wanted us to do what they told us and our teachers never talked about D.A.R.E. . . . . It seems like a lot of adults and teachers can't bring themselves down to talk to students . . . so you don't care what they think either.[20]

As part of a large evaluation study of drug education in California conducted by Dr. Brown and his colleagues, students were asked to tell "in their own voices" how much their drug use had been influenced by the drug education they had received. Only 15% felt drug education had a "large effect" on their choice of whether to use drugs, and 45% said they were "not affected at all."[21] In conversations with students, Brown also obtained their views on the entire drug education experience. Many felt it was insulting to teach so-called "decision-making skills" when it seemed obvious that the only acceptable decision was to decline to use drugs. Brown believes this basic hypocrisy undermines drug education: "When young people recognize that they are being taught to follow directions, rather than to make decisions, they feel betrayed and resentful. As long as federal mandates force this charade, drug education programs and policies will continue to fail."[22]

> **Long-term studies have found little or no difference in drug use between D.A.R.E. graduates and non-graduates.**

Fundamental Problems With Drug Education

The foundations of conventional school-based drug education are fundamentally flawed. Many programs are based on the conviction that any use of illegal drugs is inherently pathological, dangerous behavior, an indication that something is wrong. Some psychologists define drug use as deviant, aberrant behavior caused by a personality problem. Other explanations suggest a "proneness" on the part of some teenagers to problem behavior such as unconventionality (e.g., sagging pants and exposed bra

straps) and willingness to take risks (e.g., driving too fast). Sociological explanations link youthful drug use to weak ties to family religion and school, to "peer pressure," and to membership in drug-using groups. Alternative explanations, not based on the idea that experimentation with drugs is pathological, acknowledge the importance of *culture*. The American people and their children are perpetually bombarded with messages that encourage them to imbibe and medicate a variety of substances. We routinely alter our states of consciousness through conventional means such as alcohol, tobacco, caffeine, and prescription drugs. Fifty-one percent of Americans use alcohol regularly and nearly 35% have tried marijuana at some time in their lives.[23] Even in the context of school, today's teenagers have witnessed the Ritalinization of difficult-to-manage students.[24] In today's society, teenage drug use seems to mirror American proclivities.[25] In this context, some psychologists argue, experimentation with mind-altering substances, legal or illegal, might instead be defined as normal, given the nature of our culture.[26]

Another flaw in drug education is its assumption that drug *use* is the same as drug *abuse*. Some programs use the terms interchangeably; others utilize an exaggerated definition of use that in effect defines anything other than one-time experimentation and any use of illegal drugs as abuse. But teenagers know the difference. Most have observed their parents and other adults who use alcohol, itself a drug, without abusing it. Virtually all studies have found that the vast majority of students who try drugs do *not* become abusers.[27] Programs that blur the distinctions between use and abuse are ineffective because students' own experiences tell them the information presented to them is not believable.[28]

The "gateway" theory, a mainstay in drug education, argues that the use of marijuana leads to the use of "harder" drugs such as cocaine and heroin.[29] There is no evidence, however, that the use of one drug causes the use of another. For example, several researchers, as well as the federal government, have found that the vast majority of marijuana smokers do not progress to the use of more dangerous drugs.[30] Based on the National Institute on Drug Abuse Household Survey, Professor Lynn Zimmer and Dr. John P. Morgan calculated that for every 100 people who have tried marijuana, only one is a current user of cocaine.[31] Teenagers know from their own experience and observation that marijuana use does not inevitably, or even usually, lead to the use of harder drugs. In fact, the majority of teens who try marijuana do not even use marijuana itself on a regular basis.[32] Therefore, when such information is given, students discount both the message and the messenger.

A common belief among many educators, policymakers, and parents is that if teenagers simply understood the *dangers* of drug experimentation they would abstain.[33] In an effort to encourage abstinence, "risk" and "danger" messages are grossly exaggerated, and sometimes even completely false. Although the *Reefer Madness* messages have been replaced by assertions that we now have "scientific evidence" of the dangers of drugs, when studies are critically evaluated, few of the most common assertions (especially about marijuana) hold up.

Marijuana, the drug second only to alcohol in popularity among teens, has been routinely demonized in drug education today. Many "drug education" websites, including that of the Office of National Drug Control Policy "Project kNOw," include misinformation about marijuana's potency, its relationship to cancer, memory, the immune system, personality alteration, addiction, and sexual dysfunction.[34] In their 1997 book, *Marijuana Myths, Marijuana Facts: A Review of the Scientific Evidence*, Professors Zimmer and Morgan examined the scientific evidence relevant to each of these alleged dangers. They found, in essentially every case, that the *claims of marijuana's dangerousness did not hold up.*[35] Over the years, the same conclusions have been reached by numerous official commissions, including the La Guardia Commission in 1944, the National Commission on Marijuana and Drug Abuse in 1972, the National Academy of Sciences in 1982, and, in 1999, the Institute of Medicine.

The consistent mischaracterization of marijuana may be the Achilles' heel of conventional approaches to drug education because these false messages are inconsistent with students' *actual* observations and experience. As a result, teenagers lose confidence in what we, as parents and teachers, tell them. They are thus less likely to turn to us as credible sources of information. As one 17-year-old girl, an 11th-grader in Fort Worth, Texas, put it, "They told my little sister that you'd get addicted to marijuana the first time, and it's not like that. You hear that, and then you do it, and you say, 'Ah, they lied to me.' "[36]

Ultimately the problem with delivering unbelievable messages, particularly about marijuana, is that students define the entire drug education exercise as a joke. But their dismissal of warnings should not be taken lightly. A frightening ramification of imparting misinformation to them is that teenagers, like the heroin addict I interviewed over two decades ago, will ignore our warnings completely and put themselves in real danger. She did not find the negative claims about marijuana credible, discounted the entire message, and tried heroin. Today's increased purity and availability of "hard drugs," coupled with teenagers' refusal to heed warnings they don't trust, have resulted in *increased* risk of fatal overdose such as those we've witnessed among the children of celebrities and in affluent communities like Plano, Texas.[37]

> **The consistent mischaracterization of marijuana may be the Achilles' heel of conventional approaches to drug education because these false messages are inconsistent with students' *actual* observations and experience.**

Another problem with government-funded drug education programs is that they are mandated simply to *prevent* drug use. After admonitions and instructions to abstain, the lessons end. There is no information on how to reduce risks, avoid problems, or prevent abuse. Abstinence is seen as the sole measure of success and the only acceptable teaching option.

While the abstinence-only mandate is well-meaning, it is misguided. According to the government's own General Accounting Office, the expectation that teenagers, at a time in their lives when they are most amenable to risk-taking, will be inoculated from experimentation with consciousness alteration is unrealistic at best.[38, 39] In fact, more than *half* of all American teenagers have tried marijuana by the time they graduate from high school, and four out of five have used alcohol.[40] The insistence on complete abstinence has meant the inevitable failure of programs that make this their primary goal.[41]

The abstinence-only mandate leaves teachers and parents with *nothing* to say to the 50% of students who say "maybe" or "sometimes" or "yes," the very teens we most need to reach. As seasoned drug education researchers Gilbert Botvin and Ken Resnicow note:

> As mandated by federal guidelines, most current substance-use prevention programs emphasize "zero tolerance" and abstinence. Although controversial, programs that include messages of responsible use, however, may be more credible, and ultimately more effective.... The primary goal of substance abuse prevention programs should, it could be argued, be the reduction of heavy use and abuse rather than limiting experimentation among individuals unlikely to become frequent users.[42]

Increasing numbers of educators are becoming frustrated by the abstinence-only mandate of federally funded drug education. While attending a local summit on teens and drugs, a county-funded drug educator pulled me aside and whispered that he would like to give his students (whom he knew smoked marijuana) information that might help them minimize its dangers (e.g., not to smoke and drive). But for him to admit that they might use it at all would violate the abstinence-only school policy dictated by federal funding regulations. He believed his hands were tied, and he could not really educate his students at all. This

man was only one of dozens who have expressed such frustrations to me.

Safety First: A Reality-Based Alternative

A *safety-first* strategy for drug education requires *reality-based* assumptions about drug use and drug education. Whether we like it or not, many teenagers will experiment with drugs. Some will use drugs more regularly. At the same time we stress abstinence, we should also provide a fallback strategy for risk reduction, providing students with information and resources so they do the least possible harm to themselves and those around them.

We must approach alcohol and other drugs as we approach other potentially dangerous substances and activities. For instance, instead of banning automobiles, which kill far more teenagers than drugs do, we enforce traffic laws, prohibit driving while intoxicated, and insist that drivers wear seat belts. Reality-based alcohol education provides a model, with Students Against Drunk Driving (SADD), "Alive at 25," as well as many "designated driver" programs adopting a risk-reduction approach. Such "responsible use" messages are being introduced in alcohol education as an alternative to zero-tolerance.[43]

The first assumption of *safety-first* drug education is that *teenagers can make responsible* decisions if given honest, science-based drug education. Few young people are interested in destroying their lives or their health. Many already know the pitfalls, having experimented with drugs before, during, and after receiving drug education, and/or having seen its consequences in their own families and communities.

The majority of teenagers do make wise decisions about drug use. According to the 1998 Household Survey, 90% of 12–17-year-olds *refrained* from regular use.[44] In fact, studies conducted to discover the reasons why students quit using marijuana found they were motivated by health reasons and negative drug effects, *which they themselves experienced.* Thus, any form of drug education should respect and build upon teenagers, abilities to reason and to learn from their own experiences.[45]

A second assumption of a *safety-first* drug education program is that *total abstinence may not be a realistic alternative for all teenagers.* Drugs have always been, and are likely to remain, a part of American culture. To proclaim a "drug-free America by the year 2008" or some other arbitrary date is pure wishful thinking. Teenagers know this, and most parents and teachers know that they know it. Instead, a realistic perspective emphasizes safety and a reduction in drug problems rather than abstinence as the key measure of success of any program.

> At the same time we stress abstinence, we should also provide a fallback strategy for risk reduction.

A third assumption of *safety-first* drug education is that the *use of mind-altering substances does not necessarily constitute abuse.* The majority of drug use (with the possible exception of nicotine, which is the most addictive of all substances) does not lead to addiction or abuse. Instead, 80–90 percent of users *control* their use of psychoactive substances.[46] According to Professor Erich Goode, author of the best-selling text *Drugs in American Society*: "The truth is, as measured by harm to the user, most illicit drug users, like most drinkers of alcohol, use their drug or drugs of choice wisely non-abusively in moderation; with most, use does not escalate to abuse or compulsive use."[47]

Students who, despite our strong admonitions to abstain, use marijuana, need to understand that there is a huge difference between use and abuse, between occasional and daily use. If they persist, students need to know that they can and *must* control their use by using moderation and limiting use. It is *never* appropriate to use marijuana at school, at work, while participating in sports, or while driving. As the late Harvard psychiatrist Dr. Norman Zinberg stressed, users must recognize the complex interaction between the drug they are ingesting, their own mind-set, and the setting in which they use substances, which combine to form the context of drug use.[48] As with sexual activity and alcohol use, teenagers need to understand the importance of context in order to make wise decisions, control their use, and stay safe and healthy.

Some 'How To's' of Safety-First Drug Education

Communication is key in *safety-first* drug education. We must keep the channels of communication open, find ways to keep the conversation going, and listen, listen, listen. If we become indignant and punitive, teenagers will stop talking to us. It's that simple.

Safety-first drug education should be *age-specific* and begin in middle-school, when teens are actually confronted with drugs. Courses should run continuously through high school, when most experimentation occurs, utilizing both student engagement and participation (which conventional drug education acknowledges as crucial) and reality- and science-based educational materials.

Almost any discussion of drugs captures the attention of students. Teenagers often know more than we (want to) think about drugs through experience, family and the media. We must include them, incorporating their observations and experience in any drug education curriculum if we want it to be credible.[49, 50] There must be *no negative repercussions* for their input and honesty.

Safety-first drug education affords us the opportunity to engage students in the broad study of how drugs affect the body and mind. Quality drug education may provide an introduction to physiology, including the psychopharmacology of drugs (how they work), as well as their health and psychological risks (and benefits). An exceptional text is Dr. Andrew Weil and Winifred Rosen's *From Chocolate to Morphine: Everything You Need to Know About Mind-Altering Drugs,*[51] which describes nearly every drug available to teenagers in a comprehensive but objective way. Finally, students should learn about the social context of drugs in America. Drug education courses provide an opportunity to teach history, sociology, anthropology, and political science.

Students must also understand the *legal* consequences of drug use in America. Because teens are underage, *all* drugs are illegal for them. With increasing methods of detection such as school drug testing and escalating "zero tolerance" efforts, drug education must acknowledge *illegality* as a risk factor in and of itself, extending well beyond the physical effects of drug use. There are real, lasting consequences of using drugs and being caught, including expulsion from school, denial of college loans, a criminal record, and lasting stigma.

The goals of realistic drug education, as noted, focus on safety. With such an education, students will more deeply understand the concrete risks inherent in the use of drugs. But if we are to capture and retain students' confidence, we must separate the real from the *imagined* dangers of substance use. Just as drugs can be dangerous, they can also provide users with psychological and medical benefits, which explains why use has persisted around the world since civilization began. Reality-based drug education will equip students with information they trust, the basis for making responsible decisions.

As the demand for reality-based drug education grows, programs are being developed in the United States and abroad. A listing of such programs can be found at the website of the Lindesmith Center: *www.lindesmith.org.*

Summary

Drug education has existed in America for over a century. It has utilized a variety of methods, from scare tactics to resistance techniques, in the effort to prevent young people from using drugs. Nonetheless, teenagers continue to experiment with a variety of substances. Despite the expansion of drug prevention programs, it is very difficult to know which, if any "work" better than others. The assumptions that shape conventional programs render them problematic: that drug experimentation constitutes deviance; that drug *use* is the same as drug *abuse*; that marijuana constitutes the "gateway" to "harder" substances; that exaggeration of risks will deter experimentation.

> **Reality-based drug education will equip students with information they trust, the basis for making responsible decisions.**

The main reasons many students fail to take programs seriously and continue to experiment with drugs is that they have learned for themselves that America is hardly "drug-free"; there are vast differences between experimentation, abuse, and addiction; and the use of one drug does not inevitably lead to the use of others.

While youth *abstinence* is what we'd all prefer, this unrealistic goal means programs lack *risk-reduction* education for those 50% who do not "just say no." We need a fallback strategy of *safety first* in order to prevent drug *abuse* and drug *problems* among teenagers.

Educational efforts should acknowledge teens' ability to make reasoned decisions. Programs should differentiate between use and abuse, and stress the importance of moderation and context. Curricula should be age-specific, stress student participation and provide science-based, objective educational materials. In simple terms, it is our responsibility as parents and teachers to engage students and provide them with credible information so they can make responsible decisions, avoid drug abuse, and stay safe.

Notes

1. Bordin, R., *Women and Temperance: The Quest for Power and Liberty, 1873–1900*, Philadelphia: Temple University Press (1981).

2. Milgram, G. G., "A historical review of alcohol education: research and comments," *Journal of Alcohol and Drug Education* 21:1–16 (1976).

3. Rathbone, J. L., *Tobacco, Alcohol and Narcotics*, New York: Oxford Guidance Life Pamphlets (1952).

4. Beck, J., "100 years of 'just say no' versus 'just say know': reevaluating drug education goals

for the coming century," *Evaluation Review,* 22(1):15–45 (1998).

5. Goode, E., *Drugs in American Society,* New York: McGraw-Hill (1993), p. 334. Goode also cites H. S. Resnick, *It Starts With People: Experiences in Drug Abuse Prevention,* Washington. D.C.: U.S. Department of Health, Education and Welfare (1978).

6. Baum, D., *Smoke and Mirrors: The War on Drugs and the Politics of Failure* (1981), Boston: Little Brown (1996).

7. U.S. Department of Education, *Drug Education Curricula: A Guide to Selection and Implementation.* Washington, D.C.: U.S. Government Printing Office (1981).

8. Perhaps the most thorough and informative drug education book available for high school students, *Chocolate to Morphine: Understanding Mind-Altering Drugs,* by Andrew Weil M.D. and Winifred Rosen (Boston: Houghton Mifflin), was hastily removed from drug education curricula shortly after its 1983 publication because it stressed non-abusive relationships with drugs rather than total abstinence.

9. Rosenbaum, M., *Kids, Drugs, and Drug Education: A Harm Reduction Approach.* San Francisco: National Council on Crime and Delinquency (1996).

10. For an exhaustive listing of the most popular programs, see *Making the Grade: A Guide to School Drug Prevention Programs.* Washington D.C.: Drug Strategies (1999).

11. *Making the Grade: A Guide to School Drug Prevention Programs.* Washington, D.C.: Drug Strategies (1999).

12. Dusenbury, L., Lake, A., and Falco, M., "A review of the evaluation of 47 drug abuse prevention curricula available nationally." *Journal of School Health* 67(4):127–132 (1997).

13. Skager, R., "Can science-based prevention deliver the goods in the real world?" *Prevention File* Winter: 11–14 (1998).

14. Gorman, D. M., "The irrelevance of evidence in the development of school-based drug prevention policy, 1986–1996," *Evaluation Review* 22(11):118–146 (1998).

15. Kreft, I. G. G., and Brown, J. H., eds., "Zero effects of drug prevention programs: Issues and solutions," *Evaluation Review* 22(1):3–14 (1998).

16. Wysong, S., Aniskiewicz, R., and Wright, D., "Truth and D.A.R.E.: Tracking drug educa-

tion to graduation and as symbolic politics," *Social Problems* 41(3):448–72 (1994).

17. Ennett, S. T., Tobler, N. S., Ringwalt, C. L., and Flewelling, R., "How effective is drug abuse resistance education? A meta-analysis of project D.A.R.E. outcome evaluations," *American Journal of Public Health* 84(9):1394–1401 (1994).

18. Lynam, D. R., et al., "Project D.A.R.E.: No effects at 10-year follow-up," *Journal of Consulting and Clinical Psychology* 76(4):590–593 (1999).

19. Tobler, N. S., and Stratton, H. H., "Effectiveness of school-based drug prevention programs: A meta-analysis of the research," *The Journal of Primary Prevention* 18(1):71–128 (1997); Dukes, R. L., Ullman, J. B., and Stein, J. A., "A three-year follow-up of Drug Abuse Resistance Education (D.A.R.E.)," *Evaluation Review* 20:49–66 (1996); Clayton, R. R., Cattarello, A. M., and Johnstone, B. M., "The effectiveness of drug abuse resistance education (Project D.A.R.E): 5-year follow-up results," *Preventive Medicine* 25:307–18 (1996); Rosenbaum, D. P., and Hanson, G. S., *Assessing the Effects of School-Based Drug Education: A Six-Year Multi-Level Analysis of Project D.A.R.E.* Chicago, Department of Criminal Justice and Center for Research in Law and Justice, University of Illinois (1998).

20. Wysong, E., Aniskiewicz, R., and Wright, D., "Truth and D.A.R.E.: Tracking drug education to graduation and as symbolic politics," *Social Problems* 41(3):448–72 (1994).

21. Brown, J. H., D'Emidio-Caston, M., and Pollard, J., "Students and substances: Social power in drug education," *Educational Evaluation and Policy Analysis* 19:65–82 (1997).

22. Brown, J. H., "Listen to the kids," *American School Board Journal* 184:38–47 (1997).

23. SAMHSA, Office of Applied Studies, *National Household Survey on Drug Abuse: Main Findings 1998,* Washington. D.C.: National Clearinghouse for Alcohol and Drug Information (1999).

24. Knickerbocker, B., "Using drugs to rein in boys," *The Christian Science Monitor,* May 19 (1999).

25. For an excellent discussion of the role of drugs in American culture, see C. Reinarman and H. G. Levine, "The cultural contradictions of punitive prohibition," in Reinarman, C., and Levine, H. G., eds., *Crack in America: Demon Drugs and Social Justice,* Berkeley: University of California Press (1997).

26. Newcomb, M., and Bentler, P., *Consequences of Adolescent Drug Use: Impact on the Lives of Young Adults*, Newbury Park, CA: Sage (1988); Shedler, J., and Block, J., "Adolescent drug use and psychological health: A longitudinal inquiry," *American Psychologist* 45:612–630 (1990).

27. Brown, J. H., and Horowitz, J. E., "Deviance and deviants: Why adolescent substance use prevention programs do not work," *Evaluation Review* 17(5):529–55 (1993); Zimmer, L., and Morgan, J. P., *Exposing Marijuana Myths: A Review of the Scientific Evidence*, New York: Open Society Institute (1995).

28. Duncan, D. F., "Problems associated with three commonly used drugs: A survey of rural secondary school students," *Psychology of Addictive Behavior* 5(2):93–96 (1991); United States General Accounting Office, *Drug Use Among Youth: No Simple Answers to Guide Prevention*, Washington, D.C.: U.S. General Accounting Office (1993).

29. Kandel, D., "Stages in adolescent involvement in drug use," *Science* 190:912–14 (1975); Gabany, S. G., and Plummer, P., "The marijuana perception inventory: The effects of substance abuse instruction," *Journal of Drug Education* 20(3):235–45 (1990).

30. Zimmer, L., and Morgan, J. P., *Marijuana Myths, Marijuana Facts: A Review of the Scientific Evidence*. New York: The Lindesmith Center (1997); Brown, J. H., and Horowitz, J. D., "Deviance and deviants: Why adolescent substance use prevention programs do not work," *Evaluation Review*, 17(5):529–55 (1993); SAMHSA, Office of Applied Studies, *National Household Survey on Drug Abuse: Main Findings 1998*. Washington, D.C.: National Clearinghouse for Alcohol and Drug Information (1999).

31. Zimmer, L., and Morgan, J. P., *Marijuana Myths, Marijuana Facts: A Review of the Scientific Evidence*, New York: The Lindesmith Center (1997).

32. SAMHSA, Office of Applied Studies, *National Household Survey on Drug Abuse: Main Findings 1998*. Washington, D.C.: National Clearinghouse for Alcohol and Drug Information (1999).

33. Bachman, J. G., Johnston, L. D., and O'Malley, P. M., "Explaining the recent decline in cocaine use among young adults: Further evidence that perceived risks and disapproval lead to reduced drug use," *Journal of Health and Human Social Behavior* 31(2)1:173–184 (1990).

34. Office of National Drug Control Policy, http://www.projectknow.com (1999).

35. Zimmer, L., and Morgan, J. P., *Marijuana Myths, Marijuana Facts: A Review of the Scientific Evidence*, New York: The Lindesmith Center (1997).

36. Taylor, M., and Berard, Y., "Anti-drug programs face overhaul," *Ft. Worth Star Telegram* November 1, 1998.

37. Gray, M., "Texas Heroin Massacre," *Rolling Stone*, May 27, 1999.

38. United States General Accounting Office, *Drug use among youth: No simple answers to guide prevention*, Washington, D.C.: U.S. General Accounting Office (1993).

39. For an excellent discussion of teenagers and risk, see Ponton, L., *The Romance of Risk: Why Teenagers Do the Things They Do*, New York: Basic Books (1997).

40. SAMHSA, Office of Applied Studies, *National Household Survey on Drug Abuse: Main Findings 1998*, Washington, D.C.: National Clearinghouse for Alcohol and Drug Information (1999).

41. Ching, C. L., "The goal of abstinence: Implications for drug education," *Journal of Drug Education*, 11(1):13–18 (1981).

42. Botvin, G., and Resnicow, K., "School-based substance use prevention programs: Why do effects decay?" *Preventive Medicine* 22(4):484–490 (1993).

43. Oldenberg, D., "Kids and alcohol: A controversial alternative to 'Just Say No.'" *Washington Post*, March 10, 1998; Milgram, G. G., "Responsible decision making regarding alcohol: A re-emerging prevention/education strategy for the 1990s," *Journal of Drug Education*, 26(4):357–65 (1996).

44. SAMHSA, Office of Applied Studies, *National Household Survey on Drug Abuse: Main Findings 1998*, Washington, D.C.: National Clearinghouse for Alcohol and Drug Information (1999).

45. Martin, C. E., Duncan, D. F., and Zunich, E. M., "Students' motives for discontinuing illicit drug taking," *Health Values: Achieving High Level Wellness* 7(5):8–11 (1983); Skager, R., and Austin, G., *Sixth Biennial California Student Substance Use Survey*, Sacramento: Office of the Attorney General, State of California (1998).

46. Nicholson, T., "The primary prevention of illicit drug problems: An argument for decriminalization and legalization," *The Journal of Primary Prevention* 12(4):275–88 (1992);

Winick, C., "Social Behavior, Public Policy and Nonharmful Drug Use," *The Milbank Quarterly* 69(3):437–57 (1991).

47. Goode, E., *Drugs in American Society*, New York: McGraw-Hill (1993), p. 335.

48. Zinberg, N., *Drug, Set, and Setting: The Basis for Controlled Intoxicant Use*, New Haven: Yale University Press (1984).

49. Martin, C. E., Duncan, D. F., and Zunich, E. M., "Students' motives for discontinuing illicit drug taking," *Health Values: Achieving High Level Wellness* 7(5):8–11 (1983).

50. For an excellent discussion of peer education see Cohen, J., "Achieving a reduction in drug-related harm through education," in Nick Heather, Alex Wodak, Ethan A. Nadelmann, and Pat O'Hare, eds., *Psychoactive Drugs and Harm Reduction: From Faith to Science*, London: Whurr (1993); and for confluent education see Brown, J. H., and Horowitz, J. E., "Deviance and deviants: Why adolescent substance use prevention programs do not work," *Evaluation Review* 17(5):529–555 (1993).

51. Weil, A., and Rosen, W., *From Chocolate to Morphine: Everything You Need to Know About Mind-Altering Drugs*, Boston: Houghton Mifflin (1993).

For Discussion

What type of role models, if any, might we utilize in a reality-based educational approach?

Reprinted from: Marsha Rosenbaum, *Safety First: A Reality-Based Approach to Teens, Drugs, and Drug Education,* pp. 3–15, 17–20. Copyright © by Marsha Rosenbaum, Ph.D., Director, The Lindesmith Center, San Francisco. Reprinted by permission. ✦

35

Advances in Therapeutic Communities

National Institute on Drug Abuse

The therapeutic community (TC) is a drug treatment modality that uses a holistic design for creating lifestyle changes. It is characterized by a democratic philosophy with foundations in social learning theory. In the next article, the historical background regarding TCs is described as well as their organizational and ideological characteristics. TCs have changed in recent years in response to the needs of various subgroups, such as women drug users with children. This article also includes a summary of findings drawn from evaluation studies of TCs.

What Is a Therapeutic Community?

"Therapeutic community," or just "TC" as it is usually referred to by researchers and clinicians in the drug field, is a generic term used to describe a wide spectrum of residential drug abuse treatment approaches. However, fundamental to the TC concept is the necessity for a total treatment environment isolated from the drugs, violence, and other aspects of street life that militate against rehabilitation. The primary clinical staff in TCs are typically former substance abusers who themselves were rehabilitated in therapeutic communities. The treatment perspective in the TC is that drug abuse is a disorder of the whole person; that the problem is the *person* and not the drug; that addiction is a *symptom* and not the essence of the disorder; and that the primary goal is to change the negative patterns of behavior, thinking, and feeling that predispose drug use (De Leon, 1994).

History of Therapeutic Communities

1. Early Roots

The roots of therapeutic communities date back to the "no restraints" therapy for mental patients developed in early nineteenth century France. Treatment was based on work therapy and the provision of recreational facilities, within a "no violence" atmosphere (Kooyman, 1993). Similar programs appeared in other parts of Europe later in the century, but none evidenced any meaningful success. They were usually replaced with more traditional forms of treatment, given that most institutions were understaffed and overpopulated with difficult to treat patients.

During World War II, psychiatrists assigned to England's Army Selection Unit found themselves confronted with growing numbers of soldiers returning from battle suffering from mental breakdowns. Maxwell Jones, a psychiatrist dealing with soldiers at the army's Northfield Hospital, stressed the importance of patients' participation in their own successful recovery (Kooyman, 1993). He described his approach as "democratic therapy," and eventually turned his unit at Henderson into a therapeutic community. Jones made five basic assumptions for patient-staff interactions in his therapeutic community (Jones, 1953):

1. two-way communication at all levels
2. decision-making at all levels
3. shared leadership
4. consensus in decision-making
5. social learning by social interaction, here and now

2. Synanon

Contemporary therapeutic communities in the United States can be traced to Synanon. Synanon seemed to just "happen" by chance in 1958, when its founder, Charles Dederich, an unemployed recovering alcoholic, used his Ocean Park, California, apartment for holding informal therapy "bull sessions" with alcoholic and drug-using friends. Dederich found that people were drawn to him and listened to him. In time, he began to structure his gatherings with different types of group therapy that he had become familiar with at Alcoholics Anonymous and other treatment. Before long, he began to exercise rigid control over the groups, introducing methods of cross examination and ridicule that gave birth to the "encounter group"—a highly confrontational and intense form of verbal communication in a group setting.

Dederich observed that many of the substance abusers in his groups stopped using drugs while they were connected with his groups. Motivated by the idea that he might have found an answer to addiction, he established Synanon House, America's first TC for drug abusers. As the program grew, with houses in several parts of the United States, its methods and procedures evolved into a dynamic that focused on the rehabilitation of drug-involved offenders (Casriel, 1963).

Since the very beginning of its founding, Synanon faced numerous problems, including community resistance to the program. It was argued that Dederich's facility was not only in violation of zoning regulations, but was operating as a hospital without a license. The zoning wars that followed gave Synanon national publicity, both positive and negative, and by 1962 it was claimed by one of Synanon's supporters that the program had attracted more than 19,000 visitors, most of whom were professionals who wished to see Dederich's "anti-criminal society" first hand (Yablonsky, 1967). But despite the adverse publicity, Synanon grew to 500 residents by 1964, 800 by 1967, and 1,400 by 1969 (White, 1998).

3. Synanon II and Synanon III

By 1968, Dederich had shifted his vision of Synanon from rehabilitation to the creation of an alternative community. The process of restructuring one's character became more important than returning an individual back to society (White, 1998). Program graduation was abolished, and addiction was cast as a "terminal disease" that could be arrested only by sustained participation within Synanon. Loyalty oaths were introduced, and only the most committed to the concept remained.

During the early 1970s Synanon underwent yet another transition. In 1974 the Synanon Foundation was chartered as a religion. At the same time, increased paranoia regarding outsiders led to the emergence of paramilitary defense measures that included major weapons purchases and martial arts training. Quickly, Synanon's role in the rehabilitation of addicts disappeared. Its legacy, however, was a new approach to addiction treatment. By introducing the use of recovering addicts as counselors, the treatment approach stepped away from the traditional doctor-patient relationship and created an environment where former users could treat current users through role modeling. In addition, Synanon was successful in stripping the culture of addiction from the addict and replacing it with a culture of recovery.

4. Daytop Village

First known as Daytop Lodge, the Daytop experience began when Herbert A. Bloch, a criminology professor at Brooklyn College; Joseph Shelly, Chief Probation Officer for the New York State Supreme Court; and Alexander Bassin, Director of Research for the State Supreme Court, submitted a proposal to the National Institute of Mental Health for a project to establish a halfway house for drug-involved offenders (Shelly and Bassin, 1965). The project was to be modeled after Synanon, and on April 15, 1963, an initial grant of $390,000 enabled Daytop to open its doors several months later. The initial population was 25 men between the ages of 16 and 45 who had been sentenced to probation with the stipulation that they remain in the program until graduation (Shelly and Bassin, 1965).

By 1965, Daytop Lodge had evolved from its halfway house roots into Daytop Village, a well-organized and tightly structured program for both women and men with an intricate network of treatment approaches. The treatment philosophy during the early years of Daytop was straightforward: *You are an addict because you are stupid, immature, and irresponsible, and cannot bear the realities of life as an adult!* This was the only cause of drug addiction recognized by Daytop, and the program leadership would not permit residents to blame their behavior on parents, peers, neighborhood, or community (Inciardi, 1967). Or stated differently:

> In other words, the concept of the drug addict as a ill person and therefore automatically entitled to the recognized prerogatives of the role of the ill in our society in terms of sympathetic understanding, special concern, leniency, and forgiveness is vehemently fought as an ideology (Shelly and Bassin, 1965).

The new resident at Daytop was considered to be a "child," and as such was given little responsibility. As he or she developed in the program, duties of greater importance were assigned. Treatment was intended to force the "child" to act as an adult, with the resolve that he or she would eventually think as an adult and feel like an adult. When that was accomplished, the resident was ready for graduation—a process that generally endured from 12 to 18 months. Regardless of one's position, however, all had to follow the three cardinal rules: no drugs, no violence, and no shirking of responsibility. Sanctions for breaking the cardinal rules ranged from public ridicule and reduction in status to shaved heads, the wearing of diapers, or expulsion from the program.

As time passed and Daytop grew, the rigidity and severity of sanctions for rule breaking lessened, and other programs adopted the Daytop model—Phoenix House and Delaney Street in New York City, Amity in Tucson, Gaudenzia House in Philadelphia, Gateway House in Chicago, Integrity House in Newark, and Marathon in Coventry, Rhode Island. All of these new programs were started during the 1960s, many by graduates of either Synanon or Daytop.

Criticisms

During their first two decades, TCs received both praise and support. Daytop and Phoenix House, furthermore, expanded into worldwide programs. But TCs also drew numerous criticisms. For example (see White, 1998):

1. The great majority of residents were mandatory rather than voluntary placements.

2. Programs boasted of great successes, but few permitted independent evaluations or provided statistics on the number of dropouts or successful graduates.

3. The TC was an artificial environment that inhibited rather than promoted a graduate's functioning in the outside community.

4. The use of nonprofessional staff ran the risk of serious mistakes in diagnoses and treatment.

5. TCs had few links to other community-based support structures.

6. Programs placed too much emphasis on the charismatic leadership of its director. This dependence, it was claimed, made TCs unstable.

7. The fact that there were only a few key positions in a TC hierarchy made programs vulnerable to abuses of power by those in charge.

8. The costs of treatment were far too high.

All of these criticisms had some validity, and by the latter 1970s and early 1980s a number of TCs had closed, while others had fallen on hard times. Part of this, however, was the result of factors unrelated to the therapeutic community process—it was the era of the "nothing works" philosophy in correctional treatment.

The 'Nothing Works' Era

During the late 1960s and early 1970s, programs to abolish poverty and racial injustice had not lived up to their expectations. There were riots, many were angered over American involvement in Vietnam, and rates of drug abuse and crime were increasing at a rapid pace. Furthermore, there was growing opposition to the many Supreme Court decisions that some claimed, and others denied, were "handcuffing police" and "coddling criminals." During much of this period, researchers in New York had been undertaking a massive evaluation of prior efforts at correctional intervention.

The idea for the research went back to early 1966, when the New York State Governor's Special Committee on Criminal Offenders decided to commission a study to determine what methods, if any, held the greatest promise for the rehabilitation of convicted criminals, including drug-involved offenders. The findings of the study were to be used to guide program development in the state's criminal justice system. The project was carried out by researchers at the New York State Office of Crime Control Planning, and for years they analyzed the literature on hundreds of correctional efforts published between 1945 and 1967.

The findings of the project were put together in a massive volume that was published in 1975 (Lipton, Martinson, and Wilks, 1975). Prior to the appearance of the in-depth report, the article, "What Works?—Questions and Answers About Prison Reform" [appeared] (Martinson, 1974). Written by one of the researchers, Robert Martinson, the article was published in *The Public Interest*. In it he reviewed the purpose and scope of the New York study and implied that with few and isolated exceptions, *nothing works!*

There was little that was really new in Martinson's article. In 1966, Professor Walter C. Bailey of the City University of New York had published the findings of a survey of 100 evaluations of correctional treatment programs with the final judgment that "evidence supporting the efficacy of correctional treatment is slight, inconsistent, and of questionable reliability" (Bailey, 1966). The following year, Roger Hood in England completed a similar review, concluding that the different ways of treating offenders lead to results that are not very encouraging (Hood, 1967). And in 1971, James Robison and Gerald Smith's analysis of correctional treatment in California asked "Will the clients act differently if we lock them up, or keep them locked up longer, or do something with them inside, or watch them more

closely afterward, or cut them loose officially?" Their conclusion was a resounding "Probably not!" (Robison, 1971).

But the Martinson essay created a sensation, for it appeared in a visible publication and attracted popular media attention at a time when politicians and opinion makers were desperately searching for some response to the widespread public fear of drug abuse and street crime. Furthermore, as Harvard University's James Q. Wilson explained:

> Martinson did not discover that rehabilitation was of little value in dealing with crime so much as he administered a highly visible *coup de grace*. By bringing out into the open the long-standing scholarly skepticism about most rehabilitation programs, he prepared the way for a revival of an interest in the deterrent, incapacitative, and retributive purposes of the criminal justice system. (Wilson, 1980)

Martinson also created a sensation within the research and treatment communities—mostly negative. He was criticized for bias, major distortions of fact, and gross misrepresentation (Klockars, 1975; Palmer, 1975). And for the most part, his critics were correct. Martinson had failed to include all types of treatment programs; he tended to ignore the effects of some programs on some individuals; he generally concentrated on whether the particular treatment method was effective in *all* the studies in which it was tested; and he neglected to study the new federally funded treatment programs that had begun after 1967. But none of that seemed to matter. The end result was the loss of funding for many treatment programs, both in and out of correctional settings, including many therapeutic communities.

Essential Elements of Modern Therapeutic Communities

The essential elements of modern therapeutic communities consist of a series of concepts, beliefs, assumptions, program components, and clinical and educational practices that are apparent to a greater or lesser degree in every TC. A cataloguing and description of these elements was accomplished by TC researcher George De Leon with the help of a national panel of TC experts (Melnick and De Leon, 1993; De Leon, 1997).

As De Leon has explained, the quintessential element of the TC approach may be termed *community as method* (De Leon, 1997). The essential concepts that characterize community as method include:

Use of Participant Roles: Individuals contribute directly to all activities of daily life in the TC, which provides learning opportunities through engaging in a variety of roles.

Use of Membership Feedback: The primary source of instruction and support for individual change is the peer membership.

Use of Membership as Role Models: Each participant strives to be a role model of the change process. Along with their responsibility to provide feedback to others as to what they must change, members must also provide examples of how they can change.

Use of Collective Formats for Guiding Individual Change: The individual engages in the process of change primarily with peers. Education, training, and therapeutic activities occur in groups, meetings, seminars, job functions, and recreation.

Use of Shared Norms and Values: Rules, regulations, and social norms protect the physical and psychological safety of the community. However, there are beliefs and values that serve as explicit guidelines for self-help recovery and teaching right living.

Use of Structure and Systems: The organization of work (e.g. the varied job functions, chores, and management roles) needed to maintain the daily operations of the facility, is a main vehicle for teaching self-development.

Use of Open Communication: The public nature of shared experiences in the community is used for therapeutic purposes.

Use of Relationships: Friendships with particular individuals, peers, and staff are essential to encourage the individual to engage and remain in the change process.

Use of Language: TC argot is the special vocabulary used by residents to reflect elements of its subculture, particularly its recovery and right living teachings. As with any special language, TC argot represents individual integration into the peer community. However, it also mirrors the individuals' clinical progress.

The basic components of the generic TC program model include the following (De Leon, 1997):

Community Separateness: TC-oriented programs have their own names, often innovated by the clients, and are housed in a space or locale that is separated from other agency or institutional programs and units or generally from the drug-related environment.

A Community Environment: The inner environment contains communal space to promote a sense of commonality and collective activities (e.g., groups, meetings). The walls display signs that state in simple terms the philosophy of the program, the messages of right living and recovery.

Community Activities: To be effectively utilized, treatment or educational services must be provided within a context of the peer community. Thus, with the exception of individual counseling, all activities are programmed in collective formats.

Peers as Community Members: Members who demonstrate the expected behaviors and reflect the values and teachings of the community are viewed as role models.

Staff as Community Members: The staff are a mix of recovered professionals and other traditional professionals (e.g., medical, legal, mental health, and educational) who must be integrated through cross-training that is grounded in the basic concepts of the TC perspective and community approach.

A Structured Day: Regardless of its length, the day has a formal schedule of varied therapeutic educational activities with prescribed formats, fixed times, and routine procedures. The structure of the program relates to the TC perspective, particularly the view of the client and recovery.

Phase Format: The treatment protocol, or plan of therapeutic and educational activities, is organized into phases that reflect a developmental view of the change process. Emphasis is on incremental learning at each phase, which moves the individual to the next stage of recovery.

Work as Therapy and Education: Consistent with the TC's self-help approach, all clients are responsible for the daily management of the facility (e.g., cleaning activities, meal preparation and service, maintenance, purchasing, security, coordinating schedules, preparatory chores of groups, meetings, seminar activities).

TC Concepts: There is an organized curriculum focused on teaching the TC perspective, particularly its self-help recovery concepts and view of right living.

Peer Encounter Groups: The peer encounter is the main community or therapeutic group, although other forms of therapeutic, educational, and support groups are utilized as needed. The minimal objective of the peer encounter is to heighten individual awareness of specific attitudes or behavioral patterns that should be modified.

Awareness Training: All therapeutic and educational interventions involve raising the individuals' consciousness of the impact of their conduct and attitudes on themselves and the social environment, and conversely the impact of the behaviors and attitudes of others on themselves and the social environment.

Emotional Growth Training: Achieving the goals of personal growth and socialization involves teaching individuals how to identify feelings, express feelings appropriately, and manage feelings constructively through the interpersonal and social demands of communal life.

Planned Duration of Treatment: How long individuals must be program-involved depends on their stage of recovery, although a minimum period of intensive involvement is required to ensure internalization of the TC teachings.

Continuance of Recovery: Completion of primary treatment is a stage in the recovery process. Thus, whether implemented within the boundaries of the main program or separately as in special halfway houses, the perspective and approach guiding aftercare programming must be continuous with that of primary treatment in the TC.

Clinical Foundations

Little has been written on the specific clinical underpinnings of the treatment techniques applied in therapeutic communities. They tend to vary depending on the client needs, and as such, those described here are what have been found to be most appropriate for those with long histories of both drug abuse and criminality. The great majority of drug-involved offenders found in prison-based therapeutic communities tend to have little or no self-confidence and trust of others, and seem to be out of touch with their feelings. Typically, they cover their feelings of hopelessness, guilt, and worthlessness with facades of strength, invincibility, and control over their immediate situations. Frequently, attempts at control are accomplished through manipulation. In turn, they tend to be both indirect and unable to seek help or to recognize areas where help is essential. Their lives, furthermore, have been marked by chaos and the inability to assume responsibility for themselves or their actions (Kooyman, 1986).

For drug-involved offenders, interactions with police, the courts and the prison system solidify feelings of mistrust. In an attempt to gain control or even survive, drug-involved offenders become increasingly manipulative. The revolving cycle of imprisonment heightens feelings of hopelessness and worthlessness. As well, it diminishes their opportunities to take responsibility for their lives and their actions (Chaiken and Johnson, 1988). In addition, few drug-involved offenders have adequate formal education. Many are from dysfunctional homes, with parents or other family members having histories of drug abuse, criminality, and incarceration. And finally, knowledge and experiences are based on street life. As such, effective treatment techniques must consider clients' educational levels and life experiences. In other words, the representations used in therapy must be relevant to the experiences of the clients. The techniques described here have been tailored for the needs, aptitudes, and experiences of drug-involved offenders.

The fundamental goal of the TC is to create behavior change by having the clients understand their feelings and thoughts and to take responsibility for their decisions and actions. In doing this, many other treatment objectives are accomplished at the same time, including the creating of trust, the instilling of hope, and increasing self-esteem (Hinshelwood, 1986). In many TCs, the theoretical framework in which the treatment is grounded is a simple paradigm in which feelings and thoughts result in behaviors. With this paradigm it is assumed that people choose how they will behave. Thus, they have free choice and are responsible for their own actions. In traditional psychotherapy, the initial focus is on feelings and thoughts. Yet the time and energy spent on feelings and thoughts can be endless, with no noticeable changes in behavior, whereas, in a TC the initial focus is on behavior. This shift in focus is effective, since behaviors are most evident to the clients. By focusing first on behaviors, clients are more likely to become engaged in treatment because they can readily understand and assimilate the treatment plan to change behaviors. In addition, criminal and drug-using behaviors are the crucial elements to be changed in order to reduce risk to self and others.

The initial behavior change occurs through modelling and redirection. During the orientation phase of TC treatment, clients' behaviors are continually addressed by experienced clients and staff. Through daily confrontations, clients' behaviors are redirected. This process teaches clients that old behaviors are unacceptable. As a result, clients begin to adopt new, prosocial behaviors. However, in order for these newly incorporated behaviors to have lasting effects and to avoid regression, inappropriate behaviors, feelings, and thoughts—both current and past—must be addressed.

Clinical Treatment Approaches

Within the framework outlined above, specific clinical techniques tend to vary from one therapeutic community to another. In the state of Delaware, for example, seven TCs are currently operating within the correctional system, and all follow an holistic approach. Different types of therapy—behavioral, cognitive, and emotional—are used to address individual treatment needs (Hooper, Lockwood, and Inciardi, 1993). Briefly:

1. Behavioral Therapy fosters positive demeanor and conduct by not accepting antisocial actions. To implement this, behavioral expectations are clearly defined as soon as a new resident is admitted to the program. At that time, the staff's primary focus is on how the resident is to behave. The client works with an orientation manual which he is expected to learn thoroughly. Once again, the focus is on his or her behavior as opposed to thoughts and feelings. As the client learns and adjusts to the routines of the therapeutic community, more salient issues are dealt with in the treatment process.

2. Cognitive Therapy helps individuals recognize errors and fallacies in their thinking. The object is to help the client understand how and why certain cognitive patterns have been developed across time. With this knowledge the client can develop alternative thinking patterns resulting in more realistic decisions about life. Cognitive Therapy is accomplished in both group and individual sessions.

3. Emotional Therapy deals with unresolved conflicts associated with interactions with others and the resulting feelings and behaviors. To facilitate this treatment strategy, a non-threatening but nurturing manner is required so that clients can gain a better understanding of how they think and feel about themselves as well as others.

Special Population TCs

The recognition that TCs may be most appropriate for "Special Populations" is the most important modification, indeed innovation, in the use of TCs in the last decade. As De Leon has noted, "the quintessential element of the TC approach [is] *community as method. . . . The purposive use of the peer community to facilitate social and psychological change in individuals*" (De Leon, 1997:5). And when the clients in the community share an identity apart from substance abuse, they have more in common. Their identity as community is actually strengthened by the existence of other shared problems and the potential to assist each other in dealing with these issues. Consequently, the rationale for being part of the community and remaining in it is greater, and when the length [of] time in treatment increases, so does the potential for prosocial changes in other important arenas. It is not surprising that, in general, retention in special population TCs is longer than in standard community-based TCs.

In most cases, special population TCs have demographic or behavioral circumstances that identify their clients apart from their substance use. It may be adolescence, gender, family circumstances, mental health, or criminal justice involvement. Often the factor that makes them "special" is correlated or co-morbid with their substance abuse. The types of special population therapeutic communities are varied and growing—in fact, targeted TCs are the growth area in the TC movement. Here we review some of the most prevalent currently established targeted TCs.

TCs for Adolescents

There have been a significant number of adolescents in TCs since the beginning of the movement. The Drug Abuse Reporting Program (DARP) summarizing treatment modality results up to the mid-1970s found almost one-third of those in TCs were 19 or younger (Sells and Simpson, 1979). In almost all cases youth were treated right along with adults in the same community-based TCs. Such co-mingling often failed to recognize any unique circumstances of adoles-

cence—puberty, identity formation, school problems, vulnerable psychological status but often seemingly invulnerable physical risk—to say nothing of the definitional fact that addiction histories were generally much shorter. At the same time that addiction careers may be shorter for adolescents in TCs, they usually began drug use earlier than adult TC clients (Jainchill et al., 1995) and are less likely to perceive they have a substance abuse problem (De Leon, 1988).

Recently, there have been a number of TCs established exclusively for adolescents, the premise being that an age-segregated community will lead to better peer relations. Others in the TC movement have argued against this, saying that an age-integrated community is better for dealing with family issues. Outcome findings on age-integrated versus age-segregated communities for youth are not yet available (Marshall and Marshall, 1993; Jainchill, 1997), but, other than in juvenile corrections settings, most TCs with adolescents also include adults.

In a recent review of 10 adolescent TC programs, it is apparent that most adolescents do not enter TCs voluntarily. Over two-thirds were referred by the criminal justice system, and another 14% by doctors, counselors or teachers. About 10% were referred by family, and only 8% were self-referred (Jainchill, 1997). Not surprisingly, since age is a known predictor of length of time in treatment, adolescents are less likely to remain in treatment than are adults. As compared to adults, it is not known if compulsory treatment works. In fact, to the extent an adolescent TC resembles a boot camp, it probably does not work very well. Moreover, for adolescents who complete residential treatment, it is not clear what the outcome expectations should be. Even when limited outcome data has shown some reduction in substance use, this has not been true of the "recreational" drugs alcohol and marijuana (Pompi, 1994). It is unreasonable to expect adolescent TC graduates to have the outcome expected of adults—self-reliance—when job, education, and family living circumstances are unlikely to have been resolved. One exception [is] educationally focused TCs like the John Dewey Academy in

Massachusetts. This TC is a "college prepa-ratory, therapeutic, residential high school that provides intensive services for gifted, self-destructive adolescents" (Bratter et al., 1997). A combination of a professional and self-help model TC, the John Dewey Acad-emy has had remarkable success in graduat-ing its clients and placing them in college. On the whole, however, adolescent TCs, while having intrinsic appeal as an intervention with youth in crisis and in need of habilitation or rehabilitation, must still be considered an open question.

TCs for Women With Children

Traditionally women have been under served in terms of substance abuse treat-ment. A 1979 survey sponsored by NIDA identified only 44 programs in the nation that provided specialized substance abuse treatment services to women (Beschner and Thompson, 1981). Although some early TCs admitted women clients, they as well did not provide specialized programs directed at women, particularly women with children. Stevens and Glider (1994) suggest that two things changed this focus beginning in the 1980s: first, a marked increase in the num-ber of women seeking treatment, particu-larly for cocaine addiction. These women were often single parents, primary care-givers and increasingly pregnant at the time they presented for treatment. Second, the passage of the 1986 Omnibus Drug Bill led to a marked increase in interest and funding for drug treatment in special populations and drug prevention among high-risk youth. This legislation had implications for other special populations, but the effect was more pronounced for women in need of treat-ment. The federal agencies now known as the Center for Substance Abuse Treatment and the Center for Substance Abuse Prevention greatly increased the funding for programs for women with children.

As with many special population TCs, there is little outcome data on the effective-ness of TCs designed especially for women with children. However, some preliminary studies do suggest a real benefit for women in terms of retention in treatment and posi-tive changes (Stevens et al., 1997; Winick and Evans, 1997).

TCs for MICA Clients

The mentally ill chemically abusing (MICA) client is a significant and growing problem. For many years the two conditions were rarely treated together. Until the 1960s institutions effectively hid or controlled the substance abusing element among the men-tally ill. However, the movement toward deinstitutionalization of the mentally ill has had the effect of increasing the homeless population and of encouraging substance use as a means of self-treating mental illness. One important variable to ascertain in treat-ing MICA clients is whether substance use precedes or antedates the psychiatric problems (Jainchill, 1994).

TCs for MICA clients retain the peer ori-entation and, even more than in other TCs, rely on a routinized daily regimen to struc-ture clients' daily lives. They do make modi-fications in the intensity of group sessions, and allow for more attention to case man-agement needs. Psychotropic medications are allowed when medically indicated. Such TCs have been successfully introduced in both hospital (Silberstein et al., 1997) and community (Sacks et al., 1997) settings. MICA programs are also characterized by the need for a long-term aftercare and sup-port program for clients who do return to the outside community.

TCs in Corrections

The TC has had its greatest impact and widest application in corrections. Correc-tional systems have long recognized the util-ity of implementing treatment programs for their "captive" populations, over two-thirds of whom have substance abuse problems (Petersen, 1974). Prison TCs, like other ther-apeutic communities, are designed to pro-vide a total treatment environment in which a drug user's transformations in behavior, at-titudes, emotions, and values are introduced and inculcated. Throughout the 1960s and into the 1970s, TCs were the most visible type of treatment in correctional settings, but by the early 1980s, almost all of these

TCs had closed, the result of prison crowding, state budget deficits, staff burnout or blowup, and changes in prison leadership (Camp and Camp, 1990).

Despite these early failures, the correctional TC reemerged in the late 1980s and demonstrated great promise in the treatment of substance abuse (De Leon, 1985; Yablonsky, 1989). TCs modified their approaches from the earlier Synanon models. Staff had more professional training and credentials, inmates were given appropriate power and rewards without too much program control, and TC programs worked with institutional staff rather than in opposition (Wexler, 1995). At the same time, correctional approaches were again becoming more favorable to the concept of rehabilitation, no doubt spurred by the massive prison crowding accompanying the increased use of determinate and mandatory minimum sentences for drug-involved offenders (Inciardi and Martin, 1993; Wexler, 1995). Moreover, correctional administrators and clinicians found TCs useful in improving client attitudes and inmate comportment (Wexler, Falkin, Lipton, Rosenblum, and Goodlue, 1988; Field, 1989; Inciardi and Scarpitti, 1992).

TCs in corrections have moved from the early prison-only applications to a variety of programs combining in-prison, transitional and aftercare elements at the long extreme to short-term (one-to-five month programs) in prisons and jails at the short extreme. The desire to have shorter programs to treat more clients and to treat them cheaper per client is understandable, but as some of the evidence reviewed below reveals, the effects of short-term treatment, while significant, are also relatively short-lived.

Outcome Studies

Apsler (1991) listed factors that singly or jointly would improve treatment outcome research: measures on the variability among treatment programs, long project periods, objective validation of self-report measures, the cooperation of the treatment programs, large samples, multiple measures of treatment experience, and multiple measures of outcomes. Recently, Knight and colleagues (1999) have reiterated this list and added to it the need for common, or at least comparable, indicators across studies.

Because of interest in the past 10 years, particularly by the National Institute on Drug Abuse, TCs have been the subject of a number of studies of effectiveness. Many of the shortcomings noted by Apsler have been addressed through NIDA-funded research during the past decade; a number of studies began reporting encouraging initial results from the use of therapeutic community treatment programs for drug-abusers. Yet even with increased support for research and recognition of the need for outcome data, the systematic assessment of specific, promising, effective, and replicable TC programs did not advance concomitantly with the increases in the number of new programs. The dilemmas of conducting field studies that can be rigorously evaluated proved difficult to solve. Consequently, most assessments of program effectiveness were *process* rather than *outcome* oriented and did not incorporate multiple outcome criteria. Outcome research, when attempted, involved short follow-up time frames and included only limited use of comparison groups, standardized measurement instruments, multivariate models, and appropriate control variables (Forcier, 1991; Rouse, 1991; Wexler, 1995; De Leon, Inciardi, and Martin, 1995).

The great majority of these outcome studies of TC programs have been in correctional systems (Lipton, 1995; Graham and Wexler, 1997; Inciardi and Lockwood, 1994; Nielsen and Scarpitti, 1997; Knight, Simpson, and Hiller, 1996; Mello et al., 1997; Hiller et al., in press; Wexler et al., 1999). Many of the studies reporting the effectiveness of prison therapeutic communities in reducing relapse and recidivism have documented significant effects, but usually over relatively short terms—6 to 12 months after release from prison (Lipton, 1995; Glider et al., 1997; Inciardi et al., 1997). Very recently, several studies showing TC effectiveness have appeared documenting significant results three years after release from prison (Knight et al., 1999; Wexler et al., 1999; Martin et al., 1999). All of these studies show a pronounced effect of TC treatment when accompanied by transitional treatment and/or aftercare in reducing recidivism three years after release from prison. Recidivism averaged under 30% for the TC/aftercare treated versus about 70% for those not so treated.

Emerging Trends and Research

1. *Modified Therapeutic Communities. Since the 1980s, many therapeutic communities have been modified from the traditional model in a number of ways in an effort to adapt specifically to patient needs and funding limitations. TCs have been modified by using shorter lengths of stay (3, 6 and 12 months) and through establishing day treatment and outpatient programs. Obviously, many of these modifications are for cost-savings. In addition, as we noted earlier, numerous correctional settings and homeless shelters, as well as medical and mental institutions, have initiated a variety of different types of therapeutic communities. Modified therapeutic communities are also targeting adolescents. Programs have been designed exclusively for juveniles because of their emotional and treatment needs. Other TCs have adapted their programming to address the special needs of addicted mothers and their children, and prison and work release populations.*

One of the more notable developments in modified TCs has been the involvement of the client's family. Although having a strong support system has always been important, in recent years families have had extensive involvement in both short term and long term TC programs. Important, as well, has been the provision of specialized health care education. Because of the growing number of clients with HIV/AIDS, virtually almost all TCs have instituted risk reduction programs and HIV testing.

Since the majority of modified TCs have a shorter length of stay, aftercare services have been instituted. These serve to extend the period of treatment, with the purpose of providing community support, relapse prevention, and access to community service agencies that can assist in the recovery process.

2. *Multi-modality Approaches. In recent years, multi-modality approaches have emerged that include a combination of therapeutic community concepts and other types of treatment, such as methadone maintenance, family therapy, drug education, AA/NA, relapse prevention, and other treatment approaches. The programs, which often exist in a single community, are ancillary, rather than competitive with, one another.*

De Leon has examined the impact of combining TC and methadone maintenance modules in his Passages program. Many of the main components of TCs remained the same; however, certain aspects were changed to accommodate methadone clients. Although TCs are typically "drug free" programs, Passages permitted the use of methadone as an opiate substitute, provided greater emphasis on outreach, increased the flexibility of the format, and reduced the intensity of the personal and interpersonal interactions (De Leon et al., 1995). Detoxification from methadone was not seen as essential to the recovery process, but some clients voluntarily chose detoxification at some point of the program. And although the program was transformed into a day treatment rather than a twenty-four hour residential approach, like typical TCs Passages promoted a culture where clients learned through a self-help process in order to produce change. Although a twist on the usual TC treatment program, outcome data suggested that the Passages program yielded a clinically observable decrease in drug use and improvement in the level of functioning during the first six months.

An alternative form of multi-modality program was instituted at Walden House in San Francisco. Walden House established a TC day treatment program by transferring TC concepts and philosophy to a nonresidential setting (Bucardo et al., 1997). The original purpose of this type of treatment was to assist those individuals who were awaiting acceptance into a therapeutic community. As this treatment method developed, it became its own unique form of intervention. The day treatment program contains the same rules and norms of the original TC by addressing clients as members of a community. In Walden House, the central belief is that each client has the potential for growth and change.

3. *Compulsory treatment. An important corollary to the extensive and impressive data on treatment outcome being a function of length of time in treatment are the data supportive of compulsory and coerced treatment for drug offenders (Leukefeld and Tims, 1988; Hubbard et al., 1989; De Leon, 1988; Platt et al., 1988). In this regard, evaluation studies have demonstrated that the key variable most related to success in treatment is length of stay, and that those coerced into treatment do as well as voluntary commitments and in fact do better because they tend to remain longer in treatment than voluntary commitments.*

4. *The TC treatment continuum. Recently, Inciardi and colleagues have argued that an integrated continuum of corrections-based TC treatment works best for seriously drug-involved offenders. This continuum involves three stages of therapeutic community treatment, tied to an inmate's changing correctional status: prison "work release" parole or other form of community supervision (Inciardi, Lockwood, and Martin, 1991, 1994).*

The *primary* treatment occurs in a prison-based TC designed to facilitate personal growth through the modification of deviant lifestyles and behavior patterns. Segregated from the rest of the penitentiary, recovery from drug abuse and the development of pro-social values in the prison TC would involve essentially the same mechanisms seen in community-based TCs. Ideally, it should last for 9 to 12 months (Wexler et al., 1988), and client recruits should be within 12 to 15 months of work release eligibility.

Since the 1970s, work release has become a widespread correctional practice for felony offenders being released from prison: Inmates work for pay in the free community but spend their nonworking hours in an institution or a community-based work release facility or "halfway house" (Inciardi, 1999). This initial freedom exposes inmates to old groups and behaviors that can easily lead them back to substance abuse, criminal activities, and reincarceration. Even those receiving intensive TC treatment while in the institution face the prospect of their recovery breaking down. Thus, *secondary* TC treatment is warranted. This *secondary* stage is a "transitional TC"—the therapeutic community work release center—with a program composition similar to that of the traditional TC.

In the *tertiary* or "aftercare" stage, clients have completed work release and are living in the free community under parole or some other form of supervision. Treatment intervention in this stage should involve continued monitoring by TC counselors, including regular outpatient counseling, group therapy, and family sessions.

This model is for correctional clients, but the argument is appropriate to other TC settings, particularly some "special populations." For some long-term TC clients in community or MICA TCs, issues of community reintegration are not paramount because there are no short-term prospects for the client leaving the TC. For most TC clients, however, reintegration into the larger community is a real goal. The rationale for the development of special population TCs and multi-modality approaches are efforts to adapt the traditional TC approach to deal with issues other than substance use. The continuum approach is another important extension of the TC model to provide support in the process of transitions—be it back to the family, gainful employment, self-support—and to tailor that support to the particular demands and risks of the transition.

References

Apsler, R. (1991). "Evaluating the cost-effectiveness of drug abuse treatment services," pp. 57–66 in W. S. Cartwright and J. M. Kaple (eds.), *Economic Costs, Cost-effectiveness, Financing, and Community-based Drug Treatment*, NIDA research monograph 113.

Rockville, MD: U.S. Department of Health and Human Services.

Bailey, Walter C. (1966). "Correctional outcome: An evaluation of 100 reports," *Journal of Criminal Law, Criminology, and Police Science* 57(June):153–160.

Beschner, G., and Thompson, P. (1981). *Women and Drug Abuse Treatment: Needs and Services.* DHHS, No. (ADM) 81-1057. Rockville, MD: NIDA.

Bratter, B. I., Bratter, T. E., Bratter, C. J., Maxym, C., and Steiner, K.M. (1997). "The John Dewey Academy: A moral caring community (an amalgamation of the professional model and self-help concept of the therapeutic community)," pp. 179–195 in George De Leon (ed.), *Community as Method: Therapeutic Communities for Special Populations and Special Settings.* Westport, CT: Praeger.

Bucardo, J., Guydish, J., Acampora, A., and Werdegar, D. (1997). "The therapeutic community model applied to day treatment of substance abuse," pp. 213–224 in George De Leon (ed.), *Community as Method: Therapeutic Communities for Special Populations and Special Settings.* Westport, CT: Greenwood Press.

Camp, G. M., and Camp, C. G. (1990). *Preventing and Solving Problems Involved in Operating Therapeutic Communities in a Prison Setting.* South Salem, NY: Criminal Justice Institute.

Casriel, D. (1963). *So Fair a House: The Story of Synanon.* Englewood Cliffs, NJ: Prentice Hall.

Chaiken, M. R., and Johnson, B. D. (1988). *Characteristics of Different Types of Drug-Involved Offenders.* Washington, D.C.: National Institute of Justice.

De Leon, G. (1997). *Community as Method: Therapeutic Communities for Special Populations and Special Settings.* Westport, CT: Greenwood Publishing Group, Inc.

——. (1985). "The therapeutic community: Status and evolution," *International Journal of the Addictions* 20:823–844.

——. (1986). "The therapeutic community for substance abuse: Perspective and approach," pp. 14–18 in George De Leon and James Ziegenfuss (eds.), *Therapeutic Communities for Addictions.* Springfield, IL: Charles C. Thomas.

——. (1988). "The therapeutic community perspective and approach to adolescent substance abusers," *Annals of Adolescent Psychiatry* 15:535–556.

——. (1994). "Therapeutic communities," pp. 391–393 in Marc Galanter and Herbert Kleber (eds.), *Textbook of Substance Abuse Treatment.* Washington, D.C.: American Psychiatric Press.

De Leon, G., Inciardi, J. A., and Martin, S. S. (1995). "Residential drug treatment research: Are conventional control designs appropriate for assessing treatment effectiveness?" *Journal of Psychoactive Drugs* 27(1):85–91.

Field, G. (1989). "The effects of intensive treatment on reducing the criminal recidivism of addicted offenders," *Federal Probation* (December):51–56.

Forcier, M. W. (1991). "Substance abuse, crime and prison-based treatment: Problems and prospects," *Sociological Practice Review* 2(2): 123–131.

Glider, P., Mullen, R., Herbst, D., Davis, C., and Fleishman, B. (1997). "Substance abuse treatment in a jail setting: A therapeutic community model," pp. 97–112 in George De Leon (ed.), *Community as Method: Therapeutic Communities for Special Populations and Special Settings.* Westport, CT: Praeger.

Graham, W. F., and Wexler, H. K. (1997). "The amity therapeutic community program at Donovan Prison: Program description and approach," in George De Leon (ed.), *Community as Method.* Westport, CT: Praeger.

Hiller, M. L., Knight, K., and Simpson, D. D. (in press). "Prison-based substance abuse treatment, residential aftercare, and recidivism," *Addiction.*

Hinshelwood, R. D. (1986). "Britain and the psychoanalytic tradition in therapeutic communities," pp. 43–54 in George De Leon and James T. Ziegenfuss (eds.), *Therapeutic Communities for Addictions: Readings in Theory, Research and Practice.* Springfield, IL: Charles C. Thomas.

Hood, R. (1967). "Research on the effectiveness of punishments and treatments," in European Committee on Crime Problems, *Collected Studies in Criminological Research.* Strasbourg: Council of Europe.

Hooper, R. M., Lockwood, D., and Inciardi, J. A. (1993). "Treatment techniques in corrections-based therapeutic communities," *The Prison Journal* 73(September–December):290–306.

Hubbard, R. L., Marsden, M. E., Rachal, J. C., Harwood, H. J., Cavanaugh, E. R., and Ginzburg, H. M. (1989). *Drug Abuse Treatment: A National Study of Effectiveness.* Chapel Hill, NC: University of North Carolina Press.

Inciardi, J. A. (1967). *The Daytop Village Therapeutic Community.* Albany: New York State Division of Parole.

Inciardi, J. A. (1999). *Criminal Justice,* 6th edition. Ft. Worth, TX: Harcourt Brace.

Inciardi, J. A., and Lockwood, D. (1994). "When worlds collide: Establishing CREST Outreach Center," pp. 63–78 in B. W. Fletcher, J. A.

Inciardi, and A. M. Horton (eds.), *Drug Abuse Treatment: The Implementation of Innovative Approaches*. Westport, CT: Greenwood Press.

Inciardi, J. A., Lockwood, D., and Martin, S. S. (1991). *Therapeutic Communities in Corrections and Work Release: Some Clinical and Policy Considerations*. Paper presented at National Institute on Drug Abuse Technical Review Meeting on Therapeutic Community Treatment Research, May 16–17, Bethesda, Maryland.

Inciardi, J. A., Lockwood, D., and Martin, S. S. (1994). "Therapeutic communities in corrections and work release: Some clinical and policy implications," pp. 259–267 in F. M. Tims, G. De Leon, and N. Jainchill (eds.), *Therapeutic community: Advances in research and application*, NIDA research monograph 144. Rockville, MD: U.S. Department of Health and Human Services.

Inciardi, J. A., and Martin, S. S. (1993). "Drug abuse treatment in criminal justice settings," *Journal of Drug Issues* 23(1):1–6.

Inciardi, J. A., Martin, S. S., Butzin, C. A., Hooper, R. M., and Harrison, L. D. (1997). "An effective model of prison-based treatment for drug-involved offenders," *Journal of Drug Issues* 27(2):261–278.

Inciardi, J. A., and Scarpitti, F. R. (1992). *Therapeutic Communities in Corrections: An Overview*. Paper presented at the annual meeting of the Academy of Criminal Justice Sciences, Pittsburgh, Pennsylvania.

Jainchill, N. (1994). "Co-morbidity and therapeutic community treatment," pp. 209–231 in F. M. Tims, G. De Leon, and N. Jainchill (eds.), *Therapeutic Community: Advances in Research and Application*, NIDA Research Monograph 144. Washington, DC: Supt of Docs., U.S. Govt. Print. Off.

Jainchill, N. (1997). "Therapeutic communities for adolescents: The same and not the same," pp. 161–177 in George De Leon (ed.), *Community as Method: Therapeutic Communities for Special Populations and Special Settings*. Westport, CT: Praeger.

Jainchill, N., Bhattacharya, G., and Yagelka, J. (1995). "Therapeutic communities for adolescents," pp.190–217 in E. Rahdert and D. Czechowitz (eds.), *Adolescent Drug Abuse: Clinical Assessment and Therapeutic Interventions*, NIDA Research Monograph 153. Washington, D.C.: Supt of Docs., U.S. Govt. Print. Off.

Jones, M. (1953). *The therapeutic community: A new treatment method in psychiatry*. New York: Basic Books.

Klockars, C. B. (1975). "The true limits of the effectiveness of correctional treatment," *The Prison Journal* 55(Spring-Summer):53–64.

Knight, K., Simpson, D. D., and Hiller, M. L. (1996). *Evaluation of Prison-based Treatment and Aftercare*. Paper presented at the annual meeting of the American Psychological Association, Toronto, Canada.

Knight, K., Hiller, M. L., and Simpson, D. D. (1999). "Evaluating corrections-based treatment for the drug-abusing criminal offender," *Journal of Psychoactive Drugs* 31(3):299–304.

Knight, K., Simpson, D. D., and Hiller, M. (1999). "3-year reincarceration outcomes for in-prison therapeutic community treatment in Texas," *The Prison Journal* 79.

Kooyman, M. (1986). "The psychodynamics of therapeutic communities for the treatment of heroin addiction," pp. 29–42 in George De Leon and James T. Ziegenfuss (eds.), *Therapeutic Communities for Addictions: Readings in Theory Research and Practice*. Springfield, IL: Charles C. Thomas.

Kooyman, M. (1993). The Therapeutic Community for Addicts. Amsterdam: Swets and Zeitlinger.

Leukefeld, C. G., and Tims, F. M. (1988). "Compulsory treatment: A review of the findings," pp. 236–254 in C. G. Leukefeld and F. M. Tims (eds.), *Compulsory Treatment of Drug Abuse: Research and Clinical Practice*. NIDA Research Monograph 86. Rockville, MD: U.S. Department of Health and Human Services.

Lipton, D., Martinson, R., and Wilks, J. (1975). *The Effectiveness of Correctional Treatment: A Survey of Treatment Evaluation Studies*. New York: Praeger.

Lipton, D. S. (1995). *The Effectiveness of Treatment for Drug Abusers under Criminal Justice Supervision*. Washington, D.C.: National Institute of Justice.

Marshall, M. J., and Marshall, S. (1993). "Homogeneous versus heterogeneous age group treatment of adolescent substance abusers," *American Journal of Drug and Alcohol Abuse* 19:199–207.

Martin, S. S., Butzin, C. A., Saum, C. A., and Inciardi, J. A. (1999). "3-year outcomes of therapeutic community treatment for drug-involved offenders in Delaware: From prison to work release to aftercare," *The Prison Journal* 79:294–320.

Martinson, R. (1974). "What works?—Questions and answers about prison reform," *The Public Interest* 35(Spring):22–54.

Mello, C. O., Pechansky, F., Inciardi, J. A., and Surratt, H. L. (1997). "Participant observation of a therapeutic community model for offenders in drug treatment," *Journal of Drug Issues* 27:299–314.

Nielsen, A. L., and Scarpitti, F. R. (1997). "Changing the behavior of substance abusers: Factors influencing the effectiveness of therapeutic communities," *Journal of Drug Issues* 27(2):279–298.

Palmer, T. (1975). "Martinson revisited," *Journal of Research in Crime and Delinquency* 12 (July):133–152.

Petersen, D. M. (1974). "Some reflections on compulsory treatment of addiction," pp. 143–169 in J. A. Inciardi and C. D. Chambers (eds.), *Drugs and the Criminal Justice System.* Beverly Hills, CA: Sage.

Pompi, K. F. (1994). "Adolescents in therapeutic communities: Retention and posttreatment outcome," pp. 128–161 in F. M. Tims, G. De Leon, and N. Jainchill (eds.), *Therapeutic Community: Advances in Research and Application.* NIDA Research Monograph 144. Washington, DC: Supt of Docs., U.S. Govt. Print. Off.

Robison, J. (1971). "The irrelevance of correctional programs," *Crime and Delinquency* 17 (January):67–80.

Rouse, J. J. (1991). "Evaluation research on prison based drug treatment programs and some policy implications," *The International Journal of the Addictions* 26:29–44.

Sacks, S., De Leon, G., Bernhardt, A. J., and Sacks, J. Y. (1997). "A modified therapeutic community for homeless mentally ill chemical abusers," pp. 19–37 in George De Leon (ed.), *Community as Method: Therapeutic Communities for Special Populations and Special Settings.* Westport, CT: Praeger.

Shelly, J. A., and Bassin, A. (1965). "Daytop Lodge: A new treatment approach for drug addicts," *Corrective Psychiatry* 2(July):180–193.

Silberstein, C. H., Metzger, E. J., and Galanter, M. (1997). "The Greenhouse: A modified therapeutic community for mentally ill homeless addicts at New York University–Bellevue Medical Center," pp. 53–65 in George De Leon (ed.), *Community as Method: Therapeutic Communities for Special Populations and Special Settings.* Westport, CT: Praeger.

Stevens, S. J., Arbiter, N., and McGrath, R. (1997). "Women and children: Therapeutic community substance abuse treatment," pp. 129–141 in George De Leon (ed.), *Community as Method: Therapeutic Communities for Special Populations and Special Settings.* Westport, CT: Praeger.

Stevens, S. J., and Glider, P. J. (1994). "Therapeutic communities: Substance abuse treatment for women," pp. 162–180 in F. M. Tims, G. De Leon, and N. Jainchill (eds.), *Therapeutic Community: Advances in Research and Application,* NIDA Research Monograph 144. Washington, DC: Supt of Docs., U.S. Govt. Print. Off.

Wexler, H. K. (1995). "The success of therapeutic communities for substance abusers in American prisons," *Journal of Psychoactive Drugs* 27:57–66.

Wexler, H. K., De Leon, G., Thomas, G., Kressel, D., and Peters, J. (1999). "The Amity prison TC evaluation: Reincarceration outcomes," *Criminal Justice and Behavior* 26(2):147–167.

Wexler, H. K., Falkin, G. P., Lipton, D. S., Rosenblum, A. B., and Goodlue, H. P. (1988). *A Model Prison Rehabilitation Program: An Evaluation of the "Stay'n Out" Therapeutic Community.* New York: Narcotic and Drug Research, Inc.

Wexler, H. K., Melnick, G., Lowe, L., and Peters, J. (1999). "3-year reincarceration outcomes for Amity in-prison therapeutic community and aftercare in California," *The Prison Journal* 79:321.

White, W. (1998). *Slaying the Dragon.* Bloomington, IL: Chestnut Health Systems.

Wilson, J. Q. (1980). " 'What works?' revisited: New findings on criminal rehabilitation," *The Public Interest* 61(Fall):3–17.

Winick, C., and Evans, J. T. (1997). "A therapeutic community program for mothers and their children," pp. 143–159 in George De Leon (ed.), *Community as Method: Therapeutic Communities for Special Populations and Special Settings.* Westport, CT: Praeger.

Yablonsky, L. (1967). *Synanon: The Tunnel Back.* New York: Macmillan.

Yablonsky, L. (1989). *The Therapeutic Community: A Successful Approach for Treating Substance Abusers.* New York: Gardner.

For Discussion

Should therapeutic communities be expected to work for persons regardless of their drug of choice? What groups, if any, might not be suitable for therapeutic communities?

36

Methadone Maintenance

A Theoretical Perspective

Vincent P. Dole
Marie Nyswander

Whereas therapeutic communities view drug addiction as an underlying symptom of other life problems, methadone maintenance treatment sees addiction as a disease rather than an expression of a character or psychological disorder.

When administered orally, methadone serves to "block" the euphoric effects of heroin. That is, when an individual is given sufficient doses of methadone, he or she will be unable to "get high" from heroin. Vincent P. Dole and Marie Nyswander were the first in the United States to introduce methadone as a treatment for heroin addiction. In this article, these investigators discuss issues related to methadone treatment. Their study of methadone clients found that criminal activity decreased greatly when addicts were enrolled in maintenance programs. This finding, they argue, suggests that antisocial behavior, such as criminal activity, occurs as a result rather than a cause of drug addiction.

The Methadone Maintenance Research Program (Dole and Nyswander 1965, 1966; Dole et al. 1966) began in 1963 with pharmacological studies conducted on the metabolic ward of the Rockefeller University Hospital. Only six addict patients were treated during the first year, but the results of this work were sufficiently impressive to justify a trial of maintenance treatment of heroin addicts admitted to open medical wards of general hospitals in the city.

The dramatic improvements in social status of patients on this program exceeded expectations. The study started with the hope that heroin-seeking behavior would be stopped by a narcotic blockade, but it certainly was not expected that we would be able to retain more than 90 percent of the patients and that almost three-fourths would be socially productive and living as normal citizens in the community after only six months of treatment. Prior to admission, almost all of the patients had supported their heroin habits by theft or other anti-social activities. Further handicapped by the ostracism of the community, slum backgrounds, minority group status, school dropout status, prison records, and anti-social companions, they had seemed poor prospects for social rehabilitation.

The unexpected response of these patients to a simple medical program forced us to reexamine some of the assumptions that we brought to the study. Either the patients that we admitted to treatment were quite exceptional, or we had been misled by the traditional theories of addiction (Terry and Pellens 1928). If, as is generally assumed, our patients' long-standing addiction to heroin had been based on weaknesses of character—either a self-indulgent quest for euphoria or a need to escape reality—it was difficult to understand why they so consistently accepted a program that blocked the euphoric action of heroin and other narcotic drugs, or how they could overcome the frustrations and anxieties of competitive society to hold responsible jobs.

Implicit in the maintenance programs is an assumption that heroin addiction is a metabolic disease, rather than a psychological problem. Although the reasons for taking the initial doses of heroin may be considered psychological—adolescent curiosity or neurotic anxiety—the drug, for whatever reason it is first taken, leaves its imprint on the nervous system. This phenomenon is clearly seen in animal studies: a rat, if addicted to morphine by repeated injections at one to two months of age and then detoxified, will show a residual tolerance and abnormalities in brain waves in response to challenge doses of morphine for months, perhaps for the rest of its life. Simply stopping the drug does not restore the nervous system of this animal to its normal, pre-addiction condition. Since all studies to date have shown a close association between tolerance and physical dependence, and since the discomfort of physical dependence leads to drug-seeking activity, a persistence of physical dependence would explain why both animals and humans tend to relapse to use of narcotics after detoxification. This metabolic theory of relapse obviously has different implications for treatment than the traditional theory that relapse is due to moral weakness.

Whatever the theory, all treatment should be measured by results. The main issue, in our opinion, is whether the treatment can enable addicts to become normal, responsible members of society; and, if medication contributes to this result, it should be regarded as useful chemotherapy. Methadone, like sulfanilamide of the early antibiotic days, undoubtedly will be supplanted by better medications, but the success of methadone maintenance programs has at least established the principle of treating addicts medically.

The efficacy of methadone as a medication must be judged by its ability or failure to achieve the pharmacological effect that is intended—namely, elimination of heroin hunger and heroin-seeking behavior, and blockade against the euphoriant actions of heroin. The goal of social rehabilitation of criminal addicts by a treatment program is a much broader objective: it includes the stopping of heroin abuse, but is not limited to this pharmacological effect. Failures in rehabilitation programs, therefore, must be analyzed to determine whether they are due to failures of the medicine, or to inability of the therapists to rehabilitate patients who have stopped heroin use. Individuals who have stopped heroin use with methadone treatment but who continue to steal, drink excessively, or abuse non-narcotic drugs, or are otherwise anti-social, are failures of the rehabilitation program but not of the medication.

When the Food and Drug Administration asks for proof of efficacy of a new drug, it is the pharmacological efficacy that is in question. For example, diphenylhydantoin is accepted as an efficacious drug for prevention of epileptic seizures. Whether or not the treated epileptics obtain employment, or otherwise lead socially useful lives, is not relevant to the evaluation of this drug as an efficacious drug for prevention of epileptic seizures or as an anti-convulsant; similarly with methadone.

With thousands of patients now living socially acceptable lives with methadone blockade, and with many more street addicts waiting for admission, the question as to whether these patients are exceptional is no longer a practical issue. The theoretical question, however, remains: is addiction caused by an antecedent character defect, and does the maintenance treatment merely mask the symptoms of an addictive personality? The psychogenic theory of addiction would say so. This theory has a long history—at least 100 years (Terry and Pellens 1928)—and is accepted as axiomatic by many people. What, then, is the evidence for it?

Review of the literature discloses two arguments to support the psychogenic, or character defect, theory: the sociopathic behavior and attitude of addicts and the inability of addicts to control their drug-using impulse. Of these arguments, the first is the most telling. Even a sympathetic observer must concede that addicts are self-centered and indifferent to the needs of others. To the family and the community, the addict is irresponsible, a thief, and a liar. These traits, which are quite consistently associated with addiction, have been interpreted as showing a specific psychopathology. What is lacking in this argument is proof that the sociopathic traits preceded addiction.

It is important to distinguish the causes from the consequences of addiction. The decisive proof of a psychogenic theory would be a demonstration that potential addicts could be identified by psychiatric examination before drug usage had distorted behavior and metabolic functions. However, a careful search of the literature has failed to disclose any study in which a characteristic psychopathology or "addictive personality" has been recognized in a number of individuals prior to addiction. Retrospective studies, in which a record of delinquency before addiction is taken as evidence of sociopathic tendencies, fail to provide the comparative data needed for diagnosis of deviant personality. Most of the street addicts in large cities come from the slums, where family structure is broken and drugs are available. Both juvenile delinquency and drug use are common. Some delinquents become addicted to narcotic drugs under these conditions, whereas others do not. There is no known way to identify the future addicts among the delinquents. No study has shown a consistent difference in behavior or pattern of delinquency of adolescents who later become addicts and those who do not.

Theft is the means by which most street addicts obtain money to buy heroin and, therefore, is nearly an inevitable consequence of addiction. For the majority, this is the only way that they can support an expensive heroin habit. The crime statistics show both the force of drug hunger and its specificity; almost all of the crimes committed by addicts relate to the procurement of drugs. The rapid disappearance of theft and antisocial behavior in patients on the methadone maintenance program strongly supports the hypothesis that the crimes that they had previously committed as addicts were a consequence of drug hunger, not the expression of some more basic psychopathology. The so-called sociopathic personality was no longer evident in our patients.

The second argument, that of deficient self-control, is more complicated, because it involves the personal experience of the critic as well as that of the patient. Moralists generally assume that opiates are dangerously pleasant drugs that can be resisted only by strength of character. The pharmacology is somewhat more complicated than this. For most normal persons morphine and heroin are not enjoyable drugs—at least not in the initial exposures. Given to a post-operative patient, these analgesics provide a welcome relief of pain, but addiction from such medical use is uncommon. When given to an average pain-free subject, morphine produces

nausea and sedation, but rarely euphoria. What, then, is the temptation to become an addict? So far as can be judged from the histories of addicts, many of them found the first trials of a narcotic in some sense pleasurable or tranquilizing, even though the drug also caused nausea and vomiting. Perhaps their reaction to the drug was abnormal, even on the first exposure. However this may be, with repeated use and development of tolerance to side effects, the euphoric action evolved and the subjects became established addicts.

Drug-seeking behavior, like theft, is observed after addiction is established and the narcotic drug has become euphorigenic. The question as to whether this abnormality in reaction stems from a basic weakness of character or is a consequence of drug usage is best studied when drug hunger is relieved. Patients on the methadone maintenance program, blockaded against the euphorigenic action of heroin, turn their energies to schoolwork and jobs. It would be easy for them to become passive, to live indefinitely on public support, and claim that they had done enough in winning the fight against heroin. Why they do not yield to this temptation is unclear, but in general they do not. Their struggles to become self-supporting members of the community should impress the critics who had considered them self-indulgent when drug-hungry addicts. When drug hunger is blocked without production of narcotic effects, the drug-seeking behavior ends.

So far as can be judged from retrospective data, narcotic drugs have been quite freely available in some areas of New York City, and experimentation by adolescents is common. The psychological and metabolic theories diverge somewhat in interpreting this fact; the first postulates preexisting emotional problems and a need to seek drugs for escape from reality, whereas the alternative is that trial of drugs, like smoking the first cigarette, may be a result of a normal adolescent curiosity and not of psychopathology (Wikler and Rasor 1953). As to the most important point—the reasons for continuation of drug use in some cases and not in others—there is no definitive information, either psychological or metabolic. This is obviously a crucial gap in knowledge. Systematic study of young adolescents in areas with high addiction rates is needed to define the process of becoming addicted and to open the way for prevention.

The other extreme—the cured addict—involves a controversy as to the goal of therapy. Those of us who are primarily concerned with the social productivity of our patients define success in terms of behavior—the ability of the patients to live as normal citizens in the community—whereas, other groups seek total abstinence, even if it means confinement of the subjects to an institution. This confusion of goals has barred effective comparison of treatment results.

Actually, the questions to be answered are straightforward and of great practical importance. Do the abstinent patients in the psychological programs have a residual metabolic defect that requires continued group pressure and institutionalization to enforce the abstinence? Conversely, do the patients who are blockaded with methadone exhibit any residual psychopathology? No evidence is available to answer the first question. As to the latter point, we can state that the evidence, so far, is negative. The attitudes, moods, and intellectual and social performance of patients are under continuous observation by a team of psychiatrists, internists, nurses, counselors, social workers, and psychologists. No consistent psychopathology has been noted by these observers or by the social agencies, to which we have referred patients for vocational placement. The good records of employment and school work further document the patients' capacity to win acceptance as normal citizens in the community.

The real revolution of the methadone era was its emphasis on rehabilitation, rather than on detoxification. This reversed the traditional approach to addiction, which had been based on the assumption that abstinence must come first. According to the old theory, rehabilitation is impossible while a person is taking drugs of any kind, including methadone. The success of methadone programs in rehabilitating addicts who had already failed in abstinence programs

decisively refuted this old theory. Indeed, nowhere in the history of treatment has a program with the abstinence approach achieved even a fraction of the retention rate and social rehabilitation now seen in the average methadone clinic. This statement includes all of the abstinence-oriented programs of governmental institutions, therapeutic communities, and religious groups for which any data are available (Brecher 1972; Glasscote 1972).

We believe that it is a serious mistake for programs to put a higher value on abstinence than on the patient's ability to function as a normal member of society. After the patient has arrived at a stable way of life with a job, a home, a position of respect in his community, and a sense of worth, it may or may not be best to discontinue methadone, but at least he can consider this option without pressure. The pharmacologic symptoms of withdrawal will be the same, whether or not the addict is socially rehabilitated; but with a job and family there is much more to lose if relapse occurs, and, therefore, the motivation to resist a return to heroin will be strong. The time spent in maintenance treatment does not make detoxification more difficult. It has proved very easy to withdraw methadone from patients who have been maintained for one to eight years when the reduction in dose has been gradual and the patient free from anxiety.

As with heroin, the real problems begin after withdrawal. The secondary abstinence syndrome, first described by Himmelsbach, Martin, Wikler, and colleagues at the United States Public Health Hospital, Lexington, Kentucky, in patients detoxified from morphine and heroin, reflects the persistence of metabolic and autonomic disturbances in the post-narcotic withdrawal period (Himmelsbach 1942; Martin et al. 1963; Martin and Jasinski 1969): these persistent abnormalities in metabolism are clearly pharmacologic, since they occur also in experimental animals addicted to narcotics and then detoxified. Follow-up studies of abstinent ex-addicts have emphasized the frequency of alcoholism and functional deterioration (Brecher 1972). An unfortunate consequence of the early enthusiasm for methadone treatment is today's general disenchantment with chemotherapy for addicts. What was not anticipated at the onset was the nearly universal reaction against the concept of substituting one drug for another, even when the second drug enabled the addict to function normally. Statistics, showing improved health and social rehabilitation of the patients receiving methadone, failed to meet this fundamental objection. The analogous long-term use of other medications, such as insulin and digitalis, in medical practice has not been considered relevant.

Perhaps the limitations of medical treatment for complex medical-social problems were not sufficiently stressed. No medicine can rehabilitate persons. Methadone maintenance makes possible a first step toward social rehabilitation by stabilizing the pharmacological condition of addicts who have been living as criminals on the fringe of society. But to succeed in bringing disadvantaged addicts to a productive way of life, a treatment program must enable its patients to feel pride and hope and to accept responsibility. This is often not achieved in present-day treatment programs. Without mutual respect, an adversary relationship develops between patients and staff, reinforced by arbitrary rules and the indifference of persons in authority. Patients held in contempt by the staff continue to act like addicts, and the overcrowded facility becomes a public nuisance. Understandably, methadone maintenance programs today have little appeal to the communities or to the majority of heroin addicts on the street.

Methadone maintenance, as part of a supportive program, facilitates social rehabilitation; but methadone treatment clearly does not prevent opiate abuse after it is discontinued, nor does social rehabilitation guarantee freedom from relapse. For the previously intractable heroin addict with a pretreatment history of several years of addiction and social problems, the most conservative course, in our opinion, is to emphasize social rehabilitation and encourage continued maintenance. On the other hand, for patients with shorter histories of heroin use, especially the young ones, a trial of withdrawal with a systematic follow-up is indicated when physician and patient feel ready for the test, and when they understand the potential problems after detoxification. The first step of withdrawing methadone is relatively easy and can be achieved with a variety of schedules, none of which have been shown to have any specific effect on the long-range outcome. The real issue is how well the patient does in the years after termination of maintenance.

References

Brecher, E. M. *Licit and Illicit Drugs.* Mt. Vernon, N. Y.: Consumers Union, 1972.

Dole, V. P., and Nyswander, M. E. A medical treatment for diacetylmorphine (heroin) addiction. *Journal of the American Medical Association,* 193:646–650, 1965.

Dole, V. P., and Nyswander, M. E. Rehabilition of heroin addicts after blockade with methadone. *New York State Journal of Medicine,* 55:2011–2017, 1966.

Dole, V. P., Nyswander, M. E., and Kreek, M. J. Narcotic blockade. *Archives of Internal Medicine,* 118:304–309, 1966.

Glasscote, R. M. et al. *The Treatment of Drug Abuse: Programs, Problems, Prospects.* Washington, D. C.: The Joint Information Service of the American Psychiatric Association and the National Association for Mental Health, 1972.

Himmelsbach, C. K. Clinical studies of drug addiction, physical dependence, withdrawal and recovery. *Archives of Internal Medicine,* 69:766, 1942.

Martin, W. R., and Jasinski, D. R. Physiological parameters of morphine dependence in intolerance, early abstinence, protracted abstinence. *Journal of Psychiatric Research,* 7:9–17, 1969.

Martin, W. R., Wikler, A., Eades, C. G., and Pescor, F. T. Tolerance to and physical dependence on morphine in rats. *Psychopharmacologia,* 4:247, 1963.

Nyswander, M. E., and Dole, V. P. Methadone maintenance and its implications for theories of narcotic addiction. *Research Publications of the Association for Research in Nervous and Mental Disease,* 49:359–366, 1968.

Terry, C. E., and Pellens, M. *The Opium Problem.* Montclair, N. J.: Patterson Smith, 1928.

Wikler, A., and Rasor, R. W. Psychiatric aspects of drug addiction. *American Journal of Medicine,* 14:566–570, 1953.

For Discussion

1. Experts on methadone maintenance often believe that some heroin users should be treated with methadone periodically throughout their lives. Who should fund life treatment? Is it cost-effective?

2. In the first section of this book, Lindesmith argues that individuals continue to use opiates to eliminate the pain associated with withdrawal. Is the philosophy of methadone treatment consistent with Lindesmith's theory of addiction? If so, how?

Reprinted from: Vincent P. Dole and Marie Nyswander, "Methadone Maintenance: A Theoretical Perspective." In *Theories on Drug Abuse*, Dan J. Lettieri, Mollie Sayers, and Helen Wallenstein Pearson (eds.). National Institute on Drug Abuse, 1980. ✦

37
The Elephant That No One Sees

Natural Recovery Among Middle-Class Addicts[1]

Robert Granfield
William Cloud

Stereotypical perceptions about drug and alcohol dependence often assume that addiction is associated with persons from low-income backgrounds and that persons dependent on drugs need treatment if they are to recover. This article dispels those myths by examining persons from middle-income backgrounds who overcame problems associated with drugs and alcohol without the benefit of formal treatment. Robert Granfield and William Cloud explore the concept of "addict identity" among these respondents and identify reasons that these persons avoided treatment. The authors also note various lifestyle aspects that appear to contribute to natural recovery. Their research findings appear to contradict the assumptions of predominant treatment ideologies.

Introduction

Social deviance literature typically portrays drug and alcohol addicted individuals as possessing distinct subcultural characteristics that marginalize them from the nonaddicted world. Whether this marginalization occurs because of a personality profile which predisposes an individual to addiction or whether it follows from being labeled and stigmatized as "an addict," the outcome is thought to be the same. Such individuals are considered to be distinctly different from the majority of the population. Indeed, the social deviance literature has played a role in classifying addicts as "other," thereby contributing to the production of an outsider status. However, as Waterston (1993:14) has recently argued, such portrayals have contributed to the "ghettoization" of drug users and to the "construction of a false separation between 'them and us.'"

While the social deviance paradigm of addiction has produced insightful material documenting the lifestyle, experiences, and world views of drug and alcohol addicted persons, this literature has excluded groups not conforming to the image of social disparagement. For instance, the social deviance perspective has been instructive in expanding our knowledge of "bottle gangs" and other alcoholic subcultures (Rubington 1967, 1968; Wiseman 1970), "crack whores" or crack-distributing gangs (Ratner 1993; Williams 1989), and the slum-dwelling heroin addict who injects in order to either enhance his/her social status or simply to escape the hopelessness of his/her own economic poverty (Stephens 1991; Hanson et al. 1985). Although such groups can be classified as "hidden populations" due to their powerlessness and poverty as well as the fact that these groups are largely omitted from national surveys (Lambert and Wiebel 1990), their actions are frequently visible. Inner-city heroin addicts, coke whores, and skid row alcoholics often come in direct contact with social control agents such as the police, the courts, treatment programs, hospitals, and researchers. Precisely because these groups are classified as deviant and are "othered," they are subject to social inspection and identification.

Often absent from the research on hidden populations are those drug addicts and alcoholics who fail to fit into the previously constructed categories that are consistent with current models of deviance. One such group that falls into such a category is the population of middle-class addicts. For instance, some heroin-addicted women from middle-class backgrounds are often able to avoid immersion into a heroin-using subculture, and also have better chances of recovery (Rosenbaum and Murphy 1990). According to these authors (1990:125), "it is possible for them to readjust more readily, because they often possess the resources necessary to start a new life." Such limited subcultural involvement may also result in an increased ability to circumvent detection. Similarly, many high-level drug dealers may remain hidden due to the secretive nature of their activity (Adler 1986). Thus, many drug users and drug dealers avoid detection because they occupy otherwise legitimate social roles and lead basically straight, middle-class lives (Biernacki 1986). In fact, recent scholarship has removed drug use from the world of deviance and has advanced alternative perspectives including the arguments that addiction is an act of cultural resistance (Waterston 1993), or one that locates addiction in the larger social, political, and economic contexts (Waldorf et al. 1991). Such views remove the unique characteristics associated with addiction and place it within the context of conventional social life (Becker 1963).

One population that remains hidden due to the fact that they deviate from socially constructed categories regarding addiction are middle-class drug addicts and alcoholics who terminate their addictive use of substances without treatment. Research exploring the phenomena of natural recovery has found that significant numbers of people discontinue their excessive intake of addictive substances without formal or lay treatment. While it is difficult to estimate the actual size of this hidden population because they are largely invisible (Lee 1993), researchers agree that their numbers are large (Goodwin et al. 1971) and some even contend that they are substantially larger than those choosing to enter treatment facilities or self-help groups (Sobell et al. 1993; Peele 1989; Biernacki 1986). Some have estimated that as many as 90% of problem drinkers never enter treatment and many suspend problematic use without it (Hingson et al. 1980; Roizen et al. 1978; Stall and Biernacki 1986). Research in Canada has shown that 82% of alcoholics who terminated their addiction reported using natural recovery (Sobell et al. 1993).

Research on natural recovery has focused on a variety of substances including heroin and other opiates (Valliant 1966; Waldorf and Biernacki 1977, 1981; Biernacki 1986), cocaine (Waldorf et al. 1991; Shaffer and Jones 1989), and alcohol (Valliant and Milofsky 1982; Valliant 1983; Stall and Biernacki 1986). Much of this literature challenges the dominant view that addiction relates primarily to the substance being consumed. The dominant addiction paradigm maintains that individuals possess an illness that requires intensive therapeutic intervention. Failure to acquire treatment is considered a sign of denial that will eventually lead to more advanced stages of addiction and possibly death. Given the firm convictions of addictionists as well as their vested interests in marketing this concept (Weisner and Room 1978; Abbott 1988), their rejection of the natural recovery research is of little surprise.

Research on natural recovery has offered great insight into how people successfully transform their lives without turning to professionals or self-help groups. The fact that people accomplish such transformations naturally is by no means a revelation. Most ex-smokers discontinue their tobacco use without treatment (Peele 1989) while many "mature out" of a variety of behaviors including heavy drinking and narcotics use (Snow 1973; Winick 1962). Some researchers examining such transformations frequently point to factors within the individual's social context that promote change. Not only are patterns of alcohol and drug use influenced by social contexts as Zinberg (1986) illustrated, but the experience of quitting as well can be understood from this perspective (Waldorf et al. 1991). Others have attributed natural recovery to a cognitive appraisal process in which the costs and benefits of continued drinking are assessed by alcoholics (Sobell et al. 1993).

Perhaps one of the most detailed investigations of natural recovery is Biernacki's (1986) detailed description of former heroin addicts. Emphasizing the importance of social contexts, Biernacki demonstrates how heroin addicts terminated their addictions and successfully transformed their lives. Most of the addicts in that study as well as others initiated self-recovery after experiencing an assortment of problems that led to a resolve to change. Additionally, Biernacki found that addicts who arrest addictions naturally utilize a variety of strategies. Such strategies involve breaking off relationships with drug users (Shaffer and Jones 1989), removing oneself from a drug-using environment (Stall and Biernacki 1986), building new structures in one's life (Peele 1989), and using social networks of friends and family that help provide support for this newly emerging status (Biernacki 1986). Although it is unclear whether the social contexts of those who terminate naturally is uniquely different from those who undergo treatment, it is certain that environmental factors significantly influence the strategies employed in the decision to stop.

While this literature has been highly instructive, much of this research has focused on respondents' circumvention of formal treatment such as therapeutic communities, methadone maintenance, psychotherapy, or regular counseling in outpatient clinics (Biernacki 1986). Many of those not seeking professional intervention may nevertheless participate in self-help groups. Self-help groups have been one of the most popular avenues for people experiencing alcohol and drug problems. This may be due in large part to the fact that groups such as Alcoholics Anonymous (AA), Narcotics Anonymous (NA), or Cocaine Anonymous (CA), medicalize substance abuse in such a way as to alleviate personal responsibility and related guilt (Trice and Roman 1970). Moreover, these groups contribute to the cultivation of a support community which helps facilitate behavioral change.

Despite these attractions and the popularity of these groups, many in the field remain skeptical about their effectiveness. Research has demonstrated that addicts who affiliate with self-help groups relapse at a significantly greater rate than do those who undergo hospitalization only (Walsh et al. 1992). Some have raised concerns about the appropriateness of self-help groups in all instances of addiction (Lewis et al. 1994). In one of the most turgid critiques of self-help groups, Peele (1989) estimates that nearly half of all those who affiliate with such groups relapse within the first year. Peele contends that these groups are not very effective in stopping addictive behaviors since such groups subscribe to the ideology of life-long addiction. Adopting the addict-for-life ideology, as many members do, has numerous implications for a person's identity as well as ways of relating to the world around them (Brown 1991).

Somewhere between the two positions of skepticism and optimism are the findings of Emrick et al. (1993). In one of the most comprehensive analyses of AA participation to date, their meta-analysis of 107 various studies on AA effectiveness report only a modest correlation between exposure to self-help groups and improved drinking behavior. They additionally point out the compelling need for further research on the personal characteristics of individuals for whom these programs are beneficial and those for whom they are not.

Given the emerging challenges to the dominant views of recovery, research on recovery will be advanced through an examination of those who terminated their addictive use of alcohol and drugs without the benefit of either formal or informal treatment modalities. While research has provided insight into those who reject formal treatment modalities, we know little about the population who additionally reject self-help groups, particularly those from middle-class backgrounds. This paper examines the process of natural recovery among middle-class drug addicts and alcoholics and first explores the identity of previously addicted middle-class respondents in relation to their past addictions. Next, respondents' reasons for rejecting self-help group involvement or formal treatment are examined. Strategies used by our respondents to terminate their addictions and transform their lives are then examined and the implications of our findings in relation to current addiction treatment are presented.

Method

Data for the present study were collected from a two-stage research design involving 46 former drug addicts and alcoholics. The initial stage of this study involving 25 interviews explored 3 primary areas. These areas included elements of respondents' successful cessation strategies, perceptions of self relative to former use, and attitudes toward treatment. The second stage of the study sharpened the focus of the exploration within these three areas. This was accomplished by constructing a new interview schedule designed to capture the most salient themes that emerged from the first stage of the study. In each phase of this study, lengthy, semistructured interviews with respondents were conducted to elicit thickly descriptive responses. All interviews were tape-recorded and later transcribed.

Strict criteria were established for respondent selection. First, respondents had to have been drug or alcohol dependent for a period of at least 1 year. On average, our respondents were dependent for a period of 9.14 years. Determination of dependency was made only after careful consideration; each respondent had to have experienced frequent cravings, extended periods of daily use, and associated personal problems due to their use. Second, to be eligible, individuals had to have terminated their addictive consumption for a period of at least 1 year prior to the interview. The mean length of time of termination from addiction for the entire sample was 5.5 years. Finally, the sample includes only individuals who had no, or only minimal, exposure to formal treatment. Individuals with short-term detoxification (up to 2 weeks) were included provided they had had no additional follow-up outpatient treatment. Also, individuals who had less than 1 month exposure to self-help groups such as AA, NA, or CA were included. Some of our respondents reported attending one or two of these self-help group meetings. However, the majority of our respondents had virtually no contact with formal treatment programs or self-help groups.

Respondents in this study were selected through "snowball sampling" techniques (Biernacki 1986). This sampling strategy uses referral chains of personal contacts in which people with appropriate characteristics are referred as volunteers. Snowball sampling has been used in a variety of studies involving hidden populations. In particular, snowball samples have been employed in previous studies of heroin users (Cloud 1987; Biernacki 1986) and cocaine users (Waldorf et al. 1991). In the present study, snowball sampling methods were necessary for two reasons. Since we were searching for a middle-class population that circumvented treatment, these individuals were widely distributed. Unlike those in treatment or in self-help groups, this population tends to be more dispersed. Also, these individuals did not wish to expose their pasts as former addicts. Very few people were aware of a respondent's drug- and alcohol-using history, making the respondent reluctant to participate. Consequently, personal contact with potential respondents prior to the interview was necessary to explain the interview process as well as the procedures to ensure confidentiality. While there are limitations to this sampling strategy, probability sampling techniques would be impossible since the characteristics of the population are unknown.

All of our respondents in the present study report having stable middle-class backgrounds. Each of the respondents had completed high school, the majority possessed college degrees, and several respondents held graduate degrees. Most were employed in professional occupations, including law, engineering, and health-related fields, held managerial positions, or operated their own businesses during their addiction. Of the respondents participating in this study, 30 were males and 16 were females. The age range in the sample was 25 to 60 with a mean age of 38.4 years.

Forming a Postaddict Identity

Research within the tradition of symbolic interaction has frequently explored the social basis of personal identity. Central to the symbolic interactionist perspective is the notion that personal identity is constituted through interaction with others who define social reality. From this perspective, the self emerges through a process of interaction with others and through the roles individuals occupy. Symbolic interactionists maintain that the self is never immutable, but rather change is an ongoing process in which new definitions of the self emerge as group affiliation and roles change. Consequently, identities arise from one's participation within social groups and organizations.

The perspective of symbolic interaction has frequently been used when analyzing the adoption of deviant identities. For instance, the societal reaction model of deviance views the formation of a spoiled identity as a consequence of labeling (Lemert 1951, 1974; Goffman 1963). Reactions against untoward behavior in the form of degradation ceremonies often give rise to deviant identities (Garfinkel 1967). In addition, organizations that seek to reform deviant behavior, encourage the adoption of a "sick role" for the purposes of reintegration (Parsons 1951). AA, for instance, teaches its members that they possess a disease and a lifelong addiction to alcohol (Trice and Roman 1970). Such organizations provide a new symbolic framework through which members undergo dramatic personal transformation.

Consequently, members adopt an addict role and identity, an identity that for many becomes salient (Brown 1991; Cloud 1987).[2] One respondent in Brown's study, for instance, indicated the degree of engulfment in the addict identity:

> Sobriety is my life's priority. I can't have my life, my health, my family, my job, or anything else unless I'm sober. My program [participation in AA] has to come first . . . Now I've come to realize that this is the nature of the disease. I need to remind myself daily that I'm an alcoholic. As long as I work my program, I am granted a daily reprieve from returning to drinking.

Brown's (1991:169) analysis of self-help programs and the identity transformation process that is fostered in those settings demonstrates that members learn "that they must constantly practice the principles of recovery in all their daily affairs." Thus, it is within such programs that the addict identity and role is acquired and reinforced (Peele 1989).

If the addict identity is acquired within such organizational contexts, it is logical to hypothesize that former addicts with minimal contact with such organizations will possess different self-concepts. In the interviews conducted with our first set of respondents, a striking pattern emerged in relation to their present self-concept and their past drug and alcohol involvement. They were asked, "How do you see yourself now in relation to your past?" and, "Do you see yourself as a former addict, recovering addict, recovered addict, or in some other way?" A large majority, nearly two-thirds, refused to identify themselves as presently addicted or as recovering or even recovered. Most reported that they saw themselves in "some other way." While all identified themselves as being addicted earlier in their lives, most did not continue to define themselves as addicts. In several cases, these respondents reacted strongly against the addiction-as-disease ideology, believing that such a permanent identity would impede their continued social development. As one respondent explained:

> I'm a father, a husband and a worker. This is how I see myself today. Being a drug addict was someone I was in the past. I'm over that and I don't think about it anymore.

These respondents saw themselves neither as addicts nor ex-addicts; rather, most references to their past addictions were not central to their immediate self-concepts.

Unlike the alcoholics and drug addicts described by Brown (1991) and others, they did not adopt this identity as a "master status" nor did this identity become salient in the role identity hierarchy (Stryker and Serpe 1982; Becker 1963). Instead, the "addict" identity was marginalized by our respondents. Alcoholics and addicts who have participated extensively in self-help groups often engage in a long-term, self-labeling process which involves continuous reference to their addiction. While many have succeeded in terminating addiction through participation in such programs and by adopting the master status of an addict, researchers have raised concern over the deleterious nature of such self-labeling. Peele (1989), for instance, believes that continuous reference to addiction and reliance on the sick role may be at variance with successful and enduring termination of addictive behaviors. Respondents in the first stage of the present study, by contrast, did not reference their previous addictions as being presently central in their lives. Their comments suggest that they had transcended their addict identity and had adopted self-concepts congruent with contemporary roles.

During the second phase of the study, the question around identity was reconstructed. Since most respondents in the first sample often made extensive and unsolicited comments about how they currently view themselves in relation to their past experiences (former addict, recovering addict, recovered addict, or other), a decision was made to reshape this question for use with the second sample. The question then read, "How do you see yourself today in relation to your own past experiences with drugs and alcohol (e.g., addict, recovering addict, person who had a serious drug and/or alcohol problem or, do you see yourself in some other way)? Please discuss as it relates to your current identity." The solicited responses from this second sample did not differ dramatically from the unsolicited responses from the first sample. Essentially, their former identities as addicts were not currently central in their lives but rather had been marginalized, as had been the case with the first sample of respondents.

Also, during the second stage of the study, an additional question about "addict identity" was constructed and asked. The question read, "To what extent do you freely discuss your previous drug and alcohol experiences with others? Please elaborate." The majority of these respondents were quite selective about with whom they discussed these previous drug experiences. Some stated that they shared these experiences with very close friends. Others stated that they discussed these matters only with people who had known them as addicts. Still others reported that they discussed these experiences with no one. Again one could conclude, as was the case with the first sample, that this second group minimized these experiences in terms of how they presently view themselves.

The fact that our respondents did not adopt addict identities is of great importance since it contradicts the common assumptions of treatment programs. The belief that alcoholics and drug addicts can overcome their addictions and not see themselves in an indefinite state of recovery is incongruous with treatment predicated on the disease concept which pervades most treatment programs. Such programs subscribe to the view that addiction is incurable; programmatic principles may then commit addicts to a life of ongoing recovery, often with minimal success. Some have suggested that the decision to circumvent formal treatment and self-help involvement has empirical and theoretical importance since it offers insight about this population that may be useful in designing more effective treatment (Sobell et al. 1992). While research has examined the characteristics of individuals who affiliate with such groups, few studies have included individuals outside programs. Therefore, there is a paucity of data that examines the avoidance of treatment. We now turn to an examination of respondents' attitudes toward addiction treatment programs.

Circumventing Treatment

Given the pervasiveness of treatment programs and self-help groups such as AA and NA, the decision to embark upon a method of natural recovery is curious. Some of our respondents in the first stage of the study reported having had direct exposure to such groups by having attended one or two AA, NA, or CA meetings. Others in this sample, although never having attended, reported being indirectly familiar with such groups. Only two of them claimed to have no knowledge of these groups or the principles they advocate. Consequently, the respondents, as a group, expressed the decision not to enter treatment, which represented a conscious effort to circumvent treatment rather than a lack of familiarity with such programs.

In order to explore their decisions to bypass treatment, we asked what they thought about these programs and why they avoided direct involvement in them. When asked about their attitudes toward such programs, most of them commented that they believed such programs were beneficial for some people. They credited treatment programs and self-help groups with helping friends or family members overcome alcohol or drug addictions. Overall, however, our respondents in the first sample disagreed with the ideological basis of such programs and felt that they were inappropriate for them.

Responses included a wide range of criticisms of these programs. In most cases, rejection of treatment programs and self-help groups reflected a perceived contradiction between these respondents' world views and the core principles of such programs. Overcoming resistance to core principles which include the views that addiction is a disease (once an addict always an addict), or that individuals are powerless over their addiction, is imperative by those who affiliate with such programs. Indeed, individuals who subscribe to alternative views of addiction are identified as "in denial" (Brissett 1988). Not unlike other institutions such as the military, law school, or mental health hospitals, self-help groups socialize recruits away from their previously held world views (Granfield 1992; Goffman 1961). It is the task of such programs to shape [their] members' views to make them compatible with organizational ideology (Brown 1991; Peele 1989). Socialization within treatment programs and self-help groups enables a person to reconstruct a biography that corresponds to a new reference point.

Respondents in this sample, however, typically rejected specific characteristics of the treatment ideology. First, many expressed strong opposition to the suggestion that they were powerless over their addictions. Such an ideology, they explained, not only was counterproductive but was also extremely demeaning. These respondents saw themselves as efficacious people who often prided themselves on their past accomplishments. They viewed themselves as being individualists and strong-willed. One respondent, for instance, explained that "such programs encourage powerlessness" and that she would rather "trust her own instincts than the instincts of others." Another respondent commented that:

> I read a lot of their literature and the very first thing they say is that you're powerless. I think that's bullshit. I believe that people have power inside themselves to make what they want happen. I think I have choices and can do anything I set my mind to.

Consequently, these respondents found the suggestion that they were powerless incompatible with their own self-image. While treatment programs and self-help groups would define such attitudes as a manifestation of denial that would only result in perpetuating addiction, they saw overcoming their addictions as a challenge they could effectively surmount. Interestingly, and in contrast to conventional wisdom in the treatment field, the overwhelming majority of our respondents in the first sample reported successful termination of their addictions after only one attempt.

They also reported that they disliked the culture associated with such self-help programs. In addition to finding the ideological components of such programs offensive, most rejected the lifestyle encouraged by such programs. For instance, several of them felt that these programs bred dependency and subsequently rejected the notion that going to meetings with other addicts was essential for successful termination. In fact, some actually thought it to be dangerous to spend so much time with addicts who continue to focus on their addictions. Most of our respondents in this first sample sought to avoid all contact with drug addicts once they decided to terminate their own drug use. Consequently, they believed that contact with addicts, even those who are not actively using, would possibly undermine their termination efforts. Finally, some of these respondents reported that they found self-help groups "cliquish" and "unhealthy." One respondent explained that, "all they do is stand around smoking cigarettes and drinking coffee while they talk about their addiction. I never felt comfortable with these people." This sense of discomfort with the cultural aspects of these programs was often keenly felt by the women in our sample. Most women in this group believed that self-help groups were male-oriented and did not include the needs of women. One woman, for instance, who identified herself as a lesbian commented that self-help groups were nothing but "a bunch of old men running around telling stories and doing things together." This woman found greater inspiration among feminist support groups and literature that emphasized taking control of one's own life.

During the second stage of the study we decided to separate and sharpen our focus on what appeared to be three prominent overlapping themes around attitudes toward treatment. We asked these respondents why they chose not to undergo formal treatment or participate in self-help groups. We also asked about their general impressions of formal treatment, separate from their impressions of self-help groups. We then asked them specifically about their impressions of AA, NA, and other 12-step programs.

The principal reason reported for not undergoing formal treatment was that nearly all of the 21 respondents in the second sample stated directly or in some variation that they felt that they could terminate their addiction without such interventions. Some stated that treatment was not a viable option since it was either too expensive or essentially unavailable. While some of these respondents registered positive attitudes regarding varying treatment modalities, these respondents, nonetheless, reported that such treatment was not necessary in their individual case. In the case of respondent evaluation of 12-step programs, the second sample of addicts was not as critical as the previous sample. However, even among the second group, most believed that the principles espoused by these programs were at variance with their own beliefs about the recovery process.

The Elements of Cessation

The fact that our respondents were able to terminate their addictions without the benefit of treatment raises an important question about recovery. Research that has examined this process has found that individuals who have a "stake in conventional life" are better able to alter their drug-taking practices than those who experience a sense of hopelessness (Waldorf et al. 1991). In their longitudinal research of cocaine users, these authors found that many people with structural supports in their lives such as a job, family, and other involvements were simply able to "walk away" from their heavy use of cocaine. According to these authors, this fact suggests that the social context of a drug user's life may significantly influence the ability to overcome drug problems.

The social contexts of our respondents served to protect many of them from total involvement with an addict subculture. Literature on the sociocultural correlates of heavy drinking has found that some groups possess cultural protection against developing alcoholism (Snyder 1964). In addition, Peele (1989) has argued that individuals with greater resources in their lives are well equipped to overcome drug problems. Such resources include education and other credentials, job skills, meaningful family attachments, and support mechanisms. In the case of our first 25 respondents, most provided evidence of such resources available to them even while they were actively using. Most reported coming from stable home environments that valued education, family, and economic security, and for the most part held conventional beliefs. All of our respondents in the first group had completed high school, nine were college graduates, and one held a master's degree in engineering. Most were employed in professional occupations or operated their own businesses. Additionally, most continued to be employed throughout their period of heavy drug and alcohol use and none of our respondents came from disadvantaged backgrounds.

It might be concluded that the social contexts of these respondents' lives protected them from further decline into alcohol and drug addiction. They frequently reported that there were people in their lives to whom they were able to turn when they decided to quit. Some explained that their families provided support; others described how their nondrug-using friends assisted them in their efforts to stop using. One respondent explained how an old college friend helped him get over his addiction to crack cocaine:

> My best friend from college made a surprise visit. I hadn't seen him in years. He walked in and I was all cracked out. It's like he walked into the twilight zone or something. He couldn't believe it. He smoked dope in college but he had never seen anything like this. When I saw him, I knew that my life was really screwed up and I needed to do something about it. He stayed with me for the next two weeks and helped me through it.

Typically, respondents in our first sample had not yet "burned their social bridges" and were able to rely upon communities of friends, family, and other associates in their lives. The existence of such communities made it less of a necessity for these individuals to search out alternative communities such as those found within self-help groups. Such groups may be of considerable importance when a person's natural communities break down. Indeed, the fragmentation of communities within postmodern society may account for the popularity of self-help groups (Reinarman n.d.). In the absence of resources and communities, such programs allow individuals to construct a sense of purpose and meaning in their lives. Respondents in our first sample all explained that the resources, communities, and individuals in their lives were instrumental in supporting their efforts to change.

In some cases, these respondents abandoned their using communities entirely to search for nonusing groups. This decision to do so was often triggered by the realization that their immediate social networks consisted mostly of heavy drug and alcohol users. Any attempt to discontinue use, they reasoned, would require complete separation. Several from this group moved to different parts of the country in order to distance themselves from their using networks. This finding is consistent with Biernacki's (1986) study of heroin addicts who relocated in order to remove any temptations to use in the future. For some women, the decision to abandon using communities, particularly cocaine, was often preceded by becoming pregnant. These women left boyfriends and husbands because they felt a greater sense of responsibility and greater meaning in their new maternal status. In all these cases, respondents fled using communities in search of more conventional networks.

In addition to relying on their natural communities and abandoning using communities, these respondents also built new support structures to assist them in their termination efforts. They frequently reported becoming involved in various social groups such as choirs, health clubs, religious organizations, reading clubs, and dance companies. Others from this group reported that they returned to school, became active in civic organizations, or simply developed new hobbies that brought them in touch with nonusers. Thus, respondents built new lives for themselves by cultivating social ties with meaningful and emotionally satisfying alternative communities. In each of these cases where respondents formed attachments to new communities, they typically hid their addictive past, fearing that exposure would jeopardize their newly acquired status.

During the second stage of the study we further examined two of the above themes. The first theme that was revisited dealt with "specific strategies used to remain abstinent." Overwhelmingly for this group, severing all ties with using friends emerged as the most important strategy one could undertake in successfully terminating addiction.

The next theme around elements of cessation that was further examined among this second sample included "resources that were perceived as valuable in the process of recovery." After giving examples of resources discovered in the first stage of the study (e.g., family), these respondents also reported that identical or similar resources had been very useful in their own struggles to overcome addictions. They reported being able to draw upon their families, job skills, formal education, economic security, and other conditions that had been identified as instrumental resources by the first sample. Interestingly, will power and determination emerged as important internal resources during the second stage of the study. However, these should be viewed cautiously since "determination" was given as an example of a possible internal resource during the interviews with the second sample.

Given the apparent roles that severing ties with using networks and having resources play in the natural recovery process, one might draw the compelling conclusion that those individuals from the most disadvantaged segments of our society are also least likely to be in a position to overcome severe addiction problems naturally. Unfortunately, these individuals are also at greatest risk for severe drug and alcohol problems, least likely to be able to afford private treatment, and least likely to voluntarily seek public treatment.

Discussions and Implications

While the sample within the present study is small, there is considerable evidence from additional research to suggest that the population of self-healers is quite substantial (Sobell et al. 1992; Waldorf et al. 1991). Despite empirical evidence, many in the treatment field continue to deny the existence of such a population. The therapeutic "field" possesses considerable power to construct reality in ways that exclude alternative and perhaps challenging paradigms. As Bourdieu (1991) has recently pointed out, such fields reproduce themselves through their ability to normalize arbitrary world views. The power of the therapeutic field lies in its ability to not only medicalize behavior, but also in the ability to exclude the experiences and world views of those who do not fit into conventional models of addiction and treatment (Skoll 1992).

Finding empirical support for natural recovery does not imply that we devalue the importance of treatment programs or even self-help groups. Such programs have proven beneficial to addicts, particularly those in advanced stages. However, the experiences of our respondents have important implications for the way in which addiction and recovery are typically conceptualized. First, denying the existence of this popula-

tion, as many do, discounts the version of reality held by those who terminate their addictions naturally. Natural recovery is simply not recognized as a viable option. This is increasingly the case as media has reified dominant notions of addiction and recovery. Similarly, there is an industry of self-help literature that unquestionably accepts and reproduces these views. Denying the experience of natural recovery allows treatment agencies and self-help groups to continue to impose their particular view of reality on society.

Related to this is the possibility that many of those experiencing addictions may be extremely reluctant to enter treatment or attend self-help meetings. Their resistance may stem from a variety of factors such as the stigma associated with these programs, discomfort with the therapeutic process, or lack of support from significant others. Whatever the reason, such programs do not appeal to everyone. For such people, natural recovery may be a viable option. Since natural recovery demystifies the addiction and recovery experience, it may offer a way for people to take control of their own lives without needing to rely exclusively on experts. Such an alternative approach offers a low-cost supplement to an already costly system of formal addiction treatment.

A third implication concerns the consequences of adopting an addict identity. While the disease metaphor is thought to be a humanistic one in that it allows for the successful social reintegration of deviant drinkers or drug users, it nevertheless constitutes a deviant identity. Basing one's identity on past addiction experiences may actually limit social reintegration. The respondents in our sample placed a great deal of emphasis on their immediate social roles as opposed to constantly referring to their drug-addict pasts. Although there is no way of knowing, such present-centeredness may, in the long run, prove more beneficial than a continual focusing on the past.

Fourth, for drug and alcohol treatment professionals, as well as those who are likely to refer individuals to drug and alcohol treatment programs, this research raises several important considerations. It reaffirms the necessity for individual treatment matching (Lewis et al. 1994). It also suggests that individuals whose profiles are similar to these middle-class respondents are likely to be receptive to and benefit from less intrusive, short-term types of interventions. Given the extent of the various concerns expressed by these respondents around some of the possible long-term negative consequences of undergoing traditional treatment and related participation in self-help programs, the decision to specifically recommend drug and alcohol treatment is a profoundly serious one. It should not be made capriciously or simply because it is expected and available. A careful assessment of the person's entire life is warranted, including whether or not the condition is so severe and the absence of supportive resources so great that the possible lifelong identity of addict or related internalized beliefs are reasonable risks to take in pursuing recovery. Overall, the findings of this study as well as previous research on natural recovery could be instructive in designing more effective treatment programs (Sobell et al. 1992; Fillmore 1988; Stall and Biernacki 1986).

Finally, the experiences of our respondents may have important social policy implications. If our respondents are any guide, the following hypothesis might be considered: those with the greatest number of resources and who consequently have a great deal to lose by their addiction are the ones most likely to terminate their addictions naturally. While addiction is not reducible to social class alone, it is certainly related to it (Waldorf et al. 1991). The respondents in our sample had relatively stable lives: they had jobs, supportive families, high school and college credentials, and other social supports that gave them reasons to alter their drug-taking behavior. Having much to lose gave our respondents incentives to transform their lives. However, when there is little to lose from heavy alcohol or drug use, there may be little to gain by quitting. Social policies that attempt to increase a person's stake in conventional life could not only act to prevent future alcohol and drug addiction, they could also provide an anchor for those who become dependent on these substances.

Further research on the subject of natural recovery among hidden populations such as the middle class needs to be conducted in order to substantiate the findings we report and related conclusions. One important direction the researchers are presently pursuing is to differentiate the natural recovery experience of individuals who have been addicted to different substances. Such research could increase understanding of how different hidden populations overcome the addictions they experience.

Notes

1. An earlier version of this paper was presented at the American Sociological Association meetings, Los Angeles, Calif., August 1994.

2. In his study of identity transformation of alcoholics, Brown (1991) found that the conversion experience to a "recovering alcoholic" was so powerful that many individuals abandoned their previous careers to become counselors.

References

Abbott, A. 1988. *The system of profession.* Chicago: University of Chicago Press.

Adler, P. 1986. *Wheeling and dealing.* New York: Columbia University Press.

Becker, H. 1963. *The outsiders: Studies in the sociology of deviance.* New York: The Free Press.

Biernacki, P. 1986. *Pathways from heroin addiction: Recovery without treatment.* Philadelphia: Temple University Press.

Bourdieu, P. 1991. The peculiar history of scientific reason. *Sociological Forum* 5(2):3–26.

Brissett, D. 1988. Denial in alcoholism: A sociological interpretation. *Journal of Drug Issues* 18(3):385–402.

Brown, J. D. 1991. Preprofessional socialization and identity transformation: The case of the professional ex. *Journal of Contemporary Ethnography* 20(2):157–178.

Cloud, W. 1987. From down under: A qualitative study on heroin addiction recovery. Ann Arbor: Dissertation Abstracts.

Emrick, C., J. Tonigan, H. Montgomery, and L. Little. 1993. Alcoholics Anonymous: What is currently known? In *Research on Alcoholics Anonymous: Opportunities and alternatives,* eds. B. McCrady and W. Miller. New Brunswick, N.J.: Rutgers Center of Alcohol Studies.

Fillmore, K. M. 1988. Spontaneous remission of alcohol problems. Paper presented at the National Conference on Evaluating Recovery Outcomes, San Diego, Calif.

Garfinkel, H. 1967. *Studies in ethnomethodology.* New Jersey: Prentice-Hall.

Goffman, E. 1961. *Asylums.* Garden City, N.Y.: Anchor Books.

———. 1963. *Stigma.* Englewood Cliffs, N.J.: Prentice Hall.

Goodwin, D., J. B Crane, and S. B. Guze. 1971. Felons who drink: An eight-year follow-up. *Quarterly Journal of Studies on Alcohol* 32: 136–147.

Granfield, R. 1992. *Making elite lawyers: Visions of law at Harvard and beyond.* New York: Routledge, Chapman and Hall.

Hanson, B., G. Beschner, J. M. Walters, and E. Boville. 1985. *Life with heroin.* Lexington, Mass.: Lexington Books.

Hingson, R., N. Scotch, N. Day, and A. Culbert. 1980. Recognizing and seeking help for drinking problems. *Journal of Studies on Alcohol* 41:1102–1117.

Lambert, E., and W. Wiebel. 1990. Introduction. In *The collection and interpretation of data from hidden populations,* ed. E. Lambert. Rockville, Md.: National Institute on Drug Abuse.

Lee, R. 1993. *Doing research on sensitive topics.* Newbury Park, Calif.: Sage.

Lemert, E. 1951. *Social pathology.* New York: McGraw-Hill.

Lemert, E. 1974. Beyond Mead: The societal reaction to deviance. *Social Problems* 21(4):457–468.

Lewis, J., R. Dana, and G. Blevins. 1994. *Substance abuse counseling: An individualized approach.* Pacific Grove, Calif.: Brooks/Cole.

Parsons, T. 1951. *The social system.* New York: The Free Press.

Peele, S. 1989. *The diseasing of America: Addiction treatment out of control.* Lexington, Mass.: Lexington Books.

Ratner, M. 1993. *Crack pipe as pimp: An ethnographic investigation of sex-for-crack exchanges.* New York: Lexington Books.

Reinarman, C. n.d. The twelve-step movement and advanced capitalist culture: Notes on the politics of self-control in postmodernity. In *Contemporary social movements and cultural politics,* eds. M. Darofsky, B. Epstein, and R. Flacks. Philadelphia: Temple University Press. In press.

Roizen, R., D. Cahalan, and P. Shanks. 1978. Spontaneous remission among untreated problem drinkers. In *Longitudinal research on drug use,* ed. D. Kandel. Washington, D.C.: Hemisphere Publishing.

Rosenbaum, M., and S. Murphy. 1990. Women and addiction: Process, treatment, and outcome. In *The collection and interpretation of data from hidden populations,* ed. E. Lambert. Rockville, Md.: National Institute on Drug Abuse.

Rubington, E. 1967. Drug addiction as a deviant career. *International Journal of the Addictions* 2:3–20.

Rubington, E. 1978. Variations in bottle-gang controls. In *Deviance: The interactionist perspective,* eds. E. Rubington and M. Weinberg. New York: Macmillan.

Shaffer, H., and S. Jones. 1989. *Quitting cocaine: The struggle against impulse.* Lexington, Mass.: Lexington Books.

Skoll, G. 1992. *Walk the walk and talk the talk: An ethnography of a drug abuse treatment facility.* Philadelphia: Temple University Press.

Snow, M. 1973. Maturing out of narcotic addiction in New York City. *International Journal of the Addictions* 8(6):921–938.

Snyder, C. 1964. Inebriety, alcoholism and anomie. In *Anomie and deviant behavior,* ed. M. Clinard. New York: The Free Press.

Sobell, L., M. Sobell, and T. Toneatto. 1992. Recovery from alcohol problems without treatment. In *Self control and the addictive behaviors,* eds. N. Heather, W. R. Miller, and J. Greeley 199–242. New York: Maxwell Macmillan.

Sobell, L., M. Sobell, T. Toneatto, and G. Leo. 1993. What triggers the resolution of alcohol problems without treatment? *Alcoholism: Clinical and Experimental Research* 17(2):217–224.

Stall, R., and P. Biernacki. 1986. Spontaneous remission from the problematic use of substances. *International Journal of the Addictions* 21:1–23.

Stephens, R. 1991. *The street addict role: A theory of heroin addiction.* Albany, N.Y.: State University Press of New York.

Stryker, S., and R. Serpe. 1982. Commitment, identity salience and role behavior: Theory and research example. In *Personality, roles and social behavior,* eds. W. Ickes and E. Knowles. New York: Springer-Verlag.

Trice, H., and P. Roman. 1970. Delabeling, relabeling, and Alcoholics Anonymous. *Social Problems* 17:538–546.

Valliant, G. 1966. A twelve-year follow-up of New York narcotic addicts: Some characteristics and determinants of abstinence. In *Classic contributions in the addictions,* eds. H. Shaffer and M. Burglass. New York: Brunner/Mazel.

———. 1983. *The natural history of alcoholism.* Cambridge: Harvard University Press.

Valliant, G., and E. S. Milofsky. 1982. Natural history of male alcoholism: IV. Paths to recovery. *Archives of General Psychiatry* 39:127–133.

Waldorf, D., and P. Biernacki. 1977. Natural recovery from opiate addiction: A review of the incidence literature. *Journal of Drug Issues* 9:281–290.

———. 1981. Natural recovery from opiate addiction: Some preliminary findings. *Journal of Drug Issues* 11:61–74.

Waldorf, D., C. Reinarman, and S. Murphy. 1991. *Cocaine changes: The experience of using and quitting.* Philadelphia: Temple University Press.

Walsh, D. C., R. Hingson, and D. Merrigan. 1992. The impact of a physician's warning on recovery after alcoholism treatment. *Journal of the American Medical Association* 267:663.

Waterston, A. 1993. *Street addicts in the political economy.* Philadelphia: Temple University Press.

Weisner, C., and R. Room. 1978. Financing and ideology in alcohol treatment. *Social Problems* 32:157–184.

Williams, T. 1989. *The cocaine kids.* Reading, Mass.: Addison-Wesley.

Winick, C. 1962. Maturing out of narcotic addiction. *Bulletin on Narcotics* 6:1.

Wiseman, J. 1970. *Stations of the lost: The treatment of skid row alcoholics.* Englewood Cliffs, N.J.: Prentice-Hall.

Zinberg, N. 1986. *Drug, set and setting: The basis for controlled intoxicant use.* New Haven: Yale University Press.

For Discussion

1. Why might some individuals be able to recover on their own, while others struggle through a lifetime of addiction? What does this say about the nature of addiction?

2. What kinds of social policies might "increase a person's stake in conventional life" and help prevent substance dependence?

Part IX

Policy Considerations

The federal approach to drug abuse and drug control has included a variety of avenues for reducing both the supply of and the demand for illicit drugs. Historically, the supply-and-demand reduction strategies were grounded in the classic deterrence model: Through legislation and criminal penalties, individuals would be discouraged from using drugs; by setting an example of traffickers, the government would force potential dealers to seek out other economic pursuits.

In time, other components were added: treatment for the user, education and prevention for the would-be user, and research to determine how to best develop and implement plans for treatment, education, and prevention.

By the early 1970s, when it appeared that the war on drugs had won few if any battles, new avenues for supply and demand reduction were added. Federal interdiction initiatives involved charging Coast Guard, Customs, and Drug Enforcement Administration operatives with intercepting drug shipments coming to the United States from foreign ports, and in the international sector there were attempts to eradicate drug-yielding crops at their source. On the surface, none of these strategies seemed to have any effect, and illicit drug use continued to spread.

The problems were many. Legislation and enforcement alone were not enough, and early education programs of the "scare" variety quickly lost their credibility. Moreover, for most social scientists and clinicians, treating drug abuse as a medical problem seemed to be the logical answer. But treatment programs did not seem to be working very effectively, probably because the course of treatment was of insufficient length to have any significant impact.

Given the perceived inadequacy of the traditional approaches to drug-abuse control, during the late 1970s federal authorities began drawing plans for a more concerted assault on drugs, both legislative and technological. It began with the RICO (Racketeer-Influenced and Corrupt Organizations) and CCE (Continuing Criminal Enterprise) statutes. What RICO and CCE accomplish is the forfeiture of the fruits of criminal activities by eliminating the rights of traffickers to their personal assets, whether these be cash, bank accounts, real estate, automobiles, jewelry and art, equity in businesses, directorships in companies, or any kind of goods or entitlements obtained in or used for a criminal enterprise.

The new, evolving federal drug strategy considered it crucial to include the U.S. military in its war on drugs. In 1982 the Department of Defense Authorization Act was signed into law, making the entire war chest of U.S. military power available to law enforcement—for training, intelligence gathering, and detection. Beginning in 1982, the "war on drugs" had a new look. Put into force was the Bell 209 assault helicopter, more popularly known as the Cobra. None in the military arsenal were faster, and in its gunship mode it could destroy a tank. In addition, there was the awesome Sikorsky Black Hawk assault helicopter, assigned for operation by U.S. Customs Service pilots. Customs also had the Cessna Citation, a jet aircraft equipped with radar originally designed for F-16 fighters. There was the Navy's EC-2, an aircraft equipped with a radar disk capable of detecting other aircraft from as far as 300 miles away. There were "Fat Albert" and his pals—aerostat surveillance balloons 175 feet in length equipped with sophisticated radar and listening devices. Fat Albert could not only pick up communications from Cuba but also could detect traffic in "Smugglers' Alley," a wide band of Caribbean sky that is virtually invisible to land-based radar systems. There were NASA satellites to spy on drug operations as far apart as California and Colombia, airborne infrared sensing and imaging equipment that could detect human body heat in the thickest underbrush of Florida's Everglades, plus a host of other high-tech devices. In all, drug enforcement appeared well equipped for battle.

The final component added to the drug war armamentarium was "zero tolerance," a 1988 White House antidrug policy based on a number of premises: (1) that if there were no drug abusers there would be no drug problem; (2) that the market for drugs is created not only by availability but also by demand; (3) that drug abuse starts with a willful act; (4) that the perception that drug users are powerless to act against the influences of drug availability and peer pressure is an erroneous one; (5) that most illegal drug users can choose to stop their drug-taking behaviors and must be held accountable if they do not; (6) that individual freedom does not include the right to self- and societal destruction; and (7) that public tolerance for drug abuse must be reduced to *zero*. As such, the zero-tolerance policy expanded the war on drugs from suppliers and dealers to users as well—especially casual users—and meant that planes, vessels, and vehicles could be confiscated for carrying even the smallest amount of a controlled substance.

By the late 1980s, well after the newest "war on drugs" had been declared and put into operation, it had already been decided by numerous longtime observers that the more than 70 years of federal prohibition since the passage of the Harrison Act of 1914 were not only a costly and abject failure but represented a totally doomed effort as well. It was argued that drug laws and drug enforcement had served mainly to create enormous profits for drug dealers and traffickers, overcrowded jails, police and other government corruption, a distorted foreign policy, predatory street crime carried on by users in search of the funds necessary to purchase black-market drugs, and urban areas harassed by street-level drug dealers and terrorized by violent drug gangs. Many of these observations were indeed true.

Within the context of these concerns, the late 1980s also marked the onset of renewed calls for the *decriminalization*, if not the outright *legalization*, of most or all illicit drugs. The arguments posed by the supporters of legalization seem all too logical. First, they argued, the drug laws have created evils far worse than the drugs themselves—corruption, violence, street crime, and disrespect for the law. Second, legislation passed to control drugs failed to reduce demand. Third, an activity that a significant segment of the population of any society is committed to doing should not be made illegal. A social system simply cannot arrest, prosecute, and punish such large numbers of people, particularly in a democracy. And specifically in this regard, in a liberal democracy the government must not interfere with personal behavior if liberty is to be maintained. Fourth, they added, if marijuana, cocaine, crack, heroin, and other drugs were legalized, a number of positive things would happen:

1. Drug prices would fall and subsequently so would crime committed for the purpose of obtaining funds with which to support expensive drug habits.

2. Users could obtain their drugs at low, government-regulated prices and would no longer be forced to engage in

prostitution and street crime to support their habits.

3. The fact that the levels of drug-related crime would significantly decline would result in less crowded courts, jails, and prisons and would free law enforcement personnel to focus their energies on the "real criminals" in society.

4. Drug production, distribution, and sale would be removed from the criminal arena; such criminal syndicates as the Medellin Cartel and the Jamaican posses would be decapitalized, and the violence associated with drug distribution rivalries would be eliminated.

5. Government corruption and intimidation by traffickers, as well as drug-based foreign policies, would be effectively reduced, if not eliminated entirely.

6. The often draconian measures undertaken by police to enforce the drug laws would be curtailed, thus restoring to the American public many of its hard-won civil liberties.

Those opposed to legalizing drugs argued a counterposition, suggesting that making heroin, cocaine, and other illicit drugs more available would create a public health problem of massive proportions. Several moderating positions were visible as well, including what is known as the "harm reduction" approach. Although an explicit definition of "harm reduction" would be difficult, harm reduction includes a wide variety of programs and policies, including the following:

1. *Advocacy for changes in drug policies*— legalization, decriminalization, ending the drug prohibition, changes in drug paraphernalia laws, reduction of penalties for drug-related crimes, and treatment alternatives to incarceration.

2. *HIV/AIDS-related interventions*—needle/syringe exchange programs, HIV prevention/intervention programs, bleach distribution, referrals for HIV testing and HIV medical care, referrals for HIV/AIDS-related psychosocial care, and case management.

3. *Broader drug treatment options*—methadone maintenance by primary care physicians, changes in methadone regulations, heroin substitution programs, and new experimental treatments.

4. *Drug abuse management for those who wish to continue using drugs*—counseling and clinical case management programs that promote safer and more responsible drug use.

5. *Ancillary interventions*—housing and other entitlements, healing centers, and support and advocacy groups.

In the four chapters that follow, the arguments for and against legalizing drugs are thoroughly examined, as are alternative drug policy choices.

Additional Readings

Courtwright, David T. (1991). "Drug Legalization, the Drug War, and Drug Treatment in Historical Perspective." *Journal of Policy History*, 3: 393–414.

Gray, James P. (2001). *Why Our Drug Laws Have Failed and What We Can Do About It*. Philadelphia: Temple University Press.

Inciardi, James A. (1999). *The Drug Legalization Debate*. Thousand Oaks, CA: Sage Publications.

Inciardi, James A., and Lana D. Harrison. (2000). *Harm Reduction: National and International Perspectives*. Thousand Oaks, CA: Sage.

MacCoun, Robert J., and Peter Reuter. (2001). *Drug War Heresies: An Agnostic Look at the Legalization Debate* (RAND Studies in Policy and Analysis). Port Chester, NY: Cambridge University Press.

Trevino, Robert A., and Alan J. Richard. (2002). "Attitudes Towards Drug Legalization Among Drug Users." *American Journal of Drug & Alcohol Abuse*, 28(1): 91–108. ✦

38

Commonsense Drug Policy

Ethan A. Nadelmann

Ethan Nadelmann argues that current drug policy is misguided. He criticizes supply reduction strategies and notes that consumption rates would likely continue even if we were able to reduce or eliminate the supply of drugs from other countries. Harm reduction strategies that have been implemented in various European counties are described, in contrast to the United States. For example, methadone maintenance is available in the United States, but its use is more strictly controlled than in other countries. Nadelmann also describes the results from Swiss and other European studies that have examined the effects of prescribing heroin for addicted individuals. Those results and other harm reduction strategies implemented elsewhere show great promise and should be used to guide and modify U.S. drug policy.

First, Reduce Harm

In 1988 Congress passed a resolution proclaiming its goal of "a drug-free America by 1995." U.S. drug policy has failed persistently over the decades because it has preferred such rhetoric to reality and moralism to pragmatism. Politicians confess their youthful indiscretions, then call for tougher drug laws. Drug control officials make assertions with no basis in fact or science. Police officers, generals, politicians, and guardians of public morals qualify as drug czars—but not, to date, a single doctor or public health figure. Independent commissions are appointed to evaluate drug policies, only to see their recommendations ignored as politically risky. And drug policies are designed,

implemented, and enforced with virtually no input from the millions of Americans they affect most: drug users. Drug abuse is a serious problem, both for individual citizens and society at large, but the "war on drugs" has made matters worse, not better.

Drug warriors often point to the 1980s as a time in which the drug war really worked. Illicit drug use by teenagers peaked around 1980, then fell more than 50 percent over the next 12 years. During the 1996 presidential campaign, Republican challenger Bob Dole made much of the recent rise in teenagers' use of illicit drugs, contrasting it with the sharp drop during the Reagan and Bush administrations. President Clinton's response was tepid, in part because he accepted the notion that teen drug use is the principal measure of a drug policy's success or failure; at best, he could point out that the level was still barely half what it had been in 1980.

In 1980, however, no one had ever heard of the cheap, smokeable form of cocaine called crack, or drug-related HIV infection or AIDS. By the 1990s, both had reached epidemic proportions in American cities, largely driven by prohibitionist economics and morals indifferent to the human consequences of the drug war. In 1980, the federal budget for drug control was about $1 billion, and state and local budgets were perhaps two or three times that. By 1997, the federal drug control budget had ballooned to $16 billion, two-thirds of it for law enforcement agencies, and state and local funding to at least that. On any day in 1980, approximately 50,000 people were behind bars for violating a drug law. By 1997, the number had increased eightfold, to about 400,000. These are the results of a drug policy over reliant on criminal justice "solutions," ideologically wedded to abstinence-only treatment, and insulated from cost-benefit analysis.

Imagine instead a policy that starts by acknowledging that drugs are here to stay, and that we have no choice but to learn how to live with them so that they cause the least possible harm. Imagine a policy that focuses on reducing not illicit drug use per se but the crime and misery caused by both drug abuse and prohibitionist policies. And imagine a drug policy based not on the fear, prejudice, and ignorance that drive America's current approach but rather on common sense, science, public health concerns, and human rights. Such a policy is possible in the United States, especially if Americans are willing to learn from the experiences of other countries where such policies are emerging.

Attitudes Abroad

Americans are not averse to looking abroad for solutions to the nation's drug problems. Unfortunately, they have been looking in the wrong places: Asia and Latin America, where much of the world's heroin and cocaine originates. Decades of U.S. efforts to keep drugs from being produced abroad and exported to American markets have failed. Illicit drug production is bigger business than ever before. The opium poppy, source of morphine and heroin, and *cannabis sativa*, from which marijuana and hashish are prepared, grow readily around the world; the coca plant, from whose leaves cocaine is extracted, can be cultivated far from its native environment in the Andes. Crop substitution programs designed to persuade Third World peasants to grow legal crops cannot compete with the profits that drug prohibition makes inevitable. Crop eradication campaigns occasionally reduce production in one country, but new suppliers pop up elsewhere. International law enforcement efforts can disrupt drug trafficking organizations and routes, but they rarely have much impact on U.S. drug markets.

> **Drug policy should reduce the damage to users and the society around them.**

Even if foreign supplies could be cut off, the drug abuse problem in the United States would scarcely abate. Most of America's drug-related problems are associated with domestically produced alcohol and tobacco. Much if not most of the marijuana, amphetamine, hallucinogens, and illicitly diverted pharmaceutical drugs consumed in the country are made in the United States. The

same is true of the glue, gasoline, and other solvents used by kids too young or too poor to obtain other psychoactive substances. No doubt such drugs, as well as new products, would quickly substitute for imported heroin and cocaine if the flow from abroad dried up.

While looking to Latin America and Asia for supply-reduction solutions to America's drug problems is futile, the harm-reduction approaches spreading throughout Europe and Australia and even into corners of North America show promise. These approaches start by acknowledging that supply-reduction initiatives are inherently limited, that criminal justice responses can be costly and counterproductive, and that single-minded pursuit of a "drug-free society" is dangerously quixotic. Demand-reduction efforts to prevent drug abuse among children and adults are important, but so are harm-reduction efforts to lessen the damage to those unable or unwilling to stop using drugs immediately, and to those around them.

Most proponents of harm reduction do not favor legalization. They recognize that prohibition has failed to curtail drug abuse, that it is responsible for much of the crime, corruption, disease, and death associated with drugs, and that its costs mount every year. But they also see legalization as politically unwise and as risking increased drug use. The challenge is thus making drug prohibition work better, but with a focus on reducing the negative consequences of both drug use and prohibitionist policies.

Countries that have turned to harm-reduction strategies for help in alleviating their drug woes are not so different from the United States. Drugs, crime, and race problems, and other socioeconomic problems, are inextricably linked. As in America, criminal justice authorities still prosecute and imprison major drug traffickers as well as petty dealers who create public nuisances. Parents worry that their children might get involved with drugs. Politicians remain fond of drug war rhetoric. But by contrast with U.S. drug policy, public health goals have priority, and public health authorities have substantial influence. Doctors have far more latitude in treating addiction and associated problems. Police view the sale and use of illicit drugs as similar to prostitution—vice activities that cannot be stamped out but can be effectively regulated. Moralists focus less on any inherent evils of drugs than on the need to deal with drug use and addiction pragmatically and humanely. And more politicians dare to speak out in favor of alternatives to punitive prohibitionist policies.

Harm-reduction innovations include efforts to stem the spread of HIV by making sterile syringes readily available and collecting used syringes; allowing doctors to prescribe oral methadone for heroin addiction treatment, as well as heroin and other drugs for addicts who would otherwise buy them on the black market; establishing "safe injection rooms" so addicts do not congregate in public places or dangerous "shooting galleries"; employing drug analysis units at the large dance parties called raves to test the quality and potency of MDMA, known as Ecstasy, and other drugs that patrons buy and consume there; decriminalizing (but not legalizing) possession and retail sale of cannabis and, in some cases, possession of small amounts of "hard" drugs; and integrating harm-reduction policies and principles into community policing strategies. Some of these measures are under way or under consideration in parts of the United States, but rarely to the extent found in growing numbers of foreign countries.

Stopping HIV With Sterile Syringes

The spread of HIV, the virus that causes AIDS, among people who inject drugs illegally was what prompted governments in Europe and Australia to experiment with harm-reduction policies. During the early 1980s public health officials realized that infected users were spreading HIV by sharing needles. Having already experienced a hepatitis epidemic attributed to the same mode of transmission, the Dutch were the first to tell drug users about the risks of needle sharing and to make sterile syringes available and collect dirty needles through pharmacies, needle exchange and methadone programs, and public health services. Governments

elsewhere in Europe and in Australia soon followed suit. The few countries in which a prescription was necessary to obtain a syringe dropped the requirement. Local authorities in Germany, Switzerland, and other European countries authorized needle exchange machines to ensure 24-hour access. In some European cities, addicts can exchange used syringes for clean ones at local police stations without fear of prosecution or harassment. Prisons are instituting similar policies to help discourage the spread of HIV among inmates, recognizing that illegal drug injecting cannot be eliminated even behind bars.

These initiatives were not adopted without controversy. Conservative politicians argued that needle-exchange programs condoned illicit and immoral behavior and that government policies should focus on punishing drug users or making them drug-free. But by the late 1980s, the consensus in most of Western Europe, Oceania, and Canada was that while drug abuse was a serious problem, AIDS was worse. Slowing the spread of a fatal disease for which no cure exists was the greater moral imperative. There was also a fiscal imperative. Needle-exchange programs' costs are minuscule compared with those of treating people who would otherwise become infected with HIV. Only in the United States has this logic not prevailed, even though AIDS was the leading killer of Americans ages 25 to 44 for most of the 1990s and is now Number Two. The Centers for Disease Control (CDC) estimates that half of new HIV infections in the country stem from injection drug use. Yet both the White House and Congress block allocation of AIDS or drug-abuse prevention funds for needle exchange, and virtually all state governments retain drug paraphernalia laws, pharmacy regulations, and other restrictions on access to sterile syringes. During the 1980s, AIDS activists engaging in civil disobedience set up more syringe exchange programs than state and local governments. There are now more than 100 such programs in 28 states, Washington, D.C., and Puerto Rico, but they reach only an estimated 10 percent of injection drug users.

> **Prejudice and political cowardice are poor excuses for allowing AIDS to spread.**

Governments at all levels in the United States refuse to fund needle exchange for political reasons, even though dozens of scientific studies, domestic and foreign, have found that needle exchange and other distribution programs reduce needle sharing, bring hard-to-reach drug users into contact with health care systems, and inform addicts about treatment programs, yet do not increase illegal drug use. In 1991 the National AIDS Commission appointed by President George Bush called the lack of federal support for such programs "bewildering and tragic." In 1993 a CDC-sponsored review of research on needle exchange recommended federal funding, but top officials in the Clinton administration suppressed a favorable evaluation of the report within the Department of Health and Human Services. In July 1996 President Clinton's Advisory Council on HIV/AIDS criticized the administration for its failure to heed the National Academy of Sciences' recommendation that it authorize the use of federal money to support needle-exchange programs. An independent panel convened by the National Institute of Health reached the same conclusion in February 1997. Last summer, the American Medical Association, the American Bar Association, and even the politicized U.S. Conference of Mayors endorsed the concept of needle exchange. In the fall, an endorsement followed from the World Bank.

To date, America's failure in this regard is conservatively estimated to have resulted in the infection of up to 10,000 people with HIV. Mounting scientific evidence and the stark reality of the continuing AIDS crisis have convinced the public, if not politicians, that needle exchange saves lives; polls consistently find that a majority of Americans support needle exchange, with approval highest among those most familiar with the notion. Prejudice and political cowardice are poor excuses for allowing more citizens to suffer from and die of AIDS, especially when effective interventions are cheap, safe, and easy.

Methadone and Other Alternatives

The United States pioneered the use of the synthetic opiate methadone to treat heroin addiction in the 1960s and 1970s, but now lags behind much of Europe and Australia in making methadone accessible and effective. Methadone is the best available treatment in terms of reducing illicit heroin use and associated crime, disease, and death. In the early 1990s the National Academy of Sciences' Institute of Medicine stated that of all forms of drug treatment, "methadone maintenance has been the most rigorously studied modality and has yielded the most incontrovertibly positive results. . . . Consumption of all illicit drugs, especially heroin, declines. Crime is reduced, fewer individuals become HIV positive, and individual functioning is improved." However, the institute went on to declare, "Current policy . . . puts too much emphasis on protecting society from methadone, and not enough on protecting society from the epidemics of addiction, violence, and infectious diseases that methadone can help reduce."

Methadone is to street heroin what nicotine skin patches and chewing gum are to cigarettes—with the added benefit of legality. Taken orally, methadone has little of injected heroin's effect on mood or cognition. It can be consumed for decades with few if any negative health consequences, and its purity and concentration, unlike street heroin's, are assured. Like other opiates, it can create physical dependence if taken regularly, but the "addiction" is more like a diabetic's "addiction" to insulin than a heroin addict's to product bought on the street. Methadone patients can and do drive safely, hold good jobs, and care for their children. When prescribed adequate doses, they can be indistinguishable from people who have never used heroin or methadone.

Popular misconceptions and prejudice, however, have all but prevented any expansion of methadone treatment in the United States. The 115,000 Americans receiving methadone today represent only a small increase over the number 20 years ago. For every ten heroin addicts, there are only one or two methadone treatment slots. Methadone is the most tightly controlled drug in the pharmacopoeia, subject to unique federal and state restrictions. Doctors cannot prescribe it for addiction treatment outside designated programs. Regulations dictate not only security, documentation, and staffing requirements but maximum doses, admission criteria, time spent in the program, and a host of other specifics, none of which has much to do with quality of treatment. Moreover, the regulations do not prevent poor treatment; many clinics provide insufficient doses, prematurely detoxify clients, expel clients for offensive behavior, and engage in other practices that would be regarded as unethical in any other field of medicine. Attempts to open new clinics tend to be blocked by residents who don't want addicts in their neighborhood.

In much of Europe and Australia, methadone treatment was at first even more controversial than in the United States; some countries, including Germany, France, and Greece, prohibited it well into the 1980s and 1990s. But where methadone has been accepted, doctors have substantial latitude in deciding how and when to prescribe it so as to maximize its efficacy. There are methadone treatment programs for addicts looking for rehabilitation and programs for those simply trying to reduce their heroin consumption. Doctors in regular medical practice can prescribe the drug, and patients fill their prescriptions at local pharmacies. Thousands of general practitioners throughout Europe, Australia, New Zealand, and Canada (notably in Ontario and British Columbia) are now involved in methadone maintenance. In Belgium, Germany, and Australia this is the principal means of distribution. Integrating methadone with mainstream medicine makes treatment more accessible, improves its quality, and allocates ancillary services more efficiently. It also helps reduce the stigma of methadone programs and community resistance to them.

Many factors prevent American doctors from experimenting with the more flexible treatment programs of their European counterparts. The Drug Enforcement Administration contends that looser regulations would fuel the illicit market in diverted methadone. But the black market, in which virtually all buyers are heroin addicts who cannot or will not enroll in methadone programs, is primarily a product of the inadequate legal availability of methadone. Some conventional providers do not want to cede their near-monopoly over methadone treatment and are reluctant to take on addicts who can't or won't commit to quitting heroin. And all efforts to make methadone more available in the United States run up against the many Americans who dismiss methadone treatment as substituting one addictive drug for another and are wary of any treatment that does not leave the patient "drug free."

Oral methadone works best for hundreds of thousands of heroin addicts, but some fare better with other opiate substitutes. In England, doctors prescribe injectable methadone for about 10 percent of recovering patients, who may like the modest "rush" upon injection or the ritual of injecting. Doctors in Austria, Switzerland, and Australia are experimenting with prescribing oral morphine to determine whether it works better than oral methadone for some users. Several treatment programs in the Netherlands have conducted trials with oral morphine and palfium. In Germany, where methadone treatment was initially shunned, thousands of addicts have been maintained on codeine, which many doctors and patients still prefer to methadone. The same is true of buprenorphine in France.

In England, doctors have broad discretion to prescribe whatever drugs help addicted patients manage their lives and stay away from illegal drugs and their dealers. Beginning in the 1920s, thousands of English addicts were maintained on legal prescriptions of heroin, morphine, amphetamine, cocaine, and other pharmaceutical drugs. This tradition flourished until the 1960s, and has reemerged in response to AIDS and to growing disappointment with the Americanization of British prescribing practices during the 1970s and 1980s, when illicit heroin use in Britain increased almost tenfold. Doctors in other European countries and Australia are also trying heroin prescription.

The Swiss government began a nationwide trial in 1994 to determine whether prescribing heroin, morphine, or injectable methadone could reduce crime, disease, and other drug-related ills. Some 1,000 volunteers—only heroin addicts with at least two unsuccessful experiences in methadone or other conventional treatment programs were considered—took part in the experiment. The trial quickly determined that virtually all participants preferred heroin, and doctors subsequently prescribed it for them. Last July the government reported the results so far: Criminal offenses and the number of criminal offenders dropped 60 percent, the percentage of income from illegal and semilegal activities fell from 69 to 10 percent, illegal heroin *and* cocaine use declined dramatically (although use of alcohol, cannabis, and tranquilizers like Valium remained fairly constant), stable employment increased from 14 to 32 percent, physical health improved enormously, and most participants greatly reduced their contact with the drug scene. There were no deaths from overdoses, and no prescribed drugs were diverted to the black market. More than half those who dropped out of the study switched to another form of drug treatment, including 83 who began abstinence therapy. A cost-benefit analysis of the program found a net economic benefit of $30 per patient per day, mostly because of reduced criminal justice and health care costs.

The Swiss study has undermined several myths about heroin and its habitual users. The results to date demonstrate that, given relatively unlimited availability, heroin users will voluntarily stabilize or reduce their dosage, and some will even choose abstinence; that long-addicted users can lead relatively normal, stable lives if provided legal access to their drug of choice; and that ordinary citizens will support such initiatives. In recent referendums in Zurich, Basel, and Zug, substantial majorities voted to continue funding local arms of the experiment.

And last September, a nationwide referendum to end the government's heroin maintenance and other harm-reduction initiatives was rejected by 71 percent of Swiss voters, including majorities in all 26 cantons.

The Netherlands plans its own heroin prescription study in 1998, and similar trials are under consideration elsewhere in Europe, including Luxembourg and Spain, as well as Canada. In Germany, the federal government has opposed heroin prescription trials and other harm-reduction innovations, but the League of Cities has petitioned it for permission to undertake them; a survey early last year found that police chiefs in 10 of the country's 12 largest cities favored letting states implement controlled heroin distribution programs. In Australia last summer, a majority of state health ministers approved a heroin prescription trial, but Prime Minister John Howard blocked it. And in Denmark, a September 1996 poll found that 66 percent of voters supported an experiment that would provide registered addicts with free heroin to be consumed in centers set up for the purpose.

Switzerland, attempting to reduce overdoses, dangerous injecting practices, and shooting up in public places, has also taken the lead in establishing "safe injection rooms," where users can inject their drugs under secure, sanitary conditions. There are now about a dozen such rooms in the country, and initial evaluations are positive. In Germany, Frankfurt has set up three, and there are also officially sanctioned facilities in Hamburg and Saarbrücken. Cities elsewhere in Europe and in Australia are expected to open safe injection rooms soon.

Reefer Sanity

Cannabis, in the form of marijuana and hashish, is by far the most popular illicit drug in the United States. More than a quarter of Americans admit to having tried it. Marijuana's popularity peaked in 1980, dropped steadily until the early 1990s, and is now on the rise again. Although it is not entirely safe, especially when consumed by children, smoked heavily, or used when driving, it is clearly among the least dangerous psychoactive drugs in common use. In 1988 the administrative law judge for the Drug Enforcement Administration, Francis Young, reviewed the evidence and concluded that "marihuana, in its natural form, is one of the safest therapeutically active substances known to man."

As with needle exchange and methadone treatment, American politicians have ignored or spurned the findings of government commissions and scientific organizations concerning marijuana policy. In 1972 the National Commission on Marihuana and Drug Abuse—created by President Nixon and chaired by a former Republican governor, Raymond Shafer—recommended that possession of up to one ounce of marijuana be decriminalized. Nixon rejected the recommendation. In 1982 a panel appointed by the National Academy of Sciences reached the same conclusion as the Shafer Commission.

Between 1973 and 1978, with attitudes changing, 11 states approved decriminalization statutes that reclassified marijuana possession as a misdemeanor, petty offense, or civil violation punishable by no more than a $100 fine. Consumption trends in those states and in states that retained stricter sanctions were indistinguishable. A 1988 scholarly evaluation of the Moscone Act, California's 1976 decriminalization law, estimated that the state had saved half a billion dollars in arrest costs since the law's passage. Nonetheless, public opinion began to shift in 1978. No other states decriminalized marijuana, and some eventually recriminalized it.

Between 1973 and 1989, annual arrests on marijuana charges by state and local police ranged between 360,000 and 460,000. The annual total fell to 283,700 in 1991, but has since more than doubled. In 1996, 641,642 people were arrested for marijuana, 85 percent of them for possession, not sale, of the drug. Prompted by concern over rising marijuana use among adolescents and fears of being labeled soft on drugs, the Clinton administration launched its own anti-marijuana campaign in 1995. But the administration's claims to have identified new risks of marijuana consumption—in-

cluding a purported link between marijuana and violent behavior—have not withstood scrutiny.[1] Neither Congress nor the White House seems likely to put the issue of marijuana policy before a truly independent advisory commission, given the consistency with which such commissions have reached politically unacceptable conclusions.

In contrast, governments in Europe and Australia, notably in the Netherlands, have reconsidered their cannabis policies. In 1976 the Baan Commission in the Netherlands recommended, and the Dutch government adopted, a policy of separating the "soft" and "hard" drug markets. Criminal penalties for and police efforts against heroin trafficking were increased, while those against cannabis were relaxed. Marijuana and hashish can now be bought in hundreds of "coffee shops" throughout the country. Advertising, open displays, and sales to minors are prohibited. Police quickly close coffee shops caught selling hard drugs. Almost no one is arrested or even fined for cannabis possession, and the government collects taxes on the gray market sales.

In the Netherlands today, cannabis consumption for most age groups is similar to that in the United States. Young Dutch teenagers, however, are less likely to sample marijuana than their American peers; from 1992 to 1994, only 7.2 percent of Dutch youths between the ages of 12 and 15 reported having tried marijuana, compared to 13.5 percent of Americans in that age bracket. Far fewer Dutch youths, moreover, experiment with cocaine, buttressing officials' claims of success in separating the markets for hard and soft drugs. Most Dutch parents regard the "reefer madness" anti-marijuana campaigns of the United States as silly.

Dutch coffee shops have not been problem free. Many citizens have complained about the proliferation of coffee shops, as well as nuisances created by foreign youth flocking to party in Dutch border cities. Organized crime involvement in the growing domestic cannabis industry is of increasing concern. The Dutch government's efforts to address the problem by more openly and systematically regulating supplies to coffee shops, along with some of its other drug policy initiatives, have run up against pressure from abroad, notably from Paris, Stockholm, Bonn, and Washington. In late 1995 French President Jacques Chirac began publicly berating The Hague for its drug policies, even threatening to suspend implementation of the Schengen Agreement allowing the free movement of people across borders of European Union (EU) countries. Some of Chirac's political allies called the Netherlands a narco-state. Dutch officials responded with evidence of the relative success of their policies, while pointing out that most cannabis seized in France originates in Morocco (which Chirac has refrained from criticizing because of his government's close relations with King Hassan). The Hague, however, did announce reductions in the number of coffee shops and the amount of cannabis customers can buy there. But it still sanctions the coffee shops, and a few municipalities actually operate them.

Notwithstanding the attacks, in the 1990s the trend toward decriminalization of cannabis has accelerated in Europe. Across much of Western Europe, possession and even minor sales of the drug are effectively decriminalized. Spain decriminalized private use of cannabis in 1983. In Germany, the Federal Constitutional Court effectively sanctioned a cautious liberalization of cannabis policy in a widely publicized 1994 decision. German states vary considerably in their attitude; some, like Bavaria, persist in a highly punitive policy, but most now favor the Dutch approach. So far the Kohl administration has refused to approve state proposals to legalize and regulate cannabis sales, but it appears aware of the rising support in the country for Dutch and Swiss approaches to local drug problems.

In June 1996 Luxembourg's parliament voted to decriminalize cannabis and push for standardization of drug laws in the Benelux countries. The Belgian government is now considering a more modest decriminalization of cannabis combined with tougher measures against organized crime and heroin traffickers. In Australia, cannabis has been decriminalized in South Australia, the Australian Capital Territory (Canberra), and the Northern Territory, and other states are considering the step. Even in France, Chirac's outburst followed recommendations of cannabis decriminalization by three distinguished national commissions. Chirac must now contend with a new prime minister, Lionel Jospin, who declared himself in favor of decriminalization before his Socialist Party won the 1997 parliamentary elections. Public opinion is clearly shifting. A recent poll found that 51 percent of Canadians favor decriminalizing marijuana.

Will It Work?

Both at home and abroad, the U.S. government has attempted to block resolutions supporting harm reduction, suppress scientific studies that reached politically inconvenient conclusions, and silence critics of official drug policy. In May 1994 the State Department forced the last-minute cancellation of a World Bank conference on drug trafficking to which critics of U.S. drug policy had been invited. That December the U.S. delegation to an international meeting of the U.N. Drug Control Program refused to sign any statement incorporating the phrase "harm reduction." In early 1995 the State Department successfully pressured the World Health Organization to scuttle the release of a report it had commissioned from a panel that included many of the world's leading experts on cocaine because it included the scientifically incontrovertible observations that traditional use of coca leaf in the Andes causes little harm to users and that most consumers of cocaine use the drug in moderation with few detrimental effects. Hundreds of congressional hearings have addressed multitudinous aspects of the drug problem, but few have inquired into the European harm-reduction policies described above. When former Secretary of State George Shultz, then–Surgeon General M. Joycelyn Elders, and Baltimore Mayor Kurt Schmoke pointed to the failure of current policies and called for new approaches, they were mocked, fired, and ignored, respectively—and thereafter mischaracterized as advocating the outright legalization of drugs.

In Europe, in contrast, informed, public debate about drug policy is increasingly common in government, even at the EU level. In June 1995 the European Parliament issued a report acknowledging that "there will always be a demand for drugs in our societies . . . the policies followed so far have not been able to prevent the illegal drug trade from flourishing." The EU called for serious consideration of the Frankfurt Resolution, a statement of harm-reduction principles supported by a transnational coalition of 31 cities and regions. In October 1996 Emma Bonino, the European commissioner for consumer policy, advocated decriminalizing soft drugs and initiating a broad prescription program for hard drugs. Greece's minister for European affairs, George Papandreou, seconded her. Last February the monarch of Liechtenstein, Prince Hans Adam, spoke out in favor of controlled drug legalization. Even Raymond Kendall, secretary general of Interpol, was quoted in the August 20, 1994, *Guardian* as saying, "The prosecution of thousands of otherwise law-abiding citizens every year is both hypocritical and an affront to individual, civil and human rights. . . . Drug use should no longer be a criminal offense. I am totally against legalization, but in favor of decriminalization for the user."

One can, of course, exaggerate the differences between attitudes in the United States and those in Europe and Australia. Many European leaders still echo Chirac's U.S.-style antidrug pronouncements. Most capital cities endorse the Stockholm Resolution, a statement backing punitive prohibitionist policies that was drafted in response to the Frankfurt Resolution. And the Dutch have had to struggle against French and other efforts to standardize more punitive drug laws and policies within the EU.

Conversely, support for harm-reduction approaches is growing in the United States, notably and vocally among public health professionals but also, more discreetly, among urban politicians and police officials. Some of the world's most innovative needle exchange and other harm-reduction programs can be found in America. The 1996 victories at the polls for California's Proposi-

tion 215, which legalizes the medicinal use of marijuana, and Arizona's Proposition 200, which allows doctors to prescribe any drug they deem appropriate and mandates treatment rather than jail for those arrested for possession, suggest that Americans are more receptive to drug policy reform than politicians acknowledge.

But Europe and Australia are generally ahead of the United States in their willingness to discuss openly and experiment pragmatically with alternative policies that might reduce the harm to both addicts and society. Public health officials in many European cities work closely with police, politicians, private physicians, and others to coordinate efforts. Community policing treats drug dealers and users as elements of the community that need not be expelled but can be made less troublesome. Such efforts, including crackdowns on open drug scenes in Zurich, Bern, and Frankfurt, are devised and implemented in tandem with initiatives to address health and housing problems. In the United States, in contrast, politicians presented with new approaches do not ask, "Will they work?" but only, "Are they tough enough?" Many legislators are reluctant to support drug treatment programs that are not punitive, coercive, and prison-based, and many criminal justice officials still view prison as a quick and easy solution for drug problems.

Lessons from Europe and Australia are compelling. Drug control policies should focus on reducing drug-related crime, disease, and death, not the number of casual drug users. Stopping the spread of HIV by and among drug users by making sterile syringes and methadone readily available must be the first priority. American politicians need to explore, not ignore or automatically condemn, promising policy options such as cannabis decriminalization, heroin prescription, and the integration of harm-reduction principles into community policing strategies. Central governments must back, or at least not hinder, the efforts of municipal officials and citizens to devise pragmatic approaches to local drug problems. Like citizens in Europe, the American public has supported such innovations when they are adequately explained and allowed to prove themselves. As the evidence comes in, what works is increasingly apparent. All that remains is mustering the political courage.

Note

1. Lynn Zimmer and John P. Morgan. (1997) *Marijuana Myths, Marijuana Facts: A Review of the Scientific Evidence.* New York: Lindesmith Center.

For Discussion

Why has the United States traditionally been so resistant to harm reduction strategies?

39

Why Can't We Make Prohibition Work Better?

Some Consequences of Ignoring the Unattractive*

Peter Reuter

In this article, Peter Reuter describes the huge costs and punitiveness of U.S. drug policies. Government initiatives to reduce the supply of drugs have failed to produce an increase in the price of drugs—in fact, Reuter observes that street prices for most drugs have declined since the most recent War on Drugs. Moreover, perceptions among young persons suggest that drugs are more available currently than in years past. Reuter discusses this paradox. He also notes that despite the enormous amount of funds designated for reducing the supply of drugs, evaluations into the impact of these expenditures are lacking.

Introduction

United States drug policies are punitive (in both rhetoric and reality), divisive (certainly by race, probably by age and perhaps by class), intrusive (in small ways for many and in large ways for some groups) and expensive ($30 billion annually). Even more distressingly, the nation has a drug problem more severe than that of any other rich Western society, whether measured in terms of the extent of drug use, dependence on expensive drugs, drug-related AIDS cases, or the level of violence and corruption associated with these drugs.

Many contend that the problems are a consequence of our policies. Either it is the harshness of those policies that has generated the disease and violent crime that surround drug use (the standard liberal critique)[1] or it is the lack of effective stringency that explains why drugs are so widely used and available (the hawks' critique).[2] Yet this may give too much credit to the role of policy, a common fallacy in modern American discussions, particularly in the nation's capital, whose business is precisely policy. Whether or not there is an epidemic of experimentation with a particular drug; what fraction of experimenters goes on to become dependent; and the severity of health and crime consequences of dependence may all be much more shaped by factors other than policy. Certainly, when comparing America's drug problems with those of other nations, most of the relevant differences appear to be rooted in broader features of societies; e.g., the United States is characterized by greater hedonism, weak informal social controls, a higher propensity for risk taking, inadequate provision of health care for the poor, unequal income distribution, and high level of criminal violence generally; it is also more intimately connected with cocaine and opium growing regions, such as Colombia and Mexico. All these factors promote use of illicit psychoactive drugs and/or worsen the problems associated with that use.

If policy is only moderately important in controlling drug use, then perhaps we can mitigate the harshness of our policies with little risk of seeing an expansion of drug use and related problems. Reducing our drug *policy* problem (i.e., the adverse consequences of the policies themselves) is worth a good deal, though it would obviously be even more desirable if we could also reduce our drug problem.

But it is hard to be highly prescriptive here, to say what good drug policy would look like, because one consequence of politicians' treating drug control as a moral crusade has been an absolute uninterest, bordering on gross negligence, in assessing the consequences, good or bad, of the emphasis on punishment. We cannot say, even approximately, whether locking up more drug dealers or seizing lots of assets has any substantial effect on prices or whether higher prices would have much effect on American drug usage or related violence. There is no credible basis for describing a policy that would reduce, in any important dimension, the extent of American drug problems by, say, one-third in the next five years.

What I will offer is a set of reasonable conjectures, but a central message of this paper is that without systematic evaluation of the consequences of drug enforcement and punishment, the current stagnation of drug policies will almost certainly continue.

Characterizing American Drug Policies and Problems

Policies

The most striking characteristics of the U.S. response to illicit drugs in the last decade have been its scale and its punitiveness. The federal government spends about $15 billion annually on drug control. State and local governments probably spend at least as much.[3] Thus drug control is a $30–35 billion government program in the mid-1990s, massively up from about $6–7 billion in 1985. By comparison, the figure for all public law enforcement expenditures was about $110 billion in 1996.

The intended punitiveness is reflected in budgets. About three-quarters of the national drug control budget is spent on apprehending and punishing drug dealers and users, with treatment getting about two-thirds of the remainder. State and local governments are even more enforcement-oriented than the federal government; budgetarily they exhibit a disdain for prevention, even though this is primarily a school-based activity which seems most naturally to flow from local governments.

The total punishment levied for drug control purposes has increased massively since 1981, when the concern with cocaine became prominent. The number of commitments to state and federal prison have risen approximately tenfold over the same period. By 1994, there were almost 400,000 people in prison or jail serving time for selling or using drugs; the comparable figure for 1980 was about 31,000 (see Table 39.1).

At the state level, one striking feature is the number of persons being imprisoned for drug *possession* felonies. This does not include possession with intent to distribute, which is classified as a distribution offense. In 1992 50,000 were sentenced to state prison for non-distribution offenses, mostly simple possession; some may be plea-bargained down from distribution charges.

Sentencing figures are of themselves insufficient to show that enforcement has become more stringent; that depends on the ratio of sentences (or years of prison time) to

Table 39.1

Trends in Drug Enforcement, 1980–1994

	1980	1985	1990	1994
Drug Arrests	581,000	811,000	1,090,000	1,350,000
Heroin and cocaine only	70,000	240,000	590,000	635,000
	(12%)	(30%)	(54%)	(47%)
Distribution only	104,000	192,000	345,000	370,000
	(18%)	(30%)	(31%)	(27%)
Inmates [Total]	31,000	68,000	291,000	392,000
Local jails	7,000	19,000	111,000	137,000
State prisons	19,000	39,000	149,000	202,000
Federal prisons	4,900	9,500	30,500	51,800

Sources: *Uniform Crime Reports, Correctional Population in the United States*: jail figures are author's estimates.

offenses. Imprisonment may hardly have kept up with the growth of drug markets. The number of offenses might have risen as rapidly as arrests/sentences/years of prison time between 1980 and 1985, when cocaine consumption was still expanding rapidly, but from 1985 to 1995 it is very likely that the number of offenses (transactions) and offenders (sales/sellers/users) was essentially flat; the risk of being imprisoned for a cocaine or heroin user or seller went up very sharply, perhaps nearly tenfold.

How risky is drug selling or drug possession? The aggregate data suggest that in 1994 a cocaine user had an 8 percent risk of being arrested; for a heroin user the figure may have been 10 percent. For drug selling, Robert MacCoun and I estimated in a study of the District of Columbia that, in 1988, street dealers of drugs faced about a 22 percent probability of imprisonment in the course of a year's selling and that, given expected time served, they spent about one-third of their selling career in prison.[4] These figures on sellers are somewhat higher than crude calculations at the national level for more recent years.

Does this make drug selling appropriately risky? One-third of a career in prison seems quite a lot. On the other hand, the risk per sale is very small indeed; in our Washington, D.C. study a seller who worked two days a week at this trade made about 1,000 transactions in the course of a year. His imprisonment risk per transaction was only about 1 in 4,500; by that metric, drug selling is a great deal less risky than, say, a burglary or robbery. Another way to assess the risk is to look at aggregate figures. It is estimated that American users consume 300 tons of cocaine per annum. If these are sold in 1 gram units, then this represents 300 million transactions, which result in fewer than 100,000 prison sentences; that generates a prison risk for a single cocaine sales transaction of about 1 in 3,000.

The punitiveness of American drug policy is not simply captured in numbers. It is also an element of rhetoric and other programs. The 1996 presidential candidates competed, albeit briefly and unconvincingly, in efforts to demonstrate their toughness; no other aspect of drug policy merited a mention. Senator Dole accused the administration of failing to make adequate use of the military, particularly in the interdiction campaign. President Clinton responded by proposing that teenagers be drug tested when they apply for a driver's license. More recently House Speaker Newt Gingrich, in what was billed as a major address on domestic policy initiatives, proposed life sentences for those trafficking across state boundaries, and death sentences for the second offense.

Even the new federal welfare reform package includes its very own antidrug clause; unless a state affirmatively opts out, it must deny federal benefits to any applicant who has been convicted of a post-1996 drug felony. As deterrence, it presumes a peculiar long-sightedness on the part of offenders. It can reasonably be called spiteful, though it is not as mean-spirited as Senator Gramm's original version, which imposed loss of a wide range of public benefits for any drug conviction. It certainly serves no welfare goal to cut off those convicted at age eighteen for simple possession of small amounts of crack, as in California, from a right to welfare at age thirty-five.

What Has Toughness Accomplished?

Toughness should raise prices, make drugs less accessible, and reinforce messages that drugs are disapproved of and harmful. This should lead to less drug use and, eventually, fewer drug-related problems. In fact illegal drugs are remarkably expensive, not universally accessible, and generally feared. Nevertheless, it is striking that, notwithstanding sharply increased stringency, prices are declining, many of the young see drugs as quite easy to get, and the fear of the most widely used drug (marijuana) is declining.[5]

Illicit drugs are very expensive by most measures. Marijuana is a cultivated weed like tobacco, but whereas a cigarette costs, even with excise taxes, hardly ten cents, an equivalent amount of marijuana costs $5 or more. Heroin, a processed agricultural good like sugar, is vastly more expensive than gold, costing about $5,000 per ounce (wholesale), compared to gold's $400.

All the same, cocaine and heroin prices have fallen steadily since 1981; by 1995, after adjusting for inflation, they were only about one-third of their 1981 levels. For marijuana, prices rose steadily and substantially from 1981 to 1992 and then fell in the next four years back to their 1981 level. Even more surprising is Jon Caulkins's finding that crack cocaine, singled out for tough sentencing, both at the national level and in some major states (e.g., California), is no more expensive at the retail level than powder cocaine in terms of price per pure milligram.

This failure of cocaine and heroin prices to rise with tougher enforcement is a major analytic and policy puzzle. Declining demand, reduced labor market opportunities for aging drug user/sellers, a decline in violence engendered by few new entrants and lower margins, and the locking up of criminal users are just some of the possible factors contributing to this. None has been subject to systematic examination.

If enforcement did not raise prices for the drugs, then it might still have been successful if it lowered availability. The only long-term data, from the annual survey of high school seniors, suggest otherwise. For example, 80 to 90 percent of the students report that they think marijuana is very available or available to them, a figure that has been stable for two decades. The percentage of seniors reporting that cocaine was available or readily available was 46 percent in 1995, compared to 30 percent in 1980, though down somewhat from its 1989 high of 55 percent. The finding that marijuana is perceived as more available to high school students than alcohol or cigarettes has been widely reported.

Drug use is estimated to be half as prevalent in 1995 as in the early 1980s, but it is now growing, albeit very slowly; in 1995 the percentage of those over twelve who reported using an illicit drug in the previous month was 6 percent, compared to 14 percent in 1981.[6] The numbers dependent on cocaine and heroin have been fairly stable over a long period of time, at about 2.5 million. It seems likely that the severity of the nation's drug problem as measured by the related violence and health costs has also been fairly stable over that period of time, though declining somewhat since about 1990.

In some cities it appears that local enforcement has driven open air markets indoors. Driving around with police in Washington, D.C., one certainly observes much more circumspect behavior than was true in the late 1980s. This may be a major accomplishment. Open air markets not only ease access for users moving from experimentation to regular consumption but also breed violence and disorder.[7]

In summary, increasing toughness has not accomplished its immediate objectives of raising price and reducing availability. Drug use has declined, but the most proximate cause, as reported in the high school senior survey, seems to be a shift in attitudes as to the risks and approval of use of specific drugs. Though enforcement might influence those perceptions, there is no correlation between crude measures of toughness and those perceptions.

But toughness has clearly had other consequences as well.

Divisiveness

It is hard to analyze drug enforcement in contemporary America without reference to race.[8] In 1992 blacks (12 percent of the general population) constituted two-thirds of admissions to state prison for drug offenses, compared to slightly less than one-half for all non-drug offenses. A similar disproportion existed for Hispanics; 10 percent of the population, they constituted 25 percent of all those sent to prison for drug offenses.

The origins of this disproportion are a matter of controversy. The standard critique is that the population of drug users is predominantly white; differences in prevalence rates for drugs (even crack) are far too modest to overcome the vastly larger white population. Ergo, drug sellers should be primarily white. This argument is at best incomplete. Sellers are a select group of users; they are likely to be poorer and more deviant than users generally since selling is risky and widely condemned. The urban poor are disproportionately minority.

Racism may play a role but a lot is driven by the police responsiveness to concerns about drug selling and the violence and disorder around inner-city markets. Focusing on those involved in the street selling of expensive drugs (essentially anything other than marijuana) is likely to generate disproportionate numbers of arrests among central city poor young males, who are tempted into this business both by the unattractiveness of their legitimate economic opportunities and the accessibility of these selling opportunities.[9] These populations are again disproportionately minorities.

Drug selling has indeed become a common activity among poor minority urban males. For Washington, D.C., my colleagues and I estimate that over one-quarter of African American males born in the 1960s were charged with drug selling between the ages of eighteen and twenty-four.[10] Most were charged with a drug felony and most will be convicted of that offense.

But it is what happens after arrest that generates much of the controversy. In particular, the disproportion in sentences for crack offenses, for which arrests are overwhelmingly of blacks and Hispanics, has been a major political issue. This, together with the difficulty of articulating any credible grounds for maintaining the current federal disparity, has increased suspicion in the black community that drug enforcement is an instrument of continuing white oppression. Tom and Mary Edsall report that focus groups in the early 1990s found that many blacks believed drug enforcement was part of an effort by the white community to oppress blacks.[11]

Nor is this the only division in society arising from tough drug policies. For the young the growing harshness of rhetoric and policy to marijuana, arrests for simple possession having doubled in the last five years, reduces the credibility of government generally. The claims about marijuana's dangers, both in public rhetoric and school prevention programs, seem grossly exaggerated and indeed lack much scientific basis. For HHS Secretary Shalala to say, as she did in a recent meeting, that marijuana is comparable to crack in its dangerousness, is to disparage science and reason.[12]

Marijuana is not good for health but represents less threat in that respect than do alcohol and cigarettes; no one dies of the acute effects of marijuana and even the long-term effects are surprisingly modest. The negative effects of marijuana use on adolescent development are clearer but still modest. These are not arguments for legalization (indeed, they argue rather more for prohibition of cigarettes and alcohol), but they create a tension when so much emphasis is placed on the health effects of the only one of these substances that is not legally promoted, and is disproportionately consumed by the young.

Intrusiveness

A whole array of legal innovations have been justified by the need to end the "scourge of drugs," to use President Bush's memorable 1989 phrase. Drug dealer "profiling" by police has allowed police to undertake numerous searches with barely plausible cause; most of those searched are again either minority or young or both.[13] Drug testing of federal employees (such as those in the executive office of the president) for purely symbolic purposes has demeaned public service. Some states require that candidates for state office be drug tested for symbolic purposes; the Supreme Court in 1997 unanimously ruled against this requirement for Georgia. Preventive detention, a particularly chilling power, has been extended in the context of the Controlled Substances Act.

Drug policy is clearly getting harsher in this respect. Some jurisdictions are contemplating testing welfare recipients for drug use and disqualifying those who cannot remain drug-free. Abe Rosenthal of the *New York Times*, the most prominent of columnist drug hawks, quickly pounced on President Clinton's proposal that all teenaged applicants for driver's licenses be subject to a drug test, suggesting that this was not nearly enough, and that the logic and facts spoke to the need to do random tests of young adults as well, since they are the highest risk group.[14]

The Punitive Cycle

The response to emerging drug problems is invariably punitive: the first twitch is to raise the statutory penalty for some offense. This was true in 1996 when methamphetamine showed signs of moving out of its long-established western base in San Diego, Dallas, etc. It has not yet happened for marijuana at the federal level, somewhat surprisingly, but various states are moving in that direction. For example, the Virginia Senate recently passed an increase in maximum sentences for marijuana possession offenses; a second conviction can result in a four-year prison sentence.

This is truly a vicious cycle, since the argument for raising the sentence for offenses involving a particular drug are mostly that the current sentence is less than that for other drugs and hence encourages sellers to pick that drug. This systematically generates sentence inflation. Indeed, many in Congress responded to the claim of imbalance between crack and powder cocaine by suggesting dramatically increasing penalties for powder. In May 1997 the U.S. Sentencing Commission, defeated in its previous effort at reducing the crack-powder cocaine [disparity] by lowering the crack penalties, made recommendations that would indeed increase the powder penalties, while trying again to lower the discrepancy.

The intrusive and divisive elements of our policies are not inherent in prohibition. Even harsh punishment is not; consider how lightly we enforce laws against prostitution.[15] However, they arise remorselessly out of the logic of drug scares, under the assumption that tougher policies will make a difference. There is some understanding that racial disparity and loss of civil liberties are not trivial harms but this rubs up against the unquestioned assumption that another major goal is importantly served by these measures, namely reductions in drug problems.

Comparing the U.S. and Western Europe

Perhaps we suffer no more from illicit drugs and clumsy drug policies than other developed countries with more wealth than self-control. Robert MacCoun and I have been studying the experiences of ten Western European countries, all of which have had significant problems with heroin and marijuana; some have also experienced cocaine or amphetamine problems.[16]

European innovations in tolerant drug policy, such as the Dutch coffee shops and the Swiss heroin maintenance trials, attract a fair amount of attention in the United States. But most Western European drug policy is firmly in the prohibitionist legal framework and, with respect to drug selling, these countries are, by their standards, aggressive both in enforcing the laws and in the length of sentences served by traffickers. They are, with Sweden and France as interesting exceptions, very much less aggressive toward drug users than is the U.S. They are, again with the exception of Sweden and France, strong supporters of needle exchange programs and other efforts to reduce HIV risk behaviors among intravenous drug users. As the British Advisory Council on the Misuse of Drugs said famously in 1987, "Drugs are an important problem. AIDS is a more important problem."[17]

None of these countries has a problem with illicit drugs comparable to that in the U.S., mostly because they have not experienced a major epidemic of cocaine use. The highest reported figure we have been able to find for lifetime marijuana use among high school seniors is 36 percent in Spain, compared to more than 50 percent in the U.S. in recent years; for most European countries the figure is closer to one-quarter. Heroin addiction in some countries, notably Italy, Spain, and Switzerland, approaches the U.S. rate of about 2–3 per 1,000 population. But if one adds in cocaine, the U.S. figures for the prevalence of addiction are at least twice that of any European country.

Even starker is the difference in violence, though this is all impressionistic. I interviewed a senior Zurich police official during the period when that the city allowed drug sellers and buyers to operate openly in a park, called the Platzspitz, near the train station. The official was complaining about how bad the crime situation had become because of the drug market. He showed me a list of the thirty-one major crime incidents in the park in 1990. The list included a fight with a policeman and precisely one homicide. This for a park in which many hundreds of drug dealers and buyers, using heroin and some cocaine, congregated every day! In other European cities the drug market generates theft and disorder but not high levels of violence.

AIDS related to intravenous drug use has been a significant problem in some European countries, with France, Italy, and Switzerland the most badly affected. But neither in terms of the fraction of IVDU who are HIV-positive nor in the fraction of the population that is HIV positive as the result of drug use does any European country approach the U.S.

Should we attribute the smaller drug problems in Europe to their policies? MacCoun and I see little basis for this. Take the violence for example. The low level of violence in crime generally, perhaps itself the result of the small number of guns, is more plausible a factor than any policy action by police or the criminal justice system. The absence of a significant cocaine epidemic can hardly be attributed to enforcement; prices are now down near to U.S. levels despite increasing seizures. The greater strength of families in Southern Europe, the better safety net for those who are long-term unemployed, and the smaller fraction of young males growing up in poor female-headed households, are plausibly more important. It is hard to do any formal testing with the available data but this seems to us a reasonable interpretation.

Interestingly, the choice of drug policy by nations is more influenced by views about the role of government, as well as by views about what constitutes the drug problem. For example, the Swedish population accepts a paternalistic state and will tolerate highly intrusive rules, including compulsory drug treatment even without an arrest. In Spain there are no criminal penalties for the possession of small amounts of any psychoactive drug; this represents less a decision about drug policy than a response to the long experience with the authoritarian Franco regime, which has created a strong suspicion of any laws that allow the government to regulate private conduct. Europeans generally see illicit drugs as primarily a personal and health problem, a position consistent with the lower levels of drug-related violence. The U.S. public sees illegal drugs as a crime problem; almost all speeches and most newspaper articles refer to "drugs and crime." For a nation that sees crime as something to be solved by punishment, that is enough to sustain a set of laws and programs that make toughness their centerpiece.

A Role for Research

Clearly there are policy alternatives to our current regime, even if we stick with prohibition. For any proposal involving less harshness the central issue is assessing the consequences of a highly punitive approach. At a minimum it would be useful to say whether longer prison sentences, more drug seizures, or more intensive money-laundering investigations can increase prices or reduce availability, and what effect these changes would have on drug use by current and prospective users, and on drug-related problems. There is not a single empirical paper that attempts to answer that question. The closest one gets is a paper of twenty-five years ago, which found that higher prices for heroin increased property crimes in Detroit.[18] There has been a little progress lately in estimating the price elasticity of demand for various drugs and various populations[19] but that is just a baby first step.

Oddly enough, we can say a great deal more about the effects of treatment and prevention, which account for no more than 20 percent of this nation's public expenditures on drug control, than about the consequences of enforcement.[20] Even more oddly, that is the result of the dedication to punishment; any other program has to justify itself against the suspicion that it is kind to criminals (treatment) or too diffuse (prevention). Since punishment is what drug users and sellers deserve, there is little need (in the eyes of politicians and perhaps the public) for these programs to demonstrate their effectiveness. Thus the National Institute on

Drug Abuse has a research budget of $450 million; research on drug enforcement has to fight for its share of the National Institute of Justice's paltry $30 million annual budget, albeit that money is tripled by various evaluations and earmarks. Twenty million dollars is certainly far too generous an estimate of the funding for research related to drug enforcement.

One can usefully adapt a complaint of the public health research world to explain this situation. Prevention researchers object that whereas surgical procedures only have to be shown to be safe and medicines safe and effective, prevention programs have to be demonstrated to be safe, effective, and cost-effective as well. The corollary for drug enforcement is that it doesn't even have to be shown to be safe, let alone effective or cost-effective. Drug enforcement has become a crusade, and crusaders scarcely need a map, let alone evaluation.

The federal enforcement agencies sponsor no research themselves, notwithstanding federal program expenditures of about $10 billion. The DEA and FBI may generously be called non-analytic; more accurately they are anti-analytic. Not only do they lack any internal policy analytic capacity, they seem to lack even the ability to contract with external research organizations. The DEA's inability to report price data in a meaningful way, despite gathering about five thousand observations each year, is just symptomatic of this. Surely no other federal agency in the 1990s would report as a range the very highest and lowest figures, without any measure of central tendency; to report that the price range for marijuana went from $25–$450 in 1993 to $40–$450 in 1994 is to simply inform the world that these data are irrelevant.

Clearly a large research and analysis program is needed that has the depth and durability to develop more credible measures of the intensity of treatment and the size of the drug problem in a particular community. We need to take account of the enormous variation in the intensity of enforcement and severity of sentencing that seems to exist across cities and states. For example, in Texas in 1992 the median prison sentence for those convicted of drug trafficking was ten years, compared to only two years for those in Washington State. It should be possible to build on the improvements in the drug data indicators being developed by various federal agencies.

Why is there so little research on drug enforcement? Surely part of the answer is simply that there is, as James Q. Wilson noted in a recent lecture,[21] shockingly little research on crime control generally. But another factor, I conjecture, is a curious confluence of liberal and conservative interests. Those who support tough drug enforcement see no gain in evaluation; Peter Rossi's oft-cited comment, "If you don't like a program, evaluate it," is highly relevant. Liberals find the whole effort distasteful enough that they simply want nothing to do with it; in particular, they do not want to evaluate it for the purposes of making it work better. They would much rather focus on the programs in which they have faith and in which they passionately believe, namely prevention and treatment.

Conclusion

But a society that deliberately averts its eyes from an honest assessment of a massive and frequently cruel intervention that sacrifices so many other goals for the one desideratum of drug abstinence can scarcely expect to find a well-grounded alternative. I am struck by the lack of any nuanced debate about drug policy, beyond the ungrounded and polarizing legalization shouting match and the banal and marginal discussion of how the federal drug budget should be spent. Welfare reform, public housing policies, and income support generally may do more to affect drug abuse and related problems than those programs that claim to explicitly target them, yet there is rarely any serious discussion of their role in drug policy.

In John Le Carré's *The Honorable Schoolboy*, George Smiley finds some evidence that a prominent Chinese businessman in Hong Kong may be a Communist spy. Launching an investigation in Hong Kong is both politically sensitive and expensive, so he has to convene a meeting of the Foreign Office,

Treasury, and other agencies to get authorization and funds. The Foreign Office is aghast; if the investigation were to become public and the businessman were innocent, it would be a major political embarrassment. On the other hand, the governor in Hong Kong entertains and trusts this businessman, indeed may recommend him for a knighthood; it would be equally embarrassing if it turned out that he was a spy! They become increasingly panicked and press Smiley for a judgment; is he a spy? Smiley inscrutably says he cannot answer without doing the investigation. The end of the story is of course that they give him the money and the authority, because the answer must be found.

That is the situation we face with respect to drug policy. If you want to know the answer as to whether we can make prohibition less expensive, divisive, and intrusive and maybe reduce the American drug problem, then you can't expect anyone to give a persuasive answer, who is not provided the money and authority to find out what our tough enforcement actually accomplishes.

Doing less rarely attracts much support for dealing with a problem that still concerns large parts of the community. But this may be the only responsible recommendation that can be made now. Locking up drug offenders for shorter terms, worrying more about the racial disparities in sentencing policies, giving up fewer of our civil liberties for unlikely reductions in drug problems, may be the best one can do at the moment. That would mean less intrusive, divisive, and expensive policies and perhaps little increase in drug problems.

Researchers are always inclined to think that learning and understanding are important for policy. The failure of the repeated findings that drug treatment has a very high benefit–cost ratio to make a policy impact[22] is a sober reminder that the political decision making here is driven by other considerations. But we might actually see something approximating a reasonable discussion of the alternatives in front of the nation if there were a more credible base of empirical analysis available. In its absence we are doomed to rhetorical debate.

*This paper is derived from a lecture at the April 1992 American Philosophical Society 1992 meeting, which was originally published as "Hawks Ascendant," *Daedalus* 1992. This paper was updated and delivered as a lecture at the National Institute of Justice series *Perspectives on Crime and Justice* in February 1997. The research reported here was supported by a grant from the Alfred P. Sloan Foundation to RAND's Drug Policy Research Center. It draws heavily on work done jointly with Robert MacCoun, who provided valuable comments on the paper as well.

Notes

1. See, e.g., Skolnick, J., "Rethinking the Drug Problem," *Daedalus* 121.3 (1992): 133–60.

2. The most articulate statement of this position is contained in William Bennett's introduction to the first *National Drug Control Strategy* (Office of National Drug Control Policy, 1989).

3. Federal figures are published annually in the *National Drug Control Strategy* (Office of National Drug Control Policy). State and local figures are available only for 1990 and 1991; see *State and Local Spending on Drug Control Activities* (Office of National Drug Control Policy, 1993).

4. Reuter, MacCoun, and Murphy, *Money from Crime* (Santa Monica, Ca.: RAND, 1990).

5. The best data come from an annual survey of high school seniors conducted by the Institute of Social Research at the University of Michigan: Johnston, O'Malley and Bachman, *Monitoring the Future*.

6. Annual data on drug use in the general population are provided by the National Household Survey on Drug Abuse (Department of Health and Human Services).

7. On this and other enforcement effects see Kleiman, M., *Against Excess: Drug Policy for Results*, 1992, Chapter 6.

8. See Tonry, M., *Malign Neglect* (Oxford University Press, 1994).

9. The most compelling description of this world is provided in Bourgois, P., *In Search of Respect: Selling Crack in El Barrio* (University of California Press, 1996).

10. Saner, MacCoun, and Reuter, "On the Ubiquity of Drug Selling," *J. Quantitative Criminology* 11.4 (1995): 337–62.

11. Edsall, T. with M. Edsall, *Chain Reaction: The Impact of Race, Rights and Taxes on American Politics* (New York: W.W. Norton, 1991), 237.

12. This comment was reported by two participants in the meeting of the National Advisory Council of the Substance Abuse and Mental Health Administration in early 1997.

13. On these matters generally see Rudovsky, "The Impact of the War on Drugs on Procedural Fairness and Racial Equality," *Chicago Legal Forum* 1994: 23 7–74.

14. Rosenthal, A., *New York Times*, September 1996.

15. On recent prostitution enforcement policies, showing that most arrestees receive very modest penalties, see Pearl, Julie, "The Highest Paying Customers: America's Cities and the Costs of Prostitution Control," *Hastings Law Journal* 38 (1987): 769–90.

16. On the problems of comparison here see MacCoun, Saiger, Kahan, and Reuter, "Drug Policies and Problems: The Promise and Pitfalls of Cross-National Comparison," in N. Heather, A. Wodak, E. Nadelmann and P. Ohare (eds.), *Pyschoactive Drugs and Harm Reduction: From Faith to Science* (London: Whurr Publishers, 1993): 103–17.

17. Advisory Council on the Misuse of Drugs, *AIDS and Drug Misuse* (London, 1987).

18. Silverman, L. and N. Spruill, "Urban Grime and the Price of Heroin," *Journal of Urban Economics* 4 (1977): 80–103.

19. E.g., Saffer, Henry and Frank Chaloupka, "The Demand for Illicit Drugs," Working Paper No. 5238 (Cambridge, Mass.: National Bureau of Economic Research, 1995).

20. For a review see Anglin, M.D. and Y-I. Hser, "Treatment of Drug Abuse," in Tonry, M. and Wilson, J.Q. (eds.), *Drugs and Crime* (Chicago: University of Chicago Press, 1990).

21. Wilson, James Q., "What, if anything, can the federal government do to reduce crime?" *Perspectives on Crime and Justice, National Institute of Justice*, 1996.

22. The most important of these studies, which compares the costs of reducing cocaine consumption by one percent through treatment or enforcement, is Rydell, C.P. and S. Everingham, *Controlling Cocaine* (RAND, 1994).

For Discussion

What criteria should be used to evaluate the success or failure of the war on drugs?

Reprinted from: Peter Reuter, "Why Can't We Make Prohibition Work Better? Some Consequences of Ignoring the Unattractive." In *Proceedings From the American Philosophical Society* 141, pp. 262–275. Copyright © 1997 by Peter Reuter. Reprinted with permission. ✦

40

Legalizing Drugs

Would It Really Reduce Violent Crime?

James A. Inciardi

Using Goldstein's typology of drug-related violence, James Inciardi considers the implications for violence if drugs were legal. Drawing on the findings from several studies that show a strong link between alcohol use and violence, Inciardi concludes that alcohol-related violence is considerable, despite the fact that alcohol is legal. Based on this finding and others, he argues that legalizing drugs is unlikely to reduce drug-related violence.

Frustrated by evidence of only minimal progress in reducing the supply of illegal drugs on the streets of America, and disquieted by media stories of innocent victims of drug-related violence, numerous observers are convinced that the U.S. "War on Drugs" has failed. In an attempt to find a more viable solution to the "drug crisis," or at the very least, to try an alternative strategy, many proposals have been offered. The most controversial of these has been to legalize drugs. The overwhelming majority of Americans, including their political representatives as well as researchers and clinicians working in the drug field, consider legalization to be both simplistic and dangerous. By contrast, a small but highly vocal and prestigious minority argue that the benefits of legalizing drugs are well worth the risk.

Since the closing years of the 1980s, an ample body of literature debating drug legalization has accumulated (Nadelmann, 1989; Trebach and Inciardi, 1993; Wilson, 1990). Issues involving public health, ethics, freedom of choice, civil liberties, and public and private harm stir up healthy discussions. Among these, the crime issue often takes center stage, and the pro-legalization group argues that if marijuana, cocaine, heroin, and other drugs were legalized, drug-related crime, and particularly violent crime, would significantly decline (Nadelmann, 1987, 1988a, 1988b, 1988c, 1989; Trebach, 1989, 1990).

By contrast, the anti-legalization camps argue that violent crime would not necessarily decline in a legalized drug market and might actually increase for three reasons. First, removing the criminal sanctions against the possession and distribution of illegal drugs would make them more available and attractive and therefore create large numbers of new users. Second, an increase in use would result in a greater number of dysfunctional addicts who could not support themselves, their drug habits, and their drug-taking lifestyles through legitimate means. Hence, crime would be their only alternative. Third, more users would mean more of the violence associated with the ingestion of drugs (Inciardi, McBride, McCoy, Surratt, and Saum, 1995; Kleber, 1994).

These divergent points of view tend to persist because the relationships between drugs and crime are quite complex and because the possible outcomes of a legalized drug market are based primarily on speculation. However, this is an important issue that is not going to go away. As such, the intention here is to review the empirical literature on drugs and violence to determine *what*, if anything, might be inferred from existing data.

Considering 'Legalization'

How one approaches the legalization/violent crime/increase-decrease quandary depends on how "legalizing drugs" is operationalized. Would all currently illicit drugs be legalized, or would the experiment be limited to just certain ones? True legalization would be akin to selling such drugs as heroin and cocaine on the open market, much like alcohol and tobacco, with a few age-related restrictions. In contrast, there are "medicalization" and "decriminalization" alternatives (Reuben, 1994; Schmoke, 1994). *Medicalization* approaches are of many types, but in essence they would allow users to obtain prescriptions for some, or all, currently illegal substances. *Decriminalization* removes the criminal penalties associated with the possession of small amounts of illegal drugs for personal use while leaving intact the sanctions for trafficking, distribution, and sale.

But, what about *crack*-cocaine? It is clear in the literature that the legalizers, the decriminalizers, and the medicalizers avoid talking about this particular form of cocaine base. Perhaps they do not want to legalize crack out of fear of the drug itself or of public outrage. Arnold Trebach, emeritus professor of law at American University and the former president of the Drug Policy Foundation, is one of the very few who argue for the full legalization of *all* drugs, including crack. However, he explains that most are reluctant to discuss the legalization of crack-cocaine because "it is a very dangerous drug. . . . I know that for many people the very thought of making crack legal destroys any inclination they might have had for even thinking about drug-law reform" (Trebach and Inciardi, 1993, p. 110).

The story of crack is pretty well known, having been reported (and perhaps over-reported) in the media since early in 1986—the "highs," binges, and "crashes" that induce addicts to sell their belongings and their bodies in pursuit of more crack; the high addiction liability of the drug that instigates users to commit any manner and variety of crimes to support their habits; the rivalries in crack distribution networks that have turned some inner-city communities into urban "dead zones," where homicide rates are so high that police have written them off as anarchic badlands; the involvement of inner-city youths in the crack business, including the "peewees" and "wannabes" (want-to-be's), those street gang acolytes in grade school and junior high school who patrol the streets with walkie-talkies and cellular phones and handguns in the vicinity of crack houses, serving in networks of lookouts, spotters, and steerers, and aspiring to be "rollers" (short for high rollers) in the drug distribu-

tion business; and finally, the child abuse, child neglect, and child abandonment by crack-addicted mothers (Chitwood, Rivers, and Inciardi, 1996; Inciardi, Lockwood, and Potteiger, 1993; Ratner, 1993).

There is a related concern associated with the legalization of cocaine. Because crack is easily manufactured from powder cocaine (just add water and baking soda and then cook either on a stove or in a microwave), many drug policy reformers hold that no form of cocaine should be legalized. Logically, this weakens the argument that legalization will reduce drug-related violence, since much of this violence appears to be in the cocaine and crack distribution markets.

Within the context of these remarks, this chapter examines recent empirical studies of drugs and violence in an effort to begin unraveling the legalization/drugs-violence connection. And to better understand the overall relationships between drugs and violence, the analysis makes use of Goldstein's (1985) tripartite conceptual framework of psychopharmacological, economically compulsive, and systematic models of violence.

Psychopharmacological Violence

The common wisdom that violence primarily occurs either when people are desperate for more drugs or as a result of buying and selling drugs and not from the effects of drugs needs to be reconsidered. Users of drugs do get violent when they get high. (Spunt, Brownstein, Goldstein, Fendrich, and Liberty, 1995, pp. 133–134)

The psychopharmacological model of violence suggests that some individuals, as the result of short- or long-term ingestion of specific substances, may become excitable, irrational, and exhibit violent behavior. Research has documented that chronic users of amphetamines, methamphetamine, and cocaine in particular tend to exhibit hostile and aggressive behaviors. Psychopharmacological violence can also be a product of what is known as "cocaine psychosis" (Brody, 1990; Reiss and Roth, 1993; Satel et al., 1991; Weiss and Mirin, 1987, pp. 50–53). As dose and duration of cocaine use increase, the development of cocaine-related psychopathology is not uncommon. Cocaine psychosis is generally preceded by a transitional period characterized by increased suspiciousness, compulsive behavior, fault finding, and eventually paranoia. When the psychotic state is reached, individuals may experience visual and/or auditory hallucinations, with persecutory voices commonly heard. Many believe that they are being followed by police or that family, friends, and others are plotting against them. Moreover, everyday events tend to be misinterpreted in a way that supports delusional beliefs. When coupled with the irritability and hyperactivity that the stimulant nature of cocaine tends to generate in almost all of its users, the cocaine-induced paranoia may lead to violent behavior as a means of "self-defense" against imagined persecutors. The violence associated with cocaine psychosis is a common feature in many crack houses across the United States (Inciardi et al., 1993). Violence may also result from the irritability associated with the drug withdrawal syndromes. In addition, some users ingest drugs before committing crimes to both loosen inhibitions and bolster their resolve to break the law (Tunnell, 1992).

Acts of violence may result from either periodic or chronic use of a drug. For example, in a study of drug use and psychopathy among Baltimore city jail inmates, researchers at the University of Baltimore reported that cocaine use was related to assault, irritability, resentment, and hostility and concluded that these indicators of aggression may be a function of *drug effects* rather than predisposing conditions (Fishbein and Reuland, 1994). Similarly, Barry Spunt and his colleagues at National Development and Research Institute (NDRI) in New York City found that of 269 convicted murderers incarcerated in New York State prisons, 45% were high at the time of the offense (Spunt et al., 1995). Three in 10 believed the homicide was related to their drug use, challenging conventional beliefs that violence only infrequently occurs as a result of the effects of drug consumption. Even marijuana, which pro-legalizers consider harmless, may have a connection with violence and crime.

Spunt, Goldstein, Brownstein, and Fendrich (1994) and their colleagues also attempted to determine the role of marijuana in the crimes of the homicide offenders they interviewed in the New York State prisons. One third of those who had ever used marijuana had smoked the drug in the 24-hour period prior to the homicide. Moreover, 31% of those who considered themselves to be "high" at the time of committing murder felt that the homicide and marijuana were related. It might be added here that William Blount of the University of South Florida interviewed abused women in prisons and shelters for battered women located throughout Florida. He and his colleagues found that 24% of those who killed their abusers were marijuana users, while only 8% of those who did not kill their abusers smoked marijuana (Blount, Silverman, Sellers, and Seese, 1994).

In an alternative direction, a point that needs to be emphasized here is that alcohol is linked with violence to a far greater extent than any illegal drug (Miczek et al., 1994; Murdoch, Pihl, and Ross, 1990). For most addicts, the drug of choice is alcohol—because it is both legal (and therefore accessible) and inexpensive in comparison to other drugs. The extent to which alcohol claims responsibility for violent crimes compared with other drugs is apparent when the statistics are examined. For example, Carolyn Block and her colleagues at the Criminal Justice Information Authority in Chicago found that between 1982 and 1989, the use of alcohol by offenders or victims in local homicides ranged from 18% to 32% (Block et al., 1990).

Alcohol appears quite able to reduce the inhibitory control of threat, making it more likely that a person will exhibit behaviors normally suppressed by fear. In turn, this reduction of inhibition heightens the probability that intoxicated persons will perpetrate, or become victims of, aggressive behavior (Pihl, Peterson, and Lau, 1993). In this regard, consider the following comment by an anonymous physician, on the relationship between alcohol and crime: "When I see lung cancer, I'm 95% certain that cigarettes are involved; when I see a stab wound, I'm just as sure that alcohol is involved" (in Benjamin and Miller, 1991, p. 109).

A second physician, the director of emergency care at a major metropolitan hospital, was even more emphatic, stating "I have never seen a stab wound in which alcohol was not involved."

Backing up these anecdotal accounts, Douglass Murdoch of Quebec's McGill University found that in some 9,000 criminal cases drawn from a multinational sample, 62% of violent offenders were drinking shortly before or at the time of the offense (Murdoch et al., 1990). A more recent study by researchers at the School of Public Health at the University of Texas–Houston surveyed 2,075 ninth- and 11th-grade students in a large Texas school district. Their purpose was to examine the co-morbidity of violence and health risk behaviors. Findings indicated that male students involved in fighting and carrying weapons were almost 20 times more likely to drink alcohol regularly than those who were less aggresive (Orpinas, Basen-Engquist, Grunbaum, and Parcel, 1995).

Alcohol has consistently been linked to homicide. NDRI's Barry Spunt and his colleagues (Spunt, Goldstein, Brownstein, Fendrich, and Langley, 1994) interviewed 268 homicide offenders incarcerated in New York State correctional facilities to determine the role of alcohol in their crimes. Of the respondents, 31% reported being drunk at the time of the crime and 19% believed the homicide was related to their drinking. Similarly, in Blount et al.'s (1994) study of abused women in Florida, it was found that those women who eventually killed their abusers were more likely to use alcohol (64%) than those who did not (44%).

Substance use by violent offenders is often apparent to the victims of violence. For example, the U.S. Department of Justice (1992) found that 21% of victims of violent crimes believed their offender to have been under the influence of alcohol, and 7.6% believed other drugs influenced the offender's behavior. Similarly, in a study of urban violence, medical records and interviews of patients entering a small city trauma center in Youngstown, Ohio, determined that the vic-

tims considered their attackers to have been under the influence of alcohol and/or other drugs in 60% of the cases (Buss, Abdu, and Walker, 1995).

When analyzing the psychopharmacological model of drugs and violence, most of the discussions focus on the offender and the role of drugs in causing or facilitating crime. But what about the victims? Are the victims of drug- and alcohol-related homicides simply casualties of someone else's substance abuse? In addressing these questions, the data document that victims are likely to be drug users as well. For example, based on an analysis of the 4,298 homicides that occurred in New York City during 1990 and 1991, Kenneth Tardiff of Cornell University Medical College found that the victims of these offenses were 10 to 50 times more likely to be cocaine users than were members of the general population (Tardiff et al., 1994). Of the white female victims, 60% in the 25–34 age group had cocaine in their systems; for black females the figure increased to 72%. Tardiff speculated that the classic symptoms of cocaine use—irritability, paranoia, or aggressiveness—may have instigated the violence. In another study of cocaine users in New York City, it was found that female high-volume users were victims of violence far more frequently than low-volume users and nonusers of cocaine (Goldstein, Bellucci, Spunt, and Miller, 1991). Studies in numerous other cities and countries have yielded the same general findings—that a great many of the victims of homicide and other forms of violence are drinkers and drug users themselves (Collins, 1981).

An aspect of the drugs/violence connection rarely mentioned as part of the psychopharmacological model is driving while under the influence (DUI) of alcohol or other drugs. According to a 1997 National Highway Traffic Safety Administration report, alcohol was involved in nearly 39% of all fatal motor vehicle crashes. Moreover, data from the Centers for Disease Control (1997) indicate that alcohol is involved in nearly 25% of motor vehicle-related deaths among children aged 15 and under. As for driving under the influence of illegal drugs, data suggest that it is not uncommon. For example, in a

Memphis, Tennessee, study of persons arrested for reckless driving who did not appear to be under the influence of alcohol, urinalysis tests found 58% to be positive for cocaine, marijuana, or both (Brookoff, Cook, Williams, and Mann, 1994).

Economically Compulsive Violence

The economically compulsive model of violence holds that some drug users engage in economically oriented violent crime to support drug use. This model is illustrated in the many studies of drug use and criminal behavior that demonstrate that, although drug sales, property crimes, and prostitution are the primary economic offenses committed by users, armed robberies and muggings do indeed occur (Fagan and Chin, 1991; Inciardi, 1986, 1992).

Analyzing the legalization/drugs-violence connection within this model is far more complex than with the psychopharmacological pattern. The contention is that in a legalized market the prices of "expensive drugs" would decline to more affordable levels and hence predatory crimes would become unnecessary. This argument is based on several premises. First, it assumes that there is empirical support for what has been referred to as the "enslavement theory of addiction." Second, it assumes that people addicted to drugs commit crimes only for the purpose of supporting their habits. Third, it assumes that in a legalized market users could obtain as much of the drugs as they wanted whenever they wanted. Finally, it assumes that if drugs are inexpensive they will be affordable and hence crime will be unnecessary.

With respect to the first premise, for the better part of this century there has been a concerted belief that addicts commit crimes because they are "enslaved" to drugs, that because of the high prices of heroin, cocaine, and other illicit chemicals on the drug black market, users are forced to commit crimes in order to support their drug habits. Interestingly, however, there is no solid empirical evidence to support this contention. From the 1920s through the close of the 1960s, hundreds of studies of the relationship between crime and addiction were conducted (Austin and Lettieri, 1976; Greenberg and Adler, 1974). Invariably, when one analysis would support the posture of "enslavement theory," the next would affirm the view that addicts were criminals first and that their drug use was but one more manifestation of their deviant lifestyles. In retrospect, the difficulty lay in the ways that many of the studies had been conducted, with biases and deficiencies in research designs and sampling that rendered their findings of little value.

Research since the middle of the 1970s with active drug users on the streets of New York, Miami, Baltimore, and elsewhere has demonstrated that enslavement theory has little basis in reality (Johnson et al., 1985; McBride and McCoy, 1982; Nurco, Ball, Shaffer, and Hanlon, 1985; Stephens and McBride, 1976). All these studies of the criminal careers of heroin, cocaine, and other drug users have convincingly documented that although drug use tends to intensify and perpetuate criminal behavior, it usually does not initiate criminal careers. In fact, the evidence suggests that among the majority of street drug users involved in crime their criminal careers were well established prior to the onset of either narcotics or cocaine use. As such, it would appear that the "inference of causality"—that the high price of drugs on the black market per se causes crime—is simply not supported.

Looking at the second premise, a variety of studies document that drug use is not the only reason why addicts commit predatory crimes. They also do so to support their daily living expenses—food, clothing, and shelter. To cite but one example, researchers at the Center for Drug and Alcohol Studies at the University of Delaware studied crack users on the streets of Miami. Of the scores of active addicts interviewed, 85% of the men and 70% of the women paid for portions of their living expenses through street crime. In fact, half of the men and one fourth of the women paid for 90% or more of their living expenses through crime. And not surprisingly, 96% of the men and 99% of the women had not held a legal job in the 90-day period before being interviewed for the study (Inciardi and Pottieger, 1994).

With respect to the third premise, that in a legalized market users could obtain as much of the drugs as they wanted whenever they wanted, only speculation is possible. More than likely there would be some sort of regulation, and hence drug black markets would persist for those whose addictions were beyond the medicalized or legalized allotments. In a decriminalized market, levels of drug-related violence would likely either remain unchanged or increase (if drug use increased).

As for the last premise, that cheap drugs preclude the need to commit crimes to obtain them, the evidence emphatically suggests that this is not at all the case. Consider crack-cocaine. Although crack "rocks" are available on the illegal market for as little as $2 in some locales, users are still involved in crime-driven endeavors to support their addictions. For example, Miller and Gold (1994) surveyed 200 consecutive callers to the 1-800-COCAINE hotline who considered themselves to have a problem with crack. The researchers found that, despite the low cost of crack, 63% of daily users and 40% of nondaily users spent more than $200 per week on the drug. Similarly, interviews conducted by NDRI researchers in New York City with almost 400 drug users contacted in the streets, jails, and treatment programs found that almost half spent over over $1,000 a month on crack (Johnson, Natarajan, Dunlap, and Elmoghazy, 1994). The study also documented that crack users—despite the low cost of their drug of choice—spent more money on drugs than did users of heroin, powder cocaine, marijuana, and alcohol.

Miller and Gold (1994) summarized the issue of crack and crime by stating: "Once the severity of addictive use is established, the pattern of the cost of maintaining the addiction and its consequences is related to preoccupation with acquisition and compulsive use" (p. 1075).

Systematic Violence

The systematic model of violence maintains that violent crime is intrinsic to the very involvement with illicit substances. As such, systematic violence refers to the tradi-tionally aggressive patterns of interaction within systems of illegal drug trafficking and distribution. It is the systemic violence associated with trafficking in cocaine and crack in America's inner cities that has brought the most attention to drug-related violence in recent years. Moreover, it is concerns with this same violence that has focused the current interest on the possibility of legalizing drugs. And it is certainly logical to assume that if heroin and cocaine were legal substances, systemic drug-related violence might indeed decline significantly. However, there are two very important questions in this regard. First, is drug-related violence more often psychopharmacological than systemic? Second, is the great bulk of systemic violence related to the distribution of crack? If most of the drug-related violence is psychopharmacological in nature, and if systemic violence is typically related to crack—the drug generally excluded from consideration when legalization is argued—then it might be logical to conclude that legalizing drugs would *not* reduce violent crime.

Evidence from studies in New York City tend to contradict, or at least fail to support, the notion that legalizing drugs would reduce violent, systemic-related crime. For example, Goldstein et al.'s (1991) ethnographic studies of male and female drug users during the late 1980s found that cocaine-related violence was more often psychopharmacological than systemic. Among men, the greater the volume of cocaine consumed, the more violence they engaged in—most of which was unrelated to cocaine sales or distribution. Among the women, the great majority of violent events in which they were involved were not drug related.

Similarly, in the study of 4,298 New York City homicides mentioned earlier, 31% of the victims had used cocaine in the 24-hour period prior to their deaths (Tardiff et al., 1994). One of the conclusions of the study was that the homicides were not necessarily related to drug dealing. In all likelihood, as victims of homicide, the cocaine users may have provoked violence through irritability, paranoid thinking, and verbal or physical aggression—all of which are known to be among the psychopharmacological effects of cocaine.

Shifting to the alternative consideration, in a 1988 study of 414 New York City homicide events, 47% were not drug related, 10% were alcohol related, and the remaining 43% involved illegal drugs (Goldstein, Brownstein, Ryan, and Bellucci, 1989). Interestingly, 60% of the drug-related homicides involved crack, and as noted earlier, those arguing for legalizing drugs retreat from increasing the availability of crack. Going further, another 10% of the drug-related homicides were alcohol related. Thus, if alcohol, crack, and non-drug-related homicides were removed from consideration, only 87 homicides remain, or 21% of the total that potentially could have been eliminated if drugs were legal. And that is New York City, where drug use and violence rates were among the highest at the time of the study.

Going beyond this issue, there is another important question. Is all of the systemic violence we see in the drug industry actually drug-related? Some of it may be only indirectly related or not at all (Inciardi et al., 1995; Reiss and Roth, 1993). In Goldstein et al.'s (1991) study of high-volume cocaine users, it was suggested that drug use may be a symptom of a mode of living that includes violence that is not directly related to cocaine use or distribution. "Indirect" violence in the drug marketplace ranges from weapons readily accessible during disputes over nondrug matters, armed robberies targeting buyers carrying money and sellers transporting drugs, and female buyers who became victims of sexual assault (Reiss and Roth, 1993). Ansley Hamid (1990), a noted researcher and professor at John Jay College of Criminal Justice, made a striking point in this regard:

> Even among youth who are not crack users or distributors, crack continues to stimulate violence. The model it so vividly presents—extreme youth in control, adults "out of control," women exploited, the short life glorified—apparently absorbs whole neighborhoods faster than crack itself can addict. (p. 67)

A related issue is that guns contribute to violence both inside and outside the drug marketplace. In fact, firearm violence may be less related to the drug trade than is popularly believed. In a study of drug involvement and firearms possession by juveniles, Joseph Sheley of Tulane University found in 1994 that gun activity did not increase with rises in levels of drug use. Self-administered questionnaires given to over 800 male inmates in reform schools of four states (California, New Jersey, Illinois, and Louisiana) revealed that 83% had owned a gun prior to confinement and 69% owned three or more guns. Although 47% had used illicit drugs in the year or two before confinement and 25% were considered heavy users, nondrug users were equally as likely as users to possess, carry, and fire a gun. However, when broken down by sellers and nonsellers of drugs, a relationship emerged—those who sold drugs were more likely to posses, carry, and fire a gun. This certainly demonstrates a link between drug selling and firearm violence (though not necessarily a causal link), but it also shows that nonusers and nondealers are also heavily involved in gun activity.

There is evidence that the drive-by shootings that occur in our nation's inner cities have little or nothing to do with drugs. For example, in Lawrence Sherman's study in 1988 of shootings of innocent bystanders in four large cities, such shootings accounted for less than 1% of all homicides, and drug market conflicts were only one of several causes of the shootings (Sherman, Steele, Laufersweiler, Hoffer, and Julian, 1989). In a study of children and adolescents injured or killed in drive-by shootings in Los Angeles, investigators determined that those at risk for firearm violence lived in areas where gang rivalry and retaliatory shootings were frequent and that drug trafficking was not believed to be a major causative factor (Hutson, Anglin, and Pratts, 1994).

Research with gangs has also shown that lethal street violence is more often related to intergang battles over territory and other factors unrelated to the drug trade. In their study of 288 gang-related homicides in Chicago from 1987 through 1990, Carolyn and Richard Block (1993) found that less than 3% of the killings were drug related. Similar findings can be seen in studies by Klein,

Maxson, and Cunningham (1991) at the University of Southern California. After analyzing three years' worth of narcotics and homicide files at the Los Angeles Police and County Sheriff's departments, they concluded that there was only a weak association between street gangs, drug distribution, and violence. Most interesting, they found that gang violence—including homicide—did not increase with the introduction and proliferation of crack-cocaine in the mid-1980s. A subsequent study by researchers from the Centers for Disease Control came to the same conclusion—that gang violence in Los Angeles was typically unrelated to drugs (Meehan and O'Carroll, 1992). And in a study of gang-related homicides published in the *Journal of the American Medical Association* towards the close of 1995 there was a similar conclusion (Houston, Anglin, Kyriacou, Hart, and Spears, 1995). Of the 7,288 gang-related homicides that occurred in Los Angeles County from 1979 through 1994, drug trafficking was not considered a major factor. Rather, the problems were the increasing numbers of violent street gangs and gang members, greater levels of intergang violence, an increase in the use of firearms in gang violence, worsening socioeconomic conditions in the inner city, and the continual breakdown of sociocultural institutions.

Discussion

Study after study document that alcohol and other drugs have psychopharmacological effects that result in violence. Cocaine in all of its forms is linked to aggressive behavior as a result of the irritability and paranoia it engenders. Also, alcohol and cocaine have been found to be present in both the perpetrators and victims of violence. Alcohol is legal and cocaine is not, suggesting that the legal status of a drug may be unrelated to the issue of psychopharmacological violence. Hence, it is unlikely that such violence would decline if drugs were legalized.

Studies of economically compulsive violence also suggest that in a legalized market, crime would not necessarily decline. Users who engage in predatory behaviors do so for a variety of reasons—not only to obtain drugs but also to support themselves. And typically, as many studies suggest, drug-involved offenders were crime involved before the onset of their careers in drugs. Too, even when a drug is inexpensive, it still may not be affordable if there is addiction and compulsive use. This is amply illustrated in the experience with crack.

As for systemic violence, much of it is unrelated to the use of drugs. When it *is* drug linked, the overwhelming majority of violent episodes seems to be associated with the use of alcohol or crack, and this brings us to another interesting consideration. The illegal drug most associated with systemic violence is crack-cocaine, and of all illicit drugs, crack is the one now responsible for the most homicides. In a study done in New York City in 1988 by Goldstein and his colleagues, crack was found to be connected to 32% of all homicides and 60% of all drug-related homicides. What they concluded was that crack-related homicides appeared to be replacing other forms of homicide rather than augmenting the existing homicide rate.

Taking this point further, violence stems from many of the dysfunctional aspects of our society other than drug use. After studying the violence associated with crack distribution in Manhattan neighborhoods, Fagan and Chin (1990) concluded that crack has been integrated into behaviors that were evident before drug sellers' involvement with crack or its appearance on New York City streets. In other words, the crack users/dealers of today are often engrossed in violent and crime-involved lifestyles that likely exist (and previously did) independent of their involvement with crack. Furthermore, although there is evidence that crack sellers are more violent than other drug sellers, this violence is not confined to the drug-selling context—violence potentials appear to precede involvement in selling (Fagan and Chin, 1990).

It appears, then, that crack has been blamed for increasing violence in the marketplace, but perhaps this violence actually stems from the psychopharmacological consequences of crack use. *Crack dealers* are generally *crack users*, and since crack is highly addictive yet comparatively inexpensive, there is a continuous demand for it. This leads to the competition that generates violence. Legalizing crack would likely reduce the competition but increase the demand. Hamid (1990) reasons that increases in crack-related violence are due to the deterioration of informal and formal social controls throughout communities that have been destabilized by economic processes and political decisions. As such, does anyone really believe that we can improve on these complex social problems through the simple act of legalizing drugs?

As a final point here, the issue of whether or not legalization would create a multitude of new users needs to be addressed. This is important because it is at the heart of the argument of those who oppose legalization, and on this there are three issues. First, many biologists and anthropologists have argued that people have an inborn drive to alter their normal states of consciousness (Tiger, 1992; Weil, 1972). If the illicit drugs were suddenly legal, would the many who are currently suppressing this desire to experience an altered state give in to it? Second, many people do not use drugs simply because they are illegal. Or as Mark Kleiman (1992), author of *Against Excess: Drug Policy for Results*, recently put it,

> Illegality by itself tends to suppress consumption, independent of its effect on price, both because some consumers are reluctant to disobey the law and because illegal products are harder to find and less reliable as to quality and labeling than legal ones. (p. 108)

And third, although there is no way of accurately estimating how many new users there would be if drugs were legalized, in all likelihood there would be many. Currently, relatively few people are steady users of drugs. The University of Michigan's Monitoring the Future study for 1997 reported that less than 1% of high school seniors are daily users of either hallucinogens, cocaine, heroin, sedatives, or inhalants (Johnston, O'Malley, and Bachman, 1998). In fact, it is the addicts who overwhelmingly consume the bulk of the drug supply—80% of all alcohol and almost 100% of all heroin (Benjamin and Miller, 1991). In other words, there are significantly large numbers of non-users who have yet to even try drugs, let alone use them regularly. Of those who begin to use drugs "recreationally," researchers estimate that approximately 10% go on to serious, heavy, chronic, compulsive use (Grabowski, 1984). Herbert Kleber, former deputy director of the Office of National Drug Control Policy, estimated that cocaine users might increase from the current 2 million to between 18 and 50 million—which are the estimated numbers of problem drinkers and nicotine addicts (Kleber, 1994).

Restrictions on alcohol have curtailed its widespread use. During Prohibition, there was a decrease of 20% to 50% in the number of practicing alcoholics. These estimates were calculated based on a decline in cirrhosis and other alcohol-related deaths (Jellinek, 1960). After Prohibition ended, both of these indicators increased. More recently, when the drinking age was raised from age 18 to 21 across the United States, deaths from drinking and driving decreased dramatically.

What all of this suggests is that drug prohibition seems to be having some very positive effects and that legalizing drugs would not necessarily have a depressant effect on violent crime. With legalization, violent crime would likely escalate; or perhaps, some types of systematic violence would decline at the expense of greatly increasing the overall rate of violent crime. Moreover, legalizing drugs would likely increase physical illnesses and compound any existing psychiatric problems among users and their family members. And finally, legalizing drugs would not eliminate the effects of unemployment, inadequate housing, deficient job skills, economic worries, and physical abuse that typically contribute to the use of drugs.

References

Austin, C. A., and Lettieri, D. J. (1976). *Drugs and Crime: The Relationship of Drug Use and Concomitant Criminal Behavior*. Rockville, MD: National Institute on Drug Abuse.

Benjamin, D. K., and Miller, R. L. (1991). *Undoing Drugs: Beyond Legalization.* New York: Basic Books.

Block, C. R., and Block, R. L. (1993). *Street Gang Crime in Chicago.* Washington, DC: U.S. Department of Justice.

Block, C. R., Block, R. L., Wilson, M., and Daly, M. (1990). *Chicago Homicide from the Sixties to the Nineties: Have Patterns of Lethal Violence Changed?* Paper presented at the annual meeting of the American Society of Criminology, Baltimore, MD.

Blount, W. R., Silverman, I. J., Sellers, C. S., and Seese, R. A. (1994). Alcohol and drug use among abused women who kill, abused women who don't, and their abusers, *Journal of Drug Issues:* 166–177.

Brody, S. L. (1990). Violence associated with acute cocaine use in patients admitted to a medical emergency department. In M. De La Rosa, B. Y. Lambert, and B. Cropper (eds.), *Drugs and Violence: Causes, Correlates, and Consequences* (Monograph No. 103, DHSS Pub. No. ADM 90-1721). Rockville, MD: National Institute on Drug Abuse.

Brookoff, D., Cook, C. S., Williams, C., and Mann, C. S. (1994). Testing reckless drivers for cocaine and marijuana, *New England Journal of Medicine* 331: 518–522.

Buss, I. F., Abdu, R., and Walker, J. R. (1995). Alcohol, drugs, and urban violence in a small city trauma center, *Journal of Substance Abuse Treatment* 12(2): 75–83.

Centers for Disease Control. (1997). Alcohol-related traffic fatalities involving children—United States, 1985–1996, *Morbidity and Mortality Weekly Report* 46(48): 1129–1133.

Chitwood, D. D., Rivers, J. B., and Inciardi, J. A. (1996). *The American Pipe Dream: Crack and the Inner City.* Fort Worth, TX: Harcourt Brace.

Collins, J. J. (ed.) (1981). *Drinking and Crime.* New York: Guilford.

Fagan, J., and Chin, K. (1990). Violence as regulation and social control in the distribution of crack. In M. De La Rosa, E. Y. Lambert, and B. Gropper (eds.), *Drugs and Violence: Causes, Correlates, and Consequences* (Monograph No. 103, DHSS Pub. No. ADM 90-1721). Rockville, MD: National Institute on Drug Abuse.

Fagan, J., and Chin, K. (1991). Social processes of initiation into crack, *Journal of Drug Issues* 21: 313–343.

Fishbein, D. H., and Reuland, M. (1994). Psychological correlates of frequency and type of drug use among jail inmates, *Addictive Behaviors* 19(6): 583–598.

Goldstein, P. J. (1985). Drugs and violent behavior, *Journal of Drug Issues* 15: 493–506.

Goldstein, P. J., Brownstein, H. H., Ryan, P. J., and Bellucci, P. A. (1989). Crack and homicide in New York City, 1988: A conceptually based event analysis, *Contemporary Drug Problems* 16: 651–687.

Goldstein, P. J., Bellucci, P. A., Spunt, B. J., and Miller, T. (1991). Volume of cocaine use and violence: A comparison between men and women, *Journal of Drug Issues* 21: 345–367.

Grabowski, J. (ed.) (1984). *Cocaine: Pharmacology Effects and Treatment of Abuse.* Rockville, MD: National Institute on Drug Abuse.

Greenberg, S. W., and Adler, P. (1974). Crime and addiction: An empirical analysis of the literature, 1920–1973, *Contemporary Drug Problems* 3: 221–270.

Hamid, A. (1990). The political economy of crack related violence, *Contemporary Drug Problems*: 31–78.

Houston, H. R., Anglin, D., Kyriacou, D. N., Hart, J., and Spears, K. (1995). The epidemic of gang-related homicides in Los Angeles County from 1979 through 1994, *Journal of the American Medical Association* 274(13): 1031(6).

Hutson, H. R., Anglin, D., and Pratts Jr., M. J. (1994). Adolescents and children injured or killed in drive-by shootings, *The New England Journal of Medicine* 330: 324–327.

Inciardi, J. A. (1986). *The War on Drugs: Heroin, Cocaine, Crime, and Public Policy.* Mountain View, CA: Mayfield.

Inciardi, J. A. (1992). *The War on Drugs: The Continuing Epic of Heroin, Cocaine, Crack, Crime, AIDS, and Public Policy.* Mountain View, CA: Mayfield.

Inciardi, J. A., Lockwood, D., and Pottieger, A. E. (1993). *Women and Crack-cocaine.* New York: Macmillan.

Inciardi, J. A., McBride, D. C., McCoy, C. B., Surratt, H. L., and Saum, C. A. (1995). Violence, street crime and the drug legalization debate: A perspective and commentary on the U.S. experience, *Studies on Crime and Crime Prevention* 4(1): 105–118.

Inciardi, J. A., and Pottieger, A. E. (1994). Crack cocaine use and street crime, *Journal of Drug Issues* 24(2): 273–292.

Jellinek, E. M. (1960). *The Disease Concept of Alcoholism.* New Haven, CT: Hillhouse Press.

Johnson, B. D., Goldstein, P. J., Preble, P., Schmeidler, J., Lipton, D. S., Spunt, B., and Miller, T. (1985). *Taking Care of Business: The Economics of Crime by Heroin Users.* Lexington, MA: Lexington Books.

Johnson, B. D., Natarajan, M., Dunlap, E., and Elmoghazy, E. (1994). Crack abusers and noncrack abusers: Profiles of drug use, drug sales and nondrug criminality, *Journal of Drug Issues* 24(1): 117–141.

Johnston, L. D., O'Malley, P. M., and Bachman, J. G. (1998). *Monitoring the Future, 1997.* Ann Arbor: University of Michigan Press.

Kleber, H. (1994). Our current approach to drug abuse: Progress, problems, proposals, *New England Journal of Medicine* 330: 361–365.

Kleiman, M. A. R. (1992). *Against Excess: Drug Policy for Results.* New York: Basic Books.

Klein, M. W., Maxson, C. L., and Cunningham, L. C. (1991). "Crack," street gangs, and violence, *Criminology* 29(4): 623–650.

McBride, D. C., Burgman-Habermehl, C., Alpert, J., and Chitwood, D. D. (1986). Drugs and homicide, *Bulletin of the New York Academy of Medicine* 62(5): 497–508.

McBride, D. C., and McCoy, C. B. (1982). Crime and drugs: The issues and the literature, *Journal of Drug Issues* 12: 137–152.

Meehan, P. J., and O'Carroll, P. W. (1992). Gangs, drugs, and homicide in Los Angeles, *American Journal of Disadvantaged Children* 146(6): 683–687.

Miczek, K. A., DeBold, J. F., Haney, M., Tidey, J., Vivian, J., and Weerts, E. M. (1994). Alcohol, drugs of abuse, aggression, and violence. In A. J. Reiss, Jr., and J. Roth (eds.), *Understanding and preventing violence*: Vol. 3. *Societal influences* (pp. 377–570). Washington, DC: National Academy Press.

Miller, N., and Gold, M. (1994). Criminal activity and crack addiction, *International Journal of the Addictions* 29(8): 1069–1078.

Murdoch, D., Pihl, R. O., and Ross, D. (1990). Alcohol and crimes of violence: Present issues, *International Journal of the Addictions* 25: 1065–1081.

Nadelmann, E. A. (1987). *The Real International Drug Problem.* Paper presented at the Defense Academic Research Support Conference "International Drugs: Threat and Response." National Defense College, Defense Intelligence Analysis Center, Washington, DC.

Nadelmann, E. A. (1988a). The case for legalization *Public Interest* 92: 3–31.

Nadelmann, E. A. (1988b). U.S. drug policy: A bad export, *Foreign Policy* 70: 83–108.

Nadelmann, E. A. (1988c). *Legalization of Illicit Drugs: Impact and Feasibility.* Select Committee Hearing on Narcotics Abuse and Control, House of Representatives, 100th Congress, Washington, DC.

Nadelmann, E. A. (1989). Drug prohibition in the United States: Cost, consequences, and alternatives, *Science* 245: 939–947.

National Highway Traffic Safety Administration. (1998). *Traffic Safety Facts 1997.* Washington, DC: National Center for Statistics and Analysis, U.S. Department of Treasury.

Nurco, D. N., Ball, J. C., Shaffer, J. W., and Hanlon, T. F. (1985). The criminality of narcotic addicts, *Journal of Nervous and Mental Disease* 173: 94–102.

Orpinas, P. K., Basen-Engquist, K., Grunbaum, J., and Parcel, G. S. (1995). The co-morbidity of violence-related behaviors with health-risk behaviors in a population of high school students, *Journal of Adolescent Health* 16: 216–225.

Pihl, R. O., Peterson, J. B., and Lau, M. A. (1993). A biosocial model of the alcohol-aggression relationship, *Journal of Studies on Alcohol* 11: 128–139.

Ratner, M. (1993). *Crack Pipe as Pimp: An Ethnographic Investigation of Sex-for-Crack Exchanges.* New York: Lexington Books.

Reiss, A. J., and Roth, J. (eds.) (1993). *Understanding and Preventing Violence:* Vol. 3: *Societal Influences.* Washington, DC: National Academy Press.

Reuben, R. C. (1994). New president willing to speak up: Media takes note of Bushnell's drug policy comments, *ABA Journal* 80: 85.

Satel, S. L., Price, L. H., Palumbo, J. M., McDougle, C. J., Krystal, J. H., Gawin, E., Chamey, D. S., Heninger, G. R., and Kleber, H. D. (1991). Clinical phenomenology and neurobiology of cocaine abstinence: A prospective inpatient study, *American Journal of Psychiatry* 148: 1712–1716.

Schmoke, K. L. (1994). Side effects, *Rolling Stone* 38(2).

Sheley, J. E. (1994). Drug activity and firearms possession and use by juveniles, *Journal of Drug Issues* 24(3): 363–382.

Sherman, L. W., Steele, L., Laufersweiler, D., Hoffer, N., and Julian, S. A. (1989). Stray bullets and 'mushrooms': Random shootings of bystanders in four cities, 1977–1988, *Journal of Quantitative Criminology* 5(4): 297–316.

Spunt, B., Brownstein, H., Goldstein, P., Fendrich, M., and Liberty, H. J. (1995). Drug use by homicide offenders, *Journal of Psychoactive Drugs* 27(2): 125–134.

Spunt, B., Goldstein, P., Brownstein, H., and Fendrich, M. (1994). The role of marijuana in homicide, *International Journal of the Addictions* 29(2): 195–213.

Spunt, B., Goldstein, P., Brownstein, H., Fendrich, M., and Langley, S. (1994). Alcohol and homicide: Interviews with prison inmates, *Journal of Drug Issues* 24(1): 143–163.

Stephens, R. C., and McBride, D. C. (1976). Becoming a street addict, *Human Organization* 35: 87–93.

Tardiff, K., Marzuk, P. M., Leon, A. C., Hirsch, C. S., Stajic, M., Portera, L., and Hartwell, N. (1994). Homicide in New York City: Cocaine use and firearms, *Journal of the American Medical Association* 272(1): 43–46.

Tiger, L. (1992). *The Pursuit of Pleasure.* Boston: Little, Brown.

Trebach, A. S. (1989). Tough choices: The practical politics of drug policy reform, *American Behavioral Scientist* 32: 249–258.

Trebach, A. S. (1990). A bundle of peaceful compromises, *Journal of Drug Issues* 20: 515–531.

Trebach, A. S., and Inciardi, J. A. (1993). *Legalize It? Debating American Drug Policy.* Washington, DC: American University Press.

Tunnell, K. D. (1992). *Choosing Crime: The Criminal Calculus of Property Offenders.* Chicago: Nelson-Hall.

U.S. Department of Justice, Bureau of Justice Statistics. (1992). *Drugs and Crime Facts, 1991.* Washington, DC: Government Printing Office.

Weil, A. (1972). *The Natural Mind: A New Way of Looking at Drugs and the Higher Consciousness.* Boston: Houghton Mifflin.

Weiss, R. D., and Mirin, S. M. (1987). *Cocaine.* Washington, DC: American Psychiatric Press.

Wilson, J. Q. (1990). Against the legalization of drugs, *Commentary* 21–28.

For Discussion

1. What issues might be addressed that would allow for reductions in both drug use and violence?

2. Outline the arguments for and against legalization that have been addressed in this section.

41

Against the Legalization of Drugs

James Q. Wilson

In contrast to Ethan Nadelmann's position, James Q. Wilson offers a number of arguments against legalizing drugs, especially heroin and cocaine. Wilson claims that because heroin has been illegal for so many years, the actual number of users has remained relatively stable since the early 1970s. Heroin is costly and difficult to obtain, and these factors deter individuals from using it. Cocaine, and especially "crack" cocaine, is a far more serious drug, and, if legalized, a major public health problem might ensue.

In 1972, the President appointed me chairman of the National Advisory Council for Drug Abuse Prevention. Created by Congress, the Council was charged with providing guidance on how best to coordinate the national war on drugs. (Yes, we called it a war then, too.) In those days, the drug we were chiefly concerned with was heroin. When I took office, heroin use had been increasing dramatically. Everybody was worried that this increase would continue. Such phrases as "heroin epidemic" were commonplace.

That same year, the eminent economist Milton Friedman published an essay in *Newsweek*, in which he called for legalizing heroin. His argument was on two grounds: as a matter of ethics, the government has no right to tell people not to use heroin (or to drink or to commit suicide); as a matter of economics, the prohibition of drug use imposes costs on society that far exceed the benefits. Others, such as the psychoanalyst Thomas Szasz, made the same argument.

We did not take Friedman's advice. (Government commissions rarely do.) I do not recall that we even discussed legalizing heroin, though we did discuss (but did not take action on) legalizing a drug, cocaine, that many people then argued was benign. Our marching orders were to figure out how to win the war on heroin, not to run up the white flag of surrender.

That was 1972. Today, we have the same number of heroin addicts that we had then—half a million—give or take a few thousand. Having that many heroin addicts is no trivial matter; these people deserve our attention. But not having had an increase in that number for over fifteen years is also something that deserves our attention. What happened to the "heroin epidemic" that many people once thought would overwhelm us?

The facts are clear: a more or less stable pool of heroin addicts has been getting older, with relatively few new recruits. In 1976, the average age of heroin users who appeared in hospital emergency rooms was about twenty-seven; ten years later, it was thirty-two. More than two-thirds of all heroin users appearing in emergency rooms are now over the age of thirty. Back in the early 1970s when heroin got onto the national political agenda, the typical heroin addict was much younger, often a teenager. Household surveys show the same thing—the rate of opiate use (which includes heroin) has been flat for the better part of two decades. More fine-grained studies of inner-city neighborhoods confirm this. John Boyle and Ann Brunswick found that the percentage of young blacks in Harlem who used heroin fell from 8 percent in 1970–71 to about 3 percent in 1975–76.

Why did heroin lose its appeal for young people? When the young blacks in Harlem were asked why they stopped, more than half mentioned "trouble with the law" or "high cost" (and high cost is, of course, directly the result of law enforcement). Two-thirds said that heroin hurt their health; nearly all said they had had a bad experience with it. We need not rely, however, simply on what they said. In New York City in 1973–75, the street price of heroin rose dramatically and its purity sharply declined, probably as a result of the heroin shortage caused by the success of the Turkish government in reducing the supply of opium base and of the French government in closing down heroin-processing laboratories located in and around Marseilles. These were short-lived gains, for, just as Friedman predicted, alternative sources of supply—mostly in Mexico—quickly emerged. But the three-year heroin shortage interrupted the easy recruitment of new users.

Health and related problems were no doubt part of the reason for the reduced flow of recruits. Over the preceding years, Harlem youth had watched as more and more heroin users died of overdoses, were poisoned by adulterated doses, or acquired hepatitis from dirty needles. The word got around: heroin can kill you. By 1974, new hepatitis cases and drug-overdose deaths had dropped to a fraction of what they had been in 1970.

Alas, treatment did not seem to explain much of the cessation in drug use. Treatment programs can and do help heroin addicts, but treatment did not explain the drop in the number of *new* users (who, by definition, had never been in treatment) nor even much of the reduction in the number of experienced users.

No one knows how much of the decline to attribute to personal observation, as opposed to high prices or reduced supply. But other evidence suggests strongly that price and supply played a large role. In 1972, the National Advisory Council was especially worried by the prospect that U.S. servicemen returning to this country from Vietnam would bring their heroin habits with them. Fortunately, a brilliant study by Lee Robins of Washington University in St. Louis put that fear to rest. She measured drug use of Vietnam veterans shortly after they had returned home. Though many had used heroin regularly while in Southeast Asia, most gave up the habit when back in the United States. The reason: here, heroin was less available and sanctions on its use were more pronounced. Of course, if a veteran had been willing to pay enough—which might have meant traveling to another city and would certainly have meant making an illegal contact with a disreputable dealer in a threatening neighborhood in order to acquire a (possibly) dangerous dose—he could have sustained his drug habit. Most veterans were unwilling to pay this price, and so their drug use declined or disappeared.

Reliving the Past

Suppose we had taken Friedman's advice in 1972. What would have happened? We cannot be entirely certain, but at a minimum we would have placed the young heroin addicts (and, above all, the prospective addicts) in a very different position from the one in which they actually found themselves. Heroin would have been legal. Its price would have been reduced by 95 percent (minus whatever we chose to recover in taxes.) Now that it could be sold by the same people who make aspirin, its quality would have been assured no poisons, no adulterants. Sterile hypodermic needles would have been readily available at the neighborhood drugstore, probably at the same counter where the heroin was sold. No need to travel to big cities or unfamiliar neighborhoods—heroin could have been purchased anywhere, perhaps by mail order.

There would no longer have been any financial or medical reason to avoid heroin use. Anybody could have afforded it. We might have tried to prevent children from buying it, but as we have learned from our efforts to prevent minors from buying alcohol and tobacco, young people have a way of penetrating markets theoretically reserved for adults. Returning Vietnam veterans would have discovered that Omaha and Raleigh had been converted into the pharmaceutical equivalent of Saigon.

Under these circumstances, can we doubt for a moment that heroin use would have grown exponentially? Or that a vastly larger supply of new users would have been recruited? Professor Friedman is a Nobel Prize-winning economist whose understanding of market forces is profound. What did he think would happen to consumption under his legalized regime? Here are his words: "Legalizing drugs might increase the number of addicts, but it is not clear that it would. Forbidden fruit is attractive, particularly to the young."

Really? I suppose that we should expect no increase in Porsche sales if we cut the price by 95 percent, no increase in whiskey sales if we cut the price by a comparable amount—because young people only want fast cars and strong liquor when they are "forbidden." Perhaps Friedman's uncharacteristic lapse from the obvious implications of price theory can be explained by a misunderstanding of how drug users are recruited. In his 1972 essay, he said that "drug addicts are deliberately made by pushers, who give likely prospects their first few doses free." If drugs were legal, it would not pay anybody to produce addicts, because everybody would buy from the cheapest source. But as every drug expert knows, pushers do not produce addicts. Friends or acquaintances do. In fact, pushers are usually reluctant to deal with non-users, because a non-user could be an undercover cop. Drug use spreads in the same way any fad or fashion spreads: somebody who is already a user urges his friends to try, or simply shows already eager friends how to do it.

But we need not rely on speculation, however plausible, that lowered prices and more abundant supplies would have increased heroin usage. Great Britain once followed such a policy and with almost exactly those results. Until the mid-1960s, British physicians were allowed to prescribe heroin to certain classes of addicts. (Possessing these drugs without a doctor's prescription remained a criminal offense.) For many years, this policy worked well enough because the addict patients were typically middle-class people who had become dependent on opiate painkillers while undergoing hospital treatment. There was no drug culture. The British system worked for many years, not because it prevented drug abuse, but because there was no problem of drug abuse that would test the system.

All that changed in the 1960s. A few unscrupulous doctors began passing out heroin in wholesale amounts. One doctor prescribed almost 600,000 heroin tablets—

that is, over thirteen pounds—in just one year. A youthful drug culture emerged with a demand for drugs far different from that of the older addicts. As a result, the British government required doctors to refer users to government-run clinics to receive their heroin.

But the shift to clinics did not curtail the growth in heroin use. Throughout the 1960s, the number of addicts increased—the late John Kaplan of Stanford estimated by fivefold—in part as a result of the diversion of heroin from clinic patients to new users on the streets. An addict would bargain with the clinic doctor over how big a dose he would receive. The patient wanted as much as he could get; the doctor wanted to give as little as was needed. The patient had an advantage in this conflict, because the doctor could not be certain how much was really needed. Many patients would use some of their "maintenance" dose and sell the remaining part to friends, thereby recruiting new addicts. As the clinics learned of this, they began to shift their treatment away from heroin and toward methadone, an addictive drug that, when taken orally, does not produce a "high" but will block the withdrawal pains associated with heroin abstinence.

Whether what happened in England in the 1960s was a mini-epidemic or an epidemic depends on whether one looks at numbers or at rates of change. Compared to the United States, the numbers were small. In 1960, there were 68 heroin addicts known to the British government; by 1968, there were 2,000 in treatment and many more who refused treatment. (They would refuse, in part because they did not want to get methadone at a clinic, if they could get heroin on the street.) Richard Hartnoll estimates that the actual number of addicts in England is five times the number officially registered. At a minimum, the number of British addicts increased by thirty fold in ten years; the actual increase may have been much larger.

In the early 1980s, the numbers began to rise again, and this time nobody doubted that a real epidemic was at hand. The increase was estimated to be 40 percent a year. By 1982, there were thought to be 20,000 heroin users in London alone. Geoffrey

Pearson reports that many cities—Glasgow, Liverpool, Manchester, and Sheffield among them—were now experiencing a drug problem that once had been largely confined to London. The problem, again, was supply. The country was being flooded with cheap, high-quality heroin, first from Iran and then from Southeast Asia.

The United States began the 1960s with a much larger number of heroin addicts and probably a bigger at-risk population than was the case in Great Britain. Even though it would be foolhardy to suppose that the British system, if installed here, would have worked the same way or with the same results, it would be equally foolhardy to suppose that a combination of heroin available from leaky clinics and from street dealers who faced only minimal law-enforcement risks would not have produced a much greater increase in heroin use than we actually experienced. My guess is that, if we had allowed either doctors or clinics to prescribe heroin, we would have had far worse results than were produced in Britain, if for no other reason than the vastly larger number of addicts with which we began. We would have had to find some way to police thousands (not scores) of physicians and hundreds (not dozens) of clinics. If the British civil service found it difficult to keep heroin in the hands of addicts and out of the hands of recruits when it was dealing with a few hundred people, how well would the American civil service have accomplished the same tasks when dealing with tens of thousands of people?

Back to the Future

Now cocaine, especially in its potent form, crack, is the focus of attention. Now, as in 1972, the government is trying to reduce its use. Now, as then, some people are advocating legalization. Is there any more reason to yield to those arguments today than there was almost two decades ago?[1]

I think not. If we had yielded in 1972, we almost certainly would have had today a permanent population of several million, not several hundred thousand, heroin addicts. If we yield now, we will have a far more serious problem with cocaine. Crack is worse than heroin by almost any measure. Heroin produces a pleasant drowsiness and, if hygienically administered, has only the physical side effects of constipation and sexual impotence. Regular heroin use incapacitates many users, especially poor ones, for any productive work or social responsibility. They will sit nodding on a street corner, helpless but at least harmless. By contrast, regular cocaine use leaves the user neither helpless nor harmless. When smoked (as with crack) or injected, cocaine produces instant, intense, and short-lived euphoria. The experience generates a powerful desire to repeat it. If the drug is readily available, repeat use will occur. Those people who progress to "bingeing" on cocaine become devoted to the drug and its effects, to the exclusion of almost all other considerations—job, family, children, sleep, food, even sex. Dr. Frank Gawin at Yale and Dr. Everett Ellinwood at Duke report that a substantial percentage of all high-dose, binge users become uninhibited, impulsive, hypersexual, compulsive, irritable, and hyperactive. Their moods vacillate dramatically, leading at times to violence and homicide.

Women are much more likely to use crack than heroin, and, if they are pregnant, the effects on their babies are tragic. Douglas Besharov, who has been following the effects of drugs on infants for twenty years, writes that nothing he learned about heroin prepared him for the devastation of cocaine. Cocaine harms the fetus and can lead to physical deformities or neurological damage. Some crack babies have, for all practical purposes, suffered a disabling stroke while still in the womb. The long-term consequences of this brain damage are lowered cognitive ability and the onset of mood disorders. Besharov estimates that about 30,000 to 50,000 such babies are born every year, about 7,000 in New York City alone. There may be ways to treat such infants, but from everything we now know, the treatment will be long, difficult, and expensive. Worse, the mothers who are most likely to produce crack babies are precisely the ones who, because of poverty or temperament, are least able and willing to obtain such treatment. In fact, anecdotal evidence suggests that crack mothers are likely to abuse their infants.

The notion that abusing drugs such as cocaine is a "victimless crime" is not only absurd but dangerous. Even ignoring the fetal drug syndrome, crack-dependent people are, like heroin addicts, individuals who regularly victimize their children by neglect, their spouses by improvidence, their employers by lethargy, and their co-workers by carelessness. Society is not and could never be a collection of autonomous individuals. We all have a stake in ensuring that each of us displays a minimal level of dignity, responsibility, and empathy. We cannot, of course, coerce people into goodness, but we can and should insist that some standards must be met if society itself—on which the very existence of the human personality depends—is to persist. Drawing the line that defines those standards is difficult and contentious, but if crack and heroin use do not fall below it, what does?

The advocates of legalization will respond by suggesting that my picture is overdrawn. Ethan Nadelmann of Princeton argues that the risk of legalization is less than most people suppose. Over 20 million Americans between the ages of eighteen and twenty-five have tried cocaine (according to a government survey), but only a quarter million use it daily. From this, Nadelmann concludes that at most 3 percent of all young people who try cocaine develop a problem with it. The implication is clear: make the drug legal, and we only have to worry about 3 percent of our youth.

The implication rests on a logical fallacy and a factual error. The fallacy is this: the percentage of occasional cocaine users who become binge users when the drug is illegal (and thus expensive and hard to find) tells us nothing about the percentage who will become dependent when the drug is legal (and thus cheap and abundant). Drs. Gawin and Ellinwood report, in common with several other researchers, that controlled or occasional use of cocaine changes to compulsive and frequent use "when access to the drug increases," or when the user switches from snorting to smoking. More cocaine more potently administered alters, perhaps sharply, the proportion of "controlled" users who become heavy users. The factual error is this: the federal survey Nadelmann quotes was done in 1985, before crack had become common. Thus, the probability of becoming dependent on cocaine was derived from the responses of users who snorted the drug. The speed and potency of cocaine's action increases dramatically when it is smoked. We do not yet know how greatly the advent of crack increases the risk of dependency, but all the clinical evidence suggests that the increase is likely to be large.

It is possible that some people will not become heavy users, even when the drug is readily available in its most potent form. So far, there are no scientific grounds for predicting who will and who will not become dependent. Neither socio-economic background nor personality traits differentiate between casual and intensive users. Thus, the only way to settle the question of who is correct about the effect of easy availability on drug use, Nadelmann or Gawin and Ellinwood, is to try it and see. But that social experiment is so risky as to be no experiment at all; for, if cocaine is legalized, and if the rate of its abusive use increases dramatically, there is no way to put the genie back in the bottle, and it is not a kindly genie.

Have We Lost?

Many people who agree that there are risks in legalizing cocaine or heroin still favor it, because, they think, we have lost the war on drugs. "Nothing we have done has worked," and the current federal policy is just "more of the same." Whatever the costs of greater drug use, surely they would be less than the costs of our present, failed efforts. That is exactly what I was told in 1972—and heroin is not quite as bad a drug as cocaine. We did not surrender, and we did not lose. We did not win, either. What the nation accomplished then was what most efforts to save people from themselves accomplish: the problem was contained and the number of victims minimized, all at a considerable cost in law enforcement and increased crime. Was the cost worth it? I think so, but others may disagree. What are the lives of would-be addicts worth? I recall some people saying to me then, "Let them kill themselves." I was appalled. Happily, such views did not prevail.

Have we lost today? Not at all. High-rate cocaine use is not commonplace. The National Institute of Drug Abuse (NIDA) reports that less than 5 percent of high-school seniors used cocaine within the last thirty days. Of course, this survey misses young people who have dropped out of school and miscounts those who lie on the questionnaire, but even if we inflate the NIDA estimate by some plausible percentage, it is still not much above 5 percent. Medical examiners reported in 1987 that about 1,500 died from cocaine use; hospital emergency rooms reported about 30,000 admissions related to cocaine abuse.

These are not small numbers, but neither are they evidence of a nationwide plague that threatens to engulf us all. Moreover, cities vary greatly in the proportion of people who are involved with cocaine. To get city-level data, we need to turn to drug tests carried out on arrested persons, who obviously are more likely to be drug users than the average citizen. The National Institute of Justice, through its Drug Use Forecasting (DUF) project, collects urinalysis data on arrestees in 22 cities. As we have already seen, opiate (chiefly heroin) use has been flat or declining in most of these cities over the last decade. Cocaine use has gone up sharply, but with great variation among cities. New York, Philadelphia, and Washington, D.C., all report that two-thirds or more of their arrestees tested positive for cocaine, but in Portland, San Antonio, and Indianapolis, the percentage was one-third or less.

In some neighborhoods, of course, matters have reached crisis proportions. Gangs control the streets, shootings terrorize residents, and drug-dealing occurs in plain view. The police seem barely able to contain matters. But in these neighborhoods—unlike at Palo Alto cocktail parties—the people are not calling for legalization, they are calling for help. And often, not much help has come. Many cities are willing to do almost anything about the drug problem except spend more money on it. The federal government cannot change that; only local voters and politicians can. It is not clear that they will.

It took about ten years to contain heroin. We have had experience with crack for only about three or four years. Each year, we spend perhaps $11 billion on law enforcement (and some of that goes to deal with marijuana) and perhaps $2 billion on treatment. Large sums, but not sums that should lead anyone to say, "We just can't afford this anymore."

The illegality of drugs increases crime, partly because some users turn to crime to pay for their habits, partly because some users are stimulated by certain drugs (such as crack or PCP) to act more violently or ruthlessly than they otherwise would, and partly because criminal organizations, seeking to control drug supplies, use force to manage their markets. These also are serious costs, but no one knows how much they would be reduced, if drugs were legalized. Addicts would no longer steal to pay black-market prices for drugs, a real gain. But some, perhaps a great deal, of that gain would be offset by the great increase in the number of addicts. These people, nodding on heroin or living in the delusion-ridden high of cocaine, would hardly be ideal employees. Many would steal simply to support themselves, since snatch-and-grab, opportunistic crime can be managed even by people unable to hold a regular job or plan an elaborate crime. Those British addicts who get their supplies from government clinics are not models of law-abiding decency. Most are in crime, and, though their per-capita rate of criminality may be lower thanks to the cheapness of their drugs, the total volume of crime they produce may be quite large. Of course, society could decide to support all unemployable addicts on welfare, but that would mean that gains from lowered rates of crime would have to be offset by large increases in welfare budgets.

Proponents of legalization claim that the costs of having more addicts around would be largely, if not entirely, offset by having more money available with which to treat and care for them. The money would come from taxes levied on the sale of heroin and cocaine.

To obtain this fiscal dividend, however, legalization's supporters must first solve an economic dilemma. If they want to raise a lot of money to pay for welfare and treatment, the tax rate on the drugs will have to be quite high. Even if they themselves do not want a high rate, the politicians' love of "sin taxes" would probably guarantee that it would be high anyway. But the higher the tax, the higher the price of the drug; and the higher the price, the greater the likelihood that addicts will turn to crime to find the money for it, and that criminal organizations will be formed to sell tax-free drugs at below-market rates. If we managed to keep taxes (and thus prices) low, we would get that much less money to pay for welfare and treatment, and more people could afford to become addicts. There may be an optimal tax rate for drugs that maximizes revenue, while minimizing crime, bootlegging, and the recruitment of new addicts; but our experience with alcohol does not suggest that we know how to find it.

The Benefits of Illegality

The advocates of legalization find nothing to be said in favor of the current system except, possibly, that it keeps the number of addicts smaller than it would otherwise be. In fact, the benefits are more substantial than that.

First, treatment. All the talk about providing "treatment on demand" implies that there is a demand for treatment. That is not quite right. There are some drug-dependent people who genuinely want treatment and will remain in it, if offered; they should receive it. But there are far more who want only short-term help after a bad crash; once stabilized and bathed, they are back on the street again, hustling. And even many of the addicts who enroll in a program, honestly wanting help, drop out after a short while when they discover that help takes time and commitment. Drug-dependent people have very short time horizons and a weak capacity for commitment. These two groups—those looking for a quick fix and those unable to stick with a long-term fix—are not

easily helped. Even if we increase the number of treatment slots—as we should—we would have to do something to make treatment more effective.

One thing that can often make it more effective is compulsion. Douglas Anglin of UCLA, in common with many other researchers, has found that the longer one stays in a treatment program, the better the chances of a reduction in drug dependency. But he, again like most other researchers, has found that drop-out rates are high. He has also found, however, that patients who enter treatment under legal compulsion stay in the program longer than those not subject to such pressure. His research on the California civil-commitment program, for example, found that heroin users involved with its required drug-testing program had, over the long term, a lower rate of heroin use than similar addicts who were free of such constraints. If for many addicts compulsion is a useful component of treatment, it is not clear how compulsion could be achieved in a society in which purchasing, possessing, and using the drug were legal. It could be managed, I suppose, but I would not want to have to answer the challenge from the American Civil Liberties Union that it is wrong to compel a person to undergo treatment for consuming a legal commodity.

Next, education. We are not investing substantially in drug-education programs in the schools. Though we do not yet know for certain what will work, there are some promising leads. But I wonder how credible such programs would be, if they were aimed at dissuading children from doing something perfectly legal. We could, of course, treat drug education like smoking education: inhaling crack and inhaling tobacco are both legal, but you should not do it, because it is bad for you. That tobacco is bad for you is easily shown; the Surgeon General has seen to that. But what do we say about crack? It is pleasurable, but devoting yourself to so much pleasure is not a good idea (though perfectly legal)? Unlike tobacco, cocaine will not give you cancer or emphysema, but it will lead you to neglect your duties to family, job, and neighborhood? Everybody is doing cocaine, but you should not? Again, it might be possible under a legalized regime to have effective drug-prevention programs, but their effectiveness would depend heavily, I think, on first having decided that cocaine use, like tobacco use, is purely a matter of practical consequences; no fundamental moral significance attaches to either. But if we believe—as I do—that dependency on certain mind-altering drugs is a moral issue, and that their illegality rests in part on their immorality, then legalizing them undercuts, if it does not eliminate altogether, the moral message.

That message is at the root of the distinction we now make between nicotine and cocaine. Both are highly addictive; both have harmful physical effects. But we treat the two drugs differently, not simply because nicotine is so widely used as to be beyond the reach of effective prohibition, but because its use does not destroy the user's essential humanity. Tobacco shortens one's life, cocaine debases it. Nicotine alters one's habits, cocaine alters one's soul. The heavy use of crack, unlike the heavy use of tobacco, corrodes those natural sentiments of sympathy and duty that constitute our human nature and make possible our social life. To say, as does Nadelmann, that distinguishing morally between tobacco and cocaine is "little more than a transient prejudice" is close to saying that morality itself is but a prejudice.

The Alcohol Problem

Now we have arrived where many arguments about legalizing drugs begin: is there any reason to treat heroin and cocaine differently from the way we treat alcohol?

There is no easy answer to that question, because, as with so many human problems, one cannot decide simply on the basis either of moral principles or of individual consequences; one has to temper any policy by a common-sense judgment of what is possible. Alcohol, like heroin, cocaine, PCP, and marijuana, is a drug—that is, a mood-altering substance—and, consumed to excess, it certainly has harmful consequences: auto accidents, barroom fights, bedroom shootings. It is also, for some people, addictive. We cannot confidently compare the addic-

tive powers of these drugs, but the best evidence suggests that crack and heroin are much more addictive than alcohol.

Many people, Nadelmann included, argue that, since the health and financial costs of alcohol abuse are so much higher than those of cocaine and heroin abuse, it is hypocritical folly to devote our efforts to preventing cocaine or drug use. But, as Mark Kleiman of Harvard has pointed out, this comparison is quite misleading. What Nadelmann is doing is showing that a *legalized* drug (alcohol) produces greater social harm than *illegal* ones (cocaine and heroin). But of course. Suppose that in the 1920s we had made heroin and cocaine legal and alcohol illegal. Can anyone doubt that Nadelmann would now be writing that it is folly to continue our ban on alcohol, because cocaine and heroin are so much more harmful?

And let there be no doubt about it—widespread heroin and cocaine use are associated with all manner of ills. Thomas Bewley found that the mortality rate of British heroin addicts in 1968 was 28 times as high as the death rate of the same age group of nonaddicts, even though in England at the time an addict could obtain free or low-cost heroin and clean needles from British clinics. Perform the following mental experiment: suppose we legalized heroin and cocaine in this country. In what proportion of auto fatalities would the state police report that the driver was nodding off on heroin or recklessly driving on a coke high? In what proportion of spouse-assault and child-abuse cases would the local police report that crack was involved? In what proportion of industrial accidents would safety investigators report that the forklift or drill-press operator was in a drug-induced stupor or frenzy? We do not know exactly what the proportion would be, but anyone who asserts that it would not be much higher than it is now would have to believe that these drugs have little appeal, except when they are illegal. And that is nonsense.

An advocate of legalization might concede that social harm—perhaps harm equivalent to that already produced by alcohol—would follow from making cocaine and heroin generally available. But at least, he might add, we would have the problem "out in the open," where it could be treated as a matter of "public health." That is well and good, *if* we knew how to treat—that is, cure—heroin and cocaine abuse. But we do not know how to do it for all the people who would need such help. We are having only limited success in coping with chronic alcoholics. Addictive behavior is immensely difficult to change, and the best methods for changing it—living in drug-free therapeutic communities, becoming faithful members of Alcoholics Anonymous or Narcotics Anonymous—require great personal commitment, a quality that is, alas, in short supply among the very persons—young people, disadvantaged people—who are often most at risk for addiction.

Suppose that today we had, not 15 million alcohol abusers, but half a million. Suppose that we already knew what we have learned from our long experience with the widespread use of alcohol. Would we make whiskey legal? I do not know, but I suspect there would be a lively debate. The Surgeon General would remind us of the risks alcohol poses to pregnant women. The National Highway Traffic Safety Administration would point to the likelihood of more highway fatalities caused by drunk drivers. The Food and Drug Administration might find that there is a non-trivial increase in cancer associated with alcohol consumption. At the same time, the police would report great difficulty in keeping illegal whiskey out of our cities, officers being corrupted by bootleggers, and alcohol addicts often resorting to crime to feed their habit. Libertarians, for their part, would argue that every citizen has a right to drink anything he wishes and that drinking is, in any event, a "victimless crime."

However the debate might turn out, the central fact would be that the problem was still, at that point, a small one. The government cannot legislate away the addictive tendencies in all of us, nor can it remove completely even the most dangerous addictive substances. But it can cope with harms when the harms are still manageable.

Science and Addiction

One advantage of containing a problem, while it is still containable, is that it buys time for science to learn more about it and perhaps to discover a cure. Almost unnoticed in the current debate over legalized drugs is that basic science has made rapid strides in identifying the underlying neurological processes involved in some forms of addiction. Stimulants, such as cocaine and amphetamines, alter the way certain brain cells communicate with one another. That alteration is complex and not entirely understood, but in simplified form it involves modifying the way in which a neurotransmitter called dopamine sends signals from one cell to another.

When dopamine crosses the synapse between two cells, it is in effect carrying a message from the first cell to activate the second one. In certain parts of the brain, that message is experienced as pleasure. After the message is delivered, the dopamine returns to the first cell. Cocaine apparently blocks this return, or "reuptake," so that the excited cell and others nearby continue to send pleasure messages. When the exaggerated high produced by cocaine-influenced dopamine finally ends, the brain cells may (in ways that are still a matter of dispute) suffer from an extreme lack of dopamine, thereby making the individual unable to experience any pleasure at all. This would explain why cocaine users often feel so depressed after enjoying the drug. Stimulants may also affect the way in which other neurotransmitters, such as serotonin and noradrenaline, operate.

Whatever the exact mechanism may be, once it is identified, it becomes possible to use drugs to block either the effect of cocaine or its tendency to produce dependency. There have already been experiments, using desipramine, imipramine, bromocriptine, carbamazepine, and other chemicals. There are some promising results.

Tragically, we spend very little on such research, and the agencies funding it have not in the past occupied very influential or visible posts in the federal bureaucracy. If there is one aspect of the "war on drugs" metaphor that I dislike, it is its tendency to focus attention almost exclusively on the troops in the trenches, whether engaged in enforcement or treatment, and away from the research-and-development efforts back on the home front, where the war may ultimately be decided.

I believe that the prospects of scientists in controlling addiction will be strongly influenced by the size and character of the problem they face. If the problem is a few hundred thousand chronic, high-dose users of an illegal product, the chances of making a difference at a reasonable cost will be much greater than if the problem is a few million chronic users of legal substances. Once a drug is legal, not only will its use increase but many of those who then use it will prefer the drug to the treatment: they will want the pleasure, whatever the cost to themselves or their families, and they will resist—probably successfully—any effort to wean them away from experiencing the high that comes from inhaling a legal substance.

If I Am Wrong . . .

No one can know what our society would be like, if we changed the law to make access to cocaine, heroin, and PCP easier. I believe, for reasons given, that the result would be a sharp increase in use, a more widespread degradation of the human personality, and a greater rate of accidents and violence.

I may be wrong. If I am, then we will needlessly have incurred heavy costs in law enforcement and some forms of criminality. But if I am right, and the legalizers prevail anyway, then we will have consigned millions of people, hundreds of thousands of infants, and hundreds of neighborhoods to a life of oblivion and disease. To the lives and families destroyed by alcohol, we will have

added countless more destroyed by cocaine, heroin, PCP, and whatever else a basement scientist can invent.

Human character is formed by society; indeed, human character is inconceivable without society, and good character is less likely in a bad society. Will we, in the name of an abstract doctrine of radical individualism, and with the false comfort of suspect predictions, decide to take the chance that somehow individual decency can survive amid a more general level of degradation?

I think not. The American people are too wise for that, whatever the academic essayists and cocktail-party pundits may say. But if Americans today are less wise than I suppose, then Americans at some future time will look back on us now and wonder, what kind of people were they that they could have done such a thing?

Note

1. I do not here take up the question of marijuana. For a variety of reasons—its widespread use and its lesser tendency to addict—it presents a different problem from cocaine or heroin. For a penetrating analysis, see Mark Kleiman, *Marijuana: Costs of Abuse, Costs of Control* (Greenwood Press, 217 pp.).

For Discussion

Wilson argues that the number of heroin users has remained stable over the years because it is costly and difficult to obtain. Can this argument explain heroin use among individuals from middle and upper income backgrounds? Why or why not?